The Material Culture of the Tradesmen of Newcastle upon Tyne 1545-1642

The Durham Probate Record Evidence

Gwendolynn Heley

BAR British Series 497
2009

Published in 2016 by
BAR Publishing, Oxford

BAR British Series 497

The Material Culture of the Tradesmen of Newcastle upon Tyne 1545–1642

ISBN 978 1 4073 0601 8

BAR Publishing is the trading name of British Archaeological Reports (Oxford) Ltd. British Archaeological Reports was first incorporated in 1974 to publish the BAR Series, International and British. In 1992 Hadrian Books Ltd became part of the BAR group. This volume was originally published by Archaeopress in conjunction with British Archaeological Reports (Oxford) Ltd / Hadrian Books Ltd, the Series principal publisher, in 2009. This present volume is published by BAR Publishing, 2016.

Printed in England

BAR
PUBLISHING

BAR titles are available from:

BAR Publishing
122 Banbury Rd, Oxford, OX2 7BP, UK
EMAIL info@barpublishing.com
PHONE +44 (0)1865 310431
FAX +44 (0)1865 316916
www.barpublishing.com

Abstract

This book examines the material culture of middling tradesmen living in Newcastle upon Tyne between 1545 and 1642. The analysis is based on wills and inventories selected from the Durham Probate Records pertaining to Newcastle residents. The book has three major themes; people, property and objects, and covers five subject areas: firstly, a background discussion of the limitations inherent in working with probate records in material culture studies, and an explanation of the methodology employed; secondly, an analysis of inheritance practices and patterns concerning selected types of bequests, exploring issues such as primogeniture, gender and life-cycle factors; thirdly, a study of the built environment and social demography of the town, including occupational zones, based on descriptions of properties along streets and in specific locations recorded in the documents; fourthly, an extensive analysis of patterns of consumption, production and investment among tradesmen by way of categories of objects associated with the household, household production and objects relating to the practice of a trade; the final chapter explores the size of houses, the function of rooms and the nature of social relations within the home (evidenced by way of objects in named rooms).

The study shows that probate records provide an unrivalled opportunity for pursuing material culture studies, despite the difficulties presented by these primary sources. The study argues that inheritance practices in northern England conform to a national pattern as early as the mid-16th century, and that although primogeniture is an important factor, the life-cycle stage which families had reached at the death of the head of the household are central to understanding the distribution of estates. The study demonstrates that probate records can be used to recover aspects of the vanished built environment and social geography of pre-Civil-War Newcastle – a period of history suffering a paucity of sources, including the problem that very few standing structures from the epoch remain. The analysis also illustrates marked change in the material culture of middling tradesmen in the early rather than the later decades of the 17th century, a transition closely linked to the exceptional industrial and commercial growth experienced in the region associated with the coal trade, that ensured Newcastle upon Tyne was among the most advanced regions in the country by the early 17th century.

Acknowledgements

The author wishes to thank those individuals who have supported the research and writing of this study - notably my family - Peter Taylor, Buffy Heley and Paul Nieuwenhuis – my friends Robert Childs and Dr. Stuart Weeks, and my supervisor Dr. Chris Gerrard. In particular, the author wishes to thank Dr. Christopher Neville-Smith for lending his expertise in computers. The guidance provided by my External and Internal Examiners, Professor Mark Overton and Dr. Adrian Green, in the re-writing of the original version of this thesis, is gratefully acknowledged. The author wishes also to thank the staff of the Palace Green Library, Durham University.

CONTENTS Page

Chapter 3

Chapter 4

Chapter 5

Chapter 6

Appendices

List of figures

List of maps

CHAPTER 1: Introduction

1:1 Introduction

Newcastle upon Tyne in northern England lies some 19 kilometres inland from the North Sea on the northern bank of the River Tyne. The modern city occupies a site with a long history encompassing the pre-historic period, the Romans, the Anglo-Saxons, and the Normans who gave the town its modern name (Snape and Bidwell 2002; Rollason 2003, Heslop and Graves forthcoming). Today, much of the layered history of this place has been destroyed and relatively little of the built environment pre-dates the 19th century. The dominance of architecture and streets belonging to the modern era, extensively reviewed by Pevsner et al. (1992), obscures what remains of the medieval and early modern town, and belies a place with a remarkable past.

By the beginning of the 14th century, Newcastle was already a wealthy and powerful Corporation governed by an oligarchy protective of its rights and privileges. Self-centred and acutely aware of the value of the natural resources upon which the wealth of the town was based, the Corporation fought to maintain monopolies and thwart anyone who was seen to threaten their powerful position (Gardner 1655). By the middle of the 16th century Newcastle had become the second-largest provincial town in England and, by the 17th century was one of the busiest international ports in Britain (Welford 1885: 244-5; Nef 1932; Howell 1967: 2, 1978: 5; Lomas 1992:167; Ellis 2001: 15; Graves 2003: 31).Countries in Europe and the Baltic, the southern and eastern towns of England, and especially London, were dependent on the resources Newcastle could offer. By the beginning of the early modern period, trade in coal and other commodities, including the provision of ships to the monarch, had made Newcastle an important town both nationally and internationally. Newcastle coal lit the fires of both domestic and industrial London, and the French were so dependent on this commodity they could 'neither make stele-werk, or metal work … nor guns, nor no matter of things that passeth the fier' without it (Welford 1885: 36, 67; Nef 1932; Green 2003: 60). Newcastle was also strategically located, as the main roads east-west between Tynemouth and Carlisle, and north-south between London and Scotland, ran through the town. Howell described Newcastle as a 'military centre of clear importance even without coal, of supreme importance with it' (1967: 4; Langton 1974: 21).

The reputation of Newcastle in the past and in the present is bound up with the history of its natural resources, industrial production and political turbulence, and writers have not always done justice to this place. Discouraging reviews are recorded by southern visitors travelling through the north in the 17th and 18th centuries. Daniel Defoe found the town was located in an 'exceedingly unpleasant' situation (Rogers 1983), and Celia Fiennes described a people exposed to 'brutalising' conditions (Morris 1983). Some modern reviews are equally unfavourable: Houlbrooke wrote that 'Nowhere in England remained lawless and without effective government longer than the far north' (1995: 50), and Myer claimed that 'no area in England is more studded with castles or soaked in blood', and he described Newcastle as 'England's northern bastion … a place for mustering troops and a venue for royal encounters' (2001: 294). Walton's 'Bleak Northumberland', 'wild and vulnerable', was a place where a single market town supposedly served an area of 250 square miles (2000: 121; Everitt 1967: 485-90). Ellis observed that, in the 17th

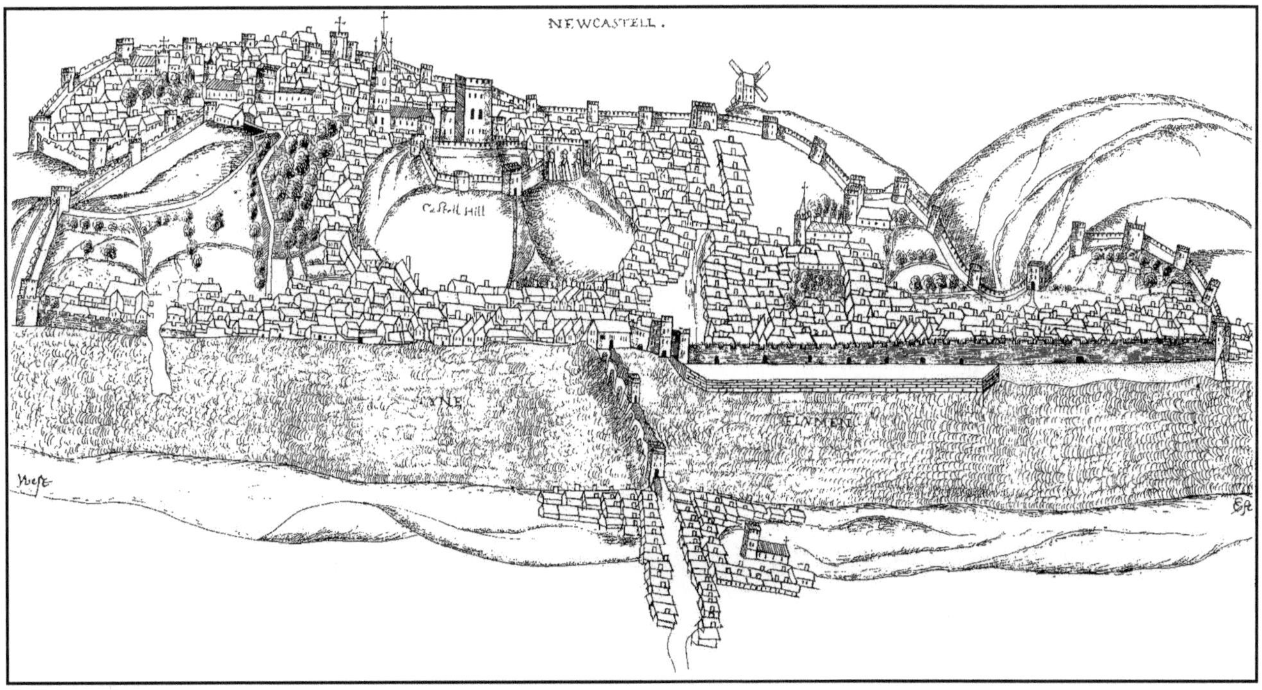

Illustration 1.1: The Cotton Manuscript – Newcastle upon Tyne c. 1590

and 18th centuries 'no-one could doubt that Newcastle society as a whole, from the great families who controlled the Corporation down to the poorest labourer on the waterfront, was noticeably competitive and aggressive, and prone to drunkenness, cursing, swearing and internal recriminations' (2001; 1, 13-14).

Such characterisations do not, of course, do justice to either the place or the people. Levine and Wrightson can find no evidence of a place 'full of ungovernable people', 'in the supposedly lawless north of England', and they believe these 'stereotypes may go deep' (1991: 275, 307; 1995: 160, 172), rooted in the attitudes of Stuart and Tudor authorities that remain largely unchallenged (Malcolmson 1980: 85-9). These writers noted just such a 'historiographical stereotype' of a 'brutalized plebeian population' imposed on the people of nearby Whickham (a village close to Newcastle on the south side of the Tyne), but say this reputation is not justified, as 'the vices and disorders attacked were the traditional fare of moralistic indigo nation', and are common to 'all places' in the late 16th and 17th centuries (Levine and Wrightson 1991: 275, 307-8). However, Levine and Wrightson acknowledge that the pursuit of coal appears to have bred 'an entrepreneurial climate ... one of ruthless opportunism and obsession with gain' (1991: 107). Ellis also examines this dimension of Newcastle where she describes a 'polarised society' in her exploration of social relations in the town after the Restoration, with a narrow oligarchy, who monopolised the coal trade, negotiating with a large and sometimes volatile workforce (1985: 203-5, 216). Green, however, noted that the substantial degree of 'social polarisation' affected 'those at the coal face', while others prospered from industrial and agricultural change (2003: 60).

While acknowledging conflict in social relations in this period, the history of the north should not be characterised as one of unremitting gloom and backwardness, dominated by civil unrest, border war and industrial production. A more balanced interpretation of the region should be sought. It is the aim of this thesis to present aspects of the material culture life of this provincial capital that have been relatively neglected, as although the north-east was a 'border zone, at the frontier between England and Scotland' (Green 2003: 57), Newcastle was simultaneously and inextricably linked to the south. The interconnectedness of north and south is reflected in remarks by the contemporary historian Thomas Fuller (1662), who recognised that social and economic life in County Durham was comparable to that in southern England (Green 2003: 59) - a view that has been confirmed by Weatherill, who found parts of the north-east as advanced as London in terms of trade links and consumption patterns (1996: 61). While such general observations on the region provide a useful background to understanding life in the north, the history of Newcastle in particular deserves greater attention.

The town has been the focus of several outstanding writers in past centuries, whose works have an abiding importance and have been very influential in guiding this writer. Some of the earliest works by Gray (1649) and Gardiner (1655) are quoted extensively by later antiquarians, as well as modern writers. Bourne (1736), Brand (1789), McKenzie (1827), Charleton (1885) and Welford (1884, 1885, 1887), are some of the best-known authors, while Knowles and Boyle (1890) have ensured the survival of wonderful pictorial representations of the old town. Very extensive collections of journals have been published since the 19th century, such as those of the Surtees Society and *Archaeologia Aeliana*, which are dedicated to understanding the long and varied history of the north. However, few histories of Newcastle have emerged in recent decades. In 1950 Middlebrook wrote a history of the town, a modest achievement by the standards of earlier writers, whereas Howell (1967) is among the most important writers of the 20th century with his detailed account of religious dissent in Newcastle among the Puritans. More recent work by such writers as Green (2000, 2003) on houses and households of the early modern period, including those in Newcastle, and King (2001, 2004) on the sociability of Newcastle guilds, have opened up new areas of scholarship. Other recent publications on the north-east include a new edited volume on Newcastle (Colls and Lancaster 2001), with studies from Ellis on the economy of the town after 1700, and by Hugman on the local book trade. A second recent contribution comprises a collection of essays on cultural identity in the north (Berry et al. 2004), which includes Schammell's latest work on consumption (2004), and Green's review of aspects of literary life in the region (2004). The volume and variety of publications on the early modern period available to the researcher is impressive.

However, many of these works, especially more recent contributions, have been primarily focused on the mid-to-late 17th and 18th centuries or later periods and, although the subjects explored have helped to inform the arguments presented in this thesis and provide useful comparative data, Newcastle's material culture prior to the outbreak of the Civil War has tended to be overlooked. Glennie highlights 'an awkward gap' between studies on medieval consumption (which have been largely ignored) and those which concentrate on the post-Civil-War era and beyond (1995:173). In this thesis an empirically based study, beginning in the mid-16th century, is undertaken through a very detailed analysis, which documents changes to the material culture of the town throughout the decades leading up to the Civil War, a period of great disruption to Newcastle and one deserving separate study (Levine and Wrightson 1991: 41-4). The principal source of evidence for this study is the Durham Probate Record Collection, which forms the most comprehensive account in existence of the ordinary people of Newcastle in the early modern period. This analysis of the material culture of a town concentrates on a small section of the population, representing middling tradesmen. The thesis examines the lives of these men and their families through inheritance practices, charts the neighbourhoods and properties where they lived and worked, and analyses their worldly possessions by way of the wills such tradesmen wrote and the inventories compiled by their appraisers. It is in the minutiae of material life documented in the surviving records of individuals that an intimate portrait of these people and their lives can be recovered.

The importance of detailed studies is recognised by Spufford in her outstanding work on Cambridgeshire villages, in which she draws attention to a need for 'microcosmic studies' in developing an understanding of the variety and complexity of each community (2000; xxix). Other writers have echoed this concern. For example, Weatherill, who has explored consumer behaviour and material culture in several regions of Britain, suggests that 'relatively small, carefully contrived samples are to be preferred' in this kind of research as they provide the most flexible results (1996: 201). This approach is evident in Levine and Wrightson's study of society in industrial Whickham (1991). The authors note that, without empirically based research there is a lack of historical depth, and that while 'closeness of focus has its limitations … it is simply the most fruitful way of pursuing social history, permitting as it does, the intensive analysis of particular sources' (1991: x). Overton has noted that, in many studies of consumption, 'theoretical speculation has run ahead of empirical research' (2004: 9).

This thesis is a microcosmic study, based on empirical data collated from a selected body of primary sources. These records contain a vast amount of very detailed information with which to pursue the aims of this thesis in depth, relating to people, property and objects. The findings concerning different aspects of the material lives of the tradesmen presented in the chapters are discussed in the context of secondary literature on probate, material culture, early modern towns and, especially, Newcastle, focusing on works of particular relevance to this study.

This thesis is divided into seven chapters covering five major subject areas. Chapter 2 provides a comprehensive background to the selection of the wills and inventories used in the study, and the methodology employed, to the law, custom and practice of probate jurisdiction in the period, and to the nature and limitations of probate records in undertaking material culture studies. The extant collections of similar records in many regions of Britain provide the basis for much comparative research, as these documents survive in their millions for the period from the mid-16th century through to the 18th century (Cox and Cox 2000: 14). There is, however, a great deal of controversy as to how the records can be employed in historical analyses. Arkell et al. (2000) have compiled an edited volume on understanding and interpreting probate records, which provides one of the best and most comprehensive guides to working with the documents; other insightful contributions are found in Spufford's article on the limitations of the source (1990), and in Glennie's work on understanding consumer society (1995: 169-171). Orlin (2002) is, perhaps, the most vehement critic of the records, uncovering so many potential difficulties with the source as to suggest that the evidence is practically inadmissible. The contributions to this debate by many writers, whose own work has involved probate records, including Thirsk (1967), Corfield and Priestley (1982), Shammas (1990), Johnson (1991), Levine and Wrightson (1991), Weatherill (1996), Colls and Lancaster (2001), Erickson (2002) and Overton (2004) are examined in the light of the methodology employed in this study. The chapter aims to show, that despite inherent difficulties, the documents are one of the most important sources in existence for the study of the early modern period, and that these unique records provide an unrivalled opportunity for pursuing material culture studies.

In Chapter 3, inheritance practices among the middling tradesmen of Newcastle are examined. Issa has found that 'powerful assumptions rather than detailed research' among 'common people' has obscured an understanding of kinship obligations (1986: 9) - a concern echoed by Erickson, who noted the impressionistic nature of evidence in the absence of comprehensive analysis of actual patterns of inheritance (2002: 18). Goose and Evans found that there are no 'full-blown studies' of inheritance practices of provincial towns (2000: 68-69). In a contribution to this subject, Chapter 3 examines patterns of bequests in relation to the law of the period and in its application in local practice in Newcastle. Factors such as primogeniture and gender, the life cycle, the age of both beneficiary and benefactor, and the occupation and wealth of tradesmen are analysed in relation to obligations to family, kin, servants and friends. Whether practices in the north were 'culturally distinct' from those in other regions (Issa 1986: 9), or whether customs echo those of the nation as a whole, are questions explored through an empirical study of the distribution of particular categories of bequests.

Drawing on the original instructions recorded in wills, a very accurate picture of how real and personal property, money, clothes, animals, and bequests to the poor were bequeathed reveals, not just practices surrounding the way bequests were made, but also the nature of social relations and attitudes of middling tradesmen towards their beneficiaries. Levine and Wrightson's (1991) study of Whickham copyholders, and Issa's (1986) study of inheritance practices in County Durham provide useful regional comparisons with the Newcastle evidence. Other important studies - by Erickson on women and property (2002), by Spufford on Cambridgeshire villagers (1984), by Cressy on kinship in Essex and Wiltshire (1986), and by Howell on Midlands peasants (1976, 1983) - provide further contributions to the discussions relating to practices in other regions, particularly in the south of England.

In Chapter 4 the focus of the thesis turns to the built environment and historical demography of pre-Civil War Newcastle. The study of early modern towns is clearly a vast subject area. Clark's comprehensive review of the literature on the subject in *The Cambridge Urban History of Britain* underlines the extraordinary diversity of studies spanning a time frame beginning with the first town history by Stow (1603), and following a progression of work through the influential contributions of Hoskins (1935, 1953) on regional and local history, to an explosion of research in recent decades on urban groups, types of towns and individual communities - studies that display a range of different approaches and examine a variety of demographic, economic, cultural and political issues (Clark 2000: 4, 22, 24). While recognising the scale and importance of the myriad of approaches to the subject, a circumspect analysis is proposed here.

As already mentioned, the topography of early modern Newcastle is hardly discernible today. Byrne describes 'an ancient place which has been remade and extended', a remaking 'so drastic ... so massive that it makes sense to see Edwardian Newcastle as a new place laid over an old' (2001: 341). The difficulties in reconstructing the environment of a relatively recent period warn of the limitations inherent in attempting to recover the town of some 350 years earlier, when this study begins. The streets of the modern city, while bearing names from past centuries, reveal little about the late medieval and early modern buildings or neighbourhoods. Archaeological excavations have contributed to understanding aspects of the development of the early town (Nolan, forthcoming; Harbottle 1981; O'Brien et al. 1988; Ellison et al. 1993), but properties occupied by tradesmen and the areas where these men once worked and lived have largely been lost to history. Standing structures belonging to these social groups are almost non-existent in modern Newcastle, although a handful of the houses that once belonged to more elite social groups of a slighter later period have survived which provide glimpses of the local architecture (McCombie 1985; Heslop et al. 1993; 1995; 2001; Green 2000, 2003: 63, 66). However, the dwellings of the poorer sections of society, and certainly those of many of the middling sorts as well, have not survived the housing demands of later generations, highlighting the difficulties of recovering information on living arrangements among these social groups (Green 2003: 66). Over the centuries, the great changes to the topography of Newcastle that began in the late 18th century were followed by relentless and unprecedented destruction in the 20th century, and little of the historical town has survived the radical transformation (Pevsner et al. 1992: 413-17).

The rarity of standing structures from the pre-Civil War period, the limitations imposed on archaeological excavations; a reliance on the few contemporary accounts of the town by Gray (1649), Bourne (1736) and Brand (1789); and on the precious early map evidence by Speed (1610), Corbridge (1723), Hutton (1772) and Thompson (1746); combined with a dearth of information on the town's middling tradesmen, underlines the importance of probate records as a source of evidence for this type of study. A failure to recognise the potential of the records for studies of the built environment is, in part, due to misunderstandings about the content of the documents (Spufford 1984: 37, 1990: 142, Erickson 2002: 23 -7), as will be demonstrated in the course of Chapter 4.

An original approach has been devised in this thesis, incorporating descriptions from wills and inventories of properties in named locations to reconstruct and map individual houses, shops, mills and land-holdings around the town and suburbs. The findings from the period between 1549 and 1642 are compared with Langton's post-Civil-War study of the social geography of the town by way of the Hearth Tax Assessments of 1665 and Freeman's Rolls of 1635–64 (1974), charting change and continuity in the town over these decades. In the more than 30 years since Langton's analysis (one of the only major studies on occupational zoning in the town, and one that relies on Welford's (1911) interpretation of Bourne's (1736) evidence for ward boundaries), no comparable studies of Newcastle have been undertaken. The scope of this analysis is necessarily narrow, because of the volume of data and the limitations that the documents impose on reconstructing the architectural layout of houses (Priestley and Corfield 1982: 100; Overton 2004: 122). In order to fully utilise the probate data, two separate approaches are pursued, enabling both external and internal aspects of the properties to be examined. The particular way that information on properties is recorded in the probate documents means that fewer than 50% of wills provide information on property location, whereas up to 95% of inventories provide information on rooms. Chapters 4 and 6 are separated by an intervening chapter on 'goods and chattels'. The findings in Chapter 5 relating to the ownership of objects are taken up in Chapter 6, providing an opportunity to examine the association between the function of space within properties and the types of objects listed in the documents.

In Chapter 5, three separate areas of material life associated, first, with the household, second, with household production, and third, with the principal occupation of the tradesmen included in the study, take the thesis in a new direction. An extensive analysis, by way of thousands of objects listed in tradesmen's inventories, reveals strategies of consumption, production and investment relating to wealth levels and valuation of objects, and to occupations, and examines how these and other factors such as emulation, identity and urbanisation, shaped the material lives of the middling tradesmen. A picture of the material culture of the town emerges in the course of detailed examinations into specific types of objects common to almost all inventories.

This kind of research is, of course, not new. Studies using inventories date back to Hoskins' (1957) pioneering study of Leicestershire. In the following decade, Thirsk used inventories in a landmark study of agricultural regions in England and Wales (1967). Overton compiled a bibliography of the growing numbers of studies in 1983. During the 1980s and 90s, research on aspects of consumption, production and material culture proliferated (Glennie 1995), utilising inventories in pursuing a debate on a supposed 'consumer revolution'. Many historians have contributed to the argument that, either in the early 18th century or slightly earlier still in the late 17th century, a significant change and a rapid increase took place in the availability and uptake of consumer and domestic goods

(McKendrick 1982; Spufford 1984; Weatherill 1996; Earle 1989; De Vries 1993; Barry et al. 2004).

This chapter looks at the evidence for a much earlier period of transition. Cox notes that 'few have seriously attempted to push back the seeds of change to the period before the Restoration in 1660' (2000: 3-4). De Vries, however, argues that the term 'consumer revolution' should be suppressed, as the emergence of a consumer society was by no means sudden, suggesting instead that an 'industrious revolution' evolved over the 17th and 18th centuries (1993: 107). Other evidence indicates still earlier origins of economic and social change. Thirsk (1978), for instance, charts increasing production (if not consumption) already by the second half of the 16th century, while Overton believes gradual change in production as well as consumption began as early as 1550 (2004: 7), although Levine and Wrightson observed 'sharp discontinuities' between the late 16th and early 17th centuries (1991: 230-1).

In this analysis, an empirically based assessment is presented that argues, as Levine and Wrightson have done (1991), that important and marked changes in material culture are visible in the early 17th century, setting these decades apart from those of the late Elizabethan era. The findings are extensively examined within the context of other studies. The most important of these include Weatherill's seminal work on eight regions of Britain, (including the north-east), exploring changes in material culture and consumer behaviour in the late 17th and early 18th centuries (1996), and Shammas' comparative analysis of consumption in England and America, in what she terms a 'pre-industrial' era (1990). Both studies provide extensive data that are usefully compared with the Newcastle findings. Overton's recent work on consumption and production in Kent and Cornwall, which examines how and when the economy moved from self-sufficiency to complete market dependency (2004), provides a third major study with which to contextualise the Newcastle data. The most important local study utilising inventories is Levine and Wrightson's study of the industrial parish of Whickham (1991), which provides further comparative material relating to the consumption patterns of copyholders and labourers. The data presented in the course of the analysis provide a way of understanding the material culture of Newcastle in the context of other regions.

Weatherill recognised that Newcastle was in the vanguard of urban development in Britain in the decades from the post-Restoration era to the early 18th century, with a growing and varied commercial and industrial basis centred on the coal trade (1996: 51-2). But the general region-wide nature of her assessment of urban and rural areas leaves many unanswered questions about the provincial capital in a period beginning some 175 years earlier. This chapter examines the evidence for a much earlier ascendancy of the town, reflected in changes to the material culture.

In the final chapter, the findings from Chapter 5 on objects are analysed in relation to named rooms and room function in properties belonging to the middling tradesmen of Newcastle, reviewed in Chapter 4, and comparisons are made with research from several regions of the country (Priestley and Corfield 1982; Schofield 1987; Shammas 1990; Johnson 1991; Overton 2004). Changes to house sizes in the wake of arguments concerning the Great Rebuilding (Hoskins 1953), and the uses of rooms among tradesmen of differing wealth and occupation, help to elucidate the extent to which the houses of Newcastle conformed to national trends (Green 2000; 2003: 66).

This wide-ranging study endeavours to compose a multi-faceted but intimate portrait of material life in Newcastle in the century between 1545 and 1642. Throughout this thesis, the place of the middling tradesmen, both as individuals and as part of this northern society is central to understanding the arguments presented. However, who these people were and why they are described as the middling sorts requires some definition.

1.2 Defining the 'Middling Sort'

The occupations claimed by the testators in their wills, and subsequently confirmed by appraisers in the accompanying inventory of the deceased (where such an inventory survives), form an important legal, economic and social framework throughout this analysis. The designation is an important contemporary assignation, one used 'above all in drawing up of formal legal documents' (Wrightson 1994: 30), which in this study comprise the probate records upon which the thesis is based.

The individuals deemed as belonging to the 'middling sorts' in this analysis do not include the merchants, or gentry, or urban yeomanry, who were among the wealthier and more powerful residents of the town, nor the poor who have left no records. They are men who are set apart from the 'lower' or 'upper sorts' of early modern Newcastle society. Writers have variously suggested the 'middling sorts' occupy 'the social space between the landed gentry … and the poor' (Barry 1994: 2), that they are 'neither at the bottom or top' of society (Weatherill 1996: 13), and have been, according to Wrightson (1995), 'gradually inserted between richer and poorer sorts' (French 2000: 279, 281). No legal definition for this social position, in fact, exists, and a myriad of possible criteria employed in seeking a definition – economic, political, religious and cultural – when 'applied too strictly … would dissolve every social category' one tries to construct (Barry 1994: 12).

French notes that apart from the landed aristocracy and those in receipt of poor relief, everyone in between is a possible candidate for middling status (2000: 281). Clearly, any categorisation must account for a social hierarchy that was constantly shifting with the cycles of life - as reflected, for instance, in marriage prospects, coming of age, acquisition or loss of property, prosperity or indebtedness - which will have altered both an individual's and society's perception and acknowledgment of rank. Defoe's distinctions in the early 18th century even include questions of moral values (French 2000: 281). Such dimensions further complicate the definition adopted here of a middling status based on occupation alone, a criterion that in turn creates difficulties.

French's examination of Gregory King's 'famous social table' cites the inconsistencies in contemporary descriptions of the middle sort resulting from 'occupational ambiguity', and concludes that the social categories constructed by Brodski–Elliot are 'the most successful' (2000: 279, 282–3). Brodski's hierarchy of trades and occupations, based on the links between marriage partners and apprenticeships, is however, problematic for the study of tradesmen, as is demonstrated in Chapter 5. Her categories result in all but two of the trades in this study being designated as 'low-status' (Weatherill 1996: 212-3). French asserted that the 'hierarchy is well established', with 'dirty' manual trades placed below shopkeepers, and weavers and shoemakers defined as 'poorly capitalised manual trades' (2000: 283–4). Brooks also identifies a 'distinct status hierarchy' for trades and crafts (1994: 60). In his assessment of Newcastle, citing Houston (1981), he finds that, whereas hostmen and merchant adventurers became leading political figures, 'At the other end of the scale, a cordwainer ... would have been one of the poorest members of the community' (Brooks 1994: 60).

Such assumptions about the social status of tradesmen in early modern Newcastle are shown in this study to be misconceived. Weatherill (1996) and Erickson (2002) have both noted the marked differences in the scale of operations and incomes among men practising the same trade. According to Weatherill, 'Understanding the position of the craft trades is crucial to appreciating the limits of the middle ranks' (Weatherill 1996: 99-10), while Erickson suggests that the social status of a man 'was defined either by his trade or by his land ownership' (2002: 41, 39). Middling tradesmen included several different kinds of people of different wealth and status, from manufacturers to wage-earners.

The tradesmen taken up in this research were not all equally well off and would certainly not have considered themselves as 'equals among equals'; one might also question whether the keelmen included in the study should be seen as belonging even to the lower middle ranks of Newcastle society. A preoccupation with those belonging among the upper limits of the middling sorts, representing tradesmen who could 'vie in wealth and standards of living with the lesser gentry' (French 2000: 279), has resulted in the lowest levels of this middle group being somewhat neglected, a problem highlighted by King in her analysis on the sociability of guilds (2001: 6). A lack of interest in defining the lower orders is exemplified by Wilson (1600), who largely ignored those below the gentry. Wrightson has observed a general tendency among contemporary authors to minimise distinctions at the lower end of the social scale, although he observes that, in the early modern period, gentlemen were as indistinguishable to labourers as the common people appeared to their superiors (1995: 21-2, 37).

Wrighton's analysis of 'Degrees of people' reviews the contemporary accounts of Harrison (1577), Wilson (c.1600) and King (1695) on social order and concludes that a 'broad pattern of society emerges clearly and consistently ... despite variations in detail or disagreement over the exact position of certain middling groups' (1995: 22). Harrison placed those citizens defined by occupation and 'possession of freedom of their cities' second among four degrees, whereas those described as 'artificers' were ranked last; Gregory King created a 'ladder of occupations', in which shopkeepers, tradesmen and artificers all appeared on the second rung, with common seamen on the fourth and lowest rung (Wrightson 1995: 22). The 'classical social hierarchy', repeatedly described by contemporary writers, was (according to Wrightson) a 'gradual ladder of subordination and reciprocal obligation', and was as such 'widely accepted as an essentially accurate account of the principal social groupings distinguishable in Tudor and Stuart society' (Wrightson 1994: 28-9; 1995: 19-21). However, the term 'middling' requires further definition still in the pre-Civil-War period.

The phrase 'middling sort' was applied first in a commercial context and was used to describe commodities, but it was rarely used in a sociological context before the 1640s (Wrightson 1994: 41). The population had been aware of the existence of a middle range of people in the social distributions of wealth, status and authority, but what Wrightson calls 'the language of sorts' was not the vocabulary of estates and degrees but of social descriptions employed to distinguish people, for example, as 'rich' or 'poor' (1994: 37-8, 42–45; Earle 1994: 141). Therefore, whether one can appropriately apply the term 'middling sort' to a study of tradesmen in the period prior to the Civil War might be questioned. Nevertheless, the expression does allow the identity of this group in Newcastle society to be explored in relation to a categorization that would have been recognisable to people of the period. The terminology was 'grounded in contemporary usage' as part of 'the evolution of the language of sorts' (French 2000: 279-280).

The occupational designations claimed by Newcastle testators and confirmed by appraisers remain an important contemporary framework that has been retained in this study, although it is recognised that, in understanding how to define the middle sort, both the context and the 'variety and complexity' of social identity must be emphasised (French 2000: 292). This complexity is bound up with changes over the life cycle and with social mobility, which in turn will alter identities, but such considerations do not detract from the importance of occupational designations as a guide to status in the early modern period.

Ultimately, perhaps 'middling sort' is a term of convenience. It signifies a group of people who were neither the wealthiest or the most powerful, nor the poor who left virtually no records of this kind, but those people in between these extremes, who include the middling tradesmen of Newcastle, whose lives are the subject of this thesis.

CHAPTER 2 - The Durham Probate Records

In a study of material culture based on the evidence presented in probate records, it is important, prior to embarking on such research, to recognise the inherent difficulties that the documents present relating to the laws, customs and practices surrounding how and why the records were made, that occasion many limitations and omissions. In this chapter the background to the creation of the documents is outlined, the perimeters of the study defined on the basis of document survival, and the methodology is explained in detail. The historical context of the records is reviewed, and criticisms made by other researchers in the field are questioned and solutions proposed in line with the aims and objectives of this thesis.

2.1 Location and selection of the sources

The Durham Probate Records are held in the Palace Green Library at the University of Durham. The collection includes wills, probate inventories, bonds, letters, commissions, codicils, accounts, interrogatories and administrations. Among these documents are those that relate to the testamentary business of residents of Newcastle upon Tyne. Records for the town survive from the 1540s. Before 1858, probate administration for the town of Newcastle was the responsibility of the Consistory Court of Durham and all probate documents were registered at Durham Cathedral. The Diocese gave the collection to the University of Durham in 1958. When this thesis was being written the records were accessible through a card file index; they are currently being compiled onto a computer database.

The dates selected for the study begin with the earliest surviving will (for a tailor, dated 1545) and continue up to the outbreak of Civil War in 1642. The war caused devastating disruption to the Newcastle economy bringing industry and trade to a standstill (Nef 1932: 69, 287, 294; Middlebrook 1950: 77; Howell 1967: 131, 155, 274; Wrightson 1991: 42), as well as having profound implications for the process of probate, as the ecclesiastical courts were abolished by the Commonwealth and a Court of Civil Commissions set up in its place by 1653. Together, these factors were decisive in confining the research to the selected period. There was a hiatus in probate jurisdiction from the early 1640s until 1660, and few probate records survive locally. With all the ecclesiastical courts abolished, the Court of Civil Commissions was given sole jurisdiction over all probate matters nationally, resulting in chaos (Erickson 1993: 35), and creating a breakdown in the system of probate jurisdiction for 'some years before 1653, as many church courts were practically closed down from the outbreak of Civil War in 1642' (See Durham Probate Records; Index 1600-1660: General Introduction; Kitching 1976: 283-93, 346-56). Cressy describes 'the splintering of the English church in the 1640s and the confusions of the 1650s' (1999: 10). However, despite the war and the imposition of new probate laws during the Interregnum, which should have resulted in a cessation of the old system, probate records for over 137 individuals survive for Newcastle from the first decade of the Civil War. These records have nevertheless been excluded from this thesis, as the disruption to life Newcastle during this period argues for a separate study. Following the Restoration, statutory changes in the law altered probate administration, necessitating different approaches to the later records. Erickson saw the gap in probate records in the mid-17th century as 'a convenient means to compare earlier with later patterns' (2002: 3, 6, 27-29, 42), and this approach is adopted in this thesis.

The documents selected for this research are limited to the wills and probate inventories, with occasional references to accounts, and concern only those probate records that were made by residents of Newcastle upon Tyne. Although other probate records collections relating to the town of Newcastle survive in two collections - one at the Borthwick Institute at York University, and the other at the Public Record Office in London - those collections have not been included because this thesis focuses on recovering a picture of the material culture of the northern provincial capital of Newcastle. People who owned property in more than one diocese and were thus registered at York or Canterbury, and whose primary residence may have been elsewhere in the country, will inevitably present a unique material culture, reflecting the areas in which they chiefly lived: their houses and households will have been influenced by circumstances distinct to other regions of the country (Weatherill 1996). Another reason for excluding those collections concerns the volume of data. The records of almost 1,700 individuals survive for Newcastle in the period of this study, and testators had up to four documents in their names. The total number of documents is in the thousands and therefore the collection provides more material than can reasonably be included here. Wrightson noted the richness of England's archival resources, and that examining 'the accumulation of detailed information' in one parish alone 'can prove enormously time-consuming' (1991: xi), and although Erickson found that records from the northern provinces, including those of the Diocese of Durham, were not readily accessible (2002: 16), this is not true. However, the handling of these vast sources presents practical difficulties which have perhaps meant that the collections have been neglected. Most of the documents pertaining to Newcastle in this period have never been used in material culture studies. De Vries has noted the extraordinary richness of the probate inventory which can draw the investigator into an archival abyss from which some never return (1993: 99). The documents selected for this study indeed provide an extraordinarily comprehensive range of material with which to pursue the aims of the thesis. How representative these records are of the population as a whole is unknown. Newcastle was home to some 10,000 people by around 1600, practising at least 50 trades in the town (Brand 1789; Howell 1967). Erickson has suggested that anywhere from 5% up to 45% of a given population wrote wills in the early modern period (2002: 32). Although just 13 guilds and by-trades have been selected in this study, the overall importance of the survival of so many records, belonging to such a wide variety of people of varying social, occupational and economic backgrounds, endorses research on the material culture of this portion of the population.

2.2 Methodology

An Access database has been created for all the Durham Probate Records dated between 1543 and 1642 relating to Newcastle residents. File cards that recorded incomplete or insufficient details about individuals have been checked against original documents, ensuring that the database is as accurate as possible. Information has been compiled on testators names, status or occupation; the types and dates of documents that survive; and whether a document has been published. The records encompass a wide cross-section of the community living in Newcastle and its suburbs, and represent people as socially disparate as servants and labourers with small inheritances, to gentlemen and aldermen with small fortunes. From the main Access database a second database has been created that groups individuals according to the information on status or occupation. This information has been collated into 19 status or occupational groups from which the 13 occupations have been selected. A minimum of 17 individuals per named trade was judged to be the requirement for inclusion in the sample which is presented in Table 2.1.

Very little systematic analysis has been carried out on individual trades of the town in the period of the study, and none (as far as the researcher can determine) on the material culture of this particular section of society. There is much argument over the usefulness of trade designations in understanding social-economic aspects of early modern society: for example, Weatherill states that trade alone does not give enough information to reveal where any one individual might be placed in the social order, although in her study, she categorised trades following the designations created by Brodsky-Elliot, King and Armstrong (1996: 177, 208-212), but precisely where individual trades featured in the consumer hierarchy she uncovers is not examined (1996: 21, 99-102, 185). Occupational designations are central to this thesis. It is argued here that the approach of amalgamating all trades and crafts into a single category results in numerous generalisations, and the importance of retaining trade designations is demonstrated in the course of this study.

Overton's study of over 8,000 inventories from Kent and Cornwall analyses occupational groups rather than individual trades, including an amalgamation of crafts (2004: 136). He argues against the use of occupation in production and consumption studies, especially concerning status descriptions (such as esquire, which he notes cannot be mapped onto occupations). However, this argument is not applicable to tradesmen, and Overton acknowledges that occupational designations prove useful in revealing production activities, such as butchering or tailoring which are otherwise hard to identify (2004: 34). No difficulty has been encountered in identifying trade-related occupations from the Newcastle data.

Shammas acknowledges that occupation does deserve consideration (1990: 105, 110, 173). Her methodology involved the creation of wealth groups, but these did not account for named occupations. Individuals were placed in a low or medium-high wealth group based on median net valuations from inventories, and such an approach resulted in, for instance, shoemaking being described as a lower-paying craft, while she concluded that 'few in the low-wealth group engaged in home brewing' (1990: 34-6). Neither assertion stands up under a detailed examination when occupational groups are examined more closely. The problem is that a designated wealth group will alter in relation to occupation depending on which objects are included in the research design and what has been recorded on the inventory. Shammas's conclusions that trade designation had 'no impact on accumulation of any category of good' is challenged in Chapter 5 (1990: 180).

In her study of social status in association with median moveable wealth, Erickson did not include tradesmen and craftsmen because their numbers in inventories are small and their wealth too disparate (2002: 41-2). Overton confirmed this, as he found the spread of wealth in each status group to be too wide to enable rank to be determined simply on the basis of wealth (1996: 38). Shammas contends that the importance of occupation can be overestimated if the sample is not first controlled for wealth (1990: 173). Spufford, however, concluded that the inventory cannot be used as a guide to relative financial standing within a social group, but maintains that occupation still acts as a good guide to a 'mans scale of operations, his social pretensions, and quite explicitly, his borrowing power' (1990: 173-4).

Occupation analysed in association with material wealth is shown in this thesis to be central to understanding the place of individual tradesmen in the local socio-economic hierarchy. A more refined understanding of the material culture of the town becomes possible, and an important contemporary social framework preserved. Retaining the occupational designations stated on the probate records also allows the individual a voice in defining their identity. Given the marked absence of voices of ordinary people in the period, their contribution should not be ignored: individuals should be given their 'moment on stage' (Cressy 1999: 8).

Nevertheless, adoption of occupation in creating social categories does present some problems. Very occasionally in the Newcastle records the occupation claimed by a testator in a will does not concur with that given in the inventory by appraisers. This finding contradicts Spufford who found documents 'frequently' revealed a difference of opinion between what the will and inventory record in her Cambridgeshire sample (1990: 144), a finding incidentally echoed by Overton in his analysis of documents from Kent and Cornwall (2004: 34). Analysis of testators in the main database shows that there was just one man who called himself a yeoman but who was described as a labourer by his appraisers, and one other man who called himself as a merchant, but was referred to as a gentleman on his inventory. There were no conflicts regarding titles among the sample group of tradesmen, but a very few men were clearly not practising the trade to which they continued to claim an affiliation, as evinced by the presence or absence of property or objects on their inventories associated with a given occupation. These men differ markedly from a clear majority of tradesmen who did record items affiliated with their trade. Although we do not know whether an individual was an active member of their relevant guild, there is much to suggest that giving up membership to a guild or by-trade was unlikely, as has been shown by King in her study of the sociability of guilds evidenced by strong ties and responsibilities among members (2004: 59-65). Most men followed a long and often costly seven-year apprenticeship, and a social support network was provided by membership, with fines for changing guilds (Dendy 1921: 46; Langton 1974: 25). Brooks describes the 'culture of the guilds', where members shared the secrets of a mystery or science and were responsible for maintaining these and passing them on, and where the chief purpose of guilds was to 'promote love, unity and charity among the members' (1994: 74-7). A continued devotion to guild membership among almost all of the tradesmen in the study suggests acceptance of these principles, although it should be noted that not all the trades in the study had the status of a guild. Incidentally, those men working in by-trades show equal loyalty to the occupation declared on their wills.

That the majority of testators were practising a single trade, underlines the importance of occupation in this analysis, although the contents of wills and inventories do indicate secondary sources of income or interests. This could be reflected, for example, in the ownership of significant numbers of animals, or in the listing of brewing equipment. However, the ownership of one or two cows, of brewing and spinning equipment, or a rig or two of land, was common to many tradesmen and by this standard, most of the inventoried population was involved in by-employment to some degree, with production either for household consumption or for sale in a market. Spufford observed that an inventory alone is a seriously misleading document regarding occupation, because dual-occupation was evident when the work of all family members was considered (1990: 144). Wrightson, however, remarked that keeping a few head of stock did not necessarily constitute a dual economy but was more a small-scale means of supplementing of family income (1991: 223). Either way, supplementing a main source of income does not negate the validity of an official trade designation. The role of by-employment is examined extensively in Chapter 5.

Wrightson's study of occupational categories in Whickham indicates that industrial workers were 'engaged wholly in their stated occupations' (1991: 212, 219, 223-4). He found that a dual-economy together with 'life cycle-related occupational mobility' certainly existed in industrial Whickham, but where specialised industrial workers were concerned 'occupational complexity was very limited and occupational mobility slight' (1991: 222, 226, 230). This finding is confirmed by Weatherill, who noted that craftsmen probably concentrated on their trade in order to survive, as they needed a great deal of commercial know-how or technical dexterity, neither of which were readily combined with any other activity (1996: 104). Although Overton stated that 'the majority of individuals in early modern England had more than one occupation' (2004: 34), most of these activities would not affect the principal occupation of a tradesman and did not apparently move a man to record the practice of a second trade in an official document.

Overton recognised that appraisers recorded the occupation that they considered to be most important, if the individual was engaged in more than one activity (2004: 65-86), and this is the case for the tradesmen included in the sample. It is clear that by-employment needs to be accounted for, while the usefulness of occupational designations can be defended in the study of urban tradesmen. In all social research, some sort of categorisation becomes necessary in analysing populations, and here the testators preferred designation has been retained.

A second criterion that defined the sample for this thesis is the number of documents surviving for the middling and lower sorts. Records belonging to the wealthier sorts, notably merchants and gentry, do survive in larger numbers than those of the poorer trades, but this analysis concentrates on the middling and lower sorts. It should be noted, however, that all those represented in the sample had a sufficient level of personal wealth to warrant them writing a will and enough 'goods and chattels' to make compiling an inventory worthwhile. They inevitably represent the better-off in society, but this assertion is relative, as is shown in the course of the thesis. Although warnings come from Shammas of a 'bias towards the affluent' (1990: 20, 23), and from Erickson that the 'wealthy are over-represented' (2002: 41), the selected sample is representative of a wide range of ordinary tradesmen, representing both the rich and poor in relative terms. The absence of any documents belonging to truly poor people without sufficient means to warrant an administration at their deaths, cannot invalidate the study of those for whom records do survive, although one can still acknowledge that the poor made up an average of close to one-third or one-half of a towns population (Ellis 1984: 197); their presence is recognised within the records, where they are named as recipients of bequests. Equally, one might note that the wealthy were under no obligation to undertake probate administration and many are, no doubt, also invisible. Interestingly, in her study of Cambridgeshire villages, Spufford found a bias towards the poorer landless peasants who wrote more wills than the richer men (1978: 169). The related problem of the potential bias in the age profile in the sample between older, and therefore potentially wealthier testators (Chaytor 1980: 32), and the younger and possibly poorer testators, will be overcome as long as similar biases exist in all of the samples (Shammas 1990: 19). The extent of bias in the research sample remains unknown; however, some clue to the age at death of testators is explored in Chapter 3 in relation to patterns of bequests.

The documents of over 200 women also survive for Newcastle in this period, but these are not taken up in the analysis, as none records a trade designation, which is fundamental to the approach employed in this study. Analysing the social position of women requires a different approach to that used in the male sample. The occupation or status of a woman's husband is not usually recorded on the widows will or inventory and a woman's social status derived from that of her husband or father (Erickson 1993: 39). However, Erickson warns that one should not attempt to write a separate history for women, and that 'whether we ought to or not, one cannot' (2002: 18). This point is illustrated by the presence of women in this study as the widows, relatives or friends of the testators and these people feature particularly in Chapter 3 on inheritance. Ultimately, Erickson found it necessary to write specifically on women and property, as women had different ideas about 'moral desert, about who was in need and about what was important', and that they had 'distinct economic values' (2002: 244-250, 226, 235-236). Overton also concludes that the position of women implied different modes of production and consumption, different patterns of earning and expenditure, 'in short, different household economies' (2004: 5), considerations that all create a case for a separate study. A woman's distinct legal status in the period also argues for separate treatment in a material culture study relating to, for example, coverture (Cox and Cox 2000: 22; Erickson 1993: 24; 27-28).

In the final selection of the sample, trades where both the will and the inventory have been preserved in the greatest numbers have been given priority. The two documents provide quite different information about economic standing and other aspects of individual's lives that are not always apparent when the documents are examined separately: a more balanced picture can be recovered when they are considered together (Spufford 1984: 41, 1990: 142 -153; Shammas 1990: 26). The records are best treated as two parts of a single legal process: wills provide information about beneficiaries and bequests, including heirlooms, and about real estate, which is excluded from inventories (Shammas 1990: 26; Spufford 1990: 142; Erickson 1993: 23 - 4; Overton 2004: 138). The inventory simply itemises the material wealth of an individual, while a social context for the analysis of objects is provided by accounting for information given by testators in their wills. This is fundamental to the study of material culture. Orlin observes that inventories should be read in tandem with wills, as these 'reveal early modern habits of material thought' (2002: 76).

One other group of documents mainly excluded from the study comprises those in which no status or occupation is recorded. A very small number of these records have been incorporated in the analysis where the inventory is so extensive as to provide clear evidence of the practice of a recognised trade, notably by the inclusion of tools and stocks. In the sample about 5% of records could not be used in this study owing to the absence of such information.

Analysis of the contents of the documents has been time-consuming and posed a number of difficulties, as the records are written on pieces of parchment or on vellum strips in Tudor and Stuart hand script. Some of the documents are large awkward squares of more than half a metre, and some are narrow strips over two metres in length. A number of the earlier documents contain passages in Latin that have required translation. The handwriting varies widely in legibility and a single letter may be formed in several different ways. The writing is often extremely small, sometimes requiring magnification, and there is no standardisation in spelling in this period (Munby 2002). Fading and mould have affected many of the documents, and ultra-violet illumination has been necessary to decipher the text. The best method of analysing the documents, though very time consuming, is to transcribe them *in toto*, which enables a much greater understanding of the unique data preserved in each folio (Orlin 2002: 76).

Despite the difficulties, there are, nevertheless, clear patterns in both the layout and overall content of these records. This analysis used specifically designed questionnaires to collect information relevant to specific lines of enquiry. Contrary to Spufford's assertion that wills are not readily broken down and do not lend themselves to computer analysis (1984: 37), this has not been found to be the case. Information from wills relating to personal details, the type and extent of bequests, the numbers and categories of beneficiaries, and details on properties and their location have been collated, together with personal instructions given by testators explaining and clarifying their priorities. The inventories have simply been transcribed verbatim. The resulting forms have enabled consistent and systematic analysis of these complex and relatively inaccessible sources. A representative sample of wills and inventories that have been fully transcribed appears in Appendix 1.

2.3 Probate jurisdiction: Law, custom and practice

Understanding probate jurisdiction is vital to any attempt at analysis of the documents. Failure to understand the legal and social context in which these records were created, could lead to misleading conclusions. Wills and their accompanying probate inventories are not a straightforward record of the goods and chattels: what is included in the documents is the residue of a legal and customary process, which incidentally forms a very detailed record of certain categories of personal property, at a specific time and in a specific place. The question of why and by whom these documents were created, what they included and, equally importantly, what they excluded must be of primary concern to the researcher.

From a legal perspective probate jurisdiction is very complex, as a glance at the lengthy works on Roman

Canon Law by Burn and Helmholz will testify (Burn 1775; Helmholz 1990). Holdsworth's *History of English Law* consists of 17 volumes; the first 12 relate to the early modern period and half of the contents of these volumes bear on probate (Cox and Cox 2000: 37). Therefore, in approaching these documentary sources several problems should be borne in mind. The first is that the history of probate jurisdiction has been too little studied for a complete picture of its operation to have emerged (Helmholz, 1990: 79). Secondly, although a uniform national pattern of church courts existed in theory, it did not operate in practice, mainly because of the differences in the ways in which bishops and archdeacons shared their work, with the result that no single uniform pattern of church administration existed throughout the 26 dioceses (Arkell 2000: 4, 9). The complexity of the system is summed up by Erickson, who notes that common law, equity, manorial law and ecclesiastical law operated jointly to produce a workable legal system, but that the result was confusing and systems overlapped (2002: 5, 23-4, 32-44).

A discussion of precisely how the Diocese of Durham administered probate jurisdiction over the town of Newcastle upon Tyne in the 16th and 17th centuries is not critical to interpretation of the documents for this material culture study, but a general background of the processes involved in probate law helps to explain how the documents were made and what motivated testators to involve themselves in these legal proceedings. Probate jurisdiction had been the responsibility of the church courts from the medieval period, and the basic framework behind probate law was contained in parliamentary Acts that applied throughout the 16th and early 17th centuries (Erickson 1993: 5-6). The system dates from early Acts of Parliament in 1357 and again in 1415, which had failed to curb the fees that the ecclesiastical courts were charging individuals for proving wills. The Act of 1529, which was primarily set up to prevent the ecclesiastical courts from overcharging for probate fees, was introduced by Henry VIIIs Reformation Parliament. The Act formalized the process of probate administration that may have been established practice for centuries. It confirmed who should administer the estate or make the inventory, and how it was to be made. An estate of any value could be administered, and the Act 'distinguished only in matters of charges' (Cox and Cox 2000: 25, 26). The Act had four principal obligations taken from the *Book of Common Prayer* (1552); the first was 'payment of their debts', the second the 'necessary & convenient finding of their wives', the third, 'the virtuous upbringing & Advancement of their children to marriage', and lastly, that of 'Charitable Deeds ... for the Health of their Souls' (Cox and Cox 2000: 24). All these criteria are reflected in the form and content of the wills and inventories of the Newcastle testators.

In 1530, a fee for probate, based on the value of the deceased's personal estate, was established and applied up to the 1640s. Personal estates worth 5li or less were exempt from any charges, apart from a fee of 6d to the registrar for copying the will, and another 6d when letters of administration were required because of intestacy. For goods valued between 5li and 40li the charge was 3s 6d, and for personal estates worth over 40li the fee was 5s. These figures represent the maximum; some courts charged less. Parliament passed a number of Acts from 1540 onwards that encouraged landowners to use written wills to bequeath their property, promoting more uniform inheritance practices that gave greater discretion to testators throughout the country (Arkell 2000: 8, 12). We see the Tudor government attempting, on the one hand, to curb the power of the clergy and, on the other, to encourage a more uniform process of the administration of probate throughout the country at a price the testator could (theoretically) afford.

The question is how testators in Newcastle responded to these directives from the government. According to Cox and Cox, local custom played a vital role in the disposal of personal property. These authors refer to what they call 'The ancient Germanic method' of transmitting property by intestate succession (Cox and Cox 2000: 19, 28). The authors maintain that intestate succession died out in the south, while in the north it remained into the early modern period as the dominant method of transmitting personal property. This custom required the man, even when he made a will, to leave one-third of his moveable property divided equally among his children, and another third to his widow. However, Cox and Cox provide no references concerning the alleged customs of northern England in this period. Contrary to their assertions, Newcastle residents wrote thousands of wills and other probate documents in the early modern period. Cox and Cox also did not mention the last third or dead part, which Erickson noted could be devised by the testator (2002: 28). According to ecclesiastical law of the period, where the testator died intestate, two-thirds of the moveables were given to the children and one-third to the widow. As the probate records of the Diocese of Durham are among the most extensive in the country, the survival of such extensive records, including those pertaining to residents of early modern Newcastle, clearly suggests that northern residents were making decisions to write wills, and administrators were following probate procedures where there was, in fact, no legal compulsion to do so. Spufford noted that anyone wanting to dispose of their estate by local custom was able to do so (1990: 142), but the law did not allow 'complete freedom' (Wrightson 1991: 283). It would appear that a basic procedure for probate administration was provided for in the law and, apparently, widely accepted. However, there was at the same time, clearly, plenty of scope for the wishes of the individual.

Examination of the processes involved with administering an estate suggests why people adhered to both a customary and legal procedure. The probate procedure began when the executor(s) and the witnesses of the will swore an oath in the Consistory Court that the will in question was the testators last. Permission was granted to these individuals to administer the deceased person's estate, and the agreement was legally confirmed by an entry of the names and occupation or status of those involved in the Probate Act Books of the relevant court. The administrators of the estate were then also required to strengthen their oath to carry out the wishes of the testator by entering into a bond for twice the value, approximately, of the deceased person's estate. They would guarantee to complete the administration of the estate within a certain period (about a year) during which time they were to make an inventory of the deceased person's goods and credits, and to account for the expenses incurred in carrying out the administration. As noted, there was no legal compulsion to adhere to the probate laws. Therefore, in whose interest was it for a written testament to be made? Cox and Cox note that probate did not operate in isolation but 'was embedded in a web of principles concerning duties, rights and obligations' (Arkell 2000: 15). According to Wrightson, the need to provide for dependents by an orderly transmission of property was of paramount importance in this most drastic of transitions (1991: 281). These observations are significant and reflect the tone of the Act of 1529 and the obligations outlined in the *Book of Common Prayer*.

The repayment of debt appears to be among the most critical incentive for the custom of writing wills and making inventories. Orlin points out that the 'interest of the state in this process of probate was that personal goods were commodities that could be held against debts' (2002: 51), and that debts were a potential source of delay in winding up the probate procedure. Debts owed to the deceased should not have been recorded since they were not assets, nor were debts owed by the deceased to be administrated, as these were liabilities (Cox 2000: 31; Overton 2004: 138). Nevertheless, many Newcastle wills and inventories do list both debts and credits, a point discussed below regarding the content of the documents. If the will was contested, the administrator had to present a detailed account of all the debts and legacies to a civil court, and show that they had all been paid up. This Civil Court was not the same as the Consistory Court, which was responsible for the completion of the probate. The legal complications arising from a disputed will would adversely affect all parties awaiting settlement. The executor(s) and administrators would therefore have very important reasons to ensure that a will was carried out as the testator had wished, and to ensure that a competent inventory was taken for all the goods and chattels belonging to the deceased.

Cox and Cox suggest that, ultimately, 'the threat to their own pocket' was the motivating factor for the administrators in the whole process, noting that if no inventory was taken, the common law courts assumed that the estate of the deceased covered all the debts and legacies and obliged the personal representatives to make up for any shortfall (Cox and Cox 2000: 28). The high proportion of tradesmen appraised suggests that it was self-interest rather than the law that moved personal representatives to take and to exhibit inventories (Cox and Cox 2000: 28). This assessment of the role of debt repayment, placed in the context of the thriving mercantile town of Newcastle, helps to explain why so many documents recording debt and credit survive in the Durham Probate records.

The Church was another highly influential force in the creation of these documents. Probate jurisdiction remained its prerogative, despite the government's determination to curtail its power and profits by the early 16th century. The non-payment of debt was a serious spiritual as well as secular concern, deeply feared by both the Church and the individual Christian. What was known as *Ars Moriendi,* or the art of dying well, was of central importance to this society (Duffy 1992: 315 - 16; Cressy 1999: 389). It was believed, even after the Protestant Reformation, that unpaid debts would imperil the soul, and although there were differences in emphasis among Catholic and Protestant writers in making preparations for death, 'what such writers shared was more important than the issues which divided them' (Houlbrooke 2000: 60). The belief that being out of charity or in conflict might ultimately place the soul in jeopardy was a notion that survived well into the 17th century (Brooks 1994: 76-7). In the *Book of Common Prayer* from 1552, the service for the Visitation of the Sick required the clergy to remind the dying it was the first duty of the Christian to make a will and pay their debts. Wrightson emphasised the spiritual significance of death in his study of Whickham, remarking that the wills imply that testators died calmly and devoutly, in accordance with the contemporary ideal of a good death, and that part of that comportment was the making of a settlement with God as well as man concerning material, emotional and spiritual obligations (1991: 291). The Church teachings and literature of the period clearly had a strong influence in the creation of so many documents. Books, tracts and sermons on preparation for death poured from the presses between the late 15th and early 18th centuries (Cressy 1999: 390; Houlbrooke 2000: 59).

On a more practical level, Arkell confirms that the Church was also 'eager to prevent corrosive arguments among families and neighbours over the division of deceased people's property and the non-payment of their debts and so usually sought to discourage intestacy' (Arkell 2000:7). Quarrels that could affect the stability and order of the neighbourhoods were clearly to be avoided. Cressy also concurs, noting that the Church sought to preserve harmony and avoid sharp polarization, and that the business of the household was also the business of the wider community (Cressy 1999: 476, 482). Many people were involved directly in the process of probate administration, including the testator, the beneficiaries, the executor(s), legatees, supervisors, administrators, assessors and witnesses. Those who were concerned with the process indirectly included anyone who owed money to, or was owed money by, the testator, as well as those who arranged the funeral rituals and the burial. The numerous people involved with carrying out a very public event suggests that it was important to administer probate procedures with care and honesty, and a written record would surely be a means to avoid unnecessary arguments.

Probate law and local custom; the influence of Church teachings concerning indebtedness in the light of consequences for the soul; and, certainly, pressure from relatives, friends and creditors, must have motivated individuals to create written records. Erickson suggests motives included 'convention, affection, guilt, need and duty' (2002: 32). It is safe to assume that the resulting wills and inventories are a very reliable indicator of the material wealth of individuals in the period, and substantiate the value of probate documents in historical studies. Reliability, however, does not equate to actual contents recorded: questions remain as to what the documents actually included and what exactly was omitted.

2.4 Wills and inventories: Contents and omissions

In spite of repeated assertions by modern writers concerning what probate records, particularly inventories, included or did not include (remarks often based on Burn's *Ecclesiastical Law* 1763), the contents continue to defy categorisation (Shammas 1990: 26; Spufford 1990: 146 – 9; Weatherill 1996: 2-3, 106; Cox and Cox 2000: 29; Erickson 1993: 4, 33; Overton 2004: 87). Erickson notes that the prescriptive evidence of the law is still taken largely as reflective of practice (2002: 4). Newcastle wills contain information about bequests of property including freehold, copyhold and leasehold lands, heirlooms, lists of a widows original dowry, objects of the trades, cash, gold, silver objects and jewellery, household objects, animals, crops, provisions, and even ships. They also reveal debts both owed by and owing to the testator, and much else besides. Inventories list household objects, referred to as the goods and chattels, objects of the trades, provisions and crops, animals, leased properties, debts and credits and various expenses such medicines, tuition fees, wages and funeral costs. There do not appear to have been hard-and-fast rules about what could be included on Newcastle documents, and any attempt to construct restricted categories is inevitably contradicted. What can be confirmed is that objects included in the documents all had some value in the settlement of the estate, with two exceptions: these were tokens, usually old coins given to those deserving special recognition, often in lieu of a share of the inheritance, and bequests to the poor.

Whatever objects were actually recorded on the wills and inventories, these were the residue of a process that eliminated possessions that had either been given away during the testator's life, or entailed away by legal contract, and also those without a useful market value. However, old, second best, worn, broken and torn items were all included in the records, contrary to Erickson's finding that cheap ubiquitous items (for example, trenchers or spoons) do not appear in inventories (2002: 33-4). Spufford also contends that low-value goods were left out, or appeared less often as articles became commoner and cheaper, citing the absence of chapbooks which, she says, had stood no chance of being listed (1990: 146, 149-150). Such findings are contradicted by the Newcastle records which listed many items worth just a penny or in the case of trenchers and spoons several for a penny, and although chapbooks were never named as such, small printed books were included. The rule seems to be that individual choice, along with financial considerations, dictated what was listed.

In the case of real property wills and inventories provide only a partial accounting of what was once owned or rented by a testator, and inventories include only leasehold land (Spufford 1990: 142, Erickson 1993: 23-7). More than half of all Newcastle testators specifically bequeath property. The most obvious omissions are lands and properties that were entailed away by strict settlement in separate legal contracts, and were therefore not at the disposal of the testator. This situation applied chiefly to those with substantial landed inheritances and does not feature in the documents of the Newcastle tradesmen. Where the wills and inventories record property, information is given on location and types of structures, whether a property was owned or rented, and who occupied the premises. In this thesis, the distinction between properties that were owned and those that were leased has not been retained, as this information was not consistently specified, and whether a property was owned or leased is not actually relevant to this enquiry. By the 16th century, according to Cox and Cox, practice regarding the transmission of property followed the Statute of Wills and subsequent legislation because the law regarded copyhold land in the same way as freehold and thus deemed it covered by the same rules of transmission (2000: 22). Discussion in Burn's *Ecclesiastical Law* on property indicated that the law attached far more importance to seissin, that is occupation, than to claims of ownership, and leases for life were regarded as a form of real estate, so transmission at death followed the same rules as those for freehold land (Cox and Cox 2000: 31, 44). Goose and Evans support these findings as 'in some parts of the country copyhold land could be freely devised by will, and freehold land was readily devisable by will (2000: 66). Therefore, all property listed in the wills and inventories, whether leased or owned, has been analysed together without legal distinction.

Apart from the problems associated with the omission of goods or real property, there is the problem of omission of debts, which could wipe out what has been accounted for on an inventory, presenting difficulties in understanding net wealth. This key problem is discussed by Spufford, who warns that 'one is moving on quicksand' to establish net wealth in any individual's estate, especially because of the absence of real property and indebtedness (1990: 151, 153, 173). Shammas suggests that estimates of realty holdings and debts would be necessary to calculate per capita wealth (1990: 19). Spufford advocates the use of accounts to redress the problems associated with the omission of debt, although relatively few of these survive for Newcastle (1990: 153-4). However, she has found that in using accounts figures moved both up and down relative to the inventoried wealth and that debt was likely to be to scale in relation to borrowing power (1990: 161, 166). She also notes that credit underpinned the whole of rural society in the early modern period (Spufford 1990: 173), a situation that certainly pertained to Newcastle tradesmen according to the extensive credit network evident from the documents. Overall, the fact that people lived with debt and that a credit network was widely exploited, does not negate the records of goods and chattels that individuals accumulated over their lifetime. The methodology employed in this study largely circumvents the problems of debt and the omission of property valuations, as in this analysis, total valuations have not been used, as these do not reflect real net wealth. Instead, objects that are common to most inventories have been selected to provide comparative data on specific categories of material wealth.

What was recorded in the documents is, *de facto*, an accurate picture of material wealth of testators, despite the ever-changing situation *vis-à-vis* debts and credits over the life cycle stages, or whether what was recorded at the death of a testator was acquired by credit or paid for in cash, inherited from family or borrowed from a friend. According to Erickson's extensive study, only about one-quarter of all accounts ended in debt (2002: 34, 38). When the debts included in inventories from the Newcastle sample are deducted from the total valuations given, it is evident that just 10% of the testators in this sample actually died in debt.

Another important aspect in analysing the contents of inventories is deciding whether the valuations given are honest and reflective of prices obtained on the second-hand market, should the goods be sold to settle the estate. The Act of 1529 does not mention the valuation of goods, but it seemed to have been understood by the community that those who competently understand the value of the deceased's goods should value them (Arkell 2000: 29). Cox and Cox state that the evidence is overwhelming that the inventories were usually made carefully and the goods valued appropriately (2000: 30), a view supported by Overton and others, who found that inventory prices for commodities were an accurate reflection of sale prices (2000: 125, 141). Creditors, legatees, and others awaiting settlement of an estate would have known the market prices, and tradesmen would have been knowledgeable about prices within their trade. The witnesses or appraisers of Newcastle wills and inventories were very often fellow-tradesmen or men of higher rank and wealth than the testator. Occasionally, a family member was included, perhaps to ensure an honest assessment. Those with large estates were as carefully appraised as those of very little worth. Erickson noted a case of a 'poore mayde' whose 'meagre estate' of £1 was appraised by four men, and such cases are also found in the Newcastle documents, particularly those of the poor keelmen (2002: 33).

In contrast to these findings, Orlin takes a very pessimistic view, highlighting inaccuracies in valuation, and argues against the credibility of those involved from evidence in cases which can be found in court records, such as where a orphaned child is defrauded of property, or where appraisers have failed to value items correctly or have concealed items (2002: 54-6). To suggest that the percentage of the population who ended up in court was representative of the population as a whole cannot be supported, as most people were clearly not involved in lawsuits. In addition, the consistency of valuations given in Newcastle inventories for hundreds of items that can reasonably be compared, such as the prices of cows, of linen sheets, or of specific wares such as frying pans or salt-cellars covering ten decades and involving thousands of people, substantiates the finding that the inventory evidence can be taken to be reliable. Erickson finds it 'difficult to think that large numbers of accountants either tried or succeeded in falsification' (2002: 36-7). Brooks noted that guilds punished dishonesty, and this observation has clear implications for tradesmen involved in witnessing wills and assisting in the appraisal of inventories (1994: 77).

Orlin continues her assault on the analysis of probate inventories for social and economic research by revealing 'fictions', which can be challenged by facts, demonstrating not just the weakness in her own understanding of the potential of the records but also in her own 'sweeping claims' (2002: 52). She informs us that most researchers do acknowledge limitations and biases, but this is apparently sometimes 'disingenuous' as (the researcher) is 'understandably eager not to invalidate their own findings' (2002: 79). As has been shown above, to argue from the exception does not invalidate a general rule, as in the case, for example, of fraudulent behaviour by some testators and appraisers, compared with a clear majority of examples where procedures were followed correctly and no one defrauded.

A second example of both bias and limitations in Orlin's own arguments can be shown in her concern regarding consumption patterns and quantitative analysis of household spaces and household goods. In the study of household spaces, for example, she identifies a problem in studying the number of rooms in houses from inventories, as those areas of a house that were occupied by third parties will not be included, because a testator will have no items in them useful to the appraisers and therefore the room(s) are not mentioned (2002: 56). The problem with this criticism is that a researcher of household space will not necessarily be interested in areas of a structure *not* used by the testator and the family. The study of domestic space does not necessarily entail reconstruction of house plans, which cannot be undertaken with probate records alone (Overton 2004: 122). In this study, the wills provide very useful information about the division of houses, demonstrating multiple occupancy with shared access to different parts of a structure, particularly in poorer neighbourhoods. In such cases the wills tend to specify rooms adjoining the testators own dwelling house, often with named occupants and leased for a given number of years. Equally, many wills give no evidence that a family's dwelling house was shared with people outside the household. Where information on rooms is provided in

Newcastle documents, there is great consistency throughout the period.

In all, Orlin suggests ten reasons why a given room may not appear on an inventory including, for example, rooms that might be empty or unused. In Newcastle this situation was most unlikely considering the number of people in an average household (husband and wife, several children, servants and, perhaps, apprentices) and given the average size of a house (Wrigley and Schofield 1989; Houlbrooke 1995: 20, 153; Weatherill 1996: 94; Overton 2004: 121–122), and the fact that totally empty unused spaces are uncommon in any domestic situation. She cites the possible absence from an inventory of unfurnished space, such as a corridor - but a corridor is not a room, it is a passageway, and the necessity of a means of access to a property and rooms can be assumed. In fact, there *are* rare examples of entrance ways containing objects among the Newcastle documents. She suggests that a woman who brought goods to her marriage could have had exclusive rights to a room entirely devoid of any other objects apart from her own belongings - a situation unlikely and impractical in the case of years of marriage, with her children and husband and servants all living in the family dwelling. Given the law of coverture, discussed above, the right to such a 'designated space' devoid of anything belonging to the household seems remote in the extreme (Orlin 2002: 59). Orlin's suggestion of the existence of a room entirely furnished with heirlooms is equally implausible in a tradesman's home, and such a situation has not been uncovered in the hundreds of inventories examined for this study, whereas the heirlooms mentioned in inventories are found in rooms cluttered with other objects, especially halls, chambers and kitchens (2002: 59 - 60). Her suggestion that rooms were not enumerated because 'scattered goods' could be brought into a single room ignores the fact that the deceased's family was usually still living and working in the family home. It is also manifestly implausible to suggest that objects were expressly moved about for appraisers, for example, that all the pewter should be taken out of a buttery (where most was, apparently, kept) and placed in another room, or that cookery items should be dismantled and 'gathered' it into a pile somewhere, let alone that larger objects such as beds or pressers should be shifted from one room to another (Orlin 2002: 60). The remarkable consistency in the compilation process of inventories argues against this sort of behaviour.

In the same vein, regarding the accounting of household goods, Orlin continues to focus on what might possibly be missing from a will or omitted from an inventory, in an endeavour to 'register their silences' (2002: 63-73, 76). However, her wearisome list of problems encountered in interpreting probate documents can be confuted by *facts* that both contradict and overcome her *fictions*. Wrightson describes such problems with inventories as patchiness of survival, inconsistency of form, casual and deliberate omissions, unreliable valuations and the variation that must be accounted for in life cycle stages (1991: 89). Nevertheless, this doyen of northern historians, in chorus with many writers, makes the simple point that these records, both wills and especially inventories, which have been (and continue to be) a source of controversy in historical analysis, must be used with discretion (Thirsk 1967; Corfield and Priestley 1982; Spufford 1990; Shammas 1990; Wrightson 1991; Weatherill 1996; Arkell 2000; Colls and Lancaster 2001: x; Erickson 1993; Overton 2004). Wrightson emphasizes that probate records remain an invaluable guide providing one of the few opportunities open to the historian to reconstruct the material culture of the age (1991: 90). The inevitability of lacunae in any body of evidence certainly does not invalidate the study of what is recorded. Cressy reminds us that 'The records are filled with exceptional cases' but 'Each act of deviance underscores the norm' (1999: 12), a point also made by Chaytor that the 'abnormal' may 'most illuminate' the norm (1980: 51).

The Durham probate records are a uniquely important source of evidence for the study of material culture. Many criticisms of the documents on which this thesis is based have been overstated. It is clear that the evidence, as it has survived and despite its shortcomings, can provide an unrivalled opportunity to reconstruct a picture of the material lives of tradesmen in Newcastle in the early modern period. That is the aim of the forthcoming chapters.

CHAPTER 3 - People

3.1 Introduction

The great ritual markers in the life cycle of people in the early modern period were birth, marriage and death (Cressy 1999). These three phases encompassed both spiritual and practical dimensions that could profoundly alter family structure and material life. This chapter explores the significance of the final ritual, that of death, by examining how individuals redistributed their accumulated 'lands, goods and chattels', and precisely what the actions of the dying meant to the material lives of the survivors. The aim is to analyse patterns of bequests that reveal a complex web of personal relationships, obligations, and demands (Cressy 1986: 67; Issa 1986; Wrightson 1991: 287-8), as well as personal intentions (Erickson 1993: 33), embodied in the material culture record of Newcastle tradesmen.

In examining material culture through the process of inheritance, questions are asked such as who in this early modern northern society received bequests and who gained most? Was the 'remote' north 'culturally distinct' from other regions (Issa 1986: 9)? Was primogeniture the norm in urban northern England and how important are family constitution and wider kinship ties to patterns of bequests? Did the age of a testator at death affect decisions, and how was this linked to the family life cycle in the redistribution of the estate? Were factors such as occupation and wealth influencing outcomes for benefactors? In pursuing these lines of enquiry, the material evidence in the wills is placed within the context of the instructions formulated by the testators concerning their estates.

Cressy remarks on the 'anecdotal nature' of much evidence on kinship which is 'not susceptible to quantification' (1986: 44), a view echoed by Spufford who has reservations about the suitability of these data for statistical analysis (1984: 37). This analysis demonstrates that wills, in fact, readily lend themselves to such investigative techniques. Selected categories of objects from the wills of some 296 tradesmen, who recorded bequests to over 2,500 people, are analysed in detail. The selected items include real property (houses, shops, mills and lands), personal property (representing household and work-related objects), money, clothes and animals. Bequests to the poor are also examined.

In terms of how representative the sample of testators is in relation to the population, it should be noted that the demography of Newcastle in the early modern period cannot be constructed from the probate evidence alone. It can be assumed, however, that the constitution of the families of testators will not have any particular biases, and none has been recognised in the analysis (Wrightson 1984: 326; Erickson 1993: 63). The age at death of testators also cannot be recovered. In theory, parish records could be consulted, as they would probably record this information, and inserting information from wills into the framework of parish records to discover the age of individuals has been successful in other studies (Howell 1978: 139). However, in this study parish records have not been consulted, principally because common surnames were widespread throughout the Tyneside region and recognisable kinship linkage cannot be assumed (Chaytor 1980: 33; Wrightson 1991: 334). Additionally, the presence at any one time of several people with the same forename makes distinctions between individuals questionable, creating an unreliable guide to the transmission of property (Dyer 1984: 305).

An indication of the age of death of a testator can, nevertheless, be estimated from wills by accounting for minor children, for those who have reached the age of majority, and for grandchildren, or (in a few cases) where parents are still living. The lack of any recorded heirs, however, is more difficult to interpret. Further clues about the structure of families can be recovered when, for example, a child is named as the eldest or youngest, or where brothers, uncles, sisters and parents and so on are specifically mentioned. Information on the precise age of an individual is not, ultimately, of immediate significance to patterns of bequests, as the greater concern here is the life cycle stage, together with the size and make-up of families – and the range of kin, which varies with one's stage in the life cycle (Cressy 1986: 58). Such information on family constitution is vital to any analysis of inheritance patterns. The life cycle stages are central to understanding priorities of both testators and beneficiaries concerning the distribution and nature of bequests. Wrightson's study of Whickham has shown that the freedom to divide an inheritance was largely a question of the life cycle stage, relating above all to the need to provide for dependants by an orderly transmission of the property upon which their future well-being would depend (1991: 281). For example, he has found that, if a testator dies in the midst of the family life cycle, the first obligation is to wives and children, while concern is also shown in small legacies given to others beyond the nuclear family such as brothers, sisters, nieces and nephews, and occasionally to more distant kin, servants and neighbours (1991: 284-5). However, if a testator is unmarried, widowed or youthful, bequests tend to be given to siblings and parents, as well as to nephews and nieces (Wrightson 1991: 284-5). In a study of County Durham, Issa found similar obligations to wives and children in the early stages of the life cycle, whereas at later periods of a testator's life obligations broadened to include other members of the nuclear family, with an apparent implicit understanding 'that the integrity of the nuclear family should be maintained' (1986: 470-2). Research elsewhere in the country has confirmed similar patterns (Cressy 1986; Spufford 2000; Erickson 1993). According to Howell a fundamental principle was that 'everyone had a claim to support' (1978: 113). How far Newcastle families fitted into such patterns is examined in the course of this chapter.

Other issues affecting inheritance patterns, besides those relating to life cycle stages, such as occupation and wealth, must also be considered. Wrightson notes that wage earning is concentrated within particular phases of the life cycle (1991: 272), implying high and low periods in working lives, and Spufford points out that, if the peak of an individual's career is reached at the end of the life cycle, the wills and inventories will be biased towards a picture of an older established population (1984: 49). However, Issa states that the life cycle and not wealth was the 'crucial factor determining patterns' of bequests (1986: 469–70). It is argued here that both occupational fluctuations and life cycle stage would doubtless have affected the size and nature of an estate. A person who died young, before or shortly after marriage, might not have accumulated as large an estate as someone dying in the prime of their working life. Someone dying in old age might already have given away much of what they once owned in anticipation of requiring little in the way of assets if younger family members were expected to look after that individual in his final stages of life (Chaytor 1980: 32).

What was eventually recorded on a will reflected an ever-changing situation as years passed and circumstances were altered. Issa noted that retirement was in fact a gradual process (1986: 468). Additionally, it cannot be known with any certainty whether approaching death at any age, would have modified a person's behaviour, priorities or financial situation and, consequently the patterns recorded in the documents (or even the entire will). Nor do we know whether the testators died at a time when they were enjoying their greatest prosperity, or if they had fallen on relatively harder times, or when these phases might have occurred over a lifetime. While acknowledging that stages in a working life would be reflected in relative gain or loss, we may wonder whether such a changing material situation would have altered the personal priorities of an individual.

Another area of interest in this study is whether middling tradesmen have any practises peculiar to their trade regarding inheritance. Goose and Evans found that in 17th century London, tradesmen tended towards primogeniture in the disposal of their real estate, but shared money and goods equitably between heirs (2000: 68-9), a practice promoted among the English gentry in the 16th century, one which caused controversy because of the harsh consequences to younger sons (Cooper 1978: 197; Thirsk 1978: 183). The question of whether such a trend is apparent among Newcastle's tradesmen in the late 16th and early 17th centuries is pursued.

Howell argues that class - which can be taken to mean sorts - was not a decisive factor in inheritance practices, whereas age and responsibilities were (1978: 140). Her work on Midland peasants did not, however, attempt to distinguish between the attitudes of the labourers, husbandmen or yeomen she studied, whereas in this analysis, the decisions of individual trades are considered. Spufford felt that both social and economic status must be studied to gain understanding of patterns of inheritance (1978: 156). Erickson states that, historically, the most important component of wealth was inheritance (2002: 3); thus, trade designations, it is proposed here, are of particular relevance. Nevertheless, Wrightson found wealth was less significant than demography and the family cycle (1984: 327), and Issa believes obligations were independent of considerations of wealth (1986: 475). Throughout this chapter all these social considerations are examined in relation to the distribution of selected bequests manifested in the material culture record.

3.2 Methodology

A short note on methodology is given here for clarification. In calculating the number of beneficiaries in the sample, each person named on a will has been counted separately as an individual, even when inheriting jointly with another person, as the exact nature and value of the inheritance is unknown. For example, two daughters jointly inheriting the family home may each have received a more valuable inheritance overall than a son who inherited a family home in his own right. Bequests to the poor are treated as one entry, although many people may have received the assistance. Where there are non-specific references to children, two entries have been added, one male and one female.

Sample sizes vary considerably for some types of bequests. Percentage figures below 5% cannot be considered significant, as these represent very small numbers of beneficiaries. However, such figures have been included as they provide a useful guide to understanding which social groups were most likely to be included in the inheritance process.

Lastly, in terms of identifying social groups, wills usually specify the relationship of the beneficiary to the testator, and although Cressy warns that the language of kinship in this period is 'limited and loose' (1986: 65-6), Newcastle testators are very accurate in descriptions of kin, differentiating, for example, between a brother or a brother-in law, and mentioning whether a child is the son or daughter of another sibling, etc. Only the category of 'friends' presents some difficulty in this respect. Wrightson identifies this group as 'the range of effective kin' that included those households linked by close ties of 'consanguinity and affinity and geographical proximity' (1991: 285). In this analysis, men, women and children who do not share the testator's family name and for whom no other clues are provided regarding their affiliation with the testator, are assumed to be friends.

3.3 Bequests of real property

Amongst the bequests in Newcastle wills are details concerning who in this society inherited real property. Those properties included in the analysis are actually named as such, or are referred to as 'lands and leases'. Real property is bequeathed in an average of 72% of the wills, a high figure relative to other regions (Erickson 1993: 66-7). The list of overall beneficiaries of all categories of property shown in Table 3.1 indicates who was first in line, and includes all houses, shops, mills and lands. Table 3.2 lists the beneficiaries of the testator's principal residence or 'dwelling house', where he lived with his wife and family (if he had one). This property contained the 'goods and chattels' listed in the accompanying inventory, where one survives. Tables 3.3 and 3.4 list the beneficiaries of shops and mills, including those that can be linked to the principal residence through the inventory. Incidentally, leased lands do appear on inventories, contrary to Erickson's finding (2002: 64).

Table 3.1 shows that some 842 properties, owned and leased by the 13 trades, are consistently bequeathed to 18 social categories, which can be divided into four groups: first, the nuclear family; second, close relatives including grandchildren, brothers, sisters, nephews and nieces; third, other relatives, including parents (although fathers were very rarely mentioned), sons and daughters-in-law, brothers and sisters-in-law and cousins. The fourth group includes non-relatives, including male and female friends and their children, executors and supervisors. The percentage of properties bequeathed decreases markedly for the latter three groups, but there is no change in the social groups who inherit property over the 100-year period: on average, wives inherit 33% of the combined family properties; sons receive 34%; while daughters inherit just less than half the number of those given to their brothers and mothers. Overall, the nuclear family receive over 80% of the testator's combined properties, leaving almost 20% of family property in the hands of a wide variety of other people. The testator's brothers and sisters, followed by grandchildren (especially grandsons), are given priority over more distant relatives; but nieces and nephews feature occasionally as principal heirs. A bias towards males is evident. However, anomalies do occur, which might be explained in terms of the age of the testator, but also possibly in association with the nature of a testator's trade. For example, in the case of mariners' families, sons receive the same percentage of property as sisters. A close examination of the wills shows that half the mariners have no children, suggesting the deceased may have been young, and the other half have a proportionately larger number of daughters who, in turn, are given land, providing an explanation for the figures.

The differences in family constitution and life cycle stages are clearly revealed in the division of bequests. For example, fewer than one-quarter to more than one-half of wives are named as the principal beneficiary, with similar figures shown for sons, whereas figures for daughters are half these. The percentage of properties bequeathed also varies considerably among trades. The shipwrights appear to have been the largest property owners (perhaps reflecting their skills in the building trade), as their bequests reflect double the number of properties, on average, relative to other trades for whom two to five properties are recorded. There are up to three recipients of property per will. Beneficiaries of real property do not usually inherit jointly, and this fact also applies to most daughters, contrary to Erickson's findings (2002: 26), and it appears that in the majority of cases younger siblings, both male and female waited their turn in order of birth to acquire the family property, although brothers were almost without exception favoured above sisters, following the norm in this period (Erickson 1993: 64).

In the case of the testator's principal residence, inheritance patterns echo the findings concerning the inheritance of property overall, with over 90% of some 154 family homes remaining in the possession of the nuclear family. The averages shown in Table 3.2 indicate that, in 57% of cases, wives inherit the family home; sons inherit in 26% of cases, and daughters in less than 9%. When no-one in the nuclear family is named in the will, 1 to 2% of family homes are passed next to the testator's brothers and sisters or to their mother, possibly indicating in these cases a youthful or unmarried testator without his own family (Wrightson 1991: 285). Other properties, less than 1%, are bequeathed either to grandsons, a daughter-in-law or a male friend.

An accurate picture of who inherits family businesses is difficult to recover because, although certain trades specifically mention their work spaces or shops (notably butchers, cordwainers and smiths), many such premises are integral to the family home (Schofield 1987: 22). Wills have shown that the beneficiary of the principal residence is usually also the beneficiary of the shop or workhouse (when this was specified); and thus, most shops are bequeathed to the nuclear family. Where businesses are separately bequeathed, Table 3.3 shows that, on average, 27% are given to wives and 31% to sons, whereas only 4% are left to daughters. All the other named recipients receive less than 1% of the total. Shops are listed by a number of trades as shown on Table 3.3, and differences among the trades are apparent. Cordwainers and butchers leave shops to wives and sons, as well as to daughters (who receive nearly 30% of the properties); however, only these trades have left shops to a daughter, which suggests the active participation of women and girls in these types of work. The 12 smiths who list shops left three-quarters to their wives and just less than 20% to their sons, and uniquely, named 8% of their brothers. The percentage figures may simply reflect periods in the life cycle where children, especially sons, were too young to take over the businesses, leaving wives and daughters to run them. However, in the case of smiths many more women were involved in what has come to be seen as a male-dominated trade than one might suppose considering the nature of the work (Clark 1919, 1992: 210, 294; Erickson 1993: 39, 53). The weavers also leave most workhouses to their wives, with far fewer going to their sons. Does this arrangement also reflect the level of participation by wives in the process of weaving? Observations concerning individual bequests of looms show that it is male apprentices who are most favoured with such bequests, as is also the case with the tools belonging to smiths (see Table 3.5). It would seem in view of this evidence that women may have overseen different aspects of business, but not always participated in production.

The figures concerning bequests of mills pertain almost exclusively to the millers, although mills are owned by men belonging to eight other trades. In total, 28 mills have been identified, bequeathed to 32 people. The average percentages in Table 3.4 indicate that 33% of wives, 20% of sons, and 3% of daughters were left mills, with a very few others bequeathed to brothers, male cousins, a mother and a grandson. However, the inheritance of mills specifically among miller's families shows that division is remarkably equitable, with about one-third given to wives and sons respectively, while 20% were given to daughters, a high figure relative to other businesses, excepting cordwainers and butchers. Several male cousins of millers also came to inherit mills, a noteworthy situation as most families have chosen closer relatives in all other categories of property analysed here. A number of documents suggest that millers tended to retain the ownership or leases of mills within families for decades. In the Appendix of Mills: Part 2, a history of how mills have been passed from one generation to another is examined in the case of the Reasley family.

All the figures on property bequests must be examined in some detail in order to explain major discrepancies in percentages between the different social groups and trades. These differences are shown to be connected to life cycle factors and the occupations of the testators, as well as efforts to devise estates equitably. Erickson's finding that widows commonly enjoyed much more property from the marital estate than the law entitled them to (2002: 19), does not appear to have been the case regarding Newcastle widows, who, on average, received a third part only, in accordance with the law. Erickson's sample reveals that three-quarters of testators gave the 'dwelling house' to the widow, whereas the average is 57% for Newcastle (2002: 162-3).

Widows consistently inherit the family property while their children are unmarried and still in their minority, or while they themselves remain unmarried, although a number are left the family home for the remainder of their natural life. Thomas Redhead, shipwright, left his wife the family home on condition that she kept it 'well & sufficiently repayred' (D.P.R. 1592). If she remarried she was to 'enter into bond for the true delyvery of my children's part unto them at their severall ages', but the widow was nevertheless allowed to retain the family home. John Holbourne, mariner, protected his wife Margaret by only allowing his son Roger the family inheritance once his mother remarried, as it seems she was expected to do. When she did, she would retain her third share as the law allowed, but on her death the remaining third was to be divided between both her son and her daughter equally (D.P.R.1622).

Sometimes a widow is allowed to live in a property for a specified number of years before the second-in-line takes possession, although remarriage affects not only widows, as the example of Cuthbert Todd, son-in-law to a cordwainer, illustrates. This man was allowed to 'have his lodging in my little chamber next the kitchen with bed and bedding' only 'so long as he keepeth him selfe unmaryed' (D.P.R. Smith 1587). The testator's daughter must have died and a new wife would not be allowed to benefit from this bequest. Many widows were perhaps older and not expected to remarry, an arrangement reflecting the law and custom of the period concerning the rights of free bench and dower (Goose and Evans 2000: 23). Erickson confirms that most women did not remarry, and when Newcastle widows did remarry, bequests were indeed often altered (2002: 72, 149, 154, 196).

Some widows were, however, allowed to decide about the disposition of property themselves, as was the case with William Reed's wife Margaret, who was to bequeath the family house 'as she shall thynke good' (D.P.R. 1570). The keelman James Wilson told his wife that, regarding the disposal of his property, 'she so to devyde them amongste my children as she shall thynke most fytt & commodius' (D.P.R. 1584). These statements indicate confidence that a wife would protect the family priorities, especially regarding children. Other wives are given clear instructions: Roger Bilton, skinner, told his wife Ann that although she was named as sole executor, he was 'not indending theareby that shee shall have anie better or greater benifitt then my said two sonnes, but onely that shee maie execute this', the said testament, 'excepting that my said wife shall have the sole and onely benifitt and advantage of the said shoppe to herself for and in regard that my said two sonnes are tender of yeares towards theare bringing upp' (D.P.P. 1623).

Where a wife is excluded from the will, the explanation probably lies with the norms of the day reflected in the law, which as we have seen allowed a woman a one-third share of all the property belonging to the testator; her rights may therefore have been assumed rather than specified by the testator. When the wives, sons or daughters of a testator are alive, it is difficult to find any examples where they have been left out of his will, a finding echoed by Issa where she found no child was totally disinherited (1986: 475). Death can be assumed to be the reason for any other silences. For example, the shipwright Jhon [sic.] Readheade the Elder, leaves all his property to his only son, also called Jhon, and all his goods not otherwise bequeathed to his three daughters. We may assume his wife is dead as he asks to be buried in All Saints churchyard 'so nighe my wife there buride as I conveniently maye be' (D.P.R. 1581).

Where the law has been strictly applied, this probably reflects fears that either a stepfather (who would come to own all his wife's possessions on marriage), might not protect the interests of the children of the deceased father, or that the wife would default on payments to the children of her first marriage. Throughout the period, guidelines were laid down in wills for the executors to follow (Wrightson 1984: 328). The will of the keelman Cuthbert Watson seems to suggest that laws concerning remarriage and inheritance were not a question of local custom. He notes 'ande if that my fore said wiff Allison Watson do marye againe I will that she shalt have no part of my godes bode (but) as the letter of this reallme will admytt' (D.P.R. 1570). Allane Clarke, shipwright, tells his wife Jannett she is 'To have her portion ... accordinge to the lawes of this Realme w[i]th favwore'. The 'favwore' is perhaps the lists of items he specially bequeaths to her, but she must be contented with this 'or else to have no legesse but as the lawe will give her' (D.P.R. 1573). The law of the period appears to have been widely recognised and followed, although a testator occasionally underlines his wishes, especially if he suspects that his wife might challenge the terms of the will. William Matlande, mariner, leaves one-third of his household goods to his wife Agnus 'in full satisfaction of her widow Right or buie (by) there title that she may or can p[re]tende to anie my said good' (D.P.R. 1608). Robert Phillipson reiterates his wishes concerning Anna his wife, saying 'I protest & trewely declare that I do geve her the said house & goodes in full satisfaction & contention of all & singular my goodes for her full portion And I will & commande that my wife shall have no more clame nor challenge unto any parte or parcel of any of my saide goodes but that which is already geven unto her' (D.P.R. 1588). However, there are also examples where the testator explicitly states that a wife was to have everything, as is the case with the skinner and glover Robert Haddocke. He writes that Ellinore is to have 'all my goods chattels debts movables & unmovables whatsoever dothe appertayne unto me in this world I give them all unto my wyffe as afore named' (D.P.R. 1616).

Erickson's studies of Cambridgeshire, Essex, Hertfordshire and Westmoreland have shown that daughters are given land only in the absence of any sons, while her work on Lincolnshire and Sussex indicates that daughters only rarely (5%) inherit land when they have brothers. In comparison, her Yorkshire sample indicates that 26% of men include daughters in property bequests (2002: 61-2). In the Newcastle sample the figure is 15% overall, including daughters with or without brothers. Erickson perceives a difference between the north and south of the country, citing a possible 'Norse influence in northern England' where, historically, daughters are given more land following a Scandinavian custom (2002: 62). An in-depth analysis of the inheritance patterns of Newcastle butchers, carried out in the preliminary stages of this research, has shown that where daughters inherit the family home in their own right, no living brothers are mentioned, or the brothers have also received separate properties. Overall, daughters in Newcastle are not, apparently, specially favoured, receiving only half as many properties as are bequeathed to their brothers.

Where families have several daughters (who were according to the common law of the period supposed to inherit jointly), a number of exceptions can be found in the Newcastle data that show elder daughters to be favoured in the same way as elder brothers, who are more often the focus of discussions on primogeniture. When Thomas Dalton wrote his will in 1599 he left his house to his wife Elizabeth. However, he had four daughters to care for; thus when his wife died, the eldest daughter was to be given the family home, but only on the condition she provided each of her three younger sisters with 20li when they in turn reached 21 years. If the eldest daughter failed to pay this money, the sisters could remain in the house until they got their money, thus ensuring the girls had a stake in the family property, and would not become homeless as well as penniless (D.P.R. 1599). In the will of Edward Jackson, a keelman who died in 1556, a man who had two sons and two daughters, the eldest daughter is, unusually, given special consideration above her brothers. The two boys, Robert and John, each receive two lighters, but have to provide their two sisters, Agnus and Alice with 3li 6s 8d 'forth of the boats for their childs portions' (D.P.R. 1556). All the children appear to have been minors and their mother must have died. However, the eldest daughter Agnus was specifically left another lighter *and* the testator's house under the supervision of the testator's close friend Bartram Anderson. The girl was to look after the other three children until she married, at which time the house was to be looked after by Bartram who would continue to care for the younger children. Here, we see the age rather than the sex of the children playing the key role in the way bequests are made.

The figures from the wills show that the occupation of a testator plays a role in what widows and daughters came to own, especially regarding businesses in which the family worked. Bequests of shops and mills certainly came to female members of the family (Spufford 1984: 53, 70, 74; Clark 1919, 1992: 293-4, 298). However, the wills also show that the daughters of keelmen, skinners, tailors and weavers (none of which are the wealthiest trades as will be shown in Chapter 5) are left significantly less property than those of the better-off butchers, master mariners and shipwrights, which suggests that daughters from families engaged in more lucrative trades may have come to own more property. This trend seems to conflict with Erickson's finding that poorer men are more likely to distribute what they had 'equally among all children' (2002: 72), although poorer men doubtless had much less real property to give.

In Newcastle some testators clearly give priority to wives and daughters in bequests of real property, even when they have sons. They also follow the canons of descent in preferring lineal females to collateral males in bequeathing property, as established elsewhere in the country (Erickson 1993: 63). Nevertheless, in general, where northern daughters may inherit more property than their southern counterparts initially, as widows they did not on average retain more than is allowed by law, whereas southern widows seem to do rather better.

In examining bequests to sons, Erickson has found that the system of primogeniture operates in the case of the main estate, as is most often the case in Newcastle. Nevertheless, when the eldest son is left the main property, he very often cannot immediately take possession. Such was the case of Christopher Fairallis, skinner and glover, who remarried after his first wife died. The testator warns his son Edward regarding the family home (which the second wife would inherit, and which would come to Edward only on his stepmother's death), 'givinge charge even as he will answere at the last day of Judgement not to wronge his mother-in-law for her life time' (D.P.R. 1638). There may have been some bad feeling, as Edward receives only a few pieces of furniture, whereas the second wife Marie is left not just the family home but also all the remaining 'goods and chattels'. In the case of another eldest son, Roger, of the mariner John Holbourne, other impediments are placed in the way of a straightforward inheritance: Roger inherits the family mill bequeathed to him by his father, only if he pays all four of his father's brother's daughters (Roger's first cousins) 10li each (D.P.R.1622).

Other documents indicate that sons who were first in line for property are not always the eldest: sometimes a second or youngest son is mentioned instead, together with sisters, especially when older sons have attained their majority. In the case of the butcher Andrew Harup, his older sons John and James have already been given 'portions equal to my estate' and the testator asks 'that neither of them disturbe my other children but that they suffer quietly to enjoy the goods' (D.P.R 1618). The older sons receive 40s each as a token of their father's love; the two minor sons and daughters are to divide the residual estate.

Erickson has found evidence of a consensus among ordinary people that eldest sons ought to be privileged, but not excessively (2000: 77). This is exemplified by the will of Richard Rowmaine, tanner, with two sons and three daughters. On his death the two family properties are to be divided. One is to go to the testator's wife, and next to the second son, then to the eldest married daughter, then to her unmarried younger sister. The other property is to go to the eldest son directly on his father's death, and is then to be passed on 'according to the custom of the cuntrey' (D.P.R. 1587). But all the children also receive 40li each for their child's portions. Even when the wills are examined for the next in line in larger families, should the principal beneficiary die, other sons invariably take priority over daughters; when the latter eventually inherit, they often, though not always, did so jointly with their sisters, following the common law of the period (Erickson 1993: 26). Interestingly, however, within smaller families the property division appears to be more equitable.

Thus far, the evidence clearly indicates that eldest sons often receive more property than their sisters and younger brothers. However, eldest sons are rarely given control of the family property if their younger siblings are still at home, and the majority of eldest minor sons inherit property jointly with their mothers until they reach the age of majority. In other examples, the family property is equitably divided between siblings, as in the case of Raiphe Totherick, a butcher whose will dated February 1615 appears to be designed to ensure that his son Robert and daughter Isabelle each get a fair share. He left this (minor) son his own house on the Flesh Market in the centre of the town and all his goods and chattels (once all the debts had been paid), thus confirming that the main dwelling house went to a male heir. However, he left his daughter a 'chamber adjoining on the south side of my dwelling house' (the same house willed to his son), together with a four-year lease on a shop and a tenement, and also 40li cash for her child's portion (D.P.R.). Such examples help to confirm Erickson's finding that in northern regions younger sons and daughters are compensated with other pieces of land (2002: 78). But as noted above, this often depends on both the extent of properties owned and on the occupation of a testator relating to the type of business premises bequeathed.

Tables 3.1 - 3.4 relating to bequests of property show that where properties are amalgamated (Table 3.1), there are two properties per beneficiary, but in the case of a mill or shop there is closer to one (Tables 3.3 and 3.4), while the principal residence is shared between 1.2 persons on average. The suggestion is that where extra properties are available these are spread more evenly between beneficiaries.

Erickson says the rapidity with which property changed hands as a result of a high rate of mortality, and the unexpected channels of diffusion, cannot be over-emphasised (2002: 63). This observation certainly applies to Newcastle in the case of diffusion of properties to many different people under a variety of circumstances. As an example of lives suddenly being altered, we have the testament of a miller called William Gray who contracted the plague that struck in 1585. This miller, besides making bequests to the poor of two almshouses, and to the curate of All Hallows, leaves all his 'goods and chattels' to his father, his brother and his brother's family, as well as to friends. All his lands are to go to Isabelle (his minor daughter) 'when she is of lawful years' (D.P.R.). We can see from the inventory that everyone else in the family - his wife, two other daughters and a son - have recently died. Their clothes are all listed individually and were bequeathed in the will. The child Isabelle has also been struck down with the plague for ten weeks (according to the costs outlined on the inventory), so it is probable that she too, has died. If so, the whole family has been wiped out. William's brother thus inherits almost everything, including all the lands. However, one of the four women who have cared for the dying family, Agnus Pearson, is included in the will: she receives a Danish chest and Danish pots, as well as the testator's wife's gown 'for her paines in kepeing them' (D.P.R. 1585, Welford 1887; 31-2). Death of the whole family in this case is the only explanation for the patterns of bequests. Incidentally, Corfield's description of the plague as a 'panic disease' (1972: 269), as differentiated from social reactions to smallpox, is wholly unfounded according to evidence from Newcastle wills, which shows careful consideration of responsibilities both among the dying in terms of recognising the help they receive, and from those caring for the ill. There is no evidence of people being abandoned.

High mortality, overall, is apparent from a number of Newcastle wills, as testators often provide detailed information on succession, extending to as many as four or five lineal beneficiaries. But most property remains in the hands of the immediate family, although as Erickson noted, parents without children are underestimated in the records, accounting for 9% of the total overall (2002: 254).

Taking the evidence together, bequests of real property seem to have been designed to promote family unity and a sense of fairness, rather than to favour individuals. Almost without exception, being an heir of any age, male or female, of real property came with qualifications and responsibilities. But were the rules the same for the family's 'goods and chattels'? This is the question posed in the next section.

3.4 Bequests of objects

Bequests of objects have left a comprehensive record relating to patterns of consumption, providing a factual account of what items have been seen as particularly valued and therefore specially selected for inclusion in the testament. Shammas notes that wills are the obvious place to look for evidence about the role of intergenerational transmission of wealth in distributing consumer goods to widows and lineal descendants (1990: 204). This section examines who received this type of bequest; whether movables acted as compensation in the absence of other types of bequests, especially real property; and the value of inheritances. Erickson notes that, in this period, movables had a value comparable to that of property (2002: 64-6), thus comparisons can be made between categories of bequests. Of the two tables compiled for this assessment, Table 3.5 summarises the percentage of recipients of all individual bequests, excluding real property, cash, clothes, animals and gifts to the poor, which are analysed separately. Table 3.6 lists the recipients of the residue of the estate, described in the documents as 'All the rest of my goods and chattels, debts, legacies and funeral expenses paid, representing the bulk of goods remaining once all debts and individual bequests have been honoured.

The most common individual bequests in wills are for work or shop gear; products of a trade, such as hides, yarn or timber; and occasionally, grains, either growing or harvested. Other items include furniture or household objects such as linen, silver vessels and spoons. Clothes, animals and ships are also all specifically bequeathed. Jewellery tends to be restricted to rings given as 'tokens'. Bequests of weapons are fairly rare, and books very rare. All these items, however, are also bequeathed as part of the residue of the whole estate.

Almost every trade includes individual bequests to the nuclear and extended family, as well as to non-family members. Table 3.5 shows that the majority of individual bequests are to wives, sons and daughters. Wives receive about one-third, sons about one-quarter, and daughters just less than one-quarter overall. Beyond the nuclear family, the next group to benefit most are brothers, male friends, and male apprentices and servants, who receive between 2 - 7% of individual bequests. With few exceptions these men are consistently given practical objects: most receive tools of the trade (where a son does not inherit these), and clothes, including 'work day apparel'. Some receive a share of products of the trade; others receive weapons. Men, apparently, never receive domestic household objects unless they are the principal beneficiary of 'all the goods and chattels' (Table 3.6). The category of male friends is treated most generously outside members of the immediate family; some of these men may be past apprentices. Certain land-based trades appear to be more generous than seafarers towards apprentices (although mariners would, of course, have no apprentices). Nevertheless, the paucity of bequests from wealthy master mariners stands out, although life cycle factors must always be considered.

The differences in patterns of bequests between the trades are more visible outside the nuclear family as a consequence of the type of business practised, which is perhaps, a more important factor than wealth. When the figures for male friends are combined with those for male apprentices and servants, discrepancies become quite clear: the poor tailors and keelmen, as well as the seafarers, provide fewer bequests than the other land-based trades. Examination of other differences between the trades shows that a high percentage (60%) of mariner's wives receive all household objects, again suggesting that mariners die younger than other tradesmen. As in the case of real property, mariners have fewer children and sisters are favoured in the absence of daughters.

Female friends, who receive 2% of these bequests, overall, are remembered less often than male friends. These women are given household objects including furniture, kitchenware, linen, yarn and grain. Women appear never to be left tools of the trades or weapons, unless they also are the principal beneficiary of 'all the goods and chattels'. Other family members, female servants, executors and supervisors are remembered in many wills, but represent 1% or less of the beneficiaries overall. Male friends tend to receive the same type of objects as men within families, and the same is true for women. An exception to this general rule is where silver objects, such as bowls and spoons, are bequeathed to selected family and special friends of either sex.

Overall, objects selected for individual bequests can only be described as practical rather than luxury items. For example, no clocks, pictures, mirrors, decorated cushions, curtains, musical instruments, fine vessels or glassware, or novelty items, are included as specific bequests, such objects being bequeathed only as part of the bulk of the household goods. Silver vessels and spoons are possible exceptions to this rule, but these objects are often listed in relation to weight and corresponding value. In this period, silver is treated in much the same way as pewter, where it is the weight and precious metal content of vessels, not the design that is important relative to the valuation (Weatherill 1996: 29, 66, Overton 2000: 125). This is illustrated in the inventory of Gavine Preston, which records about 600 objects, including a silver bowl, two beakers and a wine cup, listed last and described as 'parcel gilt' worth 6li (D.P.R. 1640). Thomas Collingwood lists silver bowls, ready money, gold 'gymes' and gold and silver rings at the bottom of his exceptionally long inventory of over 1000 items (D.P.R. 1625). Broken pieces of silver are also inventoried alongside whole vessels (D.P.R. Nicholson 1587), and the 'plate' is often valued separately (D.P.R. Steel 1634, Collingwood 1636). Even the coveted silver whistles and chains owned exclusively by the mariners, master mariners and shipwrights, and most often bequeathed to a son or brother, are listed on the inventory by weight relative to value. These are in some sense luxury items: a silver whistle on a silver chain, weighing up to 15 ounces, would have been a clear symbol of solidarity among seafarers, as well as perhaps conveying status; however, like any other whistle, these must also have had an important function, to draw attention to oneself. If a man fell into the sea in bad weather or at night, a whistle could be a means of calling for attention with a sound that might carry over the wind and waves and thus prove a life-saving device. John Holborne specifies as much, as he tells his son Roger that the whistle is 'to carry to sea with him' (D.P.R. 1622). Such bequests are made from as early as 1546 until 1623, when they disappear from the records.

Gold rings, given as tokens to special family and friends, may be the only other exception to the contention that wills of this period never include sentimental luxuries as individual bequests. In fact, in a data set containing many thousands of items, the sole example the researcher can find of a trivial object being specifically bequeathed comes from the will (dated 1622) of George Watson, a very wealthy shipwright, who became carried away with the list of bequests, including no less than 40 people. After the will had been witnessed and signed, George added five more people, some 'honest neighbours' and the children of another shipwright. The very last entry is 'to Roland Seamer a pitch pot' (D.P.R.1622). The impression is that the testator is considering whom he had forgotten: did he remember that Roland had always been troubled with a leaking boat? Thus the pitch pot is specially bequeathed on the final line of this lengthy will and was probably included with an element of good humour.

The second set of figures presented in Table 3.6 focuses on what becomes of the objects and cash left to the person who is usually the last to be named on a will, the person who receives 'all the rest of the goods and chattels'. These items were usually located in the testator's principal residence. The table shows the social categories of legatees, but not their trade affiliations; some 286 people are named. As with the other categories of bequests, the social make-up of beneficiaries shows no change over time: wives are overwhelmingly favoured as the chosen recipient to take control of the majority of the family objects, accounting for nearly 40% of the total beneficiaries. As co-inheritors with all their children, or with either sons or daughters, the figure rises to 70% overall. Where children inherit alone, sons receive four times the bequests of daughters, who do better when they inherit jointly with their brothers. The figures usually exclude children who have reached the age of majority. The testator's brothers are the only non-nuclear family members to be favoured above all other recipients, whereas sisters are never specifically mentioned. Other non-family members are, on occasion, the sole beneficiaries of this category of bequest, under exceptional circumstances relating to the survival of other family members. In the remainder of the sample, the recipients of the bulk of the family goods are not clearly specified.

The prominence of wives in the statistics is explicable on examination of the documents. Wives consistently receive all the remaining family objects, once the legacies, debts and funeral expenses have been met, when they have minor children to support, a finding echoed in other studies of northern populations (Issa 1986: 475; Wrightson 1991: 281). But such arrangements come with clear stipulations, and instructions to a wife from a husband are fairly common in the wills, such as that from the mariner Martyn Errinton to his wife to keep herself unmarried as a condition of the bequest, as the 'stuff is towards the bringing up' of their five minor children (D.P.R. 1627). If she were to remarry she would retain her legal one-third of the goods and no more. The cordwainer William Duxford also leaves all the family goods to his wife 'towards payment of my debts, and raising porcons for my younger children' (D.P.R. 1634). Thomas Sheell, smith, makes a specific agreement about his goods, saying 'and bicause mie wife hathe solemly renounsed and disclaimed all hir right, title and claime or demande of mie goods I do geive bye mie wifes co[ns]ent all mie goods and chattels to mie fyve children' (who were all minors) (D.P.R. 1603). Where a wife has already died, the objects tend to be left equally to all the younger children, especially to minors and unmarried children. The younger minor children will not have received their 'child's portions' and are therefore favoured above their older siblings. Occasionally a testator specifies that the older children have already received portions, as is the case with the daughter of Richard Jobson, tanner. He writes that Margaret his eldest has been given some money 'taken out of my holl goodes' and therefore she will receive no more 'because she is towartt the world' (D.P.R. 1552). When a wife shares the bulk of the family goods with one or more of her sons, and not with her daughters, the reason is often that the girls are given more substantial cash bequests, as is discussed below.

Overall, Erickson's finding in wills from Lincolnshire, Sussex and Yorkshire, that younger sons and daughters are compensated with moveables when they do not inherit real property, and that in particular daughters are given larger bequests of moveable goods (2002: 64, 77-8, 225), does not seem to be applicable to Newcastle. In this northern town, sons and other males appear always to be more favoured in terms of the residue of objects from the estate, compared with daughters and other females, just as they are with real property and individual bequests. Daughters are first in line for the bulk of the family goods only when they have no brothers or the sons have died. The same is true when wives and daughters inherit together: in such cases there are no male heirs at all; the reverse scenario never applies according to the evidence examined. Issa's contention that obligations to the nuclear family 'inevitably placed limits on individual choice' (1986: 467-8), does not recognise that as individuals, many male testators differentiate between daughters and sons, making choices that are deleterious to female heirs.

Nevertheless, regardless of such observations, and the impression one gains from the statistics, it seems that most testators genuinely try to be even-handed with children. Apparently, the youngest boys and (particularly) the youngest girls may not do as well as their older siblings, as portions to older children may have put strain on the family. The nuncupative will of William Duxfield divides his lands and goods to favour his wife and youngest children. The estate is to be put 'towards payment of my debts, and raising porcons for my younger children', and he tells his eldest son George that he has already 'received his full porcon and had gotten more then would fall unto three of his younger children' (D.P.R. 1634). Unfortunately for the family, the inventory indicates that William died in deep debt. Where minors do come to inherit the family 'goods and chattels', many children are treated remarkably equitably: for example, in a will of 1552, the six children of a tanner are to share the estate with their mother, she to get half and the other half 'to be dystributed emongst them by even portiones' (D.P.R Jobson). In the event of one sibling dying, it is not uncommon for this 'child's portion' to be given to the surviving children. The baker and brewer Edward Hale specifies that the portions of any dead children are 'to be divided among the living children equally' (D.P.R. 1618). Unborn children are also considered. William Cooke, cordwainer, makes a bequest 'To the child that my wife is withall', continuing somewhat awkwardly that 'if it come forward I give it 20li & if it die the mother to enjoy it' (D.P.R. 1636). Anthony Wilkinson is more optimistic, leaving his four children - Alleson, Jane, Robert and an unborn child - 'to share equally of the goodes unbequeathed' (D.P.R. 1582). The cordwainer Nicholas Ridley echoes the same arrangements for his 'goods and chatteles' saying 'I will that it shalbe apprised and my wifes due taken out which the lawe will allowe hir', and the remaining two-thirds 'to be equalie distributed amongst my foure children to everie one a like parte' (D.P.R 1622). It is not common for just one child among the siblings to be given exclusive rights to the family goods, although on occasion the eldest (or sometimes the youngest) son does seem to be selected. But this type of bequest, as with property, comes with a price in terms of responsibilities towards those not directly included in the bequests.

Non-nuclear family members are favoured with the residue of the estate only when the testator has no family. This situation is most apparent in plague years, such as when Thomas Eden's entire family succumbed in the 1636 outbreak and all the goods were sold at the testator's death (D.P.R. l636). In another case from 1585, George Armstronge, cordwainer, when dying of the plague, leaves all his goods to his only son; however, he asks his brother Henry 'yf it please god to call my sonne Henry Armstronge to his mercie in this tyme of visitacion' to 'distribut my goodes to the most needfull of my frends' (D.P.R.). No other family is mentioned and his wife had already died

Taken together, the evidence for the division of objects reveals that testators with adult children are more likely to make individual bequests and to leave the widow with just the one-third part of the goods as provided by law (Table 3.5). By contrast, widows left with minor children are often bequeathed 'all the rest of the goods and chattels', amounting to more than the law allowed (Table 3.6). Such priorities within the life cycle of families follows a national trend (Howell 1978: 141-3; Issa 1986: 473; Wrightson 1991: 284, 330, 1984: 328; Spufford 2000: 106; Erickson 1993: 69, 73). And yet despite the efforts of testators to create solutions designed around personal circumstances, overall discrepancies remain, and Newcastle testators seem to favour males over females in bequests of both real property and objects. In other parts of the country, Erickson's finding is that, by custom, boys are most often bequeathed real property and girls usually inherit personal property, but that this is not universal (2002: 19, 64). The children of Newcastle tradesmen are clearly one such exception. In the next section cash bequests are examined to assess what possible mechanisms there might be to redress the continuing imbalance between the sexes in the division of estates.

3.5 Bequests of cash

The largest percentage of bequests recorded in wills is for cash sums. Some 40 social groups are named, the widest distribution for any type of bequest, and 26% of these beneficiaries are included on a regular basis. With so many people given money, the question of who is selected, the magnitude of the sums, and what conditions apply to bequests, deserves analysis, particularly as the findings have implications for patterns of consumption.

In the case of the majority of bequests, only the nuclear family are given both money and objects, while other family members and friends tend to receive one or the other, and this division does not appear to have any relation to factors such as levels of wealth (Howell 1978: 152; Issa 1986: 469). The legatees include wives, sons, daughters, grandchildren, parents, nieces, nephews, uncles, aunts, cousins, in-laws, 'kin', half-brothers and half-sisters, friends and their children, neighbours, servants and apprentices (both male and female). Local parish ministers, churches, charitable institutions, local worthies and the poor of the town are listed, as well as supervisors and clerks; even unborn children were mentioned. Money is given to almost every category of person one could think to include.

The size of monetary inheritances varies enormously over time and between the trades, as well as among the many different social groups. The evidence from the wills indicates that bequests become larger in the second quarter of the 17th century, during which 200li, on occasion is left as a 'child's portion' (D.P.R. Hope 1632, Robinson 1627); more commonly, bequests of several pounds are left to the closest family members or particularly favoured friends. Smaller bequests consisting of a few shillings - for example 2s 6d, 5s or 10s - are given to a wide variety of friends, family, servants and the poor. 'Tokens' are usually the smallest monetary bequests given, and include coins or even half coins of gold known as 'angels' or 'nobles', 'Edward shillings', 'French crowns' or 'Jacobus pieces'. The phrase 'for a token' is repeated throughout the documents in all periods and represents a gesture of love or appreciation. Sometimes the coin is to be used to make a gold ring in remembrance of the testator (Spufford 1984: 80). For example, in 1617 a miller called William Anderson leaves his eldest daughter Elizabeth 'a ring of gold of four angels', and to each of the three supervisors of his will 'an angel for a token' (D.P.R. 1617). Edward Berwick gives his friend Robert Johnson '1 double ducket & two old angels to make in a ring' (D.P.R. 1587). He instructs Robert to pass the ring in turn to Edward, his son. Tokens are also given to women who have cared for the dying during an often protracted illness, and are also frequently given to other tradesmen who probably have been friends and colleagues, quite often men from a different trade. Such gestures are, in fact, common in the Tudor and Stuart period (Cressy 1986: 61). The word 'token', however, is never used in connection to bequests to the poor.

With such large discrepancies in the amounts of money bequeathed, and with so many recipients named, the focus here is to establish who gains most, especially in the light of the findings relating to other types of bequests. Table 3.7 gives percentage figures for the principal beneficiaries of the largest cash sum from each will. The figures include those who inherit a sum jointly with one or more person, if all parties receive the same amount. The table excludes beneficiaries of 'ready money' listed on the inventory. This money may or may not have come to the recipient of 'all the rest of the goods and chattels', as all outstanding legacies and debts had to be paid before such a beneficiary received a final settlement.

In analysing the recipients on Table 3.7, five social categories have been constructed. Among the nuclear family, wives rarely receive the largest bequests of cash. They are named in just 3% of wills, but this does not mean widows receive no money. Rather, it is counted among the 'goods and chattels' recorded on the inventories, taken up in Table 3.6. Sons are named as principal beneficiary in 18% of wills, but the figures for the majority of trades show a clear preference for daughters who receive cash bequests in nearly 30% of wills. It is difficult to decide whether the discrepancies in percentages in favour of boys, shown in the wills of shipwrights, master mariners and weavers, indicate a genuine bias in these trades, or if these merely reflect family constitution. Erickson has confirmed that, overall, daughters are likely to receive cash portions in lieu of land (2002: 94); however, as sons inherit more than twice the number of properties given to daughters, as well as more objects on average, the relatively higher percentages of cash bequests does not appear, ultimately, to compensate daughters fully. Additionally, Erickson's statement that in the first half of the 17th century, wealthy tradesmen usually provided daughters with portions of between £100 and £500 (2002: 87), does not seem to have been true even for the better-off tradesmen of Newcastle. It is interesting to note that children from previous marriages are often treated very equitably in relation to their half-sisters and half-brothers (especially in the case of minor children), while the only children of either sex who are never named in the will as the principal beneficiary are those who have already received their 'child's portion'. Nevertheless, such siblings often receive a very small sum as a token.

Outside the nuclear family, sisters receive the largest share of cash bequests (8%), whereas their brothers receive cash in only 4% of wills. In trades for which figures can be compiled, discrepancies are very marked, but overall the sample favours females. The two trades that stand out are the shipwrights, who name their sisters in 26% of the sample, and the mariners, who endow their sisters in 40% of cases. The figure for shipwrights is comparable to the overall average percentage of bequests given to daughters by members of other trades, while that for mariners is a clear anomaly. This finding is akin to that *vis-à-vis* other property, and the most likely explanation is the age profile of the men and their marital status. As already noted, youthful will-makers tended to leave bequests to parents and siblings or to nephews and nieces (Wrightson 1991: 285, 330). The wording in Newcastle wills affords some useful insights into this question, especially concerning the mariners. The mariner John Patteson left his property to one brother, forgave the debts owed by another, and gave his sister money. He 'commanded' the first brother to pay their mother and father a cash sum, and noted that his sister's son 'being fatherless' should have 'all my see apparel', 'desiring that my brother ... to be a good uncle to him' (D.P.R. 1584). Another mariner, William Matlande, mentions no children, and leaves his wife only her 'third part', giving all the rest of his objects, clothes and his silver whistle to his three brothers and money to his two sisters (D.P.R. 1608). The mariner, John Hird, married for a second time, but also mentioning no children, leaves his wife the property and goods, but gives his 'owne natural' sisters money and names them as next in line to his estate (D.P.R. 1597). The mariner Richard Herrisone asks his wife to 'deliver to my sister ... my will and testament to keep for the good of my child' (D.P.R. 1596). William Moorton, mariner, also married, leaves all his goods to his wife, but gives most of the rental income from his property to his two sisters and clothes to his brother (D.P.R. 1587). The wills of several other mariners also indicate that they are married, but they may have had fewer children. Some aspect of a mariner's profession may have often persuaded such men to leave bequests to their siblings, especially their sisters. Many mariners lost their lives at sea, a situation pertaining to a lesser extent to shipwrights. The danger of the sea is reflected in the will of mariner Martyn Errington writing in 1625 that he is 'bound forth to sea or elsewhere in his Majesties service' and is 'considering the transitorines of this life' (D.P.R.). In the case of unmarried testators from other trades, family members are also almost always named. For example, Cuthbert Nicholson describes himself as 'servant to William Dodes', a deceased tanner (D.P.R. 1575). Nicholson is, at this time, an apprentice, probably fairly young and still unmarried. According to his will his minor brother is to inherit his house and household goods, with his unmarried sister next in line. He leaves his aunt and uncle a little money so it is probable his parents are dead. No other family member is mentioned.

Outside the nuclear family, and the sisters and brothers of testators, bequests to principal recipients are somewhat more equally divided between the sexes as well as the trades. Grandchildren, parents, adult friends and cousins are all included, although a distinct bias towards males is evident. The same bias is also seen in the figures in Table 3.7 Group 4, which includes in-laws, nieces and nephews, the children of friends, servants, and apprentices. One might ask if the preference towards male beneficiaries by males testators is analogous to the fact that widows, in turn, tend to favour females in their wills (Erickson 1993: 211-217).

The inclusion of servants and apprentices as legatees is not perhaps surprising, but the fact that these people are occasionally named as the principal beneficiary of the largest sum does draw attention to the important role some of these people must have played in the lives of the testators. Erickson noted the practice of young women who saved money towards a marriage portion, or who might receive money as a gift from a master upon marriage (2002: 85-6). Brooks discusses the same priorities for young men who need money to pay apprenticeship fees, some of which are very high, depending on the profession, noting that there was a responsibility to educate young men in the interests of their guilds (1994: 53, 60). Perhaps some testators simply chose to be generous to servants and apprentices, who also required money to establish a household. It can also be suggested that such bequests may have had implications for these people as consumers.

Friends are also included in the wills, and although most receive small tokens, in nine trades a friend is selected as the principal beneficiary. These people appear most often to have been other tradesmen, often practising a different trade to the testator, or the wives of these men, although widows or neighbours in need are also often selected. Thomas Hall, a cordwainer who died in 1625, has left no doubt as to the nature of his affection towards Margaret Milburne, a widow to whom he gave 4li 'for a token' … 'for & in respect of the love I beare unto her' (D.P.R.). The tailor Thomas Clark, writing his will in 1636, left his servant 20s 'in lew of his mothers love in his entertaining his daughter Margarett att Table' (D.P.R.). In 1548 John Bullock, keelman, wished to leave his friends something to remember him by, and although the men are not the principal beneficiaries on the will, they illustrate why friends are so often included in cash bequests. Bullock asked that 'my bretherne off thocupation bayre me to church', 'And any one off them to have 4d to make mery withall' (D.P.R.).

There are two other groups of people to be considered in monetary bequests, although the amounts can not be calculated, and therefore whether any of these people is a principal beneficiary is unknown. The first includes a handful of women who receive an annuity for life. Examples of such arrangements include one concerning Robert Shaldforthe who leaves his mother '10s for lyfe' in 1549 (D.P.R. 1549), another of a master mariner, John Peacock, who leaves his wife '2s a week for lyfe' (D.P.R. 1629), and a third where the master mariner John Michaelson leaves his sister '2d each week for lyfe' (D.P.R. 1595). In a period when the family might be required to provide where the state would not, and poor relief came with a social stigma attached (Wrightson 1991: 347), this was a lifeline for those who were lucky enough to benefit from such an arrangement. Annuities are apparently not evident until 1690 according to Wrightson's research of Whickham, and Erickson finds that they were rare in this period (2002: 164). The only other group not represented in the figures are those people who are released from debts by the testator, as the nature and extent of the debts are not always specified.

Overall, the nuclear family, the testator's siblings, grandchildren and parents, together represent about two-thirds of principal beneficiaries of cash bequests, but this leaves another third of this society, including those beyond close family, benefiting extensively as individuals. Cressy's claim that 'relations outside the nuclear family were likely to be ignored' and that 'only a minority took pains to acknowledge selected members of their wider circle of kin' (1986: 56, 61) appears too pessimistic in view of the Newcastle evidence.

A clear bias in cash settlements is evident towards females among the immediate family, but the bias is reversed outside this group, where the ratio was two to one in favour of males. Daughters and sisters in Newcastle society recover to an extent from the discrimination shown towards them in relation to bequests of real property and objects, as such women receive the largest cash bequests. Widows, whose husbands have not died in debt and where legacies and portions have not reduced the estate too much, may well have enjoyed the 'ready money' listed on the inventory.

Overall, however, a trend has emerged showing that cash bequests to women in general are given a lower priority than cash bequests to men, the same trend as that seen regarding property and objects. Interestingly, such a bias was not evident in Cressy's study of Essex and Wiltshire tradesmen in the 1680s, although he tended to combine the genders in the sample (1986: Tables 1 and 2). Such discrimination against females must have contributed to the proportion of widows and other women who became dependent on poor relief at critical stages of their lifecycle. According to Wrightson, men figure far less frequently in the records of those in receipt of regular allowances from parish funds (1991: 351), even accounting for the preponderance of widows in this society (Erickson 1993: 154). The laws, customs and practices surrounding inheritance seem ultimately to have worked against women in general, and the resulting poverty will certainly have had implications for the distribution of wealth in society.

In a final analysis, Table 3.8 looks at amalgamated figures for recipients of monetary bequests, large and small, and at changes over three time periods for bequests to combined social groups. Prior to 1600 an average of 55% of the beneficiaries receive monetary bequests, whereas in the final period from 1626 to 1642 the figure increases to 70%. Looking at the trades individually, the figures suggest that priorities among trades change over the decades, even if allowances are made for life cycle stages. Cash bequests made prior to 1600 are common to all trades, but the percentages are significantly lower, overall, than is the case by the second quarter of the 17th century, where figures up to 80% are recorded more frequently, suggesting monetary assets are increasing. Over the same time frame, a steady polarisation between trades emerges with some trades in a better position to give monetary bequests, especially those dealing in food or commodities. The low figure for the shipwrights is notable, but these men have invested in many more properties than other tradesmen, as well as in ships (see Chapter 5: 5.10.8). Bequests from the keelmen and mariners fall behind the other trades at the start of the new century, and then begin to disappear from the records. A widening gap between rich and poor farmers in their ability to provide cash bequests has been observed in Kibworth Harcourt (1983: 266-7), and the situation in Newcastle is probably similar. Interestingly, however, the possession of greater wealth is not apparently the motivating factor in leaving cash bequests in wills, as conclusively shown in the comparison between, for example, the well-off master mariners and the much less well-to-do tailors, who make similar numbers of bequests, but who cannot give as much. Issa notes that in terms of obligations to kin, this is a 'matter of choice', and that wealth is of 'limited importance' (1986: 469-70).

Overall, the records confirm that more than half the beneficiaries, representing more than 40 different statuses, trades or professions, are provided with some cash money by way of inheritance. Howell has found, among peasants at Kibworth Harcourt in the 16th and 17th centuries that larger cash bequests indicate a strong economy (1978: 140), and the Tyneside economy, and especially that of Newcastle, goes from strength to strength over these decades (Wrightson 1991: 24; Ellis 1984, 2001). The evidence from this study contradicts Weatherill's finding that the middling ranks do not receive regular sums in cash (1996: 96). Cash bequests are common, and monetary transactions from the Newcastle inventories, include debts for goods and services, tuition fees, servants' wages, funeral expenses, medical bills, etc., all given in cash figures. A more cash oriented society than Weatherill suggests seems to be very much the reality for the tradesmen and their families in this period. The existence of a widespread money-lending system is also well attested in the period, despite much trade being conducted on credit (Spufford 1978: 163).

With such a wide variety of people who were personally known to the testators benefiting from cash bequests, the question of whether these tradesmen were also disposed to share their wealth with those beyond family and friends, to include the 'nameless' poor, is the theme of the next section.

3.6 Bequests to the poor

Howell tells us that the Puritan corporation of Newcastle inherited from its predecessors a social obligation to help the poor, but that the amount of co-ordination between the charitable efforts of the town and the machinery of the parishes was by no means really effective, and there seems to have been no attempt at all to combine these two sources of assistance with the small amount of poor relief provided by the town companies (1967: 314, 319). Given such a situation, it is of interest to know how far individual tradesmen felt a responsibility to contribute to the cause.

Bequests to the poor, to parish churches and to institutes for the care of the poor, were fairly common to wills of the period. In Chapter 2, the significance of preparing for death was outlined in relation to the four principal obligations of a testator taken from the Book of Common Prayer. The last of these obligations was that of charitable deeds, performed for the health of one's soul (Cox and Cox 2000: 24). Charitable donations were part of the purchase of 'a good death'. The *Ars Moriendi*, or the art of dying well, and the teachings in the Book of Common Prayer were central to Christian beliefs of the period (Duffy 1992: 315-16). Yet despite the teachings and the social obligations highlighted by the efforts of the parish, and by the guilds (King 2001: 34), by no means everyone was inclined to give to the poor.

Fewer than one-quarter of Newcastle tradesmen, on average, over the period of study specify donations in wills, although whether this figure should be taken as accurate is debatable. It is sometimes unclear whether the total figure given on a will or an inventory for funeral expenses includes or excludes gifts to the poor, as this is often unspecified. Occasionally, documents list all expenses involved in the funeral arrangements in sufficient detail as to suggest that many more donations may have been made to the poor than are specified. The example of William Billingham, a tailor who died in 1625, shows why omissions are probable. The first item on his will combines the donation to the poor with the other funeral expenses, totalling £8 (D.P.R. 1625), and this sort of figure is not untypical of the cost recorded for a funeral on a fair percentage of Newcastle inventories, where sums varied between £1 and more than £10. The poor took part in funeral processions, as demonstrated in the case of Mathew Sheel, cordwainer, who left 20s 'to the poor att the church door where & when I [shall]be buried' (D.P.R. 1634). Although Thomas Draver, a shipwright, left no bequest to the poor in his will, the appraisers of the inventory included a payment of 3s 4d 'to the vicar for his mortuarie' in addition to the 21s recorded for unspecified 'funeral expenses' (D.P.R. 1587). The figures presented here can therefore be seen as only a guide to patterns of bequests.

Testators specified who was to receive a donation, the amount to be given, and who was responsible for ensuring that the terms of the will were carried out. There appears to have been a strong correlation between the parish where the testator was buried and where the recipients lived, but there were also exceptions. Table 3.9 shows the divisions of bequests over three periods, with a separate table giving the combined figures for the whole period which also specifies trades. In the sample of 296 wills, 69 men provided over 100 bequests. Several groups of recipients were identified – namely, the four parish churches, the clergy, the poor (including widows and neighbours living locally and in the surrounding region), and several institutions. A change in the distribution of bequests over the decades was apparent, but some beneficiaries were consistently favoured.

Among the donations to parish churches, the majority went to All Saints, also known as All Hallows, which received up to six times the overall average of the other three parish churches of St. Andrew, St. John and St. Nicholas. A sharp increase in the number of gifts to All Saints was visible in the early 17th century, which declined in the later decades. Men from all but two of the trades left money to this church. The majority of the poor of the town lived and worked around Sandgate and the quayside and were thus likely to be parishioners of this church, located on the high cliff above the river overlooking these neighbourhoods (Gray 1649; Brand 1789; Bourne 1736; Langton 1975: 16; Ellis 1984: 197). The tables provide evidence that the neighbourhood where tradesmen lived, (discussed in Chapter 4), affected the choice of parish church selected for a donation. For example, the tanners and weavers, who lived to the west and the north of the town tended to select St. Johns and St. Andrews, whereas bakers, master mariners and shipwrights selected All Saints.

Clergymen, (who were variously referred to as vicar, curate, minister, parson or preacher, with a single reference to a 'Right Worshipful Doctor'), were left nearly a quarter of bequests overall by the early decades of the 17th century. Some of these men belonged to local churches, some to a church elsewhere in the region. The distribution of the remainder of bequests, comprising an overall average of over 30%, was more widespread. In the period prior to 1600, over 40% of recipients were included in this group, and the bequests were described in more detail than was the case by the 17th century. By this later period, the figure had halved, apparently in favour of the clergy and to a lesser extent the local parish churches.

Where institutes were named, most notably in the earlier decades, they included bequests by a miller 'To the Almshouse besyde my house' and to the 'Poor of the Spittel Almshouses' which stood on Westgate Street opposite St. Johns Church (D.P.R. Grey 1585). This man was a parishioner of St. John where a number of millers lived (D.P.R. Grey 1585). A tailor left 12d 'to the tow pore womene in the Maysing dew', the Maison Dieu on the quayside (D.P.R. Swyneborne 1549). A mariner left 20s 'to the poor of Trinity House - to be divided amongst them', Trinity House being the seamen's guild (D.P.R. Holborne 1622; McCombie 1985). A tanner left 6s 8d 'to the preparing of the house of provition for the poor' (D.P.R. Rowmaine 1587). In 1590 a keelman left money to the poor of Sandgate Ward, the neighbourhood where most of these tradesmen lived. A 'poor man's box' was mentioned in the later 16th and early 17th century, probably held by the Corporation of Newcastle. Funds were mentioned which were 'to be letten by Mr. Mayor that is now ... put in good surety in the towne chamber' (D.P.R. Frier 1591), indicating sustained efforts in caring for the poor by the town officials, supported by private donation, a finding somewhat at odds with Howells's conclusions, discussed above (1967: 314, 319). A bequest of 20s was given by Oswald Chater, weaver, who lived on Westgate Street, and who lies buried in St. John's church. The money was 'for or towards the buying of A Carpett for the Communion table of St. John's Church', showing that after the turmoil of the Reformation, gifts to the infrastructure of a church continued, now in accordance with a changed ideology (D.P.R. 1623; Bourne 1736, 1980: 26-7).

The most prominent recipients of bequests overall are poor neighbours and poor widows, often people known to the testator, and contrary to Cressy there is no evidence that those 'without issue' are more likely to leave money to charities, friends or neighbours (1986: 64). The decline in donations to the poor in general by the second quarter of the 17th century, a much earlier date than observed by King (2004: 62), was perhaps, compensated to some extent by bequests to particular named individuals known personally to the testators. Wrightson observed that neighbourly interaction was structured by occupational solidarity (1984: 331-2), a finding also discussed by King in regard to charitable giving within trades (2001: 42; 2004: 59, 65), and this closeness of community is evident in the documents. However, the provision of bequests does not appear to have been restricted in any way by occupational affiliation, as tradesmen were very generous to members of other trades and their families. Most such neighbours and widows are not, however, included in this section as they were not referred to directly as 'the poor' in wills. In one of the earliest documents (dated 1548), a keelman, a poor man himself, left a bequest to the children of a friend (D.P.R. Bullok). In 1571, a skinner and glover left 20s 'to be bestowed amongste my neighbours poore householders' (D.P.R. Moyser). A smith gave over 3li to the poor 'whereof 20s shalbe to the poore widowes that dwelles besides us' (D.P.R 1585). In subsequent decades 1620-1640, there are references to money bequeathed to poor 'widows and neighbours', 'kind friends' and 'loving neighbours'.

It appears that some testators felt more conscious of responsibilities to the poor than others. Richard Kell, tailor, left bequests to All Saints church, to the 'poor of the town', to two preachers and two curates of St. John's and St. Andrew's parish churches. He also left a shilling to 'every childe now living which I was witness unto at there Baptisme', to several servants and friends and to a boy 'to get him a master' (D.P.R. 1604). In all, Kell gave 20 bequests to over 25 people

Annuities for the poor were also set up from the revenues of rented properties. Thomas Smithe, blacksmith, bequeathed his wife the revenue from rents 'whereof I will the halfe that it be distributed to the poore yeareley during hir life and after hir decease the whole out rent for ever I will shale be given to the poore' (D.P.R 1585). A weaver, Cuthbert Woodman, 'being visited with the plague of pestilence', bequeathed the poor of All Saint's parish 12s per year to be paid to the churchwarden by his wife from the revenue from their property. However, if the money was not paid, then the churchwardens were 'to enter and distraine from time to time or otherwise take such course by disposing of the tenements to the use aforesaid as they shall think good' (D.P.R. 1636). Poor women appeared to have been particularly remembered as testators seemed to recognise that women may have been in greater want than men. For example, the tailor who bequeathed money to the two poor women in the Maison Dieu, also gave the four children of a widow 16d, and three other children of another woman he knew 13d, and three more women 4d each 'for want'. Lastly, he bequeathed one poor friend 'a half an angel for a token' (D.P.R. Swyneborne 1549). The documents also contained bequests to parish churches outside Newcastle - in Ponteland and Ovingham and to a chapel in Arrendale, all located in Northumberland - perhaps given in acknowledgement of places where the testators had some personal connection.

The data in Table 3.9 suggests that over the decades, fewer testators were providing a larger number of bequests per person, with the average numbers of bequests increasing from 1.3 per testator before 1600, to 1.5 in the first quarter of the 17th century, to 1.8 in the final period. The percentage of testators in each trade who included bequests varies widely, with no clear distinction evident between the richer or poorer trades, perhaps with the exception of keelmen and mariners who were some of the least affluent men in the sample. These figures may, however, be misleading because when the number of bequests per person was compared with overall percentage figures, the lower percentages for a given trade did not correlate with the generosity of individuals. In addition, the size of donations varied considerably, ranging between 12d and several pounds, and wealthier men do seem occasionally to have provided more generously than others. A well-to-do smith left 5li to All Saints church in 1641, but in some cases the amount seems very small in comparison with the size of other types of bequests, and especially in relation to the overall wealth reflected in the will and inventory. Taking the evidence together, one cannot help feeling that the poor were not helped as much as they might have been, and that secular family concerns rather than spiritual matters were the greater priority for the majority of the population. Erickson noted that few will-makers, regardless of their family situation could not have afforded a shilling or two in charity, and that giving was not dependant on the life cycle stage (2002: 211), although receiving relief was certainly related to life cycle poverty (Wales 1984: 353, 378).

The Newcastle evidence shows that testators were often inclined to be specific about how their gift was to be used, and donations were indeed becoming rarer, but only in the sense that fewer men were giving more. The finding has confirmed that this trend began earlier than Wrightson's evidence for Whickham had indicated, where he had found that after the third quarter of the 17th century bequests were becoming both rarer and more directed to specific purposes (1991: 341). Erickson's research on Yorkshire, Lincolnshire and Sussex also indicated that charitable bequests in wills declined in the latter 17th century, where prior to the mid 17th century 29% of men and 32% of women gave to the poor, the figures dropping to less than 20% in the latter half of the century (2002: 211). Although Newcastle tradesmen may not have been as generous collectively as those in other parts of the country, as individuals, many showed concern. Marsh discussed the duty to settle an estate in order to procure a degree of spiritual tranquillity as essential if one were to die 'Chrystyanlye' (2000: 174), and Duffy wrote 'Justice and charity alike demanded that the dying Christian should be reconciled not only to God, but to neighbour also' (1992: 322). Perhaps those who chose to help the poor, especially those personally known to them, sought more than others to follow the Christian teachings of the day, although their generosity was not always visible in the records. Erickson's observation that widows were more generous to the poor than male testators, suggesting they had a greater awareness of the poverty of women in this society, may underestimate the contributions men made to poor friends and neighbours (2002: 211, 228). However, cash was not the only type of bequests that could assist the needy, and it is to other types of bequests that we now turn.

3.7 Bequests of clothes

Acquiring new clothing in the early modern period involved substantial financial outlay, and in terms of household expenditure, clothing was second only to food (Weatherill 1996: 119). The value of these items was also high relative to other types of bequests in wills (Erickson 1993: 65), and as one of life's absolute necessities, it is not perhaps surprising to find second-hand clothes recorded in the documents. Clothing (but not usually shoes), belonging to testators, often the 'best' or 'second best' they owned, and clothing specifically designed for work in a trade, was bequeathed in about 10% of wills to selected family and friends among all the 13 trades throughout the period, although such bequests were rather inconsistently recorded.

There were marked changes in the practices relating to bequests of clothes (shown in Table 3.10) between the 16th and 17th centuries. Such bequests were most common prior to 1600, although a close analysis of the records indicated that these were already declining in the late 1580s and the beginning of the 1590s. By the first half of the 17th century, even fewer bequests were recorded (although one man who gave away a disproportionate number of these buoys up the figures). In the second quarter of the 17th century, bequests decrease again for all but three trades - the cordwainers, tailors and tanners.

Cordwainers were among the more affluent tradesmen in Newcastle, which may explain why they owned more clothes that were of a quality worth passing on to others. The majority were given to sons and brothers and descriptions include items with buttons of silver or stitched with silk. However, wealth did not influence the bequests of master mariners who, as will be shown in Chapter 5, invested in more clothes than any other trade, but did not include them in wills (except in the earliest period). The tailors listed a great variety of clothing in their wills, including those dated to the plague year of 1636. At this time several other trades also included bequests to non-family members as a result of widespread deaths within families. The descriptions of clothes in plague years were often elaborate, possibly indicating a necessity to make clear to the executors what exactly was being bequeathed, as sometimes no family members survived to administer this. The higher percentage of bequests of clothes by tailors may relate to the wide range of clothing created by men of the trade, although evidence from inventories contradicts this as clothes were rarely listed, where yards of cloth were, and most tailors worked to order (Weatherill 1996: 145). Bequests of clothes by tanners appeared to focus more on the need of an individual than on descriptions of the item - the most favoured recipients were brothers, male friends and (particularly) apprentices.

The decline in bequests of clothing over the decades does suggest changing norms regarding what people chose to include on wills, although Erickson pointed out that women continued for longer and with greater frequency with these bequests than did men (2002: 216). Spufford suggested that the steady decline of such bequests in wills may have been the result of clothing becoming cheaper and more readily available; thus, the appraisers tended to ignore such items (1990: 150, 1984: 126). She found that ready-made clothes were becoming easier to acquire in the late 17th century, although she does not discount the continuing importance of second-hand apparel (1984: 125, 148).

From the Newcastle evidence it appears that clothes were becoming more readily available, and second-hand items were not so much desired by the early 17th century as they had been in the decades before 1590, arguing for a much earlier change in consumption patterns than the late 17th century. But the clothing recorded in wills, while providing some insight into inheritance patterns, is also very incomplete as almost 90% of Newcastle inventories included the testator's clothing (Table 5.6, Arkell 2000: 92), precisely the opposite finding to that of Trinder and Cox that clothes were often listed on wills, but subsequently often removed from inventories (1980: 34-5; Spufford 1984: 129). The recording of clothes in Newcastle inventories is much higher than elsewhere in the country (Wrightson 1979: 38; Spufford 1984: 129), and most came to members of the nuclear family as part of the 'rest of the goods and chattels' (Table 3.6). Clothes were never left to the poor. Overall, the findings suggest that while bequests of clothes declined, a corresponding growth in consumption of apparel appears to have been evident by the early 17th century, a situation discussed further in Chapter 5.

3.8 Bequests of animals

Individual bequests of animals were not particularly common to Newcastle wills, a finding echoed in Yorkshire, Lincolnshire and Sussex wills (Erickson 1993: 68). However, the evidence from Newcastle wills is misleading, as ownership of livestock was widespread among most urban tradesmen, although members of land-based trades owned more animals and were more likely to make bequests than were seafarers. Animals were recorded in anywhere from 16% to over 90% of inventories, bequeathed as part of the 'rest of the goods and chattels', most often to the nuclear family (Tables 3.6, 5.10a, 5.10b), although some animals may have been sold or given away prior to the writing of the will - notably horses, as they were both expensive to keep and easy to sell (Spufford 1984: 40).

Table 3.11 examines types of bequests to 17 social groups, in all 89 people, representing just 3.5% of the total beneficiaries in the wills overall. Of the 39 wills listing animals, 21 of these were dated earlier than 1600, 14 fell in the first quarter of the 17th century, with just four bequests dated to the second quarter of the 17th century. This decline in bequests was similar to that seen in bequests of clothing. Such changes suggest altering priorities as to what was included in wills, but a decline in livestock ownership is evident in the 17th century, and is discussed below.

Over 250 animals, including cattle, sheep and horses were recorded over the period but the distribution figures were skewed by three large bequests for herds of sheep. When these anomalies were removed from the calculation, about 60% of animals listed were cows, many about one year old, one-quarter were sheep, and 14% were horses. Pigs were virtually absent from wills as were poultry. The nuclear family received over 40% of the bequests, such bequests being mainly of young cows, and these were fairly equally distributed between wives, sons and daughters. Two girls were left fair-sized herds of sheep, and the wife of a miller was the only women in the data set to be specifically bequeathed horses, which belonged to the family mill (D.P.R. Reisley 1604), underlining the participation of women in trade within the town, a subject discussed in Chapter 5.

Other recipients of bequests were divided into four groups. Group 2a includes male relatives and Group 2b female relatives, each gender group comprising siblings, parents, grandchildren, nephews and nieces, and one father-in-law. Bequests to these groups were again fairly equally divided in relation to the number of bequests recorded, although nieces were favoured over nephews and female relatives received about twice the number of animals bequeathed to their male counterparts, *excluding* the anomaly of a single bequest of 81 sheep to a shipwright's brother. Groups 3a and 3b included male and female friends and their children and a single male servant, and bequests here were slightly biased in favour of males in terms of the percentage of recipients. However, the actual number of animals bequeathed to male friends was double that given to female friends. This is the reverse of the figures indicated for female relatives (Group 2b).

If the ratios of different types of animals given to legatees are examined, the results show women received marginally more cows than men, whereas there was a strong bias towards males receiving horses. Evidence from Yorkshire, Sussex and Lincolnshire also showed male testators favoured sons regarding bequests of horses (Erickson 1993: 215). Overall, sheep were the most commonly listed animal. Erickson discusses the omnipresence of bequests for lambs and ewes in wills, noting that animals were not merely tokens of affection but benefited recipients with their wool, meat and even rent, and that they were often given to grandchildren, godchildren, nieces and nephews (2002: 85). This was also the case within Newcastle families.

The decline in individual bequests of animals can be linked to wider evidence of a steady decline of livestock ownership in the north in the 17th century (Everitt 1967: 417; Shammas 1990: 41-2), a change also evident from inventories and discussed in Chapter 5. However, importantly, children appear to have continued to receive bequests of animals in Newcastle, in contrast to the findings of Erickson in the 17th century for Yorkshire, Sussex and Lincolnshire (2002: 68), and Howell in the 16th century for Kibworth Harcourt (1978: 151, 267, 1983: 265), where cash bequests were replacing gifts of lambs or ewes (although cash bequests were also increasing in Newcastle (Table 3.8). Overall, of 89 recorded recipients of animals, 52 were children, both male and female, a figure clearly suggesting that such bequests continued to be seen as important to the welfare of the young.

3.9 Circumstances affecting bequests

It has become clear in following the evidence presented in Newcastle testaments that the division of estates usually followed the laws and customs of the time. But what befell estates when a family quarrelled, or unforeseen circumstances occurred, or when plague wiped out an entire family? This section explores the responses of testators to difficult situations. In examining the wording of wills written in times of trouble or conflict, the continued efforts that testators made to arrange a settlement to the advantage of all concerned, can be underlined.

A marked worry for some testators was that their wishes might be overridden by unruly children, although threats to disinherit a family member were rare. However, Issa's contention that conflict more often concerned those related by marriage, rather than by blood, appears to be misconceived (1986: 472). One example of a thinly veiled warning to children came from the shipwright Thomas Smithe, who referred to his two daughters as 'wenshes & maids'. The girls had perhaps worried their father as he warns them not to marry without the consent of their mother, their uncle and the partner of the testator, 'nor make anie contr[ac]t w[i]th anie man' or they would not receive a child portion 'nor anie pennie worthe of my goods' (D.P.R. 1585). However, if they consented to their father's wishes, they would receive their fair share. Richard Bulman, shipwright, was blunter still with his siblings, saying 'that if my brother and sister or any of them be not contented with theis thinges w[hi]ch I have given them ... or maike my question about any my goodes', then their bequests 'to be voyd and they to have nothing att all' (D.P.R. 1604). The miller Thomas Reade was clearly worried about his eldest son Bartram. This son was left the family mill and, when his mother died, he was first in line for the family home that was adjoined to this mill. The father informed the son that he 'may not lett, sett sell mortgage or put away the premises' nor 'buy part to another person' without the supervisor's consent, and that if he 'will not here after order and behave himself as an honest man ought to in every respect' that the supervisors 'shall use and dispose of the said lands and goods by me formerlie bequeathed unto him'. The inheritance would go instead to Bartram's two 'cousins as he calls them' (D.P.R. 1613). The will was not witnessed, which suggests that perhaps it had been drawn up with the express intent of threatening this unruly son. Testators were clearly prepared to go to some lengths to try to enforce their wills, even from beyond the grave. Cressy notes that, although a patriarchal ideology prevailed, parents did not always control their children or husbands their wives (1999: 10).

Unruly offspring or siblings were not the only concern of testators. The weak and venerable required protection and this was also specifically requested by benefactors, most notably regarding those who were not directly included in the division of the estate, and asked of those who would inherit. Thomas Pearson, a weaver, whose first wife and all his children had died, asked his second wife to look after his sister, 'to be good to hir & keep hir so longe as she lyvethe' (D.P.R. 1607). Perhaps this sister was elderly and the rest of her family had passed away leaving her at the mercy of people to whom she was not related. John Patteson, mariner, left his mill on Broad Chair to his brother William, as he had no wife or children of his own. John 'commanded' his brother to pay their mother and father 40s, but also mentioned their nephew Oliver Sharper, son of their sister Margaret, the boy 'being fatherless', and 'desiring my brother William for to be a good uncle unto him' (D.P.R. 1584). John Sayre, an unmarried miller, left his two properties to his sisters, Elizabeth who was married, and Agnus the younger, described as a 'spinster'. John clearly worried about the fate of his youngest sibling and asked his friend Robert Hope to take 'special care' of her to see that she 'be in noe way wronged of what shalbe hereby due unto her' (D.P.R. 1624). In such cases, threats of disinheritance were replaced by pleas for kindness from those who would materially benefit from the testators generosity.

Circumstances which could lead a testator to bequeath his 'worldly goods' to someone, other than his immediate family, might involve debts. One such example comes from Lancelot Wilkinson, a cordwainer, who left all his goods to 'my servant and apprentice' John Toore, who he names as sole executor. John was 'to pay him selfe out of my said goodes provided all wayes that my said executor shall be countable and give unto my wife Allyes Wilkinson all the surplus of my goods'. Lancelot owed his apprentice John 20li 'at the exsperacion of his yeares the which he hath bound for (and) in consedderacon thereof do make him my full and holle executor as I assuredly trust him and as he hath promised unto me' (D.P.R. 1623). The inventory revealed the extent of debt that Lancelot was faced with on his deathbed, and explains why his apprentice is named as principal beneficiary instead of his wife. Although the testator himself was owed enough money to cover the debts due to the apprentice, he owed another 22 people money and he had 'desperate debts', which had to be written off as there was no hope of repayment. Once the administration of the testament was complete, the executor appears to have been left l5s in debt. John will have got most of his money, but Allyes (Lancelot's wife) was left with nothing. Apparently, the consideration of debt repayment in the light of the fear surrounding dying in debt and the consequences on Judgement Day outweighed family considerations, at least in this case, though similar attitudes prevailed throughout the country in the early modern period, for example in the case of chapmen (Spufford 1984: 53).

There were rare examples in wills that illustrate how this society reacted if a testator chose not to adhere to the law, traditions or expectations concerning an inheritance. In an exceptional nuncupative testament dated August 1625, William Collingwood, a cordwainer, was according to those who witnessed his testament 'sicke of the plague in a lodge in the fields nigh upon Newcastle upon Tyne which sicknes he shortely after dyed'. There were five witnesses present who 'had just felt oportunitie then to commit the same to writinge', 'for the better and more fully clearinge explaining and declareing the ambeguitye and doubtfulness of the said deseaseds will and mind'. When William was 'demanded by Leonard Carr of Newcastle Merchant howe hee would disposse of his howses and his estate' the dying man left everything to Margaret Robinson, wife of John Robinson, tailor. This seems to have caused quite a stir. The will continues 'And being further tould by the said Leonard Carr that hee had poorer bretheren and sisters hee might doe well to remember them w[i]th some p[ar]rte of his estate hee answeard againe and said Noe for as I tould you before soe I saie againe all my goods & howses whatsoever I give and bequeath unto the saide Margaret Robinson' (D.P.R. 1625). An allegation was made some months later by three people who questioned whether the testator's intention was that Margaret would inherit the estate 'for & during her life naturall', or whether he meant she could also pass the estate to her own heirs, that this was the 'intent' of the deceased. The evidence suggests that a strict line of inheritance was considered the norm and that deviation could be seen as a sign that the testator was not in full control of his mental faculties, a situation that led to a legal dispute in this case. Taken together, these findings are supported by Issa, who says that the strength of implicit obligations should not be underestimated, as even in conflict there was no departure from 'normal patterns of recognition' (1986: 474).

Wills of the period record thousands of very individual arrangements, outlining precisely what should be done with an individual's estate. Each tells a unique story, reflecting the priorities made for the care of the testator's closest family and friends. In times of crisis, the methods by which this northern society tried to assist those left to cope, by way of bequests, tells us much of the mentality of people from the period and illustrates how even adversity could not change the basic tenets of inheritance practices.

3.10 Conclusions

Newcastle testators of the 16th and 17th centuries form part of a nationwide pattern concerning priorities in the division of estates associated with the life cycles of both individuals and families. The responsibility towards a spouse and children was paramount, and where there were no immediate heirs within a nuclear family, close relatives and good friends came to inherit the residue of an estate (Everitt 1967: 455; Howell 1978: 14, 1983: 257; Wrightson 1991: 284; Spufford 1978: 172, 2000: 112-3, 119; Erickson 1993:73). There was a broad structural homogeneity within English society by the early modern period, and a common kinship system, and the north was integral to this system (Issa 1986: 473). It was rare for any nuclear family member to be excluded from bequests, excepting in cases of widespread deaths (especially in times of plagues), or in the event of serious debt. There were clear divisions, relating to age, sex and marital status, as well as wealth and occupation. Certain distinct practices were apparent in the settlement of estates among trades.

Erickson's conclusion, that a tradition of partible inheritance was more common than primogeniture in the north, has been questioned (2002: 68). Primogeniture was evident in the case of bequests of real property, which usually went to a son, often the eldest, but this was not a straightforward system whereby the eldest son was particularly privileged. Instead the marked responsibilities of any principal heir militated against the idea of favouritism, a finding supported by Issa's work on County Durham (1986: 476). Both Issa (1986: 476) and Spufford (1978: 157) also noted that a distinction between primogeniture and partible inheritance was a very blurred one, a conclusion also echoed by Howell in her examination of the legal distinction between unigeniture and partible inheritance (1978: 146, 1983: 262). While acknowledging that the custom of primogeniture was undoubtedly influential, it is a wholly inadequate description of the system of inheritance in early modern England (Everitt 1967: 456; Erickson 1993: 78). In evidence from the nearby town of Whickham, Wrightson found that, although practices showed a clear bias in favour of sons, to suggest that this constituted a primogeniture system would be crude and erroneous (1984: 329). Cressy confirms a 'patrilineal lineage bias' in property transmission but notes that in other regards the system was fluid and flexible (1986: 67). The testators of early modern Newcastle struggled to find ways to devise their estates equitably; nevertheless there was an apparent predilection towards male legatees throughout the period in the region.

Where a wife, son or daughter was first in line for real property, those who were not would be compensated as much as possible with other properties or, in lieu of these, with some other category of the family's wealth. In Newcastle, up to 90% of real property was bequeathed to the nuclear family. Beyond the immediate family, brothers and grandsons were slightly more favoured than all other groups. Throughout the decades included in this study, there was no evidence that widows received more land than the law entitled them to, except where the care of minor children gave them custody of the property until the male heir reached majority, a pattern similar to that found by Howell in Kibworth Harcourt (1983: 256-7), and by Issa in County Durham (1986: 475). Nor were daughters given any special privileges to land in accordance with a so-called Norse influence in northern England, as was apparent in Yorkshire (Erickson 1993: 63). Within the nuclear family, the divisions of bequests tended to be shared out in such a way that whoever came to be heir of the family property had to assist the other children, especially if they had not yet received their child's portion. The heir was either to make payments from property revenues until the portions were paid, or to support siblings, who sometimes retained a right to continue to live in the property until payments were forthcoming. Such arrangements were evident in Leicester in connection with land shortages (Howell 1983: 261), whereas in Newcastle the problem seemed to be a case of straightforward necessity in providing accommodation in a growing town.

Whether richer or poorer testators devised property more equitably is not easy to assess, such choices being markedly individual. In Yorkshire, poorer tradesmen did not apparently divide their estate more equitably than richer tradesmen (Erickson 1993: 72). In Newcastle, examples can be found of both wealthy testators devising several properties between several children, and the poorer testators of crowded Sandgate dividing up single properties to accommodate the family. In other cases the main holding was passed to a son and was not divided, as was the norm in Terling, Essex (Wrightson 1984: 328-9). In the case of Newcastle beneficiaries, there was no evidence to support Howell's finding that primogeniture tended to become associated with the more affluent sectors of society and partible inheritance with the poorer (1983: 269), while it was apparent that if a family owned more than one property, these were often equitably divided, a situation that clearly pertained more to those who had greater wealth tied up in properties.

Bequests of objects from Newcastle wills echo inheritance patterns found elsewhere in the country, with 70% of objects bequeathed to the nuclear family, while the remaining 30% was shared out between other family and friends. However, differences were apparent in the treatment of daughters who were not compensated with more movable goods than sons, in lieu of property, as had been found to be the case in Lincolnshire, Sussex and Yorkshire (Erickson 1993: 19). Sons in fact inherited marginally more objects than daughters, and this partiality continued in the treatment of male relatives, male friends, and male apprentices and servants, all of whom received a greater share than their female counter parts. In particular these men received tools and clothes associated with the various trades suggesting a gender bias in wills, one perhaps countered by widows in turn who gave preference to female legatees (Erickson 1993: 215).

Patterns of monetary bequests to principal beneficiaries, encompassing the largest number of recipients overall, were distinct from those of other bequests. Around 60% of the principal cash bequests went to the nuclear family, most notably in favour of daughters, who received one-and-a-half times the overall figure given to sons. The sisters of testators were also recognised, receiving four times the bequests given to brothers. Erickson confirmed that, normally, in other parts of the country, daughters received cash in lieu of real property (2002: 94), and Issa found that in County Durham younger children, in general, were compensated with cash in lieu of property (1986: 476). However, daughters would have had to receive more than double the amount of cash bequeathed to sons to compensate for discrimination relating to bequests of real property and, to a lesser extent, moveable goods, depending on the relative size of the various bequests. Sisters of testators also tended to receive much smaller bequests than their brothers overall. Widows had to await the settlement of the estate to know what cash would come to them, as they were rarely named as legatees for individual cash bequests on wills. In the eventual settlement of the estate, the 'ready money' listed in the inventories might be used to settle debts and, would therefore never come to the family at all, as dying in debt was not uncommon, affecting about 10% of testators in the sample. This figure is, however, lower than that in other regions, where according to Erickson

25% of men left their widows in debt, or with a much reduced estate once all legacies had been honoured (2002: 200-1). Nevertheless, it is rarely known what became of the inventoried goods, as very few of the final accounts submitted to the Durham Consistory Court by the executors survive, but a sizable majority of testators had evidently accumulated money, and the increased prevalence of cash bequests in the wills can be linked more generally to the economic prosperity of the town connected with the ever-expanding coal markets (Howell 1978: 152; Wrightson 1991: 24; Ellis 2001).

Taking the evidence together, regarding the distribution of bequests of real property, movables and cash, a hierarchical pattern has emerged, that shows different strategies were employed for each type of bequest. The range of beneficiaries broadened for each of the three categories. The selection of beneficiaries for property was the most restricted category, with nuclear families inheriting up to 90% of properties overall. In contrast, those outside the family, who received cash bequests, constituted about 40% of recipients. Newcastle testators designated a wide range of legatees, and extended their generosity even to those who were brought in as administrators. Contrary to Erickson's finding that supervisors were virtually unknown in the north, these men were frequently named in wills, even as beneficiaries (2002: 71). Wrightson described the range of recognised kin in Whickham as 'genealogically both narrow and shallow', but he noted that 70 - 80% of testators recognised kin beyond the immediate family (1991: 330). Among Newcastle testators, the consistent inclusion of a very wide range of beneficiaries for assorted bequests differs from Issa's finding in County Durham that involvement beyond the nuclear family was largely confined to siblings, nephews and nieces (1986: 472). The Newcastle evidence confirms that, indeed, the immediate family were given priority and that the line of inheritance was (in the majority of cases) narrowly defined. The family received a clear majority of all types of bequests, but recognition was given to friends and their children, apprentices and servants and, in the case of cash bequests many more friends, clerks, supervisors and unrelated executors, clergymen, the poor and various charitable institutes. Erickson's finding that women gave to a wider circle of unrelated legatees than men could be questioned in the light of the Newcastle evidence (2002: 212). In either case, given the breadth of the groups of legatees, and mindful of the observation by Erickson that moveable goods and cash bequests were of a comparable value to bequests of real property in this period (2002: 77) (although disputed by Howell, who found bequests in kind were more valuable than cash bequests (1983: 267)), an overall bias by male testators in favour of male legatees was unmistakable.

An examination of bequests to the poor indicated that only one-quarter of testators specifically mentioned the poor in their wills, and a decline in these bequests by the second quarter of the17th century was observed. The change, however, only affected the distribution of bequests and did not signify the demise of legacies to the poor. Poor people specifically known to the families of the testators were increasingly preferred to institutes, resulting in fewer bequests to the poor being included in wills by the early 17th century. Wrightson noted such a trend in Whickham by in the late 17th century, but the practice clearly began much earlier (1991: 341). Women - especially poor neighbours, widows and their children - were particularly recognised by testators outside bequests designated for the official poor. The struggle faced by single mothers with young children and aged women at these critical stages in the life cycle were well known to those living in this period (Wrightson 1991: 268, 351). Smith noted that poor women outnumbered men two to one in the early modern period (1984: 77), and Newcastle testators clearly recognised these problems in their own town, as individuals and as members of guilds (King 2001: 42). The needs of the town's poor masses were not neglected, as more bequests were directed to All Saint's church than any other, as this parish supported the largest number of poor people at that time.

Although bequests of clothes showed a declined by the 17th century, this was not, apparently, linked to any change in ownership patterns, as clothes were almost always included in inventories, and were among the most valuable items listed, and investment was rising in this period (Everitt 1967: 449; Shammas 1990: 169; Spufford 1990: 150; Wrightson 1991: 104; Weatherill 1996: 134-5; Arkell 2000:92). The change reflected what was being recorded on wills. Individual bequests of animals also declined by the 17th century, a trend which was also evident from inventories. In this instance, the decline of bequests probably reflected a more general decline in animal ownership in England in this period (Everitt 1967: 417; Shammas 1990: 40), although this trend was not universal among all trades, as will be shown in Chapter 5. Importantly, bequests continued to be given to children, including those of friends and widows, who made up the majority of legatees of animals throughout the period.

In answering the question of how important trade affiliation was to the division of estates, the evidence suggests that the specific circumstances associated with different trades, both in terms of profitability and type of business, led to different strategies being employed in determining the nature and extent of bequests. For example, shipwrights, who owned the largest percentage of properties in the town, were in a better position to devise these more equitably than those trades with far fewer properties. Many mariners, who may have died younger than other testators, and had fewer children, exhibited markedly different inheritance strategies concerning their sisters, who, unlike the sisters of men from other trades, were frequently named in wills. Butchers, cordwainers and millers were more likely to leave businesses in the hands of their daughters than other tradesmen. Such information on bequests of businesses to women helps to refute claims that women of the period lacked experience and training in the trades (Earle 1994: 154), as wills make clear that many women of all ages and trades were expected to continue running family businesses to support minor children, as well as themselves, a finding highlighted by Spufford's work on chapmen, whose wives frequently continued the family business out of pure necessity (1984: 54, 70, 74). The situation is also well attested to in Clark's earlier study of working lives of women (1919, 1992). Although life cycle factors cannot be ruled out in any of the observed patterns of bequests, especially those concerning the importance of trade designations, the discrepancies among trades were unambiguous. A connection between trade affiliation and wealth has also been established in terms of inheritance as the most important component to wealth, which broadened options in the types and scale of bequests (Wrightson 1984: 327), with clear implications for material culture (Shammas 1991: 104, 173; Erickson 1993: 3; Overton 2004: 139). Weatherill confirmed that the intergenerational transmission of wealth through the wills provides a means of better understanding consumption and material culture (1996: 105).

Whereas it is clear that personal situations *vis-à-vis* wealth and occupation created the possibility for tradesmen to devise estates on a very individual basis, these factors must be placed in the context of the overwhelming importance of the family life cycle. Issa found that for the vast majority of the population in this period, life cycle rather than wealth was the crucial factor determining patterns of kin recognition (1986: 469-70). Spufford noted that three-quarters of testators made a will not because they were rich or poor, but because they had to provide for children (1976: 171-2), and that it was these family responsibilities rather than wealth which increased the likelihood of will-making in the first place (1976: 170). Wealth and occupation can be shown to have influenced what was included in a will, but did not necessarily dictate the need to create such a document in the first instance. Cressy noted that only those with property to dispose of or minor children to safeguard had the need to make a will (1999: 392-3).

In Newcastle, as elsewhere, the presence of minor children was a key factor in the decisions made by testators in devising their estates; however, in terms of bequests, older siblings who had reached the age of majority and who had already been given their child's portion, were sometimes in a better position than the youngest children, because as a testator aged or became ill, and as portions were paid out, the financial situation in a family sometimes worsened. For example, Wrightson found that wage-earners were at the greatest risk of impoverishment in the later stages of the life cycle (1991: 161), while Wales focused on the cyclical nature of poverty in 17th century Norfolk where aged, ill, unemployed, underemployed people, orphans or widows with small children were all pushed into a precarious situation at different stages of their lives (1984: 353).

The wording of, and information provided by, wills often makes it very difficult to detect the conditions faced by a family, except in times of crisis. The documents reveal that death may have come upon a family quite suddenly, as most testators died within a few short weeks of making a will, and sometimes within days. However, transition in the life cycle at the death of the head of the household revealed clear strategies designed to protect all survivors, which also included people outside the family. Bequests were ultimately tied to particular social circumstances, which might change at any point in the life cycle. When family constitution was altered through deaths or because children reached the age of majority (usually at 21 years), when a widow remarried or there was a lack of any heirs within the immediate family, all parts of the inheritance were redistributed among other social groups according to personal wishes, perceived need, as well as practical considerations. Examples of this can be found among all trades and form a consistent pattern throughout the period. Wrightson confirms these patterns in Whickham where, in the absence of children, patterns changed as testators turned to their nearest kin, especially siblings, or to distant kin for those with no close family at all (Wrightson 1984: 325). Early in this discussion it was pointed out that the age of a testator was not ultimately of great importance, although much emphasis in understanding inheritance patterns focuses on this factor. In view of the findings here, the emphasis should perhaps be reversed to focus instead on the age of the beneficiaries, which is of at least equal, if not greater, importance.

The contents of wills reflect law, custom, practice and notions of religious duty, while it is clear that individual choice was perfectly possible and testators exercised their right to devise wills as they thought best. Cressy confirms that the system was selective, voluntary and flexible, although his assertion that the system was 'informal' must be questioned in the light of the numerous references in wills of the period to the law, and the willingness of testator's to use the principals in guiding their decisions (1986: 67 -8). Wrightson described the time of will-making as one of dramatic transition, a 'last act of social recognition and the final exercising of personal authority' (1991: 284). The emphasis in all testaments is on the practical survival and well being of the family and closest friends, both in the secular and in a hoped-for spiritual world yet to come. Bequests were never devised on grounds of novelty or fashion; such trivial concerns appear to have had no place in the serious business of setting people up in life or easing personal difficulties. The inclusion of so many people in bequests suggests a close-knit community where members felt bound to help one another, resulting in a fairer society, one where primogeniture, where it did apply, was marked by very definite responsibilities towards others. Issa says that the transmission of property must be understood within the context of obligations within the family, which were structured by both needs and emotions (1986: 477), a view echoed by Cressy who says that 'Depending on necessity and circumstance even latent kin could become effective and peripheral kin could become close' (1986: 67).

The evidence presented here, suggests the obligations of individuals and families should be seen in a wider context. A communal approach to inheritance is evident, reflected in the ritual markers of the life cycle - most particularly the birth of children, marriage and death - which were subject to scrutiny by family and friends, neighbours and associates, by officers of the church and state, because the business of the household was also the business of the wider community (Cressy 1999: 476). Henry Misson had written in the early 18th century that it was from middling people that the customs of the nation are most truly to be learned (Cressy 1999: 453-4), and such an observation must surely apply to the customs of inheritance of this study of an earlier period.

Howell sees inheritance as a dynamic process, a case of stewardship rather than ownership (1978: 141). The constant and inevitable changes within the family life cycle engendered a variety of socially responsible solutions to situations which were sometimes dictated by circumstances beyond the control of the testators. The cycle of life, reflected in the division of inheritances, in part at least, dictated who would have the opportunity to participate in the consumer society of early modern Newcastle, at least for those with the right social as well as economic connections gained by way of a bequest, however those bequests were ultimately made.

In this chapter, how people made decisions in relation to their worldly goods at the time of their deaths (not just cultural or legal motivations, but also the personal priorities, vulnerabilities and prejudices of individuals) has been analysed. In Chapter 4, the focus moves to other material sides of life.

CHAPTER 4 - Property

4.1 Introduction

Probate records contain extensive information concerning property. About half the records utilized in this chapter provide sufficient details about the location of houses or tenements, shops, mills, closes, garths and land holdings to analyse and to partially reconstruct the historical demography and built environment of early modern Newcastle. Information on over 520 properties recorded in 70 locations around the town and suburbs have been found in the wills and inventories. As very few structures dating from the medieval or early modern period survive in modern Newcastle, and the intense urbanisation of the city has meant that large-scale archaeological excavations have been restricted, the documentary evidence can make an important contribution in locating and reconstructing the early topography.

The probate records provide information on residential patterns, revealing in the most detailed instances, the location of properties along streets belonging to different tradesmen; the plan, orientation, size and number of storeys of structures; how a building was accessed; and who leased, owned or occupied the premises. Information on regional holdings has been excluded from this analysis, which concentrates on the intra- and extra-mural parts of the town (although some regional properties are mentioned in relation to by-employment activities in Chapter 5). It should also be noted that many more properties are listed in the probate records than are referred to in this chapter, as only those properties of a named location are included here. It has been necessary to design two approaches to the data in order to fully utilise all the information contained in the records. Just less than 50% of wills provide information on property location; 37% of the accompanying inventories also providing information on rooms; whereas, overall, up to 95% of inventories provide information on rooms. In Chapter 6 the combined information on all properties, whether pertaining to named or unknown locations will be examined in relation to house sizes, room layout and function, providing the opportunity for a more extensive enquiry.

The great potential of probate records for this kind of study will be demonstrated in the course of this chapter and subsequently in Chapter 6. According to Walton, there is a dearth of plausible sources for the analysis of urban populations of the 16th century, the Hearth Tax Records of the 1660s and 1670s being the first figures to provide reliable indications of patterns of urban growth and change, and of an evolving urban hierarchy (2000: 121, 123). The extensive survival of probate evidence with which to reconstruct the social and built environment of a town provides an opportunity for new approaches to earlier periods.

In this chapter, a comparative analysis between the early probate evidence, dated from 1549 to 1642, and the later hearth tax data will be undertaken, utilising Langton's post-Civil War study of the social geography of Newcastle, by way of the Hearth Tax Assessments of 1665 and the Freeman's Rolls of 1635-64 (1975). Langton's analysis is one of the only major studies on occupational zoning in the town. His work on the development of cities in the 17th century includes an examination of residential patterns within Newcastle wards among different occupations and wealth groups, based on tax liability, numbers of hearths in a household, and information on houses with more than six rooms (Langton 1975: 8). Langton recovered the town's ward boundaries from Welford's descriptions (1911) (although these were, in fact, based on Bourne's earlier work of 1736), employing map evidence from Speed (1601), Armstrong (1769) and Thompson (1746) to clarify the written descriptions, thus providing a geographical framework for his study.

In commencing this analysis, certain limitations must be considered. Langton's evidence is biased towards the wealthiest inhabitants - those liable to tax and of known occupations - presenting difficulties in interpreting the significance of correlations between occupations and wealth on a ward basis, and there is a problem of 'massive under-representation' of master mariners and the absence of by-trades for comparative purposes (1975: 13, 16; Ellis 1985:197). The probate data present the difficulty that, as with tax liability, the sample is somewhat biased towards those with greater wealth (Shammas 1990: 20, 23, Erickson 1993: 41), even accounting for the exclusion of such groups as merchants, hostmen, gentry and urban yeomanry, and the inclusion of poor keelmen. Where Langton felt confident in recovering wealth levels, despite the difficulty of both over and under-representation of hearths in these documents (Green 2000: 66), wealth levels cannot be as confidently recovered from properties recorded in probate documents. What was included in testaments is known to be an incomplete accounting of both total properties owned and total wealth. However, references are made to wealth levels (relating to the analysis undertaken in Chapter 5). Information on the size of properties in known locations given in wills also presents some difficulty, as the accompanying inventory may not necessarily reveal all the rooms in a house (Orlin 2002: 57-60), whereas in the Hearth Tax evidence the size of properties may be misjudged in the case of unheated (and thus unrecorded) rooms. Information of numbers of hearths recorded in rooms from probate records could be useful in analysing wealth levels and house size, but the numbers of hearths recorded may also be underestimated, first, because (as with tax assessments), not all rooms were heated, and secondly, because the main sources of heating in Newcastle homes were moveable 'iron chimneys', which were occasionally removed from properties as, for example, when they were separately bequeathed in wills.

Another problem with comparing the data sets relates to the fact that testators never recorded which ward they belonged to, nor the ward in which their property was located. Wards often followed or bisected streets, just as parish boundaries had done (Langton 1975: 18). Therefore concentrations of a given trade could be dispersed between contiguous wards within the neighbourhoods constructed from probate data. For example, the adjoining wards of Gunner, Plummer, Austin and Corner Towers cover areas that include several chares running down to the river in the neighbourhood of the Lower East Side (see below). It is also recognised that the inclusion of more social groups, together with the 'absent poor', and the use of further documentary sources, such as collections of deeds and, in particular, findings from the archaeological records of the town, would strengthen future research (Graves and Heslop, forthcoming; Welford 1902: 247-67, 1903: 128-77).

Despite such limitations, comparative analysis can be usefully pursued. Langton has considered economic models of pre-industrial and pre-capitalist towns, reviewing the ideas of Sjoberg (1960) and Vance (1971), in understanding changing social attitudes and their impact on residential patterns, particularly concerning wealth and status of Newcastle merchants and guildsmen (Langton 1975: 6). The probate evidence for property ownership provides few clues to social attitudes, and, as alluded to above, wealth and status are only examined in relation to the ownership of appraised objects in this study (Chapter 5). However, the records do provide a means to recover occupational zones in neighbourhoods and uniquely, to reconstruct the material infrastructure of the town. Taken together, the different sources and aims of this study and of Langton's Hearth Tax analysis provide an opportunity for an enriched interpretation.

This chapter is divided into four sections. In section 4.2 the methodology is outlined and clarification given concerning the maps, figures and tables that present important visual references to accompany the discussions. In section 4.3, an account of the properties listed by each of the trades provides a comprehensive review of the documentary evidence, including contemporary descriptions given by the testators and their appraisers. Section 4.4 provides a comparative analysis of Langton's occupational zones, relating to historic ward boundaries, and the neighbourhoods constructed from the probate data, which highlights both change and continuity in the town's development between the pre and post-Civil War periods. Section 4.5 collates the findings on properties and occupational zones from both the probate records and Langton's Hearth Tax data to construct a picture of the social and the built environment of ten neighbourhoods in the pre-Civil War town.

4.2 Methodology

Owing to changes and the destruction of the layout of early modern Newcastle, it is difficult to plot information from probate records directly onto a modern city map. Instead, a template has been created from Hutton's map of Newcastle, providing a means of identifying streets and locations for named properties. Hutton's map is one of the most comprehensive maps in existence, and is described by the author as being 'Taken from an accurate survey' (1772). Information on properties has been plotted onto multiple templates based this map. Maps 4.1 to 4.14 illustrate all types of properties recorded by testators, including houses or tenements, shops, mills, closes, garths and landholdings. The black encircled numbers on the maps represent the number of properties owned or leased on a street or at the location given in the documents. An arrow with an encircled number indicates a specific location described in a document. All properties are calculated separately: so, for example, a baker listing a mill, a house and a close count as three properties if each structure or piece of land is specifically and separately described. This is also the case where properties are described as 'adjoined' to one another, as parts of one property were sometimes occupied by different people. The numbers appearing next to the black encircled numbers record those properties where the records very specifically *confirm* that a tradesman was living and or working at this location, whether the man owned or let the property. It is clear from the context of the documents that tradesmen lived and worked in a higher percentage of properties than the second set of numbers suggests, but the distinction has been retained for purposes of analysis. A separate map has been produced plotting all mills recorded in the documents (Map 4.14), including those belonging to the millers, whose properties have also been mapped separately.

A summary map amalgamates information from all listed properties. Map 4.15 shows ten neighbourhoods defined according to the documentary evidence in relation to the local topography. The cliffs above the quayside, the denes running through the town and the land along the river edge all formed natural boundaries (O'Brien 1988). The three main north - south arteries of the town - Westgate, the central markets and Newgate Street, and Pilgrim Street - were linked by the smaller east-west streets, creating distinct quarters to the west, in the centre and to the east of the town, with separate neighbourhoods along the river and on the steep banks descending from the upper parts of the town. The precinct of the Norman castle and the town wall imposed further boundaries, while the suburbs to the west, north and east of the town were separated by the town gates. The delineations represented on Map 4.15 by a fine dashed line indicate the approximate ward boundaries originally described by Bourne (1736), and used by Langton in his analysis (1975). Errors on Langton's map (1975: Figure 3) have been rectified on Map 4.15, following Bourne's descriptions.

Table 4.1 clarifies details on the maps, providing an A - Z indexed list of all trades, place names and streets recorded. The properties let by a tradesman to another tradesman within the study group are shown in brackets. Table 4.2 records the number of properties where the text very specifically *confirms* that a tradesman was living and or working, whether the man owned or let the property - (these figures represent those shown next to the black encircled numbers giving total recorded properties). The bracketed numbers are the same properties that appear in Table 4.1. Table 4.3 amalgamates details of all properties into ten neighbourhoods. These data are used in Figures 4.1a - 4.1m showing the distribution of individual trades over the ten neighbourhoods, and in Figures 4.2a – 4.2j which show the occupations represented in each separate neighbourhood. Figure 4.3a shows the percentage of tradesmen listing properties and Figure 4.3b shows the overall occupational density of neighbourhoods according to properties recorded in the documents.

In order to facilitate comparisons with Langton's data, Table 4.4 indicates which wards corresponded to which neighbourhood, and for clarity, which neighbourhoods embraced which wards. Table 4.5 provides comparative data on concentrations of trades in neighbourhoods and corresponding wards, and Figure 4.4 illustrates the distribution of trades in neighbourhoods according to Langton's sub-groups (1975: 27). Keelmen (who do not feature in Langton's study), will nevertheless be included in this analysis.

Copies of two of the earliest maps of Newcastle are included for reference. James Corbridge's map dated 1723/4 (Map 4.16), and John Speed's map dated 1611 (Map 4.17) convey useful information relating to the discussions. For example, street furniture such as pants and crosses are marked, as well as burns running through the town, which are not depicted on later maps. The earlier street layout also provides a guide to the prominence of certain arteries, which fade further into the background as the town developed. Certainly alterations and developments took place in the town and its suburbs over the decades between the later 16th century, when the study begins, and the second half of the 18th century, when Hutton made his map. However, the medieval street plan of Newcastle remained virtually intact until the early 19th century changes brought about by the developers Dobson and Grainger, and the subsequent near-destruction of the old town in the 1960s and 1970s (Pevsner et al. 1992).

The documents included in the study date to between 1549 and 1642. However, most records pertain to the period after 1580, thus concentrating the evidence within a period of about 60 years. Where comparative analysis is undertaken, it is important also to note that Langton's assessment is based on Hearth Tax figures for individuals (1975), while the probate evidence examines numbers of properties recorded per tradesman. With respect to terminology, the testators regularly interchanged the terms 'house', 'tenement', 'burgage' or 'messuage' without discrimination. In this study, the terms 'house' and 'tenement' have been used, the latter indicating a smaller property.

4.3 Properties of the trades

4.3.1 Bakers and brewers 1549 – 1639 *(Map 4.1)*

Over 50 properties were recorded by bakers and brewers, and most of these men appear to have lived and worked in the lower east and the upper east side of Newcastle, with other holdings recorded in the northern suburbs (Fig 4.1a). Cuthbert Wymphery was the only man to record property on the west side of town in the form of a lease 'beside the westgate'. He also owned property in the centre of the town, including tenements on Denton Chare and on Newgate Street (D.P.R.1605). Another man had a tenement on Low Friar Chare, but no details survive about these properties, which were let to unknown people. John Byers listed two houses: one, let to an unknown man, stood on the High Bridge which linked the market area with Pilgrim Street where the testator's own house was located which had three rooms - a hall, a kitchen and a parlour. The will and inventory mention that he had 'work gear in the bake house', together with stocks of wheat and animals, suggesting the location of a 'bake house' or stables in the rear of the property (D.P.R.1629). Three other bakers and brewers listed properties on Pilgrim Street, but two were leased to a locksmith and a minstrel. Richard Browne the Elder, confirmed he lived on this street in a large house containing nine rooms, with a stable and loft 'in the backside' of the house. He also had a separate barn with very substantial stores of grain. The main house had a hall, a chamber over the hall with a side chamber, a chamber over a kitchen, a little buttery 'att stair head', and a bake house where the presence of a 'cole rake' suggests a coal-fired oven. There was also a brewhouse and a cellar with the kiln for drying the grain. A 'silver salt in the studdy' was added to the bottom of the list, indicating either the presence of a separate room or perhaps a side chamber of some sort. The mention of an internal stair is rare but not unknown in other documents from the town in this period. Taken together, we may conclude that the testator's main house would have been at least three storeys high, with substantial sized structures at the back of the house for baking, storing objects, as well as for keeping animals. This man also had a lease of 'arable ground ...adioning upon the Shieldfield' with a house and 'close of arable ground upon the back off the same' also adjoining the Sheildfield. This property lay outside the town wall to the east of Pandon Dene but was relatively close to his Pilgrim Street house (D.P.R.1587).

Several other bakers and brewers list property in the vicinity of All Saints Church and along the chares leading to the quayside. Hornsby Chare, where two bakers and brewers list property, was directly linked to the foot of Pilgrim Street. One man lived here in a house with a waste ground. The other had three tenements let to a mariner and two unknown men. In the next chare to the east, William Peacock owned a 'mansion house situate in a certen place or lane called plumber chare' with a 'brewhouse adioyening unto my said mansion house'. The inventory lists six rooms: a hall with a chamber overhead, a chamber over the kitchen, a 'little room over the entrie', and a well stocked brewhouse. The last items on the list were a cow and hay, which might suggest a byre to the rear of the property. The house was probably two storeys high, possibly with a timber-framed jetty over the entry to the house creating the 'little room over the entrie'. The brewhouse may have been quite large judging by the extensive list of brewing equipment it contained, along with equipment for baking and 11 barrels of herring (D.P.R. 1625). Another baker, Cuthbert Wymphery, who also had properties elsewhere in town, lived and worked on the Broad Garth, which led to Trinity House. The testator describes a mill in his own occupation that was adjoined to a tenement let to a widow, with two other 'little tenements before the said mill' let to two other people, with a stable also 'adjoyning the said mill'. As the tenants lived in such close proximity to the mill, they may have had something to do with running the business: the whole property was left to the man's wife. The mill and tenements together with the stables appear to have shared a courtyard or some other common access way. The testator listed two more tenements on the same street let to two unknown people (D.P.R. 1605). Robert Hoope also recorded two properties on Broad Garth, a tenement let to a barber surgeon, and his own eight-room house with a cellar, mill and lofts, which were stocked with malt and hops. The main residence had a hall, a parlour and a kitchen on the ground floor, with three chambers over each of the lower rooms. The house had a cellar stocked with butter and beer and a well-equipped brewhouse. The complex must have been extensive, consisting of a three- or four-storey house, outbuildings and a mill. This man also had two other tenements which he 'buylt upon a p[ar]cel of waist ground belonging to the church of All Saints', which was located just above the Broad Garth (D.P.R. 1632).

Further to the east, two bakers and brewers listed property on Pandon Street. A tenement with lands owned by George Straker, who also had property on Hornsby Chare, above, was bequeathed to a friend who was a skinner and glover by trade. The other man, Thomas Hayton, owned a group of tenements comprising a 'lowe house or lowe roomes', with 'a new building in the backside' and a 'little yard' 'all situate in a streat or place there called Pandon'. One tenement was let to an unknown man, and more 'roomes or tenements' were let to a mariner and a schoolmaster called Daniell Hancock, with the other tenement occupied by the testator and his wife. Although Hayton's inventory does not survive, that of his wife's records a hall, a parlour and a brewhouse. Both partners noted on their testaments that they lived 'upthorough and downthorough' the house, which suggests the property had at least two storeys, which they did not share with anyone else (D.P.R. 1637). Another baker, Robert Shattoe, who let a property to the minstrel Edward Davyson on Pilgrim Street, also let two tenements to a widow and to an unknown baker and brewer down on the Newcastle quayside.

William Hall was the only baker and brewer to record property in the suburb of Sandgate, where he had a 'tenement and brewehouse wherin I now inhabit' together with the 'lands' on which the house stood. The inventory records seven rooms: a hall, a buttery chamber, a kitchen next to the brewhouse, an upper hall, an inner chamber and an upper chamber, suggesting the building was at least two storeys high (D.P.R 1636). Cuthbert Wymphery, who we meet for the third time, recorded no less than 14 properties in all, and was the only man in the trade to record property in the northern suburbs. This testator occupied a tenement and a close of land 'without Pilgrim Street gate', and a second close in the same location 'lying in the suburbs [near] the Mayd[i]llins', the Magdalene or Maudlin Meadows, located at the intersection of the roads which ran north of the town towards the Barras Bridge. Wymphery also owned a 'Close called the Darke close' & tenements in the same suburb, but the location cannot be identified (D.P.R. 1605).

Overall, the bakers and brewers appear to be among the wealthier tradesmen in the study, leasing property to a number of other people including mariners, a barber surgeon, a schoolmaster, a minstrel and a locksmith. Other men of the same trade who are mentioned in the records, but whose own documents do not survive, included Thomas Kaie, who leased a tenement and horse mill on the upper part of Hornsby Chare from successive generations of the Gray family, whose members included a mariner and a tailor. Another unknown baker and brewer let a property from a master mariner on Cowgate, located to the east of All Saints Church, and a third baker and brewer let a tenement from a miller in Trinity House Chare confirming a strong presence of the trade in the lower east side of town.

4.3.2 Butchers 1592 - 1641 *(Map 4.2)*

Among nearly 60 properties held by butchers, most were concentrated in the lower east side, the central markets and the northern suburbs (Fig. 4.1b). On the west side of the town two butchers listed properties: one of these men lived outside the Westgate, but no other details of his property survive. The other, John Smith the Elder, listed four tenements on Westgate Street 'in St. Johns churchyardthere', which were probably located on the periphery of the cemetery, and let to a yeoman, a chapman and a widow. This man had numerous other properties, but the butcher himself lived on the Meale Market in a house with at least seven rooms, including a hall, a parlour, a chamber, a loft over the parlour, a combined 'kitchen & brewhouse' and a 'Candlehouse' containing a variety of objects including barrels of tallow. He lists a stable with a hayloft, a slaughterhouse and a shop that may have been separated from the main house. 'Adjoining' the testators house was another house where his daughter and son-in-law, also a butcher, were living. The property appears to have been a complex of buildings, some joined together but mainly single-storey with loft spaces overhead. In the same location the testator had two other 'little tenements' let to a cordwainer and a yeoman. In the centre of the market, on Middle Street, the butcher also let 'one tenement with a shopp under the same' to another cordwainer, while to the north, on the Nolt Market, the testator let a tenement with brewing equipment and a close to a gentleman, though the close was 'owned by lease from Sir Richard Tempest, knight'. This testator's other properties are discussed below (D.P.R. 1614). Another butcher had a house and shop on the Middle Street. The man let the house to a joiner but he occupied the shop himself.

Immediately adjacent to Middle Street to the east was the Flesh Market where two butchers listed property. Raiphe Tothericke had two houses and a shop here. He leased out one of the houses which had a 'shopp there unto belonging' to unknown people. He rented his own house from Robert Atkinson who lived next to the testator in a 'chamber adioning on the south side of my dwelling house' (D.P.R. 1615). William Wilkinson lived just south of the Flesh Market 'att the head of the side' in a house with at least three rooms on ground level. The inventory records a hall, a parlour, and a kitchen, the latter apparently quite large as the contents suggest it was used for cooking, sleeping, food stocks and brewing. Work gear and animals were listed at the end of the inventory, perhaps indicating these were kept elsewhere. The testator also leased two shops in an unknown location, and he held a lease for a 'staleroome in the market', probably one of the butcher's stalls that stood in the Flesh Market (D.P.R. 1617; Bourne 1736: 51).

Several butchers listed property in the vicinity of All Saints Church and the lower east side of the town. John Smith the Elder, mentioned above, let a tenement to a widow on 'Silver Street near All Hallows Church'. Another butcher had two houses on All Hallows Bank, a street also known as the Butcher Bank, running along the south side of the church: one of the houses was let to his brother. The testator's own house had at least seven rooms including a hall, a parlour, a chamber, a loft, a shop and a kitchen and was probably two storeys. The inventory was taken by John Smith the Elder and his brother-in-law, the butchers who lived on Middle Street (D.P.R Stock 1613). Intersecting the Butcher Bank was Pepper Corn Chare, where another butcher let two houses to unknown men. Further east on Plummer Chare a butcher called Nicholas Ridley owned a very substantial house that he had bought from a merchant in 1623. The premises must have been one of the grandest in the street making up a complex of domestic and commercial structures. The inventory indicates that the main house had at least 11 rooms, excluding the stables, and was at least four or five storeys high. The detailed description of the rooms in the house is unusual for an inventory, as some rooms were actually given names. The house had a hall, three parlours, a kitchen, a room 'over the staire head', and a forechamber with a window cushion (indicating an upper room overlooking the street). In the upper levels of the house was a room called the 'Scarborough Castle', and above this room was an 'Upper corn loft', and a second hall called the 'Birlington Hall', used as a sleeping chamber. There was a separate shop and cellar 'with roomes over the same', occupied by a barber surgeon. The inventory records objects 'lying before the shop doore and on the key', so it is possible the main house was located on the corner of Plummer Chare and the quayside. Further rooms are recorded with references to goods kept 'In the lofts in Plummer chaire', 'In the lowe Celler' and 'In the Fish Loft'. If these rooms were not part of the main house, they were probably in very close proximity to it. The whole premise was given to the eldest son. The same butcher owned another tenement on the street let to two unknown people, and one other tenement on the Blynd Chare further to the east (D.P.R. 1623). Another butcher had two tenements that he had also purchased from a merchant, let to two tailors. The property was situated 'in & near the keyside' (D.P.R.Priarmar 1605).

The butcher Henry Scott left a detailed description of his property beside Pandon Gate which included his 'lands, houses, tenements and Mylnes', 'in a certaine street or place there called Pandon neare Pandon Gate there', 'together with one [par]cell of ground or garden plot lyeing without Pandongate aforesaid adjoining upon the water race or water course of the water milne within Pandongate'. The description continues by identifying that the mill was situated 'towards the west' side of the water course, with 'the King's street towards the east part', and extending 'from the towne wall towards the south unto a ten[nemen]te and p[ar]cell of bad ground belonging to Will[ia]m Gray M[e]rchant towards the north'. The inventory indicates that the main house had at least five rooms including a brewhouse and a 'roofe loft', suggesting a two-storey structure. No details of the mill were given, but a 'little horse', perhaps used to help power the mill, is listed on the inventory (D.P.R. Scott 1641). The description of the location of this property is the most detailed given in the documents and can be compared with descriptions of a mill in this location. Bourne quotes the Milbank Manuscript that mentions 'the mills at Pandon - Gate' beside 'a waste Piece of Ground ... formerly called the Stones' located at Stockbridge and marked on Hutton's map (1736, 1980:138). The bad ground described in the will is probably a reference to this stony area south of the mill. Speed's map of Newcastle shows the Pandon Dene flowing through the wall beside Pandon Gate and under a group of structures located in front of the gate (Map 4.17, Illustration 4.1a).

Only one butcher recorded property 'in a streat called Sandgate w[i]thout the wales', which consisted of five houses 'with a key or wharf goeing & extending itself to the watter of the Tyne & belonginge to the neyther twoo houses'. The properties were occupied by two unknown men (D.P.R. Hodchon 1628). Three butchers recorded property to the north of the town. Andrew Harrup recorded living in 'tenements with a shop' in Gallowgate. The inventory suggests a three-room house with a hall, a kitchen and a chamber. The inclusion of 'work tools belonging to the trade of a butcher' following the kitchen

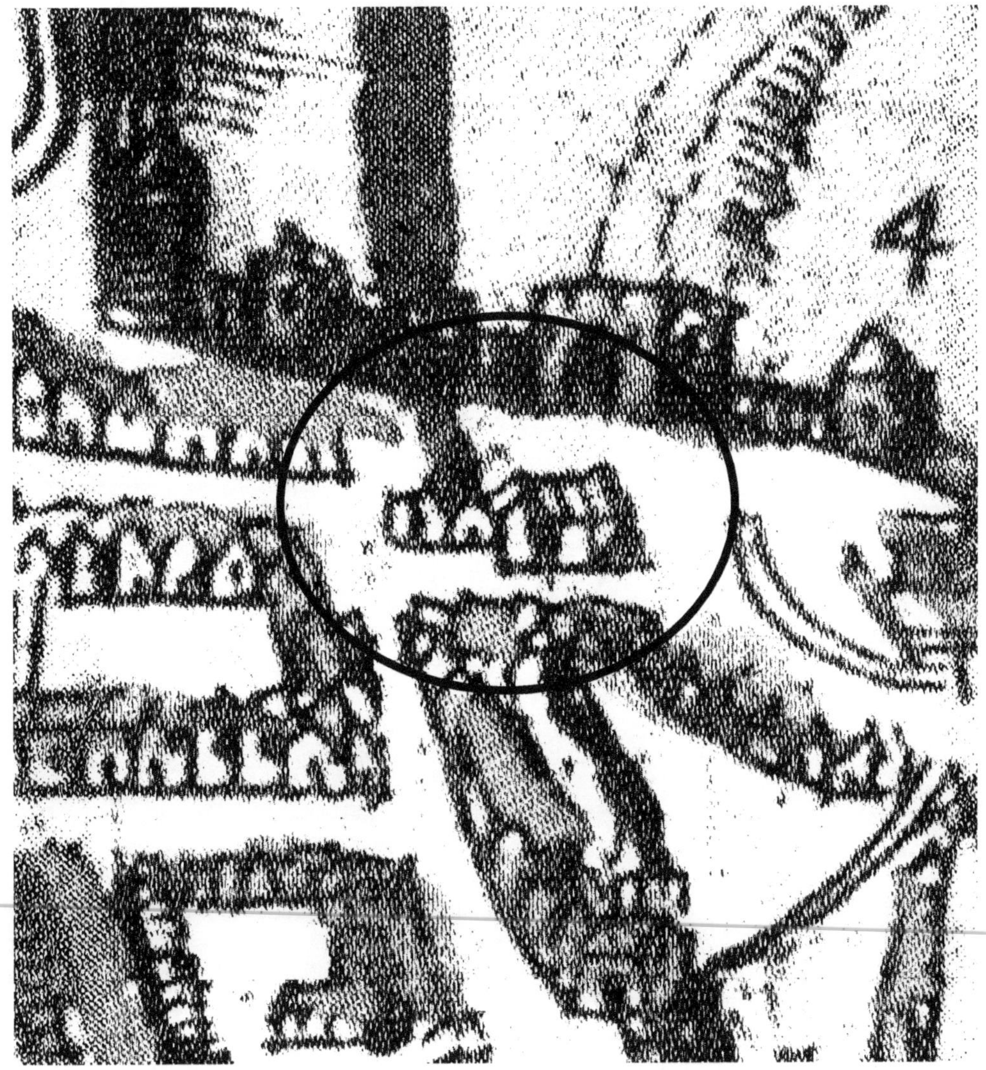

Illustration 4.1a: 'Pandon Mill' at Pandon Gate from John Speed's map of Newcastle upon Tyne (1611)

objects, suggests a shop in close proximity to the domestic parts of the house. The testator had a further four tenements and a close on Sidgate, the street north of Gallowgate. Who occupied these properties is not recorded (D.P.R. 1619). John Smith the Elder, who owned many properties, also owned a meadow close 'in a street called Gallowgate together with 2 rigges of meadow ground there unto adioning at the upper end of the said close', and 'one other meadow close' of '7 rigges . .. lying in the Castlefield'. One other butcher, William Wilkinson who lived at the Head of the Side in town, above, also had '9 riggs of land lying in the Castle field'. Additionally, the butchers leased properties to a number of other tradesmen including tailors, cordwainers, and a glover, as well as a gentleman, a chapman, a joiner, and a yeoman. They rented property themselves from a weaver and a tailor.

4.3.3 Cordwainers 1549 - 1639 *(Map 4.3)*

The cordwainers record nearly 80 properties distributed in the northern suburbs, Sandgate, the eastern side of the town and most particularly in the central market area (Fig. 4.1c). The trade dominated Middle Street and the lower markets. In the period of this study the guildhall for the trade was located on High Bridge, a street linking the eastern artery of Pilgrim Street to the central markets.

The analysis of cordwainers properties begins on the Sandhill beside the Tyne Bridge, moving north up the central artery of the town. Valentine Baker owned a property 'in or neare the Sandhill with shoppes', which he called his 'dwelling' house. His inventory records five rooms including a hall and a kitchen, with two chambers above these rooms and a separate shop. The house was at least two storeys high. This man also recorded 'A lease of 8 years yet to come of a house and shop in Maisondieu' (D.P.R. 1620). The Maison Dieu stood on the south side of the Sandhill next to the river and was built as a hospital or almshouse by Roger Thornton in the early 15th century. Gray confirms that 'next to the Town-court, or Guild Hall is an Almeshouse, called the mason de Dieu ... Above which is the stately Court of the Merchant Adventurers' (1649, 1970: 24). The designation as a hospital dedicated to St. Catherine for the care of 'nine poor men and four poor women' was maintained until the

1580s (Brand 1789: 28). It appears that at least some part of the building was being leased to tradesmen as a commercial premises prior to 1620 and for eight years thereafter. Bourne confirms the sale of the Maison Dieu, noting that 'In the Year 1629, Sir Richard Lumley, in Consideration of 100 li. convey'd to the Mayor and Burgesses of Newcastle, ... all that Building of Stone covered in Lead ... being about 16 Yards in Length, and anciently Part of the *Hospital* of St. Katherine the *Virgin*' (1736, 1980: 124; Middlebrooke 1950: 59).

The same cordwainer also owned a tenement further up the street on the Side, let to a saddler. He recorded a fourth property 'wherein I lately dwell in the meale Market and Middle Street with the shoppes roomes and appurtenances'. Three men occupied the property but, according to the inventory, Valentine only kept a bed, a table and an iron chimney in the house. The cordwainer Richard Kirkehouse the Elder also had a house with two shops on the Side above the Sandhill. The inventory lists one shop (full of merchandise), a hall, a parlour, and a kitchen with a chamber overhead, suggesting a two-storey structure. This man had another house in Denton Chare which led west from the bottom of the market street, and other property north of the town, discussed below (D.P.R. 1633).

At the top of the Side and north of St Nicholas' Church on the west side of the markets was the Meal or Groat market, where two cordwainers list property. One belonged to Valentine Baker, mentioned above, and the other was the home and shop of Thomas Potts the Elder whose inventory records three rooms, a hall, a very well-tocked parlour and the shop. The inventory also mentions a chamber, brewing vessels and a cow, indicating there that were other rooms connected to his house. A two-storey structure is suggested (D.P.R. 1588). Thomas Spoor's inventory recorded what must have been either a large or a very crowded 'shop in Middle Street', which stocked 324 pairs of shoes and boots, quantities of tallow, along with all the work gear. The family house was probably attached to the shop, but this is not specified in the records (D.P.R. 1587). The inventory of another cordwainer also records 'The shop in the Middle Street', but the whereabouts of his house is likewise unclear. Roger Gofton had a house in Middle Street 'ioyning (joining) upon the tenement' of a merchant, but he himself lived across the street in the Flesh Market in a house with a hall, a chamber and a shop. No upper rooms were specified (D.P.R. 1615). John Armstrong left a very precise description of the location of his house and shop that was 'bound by the Kings high streete called middle street on the west and a streete called the Cloath Market on the east which the other right meets and bounds together' (D.P.R.1625). Just two rooms were inventoried: a hall and shop, but there may have been others. This man also had tenements and a close in the northwest part of the town 'situate & adjoining to a street called the Frier Chaire neere adoining the place called the [white] Friers', a street running to the south of Black Friars. The remains of the Blackfriars Monastery are standing today (Harbottle 1987). Thomas Collingwood the Elder recorded several properties including his own house on the 'Pullen Market' or Poultry Market, located beside the Flesh Market on the east side of the street. The house had at least 14 rooms including a hall, a large parlour, with two chambers over these rooms, a 'Middle Chamber', a 'little chamber at the stare head', a second parlour next to a kitchen, a guile house and a brewhouse, a cellar, a hay loft with a second hay loft above it, and a shop with over 60 pairs of shoes as well as tools, tallow and stacks of leather. The property was clearly very substantial and at least two storeys high. Collingwood also had 'two little tenements standing together', 'in the Middle Street', one let to a tailor called Raphe Nicholson and the other to another cordwainer, John Hirst. Further up the street Collingwood also had a house in the Noult Market, or horse market, 'near unto the whit cross', which is clearly shown on both Speed's map of 1611 and James Corbridge's map of 1724 (D.P.R. 1625). Christopher Nicholson had a house and shop on Middle Street, which he leased from Robert Musgrave, 'House Sergeant of Newcastle'. However, this cordwainer recorded that he lived on Byker Chare near the quayside where he had another shop together with five other properties let to unknown people. Details of the house were not recorded, but it is possible this man ran shops in two parts of the town. Nicholson also recorded property in Sandgate, which he let to a widow, while one other cordwainer (for whom no documents survive), also had a tenement in the suburb, which was leased from a wealthy master mariner, indicating the presence of the trade in the suburb (D.P.R. 1587). Thomas Phillipson is another cordwainer who listed a shop in Middle Street, but he seems to have had a second house and shop, the location of which is not recorded. He also let property to several unknown people on Hornsby Chare near the quayside, as well as four other tenements 'neare unto St. John's church' (D.P.R. 1593).

Two cordwainers record living on Pilgrim Street east of the markets. Henry Atkinson had a house with at least 14 rooms. The inventory lists a hall with a buttery and 'little parlour within the hall', a 'forechamber over the hall', a porch chamber, possibly meaning a jettied room, a middle chamber and a high parlour, a chamber over the kitchen and a room called 'the Barrons Chamber' which may have been on a third storey. A room is recorded above the cellar, and a 'lowe parlour' with beds is listed, which might suggest a *sousterrain* level. The house also had a stable. The property may have been four storeys in height, including the cellar or *sousterrain*, with a stabling area to the rear of the property. This man also owned a tenement in the Noult Market, one of several properties listed in the area as owned by cordwainers, where his father-in-law lived. However, the cordwainers do not appear to have lived in this upper market area near the White Cross. Atkinson's properties outside the walls of the town are discussed below. A second cordwainer, Gavin Preston also had a house in Pilgrim Street with brewing equipment including a 'Brewlead & steep lead' listed on the will. The house had six rooms including a hall, fore chamber, a back chamber, a roof loft, a kitchen and the brewhouse where the testator seems to have kept his shoes and leather along with the brewing equipment

(D.P.R. 1640). Richard Swan listed 'houses & lands' on 'Upper Dean Bridge', or High Bridge, the street that linked Pilgrim Street to the central markets and where the Cordwainers Hall was located. The house in which he lived in had more than 11 rooms, including a hall, a parlour and a kitchen; with a second parlour described as located 'to the forestreet', suggesting that it was on the second floor overlooking the street, a room called 'the first fore chamber'; an 'inner chamber' and a 'garret'; and 'one other chamber'. There was also a cellar and a 'little cellar' and, lastly 'the Brewhouse and other Roomes Adioyeing'. The structure must have had three levels, with buildings to the rear of the premises. The testator also owned houses and land on the Long Stairs leading to the Close and property outside the walls of the town. Although none of the cordwainers recorded living in the suburbs to the north of the town, a total of four men owned or leased property in the neighbourhood. These included houses 'without the Pilgrim Gate', 'closes and parcells of ground lying in Sidgate', 'a little house without the Newegate in Sidgate', and a house and close in Gallowgate.

The findings from the probate records confirm that the cordwainers lived almost exclusively along the central artery of the town between the Sandhill and the lower market areas, with the majority of the shops being located in and around the Middle Street, often incorporated within part of the family house. Tradesmen also lived on the High Bridge near the Cordwainer's Hall and on Pilgrim Street. Cordwainers rented properties from other trades including butchers, and a tailor, and a skinner and glover who actually lived with the cordwainer, all in the centre of the town; as mentioned above, just one cordwainer rented in Sandgate from a master mariner.

4.3.4 Keelmen 1548-1636 *(Map 4.4)*

The famous keelmen of Newcastle who rowed and sailed their keels or lighters on the River Tyne from medieval times, have left little evidence of the properties they once owned. The men were among the poorer tradesmen of the town, as shown in Chapter 3 on inheritance patterns. Of the 17 men whose records survive, just nine left details on 26 properties. The majority of these were in Sandgate, with two tenements listed in Pandon and approximately six others located across the river in 'Gateside', (Gateshead today) (Fig. 4.1d). About one-quarter of the recorded properties, all located within Sandgate, specify they were let to the keelmen exclusively by the better off shipwrights, who shared this neighbourhood. A single keelman recorded letting his house in Sandgate to a carpenter. The percentage of property rented by the keelmen is high, relative to the other trades.

The two earliest properties recorded were both located in Pandon and dated 1548 and 1582, but details of these houses were not recorded, and just one keelman actually lived here. No keelman lists property within the town after this date. By the last decade of the 16th century Sandgate appears to have become the preferred neighbourhood of the keelmen, with half of the men for whom records survive confirming that they lived in this riverside suburb. After 1608, all the keelmen, without exception, actually specify on their wills that they live in Sandgate. Details of structures in the area include a description by Henry Robinson of two of his houses being roofed with slate and another four roofed with thatch (D.P.R. 1592). The inventory suggests that his home was a single storey dwelling with a loft. James Bell lists a house with at least four rooms, probably all on ground level; no upper rooms are recorded. He has a second house described as being 'in James Bell his chair' indicating private ownership of a chare, described as being 'towards the water' perhaps standing along the river's edge (D.P.R. 1608).

Henry Lawson owned properties in Gateshead described as 'houses, tenements, garths, gardens, staithes and warfes'. He leased out four houses, three 'standing together', with one separate structure. The property must have been located along the riverside with the privately owned 'staithes' and wharves jutting out into the Tyne. Lawson must have been a kindly landlord, as he willed 'every of the tenants that shall be dwelling in any of my said houses att the time of my death a quarters rent to be allowed them in remembrance of my good will to them' (D.P.R. 1609).

Most inventories pertaining to keelmen give no division of rooms, probably indicating that most men lived in houses with single cells with loft spaces above a hall. Just one property listed a kitchen and a fore chamber. The analysis shows that keelmen lived exclusively in the areas of the town that were close to the river. There is only one reference to a keelman letting property to another tradesman, while many others lived in property leased to them by other tradesmen.

4.3.5 Mariners 1584 - 1627 *(Map 4.5)*

The mariners, like the keelmen, tended to live and work in parts of the town that were most accessible to the river and quayside, towards the east and lower east side of the town and in Sandgate (Fig. 4.1e). Properties were listed along Pilgrim Street, the quayside chares, Pandon and Sandgate, with just two houses let to unknown parties in the west of the town described as lying 'in the Castlemoat & Baileygate' (D.P.R. Holbourne 1622). Eight mariners leave details relating to nearly 50 properties, but the numbers owned by the men were very unequal. About half the mariners appear to have had houses with several rooms, the remainder possibly living in single rooms. Three mariners owned mills, and two of these men had markedly more property than average.

William Crawfoot owned several properties on Pilgrim Street. He lived in one of the houses but leased the others to tenants of unknown trades. His own house had at least six or seven rooms, with a 'Parlour or Chamber next unto the hall', an 'Inner Rome' and a kitchen, a separate 'Entry' where goods had been left standing, as well as 'Malt Loftes', indicating a single-storey house with loft spaces (D.P.R. 1610). This same man had a further four tenements 'lying behind All hallows church', probably bordering on Silver Street. Another mariner also recorded living in his own house that was behind this church. No information on room division was recorded for any of these properties. Directly linking Pilgrim Street and All Saints Church was Hornsby Chare, where a mariner called Thomas Gray had nine properties, including a horse mill and tenement which he let to a baker and brewer. The mill and tenement is described as being located 'at the upper parte of hornsbie chair' (D.P.R.1623). None of the other properties provide clues about layout, except that four were described as 'small tenements', and one was let to a yeoman. A baker and brewer let a tenement to one other mariner on the same chare. A shipwright let another tenement to a mariner on Plummer Chare, one street to the east. The close proximity of all these properties to one another suggests a community of mariners living in the area around All Saints Church. A mill on the Broad Chare was owned by a mariner, which he bequeathed to his brother, a miller, who subsequently left it to another brother (D.P.R. Patterson 1584). A third mill standing on the Wall Knoll behind Pandon Street, was recorded by the prosperous mariner John Holbourne. The same man owned tenements and a cellar on Bourne Bank, as well as the tenements in Bailiff Gate, mentioned above, but no details survive for any of the properties (D.P.R. 1622).

Two mariners list properties in Sandgate and in Gateshead. Humphery Coward left a detailed account of the way his house in Sandgate was divided. In his will he records that his 'dwelling house' was divided into at least three separate areas. The property stood on the south side of the main street that ran east-west through the neighbourhood, and extended southwards down to the river's edge. The upper part of the house was rented to a mariner and was located 'in a streete there between other certain tenements now in my owne occupation and the said forestreete'. A yeoman rented the lower part of the house 'between certain ther tenements and appurtenances now in my own occupation and the lowe water mark of the tyne river'. Thus Coward occupied the part of the house sandwiched between the upper and lower ends of his property, which spanned the land between the main street and the low-water mark on the river edge. His wife inherited both the far ends of the house, which in turn were to be divided between her two sons on her death, while the middle area, in which the testator was living, was divided between his two daughters. One girl was given 'the hall house being part of the nowe dwelling house', 'w[i]th one loft or chamber above the same', 'and the kitchen': the other girl was given 'all that p[ar]te of my nowe dwellinge house used for a kitchen, one brewhouse adioininge thereunto w[i]th two chambers or lofts above the same standinge betweene the said howse, now a hall howse, and the said Cow Howse or stable'. A waste ground and stable, belonging to the upper part of the house, was located near the 'forestreete'. The description suggests a complex of buildings on the ground sloping down to the river, with loft spaces used for sleeping chambers, making this a two-storey property with at least ten rooms, including the stable. Room function was clearly flexible: two areas were designated as kitchens; one formerly a hall, indicating that use of space was a question of social and not architectural considerations. The testator's inventory records just four rooms, including the hall, a chamber above a brewhouse and a kitchen. He incidentally includes a note which tells us how the multiple-occupancy property was accessed. Coward informs all his children that 'each and evrie of them have and inioy [unreadable fragment] and accustomed passage way with free ingresse egresse and regresse into and from the peremisses to each of them severally bequethed without hindrance or molestacon one of another' (D.P.R. 1624). Just one other mariner had properties in both Gateshead and Sandgate, but no details were recorded.

The analysis confirms that the majority of mariners lived in Sandgate, in the lower east part of the town or across the river in Gateshead. Just over one- third of all properties occupied by mariners were let to the trade by master mariners and shipwrights, with two properties let to the mariners by bakers and brewers.

4.3.6 Master mariners 1569 - 1639 *(Map 4.6)*

Seventeen master mariners have recorded details concerning more than 40 properties. These men preferred property close to the river in the lower east side of the town, in Sandgate and across the Tyne in Gateshead, but a few men held properties in the central market areas in the upper parts of the town (Fig. 4.1f).

The only property on the west side of the town listed by a master mariner was located on Westgate Street, bequeathed to a son who was paying a mortgage on the property. In the centre of the town, a man let a tenement to a yeoman on the Cloth Market. Across the street, John Hawton owned a horse mill 'in the market & Pudding Chair' at the north end of the Groat Market. He also owned two halves of a house on the Side, leased to two merchants, and a shop 'standing & being on the bridge end in Newcastle' let to a third merchant, as well as properties in Gateshead and Sandgate, of which no details survive (D.P.R. 1569). Two master mariners were recorded as living on the Close, the riverside area popular with merchants in the late 16th century, but details about these houses were not given (Langton 1975: 16).

In the east part of the town, on All Hallows or Butcher Bank, one master mariner had a property with at least three rooms including a hall with a chamber overhead, and a kitchen, suggesting a two-storey structure (D.P.R. Nicholson 1623). Two master mariners listed property at the east end of all Hallows Bank on Cowgate: one house was let to a baker and brewer, the other master mariner lived in his house with a hall, a kitchen, a chamber over the hall, another 'Upper Chamber over the hall' and a chamber over the kitchen, suggesting a three-storey structure (D.P.R Smart 1622). Below these properties, master mariners listed property in close proximity to Trinity House, which still stands to the west of Broad

Chare, and which was the location of their guild (McCombie 1985; Knowles and Boyles 1892).

In 1577, a master mariner asked his friends to sell his house 'lying in a streat or lane called Broad Garth', 'for the greatest price that can be gotten' (D.P.R. Anderson), while another master mariner let his house on this street to unknown people. No details survive about either of the houses. Two master mariners recorded keeping objects in the cellars of Trinity House. One was Robert Johnson who claimed to live in a 'Mansion House' with at least ten rooms according to the inventory, but unfortunately no location was given. He listed keeping cables, timber, oars and anchors in the cellars belonging to the guild (D.P.R. 1592). The inventory of another master mariner records that he kept wood, pumps, buoys, barrels of tar and pitch, 'amyshe iron' and tiles 'In the seller in the trynitie house' (D.P.R. Taillor 1580). Two master mariners listed property in the Broad Chare, which still has a direct access to the Trinity House. One testator who lived on the street also had two houses close by on Pandon Street. The other testator let his property to a widow, but he had another property 'standing in a streate called the keyside' let to the fishmonger Robert Carr (D.P.R. Johnson 1582). No details for any of the properties were recorded. Further east, two master mariners listed property on the Byker Chare, where they both also lived. One of the men described his residence as 'all those roomes and houses situate in a lane or chair called Byker Chair', and he recorded that he shared the premises with a mariner. He also had three further tenements on the same street, let to three widows (D.P.R. Chambers 1626). Details were not recorded for any of the other houses.

Across the river in Gateshead, three master mariners listed properties, including one man who also listed a house 'in a lane or chair there called Lowe Kirke Chaire' occupied at different times by himself or his tenants, and left to his daughter for the period 'from 28th of June last past unto the full end and term of one thousand years from there next ensueing and fullie to be compleat and ended' (D.P.R. Nicholson 1623). Low Kirk Chare led to St. Margaret's Church (which still stands), on the east side of the Great North Road. The second master mariner, who lived on the Close, had another house in Gateshead let to an unknown man. The master mariner John Hawton (see above) had several properties on this side of the river, including half a close let to merchants, and three houses with waste land let to a mariner, a yeoman and a widow, respectively. He also had property in Sandgate including a house and four tenements 'there unto adjoining with a key', indicating that the properties were next to the river. The house was let to a blacksmith, while the other four 'adjoining' tenements were let to two mariners, a yeoman and a widow. He leased a separate tenement to a cordwainer (one of the few men of that trade to live somewhere other than the central market area of the town), and another to a mariner (D.P.R. 1569). Two other master mariners list property in this suburb. Oswald Nixon was the only master mariner to confirm he lived in his house 'in a streete there called Sandgate': he had let his other property on the Cloth Market to a yeoman. His inventory suggests a well-equipped house with six rooms, including a hall, a kitchen, a brewhouse, with two upper chambers (one over the hall and the other over the kitchen), and a roof loft. The structure was thus at least three storeys high, one of the taller houses in the neighbourhood (D.P.R Nixon 1636). The other master mariner only listed supplies of grain that he stored at the Stackgarth near the Ouse Burn.

A social distinction is apparent, between the master mariners on the one hand and the shipwrights, mariners and keelmen on the other, despite the fact that they all had interests in the river and sea trade. The master mariners did not generally share the same streets or neighbourhoods with the other tradesmen, with the exception of mariners. The men record leasing properties to several tradesmen including a baker and brewer, a cordwainer, a smith, and several mariners. They were also landlords to several affluent merchants, whereas there are no records of them leasing property themselves from any other tradesmen.

4.3.7 Millers 1577 - 1637 *(Map 4.7)*

The location and types of the many mills that once operated in the town and suburbs of Newcastle deserve special attention as a unique category of property. Mills owned or leased by millers will be discussed in this section, along with other types of property listed by these tradesmen. In the final part of the first section of this chapter, a more in-depth analysis will examine mills more generally, including those belonging to other tradesmen. Millers alone recorded some 45 properties distributed very widely around the town and suburbs (Fig. 4.1g), but only a few of the documents record the location of their mills.

On the west side of town, Thomas Reasley had 'one horse myllne with two little tenements adioyning all to gether in a place called the pow[ ]trone', 'in the hygh waye to the whitt freare tower'. The mill was located on the Postern to the north of White Friars Tower, which adjoins the foot of Westgate Street. The inventory gives no clues about the layout of rooms, providing only a short list of objects (D.P.R. 1611). John Reasley, who inherited the house and mill, described the location as being 'at the end of waistgate [in] the poulstren'. He left no other description but mentions owning two horses, which must have worked the mill (D.P.R. 1630). John Huntrish listed a house in Westgate Street, and although he does not specifically mention a mill, he bequeathed 'a white suete of Apperill being my work Dayes apperill'. His inventory included large stores of grain and malt as well as two horses, so the presence of a mill is implied. Huntrish also owed money to Thomas Reasley, above, who was his neighbour, and he acted as one of the assessors on Reasley's inventory, a year before his own death (D.P.R. 1612). The miller Thomas Reade had several properties on the west side of the town, including a house 'Lying in Westgate next adioyning' a house belonging to an unknown man, a tenement and a close 'lying without the westgate', let to an unknown woman, and a 'meadow close lying in the forth'. The Forth was an area of fields to the west of the town. No other testator in the study listed lands in this area. In the centre of the town, on Pudding Chare, the same miller also owned a 'Milne House & Malt Milne therein errected', with another house adjoined to the property. The inventory suggests a six-room house with three storeys, including a stable 'without the house'. The house had a hall, a parlour and a lower parlour primarily for sleeping and storage, a good-sized brewhouse and lofts full of hay and grain that also contained drying kilns. There is no description of the mill itself except that mill horses were recorded. The miller also leased a house on Middle Street to a merchant (D.P.R 1613).

A remarkable group of properties owned by another miller were described as the 'Middlemoste', the 'Northemoste', and the 'Southemoste of my three houses wh[i]ch are in the Hoockster Boothes'. Unfortunately no details were recorded about these houses, but Bourne mentions that 'A Part these Houses are still to be seen, they stand by themselves almost in the middle of the street, nigh the White-Cros cross' (1736, 1980: 39, 47). Gray says that 'This part of town is called to this day, the Hucksters Booths' ... 'where are many old houses and cottages', and that 'People in those dayes, had their livelihood from those Fryers and Nuns that lived in that part of the Town' (Gray 1649, 1970, 1970: 22). The occupation of these properties into the late 1570s by food retailers attests to an interesting historical continuation (D.P.R. Herrisone 1577). The houses have disappeared from Hutton's map but a small block of properties still appear on Corbridge's map (Map 4.16), and are clearly visible on Speed's map of 1611 (Map 4.17). No other miller lists property in the upper market area.

On the east side of the town, five millers recorded owning and leasing property. James Dunne had a house and garth in the 'Carlell', probably a reference to the Carliol Croft, the open lands behind Pilgrim Street (D.P.R. Dunne 1637). George Reasley, who had eight children including Thomas (the father of John, see above), recorded a house on Silver Street to the north of the All Saints Church. He also owned three mills but does not record their locations (D.P.R. 1581). However, 20 years later, one Robert Reasley, possibly a relative, recorded a 'Milne on the West end of All Hallows Church and all houses belonging to it' together with 'a waist in the Head of Plumber chair', located across the street from the mill (D.P.R. 1603). Below the church, Thomas Reade had three more properties on 'a lane or chair called the Trinitie House Chaire neere the keyside' including a 'tenement with the seller and shopp there unto belonging' let to a scrivener, a tenement let to an unknown baker and brewer, and a third property 'adioyning to the same tenement ... northwards' let to a yeoman. A mill on Broad Chare is recorded in 1584 by William Patterson, who inherited it from his brother the mariner (above), but no other details survive. In 1617 William Anderson also recorded a 'horse mill' on Broad Chare, and it is possible that this is the same mill in new hands. This miller also had a house on Pandon Street leased to a widow. Two millers, already mentioned above, also owned lands to the north of the town outside the wall. Thomas Reade recorded 'riggs of meadow ground lying in the Castle field' as well as a house and close in Sidgate which bordered the Castle Leazes to the southeast. George Reasley had a house in Gallowgate leased to unknown people.

In the suburb of Sandgate, three members of the Reasley family listed property. Robert Reasley recorded a house and 'water Milne' in Sandgate. The inventory lists no rooms, and the only clues to the design of the water mill are a millstone, a 'sayle' (sail), and a 'wind mill horse'. The mill was subsequently bequeathed to two other family members who provide no further details except that the mill was also referred to as a horse mill. This same miller left his son Walter another house and mill, in which the son was already living, located in the Stackgarth to the east of Sandgate. Walter, who subsequently left the property to his own two sons, described the property as a 'Water Corne Mill' listing a 'pair of mill stones' and two horses. Thomas Reasley, one of the sons, later recorded his own part of a 'half of a water corne mylne lyinge and being in a place called Ewes (Ouse) burne being the lowest mylne of and in that burne', providing a relatively accurate location for the mill (D.P.R. Robert, Walter and Thomas Reasley 1603, 1604, 1611). The miller John Reay had a house in Sandgate which had an 'under room in the back part' of the house and an 'upper room over and above the above bequeathed low room', probably indicating three areas of occupation in one property, located on the lands sloping down to the river. No mill or other property details were recorded (D.P.R. 1636).

Only one miller recorded leasing properties to a baker and brewer, and one tailor recorded leasing a mill to a miller. Evidence from the documents suggests that millers tended to own their own mills or to secure long leases and thus to keep them within a family for decades. The Reasleys who recorded mills in this section are also discussed in the Appendix of Mills: Part 2.

4.3.8 Shipwrights 1573 - 1642 *(Map 4.8)*

Shipwrights recorded nearly 70 properties, choosing overwhelmingly to live and work in the suburb of Sandgate among the poorer keelmen, mariners, joiners and carpenters, to whom they let substantial numbers of properties - more properties, in fact, than were let by any other trade (Table 4.1). Besides Sandgate, the tradesmen listed properties in the east and lower east side of the town, and in Gateshead, a pattern similar to the mariners, with just two properties listed on Middle Street (Fig. 4.1h). Where the documents actually confirm where shipwrights lived, Sandgate was the only neighbourhood mentioned (with the exception of one man who lived in Pandon in 1573). After this date, no shipwright recorded living in the area, as was also true for the keelmen, who also appear to have abandoned the walled part of the town in the early 1580s. Concerning properties recorded within the town, two shipwrights owned houses somewhere on Pilgrim Street, one being let to a joiner. Another shipwright let a house to a mariner on Plummer Chare. The shipwright Henry Temple owned a large number of properties: two on Middle Street were let to cordwainers, while his tenements on Grinden Chare were let to Alderman Robert Atkinson some time before his death in 1598 (D.P.R. Temple). Two other shipwrights list property on Byker Chare, one being let to a chapman. The other house had a parlour and substantial brewing equipment. These were all the properties recorded by shipwrights within the walls of Newcastle.

Detailed information survives about the shipwrights living in Sandgate. One man who lived in Pandon before 1573, let three tenements in this neighbourhood to unknown men. One Thomas Smith recorded three houses: one was 'by the key', let to a third party, but the testator used the 'sellor above' the house to store his own shipbuilding supplies. The location of the cellar above the living quarters suggests a structure built on ground sloping down to the river. An account of the layout of the testator's own house indicates that the property was divided into two separate residences. When he bequeathed the house to his wife, he told her that she could give the part where the family lived 'where she shall thinke best provided alwais that the howse wherein Anthonie Smithe (his tenant) doeth dwell and the howse wherein I myselfe doeth dwell shalbe equally divided by the entrie of my howse, that is to say upp throughe and downe throughe'. The inventory lists seven rooms including a hall, a parlour, a chamber and a forechamber, a stable, a back chamber and a 'sellor of the backside' (D.P.R. Smith 1585). There is no specific mention of upper rooms, but there would have been at least two storeys with the cellar. The impression is of a multiple-room low house with a shared entry.

Henry Temple owned at least 20 properties in Sandgate besides those he recorded in Newcastle town and Gateshead. Ten of the properties were let to third parties including another shipwright, two carpenters and several mariners. He had purchased four houses and 'other litle houses' from the miller Robert Reasley who lived in Sandgate in 1604 (see above). The other properties were occupied by family, including a tenement with a 'garth & keye' on the river's edge, occupied by his brother-in-law, yet another shipwright. Details of his home in Sandgate unfortunately were not recorded. Temple is the only shipwright with property in Gateshead. He listed two little tenements in the occupation of an unknown woman (D.P.R. 1598).

Thomas Wailes, who called himself a ship carpenter, but whose appraisers called him a shipwright, was another wealthy man with several Sandgate properties. He had five houses: one let to a widow was 'adjoining' another let to a keelman. A third house with a 'Great Celler' was let to an unknown man. The fourth, where his married daughter and family lived was described as 'my house wherin they now dwell'. The fifth house was called the 'heade house', bequeathed to his daughter Jane. His own home, which he calls 'my new indwelling house' was connected to this house and had two more houses 'adjoined' to it, so the one property was divided into four separate dwellings. The testator's inventory records just three rooms, including a hall, a kitchen and a loft. The structure appears to have been made up of adjoined single-storey tenements with lofts. Thomas also left rental revenues for his son from a 'new house yett to be buylde' and from at least five other houses all occupied by unknown people (D.P.R. 1609). Another shipwright recorded two houses in Sandgate, although the inventory recorded only three rooms, a hall with a chamber above and a kitchen, indicating a two-storey structure. George Garret had three houses in Sandgate, including his own. One was described as being 'in the forestreate', the upper main road running east - west through the suburb (D.P.R. 1615). Thomas Cloughe also described his house as being 'in the highstreate', 'adioining upon the house or tenement of Richard Readhead on the west-south-west p[ar]te and upon the tenement of Robert Browne on thest north east parte' (D.P.R. 1612). These houses apparently shared common walls. One other shipwright, who also had a house in Byker Chare, recorded land in Sandgate, and another 'ship carpenter' leased a house in Sandgate: the inventory of the second man lists almost nothing but his work tools.

The shipwright George Watson owned at least seven houses in Sandgate, besides his own. He let what he described as six 'little tenements' to six keelmen. As one of these houses had a quay, they must have been built next to the river. Another house, leased to a rope maker, is described as lying 'nere the pant there'. The property was later bequeathed to family and was again described as lying 'neare the pant in Sandgaite'. The inventory suggests a four-room house with a hall, a chamber, a back chamber and a kitchen. No upper rooms were mentioned so the structure was probably single storey. The Sandgate pant was located outside Sandgate Gate beside the Milk Market on the west end of the upper road through Sandgate (Charleton 1885: 328, 331), but the pant is not marked on early maps. George Watson's own house 'with the key or wharf thereto belonging and the waist at the upper end of the said house towards the fforestreat of Sandgaite', indicates that the property spanned an area from near the high street to the river edge. The testator also recorded 'timber & planks upon the key before my house'. The inventory records three rooms, a hall, a 'forechamber' and a kitchen, all at ground level (D.P.R. 1623). The inventory of William Cooke records a house which his wife added to the document on the day of the appraisal in November 1624. The house had at least four rooms - including a hall, a kitchen, a chamber over the hall, and another chamber 'over the doors' - indicating a two-storey structure with a chamber over what may have been double doors, creating a reasonably wide jettied upper room (D.P.R. 1624). William Reasley listed property 'in Sandgaite in the forestreet upon the north sidd of the said street theare' and a 'horse mylne', 'situate in Sandgaite in the occupation of Jane Browne, widow'. William, a member of the family of millers described above, who died in the autumn of 1633, had been third in line after his brothers for this mill, once his uncle's property back in 1604. The inventory records a hall, a chamber and a high chamber, suggesting a two-storey structure. No other details are recorded on any of the other earlier documents concerning this house or mill. In 1642, John Colyer recorded three houses in Sandgate: he let one tenement 'in the forestreate in Sandgate' to a widow, and a second tenement with a 'key thereunto belonging att or neare the key in Sandgate' to an unknown person. The testator's own 'dwelling house' was a large two-storey property. The inventory lists six rooms including a hall, a parlour, a kitchen, an upper chamber, a back house serving as a brewing area and stable, and a large cellar stocked with work gear and anchors, and also housing a keelboat. The testator also recorded 'planks, trees & timber lying & being upon his key or wharfe in Sandgate', indicating a large private wharf substantial enough to support the weight of felled trees (D.P.R. Colyer 1642).

Shipwrights were well represented in the neighbourhood of Sandgate and, although some men owned property within the town itself, the tradesmen do not seem to have lived in other parts of Newcastle in this period. These men also do not record renting properties themselves, but some certainly acted as landlords to quite a number of other men, especially to those in the building or river trades.

4.3.9 Skinners and glovers 1570 - 1634 *(Map 4.9)*

Among the 18 skinners and glovers whose documents survive, two-thirds include information on property. The records show that the men of the trade tended to live and work in the centre or the west side of the town (Fig. 4.1i). Thomas Dodds had a shop 'one (on) the Tyne Bridge' where he sold the 'comodytie therof' (D.P.R. 1597). The inventory is very brief, but includes 70 purses. Roger Bilton also kept a 'shop on the east side of the Tyne Bridge'. The small inventory suggests that the shop was probably part of the family house. Only two rooms were recorded - a hall and a chamber containing beds - along with substantial quantities of leather, pelts, wool, 66 purses and work tools (D.P.R. 1623). Further into town, Thomas Davison had a house 'in the heade of the Side'. He noted that he shared the property with a widow, a cordwainer '& myselfe'. No other details survive (D.P.R. 1628). Towards the west side of town, four properties were recorded in the vicinity of the Bailiff Gate, or Bailey Gate, which led to the Castle precinct. William Whitfeild had a house 'in Baylifgate' with a 'hall house', two chambers, and a kitchen. There are no clues to the number of storeys (D.P.R. 1618). Thomas Stokoe had two houses 'both in a street called Bailliffe Gate'. One house was let to a John Whitfeild 'for life, to the bringing upp of my children'. The other house, for which a small inventory survives, gives no rooms and lists no work objects or tools (D.P.R. 1614). A single house was recorded on Westgate Street. The inventory records two rooms, a hall and a chamber, along with brew vessels and a kiln for drying grain, as well as animals. No work objects are recorded, but the bequest on the will of a 'Flanders chyste & a Dansk chest 'which was my shope chest' suggests the testator had a shop on this side of town (D.P.R. Armstronge 1588). Francis Nicholson recorded a 'p[ar]cell of wasteground', 'situated att the foot of Westgaite neare adioning to Baylife Gaite', but the testator's house was 'in a streate theare called Pandon'. The inventory mentions four rooms, a hall, a 'little chamber', a second chamber 'over the hall' and a 'low cellar', suggesting a three-storey structure. No work objects are listed (D.P.R. 1623).

Henry Shevell recorded a house 'in a place or street called the Over Dean Bridge upon the north side of the said street there'. This is High Bridge where the Cordwainers Hall stood. The inventory records four rooms, including a hall with a loft overhead, a parlour, a brewhouse and a 'workhouse', probably located to the rear of the premises. The workhouse seemed to have been a multipurpose room, accommodating beds, a stable, as well as stockpiles of skins and leather bags. The number of objects suggests a large-scale business on ground level adjoined to a single-storey house with a loft (D.P.R 1634). A house and close 'without Pilgrim Street Gate' was owned by a skinner and glover, but was 'in the occupation' of an unknown woman. The skinners and glovers do not record renting properties to other tradesmen and the documents suggest they generally occupied small houses.

4.3.10 Smiths 1554 - 1641 *(Map 4.10)*

Information provided by 11 smiths regarding 26 properties indicates that their houses and shops tended to be located either in the town close to the walls and gates, or in the suburbs, especially Sandgate (Fig. 4.1j). Two smiths recorded property at the north end of the central market. William Johnson described his house as 'sett lying & being in Freer Chair (High Friar Chare) nigh unto the Newgate', with three other houses that 'do adjoin unto my said dwelling' (D.P.R. 1572). The location of houses close to the Newgate is illustrated on Speed's map (Map 4.17), which also shows the Lort Burn flowing through the properties. Bourne says, 'on the East-side of this Street of Newgate is a little running water which goes into Lorkburne' (1736, 1980: 47). The proximity of running water to a smith's shop is noteworthy. Who occupied the three houses is not specified. The testator's inventory does not record rooms, but a 'stothe with belles' (anvil and bellows) is listed, suggesting a shop somewhere on the premises (D.P.R. 1572; Speed 1611). Thomas Nicholson the Elder leased property to a widow 'in the Nolt market hard by the white crosse', but records that he lived in a 'Mylne called the Chymney Mylne and house and meadow close there unto belonging'. The inventory lists no smith tools, suggesting he was not practising his trade (D.P.R. 1638). Bourne locates the mill in the Castle Leazes and noted it was 'Commonly called Chimley Mill, upon the Syke or Rivulet called Bailiff Burn', located to the northwest of Barras Bridge - the Bailiff Burn becomes the Pandon Burn below the bridge (1736: 148). The mill, apparently still in operation in 1891, is depicted in a drawing by an unknown artist

Illustration 4.1b: 'Chimley Mill' on the Bailiff Burn in the northern part of Castle Leazes (1891) from 'Windmills', The Monthly Chronicle of North-Country Lore and Legend, Vol. V, No 58, Dec. 1891, pp 530.

shown in Illustration 4.1b (Clephan 1891: 530). Another smith owned a house and shop on the Middle Street, which he let to an unknown man, and two further houses on Pandon Street, but he does not tell us where his own house and shop were located. The inventory of Edward Holbourne confirms he also leased out a tenement in Pandon Street and a waste ground in Wall Knoll, but says nothing of the whereabouts of his own eight-room house which contained a very extensive shop (D.P.R. 1613). The story is much the same in the case of Thomas Bates who recorded a tenement 'in a street called the keysyde at the end of the Brode chayre', but he lived elsewhere in another 'house together with the house that I buldyde'. He gives no location for these properties, recording only that his tools stood in both his kitchen and in the shop (D.P.R. 1554).

Edward Lawson, an anchorsmith, recorded owning three tenements on Silver Street behind All Saints Church let to three unknown people, but tells us nothing about the house and shop where he lived with his large family (D.P.R. 1640). William Reed recorded a 'house and shop within Sandgate Gate', meaning either the smith lived in a part of the gate itself or just inside the gate beside the quayside. The location will have been a busy thoroughfare between the Newcastle quay and the suburb of Sandgate where so many keelmen, shipwrights and carpenters were living. The inventory does not name rooms but records numerous tools, such as bores, tongs, hammers, punches, several anvils and bellows, stocks of iron, a grindstone and hundreds of assorted types of nails, suggesting an extensive business (D.P.R. 1570). William Haresone recorded a 'house and shope wherin I nowe dwell' in Sandgate 'in the forestreet', confirming the property was located on the upper main road away from the river edge. The inventory lists five rooms: a hall, a kitchen, a 'Servants Chamber', a chamber above the hall, a 'kitchen loft' and a well-stocked shop which appears to have been an integral part of a two-storey structure. The smith had numerous tools, 'nails of all sorts' and specialised in horse shoes and anchors. The inventory includes a description of 'soe much old workgear in the wyndowe for shoes' suggesting a display of goods behind a glass window in the shop on the main street (D.P.R. 1614). The documents of 'Thomas Dagg of Sandgate' recorded 'a lease of the shop wherein the testator dwelt'. The inventory indicates a well-stocked shop (D.P.R. 1610). One smith owned two houses in the Lime Kilns to the east of Sandgate on the Ouse Burn, but he lived on an unspecified 'chair', possibly the nearby Kirk Chare described below by a tanner who lived in the same area, who described the location of his house as being 'from the Lyme Pytte there downwards to the Kirke Chaire' (D.P.R. Wilkinson 1582; Dalton 1599).

There is no record of the smiths letting property to other tradesmen within the study, and just one man, for whom no documents survive, leased a property in Sandgate from a master mariner.

4.3.11 Tailors 1587 - 1640 *(Map 4.11)*

Half the tailors whose documents have survived provide information on over 30 properties. These were located primarily along the main arteries of the town, particularly in the central markets and the lower east side, but tailors are not represented in the northern or eastern suburbs (Fig. 4.1k).

On the west side of town, one tailor lived 'without the westgate', but no other information survives. Jasper Fairallis, who owned six properties, gave just two locations: one house was on Westgate Street and another was in Pandon, but no details were recorded (D.P.R.1600). However, in 1640 some 40 years later, Oswald Fayrallis, the namesake of one of Jasper's sons, recorded three houses at the foot of Westgate Street: two were on Bailiff Gate, and the other, occupied by a mason, was on the street above called Back Row; both these small streets led into the Castle precinct. The testator lived in one of the houses on Bailiff Gate, which had six rooms spread over three floors. The inventory lists a hall, a kitchen, a chamber over the hall, a 'roofe lofte' and an 'inner room', as well as a 'backehouse belowe'. His other house was 'boardering on a house … in the occupation of Mr. Thirlway', likely a gentleman in view of his title (D.P.R. 1640). In the Upper Central Markets in the 'Nowtmarket' (Nolt Market) beside the White Cross, Robert Gray had his 'Head House', probably of three storeys, with 'ffive smale tenements therunto adioning lying in the ffrier chair' (Low Friar Chare). His inventory lists four rooms: a hall, a chamber above the hall and 'another Upper chamber', together with a kitchen that contained brewing tubs. His second house, also in the Nolt Market, was bequeathed to his son, a tanner, 'with the upper parte of the yarde as now yt is devided' occupied by a 'silkman' (D.P.R.1622). John Robinson lived in a house on the Bigg Market that he divided between two grandsons, each of whom received 'half' the property, though how this was achieved is not recorded and no room division is given on the inventory (D.P.R.1627). George Brown had a house on the Cloth Market about which no details were recorded (D.P.R.1578). Another tailor owned a property opposite this location on Middle Street but it was let to a cordwainer and a butcher (D.P.R.Baker 1640). William Harrison lived on the Flesher Rawe, the name given to the lower eastern side of the Lort Burn, a street more often called the Side. The inventory records a four-room house containing a hall, a parlour with a buttery, a kitchen containing brew vessels, and a chamber, the latter probably being on the upper floor as it contained stocks of corn. A horse and cow are also listed, indicating a stable area. A two-storey structure is suggested. The same testator listed a 'parcel of waist ground situate near unto the Flesh Market' located just north of his house on the other side of St. Nicholas' Church. He also had two tenements 'in Silver Street before all Hallows Church' (D.P.R.1618). Thomas Clarke is the only tailor to confirm he lived on Pilgrim Street. The inventory lists three rooms, a hall with a chamber overhead, which boasted an expensive 'London bedstead', and a brewhouse with very substantial equipment. A two-storey house containing numerous of objects was indicated, but subsequently the testator died in debt, having been 'visited w[i]th plague of pestilence' (D.P.R. 1636).

In the lower east part of town Richard Kell listed 'tenements in Pandon extending from the streat called the keyeside unto the walkenowle' (Wall Knoll), let to three unknown people, together with 'the horse mill over the backside thereof ... in the tenure of Edward Graye, miller'. The mill probably stood to the north of Wall Knoll, an open area in this period according to the contemporary map evidence. Bourne describes the Wall Knoll as 'a very great Ascent and high Hill', noting that the Monastery of the Carmelites 'was at the Top of the Wall-Knoll'. The site later passed to the Trinitarians, and the hill became known as St. Michael's Mount. However, an inventory of property made at its surrender to Henry VIII does not mention a mill (1736, 1980: 139-142). Kell also recorded a house 'with all the shops thereunto appurtayning', and a second shop run by his son, but unfortunately the whereabouts of the properties is not recorded in either case (D.P.R.1604). John Holbourne, a mariner, also recorded leasing 'the Walke Mill' some 20 years later, and this mill may well be that property previously in the hands of Edward Graye, the miller (D.P.R.1622).

Robert Gray, who lived on the Nolt Market (see above) owned three houses as well as the horse mill on the Hornsby Chare, inherited from his brother Thomas. The first house, previously left by Thomas to his wife Agnes, subsequently reappears in Robert's will, this time referred to as the 'Popper House in Hornsbie Chair'. Agnes was still living there when Robert died. Robert's second house on the same chare was let to an unknown man. The third house and the horse mill located at the 'Head of Hornsbie Chaire', were leased to the beer brewer Thomas Kaie. This brewer obtained the original lease from John Gray (father of both Thomas and Robert). When Thomas bequeathed the house and mill to Robert, Thomas Kaie continued to hold the lease. The property must therefore have been in the Gray family for some years, let to the same tenant.

The existence of shops or work houses is not well represented in the tailor's documents, but such rooms certainly existed, as they were recorded in some wills and inventories where the property location is unfortunately not specified. There are a few references to tailors who rented property from other tradesmen in the study. A butcher let 'tenements in & near the keyside', a property 'late bought of Richard Stott merchant', to two tailors, (D.P.R.Priarmar 1605). Another tailor shared 'two little tenements standing together' on Middle Street with a cordwainer (D.P.R.Collingwood 1625). In turn, the tailors leased property to a miller, a butcher, a brewer, a yeoman, a silkman, a mason, a gentleman, a cordwainer, and several widows.

4.3.12 Tanners 1570 - 1641 *(Map 4.12)*

Eighteen properties have come to light owned by just seven tanners who, according to the surviving evidence, lived and worked primarily on the north and west parts of

Newcastle, although they held other properties in the suburbs to the north, south and east of the town (Fig. 4.1l).

Properties were recorded on Westgate Street and 'without' the Westgate, owned by four men. In 1570, John Newton recorded a house in Westgate, let to the tanner Thomas Dodds, although the house was, in fact, bequeathed to his eldest son who was at the University of Cambridge at the time (D.P.R.1570). James Doddes, possibly a relation of Thomas Dodds, listed property in five areas of the town, including two houses on Westgate Street; one being let to a weaver, and the other being his own home. His inventory lists a 'House Hall', a kitchen, a chamber and a 'Tannhouse'. The tan house had ten 'vats' and large stocks of leather and was also used as a stable. The impression is of a single-storey house attached to a large structure. The testator also had a tenement 'without westgate' leased to three people, one of whom was a weaver, and further lands to the north - west of the town in the 'Tempest Leases' or Castle Leazes (D.P.R.1594). Henry Wouldhave left his 'dwelling house' on Westgate Street to his 'loving mother' but no other details survive (D.P.R.1641). Thomas Dalton listed a tenement 'without westgate', let to an unknown man (D.P.R 1599). Two tanners recorded property on the Nolt Market. James Doddes, above, recorded a 'newe house at the whit crosse ... a waste joining unto it & with a close called the ponde close or pond garth' let to another tanner, John Boutflower, for whom no documents survive. The tanner Raiphe Rowmaine also lived in a house on the Nolt Market which had at least six rooms. The inventory lists a hall, a parlour, a loft, followed, unusually, by a chamber, a kitchen and a brewhouse. The structure had either two or three storeys; there was no evidence of any work-related objects on the inventory. This tanner also had '2 cottage houses situate att the Sworrell' (Swirl) in Sandgate see map 4.12). The occupants were not specified but a tanner could have made use of the stream (D.P.R.1636). Thomas Dalton, above, lived to the east of Sandgate at the 'Lime Kilns', situated on the Ouse Burn. He described his tenement as lying 'from the Lyme Pytte there upwards', with a second tenement 'annexed to my said dwelling house from the Lyme Pytte there downwards to the Kirke Chaire and a little garden which I hold of St. Johns church' (D.P.R.1599). Lime Street is shown on Oliver's map (1838), just above the bridge to Shields on the west bank of the Ouse Burn, where Charleton confirms that lime kilns were located by the water side (1885: 375). James Doddes, above, was the only Newcastle tanner to list 'tenements in a street called Pipergate in Gatesyde' (Gateshead), a long street running west parallel to the river.

The tanners let properties to weavers in the Upper West Side, where they themselves also lived, but they do not record leasing property from other trades. Besides the one tan-house listed by James Doddes on Westgate Street, no other clues to the location of tanning facilities were actually specified in the documents, excepting the lime pits at the Ouse Burn. A number of the inventories have references to work houses, bark houses, tan houses and back houses, tanning vats, bark and bark vats, and stocks of tanned and 'un-tanned' leather, skins and 'work gear', indicating that many tanners had these facilities; unfortunately the locations were not recorded.

4.3.13 Weavers 1577 - 1641 *(Map 4.13)*

Among 29 weavers for whom documents survive, 16 record details about the location of their properties. According to the records, the weavers lived and worked almost exclusively in the western side of the town, with some holdings in the northern suburbs (Fig. 4.1m).

Mathew Milbourne is the only weaver to record property 'In a streate theare called the Close'. The testator must have been well connected, as his supervisors, witnesses and appraisers included both merchants and gentlemen. Among the trades included in this study, the master mariners were the only other men to record property here. The inventory lists seven rooms, including a hall, a kitchen that contained brewing vessels, a fore chamber, a little chamber, an inner chamber, an upper chamber and a high chamber. There is no mention of a back house or any work-related equipment. The house was probably three or four storeys high. However, this apparently well-to-do weaver died in serious debt, owing half the money to his supervisors (D.P.R.1627). On the high bank above the Close, ascended by way of the Castle Garth Stairs, Thomas Pace 'of the Castle Garth' recorded just two rooms in a house that stood somewhere within the Castle Precinct. The house may have had a stable to the rear of the property as the will records '1 kow in the house' (D.P.R.1637). Oswald Chater recorded a house on Westgate Street, and owned another 'on thother side of the streate there, adioining on a tenement belonging to Jane Rowmaine', widow of a tanner called Anthony Rowmaine. The testator's first house had 12 rooms with a hall, a parlour, a substantial buttery (a room, not a cupboard), a chamber over the hall, a study with books and bolts of cloth, a chamber above the parlour, a room called 'the Upper Most Chamber', a chamber above the buttery, a 'Servants Chamber', and a kitchen with a workhouse containing 'all the work gear', kilns and other brewing equipment, probably located to the rear of the property. A hayloft is listed, which must have been above a stabling area as cows are included in the inventory. This substantial property was at least three storeys high. The testator's second house across the street, either one or two storeys high, had just four rooms - a hall, a chamber, a kitchen and a brewhouse (D.P.R. 1623). A record of Oswald Chaytor is given by Bourne, who describes him as 'Linen Weaver, 38 year Clerk' of St. John's Church. He died on July 21st 1623 aged 68 and was buried in the Chancel among merchant adventurers, gentlemen and other notables (1736, 1980: 26-7). Edward Steavenson lived on Westgate Street in a house with at least three rooms, including a hall, a chamber and a kitchen. The kitchen incorporated an area for the brewing equipment, work gear and two linen looms. The inventory lists cows and pigs, suggesting a stabling area to the back of the property. The house appears to have been entirely at ground level (D.P.R. 1641). The weaver William Ridley leased a tenement on Westgate Street to a butcher, and had a second property 'in the Groat Market neare unto the Pudding chair', let to a yeoman, but he does not record where he lived himself (D.P.R. 1625). Across the street from the upper end of the Groat Market, a weaver lived and worked in a property on the 'Upper Dean Brigg' (High Bridge). The will records that the testator's house was part of the 'Working house' with 'one little backhouse & such therto belonging right amongst my said working house & a garth'. This description indicates that the 'backhouse', to the rear of the main house, was connected to the workhouse, with a garth giving access to the buildings (D.P.R.1627). Another weaver had a house in 'Newgate Street or the Noote Marketh (Nolt Market) near the Newgate'. The inventory lists four rooms - a hall, a parlour, an 'Inner Chamber' and a 'workehouse' where the testator had a 'coverlet lombe' with all the 'furniture belonging to it'. The whole house was apparently at ground level (D.P.R Watson 1628).

Two weavers recorded property to the north of the town. Anthony Forster recorded 'Ren[t]con (Rents on?) the barrow myles' (D.P.R.1634). It is probable that these mills are the 'Barrows-Mill' identified by Bourne, located in the 'Maudlin-Barrows', or burial ground of the hospital of St Mary Magdalen, which was 'seated at the Summit of an Hill' and 'nigh to the (Barras) Bridge' at the top of Sidgate (now the grounds of the Chapel of St Thomas) (1736, 1980: 151-3). Another weaver had a 'Title of lease in the castle field' or Castle Leazes (D.P.R. Birdes 1577).

Just one weaver recorded leasing property to other tradesmen, although other weavers leased property from tanners on Westgate Street and 'without the Westgate'.

4.3.14 Mills 1548 - 1642 *(Map 4.14)*

Having reviewed the properties of individual trades, the discussion will now turn to the mills that have come to light among the documents. Among approximately 30 mills mentioned in the probate records, 17 of those described in the above sections, dated to between 1584 and 1641, have been plotted separately on Map 4.14. The locations can be cross-referenced with Appendix 2: Part 1.

Besides millers, trades as diverse as bakers, butchers, mariners, master mariners, shipwrights, smiths, tailors and weavers recorded owning or leasing mills. The evidence is almost certainly incomplete. Wills and inventories published by the Surtees Society includes a reference to a windmill at Painter Heugh, near the Side, recorded by Alderman Mark Shafto in his will dated 1592 (Clephan 1891: 533), and further references will no doubt come to light in other records of the town. Growth in the numbers of mills in the town and suburbs is not apparent over the decades included in this study, and although references to long-term leases indicate that the properties were valuable assets, large-scale commercial mills do not appear in the period (Overton 2004: 54).

Mills were widely distributed around the town and suburbs according to the probate data. The maps of Corbridge (1723) (Map 4.16) and Speed (1611) (Map 4.17), along with the Cotton Manuscript (c.1590), do not accurately record mills as they show only one large windmill north of Pandon Gate on the road to Shields. Hutton (1770) locates mills in the grounds of Black Friars, with two along the course of Pandon Dene to the north and west of the town, and one north of St. Ann's Chapel, to the west of the Ouse Burn. The drawings indicate all these mills had sails. Thompson's map (1746) shows seven mills, but all are located in the surrounding countryside on burns coming down to the Tyne. In the 1890s the higher ground surrounding Newcastle was described as being 'crowned with an array of wands' (Clephan 1891: 533), a description echoed a decade earlier by Charleton (1885: 372), but none of the map evidence seems to account for the intra-mural mills of the town.

Three sorts of mills were described in the records - wind, water and horse-powered - the majority being operated by horses, often in conjunction with wind and or water. Horse mills were found in the central market, along the chares in the Lower East Side, high on the Wall Knoll, on the Postern, on Westgate Street, in the suburbs to the north and in Sandgate. Harrison notes the introduction of horse-driven flour and malt mills in the 16th and 17th centuries, but says there are relatively few documentary references to horse-driven corn mills in England, and he suggests that this may mean that few were actually built (2001: 56). The probate evidence, however, presents a rather different picture.

Together with references to horse mills, expensive and highly valued mill horses were also listed. It is of interest that millers alone record blind horses; they were specifically described as such and were listed separately from other horses. For example, the Pudding Chare 'Milne house & malt milne therein' was worked by 'a black blind mare & white mare' (D.P.R. Reade 1613). Although it is unclear whether the horses always worked in pairs, the inventory for another horse mill, either the same mill or a similar one 'in the market & Pudding Chair', listed four horses (D.P.R. Johnson 1592). One of the mills in Sandgate must have been worked with the '2 best horses for the said mylne', as the animals were bequeathed with the mill. The testator listed '1 blind mare ... black colour' and '1 little fille' (D.P.R. Reasley 1603, 1604). The descriptions suggest that a sighted horse worked together with a blind one. Horses were apparently also owned cooperatively: for instance, Robert Hoope owned three horses 'in cop[ar]tnershipp' (D.P.R.1632), and the assessors of one miller's inventory noted 'horses at another mill his part 33s 4d' (D.P.R. Reasley 1603). Harrison does confirm that horse mills tended to be located in or near the towns they served, as was the case in Newcastle, but his assertion that these mills were associated with bakers and maltsters rather than millers is contradicted in the case of this town (2001: 56-7).

Illustration 4.1c: 'Old Mill, Windmill Hills, Gateshead (1891) from 'Windmills', The Monthly Chronicle of North-Country Lore and Legend, Vol. V, No. 58, Dec. 1891, pp533

There were four water mills named in the documents. The Pandon Gate mill on Pandon Dene (Figure 4.1a; D.P.R. Scott 1641), the 'Chimley Mill' on the Bailiff Burn in the northern part of Castle Leazes (Figure 4.1b; D.P.R. Nicholson 1638), the 'water Milne' at Sandgate, and the mill on the Ouse Burn described as the 'lowest mylne of and in that burne' (D.P.R. Reasley 1603; Reasley 1611).

The mill located in Sandgate may have stood on the Swirle, a small stream that once marked the eastern boundary of the town, cutting through both the high and low roads before entering the Tyne (Charleton 1885: 329). The inventory included '1 sayle' and 'all furniture belonging to the water Milne & wind mill horse', indicating that the mill was powered by a flexible combination of wind, water and horse power (D.P.R. Reasley 1603). Other mills may also have used water as well as horse power. Welford noted there was a 'rivulet running under (a) messuage' on Broad Chare where two mills were recorded, but whether this helped to turn one of the mills located on the street is unknown (1885: 58). The lowest mill on the Ouse Burn, was a 'Water Corne Mill', bequeathed 'with appurtances & hay', suggesting the presence of horses (D.P.R. Reasley 1604). This is one of the many mills owned by the Reasley family of millers described above (D.P.R. Reasley 1604, 1611). The manner in which this particular mill was bequeathed suggests it may have been a 'double mill' whereby two separate sets of corn-milling machinery were set side by side with separate sluice gates each driving a single set of millstones. Water-driven corn mills were being rebuilt in the late 16th century and during the 17th century to accommodate more than one waterwheel within a single building (Harrison 2001: 59).

There are no direct references in the probate records to windmills, although the 'Barrow myles' located in the Magdalene or Maudlin Meadow indicates the use of tumuli, a good place to catch the wind (D.P.R. Forster 1634), and the same observation can be made of the mills high on the 'Wall Knoll' (see above) (D.P.R. Kell 1604, Holburne 1619). However, the Wall Knoll mill was also worked by horses (Bourne 1736, 1980: 139; Charleton 1885: 223-5).

Descriptions of properties suggest that mills were either separate from houses or they were 'adjoined' to parts of the property. For example, a mill in the Broad Garth was 'adjoined' to the testator's tenement, with a stable 'adjoined' to the mill with two more tenements 'before the mill' (D.P.R.Whymphery 1605). Thomas Reasley described 'our horse mylne w[i]th a tenement therto belonging' and 'one horse myllne with two little tenements adioying all to gether' (D.P.R.1611). Clephan's article includes a drawing by an unnamed artist, dated 1891, of an 'Old Mill, Windmill Hills, Gateshead', (Illustration 4.1c), across the Tyne, and the buildings are reminiscent of the descriptions from Newcastle records (1891: 533). Concerning the interior spaces of the mills, the inventories reveal very little, with scant information about rooms or their contents. However, valuations for what were sometimes long leases were often quite high in relation to inventoried wealth.

4.4 A comparative analysis: Occupational zones before and after the Civil War

Having examined the evidence from the probate records relating to properties belonging to individual tradesmen (Section 4.3), the findings can be collated for a comparative analysis of the decades between the 1550s and 1642 and the post-Civil-War period.

In order to facilitate an analysis with Langton's study, the trades given in the probate records have been amalgamated into categories based on the occupational sub-groups given in his Appendix (1975: 27). Langton also mapped location quotients, represented on his Figures 5C and 5D (1975:17), showing concentrations of specialized occupations in wards which were either 'marked' or 'significant' (1975: 16), and this methodology has also been adopted in the probate sample to highlight comparable concentrations of properties belonging to given trades.

Map 4.15 and Table 4.4, together with Figure 4.2, illustrate correlations between neighbourhoods and ward boundaries. Within these delineations, occupational zones are apparent relating to property ownership among the trades. Some trades are clearly concentrated in certain areas, while others are dispersed more widely around the town. Five occupational sectors are reviewed.

4.4.1 'Shipping trades' - Mariners, master mariners, shipwrights and keelmen

According to the probate evidence those men whose lives and livelihoods were bound up with the sea and river tended to live and work in parts of the town that were most accessible to the river and quayside. Findings in Section 4.3 show strong affiliations between mariners, master mariners, keelmen and shipwrights based on shared neighbourhoods, shared properties, and from lease arrangements. These 'shipping occupations', excluding the keelmen, are represented in Langton's category B1 (1975: 27). In this analysis the keelmen have been included.

According to the probate evidence, mariners listed properties in five areas of the town (Figures 4.2a,b,f,i,j), but were concentrated in the neighbourhoods of the Lower East Side and Sandgate (Figures 4.1e), which embraced respectively Plummer, Austin, Wall Knoll and Sandgate wards (Table 4.5). The master mariners, (who Langton pairs with the mariners), registered properties in seven neighbourhoods (Figures 4.2a,b,c,d,f,i,j), but most lived in the Lower East Side within Pandon, Austin and Wall Knoll wards (Table 4.5), with some owning properties in Sandgate and Gateshead across the river (Figure 4.1f). The shipwrights listed property in four neighbourhoods (4.2a,b,d,i,j), but a very marked majority lived and worked in Sandgate, with a small number of these men listing, but not living, in properties in the Lower East Side, most of which were probably within the ward of Wall Knoll (Figure 4.1h). The keelmen recorded property in three neighbourhoods, but almost all resided in Sandgate and others in Gateshead (Figures 4.1d, 4.2a,i,j).

On examining Langton's Figure 5C and Table IV (1975: 17, 18) for sub-group B1, it is clear that the high location quotients, indicating marked or significant occupational specialization in wards, correlate well with the probate evidence, most notably in the case of shipwrights. However, even accounting for those trades that were concentrated within three or fewer neighbouring wards, and where statistical data is strongest according to Langton's Table IV, which underlines his Figure 5C (1975: 17, 18), the probate evidence suggests that mariners and especially master mariners were well represented in Austin and Plummer wards, as well as in Pandon, Wall Knoll and Sandgate wards.

An overview of the findings is shown in Figure 4.4a for sub-group B1. The majority of master mariners lived in the lower east, upper east and lower west sides of town, areas that Langton has described as the abodes of the wealthier merchants (1975: 7,16, 17), confirming Gray's account (1649, 1970; 25), although several men also had properties across the river in Gateshead and in Sandgate. The majority of the poorer mariners also lived in the lower and upper east sides of town, a few in Gateshead, with a proportionately lower number residing in Sandgate. The property-owning shipwrights dominated the area of Sandgate, along with the poor keelmen, who lived both in Sandgate and in Gateshead. Langton's assessment of concentrations of occupations in wards for this group of trades from the 1665 data accords with the earlier evidence in the case of shipwrights, but appears to be contradicted in the case of the master mariners and, to a certain extent, in the case of mariners, who both tended to reside principally in areas dominated by merchants (1975: 18).

4.4.2 Victualling trades – Bakers and brewers, butchers and millers

Those tradesmen who earned their living selling food were not (according to the probate evidence) affiliated in any extraordinary ways, although they shared neighbourhoods to differing degrees in several parts of the town. Bakers and brewers, butchers and millers formed Langton's B2 sub-group (1975: 27). The bakers and brewers were found to have held properties in seven neighbourhoods (Figures 4.2a,b,d,e,f,h,i), but half of these were located in the Lower East Side, with fairly good representation in the Upper East Side and the Northern Suburbs (Figure 4.1a). These properties are in the wards of Austin, Pandon, Pilgrim and Carliol (Table 4.5). The butchers are represented in nine out of ten neighbourhoods (Figures 4.2a,b,c,d,e,f,g,h,i), although most of their properties were in three fairly evenly distributed areas covering the Lower East Side, the Central Markets and the Northern Suburbs (Figure 4.1b), representing the wards of Austin, Newgate and Mordon and, in the northern area, within the contiguous wards of Ficket, Andrew and Ever (Table 4.5). The millers, like the butchers, were found to own property in several neighbourhoods, eight in all (Figures 4.2a,b,d,e,f,g,h,i). The highest percentage was found in the Lower East Side, with slightly lower, but evenly distributed percentages in the Upper East Side, the Upper West Side and in Sandgate (Figure 4.1g). The millers were thus found in Plummer and Pandon wards, in West Gate, and in Sandgate (Table 4.5).

Langton's findings (1975: 17-18, Figure 5C, Table IV) for sub-group B2 correlate well with the probate data in the case of bakers and brewers, and to some extent with those for the butchers, where significant concentrations were found in the eastern wards of the upper and lower parts of the town, though none were found in Gunner ward in the probate evidence. Millers occupied the wards in the lower east side of town, where mills have been clearly identified in Section 4.2, but were also represented, contrary to the evidence from 1665, in the wards of Westgate and Sandgate.

Figure 4.4b showing sub-group B2 indicates that, as was the case in the 1665, bakers and brewers were present in marked numbers in the lower east parts of the town in the interstitial wards of Austin and Pandon, and were also present along the long eastern artery of Pilgrim Street and beyond the Pilgrim Gate in Pilgrim and Carliol wards (Langton 1975: 18). The evidence for the butchers suggests a more dispersed pattern of occupational zoning than found by Langton (1975: 18, Table IV), and not apparently concentrated on Butcher Bank as described by Gray (1649, 1970) and Langton (1975: 16). There was no evidence for a single 'quite separate victualling ... quarter' for butchers in the lower east of the town (Langton 1975: 16), although significant numbers of butchers were found (as described by Langton) in the interstitial ward of Pandon, but they were equally prominent in the Central Markets, and had significant holdings in the Northern suburbs. The millers, even more than the butchers, were dispersed in many parts of the town - showing up in the lower and upper east sides and upper west side of the town, and in Sandgate. However, if all mills are accounted for collectively, including those in the hands of men claiming another occupation, a concentration is apparent in the Lower East Side and on the periphery of All Saints Church, covering the wards of Wall Knoll, Pandon, Plummer and Austin, and thus indicating a partial agreement with Langton (1975: 17, Figure 5C).

4.4.3 – Metal trades – Smiths and anchorsmiths

The smiths, including one anchorsmith, were the only metal workers in the probate sample in Langton's C1 sub-group, but these men feature separately in Langton's Table IV (1975: 18, 27). The smiths recorded property in six neighbourhoods (Figures 4.2a,b,d,e,h,i), with most properties recorded in the Lower East Side, Sandgate and in the Upper Central Markets (Figure 4.1j), correlating with the wards of Wall Knoll, Pandon, Sandgate and Ficket. The wards identified by Langton (1975: 18, Table IV), as those with localised populations of blacksmiths, were Mordon, Pilgrim and Carliol. The differences in findings are striking. Although a few properties recorded by smiths in the upper east parts of town and on the central markets verify Langton's findings, these did not constitute occupational concentrations and include no references to shops. The probate data indicates shops were located at the main gates of the town, at Newgate, near the Noult (horse) Market, at Sandgate Gate and in the suburb of Sandgate close to the ship building areas. The inventories support the idea that smiths worked in areas where customers were to be found; they listed large quantities of nails, horseshoes and anchors in their shops (Sections 4.2.10, 5.11). As the sample of probate data is small, it is clear that the picture is incomplete. Langton's evidence for smiths in Mordon ward could be associated with the location of the Iron Market (Map 4.16).

4.4.4 Clothing and textile trades – Tailors and Weavers

Langton's C3 category includes tailors and weavers. The tailors were found to own property in all seven neighbourhoods located within the walls of the town and in the suburb of Westgate (Figures 4.2a,b,c,d,e,f,g). Figure 4.1k indicates concentrations of the trade in the Lower East Side and the Central and Upper Markets, but Map 4.11 suggests that tailors were widely dispersed along the three main arteries of the town and on the busy quayside. Weavers were found in six neighbourhoods (Figures 4.2c,d,e,f,g,h), but showed marked preference for the Upper West Side and the Central Markets (Figure 4.1m), corresponding primarily to the ward of Westgate, with a few properties located on the Upper Dean Bridge, which bisected the wards of Bertram Monboucher and Pilgrim (Table 4.5). Langton's Figure 5D located concentrations of tailors and weavers in Denton, West Spittle, Mordon and Pilgrim wards (1975: 17). Figure 4.4d shows some evidence of both trades in the Lower West Side which covers the wards of West Spittle and Denton, as well as Stank, but more significant numbers were found in the central market area of Mordon ward, evidence that agrees with Langton's later data. Westgate ward is not featured in the 1665 data. In the earlier years, weavers were also not living in the upper central areas of town associated with Pilgrim ward as proposed by Langton, whereas tailors were present in the area at this time. Tailors also show a significant presence in the lower eastern part of the town which is not mentioned in the 1665 data. This suggests, therefore, that weavers and tailors shared neighbourhoods in the centre and west of the town, but only tailors were widely dispersed into other areas.

4.4.5 Leather trades – Cordwainers, skinners and glovers, and tanners

Whereas it might be envisaged that men who worked with leather had through the medium an association of sorts, the probate evidence does not suggest that they shared common neighbourhoods. The cordwainers recorded properties in eight neighbourhoods (Figure 4.2a,b,c,d,e,f,h,i), but were markedly concentrated in the Central Markets, as well as holding significant numbers of properties below these markets in the Lower West Side, as well as in the Northern Suburbs (Figure 4.1c). Cordwainers dominated Mordon ward, especially Middle Street. Their other holdings crossed the four northern contiguous wards of Pilgrim, Carliol, Ficket and Andrew, and the five southern contiguous wards of Plummer, Pink, Gunner, West Spittle and White Friar (Table 4.5). The skinners and glovers listed properties in five neighbourhoods (Figure 4.2a,c,d,f,h), but were most concentrated in the Upper West Side and Lower West Side, covering the three contiguous wards of White Friar, Denton and West Spittle (Table 4.5), with a few properties held in the Northern Suburbs (Figure 4.1i). The tanners held property in six neighbourhoods (Figure 4.1e,f,g,h,i,j), the majority in the Upper Central Markets, a location possibly associated with the four fairs held yearly on the Noult Market for horses and 'black cattle' (Bourne 1736, 1980: 48), in the contiguous wards of Durham, Ever and Andrew. They also resided in the Upper West Side and in Sandgate (Figure 4.1l), within the wards of Westgate and Sandgate (Table 4.5).

Langton's amalgamation of the three trades results in all categories being concentrated in the wards of Pandon and White Friar (1975: 27 and Figure 5D), a finding that largely disagrees with the probate evidence. Figure 4.4e shows the three trades shared the ward of White Friar, which was included within the neighbourhood of the Upper West Side, but the property listed by tanners was on Westgate Street, which was not in fact within White Friar ward. The skinners and glovers were found to have owned shops on the Tyne Bridge within White Friar ward, and most of their properties were located in the west of the town, but the trade was, according to the slight evidence available, dispersed quite widely. A link between those skinners and glovers who sold wares on the Tyne Bridge and those working around the Castle is possible, as the Castle Stairs ran directly up from the bridge end. Langton's findings concerning cordwainers seem to be quite at odds with the earlier probate evidence, with a clear pattern emerging of the trade distributed all along the central artery of the town from the Maison Dieu up the Side, through all the central markets and out Newgate to the Northern suburbs, with just four properties, but no shops, listed on the Long Stair which marked the boundary between Denton and White Friar wards. The tanners were entirely absent from the eastern parts of the town, but one skinner and glover confirmed living on Pandon Street within Pandon ward, and although one cordwainer had properties and a shop in this part of town, these were on Byker Chare in Wall Knoll ward.

4.4.6 Conclusions - Occupational zones

It is clear that, in the period between the 1550s and 1642, neighbourhoods comprised some areas with concentrations of the same trade and other areas in which trades were more dispersed. This corresponds to the picture revealed by Langton's 1665 data (1975: 18).

However, Langton found it difficult to determine the degree to which this 'concentration and segregation of economic activities percolated down to the level of individual crafts' because his sample of population per ward is often small, and ward boundaries follow and transect streets (1975: 18, Table III); however, the crux of the problem is largely the way in which he amalgamated trades into sub-groups. The problem of small sample size also applies to the probate evidence (Figure 4.3), more so for some trades than for others, and it is difficult to recover precisely where individuals live in neighbourhoods where streets are very long. Overall, however, the approach of examining individual trades on identifiable streets and at specific locations given in the probate records was a reasonably accurate guide to where people lived and worked - perhaps a more accurate guide than could be accomplished utilising amalgamated occupational sectors and ward boundaries.

Langton found that Newcastle did not have a single centre around which the town was organised, as had been suggested in the models of Sjoberg (1960) and Vance (1971) (1975: 21). Instead, occupational groups were both concentrated and segregated, with broad quarters evident among the merchantile, shipping, victualling and manufacturing sectors (1975: 18). This multi-centred zoning of the town was also very clear from the probate records for the earlier decades from the 1550s to 1642, but the occupational groups constructed by Langton did not concur with the occupational zones assigned to them in every case.

In 1665, a pronounced service sector existed in the south eastern part of the city, represented by the neighbourhood of the Lower East Side (1975: 16). According to Langton, service trades 'tended to be the most localised' and the 'service crafts' were strongly concentrated in quite separate victualling and shipping quarters which overlapped in Pandon ward (1975: 16, 18). Such separate quarters for shipping and victualling are not apparent from the probate evidence. Figure 4.2a shows that master mariners and mariners (but not shipwrights and keelmen), together with butchers, millers, and especially bakers and brewers shared the streets and chares in many parts of the Lower East Side (Table 4.1). Langton found butchers concentrated on the Butcher Bank, as confirmed by Gray (1649, 1970: 25), but few were recorded in the probate records. Butchers were not confined to a single 'victualling quarter' on this street, but were well represented in the Flesh Market and Flesh Stalls of the Central Market (Bourne 1736: 51), corresponding to the wards of Mordon and Newgate, as well as in the Northern Suburbs.

According to Langton 'craft quarters' were not as pronounced as was the case for 'service trades' – and the degree of segregation among crafts was quite high (1975: 16-18). He found that only Mordon and Pilgrim wards had concentrations of more than one of these sub-groups. This evidence does not entirely agree with the probate findings as there were significant concentrations of manufacturing trades in several areas of the town in the earlier period, besides those identified by Langton. For example, tanners, skinners and glovers, and weavers lived together in the Upper West Side and Western Suburbs (Figure 4.2c,f,g,h).

Although Langton's description of 'loosely articulated quarters' for manufacturing sectors was applicable in the case of smiths (as members of the 'metalworking' sector), leatherworking, embracing cordwainers and skinners,

clearly did not fit Langton's pattern (1975:18). Cordwainers, in particular, were highly concentrated in Mordon ward.
The textile and clothing manufacturers, according to Langton, 'were widely separated', 'dispersed through non-contiguous wards' located in the 'merchant and service' sectors of the city (1975: 18, 27). Such descriptions accord in the case for tailors but were not true of the weavers.

Clearly, there are limitations to the findings in this analysis which should be acknowledged. Langton's amalgamation of trades into sectors presents a confused picture of 'occupational zones' (1975), whereas delineation between occupations does clarify distribution patterns. However, tradesmen of given occupations may not have always worked and lived in the properties they listed in the locations named in the probate records. The Hearth Tax data presents other complications, as Langton points out that a second Revising Act of 1664 held that a poor man who leased a property, and who was not able to pay a hearth tax, was personally exempt, but the wealthier owner of the property was required to pay the tax for the tenant (1975: 25).

While accounting for these problems, explanations for the differences in the earlier and later patterns of occupational zones can be suggested. Langton's proposal that the segregation of trades was the result of an expanding population by 1665, which might have been forcing people of one trade into the areas traditionally dominated by other trades (1975: 22), however, cannot be sustained in view of the earlier probate evidence. Langton believed that occupational concentrations were all located in crowded and completely built-up parts of the city, notably in the wards of Austin, Pandon, Wall Knoll and Sandgate (1975: 22, Figure 4). The pre-Civil War data confirms that the neighbourhoods of Lower East Side and Sandgate (Figure 4.3a), were, in fact, already the most densely occupied parts of town, together with the Central Markets, particularly Mordon ward. However, concentrations of trades, such as weavers and tanners, were also already apparent in other parts of the town which were less built-up, such as the Upper West Side, a finding supported by the probate map evidence (Maps 4.12, 4.13, 4.15).

The concentrations of trades seems to be linked to what Langton has termed 'strategic facilities', such as meeting houses and markets (1975: 16); however, this was also true for segregated trades, such as tailors, whose businesses were located along main arteries, as well as in built-up wards, and smiths, who took advantage of the traffic flowing through the gates of the town. Langton also argued that affiliations between guild members were clearly related to occupational concentrations in zones (1975: 22), and this was seen, for instance, with the cordwainers, but one cannot argue by extension that segregated occupational zones indicated weaker guild or by-trade affiliation.

The analysis has shown that distinct occupational zones existed in Newcastle in both the pre- and post-Civil-War periods; both change and continuity in the social geography of the town has been highlighted. In the final section of this study a detailed examination of the properties in ten neighbourhoods, identified from the probate records, draws together data on occupational zones and information on the nature and scale of the properties identified in Section 4.3.

4.5 The buildings in ten neighbourhoods

Langton found that the occupational zones of Newcastle were quite clearly related to distribution patterns of houses (1975: 18-19). He based his analysis of average household sizes on average numbers of hearths per sub-group (1975: 8, 19, 27), and he found that 'evidence of hearth figures' can be used to deduce 'house size data' (1975: 15, 19, Tables II, III). Langton's map showing the distribution of houses of the service and manufacturing trades (1975: Figure 6) can be compared with evidence from the probate records. To facilitate this comparison, Map 4.15 shows the correlation between boundaries of probate neighbourhoods and the historic ward boundaries represented in Langton's article.

In undertaking this analysis, however, both Langton's data and the probate evidence present certain problems that should be considered. The first problems concerns defining the size of a house in relation to numbers of hearths listed, as only about half the rooms (at most) in any house were, in fact, heated, so there is a difficulty in assuming a correlation (Schofield 1987: 17). The second problem is whether all rooms (including those to the rear of properties used for work associated activities, which were often unheated) were considered in Langton's sample. All such rooms listed in the probate records have been included in the calculations – namely, back, work and brewhouses, and outbuildings adjoined to properties. Some of these rooms were heated; some were not. As noted already, only 37% of probate records provide information on both location and number of rooms in a property, whereas overall up to 95% of documents provide information on rooms; subsequently a more extensive analysis of house size is taken up in Chapter 6.

Langton was also able to consider wealth levels relative to house size within zones, but the probate data is too limited in this particular context. It is noted here that Howell examined the numbers of hearths per household for Newcastle using the 1665 Hearth Tax evidence relating to the distribution of wealth (1967: 8-13), and his observations will be taken up in Chapter 5 in a detailed analysis of the heating of homes, where the location of the property is not central to the enquiry. Another problem inherent to probate records is that the numbers of rooms may not, in fact, correlate to wealth at all: this question is also examined in Chapter 6.

Langton found, as with other towns he analysed, that houses of various sizes were unevenly distributed. He mapped the deviations for the mean average household size, based on numbers of hearths per household, showing where the houses of practitioners of each trade were larger or smaller than the average for their trade (1975: 19, Figure 6), but he does not reveal the actual number of heated rooms per household. He found, unsurprisingly, that the larger houses were located in wards where the wealthiest part of the population was 'over-represented' (1975: 18-19).

Some observations can be made from probate data about the size and types of structures within neighbourhoods, relating to occupational zones, as Langton has done in his Hearth Tax analysis (1975: 19). In terms of the period covered in this analysis, it is acknowledged once again that the properties discussed span at least six decades. However, observations about the built environment of neighbourhoods are nevertheless useful in recovering a picture of the town during the late 16th and early 17th century, especially in the light of evidence suggesting the survival of buildings for not just decades but centuries (Pevsner 1995: 70, 412), and the continuity of occupational zones after the Civil War (Langton 1975).

4.5.1 Neighbourhood 1: The Lower East Side 1548 - 1641

The neighbourhood of the Lower East Side comprises the quayside and chares, and the streets in Pandon, and correlates to the contiguous wards of Austin, Pandon, Corner and part of Wall Knoll. Figure 4.2a shows that 11 of the 13 trades were present in the neighbourhood, and people practising many other occupations leased property here, although bakers and brewers, butchers, mariners and master mariners were dominant in the area. Several mills were also operating in the quarter.

On Grinden Chare, a shipwright let property to an Alderman, and a butcher leased out property on the Pepper Coleman Chare. At the head of Hornsby Chare, was a horse mill owned by a mariner, but let to a baker and brewer. Tailors and one cordwainer owned property here. On Plumber Chare, a baker and brewer and a butcher both owned substantial houses. The baker and brewer recorded a 'mansion house' with an adjoining brewhouse, and at least six rooms over a minimum of two storeys. A timber-framed jetty above the front door is suggested by the description of a 'little room over the entrie'. Green noted that 'projecting porches' were a sign of status and of more elite styles in architecture, and this accords with the description of a 'mansion house' (2000: 322; D.P.R. Peacock 1625). The butcher's house had at least 11 rooms and was four or five storeys high, some rooms being well decorated. A window cushion in an upper chamber suggested views from an upper storey, but the house also had fish lofts, a shop and a cellar (D.P.R. Ridley 1623). Nineteenth-century illustrations of houses resembling this description along the quayside chares were recorded by Boyles and Knowles (1890: 185, 187). A miller had a waste ground at the head of the street, and a mariner leased a property here from a shipwright. Plumber Chare would appear to have accommodated tall structures - abodes of the wealthier sorts. The butcher, who lived on this chare, had bought his house from a merchant, but the presence of shops suggests the street was also a commercial zone.

On the Broad Garth, linked to Trinity House, master mariners and bakers and brewers lived and worked. Two mills were operated on the street owned by two bakers and brewers, one of whom also let a tenement to a barber surgeon. One mill consisted of a complex of adjoined buildings, including stables, and apparently had a common courtyard or access way; it appeared to be a low level structure. The other mill, adjoined to the house, had at least eight rooms, including a cellar, and was three or four storeys high (D.P.R. Hoope 1632; Wymphery 1605). On the Trinity House Chare, two more millers recorded property: one included a cellar and shop leased to a scrivener and a tenement let to a yeoman; the second miller let a property 'neere the keyside' to a baker and brewer. Two master mariners listed objects in cellars belonging to Trinity House. Cellars appear to be a feature of this street and perhaps also of the Broad Garth.

A butcher owned property on Blind Chare, but does not indicate whether he lived there. Property on the Broad Chare, so named as it was wider than other chares in the area, was recorded by master mariners, a mariner and a miller. The mariner and the miller ran mills on the street: one was confirmed as a horse mill. There was a direct link from the Broad Chare into Trinity House. A community of master mariners, of bakers and brewers and of millers were well established in the streets surrounding the Trinity House.

Further east were the wards of Pandon, Wall Knoll and Corner Tower. On the Bourne Bank, a mariner had property with a cellar. On Byker Chare, at the foot of Pandon Street, a cordwainer owned several properties where he lived and ran a shop; he is the only man from the trade to confirm running a business in this part of town. Two shipwrights owned, but did not live, in property on this street: one house was leased to a chapman. Two master mariners also lived here: one shared his house with a mariner. Pandon Street, often referred to as 'a place called Pandon or Pandon Street', was a mixed neighbourhood. Two keelmen had lived here prior to the 1580s. Mariners leased, but did not own, property in the area. A shipwright lived here in the 1570s. A master mariner and a smith owned houses in the street, but neither trade recorded living here. One skinner and glover owned a house with four rooms including a 'low cellar', being about three storeys, but there was no evidence of a shop. A baker and brewer had bequeathed another house on the street to a second skinner and glover, who was already residing here in 1639. A baker and brewer owned several properties on the street, including his own house, which he described as a 'low house', with 'a new building on the backside' and a little yard, suggesting a group of single-storey structures around a courtyard; he also leased another house here to a mariner, which the latter shared with a schoolmaster (D.P.R. Hayton 1637). At Pandon Gate, a butcher owned a house with a water mill, which is attested to historically (Section 4.3.2; Illustration 4.1a). Details of the mill were not recorded, but the house had at least five rooms and was probably of two storeys high. Two tailors recorded properties on Pandon Street: one listed a house with a parlour and brewhouse but no other details were given; the other tailor recorded several tenements, including a horse mill in the lands behind Pandon Street in the Wall Knoll, which was leased to a miller, but later bequeathed to a mariner. A smith also had a waste ground in this open area between the Wall Knoll and the eastern town wall. Below this land, another smith recorded 'a shop and house within Sandgate gate' (D.P.R. Reed 1570). Along the quayside, a master mariner let a property to a fishmonger, and a baker and brewer let one of his properties to another baker and the other to an unknown widow. Lastly, a butcher let tenements, bought from a merchant, to two tailors.

The probate records reveal that properties belonging to the shipping and victualling trades - Langton's sub-groups B1 and B2 (Table 4.5) - lived in houses of various sizes in this neighbourhood. The largest houses, with over seven rooms, were on Plumber Chare and Broad Garth, and these were also the tallest structures listed. Houses with four to six rooms were also found on Plumber Chare, as well as on Broad Garth and at Pandon Mill, whereas the smallest houses (with one to three rooms and fewer storeys) were found on Pandon Street and Byker Chare. Langton's evidence showed the largest houses were located in Austin and Pandon wards and smaller houses in Corner, Pandon and Wall Knoll wards, indicating a good correlation in data and continuity of housing patterns from the later 16th century to the Post-Civil-War period (1975: Figure 6). Men of the manufacturing trades (Langton's sub-groups C1, C3 and C4) provide no details about house sizes, but they were not absent from the area. A great variety of buildings existed along the streets and chares in the Lower East Side; the area was socially and occupationally mixed both before and after the Civil War, with rich and poor, landlord and tenant living, side by side.

4.5.2 Neighbourhood 2: The Upper East Side 1549 - 1641

The area to the north of the natural cliff edge above the quayside chares forms the Upper East Side. The neighbourhood includes the Butcher Bank, Cowgate, the properties surrounding All Saints Church, Silver Street (bordering the church to the north), Pilgrim Street, and the Carliol Croft - an open expanse of meadow and gardens, occupying the land behind Pilgrim Street towards the eastern wall. The area takes in Pilgrim and Carliol wards and the upper part of Plummer ward. Bakers and brewers, mariners and millers list the majority of properties in the area (Figure 4.2b).

According to Gray the Butchers Bank was 'where most Butchers dwell', but only one butcher recorded property here (1649, 1970: 25). This man let one tenement to another butcher. His own house had at least seven rooms and a shop, and was perhaps of two storeys. A master mariner also lived on the street. The inventory lists just three rooms in a two-storey house. Further east, on Cowgate, two other master mariners recorded property: one man let his house to a baker and brewer; the other man listed a five-room property of three storeys. A number of people recorded living and working in properties in or around the grounds of All Saints Church. Speed's map clearly shows how properties virtually encircled the church (Map 4.17). Two mariners recorded five properties 'behind' the church, but just one confirmed he lived there. A baker and brewer had two tenements, which he built on a piece of ground belonging to the church, let to a widow. A family of millers had a mill on the west end of the church with an unspecified number of houses belonging to it, and another house behind the church on Silver Street. A butcher leased a house to widow on Silver Street, and a tailor let two tenements to unknown people here. A smith also had three tenements on the street leased to other people. The community of master mariners and mariners which appeared to have been living and working in close proximity to Trinity House (see above), also seems to have had a close historic association with nearby All Saints Church, where the guild maintained a chantry (Middlebrooke 1950: 56-7). The presence of seafarers in Austin and Plummer wards (Figures 4.2b and 4.4a) is not well represented in Langton's data on occupational groupings (1975: Figure 5C).

On the long wide artery of Pilgrim Street, members of five trades recorded properties. Of the four bakers and brewers who list property here, two leased their houses (to a locksmith and to a minstrel). A third baker and brewer listed a property, probably of two storeys, with three rooms, and a bake house with grain stocks located to the rear of the premises. A fourth baker and brewer had a very large house, apparently of at least three storeys, comprising nine rooms plus cellars, stables, and lofts, and a separate barn with very substantial stores of grain. Two cordwainers also recorded substantial properties along this street. One house had 14 rooms, with a stable and a cellar, and was perhaps four storeys high, but with no evidence of a shop. The second cordwainer recorded a six-room house with substantial brewing facilities. Leather and shoes were stored in the brewhouse. The structure was mainly on ground level, with a roof loft. A tailor also confirmed living on Pilgrim Street in a house with at least three rooms in a two-storey house. A mariner had several properties on the street: his own house had at least six rooms, including two lofts. Two shipwrights owned houses on the street that were let to various people, including a mariner. On the east side of Pilgrim Street, a miller had a house and close let to a widow in the Carliol Croft, the only reference to property in this location.

Gray remarked on the 'Market for Wheat and Rye held every Tuesday and Saterday' on the street, attesting to the strong presence of bakers and brewers and millers, who, according to the probate data, used their premises for baking and grain storage (1649, 1970: 27). Gray also noted that 'both East and West of this street is many passages into other parts of the Town: as the neither and higher Deane-Bridge into the West' and 'also a street called Silver Street, having a passage down to Pandon' (1649, 1970: 27), confirming Pilgrim Street as a very busy artery.

Langton found that large properties belonging to the service trades (sub-groups B1 and B2), were concentrated in upper Plummer ward, but none are shown for the manufacturing trades in this area (1975: Figure 6). The probate data suggests that, although fairly large houses were found on Butcher's Bank and on Cowgate, the properties bordering All Saints Church, and those on the surrounding streets, were made up both of small tenements, leased to a wide variety of people, including poorer sorts, and moderate-sized houses of two or three storeys and occupied by the same trades that lived in the Lower East Side. A concentration of large houses in the ward is therefore not apparent in the earlier period.

The precise location of the very large houses recorded on Pilgrim street by the baker, the cordwainers and the mariner is not known, but the probate evidence disagrees with Langton's finding that no manufacturers owned big houses in the Plummer, Pilgrim or Carliol wards (1975: Figure 6). It is possible that the large houses owned by the cordwainers were close to the Upper Dean Bridge, where their guildhall stood, especially in the light of Gray's observations about 'passages' above. If the huge house belonging to the baker lay outside Plummer ward, then Langton's evidence (that the houses of victuallers were smaller outside this ward and Austin ward) would appear to disagree with evidence from the earlier period (1975: 19).

Langton found that house sizes in the wards of Pilgrim and Carliol were below his mean average for both the victuallers and service trades (1975: Figure 6). The probate evidence suggests that such buildings were not as tall as those in the Lower East Side of the town; however, small properties with fewer than three rooms, houses with four to six rooms, and several very large structures with substantial buildings to the rear, were all found on Pilgrim Street. This area of town must have been relatively prosperous. According to Gray, Pilgrim Street was 'the longest and fairest street in the town' (1649, 1970: 27), and living conditions were it would seem more spacious than most other parts of town, an observation confirmed by all the early maps.

4.5.3 Neighbourhood 3: The Lower West Side 1569 - 1635

The neighbourhood of the Lower West Side includes the Tyne Bridge, Sandhill, the Side, the Close and the Long Stairs that led to the top of the river bank beside the Bailiff Gate. The area takes in seven wards including the Close and parts of White Friar, West Spittle, Gunner, Pink, Plummer and Denton. Of the six trades who listed properties here, cordwainers were dominant, with master mariners and skinners and glovers also well represented (Figure 4.2c).
Two skinners and glovers, selling both purses and gloves, recorded shops on the Tyne Bridge. The inventory of one included only two rooms, apparently used for both domestic and commercial purposes. A master mariner let a shop (that also stood at the end of the bridge) to a merchant. The Tyne Bridge had 'many houses and shops' according to antiquarian accounts (Gray 1649, 1970: 12; Bourne 1736, 1980:130-32). Two master mariners lived on the Close but no details were given about their houses. A weaver also records living in a three- or four-storey house on the Close with at least seven rooms; none containing any work-related objects. Cordwainers recorded owning and letting houses and lands on the Long Stairs. The trade also had property on the Sandhill, where one cordwainer listed five rooms in a house of at least two storeys, together with two shops. The same man listed another house and shop in the Maison Dieu, indicating the private and commercial exploitation of a once-renowned almshouse (Gray 1649, 1970: 24), which clearly had not 'remained untouched' in this period (Graves 2003: 41). The shops on the Sandhill were said to be 'almost altogether those of Merchants', with markets for 'Fish, Herbs, Bread, Cloth, Leather, &c.' (Bourne 1736, 1980: 123). Gray states that 'In this Market place is many shops and stately houses for merchants'; however, clearly, tradesmen other than merchants lived as well as worked here (1649, 1970: 23). Above the Sandhill on the Side, one cordwainer had a tenement leased to a saddler, and another had a house with five rooms and two shops; one shop contained over 100 pairs of shoes and boots, as well as prepared hides. A tailor also owned a house on Flesher Raw (the east side of the Side), with at least five rooms, possibly with stables to the rear. Both these houses were probably two storeys high. Gray confirms that 'In the Side is shops for Merchants, Drapers, and other trades (1649, 1970: 25).

Both domestic and commercial buildings, offering a wide variety of consumables to traffic moving over the bridge and into town via Sandhill, were located in the lower west part of the town. Although the Lort Burn, full of stinking rubbish in the period, ran through the area, this clearly did not hinder business or discourage wealthy merchants, who were well represented (Charleton 1885: 198; Gray 1649, 1970: 24; Langton 1975: Figure 5A). The largest house recorded in this neighbourhood was on the Close, owned by a weaver. Langton records no manufacturing trades in the Close ward, but the Close also ran through White Friar ward (1975: Figure 6C). Langton locates the largest houses in Pink ward, where the probate records list a modest two-storey five-room house, and shops (1975: Figure 6C). The houses on the bridge were clearly not large, but are absent from Langton's map. The four- and five-room houses, both of two storeys, located at the Head of the Side and on the Side, suggest properties similar to the average house sizes in Gunner and West Spittle wards, but these were smaller than any in Pink ward (Langton 1975: Figure 6C). No information on house size survives for Langton's service trades in the neighbourhood.

4.5.4 Neighbourhood 4: The Central Markets 1578 - 1640

The Central Markets encompass the Meale Market, Middle Street, the Poultry Market, the Cloth Market, the Flesh Market, and the Bigg Market to the north, and Denton Chare, Pudding Chare and Upper Dene Bridge, which were streets that linked the east and west parts of the town to the markets. The neighbourhood encompasses the wards of Mordon, Herber and Newgate, and parts of Stank, Durham, Bertram Monboucher and Pilgrim. Cordwainers, and secondly butchers, listed a clear majority of properties in the area.

Property on Denton Chare, owned by a baker and brewer and by a cordwainer, was let to unknown people. A butcher, two cordwainers and a weaver all recorded property on the Meale Market: one of the cordwainers described a five-room property, with a well-stocked shop, all at ground level; the weaver let a property here to a yeoman; the butcher had a substantial seven-room house, plus a stable and loft, a slaughter-house and a shop, all part of the same premises, with a second house 'adjoined' to his house occupied by another butcher, the entire property being mainly at ground level. The same butcher let two further tenements on the Meale Market to a cordwainer and a yeoman. Adjoining the Meale Market was Pudding Chare, where a master mariner and a miller operated mills. It is possible that the two mills, recorded 20 years apart, were one and the same property, but this cannot be determined from the probate evidence. A description of one of the mills, with 'a malt mill therein', indicated that it was adjoined to the house which comprised at least six rooms, including a large brewhouse with kilns, and was three storeys high (D.P.R. Reade 1613).

There are numerous references to properties owned and leased on Middle Street - two-thirds by cordwainers and the rest by butchers, a smith, a shipwright, a miller and a tailor. One cordwainer leased his house and shop from a sergeant. Few details are given about the size of the premises but the impression is that most were fairly small and rather crowded. The largest recorded property on the street, probably of two storeys, had four rooms, and a shop which contained more than 324 pairs of shoes (D.P.R. Spoore 1587). Two other cordwainers listed shops in Middle Street, but not their houses. One cordwainer recorded tenements adjoined to those owned by a merchant, and another leased two tenements to a tailor and to another cordwainer. A butcher leased 'one tenement with a shopp under the same' to a cordwainer (D.P.R.Smith 1614). Another butcher, with a house and shop, leased the house to a joiner but occupied the shop himself. A shipwright had two tenements let to a cordwainer; a smith leased a house and shop to an unknown man; and a tailor leased his tenement to a butcher and another cordwainer, who seem to have shared the premises. One miller left a house to his son, a merchant. Gray described Middle Street as a place 'where all sorts of Artificers have shops and houses' (1649, 1970: 26), and this is certainly confirmed by the probate evidence.

Across the street on the Cloth Market, a master mariner let a tenement to a yeoman, and a tailor owned a house here. Two butchers had property on the adjoining Flesh Market; one had a house and two shops, but leased a chamber on the south side of his house to a third party; the butcher lived at the Head of the Side, but leased a 'flesh stall' on the market. A cordwainer listed two rooms in a house with a shop on this market, and a tailor recorded a piece of waste ground situated near the Flesh Market, where he may have kept animals, indicating that some open areas existed even in crowded urban areas.

Next to the Flesh Market, a cordwainer recorded a 'Great House' standing on the Poultry Market. This house had 14 rooms, lofts and a cellar, as well as a well-stocked shop with leather, tools and 60 pairs of shoes, indicating both the sale and manufacture of objects. Near to this property, was a house owned by a tailor (the only man to list a property on the Bigg Market), which was bequeathed to two grandsons, each of whom was to receive one-half of the house. It was presumably a large property, as the tailor was a wealthy man who recorded substantial sums of money, silver, grain and cloth.

Along the Upper Dene Bridge, which led east off the market towards Pilgrim Street, a baker and brewer, a weaver, a cordwainer and a skinner and glover all listed property. The baker and brewer leased out two houses here to unknown people. A skinner and glover owned a two-story house on the north side of the street, with at least four rooms including a loft, a well-stocked workhouse and a stable. A weaver had a substantial house with a workhouse and backhouse, with a garth to the rear of the premises. A cordwainer had an unspecified number of houses, together with lands, on this street. The main house, of at least four storeys, had 11 rooms, including two cellars, an adjoining brewhouse and lofts.

The probate records reveal a number of fairly small houses with shops (mostly one or two storeys high) in

Middle Street belonging to manufacturing and service trades (sub-groups B1, B2, C3, C4), mostly selling clothes, shoes, meat, beer and grain. The evidence supports Langton's finding for Mordon ward that the houses were smaller here than those belonging to the sub-groups in the lower merchantile part of town (1975: 19). However, very substantial low-level properties also existed in the Meale and Poultry markets in the wards of Herber and Newgate, respectively, occupied by both the service and manufacturing trades, although Langton found that only the service trades in Newgate ward had large properties (1975: 21).

The presence of very large properties belonging to both manufacturers and service trades on the Pudding Chare, the Bigg Market, and the substantial workshops on Upper Dean Street within Durham and Monboucher wards, are not altogether substantiated by Langton's findings of rather smaller houses in the area (1975: Figures 6B, 6C). Gray's statement that in the medieval period there had been 'many faire houses in the Flesh Market', and that 'Merchants had their shops and warehouses there, in the back parts of their houses', but they had 'removed lower down towards the River' in his time (1649, 1970: 22), appears to be corroborated by the probate evidence. It appears that, if former merchant houses came to be owned by other tradesmen, that these will be the same 'faire houses' described in the probate records - such as the 'Great House' on the Poultry Market recorded in 1625. In 1736 Bourne described the Bigg Market as 'broader than almost any street in the whole Town, and adorn'd with good Houses' (1736, 1980: 51). Langton's 1665 data also confirmed that the houses in Newgate ward were 'larger-than-average' (1975: 21), indicating the long-term survival of large buildings of medieval origin in this part of town. The remains of the late medieval White Hart Inn on the Cloth market provides rare testimony to the substantial structures which once adorned the street (Pevsner 1995: 465-66; Website: Images of England – Number 304504).

4.5.5 Neighbourhood 5: The Upper Central Markets 1572 – 1638

The Upper Central Markets, to the north of the Bigg Market, include Newgate Street (where the 'Noult' or horse market and the 'White Cross' were located), the Low Friar Chare and the High Friar Chare. The area encompasses Andrew ward, part of the Durham ward, and the intra-mural parts of Ever and Ficket wards. Figure 4.2e suggests property ownership was dominated by cordwainers, smiths, tailors and tanners.

On Low Friar Chare, a baker and brewer owned a tenement with substantial brewing equipment, and a cordwainer recorded a tenement and close leased to unknown people. A tailor lived on the corner of this chare and the Noult Market, in a house with at least four rooms over three floors, with five adjoining tenements leased to unknown people. The tailor also had a second house with a 'yard' on the Noult market, which be bequeathed to a tanner. Two other tanners also had houses here; one man had built a new house at the White Cross - the property included a close, a piece of waste ground and a pond, all leased to another tanner. The house of the other tanner contained six rooms over three storeys. Neither of these records mentions work-related objects. A weaver recorded a house close to the Newgate, with at least four rooms including a workhouse; this property seems to have been all at ground level. Two cordwainers also listed houses on the Noult Market; a smith leased a property to a widow; and a butcher leased a 'messuage' and house with a close to a 'gentleman'. No details of these properties were recorded. A baker and brewer recorded two tenements let to unknown persons on Newgate Street. A miller owned three adjoined properties located at the site of the Huckster Booths, which stood in the middle of Newgate Street above the White Cross, described as the 'northern most', the 'south most' and the 'middle most' houses (D.P.R. Herrison 1577). On High Friar Chare, very close to the Newgate and the Lort Burn, a smith recorded four houses, three were leased to unknown people. His own house contained bellows and tools of his trade, indicating a shop close to the Newgate.

Little detailed information survives about property in the Upper Market area to compare with Langton's findings. Properties beside the Noult Market, belonging to the manufacturing trades (sub-groups C3, C4), lying in either Durham or Andrew ward, were larger, according to the probate evidence, than indicated by Langton. The tanners were apparently living in houses with between four and six rooms, perhaps more, some with closes or yards. However, the three houses located at the site of the Huckster Booths, owned by a miller (sub-group B2), indicates some smaller than average sized houses on Newgate Street. As the houses were termed 'booths', and were located in the middle of this busy thoroughfare, they must have been of modest proportions, and Speed (Map 4.17) indicates small buildings (Charleton 1885: 152; Langton 1975: Figure 6B).

The concentration of large properties, belonging to manufacturers, which Langton found in Ficket ward, was not visible in the probate sample. Although the size of the house belonging to the smith, (sub-group C1) in Ficket ward was difficult to assess (as he had leased out three of his four adjoined tenements), when the tenements, his own living space and shop are considered together, a larger than average property is suggested, agreeing with Langton's evidence (1975: Figures 6B, 6C). However, the division of larger properties between several families is noteworthy. The neighbourhood seems to have comprised many small tenements, often linked together to provide residences for a variety of people, including those purveying grain, bread and beer, as well as those manufacturing clothing, leather and metal wares.

4.5.6 Neighbourhood 6: The Upper West Side 1570 - 1641

The neighbourhood of the Upper West Side includes the Castle Garth, the Bailiff Gate leading into the Castle Precinct, the Back Row, the Postern, and Westgate Street, including the properties in the grounds of St John's Church. The area takes in all Westgate ward and parts of Herber, Denton, Stank, West Spittle and White Friar wards. Weavers, tanners, millers and skinners and glovers listed the majority of properties in these wards (Figure 4.2f).

Within the Castle Garth, one weaver lived in a small two-room house, with an area to the rear of the property where he kept animals. Two skinners and glovers and a tailor recorded property on the Bailiff Gate, 'a street which in former times belonged unto the Castle' (Gray 1649, 1970: 28). One skinner and glover had a house with four rooms, over one or two storeys, with stocks of leather in his chamber indicating a workshop. The other skinner and glover recorded two houses at this location, but gives no other details except that the second house was bequeathed to another member of the same trade. The tailor's house was extensive, having at least six rooms over three floors, with a workshop somewhere on an upper storey. He owned a second house bordering his own, leased to a gentleman, and on the Back Row (the small street to the north running parallel to Bailiff Gate), this tailor leased another house to a mason. A mariner recorded two houses, described as lying 'in the Castle Moat' and the Bailiff Gate, leased to unknown occupants.

On the Postern, a miller owned two small tenements adjoined to a mill. A second miller listed two houses on Westgate Street, one let to an unknown man. His own house had four or five rooms on ground level. The presence of work clothes, grain and mill horses on the inventory indicated a mill on the premises. Three weavers recorded property on Westgate Street: one man had a very large, deep house of three storeys, with at least 12 rooms and a separate workshop. He owned a second four-room house with two storeys, let to a tanner. Another weaver had a house with three rooms: he kept work gear and linen looms in the kitchen and a few animals in the rear of the premises. One other weaver leased a house to a butcher. Several tanners also lived on Westgate Street: one man had a house with at least four rooms, including a large separate 'Tannhouse' with ten vats and large stocks of leather - the property appears to have been all at ground level (D.P.R. Doddes 1594). This tanner had a second house, let to a weaver. A third tanner let his house to another tanner, while a fourth tanner lived here but left no details about his house. A baker and brewer held a lease beside the Westgate, and a master mariner and a tailor listed houses on the street, but no details about these properties were provided.

Several properties were listed on land around St John's Church - four owned by a cordwainer and let to unknown people, and four owned by a butcher, let to a chapman and a widow. No other details were recorded. Speed shows properties in very close proximity to the church, and Bourne describes the church as surrounded by houses 'being situated in the Middle of Fields and Gardens and more retir'd being at some Distance from the Street' (1736, 1980: 22, Map 4.17).

Langton had found that all the houses in the wards covered by the Upper West Side, belonging to the service and manufacturing trades, were smaller than average, excepting those in White Friar ward. It is probable that the larger houses, however, were located on the Close rather than within the Castle Garth, where the probate records reveal a small single-story property. Moderate-sized houses with chambers used as workplaces (only one man recorded a house with seven rooms), were found on Bailiff Gate within Denton ward, belonging to the skinners and glovers and the tailors (sub-groups C3 and C4).

Langton's findings for Westgate Street and Westgate ward indicated that only the merchants (sub-groups A1 and A2) owned larger houses in the neighbourhood (1975: Figures 6A, 6B, 6C). According to the probate data, weavers and tanners in particular, but also millers (the only service trade found to have lived here), occupied quite substantial properties here and on the Postern, although houses sizes varied, some were three storeys, others were low-level.

That the tanner mentioned above had workhouses and numerous tanning vats behind his house suggested a quite different aspect to the neighbourhood than the one given by Gray, who described Westgate as 'a broad street, and private: for men that lives there hath imployment for Town and Country', accommodating 'houses of Gentlemen' (1649, 1970: 27). The Spittel Hospital and almshouses, also referred to as the Hospital of St Mary the Virgin, were also located on Westgate, serving 'Poor and way-faring People', providing a place to bury the dead and to distribute 'Coals among poor People' (Bourne 1736, 1980: 31; Oliver 1924: 1-2; Knowles and Boyle 1892: 192). The evidence alludes to a socially mixed area, which clearly did not exclude the poor, with a great variety of buildings, and although shops were probably absent, the manufacturing trades clearly were not.

4.5.7 Neighbourhood 7: The Western Suburb 1586 - 1620

A neighbourhood often described in the probate records as 'without Westgate' appears to have been an extension of the neighbourhood of Westgate within the walls, and was part of Westgate ward. Although Figure 4.2g show that millers owned most of the properties here, weavers and tanners appear from the records to have been the most numerous of the tradesmen living in the area.

Unfortunately, no detailed descriptions about properties situated here were recovered. Langton found that house sizes were all below the mean average for both service and manufacturing trades (1975: Figures 6B, 6C). A miller recorded a tenement and close let to an unknown woman, and another property in the Forth where he had a 'meadow close'. There are no other references in the documents to properties in the Forth, described as 'a place of recreation' by Gray and other antiquarians (1649, 1970:10; Bourne 1736, 1980: 145; Charleton 1886: 347). A butcher and a tailor lived here, but no other details were given. Two weavers lived in this area, both of whom leased their houses from tanners, and a third tanner leased a tenement to an unknown man. The limited evidence suggests a community occupying small tenements, closely connected to the trades which populated Westgate Street, particularly weavers and tanners.

4.5.8 Neighbourhood 8: The Northern Suburb 1577 - 1635

The Northern Suburbs beyond Newgate and Pilgrim Street Gate encompass north-west Gallowgate, the western artery of Sidgate, the Maudlin meadow, and the Castle Leazes, covering the extra-mural parts of Ever, Andrew and Ficket wards, and to the north-east, the eastern artery of Sidgate (a street referred to as 'without the Pilgrim Gate'), and the Shieldfield, covering the extra-mural parts of Pilgrim and Carliol wards. Butchers, bakers and brewers and cordwainers listed more properties in this suburb than other trades (Figure 4.2h).

Two butchers listed property on Gallowgate; one had two tenements and a shop. This man lived in one tenement containing three rooms with a butchering area towards the rear of the property, all at ground level. On the same street, the other butcher had a 'meadow close', a meadow in Castle Leazes and rigs of land to the north of his property. A miller and a cordwainer also leased out houses and a close on Gallowgate to unknown people. To the north west of Gallowgate, in the Castle Leazes, two other butchers, a miller, a weaver and a tanner all recorded leasing lands or 'rigs' of meadow on these commons for animals and crops. A smith leased the Chimley Mill on the Bailiff Burn in the northern part of Castle Leazes. Gray confirms that the 'large fields of meddowes, called the Castle Leases' belonged to the town (1649, 1970: 39). However, Bourne says 'This Place was formerly the Inheritance of divers Persons, Owners thereof, who were accustomed from ancient Time, to take the fore Crop thereof yearly, at or before Lammas-Day, and after that, by ancient Custom, all the Burgesses of this Town used to put in their kine, and used the same in pasturing of them 'till Lady-day in Lent yearly, and then to lay the same for Meadow again till Lammas' - and it was not until 1679 that 'the Town purchased the Sweepage of the Castle Leases for the Benefit of the Burgesses' (1736, 1980: 147-8). The probate evidence suggests private use of the commons for cultivation and pasturing was well established prior to 1642.

One of the butchers mentioned above, a miller and three cordwainers all leased multiple tenements, houses, closes and garths to unknown people on Sidgate on the eastern boundary of the Leazes. At the north end of this street a weaver leased the 'Barrow Mills', located in the Magdalene or Maudlin Meadow in the grounds of the old hospital of St Magdalene. A baker and brewer owned a 'close of land' near these meadows but lived closer towards town in tenements with a close 'without Pilgrim Gate'. He leased other tenements with closes to unknown people in the same location. Further east another baker and brewer leased a house and close of arable ground in the Shieldfield to an unknown person.

Few details about houses in the northern suburbs were given in the probate records, besides the small house and shop listed in Gallowgate by a butcher. From the brief descriptions of 'tenements' rather than 'houses', most appear to have been modest premises, but the majority feature little closes and garths, as attested to by Gray, who described 'many closes' in the suburbs of Newgate and Pilgrim Street (1649, 1970: 39). Langton's evidence shows small house sizes for the service trades in the extra-mural wards of Ever, Pilgrim and Carliol, as well as for the manufacturing trades in extra-mural wards of Carliol, Pilgrim and Gallowgate (1975: Figures 6B, 6C).

Above average-sized properties were evident along the west artery of Sidgate for both the service trades and especially the manufacturing trades, which was bisected by the wards of Andrew and Ficket, although this division was not reproduced on Langton's map, which omits the extra-mural part of Andrew ward (1975: Figure 3; Charleton 1886: 367; Welford 1911: 67).

The high deviation for mean house sizes in the extra-mural part of Ficket ward is difficult to assess. Langton's data for Ficket ward shows that it contained half the average number of taxpayers compared with the lowest figures for other wards, and is one of three wards where non tax-payers out number tax payers, the others being Ever and Sandgate, where house sizes were below average (Langton 1975: Figures 6B, 6C; Welford 1911: 76). Considering the probate findings, contemporary descriptions, and the hearth tax evidence, the deviation in the sample means indicating larger houses, may be incorrect. Properties listed in other wards by sub-groups B2, C1, C3 and C4 were certainly larger than those which came to light for the Northern Suburbs.

Bourne described Gallowgate in his own day as 'a very tolerable Street, and a very pleasant place, having in it some good Houses, which are situated in Gardens and Fields'; in contrast Sidgate was described as 'Houses very indifferent, most are inhabited by poor People: but very sweetly situated, having the Leazes or Gardens behind them' (Bourne 1736: 147). The gardens and fields were well attested to in the probate records in the earlier period, and the poor are apparent from the1665 Hearth Tax. Despite the possibility of some large properties in the suburb, overall, the evidence suggests the majority were small tenements with ample gardens, where a great mix of middling tradesmen lived or worked lands, among their poorer neighbours.

4.5.9 Neighbourhood 9: Sandgate and the Eastern Suburbs 1569 - 1642

Sandgate and properties further to the east on the Ouse Burn fell within the wards of Sandgate, and the extra-mural part of Wall Knoll, which took in the north side of Sandgate's upper main street. Although 10 trades list properties in the neighbourhood, mariners, keelmen and especially shipwrights predominated (Figure 4.2i).

There is very little recorded information on properties owned by keelmen and mariners. One keelman described four houses, two roofed with slate and two with thatch which appear to have been single-storey dwellings with loft spaces. Inventories pertaining to keelmen suggest they almost all lived in single-cell properties with halls and lofts. Only one document listed a fore-chamber and a kitchen in a keelman's house. One mariner described his house in detail: it was divided into three separate residences and ran from the fore or main street down to the low-water mark at the riverside. The building comprised a complex of at least 10 rooms, with a stable and waste ground near the main street. The use of the internal space was flexible, with rooms changing hands between various family members, providing living spaces designated by function rather than design. The structure was single storey with loft spaces.

The properties of shipwrights were frequently described as situated either on the high street or by a quay, with a number occupying all the land between the road and the river. Many properties were adjoined to other houses and these arrangements, indicating shared walls and boundaries, were sometimes expressly related in the records in relation to orientation, roads or street furniture. People appear to have lived together in a complex of closely built quarters that required clear explanations regarding access. Houses with four to seven rooms standing one or two storeys high seem to have been common to shipwrights. One house had a chamber over the doors suggesting a timber jetty on the front of the property. Such a projecting porch, associated with elite status, and similar to the one for the mansion house on Plummer Chare (described above), is an interesting finding in a neighbourhood so often portrayed as the abode of the poor (Ellis 1984: 197; Green 2000: 322). The presence of such building forms in Sandgate (and Plummer Chare) argues against notions that projecting porches are 'integral to participation in civic ceremonials' in the more elite parts of town (Graves 2003: 39-40). Large cellar spaces were also a feature of the shipwrights' residences. One was described as being above the testator's house and this makes sense, as the ground was drier towards the high street owing to the steepness of the riverbank. Many 'little tenements' were leased to keelmen, carpenters and mariners, especially by shipwrights. The houses belonging to shipwrights are reminiscent of those in the suburbs of London described by Stow, who noted that the trade 'built ... large and strong houses for themselves, and smaller for sailors' (1589, 1987: 376).

Despite owning a number of properties in Sandgate, only one master mariner confirmed he lived in the neighbourhood, in a well-equipped house with at least six rooms over three storeys, indicating a taller than average house. Other master mariners let multiple- occupancy properties to mariners and to a smith: several were located adjacent to the river. A butcher also owned several adjoined houses with a wharf, let to unknown men. Two smiths list property in the suburb. One man listed a two-storey, five-room house 'in the fore street' and a well-equipped shop with a window display. A house and watermill, complete with sails and worked by horses appears to have stood on the Swirle, a stream that at one time marked the eastern boundary of Newcastle, cutting through the middle of the suburb and becoming a 'broad opening from the main street to the river' (Bourne 1736, 1980: 154; Charleton 1885, 329). A tanner recorded two cottages at the Swirle, but does not specify who occupied them. Such a location next to flowing water suggests a useful facility for tanners. Another miller described a property divided into three separate living spaces, with rooms above and below a central tenement, with shared walls. Two cordwainers leased property in Sandgate, one from a wealthy master mariner, but no details were recorded. A baker and brewer confirmed living and working in Sandgate: he had lands and a two-storey house with seven rooms, including a brewhouse with extensive, costly equipment.

Stables and wastes appeared to be a feature in the neighbourhood, located on the higher ground close to the main road. Several private wharves or quays stood in or next to the river, often piled with wood and trees owned by the shipwrights (Chapter 5).

Three trades record property on the Ouse Burn. A tanner lived in two adjoined tenements at the 'Lyme Pytte there downwards to the Kirke Chaire' (D.P.R.Dalton 1599). A smith leased property to unknown people at the Lime Kilns and also had a house possibly on the Kirk Chare nearby. The lime pits were situated on the Lime-Kiln road, mentioned by Bourne as a place where ballast was delivered (1736, 1980: 154). Charleton records that 'Where Lime Street now is, on the right bank, used to stand the lime kilns by the water side' and he also mentions 'spent bark heaps which crowd the banks', but says nothing of tanning in the area (1885: 375-6). The evidence suggests that lime kilns associated with tanning were functioning in the area for decades, if not centuries; Lime Street is shown on John Tallis's map of c.1851. A 'water corne mylne' described as 'lyinge and being in a place called Ewes (Ouse) burne being the lowest mylne of and in that burne', provides a relatively accurate location for what was probably a 'double mill' (see

Section 4.3.14), worked by generations of the Reasley family, whose history is told in Appendix of Mills: Part 2 (D.P.R. 1603, 1604, 1611).

The size of properties in Sandgate varied considerably. Several large houses, with over seven rooms and auxiliary buildings such as cellars, shops, back and brewhouses, and stables were recorded, a very few up to three storeys high. Unique to Sandgate were multi-occupancy properties, running between the high street and the river edge, with up to ten rooms divided between extended family or leased to tenants. A number of other two-storey houses had three or four rooms. There were also many small single-cell tenements with chambers in the lofts. Langton's amalgamation of manufacturing and service trades, which showed that houses in Sandgate were below average size, has proved unsatisfactory: the situation was far more complex than his map evidence suggests (1975: Figures 6B, 6C). Langton also omitted the extra-mural part of Wall Knoll ward, which encompassed 'all that dwell upon the north rawe in Sandgate' (1975: Figure 3; Welford 1911: 73). As houses in the intra-mural section of Wall Knoll ward, occupied by service trades who made up the majority of residents in Sandgate, were above average size, it is possible that some of these householders actually lived in the larger properties in the extra-mural part of Wall Knoll ward.

Sandgate was clearly an intensely urbanised, autonomous community. Most trades are represented, excepting skinners and glovers, tailors and weavers. Living conditions for many (if not most) people appears to have been confined, but Graves' contention that conditions were 'congested and filthy' appears to underestimate efforts by householders to create liveable, legally defined, spaces, despite the crowding (2003: 51). A demarcation is apparent between those trades occupying property on the drier ground along the fore-street, notably a baker and brewer, cordwainers, millers and a smith, and those who monopolised the lower area towards the river with access to the quays, rather exclusively the river- and sea-farers and shipwrights. The division echoes the ward boundaries and Gray's portrayal of the neighbourhood as having 'many houses, and populous, all along the waterside: where shipwrights, sea-men and keel-men most live, that are imployed about ships and keels' (1649, 1970: 12). The keelmen were still dominating this part of town 200 years later (Ellis 1985: 208, 2001: 6).

4.5.10 Neighbourhood 10: Gateshead 1569 - 1627

Gateshead, in the Palatine of Durham, was not part of Newcastle - the counties being divided by 'a blew Stone about the middle of the Bridge which is the bounds of Newcastle Southwards' (Gray 1649, 1970: 12). However tradesmen, especially keelmen, mariners and master mariners, and to a lesser extent tanners and shipwrights, all claiming residency in Newcastle, were found to live here or to own property in the neighbourhood (Figure 4.2j). Three master mariners recorded property in Gateshead, including one man who lived on Low Kirke Chare close to St Margaret's Church. A second man leased houses, lands and a close to various people including merchants and a mariner, while a third master mariner leased a house to unknown people. A tanner leased two tenements to an unknown man on Pipergate which ran west, parallel to the river. A keelman owned a group of houses with gardens, staithes and wharves located at the river's edge and leased to several people. A mariner and a shipwright also listed property here, which was leased to unknown people.

Although no details of the Gateshead properties survive, the probate documents provide clear evidence of the social and economic links between these communities, presenting a picture differing from that highlighted by the historic quarrels between the Corporation of Newcastle and the Bishops of Durham for possession of Gateshead (Gray 1649, 1970: 21). It would seem that tradesmen moved freely between the two towns, living, working and owning property on both sides of the river.

4.6 Conclusions

In coming to understand the vanished historical demography and built environment of early modern Newcastle, by way of an empirically based study, the potential of the probate records has been clearly demonstrated. Occupational zones unquestionably existed, with trades both concentrated and segregated around the town and suburbs. Langton maintained that the spatial groupings of people following the same occupations, in an economy where workplace and home were congruent, was still based on guild or trade affiliation in 1665 (1975: 22), a view confirmed by Vance's assertion that guild associations were among the most powerful forces shaping the morphology of early towns (1971: 105). The finding is echoed by King who stresses the vital role of the guild both economically and socially in the early modern town (2004: 59). For many Newcastle trades in the period of this study, guild association was evident in patterns of property distribution, often tied to the nature of the work or the proximity to markets associated with the requirements of businesses and clients. The same observations pertained to men practicing by-trades. Nevertheless, trade affiliation did not necessarily translate into density of a trade in a single occupational zone, and tradesmen did not necessarily live close to 'strategic facilities' such as their guilds, as Langton had found in the case of the wealthiest merchants (1975: 16). Proximity to guildhalls was evident particularly in the case of cordwainers, whose guild was located on High Bridge close to the Central Markets, and in the case of master mariners and mariners who lived and worked near Trinity House.

Some degree of specialization along streets was evident, but most accommodated a mix of people, in some instances providing one another with reciprocal services, as was the case of shipwrights, keelmen and mariners in Sandgate. In other trades, such as butchers and cordwainers, who crowded around Middle Street and the Flesh Market, the focus was apparently on the client base. Evidence of where the poorer or 'dirtier' trades were located showed that these were not exclusively found on the periphery of the town (Langton 1975: 2). Any assumptions that trades that created smells (the familiar culprits being tanners and butchers) were necessarily banished to the outer reaches of a community are not borne out by the Newcastle evidence: tanners lived on the streets in Westgate ward along with weavers and gentlemen, and butchers lived and ran shops in the very centre of town. Overall, the occupational zones seemed to reflect (a) business opportunities provided by traffic along main arteries or on markets, (b) topography, in the case of shipwrights who required space to construct ships, or convenience in the case of master mariners, mariners and keelmen, who chose to live beside the river in close proximity to their ships and boats, (c) the need for sufficient space to manufacture and store goods, as evidenced by auxiliary buildings to the rear of properties listed, for instance, by bakers and brewers on Pilgrim Street and tanners on Westgate and, (d) historical continuity, such as that seen in the case of the occupation of the medieval Huckster Booths by bakers and brewers (Gray 1649, 1970: 22).

Notwithstanding clear evidence for occupational zones, presumed differentiation in status, and certainly in wealth, did not equate to exclusivity of neighbourhoods. For instance, property-owning shipwrights lived next to their poor keelmen tenants in Sandgate; master mariners shared houses with ordinary mariners along chares in the Lower East Side; tailors lived in rented tenements among merchants and hostmen on the quayside; and skinners, owning both large and small premises, lived along the Back Row and Bailiff Gate in close proximity to gentlemen.

Levels of wealth, as has been discussed, could not be ascertained accurately from listed properties, but the significance of house sizes in connection to occupational zones has been examined. Langton has suggested that there is, perhaps, some evidence for 'class-zoning' based partly on house sizes, observing that the core areas settled by the wealthiest trades, notably merchants, embrace the wealthiest members of other trades, and that in turn, poorer areas include the less wealthy members of otherwise wealthy trades, but he wonders whether this phenomenon is more a matter of the growth of the town, rather than the beginning of a class affiliation based on wealth (1975: 21-22). Overall, he is sceptical. In evidence from probate records, examples are found of wealthier tradesmen - notably, master mariners - living in areas inhabited by the wealthier merchants, and not in poorer Sandgate, but these areas are also convenient to the Trinity House, and are the same neighbourhoods shared by poorer and richer tradesmen alike. There is no evidence that other tradesmen, listing the largest properties, are especially affiliated to the wealthy merchantile sectors of the town. Substantial houses within quite specialised occupational zones can be found on Westgate Street, on Pilgrim Street and in Sandgate, alongside much smaller tenements let to a wide variety of people. Langton's observation that very large houses are related to main street frontages in the post-Civil-War period (1975: 16), can be contrasted with the extensive properties, often with both domestic and commercial rooms attached, that are situated on very narrow chares or streets in several parts of the town, such as Plummer Chare, Upper Dean Street and Pudding Chare in the earlier period. It is also of interest to find that large, stone-built medieval houses were also wide-spread across the town, suggesting that large properties had always been built in various parts of the town (Graves 2003: 38). At the other end of the scale, smaller houses, often represented by adjoined tenements, are found mainly in the upper areas of the town on streets leading off the upper central markets, around St John's Church, and in all the suburbs, a situation that continues into the post-Civil-War period (Langton 1975: 21, Figure 6). However, a record of 'six burnt' houses in the Hearth Tax returns of 1670-71 may indicate further examples of rows of small tenements in Denton ward, a wealthier central area noted for some very large houses (Green 2000: 240, 246). A number of the smaller tenements found in the probate records are occupied by poorer people, notably the tenants of the shipwrights in Sandgate, but a wide assortment of other people are mentioned - from yeomen to widows - arguing against an exclusively poor periphery to the wealthier intra-mural neighbourhoods. Green's observation, that it is a mistake to correlate small properties to relative poverty, seems to be borne out by the probate evidence (2000: 75).

Caution should certainly also be exercised in equating the size of a house with occupational affiliations or wealth in specific parts of the town, as what is recorded about the property does not necessarily provide an accurate guide to either. Discussions on wealth and occupation relative to house sizes are taken up in Chapter 6.

Langton has found that the most densely occupied wards in post-Civil War Newcastle are Austin, Pandon, Wall Knoll and Sandgate, and, to a lesser degree Mordon ward (1975: Fig. 4). The probate data for the earlier decades reveals similar findings, although Plummer ward is also very crowded, as are the Central Markets (Fig.4.3b). Concentrations of occupations tend to coincide with a marked variety of services in a neighbourhood, and this is especially true of the Lower East Side, with shops offering meat, fish, grain, beer, ales and baked foods, clothing and leather goods, the services of scriveners and barber surgeons, and many others. Most of these services are also offered on the Central Markets, as attested by Gray (1649, 1970: 22, 26). According to Bourne, by the early 18th century the central market area supplied 'the Town in a great Measure, but ... it also furnishes the Country for several Miles round'. 'Thousands of people ... have their provisions from this market' and 'The provision also for Ships, is got from this Market' (1736, 1980: 54). Decades earlier, these markets were already well established, according to the probate findings. Sandgate also appears to have been a relatively autonomous district, described by Bourne as 'being perhaps one of the largest Parishes in the whole Kingdom', 'The Number of Souls ... computed to several Thousands', the streets 'crowded with Houses' (1736,

1980: 154). Such density of occupation along the riverside echoes patterns in later 17th century East London (Powers 1972: 244), and in Norwich, where the population was 'crammed into houses in a maze of courtyards and alleyways' (Corfield 1972: 270; Priestley and Corfield 1982: 100). The probate evidence for Newcastle confirms that this sort crowding was already apparent by the early 17th century.

Langton's calculations on occupational density, based as they are on numbers of householders, poses the problem that the figures do not always allow for how a house is occupied, and numbers of householders do not necessarily equate to numbers of houses (1975: Figure 6; Power 1972: 242, 251). Properties in Sandgate clearly illustrate this problem: a property could be divided between generations of grown-up family and tenants into separate accommodation, made possible by the flexible use of rooms, although the house would still be counted as a single household owned by one man. House sharing in Newcastle conforms to the wider practice in the early modern period (Green 2000: 161; Houlbrooke 1984: 189-92), contrary to Power's finding that multiple-occupation is an exception (1972: 251). Adult offspring may not have actually lived together in the same rooms as their parents, but they were apparently accommodated in specific rooms within, or adjoined to, the parental home. Actual occupational density - in both crowded Sandgate, as well as within the large houses in the centre of town with adjoined chambers, occupied by various people - may have been even greater than the figures reveal. The associated problem posed by the Hearth Tax figures on density relating to house numbers, rather than household numbers, could result in too few properties being accounted for because hearths used by individual households living in shared houses are all ascribed to a single owner, a problem also discussed by Green (2000: 70-1). This difficulty is illustrated by a cordwainer, 'dwelling' with two other men in a house with shops on the Meale Market. He specifically lists his own iron chimney together with his bed and table in a room in this shared residence which he alone owns. However, he also records another 'dwelling house', with more shops, which is on the Sandhill, indicating that he has two places of residence - one that he shares and one that he does not (D.P.R. 1620). There are, however, occasions where testators have made it very clear that they occupy only a part of the house: phrases such as 'up through' and 'down through' indicate occupation on two storeys on one side of a house, and there are also descriptions of shared access to separate properties.

Properties listed in the probate records provide accurate data both on densities of houses on streets and on occupants, and descriptions are sufficiently comprehensive to provide a good indication of the types of structures in the neighbourhoods. Building materials are, unfortunately, almost never mentioned, apart from a single reference to slate and thatched roofs in Sandgate. Glass windows were being produced locally in quantity by at least the 1620s (Howell 1967: 286-87), and must have been widely available to builders, but these are only suggested by the references to 'window cushions' in the upper storey of a house on Plummer Chare and by shop window displays in Sandgate. The use of glass was not apparently, as has been suggested by Graves, restricted to the houses of elites in the vicinity of the Guildhall (2003: 41) There are occasional references to internal stairs, contrary to Power's findings (1972: 256), notably in large houses on Pilgrim Street (1587), on Plummer Chare (1623), and on the Poultry Market (1625). Some slight evidence for new dwellings is recorded, with some references to extending existing properties. These are built for the use of the testators themselves, and do not appear to have been associated with marriages as proposed by Green (2000: 168). The question of whether the probate data can contribute to the debate on the 'Great Rebuilding' (Hoskins 1953; Shammas 1990: 158-9; Green 2003: 61) is taken up in Chapter 6.

In summary, the probate records reveal that taller structures, up to four or five storeys, stood along the chares running down to the quayside in the Lower East Side of town, a finding which is echoed in the last surviving structures of near contemporary date, namely Bessie Surtees House (Heslop et al. 1995), and in drawings of the quayside by Knowles and Boyle (1890). However, this neighbourhood also had many lower level properties, often with adjoining tenements. Properties also tended to be lower level along the streets of Pandon. Houses of up to four storeys were found in several other parts of town, including the Close, the Bigg Market, Upper Dean Bridge, Westgate and Pilgrim Street, but in the neighbourhoods of the higher parts of town most properties were between one and three storeys. The largest houses had up to 14 rooms, whereas the majority of houses had anywhere from two to five. Many properties appear to have had lofts, used as both living and storage spaces. Open areas of waste were found in many parts of the town, even in the crowded chares in the Lower East Side. The houses in the extra-mural western and northern suburbs tended to be quite modest; in Gallowgate and beyond Pilgrim Gate several tradesmen listed closes, rigs and meadows. The probate data echoes descriptions by Gray who described the many closes, meadows and large fields, but who noted that the area was 'ruinated in these late warres' (1649, 1970: 39). The crowded conditions in Sandgate, described by Gray in the mid 17th century (1649, 1970: 12), were already apparent decades earlier, with multiple-occupancy of low-level properties and numerous little tenements predominating, especially on the lands sloping down to the river, while shops and a mill occupied the higher ground to the north. Descriptions by Knowles and Boyle (1890), and studies, such as that on the Cooperage (Heslop et al. 1993), on Bessie Surtees House (Heslop et al. 1995), and Alderman Fenwick's House (Heslop et al. 2001), provide guides to the early modern buildings in the town which will help to contextualise the probate descriptions. More comparative analysis between published findings on the town and the extensive, but largely untouched, probate data could usefully be pursued.

The comparative analysis of the early modern probate records and Langton's post-Civil-War Hearth Tax analysis (1975) demonstrates the extent of information that can be found on a historic town where so much of the built environment and early topography, together with the social geography, has been lost. Such detailed research has more than local significance, as many of the findings and the research design could be useful in future studies, in view of the extant collections elsewhere of sources such as those employed here.

In the next chapter the probate evidence is used to explore the material lives of the people encountered in Chapter 3, who lived and worked in the neighbourhoods recovered in the course of this chapter.

CHAPTER 5 – Objects

5.1 Introduction

The Durham probate records have thus far revealed detailed accounts of the personal priorities of people in the dispersal of their worldly goods on their deaths, as well as providing information with which to recover a picture of the social and built environment of early modern Newcastle. In this chapter a comprehensive study is undertaken of objects listed both in wills and, particularly in inventories, recorded between 1549 and 1642, with the aim of tracing patterns of consumption and material culture in this northern provincial capital.

Such aims are often associated with the question of when, or even if, a so-called 'consumer revolution' can be shown to have occurred over the 'long eighteenth century', the origins of which are sought in the latter 17th century (Berry and Gregory 2004: 7), and whether a dramatic transition in material life took place in this period and how this is evidenced (Glennie 1993: 164). Shammas has noted that there is tremendous pressure to locate origins and revolutions in whatever time period one is studying (1990: 291). This chapter does not set out to discover the origins of a consumer revolution in a pre-industrial period.

Instead, the question of change over time, central to any historical enquiry, is explored by comparing evidence from the period prior to the Civil War with findings from other research, including work on the post-Restoration era (Shammas 1990, Weatherill 1989, 1996). Although there is now general agreement among early modern historians of consumption that gradual but important changes occurred between 1550 and 1750, 'deflating any suggestion of revolutionary change thereafter' (Overton 2004: 7), questions are asked relating to how early changes in material life came to the tradesmen of Newcastle and how these changes were manifested. Corfield saw an expansion of domestic demand in the late seventeenth century (1972: 295), and Spufford also dates the increased flow of consumables and increased comfort to this period, although she found that the beginnings of the growth were 'much earlier' (198: 3-4, 114, 125; McKendrick 1982). Weatherill confirms that the late 17th century was a period of increased domestic consumption and change in regions throughout Britain (1996: 25). This study examines the evidence for marked change at least a half-century earlier.

The body of evidence with which to commence the investigation is enormous, encompassing thousands of objects owned by hundreds of individuals. Selected categories of objects common to households of tradesmen in the study period are analysed to understand where consumer priorities lay in acquiring objects, and whether criteria such as wealth, status, occupation, prices, or even emulation were factors in ownership patterns. Changes in domestic comfort, the adoption of new goods, and the disappearance of objects, and how this may have affected both social and consumer behaviour are all examined.

The issue of whether living in a town would have provided an enriched opportunity to acquire consumer goods, and whether those in trade or merchandising would have been closer to the source of consumer commodities, as Shammas has suggested (1990: 180), in the light of Newcastle's location as a regional market capital, is of particular significance in this analysis. Weatherill found that, after 1660, Newcastle's trade in coal brought a return trade in many household and consumer items that meant such objects were more readily available in this area than almost anywhere else in England (1997: 52). Writing in 1770, local map-maker Charles Hutton observed that 'The Great Quantity of Coals sent to London so far exceeds in value all returns from thence hither, that there is always a considerable exchange in favour of Newcastle & its environs which occasions a greater circulation of real specie here than any other Town of equal extent in his Majesties Dominions' (Hutton 1772). The early probate evidence provides an opportunity to trace the roots of this great trade back to a period beginning some 200 years earlier.

It is particularly important to the aims of this study to discover whether differences in consumption patterns are evident amongst the various trades, which in many studies are amalgamated into a single social-status group, divided into those of low or high status based on total inventoried wealth (Brodsky-Elliot 1978; Shammas 1990; Weatherill 1996), or into trade sectors (Langton 1975). By examining selected categories of objects that belonged to distinct trades, rather than amalgamating groups defined only by total inventoried wealth, a more detailed analysis becomes possible. Differences in patterns of ownership of goods between people living in the same town with equal access to markets, but practising different trades, should be explored (Weatherill 1996: xviii-3; Overton 2004: 88, 139). The detailed examination of tradesmen of very differing occupations also shows that the social history of consumerism does not have to be confined to wealthier groups (Weatherill 1996: 16), as numerous individuals in this study who have left records cannot be embraced in such a description. A more accurate accounting will add important factual evidence to the debate on consumption and material culture at a time and in a place that has been relatively under-researched in comparison with studies from the south of England, allowing regional and national comparisons to be made, most especially concerning the pre-Civil-War period (Shammas 1990: 28, 93).

Overton highlighted the problem of theoretical speculation running ahead of empirical research, noting there have been no major studies for the period before 1660 with which to compare probate findings from studies of the later 17th and early 18th century (2004: 9-10). His own work on the counties of Cornwall and Kent begins in 1600 (2004: 166), and he makes particular reference to the important work of Weatherill (1996) and Shammas, who also noted the dearth of earlier studies from specific locations (1990: 93). The findings from all these writers are taken up in this chapter. Weatherill has written that, ideally, we require lists of goods owned by households every few years, so we can trace who owned what, allowing changes to be clearly demonstrated (1996: 22). This is precisely the approach taken here. Fortunately, goods have usually been more frequently recorded in the North East than in other regions, augmenting the evidence available for Newcastle (Weatherill 1996: 47, 51-2).

The thousands of objects recorded in the documents can analyse material culture over decades of consumption and investment activity. Overton argues that inventories represent a 'snapshot in time' rather than 'continuous consumption', measuring 'stocks not flows of goods' (2004: 9, 87-8) - an idea that echoes Earle's notion of inventories as embodying a 'frozen moment', when a man dies and his goods are appraised (1994: 150). The issue is also discussed by De Vries who differentiated between material culture reflected on an inventory, which he sees as a 'snapshot of that world', and consumer demand which he sees as a 'dynamic concept' (1993: 102). However, Overton argues that stocks of goods do imply consumption choices within a cyclical process of the acquisition and disappearance of goods (2004: 88). Inventories, together with wills, can perhaps be best seen as catalysts for change in the objects of a household, which pass to successive generations, with things added and things taken away. With a sufficiently large sample of documents, transition over years and then decades is revealed, and observations can be made along a time-line, extending in this study to a century.

Three categories of objects are examined in the course of this chapter: those belonging to the household; those associated with household production; and those objects specifically related to the practice of a guild or by-trade. Within the three categories, specific types of goods are individually analysed. The basis for the selection relates to the consistency with which the objects have been recorded and how the objects have been valued (as some objects were almost always appraised separately, whereas others were valued collectively). The way the appraisers originally recorded objects will normally provide the format for this analysis. This approach, using only those categories of goods that are consistently included in the majority of documents, allows comparisons to be made between similar assemblages relating to distinct trade associations. The methodology seeks to avoid the problem of selective accounting by appraisers, who moved through houses and shops singling out what was deemed useful in the settlement of the estate, creating fairly random wealth totals. The valuations of selected goods also give a better indication of living standards than total inventory valuations (Levine and Wrightson 1991: 158; Arkell 2000: 95; Weatherill 2004: 17), although it should be noted that neither incomes nor wages can be recovered from inventories (Weatherill 1996: 96). The wealth in inventoried goods does represent expenditure in connection to consumption (Shammas 1990: 100-101), although the way people came to own the objects on their inventories and what motivated their choices is difficult to recover. What has been recorded probably represents the accumulated material cultural choices of more than a single generation. While changes in the composition of objects through the decades can be observed, it is difficult to say when any particular object was acquired. For example, objects may have been kept for generations, as in the case of heirlooms, the acquisition of which, Overton argues, cannot be seen as a deliberate act of consumption, noting that an inclination to consume cannot be assumed to equate to a proportion of wealth in goods (Overton 2004: 10, 87, 139). However, there is no reason to assume that a person had no opinion (either positive or negative) concerning the objects they owned at their death. If an object had no function or meaning to an individual, perhaps it would not have been retained. The inventoried goods therefore represent a lifetime's accumulation of objects, including those that were inherited - and inheritance was a very important component of wealth (Weatherill 1996: 105; Erickson 2002: 3), as wealth, in turn, was the most important determinant in the value of consumer durables (Shammas 1990: 104, 173).

While acknowledging these considerations and limitations in an understanding of the precise means or motives behind consumption, the inventories are, *de facto*, a list of personal possessions, whenever and however they were acquired, and any limitations do not detract from the many insights that they provide about the material lives of early modern households of Newcastle, as will be demonstrated in the course of the chapter.

The Household

5.2 Heating and cooking

Evidence of heating and cooking arrangements in the early modern houses of Newcastle can be found in almost every inventory belonging to the tradesmen of the town. There were two types of fireplaces common to all households throughout the period: the first was called an 'iron chimney', and the other was referred to as 'pairs of iron bars'. Both were listed together with various fire-irons and cooking implements, depending on whether the fires were solely for heating or for both cooking and heating. There are no direct references in the documents to hearths, and precisely how these fireplaces were incorporated into the chimneys of properties is unknown.

The O.E.D. defines iron chimneys, in references from the 16th century, as braziers. There are no surviving images, or archaeological information, illustrating exactly what they looked like, but information from the documents reveals that they were always made from iron, and that they do not appear to have been built into a chimney stack. This can be established, as they were occasionally bequeathed in wills, often together with other valuable pieces of furniture. For example, a tanner bequeaths 'one round cubbord standing in the hall of my dwelling house & 1 iron chimney w[i]th a pair of standing racks standing in the kitchen' (D.P.R. Errington 1634). The daughter of a miller is given an almery and an iron chimney, while her mother and two brothers are to share 'all the rest of the goods' (D.P.R. Graye 1589). Iron chimneys can also be seen as belonging to the property: for example, one testator states that 'the chimney in the kitchen, the great bedstead & a great presser in the loft' were to be left 'as hiereloomes of the same house', meaning that their possible removal is expressly contrary to the terms of the will (D.P.R. Swan 1635).

In relation to how an iron chimney was constructed, the documents give occasional references to parts, such as 'an old pare of chimney ribbs' (D.P.R. Readhead 1592), or 'a piece of an old chimney' (D.P.R. Nicholson 1587). The reference to 'ribs' may confirm the O.E.D definition that iron chimneys are a form of brazier. An illustration by David Allen of the interior of a house belonging to the middling sort in late eighteenth-century Scotland shows a free-standing ribbed brazier on a hearth stone, beneath a smoke hood or chimney, and this may be what the iron chimneys of Newcastle looked like (Illustration 5.1). The influence of the Scots in the town is well recognised (Graves 2003: 44). Priestley and Corfield have suggested that portable braziers are used in rooms with no built-in hearth (1982: 101), but this pictorial evidence suggests otherwise. The O.E.D. does not include a reference to 'iron bars', but these came in pairs and were clearly used

Illustration 5.1: Brazier beneath a smoke hood from 'Claude and Peggy' by David Allan, c. 1780, National Galleries of Scotland, Edinburgh

to support a fire, perhaps placed over a hearth like fire-dogs; however, they may not have been moveable as, unlike iron chimneys, they are not specifically bequeathed in the wills. The design of both types of fireplaces must have had to accommodate the use of coal, which requires a strong draught and an efficient flue (Overton 2004: 98), and coal was the most likely fuel for all such home fires. By the late 16th century Harrison had noted that the use of coal was expanding 'from the forge into the kitchen and hall', especially in coastal towns and cities (Furvinall 1877: 68), and coal was plentiful on the domestic markets in Newcastle, according to Hutton who confirmed 'Landsale Colleries for the Town & Country supply' (1770). The inclusion of 'coal rakes' among kitchen wares on inventories confirms that coal was used for cooking in the North in the 16th and 17th centuries, although its use for cooking in other parts of the country may have come later, evidenced by the increasing presence of grates in inventories as the 17th century progressed (Priestley and Corfield 1982: 101; Overton 2004: 98).

Where a pair of iron bars or an iron chimney was used solely for heating, a 'por' or fire poke, together with a pair of tongs (probably to lift pieces of coal) were often the only implements listed. In contrast, there appears to have been a fairly elaborate but standard set-up for cooking, which included a 'por', tongs, fire shovel and rake and a 'setting' or 'testing stick'. There were up to four spits, iron racks, lying or rest irons, pairs of cranks, toasting and grid irons, fire or flesh crooks, 'racking', 'jeb or 'geb' crooks, pot clips and flesh hooks. Many households had dripping pans and frying pans. Some households listed chaffing dishes and warming pans. Other fairly common implements were brass ladles, with occasional references to basting ladles, and shredding and chopping knives. Not every household had such a complete set of cooking implements, but a sizeable majority had most of them, and the composition of the objects shows no change over the decades. Interestingly, metalwares sold in shops in the early 18th century comprised items similar to those found in the average kitchens of tradesmen as early as the mid-16th century, evidencing the durability of basic kitchen wares over decades (Spufford 1984: 85). This finding is echoed in evidence from Cornwall, where the variety of equipment showed little change between 1600 and 1750 (Overton 2004: 102). The type of equipment incidentally suggests that fried and roast meats must have been a common part of the Newcastle diet. Harrison observed that the English were noted for 'devouring less bread, but more meat, which they roast in perfection' (Furvinal 1877: lxv), an opinion echoed by Henri Misson and Gregory King (Weatherill 1996: 146-7). The common use of spits is also attested in 17th century inventories for Kent (Overton 2004: 102). Items such as pots, pans, kettles and cauldrons were not included by the appraisers as 'appurtenances' of the fireplaces, but were frequently listed, indicating other methods of cooking such as boiling, which was also common to Cornwall in the period (Overton 2004: 102). These objects are examined separately in Section 5.2. The volume of cookware in

Newcastle inventories seems to be in marked contrast to Earle's finding for late 17th century London, where he observed that few people had the 'space or equipment to do much cooking for themselves' (1994: 171).

Evidence for where people cooked and for rooms with fires can be traced through the inventories. In *The London Surveys of Ralph Treswell*, Schofield comments that 'the small and medium-sized houses of London in 1612 seem to have had fireplaces in about half their rooms, a luxury not found in other English cities' (1987: 17). The Newcastle evidence appears to contradict this finding, as the numbers of hearths listed in inventoried rooms (for most households, depending on their size), show very similar figures to those for London. In Tables 5.1a and 5.1b the location and number of iron chimneys and iron bars in specified rooms are shown. The figures are probably underestimates as many more fireplaces are listed in the documents, where rooms are not specified (see Table 6.1).

Halls, chambers, parlours, kitchens and lofts are consistently mentioned as locations for fireplaces, a situation that had not apparently altered by the latter 17th century for East London homes, where a similar distribution of fireplaces is evident, most being located in halls, chambers and kitchens (Power 1972: 255). Whereas Levine and Wrightson's evidence from Whickham suggests that poorer households very rarely list iron chimneys (although fire irons are near universal) (1991: 235), both types of fireplaces are common in all Newcastle tradesmen's homes. There is usually just one fireplace in a room, but occasionally two iron chimneys are found together. For example, a mariner has two iron chimneys in his parlour and a cordwainer has two in a hall (D.P.R. Herrisone 1596; Robeson 1622).

Preference is shown in the selected location for either iron chimneys or iron bars for different rooms: Table 5.1a shows that six times as many halls have iron chimneys as those with iron bars. A clear majority of iron chimneys are listed with the cooking implements, whereas far fewer iron bars have been set up for cooking purposes. Parlours have twice as many iron chimneys as iron bars, listed almost without exception with just a poke and tongs. The set-up suggests that parlours were not normally used for cooking, the exception being when appraisers appear to have used the term 'parlour' rather than 'kitchen', where function according to the room content was much the same. Kitchens have three times the number of iron chimneys relative to iron bars, together with a wide range of cookware, while chambers show somewhat the opposite trend, with about one-third more iron bars being used in these upper rooms in preference over iron chimneys. Fireplaces in chambers usually have a poke and tongs, but never cooking implements.

In Table 5.1b the distribution of fireplaces in homes is examined, which shows that 80-100% of households have fireplaces in halls, some for cooking and some only for heating. When the iron chimney is missing from a hall, it has probably been bequeathed, or the family is cooking in the kitchen or using the parlour for this purpose. About half the tradesmen list a kitchen for cooking, but many homes are too small to accommodate such a room, and very few millers, skinners and glovers, or weavers, and no keelmen have this facility. Heated parlours are found in about one-third of homes overall, but averages varied widely, as keelmen had none whereas more than two-thirds of cordwainers listed such rooms. Heated chambers are recorded in over half the inventories. The highest figure is recorded by mariners at over 90%. The lower figures for other trades do not necessarily indicate that these households have few heated chambers, but that larger houses with more rooms have proportionately more chambers that are unheated (Schofield 1987: 29). Mariners tended to have two-room houses (see Chapter 4), indicating small but warm abodes. No millers list a heated chamber, but these men record the highest percentage of heated lofts and miscellaneous rooms, which are associated with grain-drying facilities.

Valuations of iron chimneys and bars depend to a large extent on the number of implements listed with them. Some appraisers use the term 'with appurtenances', but give no other details about what is included in the valuation. Over the whole period iron bars are often priced at 12d for small pairs, rising to 4s a pair for those listed with implements. Little or old iron chimneys with a poke and tongs in chambers are priced as low as 3s, whereas most iron chimneys in halls and kitchens are valued from about 1li to just over 3li if a wide range of cooking implements is included.

The valuations of iron chimneys or iron bars, together with the number and type of cooking implements, can be used as a guide to where the largest cooking set-up is located. The majority of people cooked in the hall during the period of this study, as confirmed by Harrison (Furvinal 1877: 239). In larger houses, where more rooms are specified, cooking wares are divided between the hall and the kitchen. Changes in room function can be detected over the decades. Documents dated prior to 1600 confirm just two testators use the kitchen as the main room for cooking instead of the hall. Between 1600 and 1625 the figure rises, and by the beginning of the second quarter of the 17th century, kitchens in larger houses are slightly more popular as the primary area for cooking than are halls, with the trend growing in the last years running up to 1642. (In Chapter 6 room function is discussed in more detail in connection to the location of cook wares, excluding appurtenances of the fireplace).

In terms of the numbers of fireplaces in the homes of tradesmen, Table 5.1a shows that averages vary between a low of 1.33 for the poor keelmen to the highest figure of 2.72 for the cordwainers. The figure for the keelmen is probably slightly high, as most inventories for the trade do not enumerate rooms, and a single iron chimney was common to almost all these householders. Most of these men appear to have had small houses with a heated hall and an unheated loft (see Chapter 4). The evidence confirms Howell's finding, in 1665, that most houses in Sandgate (the poorest part of town), had a single hearth, and this was where a clear majority of keelmen made their home (1967: 11-12; Langton 1975: 15; Ellis 2001: 6). The millers, and the skinners and glovers also list fewer fireplaces than other tradesmen, recording an average of less than two per household, whereas all other trades averaged more than two fireplaces, with an overall average of 2.36 hearths per household. The low figure for the smiths may be indicative of rooms that did not require heating if the shops were in close proximity to the home, making extra fireplaces redundant. In Langton's 1665 Hearth Tax data smiths had the lowest number of hearths among all 17 occupations included in the sample (1975: Table III).

Howell has calculated an average of 2.06 hearths per household for the whole population of Newcastle, according to the 1665 Hearth Tax evidence, and has compared the figures with those for Exeter, York and Leicester, which he has found to be slightly higher (1967: 9). Power's figures from 1664 put the average number of hearths for East London at 2.7 (1972: 255). In Norwich the average number of hearths rose from 1.8 prior to 1600 to 2.6 by the late 17th century (Priestley and Corfield 1982: 101, Table 3). For Newcastle, Langton's refined analysis using the 1665 Hearth Tax data shows that only the bakers, master mariners and mariners average over three hearths per household, a higher figure than the inventories reveal, whereas all the other trades relevant to his study showed lower averages than the inventories revealed (1972, Table III). Although Langton does not include keelmen, skinners and glovers, or millers in his sample, his figures take much better account of the huge discrepancies in hearth figures than does Howell's amalgamated average for the town, but overall the figures appear too low.

In interpreting how these figures relate to wealth and, by extension, to levels of comfort in the home, Howell has equated those households with fewer than two hearths with the 'poorest sector', noting that those who had only two hearths had an economic position not much better than that of the poor class (defined as those with just one hearth), whereas those with three to five hearths - including shopkeepers, master craftsmen and small merchants - were defined as 'probably more or less comfortable in their economic situation' (1967: 11-12). Langton makes a similar inference in correlating levels of wealth to numbers of hearths, relating them to status and occupation (1972: 8), a finding echoed by Green, who also notes the contemporary recognition of chimneys as a signal of wealth and social standing (2000: 55-6, 240). However, Levine and Wrightson caution against making such assumptions, arguing that 'the number of hearths does not directly equate to the wealth of individuals' and that even exempted householders 'cannot simply be categorised as paupers' – the authors provide examples of one-hearth households with very substantial quantities of household equipment in 1666 (1991:161), a finding echoed in the Newcastle inventories of the earlier period. Therefore, the financial situation of exempted households, identified by Howell as including at least 41% of the population in the 1660s, must be interpreted with caution (1967: 9-10). Both Howell and Langton, among others, argue that the low figures for numbers of hearths, revealed by the Hearth Tax evidence, suggest that Newcastle suffered from problems of poverty to a greater extent than many other provincial towns in the period. In the next sections, the relative poverty or well-being of tradesmen is analysed by way of other categories of objects beyond the number of hearths, and assumptions regarding the extent and definition of poverty in Newcastle in the early modern period are questioned.

5.3 Furnishings

Three categories of household objects are examined in this section. The first category includes furniture and soft furnishings; the second, beds, bed-coverings and curtains, combined with table linen and towels (as these items were usually appraised together); the third, cookware, tableware, and decorative objects. The objects making up the three categories, listed in Appendices 3 and 4, confirm Harrison's observations concerning the increase in amenities that began in the late 16th century. Many pages of Harrison's books are devoted to describing the great increase in consumption (as well as prices), that go far beyond the frequently quoted remarks concerning the appearance of chimneys, featherbeds, pewter and carpets, etc. (Spufford 1984: 114). Harrison is also very critical of the merchants behind the expanding consumerism he witnessed, declaring 'wherefore it is to be wished ... the [huge] heape of them were somewhat restrained' (Furvinal 1877: 131).

Although Harrison believed that these changes in consumption 'were not verie amended as yet ... further off from our Southerne parts', his observations concerning artificers in the southern counties who 'garnish their cupboards with plate, their [ioned] (joined) beds with tapestrie and silke hangings, their tables with [carpets &] fine napery', are equally relevant for the inventoried households of tradesmen in Newcastle in the period (Furvinal 1877: 239-40). Harrison describes furniture as 'growne in manner even to passing delicacie', and that, in this pursuit of home comforts, he did 'not speak of the nobilitie and gentrie onelie, but likewise of the lowest sort ... unto the inferiour artificers'. And the cost of objects apparently was not hindering these trends as, even 'in a time wherein all things are growen to most excessive prices ... we doo yet find the means to obtain & atchive such furniture as heretofore hathe been unpossible' (Furvinal 1877: 237-9).

The marked expansion in consumerism, witnessed by Harrison, which pertained to the households of Newcastle tradesmen, beginning in the latter 16th century continued apace in the early decades of the 17th century. In illustrating these trends, the first analysis looks at objects selected from among those in the three categories, which represent items that were both functional and common to all households, such as salt sellers and towels, as well as objects that can be seen as decorative or even luxury items such as flower pots or footstools to get into a bed.

The objects are also those that are consistently enumerated by appraisers and thus useful in charting change in consumer patterns.

The 28 objects listed in Table 5.2a show conclusively that, between the 1550s and 1642, the ownership of some objects has greatly expanded. For instance, the number of carpet cloths and cushions more than doubles; the number of imported Danish pots triples (reflecting a much earlier increase in the growth of pewter than is seen with plates in the latter 17th century) (Weatherill 1996: 30-1), and there is a sixfold increase in the ownership of flower pots, some also made from pewter. A tenfold increase is recorded in the numbers of mirrors, an item that was steadily increasing in other areas of the country, despite being imported in this period (Overton 2004: 112). Other objects show the same patterns to differing degrees, beginning in the early years of the 17th century.

Ownership of basins and ewers, and glassware, including drinking glasses and 'glass cases' continues to rise steadily. Newcastle had an important domestic trade in glass, associated with the coal industry, dating back to the 1570s, with production growing rapidly after the opening of Robert Mansell's first works in 1615. Mansell claimed to be shipping 4,000 cases of glass from Newcastle each year in 1624, and he had erected three works by 1640 (Howell 1967: 20-1). Given the cheapness and availability of glass in Newcastle, one would expect to see even more listed than appears on inventories. Evidence from elsewhere in the country suggests that glass vessels and bottles were relatively expensive and uncommon until the late 17th or 18th centuries (Shammas 1990: 173, 181; Overton 2004: 105), although Harrison confirms that 'the poorest also will have glass if they may ... made at home of ferne and burned stone', and that window glass was 'plentiful' and 'cheap' (Furvinal, 1877: 147, 237). Desks, first listed in 1592 by a master mariner, are rare in the early period, but numbers increase in the early 17th century, as is the case with footstools, which are usually listed with the most expensive beds. At the same time, closet stools make an appearance.

Pictures first appear in the inventory of a mariner in 1616, and seem to gain rapid popularity in the following two decades. Although most are in the hands of the master mariners, suggesting a connection with the wealthier elements of society, pictures were cheap items and ownership was clearly on the rise well before the second half of the 17th century (Overton 2004: 113). The only details given about pictures, (apart from the size, and whether they are in a frame) comes from a butcher, who records '6 little Holland pictures in frames' valued at 6d each, confirming imports (D.P.R. Scott 1641). Window cloths, which are listed in the earliest inventories and were probably used to exclude draughts, disappear by the early 1600s. Spufford describes window curtains as extremely rare before 1600, but saw the fashion spreading by the late 17th century (1984: 110). A master mariner lists '1 pair of fleers for a wyndow' as early as 1580 (D.P.R. Taillor), but curtains are specifically recorded first in 1623, when a well-off weaver lists them in both of his two houses (D.P.R. Chaitor). By the later 1620s, individuals in half the trades list them, most notably the cordwainers, many of whom lived in the very crowded central market of town (Chapter 4). Ownership was not confined to the well-off as has been suggested (Overton 2004: 113), and they were no longer rare in the latter decades of this study (Weatherill 2004: 19-20).

In 1623 the term 'china' makes its first appearance, as a shipwright lists a 'china cuboard', the first and only such description in the sample (D.P.R. Watson). In the following decades, two master mariners list chinaware consisting of five 'chaney platters' and ten 'cheina dishes' (D.P.R. Nixon 1634; Reed 1636). According to Weatherill, chinaware was unknown in 1675, becoming a normal part of household equipment only by 1715, although it was more common in the north-east and had long been imported in small quantities (1996: 31; 2004: 20, 22). It is not impossible that the master mariners had acquired a few rare pieces. Levine and Wrightson had also found evidence for 'chieny dishes' in the 1660s in Whickham (1991: 233, 236). However, Overton suggests that, in the 17th century, the term 'china' may have referred to either imported or English tin-glazed ware (which imitated Chinese porcelain), but that even these items were very rare as late as 1740 (2004: 103). Two other notable items of furniture - livery and court cupboards - appear in increasing numbers from the mid 1620s onwards. Court cupboards, designed for display, appeared in Kent around the same time (Overton 2004: 90-1).

Clocks and watches appear in 1619, but these are very rare objects. The first are listed by a mariner, who owned both a watch and a clock. Three other clocks are listed in 1629 and 1636, owned by two tanners and a master mariner. The supply of clocks (and chinaware) was centred on London, and these items were most common in places that traded with the capital, where Newcastle had well-established trade links. However, these objects remained both rare and expensive even in Kent until the 18th century (Levine and Wrightson 1991: 233; Weatherill 1996: 31, 63; Overton 2004: 111). Hourglasses are listed in the inventories in all decades, and these items were very inexpensive: half-hour, one-hour and even four-hour versions cost from 6d to 4s - a much cheaper form of time-keeping than purchasing a clock. Window cushions and 'long' cushions, indicating new seating arrangements, are recorded first in 1616 in the home of a master mariner, but remain rare in the following decades.

After 1625, just two new objects appear on inventories. In 1629, covered or upholstered chairs and covered stools begin to be listed, although these were available in Kent as early as 1600 (Overton 2004: 96, 118). This type of (mostly green) furnishing was the preserve of the wealthiest tradesmen - primarily the cordwainers and the master mariners - although one butcher also owned a few pieces. Covered leather chairs also make their first appearance at the same date. Overton associates a decline in ownership of cushions and carpets after the 1650s in the south, with the appearance of better-made furniture, but such a link is not apparent in Newcastle by 1642 (2004: 95). Pairs of virginals are recorded in 1636, owned by well-to-do tradesmen - including a tanner, a baker and brewer, a cordwainer and a master mariner. The only other reference to musical instruments is to two lutes owned by a master mariner in 1596. Interestingly, virginals and clocks are not recorded until the late 17th century among the wealthy staithmen of nearby Whickham (Levine and Wrightson 1991: 212).

The steady augmentation of these more decorative objects, which must have added comfort, colour and a little luxury to life, provides a notable contrast in consumption patterns to several other items that were selected for this analysis. Among the imported objects listed on Newcastle inventories are Danish chests. Unlike the Danish pots mentioned above, the numbers of which continued to rise in the first decades of the 17th century, a downturn in the popularity of chests is evident. Danish chests, some with frames, are listed as early as the 1570s by a cordwainer, but it is the master mariners who dominate ownership in the earliest period. By the first quarter of the 17th century, fewer master mariners are recording them, while the number owned by mariners have increased markedly. Cordwainers, bakers and brewers and millers in particular also seem to have found a use for them in the later decades, although in 1588 a skinner and glover bequeathed his son his 'Best Flanders chyste & a Dansk chest which was my shope chest' indicating their use could be work-related (D.P.R. Armstrong). Playing tables for card or dice games, which are included in all periods, show no change in recording patterns, but they were very inexpensive so the numbers may be under-represented. Spice boxes, with unknown contents, are listed in all periods, notably by master mariners. With the ever-increasing volumes of trade, one might expect to see an increase in such items, but the numbers remain very small. Ownership patterns of other household objects - such as hand towels, pepper and mustard querns, mortars and pestles, and salt sellers, do not change over the decades and were clearly not regarded as special objects as, for example, almost every household listed two salt sellers; mustard, associated with refined forms of sauce cooking after the Restoration (Overton 2004: 62), was apparently consumed in the lowly home of a keelman who lists a pair of wooden mustard querns in 1570. Investment in silver spoons also remained steady, but some men were clearly more inclined to invest in them than others. A more detailed analysis of ownership patterns for this sort of precious object, acquired for investment, is taken up in the final section of this chapter.

The close examination of selected objects demonstrates clear differences in consumption patterns, with significant expansion of ownership in certain more decorative household objects contrasting sharply with unchanging consumption patterns of objects with a more pedestrian function - a situation that continued after the Civil War (Weatherill 1996: 39). Table 5.2b shows that, over three time frames, levels of consumption reflected in numbers of selected objects per household appear most marked in the second quarter of the 17th century. The overall mean average more than doubles between the period prior to 1600 and that after 1626, although ownership of certain objects (such as cushions, carpet cloths and Danish pots) shows the most substantial gains in the intervening decades. The differences in mean average consumption totals between the trades must be interpreted with caution, as the sample sizes are individually relatively small; nevertheless, significant gains are apparent in every trade apart from the keelmen. The overall mean average for the combined periods is 23.3 objects per tradesman. But the bakers, cordwainers and, especially, the master mariners own the greatest percentage of the 28 named items, whereas the homes of millers, skinners and smiths and, particularly, the keelmen are notably less well endowed.

In Table 5.3, mean average valuations for amalgamated categories of household goods are examined. These show that overall investment levels had at least doubled, just as numbers of objects had done, but that the increase in investment levels differed depending on the category of goods. Overall mean average valuations for 'Furniture etc.' remain much the same until 1625 and then double in the last period, partly reflecting the new types of furniture being acquired by better-off households. Figures for 'Beds etc.' rise steadily, more than doubling over the whole period, whereas those for 'Tableware etc.' remain quite steady in all periods with only a slight rise evident in the last period. In contrast to investment levels reflected in valuations, the percentage of objects recorded in each category over three time frames remains fairly constant. Percentage figures for 'Furniture etc.' rise slightly in the last period, whereas the figure for 'Beds etc.' remains more or less steady, while there is a corresponding decline apparent in the relative proportion of 'Tableware etc.'. Over the time frames, valuations rise for all trades, although, again, certain trades, notably millers, skinners and tailors, and especially the keelmen, show much smaller gains. The hierarchy of investment does shift over time, as 'Tableware etc.' loses ground to 'Furniture etc.', but 'Beds etc.' always take priority. Shammas' 17th century 'Age of the Bed' is evident from the latter 16th century in the homes of Newcastle tradesmen, as virtually everyone has spent more on 'Beds etc' than on the two other categories of goods; although descriptions are insufficient to judge the quality of the items, the bedding is probably becoming more elaborate, as Shammas has suggested (1990: 169, 181, 293). The only exceptions to these trends are the poorest keelmen and weavers in this early period, whose tableware, rather than beds, is their most valuable asset. This situation is similar to that found among the poor in Oxfordshire in this period, whose most valuable assets were their furniture as they lacked resources to acquire bedding (Shammas 1990: 172). Such differences in ownership patterns between the wealthier and the poorer sections of society are further underlined in the case of wealthy Kent and poorer Cornwall, where a very large discrepancy in favour of the former was apparent in this period (Overton 2004: 119). In terms of what is motivating the upward trends, aside of relative wealth, Overton has found that personal comfort appears to be the primary reason and that the increase in expenditure is not driven by emulation or fashion (2004: 118-9).

The combined mean average valuations for all periods and objects give the master mariners and cordwainers, followed by the bakers, distinctly higher figures relative to an overall average of 18.1li per trade. Valuations for most trades fall below this figure. However, when the range of valuations is considered in Tables 5.4a and 5.4b, the distribution of wealth among trades is more extensive than Table 5.3 indicates. With the exception of the skinners and keelmen, individuals from all other trades owned more than 20li of the selected household objects. Just over 30% of the sampled tradesmen fell into this higher wealth category, but more than 40% of the sample had less than 10li invested. Table 5.4b clearly illustrates the wide range of valuations, a pattern that echoes Weatherill's finding that inventory valuations were extremely variable, with a long tail to the highest valuations in the sample (1996: 185).

The question of prices and the effects of inflation have yet to be considered in the patterns of consumption that have so far emerged. Shammas reminds us of the sharp fall in real wages during the 16th and 17th centuries, and rampant inflation in the late 16th century (1990: 130, 296). The question is, whether these factors are apparent in prices from inventories? Weatherill found that goods could be acquired in the later 17th century for modest sums (1996: 111). The same finding applies to the earlier data in this sample.

Table 5.5 shows the range of prices over four time frames for items that have been valued individually. Valuations can be divided between those at the low and high ends of the second-hand market. The table shows that prices of most household objects remain stable over several decades. In fact, many second-hand household items could be bought for much the same price throughout the whole century. The most significant price rises appear to have been limited to better-quality items or newer objects when they first appeared on the inventories, particularly in the second quarter of the 17th century. For example, descriptions of carpet cloths become more detailed in the first decade of the 17th century, and price increases can be seen after 1626. The most common colour of carpet cloths is green, but others are striped, plaid, or mixed colours. Spanish carpets are also listed. Those warranting the most description tend to be more expensive. Cushions are listed from the earliest period, but from the late 16th century a very wide variety appear, including gilded, leather, tapestry, 'thrumb', carpet work and Spanish cushions, all of which continue to be listed in the following decades (excepting Spanish cushions, which disappear after 1600). After 1600, embroidered, velvet, satin, cotton and printed cushions make an appearance. The most expensive cushions are from Spain, or are embroidered, satin or gilded, but the new window cushions are the most expensive of all. The most frequently named colour for most cushions is also green.

The prices of bed and table linen are remarkably stable, with two very clear markets for different budgets. For instance, in the late 16th century, linen sheets cost between 1s and 10s 8d and hand towels between 2d and 6s 8d, and these prices hardly alter over subsequent decades. The evidence suggests that prices are actually falling and, in the case of linen, such change is evident at a much earlier date than 1660 (Spufford 1984: 116-7; Shammas 1990: 95, 100). The trends for prices of cookware, tableware and decorative objects are much the same as for other household items. There are cheap and expensive versions of most objects, and price rises are most apparent, as is the case with furniture, in the period after 1626. Expensive mortars and pestles can be acquired, while most glassware is very inexpensive, although pieces held in wainscot cases more than double in price between the first and second quarters of the 17th century. An increase in the price of window curtains over the same time frame is also apparent. A new type of flower pot appears in the latest period, as is evident from the fact that most flower pots are valued at around 4d to 10d, whereas new, later, models cost as much as 10s. Overall, there is no clear evidence of dramatic price rises or falls, and the inflation of prices in the country as a whole does not apparently affect consumption of household objects in Newcastle, a situation confirmed by Weatherill in other regions where ups and downs in the economy are not linked to change in patterns of ownership (1996: 39-40).

The findings concerning the three categories of household objects suggest that the proportion of wealth in these consumer goods increased in the period of this study. Shammas' evidence from Oxfordshire and Worcestershire confirmed that there was a considerable increase in the real amount spent on consumer goods between the late 16th and late 17th centuries, but she states that households in the period seldom invested much in furnishings other than beds (1990: 89, 209). In Newcastle, investment is indeed primarily focused on beds, but furniture is a priority for some trades by the second quarter of the 17th century.

Clear differences in consumption patterns for household goods have emerged for the diverse tradesmen, contrary to Shammas' assertion that being in a craft or trade discouraged, or had no impact on, the accumulation of any category of good (1990: 180). While a higher mean average figure for ownership of objects, and higher investment levels relative to prices, clearly show that some tradesmen had better decorated and more comfortable abodes, certain trades led the trends. Setting aside those objects recorded in all periods, it is the master mariners who are the first to list about half the items selected for Table 5.2a, probably reflecting the trades' unique position *vis-à-vis* access to markets through their travels. Items these particular men have acquired include Danish pots, desks, glass bottles, lutes, spice boxes, window curtains, livery cupboards, pictures, window cushions, chinaware and upholstered furniture. A mariner is the first to list a clock. Cordwainers also lead the new trends, being the first to acquire footstools for their beds and close stools. They also have more window curtains than other tradesmen and generally appear to have devoted a high percentage of their wealth to making their small Middle Street houses comfortable.

Shammas does, in fact, acknowledge that occupation deserves consideration 'as a possible influence on consumer expenditure', but she also maintains that this did not have a very big impact on the amount devoted to consumer goods once wealth was held constant, and that, as a determinant, occupation had a minimal effect on the visible rise in expenditure (1990: 105, 110, 112). The Newcastle evidence suggests that retaining trade designations is important, as clear differences are apparent in both consumption patterns and wealth levels between occupations (Overton 2004: 88). Inventoried wealth is a key factor to consider in these patterns and this issue is discussed in further detail in the concluding section of this chapter, taking account of the other categories of objects yet to be analysed. Considering the types of objects already reviewed, Weatherill's findings that even trades belonging to lower-wealth groups were in possession of new items, such as mirrors or glassware, suggests that a direct link between wealth levels and consumer patterns is not always apparent (1996: 109).

Detailed analysis of specific regions is also important, and Shammas has highlighted the need for studies on the mean amounts devoted to consumer goods within specific areas (1990: 93). For example, her findings that expenditure on linen, brass and pewter had peaked in the late 16th century in Oxfordshire, and that other southern households only began using tin and glass in the mid-17th century (Shammas 1990: 172-3), clearly do not apply to Newcastle households. Distinct regional variation concerning consumption patterns of household objects is confirmed by Weatherill (1996: 60-1), and is apparent from the Newcastle data. The demonstrable expansion in the ownership of household objects has also been witnessed by Levine and Wrightson for Whickham in the period between the 1570s and the 1620s, underlining the unique situation of this northern provincial capital (1991: 24). Such considerations are taken up again in the overall conclusion.

Thus far, the evidence clearly indicates that consumption patterns of Newcastle tradesmen appear to have been part of a national trend. Harrison has criticised a 'desire of noveltie', reflected in 'half penny cockhorses for children, dogs of wax (or cheese) ... leaden swords, painted feathers, gewgaws for fooles ... and such like [trumperie]' (Furvinal 1877: 64), but such items were no doubt part of a general improvement in domestic comfort, including some luxury. Levine and Wrightson have found that, despite differences in the quality and quantity of domestic goods owned by people of differing levels of wealth in nearby Whickham, there was a shift in the material culture of the household, from the relative simplicity of the mid-Elizabethan period to a situation of 'enhanced comfort and amenity' in later decades (1991: 231). Such change, beginning in the late 16th century, is observed among the middling tradesmen of Newcastle, change that is consolidated and maintained in the second quarter of the 17th century.

In the next section further categories of objects are examined in an endeavour to expand and to refine these conclusions.

5.4 Apparel

In a study of material culture, clothing deserves attention as it was highly prized by the tradesmen of early modern Newcastle. Between the 1550s and 1642, almost 90% of inventories record apparel. When this is missing, it has probably been given away either on the will, or before the will was made, as is the case with the cordwainer Valentine Baker whose appraisers note that 'His wearing apparel ... he gave all awaie in his life tyme' (D.P.R. 1620). The high percentage of inventories listing apparel may be unique to Newcastle, as this is not common to other areas in this period (Wrightson 1979: 38; Tinder and Cox 1980: 34-5; Spufford 1984: 129).

The inventories occasionally contain quite detailed descriptions of apparel (shown in Appendix 5), which provide information on materials, colours, imported items and the trade listing the garment. Some 25 types of fabric are listed, including coarse materials such as broadcloth, canvas and russet, along with linen and wool, and fine fabrics like damask, velvet, satin, silk and taffeta. Other garments made of skins or leather included those of friese, chamlet, black lamb, rabbit, fox and even 'wild leather'. Colours range from plain black, 'beggars' grey and ash, to garments of violet, red or blue, some decorated with lace or silver thread. White apparel is also quite popular. Some items have been imported from Denmark, Spain and London, with lace arriving from Belgium. Harrison describes fashions in the late 16th century as diverse in style and costliness, noting 'the fickleness and the follie' of 'all degrees' of people 'in somuch that nothing is more constant in England than the inconstancie of attire' (Furvinal 1877: 168-9).

However, while the wills and inventories do suggest great variety in materials and colours, the type of clothes listed is quite restricted, consistently comprising shirts, neck cloths, shirt ties (for around a man's waist), doublets, 'britches', hose, gowns, cloaks and hats (often of felt or lined with velvet), and handkerchiefs. No radical change in dress style is indicated over the decades of the study. Shoes are occasionally mentioned, as are silver buttons or other decorative elements. Whether an item was old or worn, or the best or second-best of two similar articles, is often noted, although detailed descriptions are more common in the period prior to 1600. Clothing specifically for work is listed separately, suggesting that some of the trades may have had a distinct type of dress code relating to a trade affiliation - contrary to information from museum collections, where evidence of working clothes is virtually non-existent for the latter 17th century (Spufford 1984: 130). Work clothes have been taken up separately in discussions about trade below. Overall, recording of apparel is patchy, so following consumer trends by way of inventories is not possible.

Apparel is often appraised separately from other objects, usually itemised at the very end of an inventory, sometimes along with ready cash (Spufford 1984: 125-6; Arkell 2000: 92). The room where the clothing has been kept is not always specified, but where this information has been included, this was almost always a chamber, with some references to a hall or parlour. Very occasionally, lofts or kitchens are mentioned.

Table 5.6 examines evidence for apparel for each of the trades over three time frames. Spufford has found that the increasing cheapness and spread of garments in the 17th century made them objects for appraisers to ignore, and thus clothes should appear less often in the records (1990:150). This trend is not apparent in the Newcastle sample, where the percentage of inventories listing apparel remains very steady throughout the period. Tracing the prices of individual pieces of clothing is not possible as apparel in the majority of all inventories is given a collective valuation (Spufford 1984: 125-7). But overall average levels of investment were rising steadily in each of three time frames, more or less doubling in each generation. When individual trades are examined, it appears that prior to 1600 the master mariners and cordwainers, and a single baker, spent significant sums on clothes. Between 1601 and 1625 the master mariners stand out, along with the mariners, as the heaviest investors, while the figures for most other trades double. After 1626 the master mariners again show the highest figure, along with smiths and tanners, but a divide becomes apparent between those trades who continue to invest higher sums and others who make no further gains beyond the figures given in the previous period. At the other end of the social scale, the keelmen stand out as being particularly poorly dressed, much more so than any other trade. The overall averages per trade for the combined periods suggest that master mariners have spent almost double the amount on apparel compared with the other trades, while the bakers and mariners invest more than the combined overall average over the whole period. Such differences in expenditure on apparel between trades suggest that wealth factors alone are not dictating consumption patterns. Arkell has also found that social standing could not be inferred from expenditure on apparel, because of the great variation in individual wardrobes (2000: 93). However, the unique levels of expenditure by master mariners do suggest that display may have been an important social factor, an observation emphasised by the patterns of ownership of weapons, discussed below.

The valuations recorded for the Newcastle tradesmen over the three periods indicates that, relative to other regions in the south, the average investment was relatively high (Arkell 2000: 92). This may relate to Newcastle's close trading ties with the capital (Earle 1989: 284-5), as a tripling of investment on apparel is also seen in Whickham copyholders between 1557 and 1619 (Levine and Wrightson 1991: 104). In comparison with other types of consumption, apparel is among the most valuable things owned by a man, especially by those with little in the way of household objects (Everitt 1967: 449; Shammas 1990: 169), and expenditure on clothing is second only to that on food (Weatherill 1996: 134-6). Over the course of the 17th century, expenditure on clothing may have risen appreciably (Spufford 1984: 129-30). This finding is borne out by the Newcastle evidence where, from the early decades of the 17th century investment in clothing increases for all trades to varying degrees, a conclusion underlined by the fact that there is no clear evidence that the actual number of items of clothing recorded in individual inventories is increasing, although prices of individual items can also not be traced. Spufford observed an increase in the spread of better and more comfortable clothing even among poorer people in rural England by the late 17th century, just as an increase in domestic comfort had been demonstrated (1984: 125). Similar observations can be made concerning the tradesmen of Newcastle. Changes and augmentation in investment in apparel are clearly evident by the *early* 17th century, just as has been seen in relation to objects in households.

5.5 Weapons

In the light of an often-repeated presumption that northern England in the early modern period was plagued with troubles from marauding Scots and other lawless groups, the expectation might be to find the local population of Newcastle fairly well armed (Houlbrooke 1995: 50, Myer 2001: 294). However, Harrison tells us that in his own day every village or town had an armoury, that almost all men above the age of 18 carried daggers as did 'burgesses and magistrates of anie citie' and that 'no man travelleth ... without his sword, or such weapon' (Furvinal 1877: lxviii, 282-3). The probate records suggest a rather different picture, although the paucity of arms in inventories dating from immediately after the Civil War (Arkell 2000: 94), and the possible secreting of weapons during the war (Overton 2004: 114), could suggest that an unknown number of weapons may also have gone unrecorded in Newcastle documents in the pre-Civil War period.

Despite such possible limitations, Newcastle inventories (and a few wills) record a wide variety of weaponry and some armour between the 1550s and 1642, and there does not appear to be a decline in references over the period - as was the case in, for example, Sussex (Kenyon 1958: 71; Arkell 2000: 93). Additionally, although there are few references to weapons in wills, this cannot be interpreted as evidence of limited ownership, as suggested by Shammas (1990: 207). The documents record bows and arrows, armour, handheld weapons and firearms. The assemblage is similar to that found in probate records of the same period in Banbury, Oxfordshire; but as Arkell has noted, no regional studies concerning the pattern of ownership of weapons has yet been undertaken (2000: 94).

Table 5.7a gives a breakdown of types and ownership patterns for weapons. Information from the inventories indicates that bows and arrows or shafts, often twelve to a quiver, are not recorded after 1593. These weapons were stored together with bill staffs and swords, but are not listed with firearms. Stuff jackets - clearly a padded jacket of an unspecified material - are only recorded in inventories dated to the 1570s. The demise of the stuff jacket appears to have coincided with increased recording of firearms for which such protective wear would have been of little use. Steel or iron capes are mentioned as early as 1563 and continue to be recorded into the late 1630s. No bowers are listed in the Durham probate records after 1587, whereas armourers are found in all decades in this study and their Company survived into the 20th century (Tyne & Wear Archive: GU.CF).

Bill and halberd staves were among the most popular hand-held weapons, making up a quarter of the overall sample. Bill staffs are recorded between 1570 and the first quarter of the 17th century, and halberds are listed from the 1580s. A 'French Halbert' is recorded in 1584. The term 'bill' applies to various cutting weapons and other implements according to the O.E.D., which says 'the relations of which to each other are not satisfactorily ascertained'. This ambivalence is seen in the inventories where, for example, a miller lists three bill staves together with a shovel and a muck fork in the same room where he also kept a dagger and a sword among his apparel (D.P.R. Grey 1585). Swords, daggers and rapiers make up another quarter of total weapons and are listed throughout the period, although rapiers are recorded only after 1600.

Calivers and muskets, which are sometimes listed with a flask for powder and a touch-box for igniting the powder, make up another quarter of the sample. The caliver, the lightest form of musket, is listed from the 1580s to the 1630s. Other muskets are recorded from the 1590s to 1642. 'Birding pieces' or 'fowling pieces' are owned by a small number of men throughout the time frame and are not restricted to the later decades as suggested by Arkell (2000: 94). A few pistols and unspecified guns are also recorded, including a 'German piece' belonging to a tanner (D.P.R. Rowmaine 1615). Some of the guns had 'rests' to stand on. Bandoliers, the belts worn over the shoulder to support a heavy musket, are also listed. Other items such as a mace, a lance, a 'partiza', a 'fueling' piece, shot, munitions, a buckler, a javelin, a bore spear, a cross-staff and a powder horn are mentioned incidentally. The majority of arms were kept in the halls, some in parlours, no doubt partly for display, but others are recorded in chambers, with a few in lofts, kitchens and backhouses.

Table 5.7b shows a range of prices for weapons and armour over three periods. Information on individual prices is limited, as these objects are sometimes grouped together and given a single valuation or listed together with other objects. Where prices can be retrieved, wide discrepancies are apparent. Prices must have been very dependent on the quality and the age of the weapon or armour, which is often specifically noted by appraisers. Bows and arrows range from 2s to over 6s before the 1590s. The valuations for bill and halberd staves remain steady in the first and second timeframes, but after 1626 the low range rises while the high range falls, with overall valuations ranging from as little as 4d to over 4s. An old sword could be had for 8d, but other examples range from under 2s prior to 1600 to over 10s in the first quarter of the 17th century. Two daggers are valued at 6d, and 1s for a long version before 1625. The better-quality muskets appear to rise in price, with a corresponding decline in the price of other examples, and the prices of calivers may also have declined. Such guns could be acquired for as little as 1s to over 25s.

Table 5.7a shows that, on average, 46% of the total sample of 257 inventories list weapons, a figure suggesting that about half of the testators either participated in civic duties or held weapons for personal defence, hunting, or for other reasons, perhaps associated with display (Overton 2004: 8). The figures are higher than those for Kent and Cornwall (Overton 2004: 114, Table 5.4). The life-cycle factor may also have played a role in the patterns, where weapons were sold or given away prior to the making of the will. Percentage figures vary from as low as 17% to over 60%, with bakers, master mariners, smiths and tailors owning a significantly higher percentage than the average.

Wealth may have been a factor in ownership, although a figure of 60% recorded for tailors must account for men who, in fact, carried fewer, less expensive weapons (the lowest number next to the keelmen). The opposite trend is apparent in the case of the weavers, where 29% list weapons but for whom the average valuation is second only to the master mariners at 12s. Neither the tailors nor weavers appear so far to have been among the better-off trades, according to the findings in the previous section relating to household objects. Keelmen clearly show a significantly lower percentage figure, as do millers to a lesser extent. In terms of expenditure, an average valuation of 9s has been calculated per trade, but sums vary from as low as 2d for the two keelmen who carried handheld weapons to the 17s recorded by the master mariners.

Occupation must play a role in ownership: master mariners have many more swords than other tradesmen, and a large share of the calivers and muskets. As these men have invested the largest sums in weapons of all the trades (as has also been found to be the case in the section on apparel), display may have been very important both on land and sea in signalling status and rank by being exceptionally well attired and heavily armed. Although mariners carry almost as many arms as the master mariners, these are of half the value; nevertheless, together these trades are the most heavily armed, with an average of four or more weapons per man. Smiths own a disproportionately large number of halberd and bill staves, perhaps having made the weapons themselves. The overall average figure for weapon ownership is 3.2 weapons per person.

The evidence suggests that potentially about half the male population reflected in the inventoried sample carried weapons. Overall, the most popular weapons were firearms, swords and halberd staves. Further observations of patterns of ownership in inventories indicate that a number of testators tended to own several types of weapons (if they owned any at all), whereas a sizeable number of testators do not appear to have owned any. Overall, weapons and armour do not appear to have been a priority for most tradesmen, as the average investment was small relative to other categories of consumables.

5.6 Books and maps

By the 18th century, Newcastle had acquired a national reputation as a centre for printing, but this was many decades in the future when this study of book ownership commences (Claire 1965: 197; Hunt 1975: xii; Hugman 2004: 117). The town would not obtain its first printing press, as far as we know, until May of 1639, when Charles I needed a printer to put into type his orders and proclamations (Welford 1907: 1, Hunt 1975: 7). It was 1642 before Buckley, the first genuine resident printer, arrived (Hunt 1975: 18), and Hunt's bibliography of Northumberland and Durham printers records just 12 book traders in the region prior to 1700 (1975).

The earliest of these traders was William Corbett (d.1626), Newcastle's first known stationer, bookseller and bookbinder (Hunt 1975: xi, 26; D.P.R. 1626). Corbett's presence in the town signals a *terminus ad quem* of a market for books which can be usefully explored in relation to the early ownership of books, as recorded in wills and inventories. The documentary evidence suggests that, by the 1580s, a market had already come into existence - one linked, perhaps, to the proliferation of printed matter centred on London dated to the mid-16th century, when John Foxe (d.1587) observed that 'bookes now seem rather to lacke readers, then readers to lack bookes' (Wheatley 2002: 183).

Between 1580 and 1642, tradesmen list bibles, religious texts, and secular works for which titles are not always recorded, and maps or 'cards' and globes, which have been included in this analysis as their use certainly requires a degree of literacy, and they are often accompanied by written manuals. For example, one master mariner lists 'my sea carde with other books' (D.P.R. Nicholson 1595), and another lists 'Compasses & a book for these' (D.P.R. Cheken 1587). Where the titles of books are given, these details can be found in Appendix 6. Where rooms are recorded on inventories, three-quarters of the tradesmen who owned books and maps kept them in the hall. A few books are listed in upper chambers, parlours and even a kitchen. These rooms are often heated and have seating and candlesticks. The location of the hall for most of the books suggests that reading aloud to the household is probably part of both the education and entertainment for the family, especially as it is unlikely that all members could read for themselves.

Evidence from the Newcastle inventories contrasts markedly with that from other regions, which shows low levels of book ownership (Arkell 2000: 94-5, Spufford 2000: 210-11). In addition, book ownership is not restricted to the clergy and gentry - as is the case before 1660 in, for example, nearby Whickham, where it is the early 18th century before books are found at every social level (Levine and Wrightson 1991: 233, 235). Spufford's contention that, in the 17th century almanacs, chapbooks and ballads worth 1d-3d 'stood no chance of being listed', and that reading habits among the barely literate are untraceable, does not appear to be entirely true (1990: 149). Cheap books are listed, and one might also question where the ballad sheets, so integral a part of the Newcastle street scene since the 16th century, were acquired (Myer 2001: 296).

Myer's claim that there is no evidence in the early decades of the 17th century, let alone in the 16th century, for an 'indigenous Newcastle literary life' (2001: 294), is contradicted both by the probate evidence and by the presence of Corbett's two shops, one called the East Shop and one the West Shop. The volume and variety of the inventoried stocks in his shops is remarkable with some 1200 items listed. The more extensive premises appears to have been the East Shop, but no clue survives in the records as to where either shop was located, although one can surmise that they were perhaps in the west and east parts of the town, respectively. Both shops contained religious works encompassing testaments (including a few in Latin and one in Greek), prayer books, the Common Prayer Book, Psalters, and primers. There are very few bibles listed, but these came in two sizes, small and great. Titles including 'The Neccessity of Conformatie' and 'The Popish Doctrine' suggest anti-Catholic works. A selection of histories was on offer, such as works on the Romans, Caesar, Constantine, Socrates and Virgil, a 'History of Woman' and a 'History of Tythes'. There was an assortment of books on such subjects as 'physic' or medicine, flora and even on sports, a work entitled 'The Survey of London', possibly written by John Stow (1598), and copies of 'Elliot's Dictionary'. About 250 titles were provided, or 20% of the collection, with about 70% of the items consisting of unnamed volumes great and small, or works in quarto, octavo and decimo-sexto. There were also dozens of almanacs and 'pamphlets about the shop'. Items were variously made of paper, vellum or parchment or combinations of these - for example, where paper books were bound in parchment. Some works were gilded. Besides all this, Corbett stocked 'rims' of white and whiter paper, dozens of horn books and table books, together with inkhorns and even spectacle cases, although not, apparently, spectacles (D.P.R. 1626). The ready availability of such a wide variety of literature; of table books, paper and pens; and of hornbooks, specifically for teaching the alphabet, numbers, and even spelling, and retailing at just 2d a piece, provides unequivocal evidence of both a literate community and of opportunities to acquire literacy skills among the town's population.

The tradesmen's inventoried books and related items are representative of those found in Corbett's shops. For example, a mariner, who could clearly read and write, owned a small bible, four small printed books, a paper book and three table books, listed together with a 'penhorne' (D.P.R. Harrison 1618). A cordwainer listed 'A historie Booke' in 1625, and a master mariner had a copy of 'Mr. Dod upon the Commandements' in 1627, the same work recorded in Corbett's East Shop. Another mariner listed an 'Engleshes bowke', rather than a Latin work one would suppose, suggesting that he read in the vernacular (D.P.R. Gamsbie 1583). A baker and brewer owned 'A booke of pres[i]dentes for wills' in 1628, confirming the use of formulaic wills (D.P.R. Hall), and although the title was not among Corbett's stock, a search for this work and several others confirms that, while early versions of some books have not survived, later works on the same themes can be found (EEPO). What is absent from Corbett's inventory are maps. Just one title relating to matters connected with the sea is included, although some of the dozens of unnamed almanacs may well have been on the subject, as suggested by manuals owned by master mariners.

It appears that, although the centre of the book trade in the late 16th century is clearly in London (Weatherill 1996: 51; Wheatley 2002: 183), with other concentrations of booksellers in places such as York (Barnard 1994: 2), the proliferation of printed matter in the period must have been influencing the availability of books in Newcastle, which was in the vanguard of urban development in the region (Ellis 1984: 193; Weatherill 1996: 51-52).

Table 5.8a examines ownership patterns for bibles, religious works in general, unnamed and secular works, and maps and globes. Bibles make up the greatest number of named works. The composition of items does not appear to alter between 1580 and 1641, a finding similar to that from Kent and Cornwall, and one which continues into the early 18th century (Overton 2004: 113). The overall percentage of Newcastle tradesmen listing works is 28%, double the figure suggested by Weatherill, who noted that by 1675 books are known but not common (1996: 28). Her figures for urban inventories from the North East is just 14% in the period between 1675 and 1715, compared with 31% for London, while an overall figure of 22% is given for all major towns. Weatherill's conclusion, that books were three times as common in London as in the North East - one repeated in subsequent publications (Schammel 2004: 8, 13, 19, 22) - does not apply to Newcastle, where ownership rates are closer to those of the capital than to other towns, as is the case, for example, with clocks and china in the post-Civil-War era (1996: 29, 43, 52, Table 3.3, 4.3). Shammas, who examines book ownership in relation to education and market accessibility, concludes that those living in towns would have better exposure to these consumer commodities, a finding borne out in the case of Newcastle (1990: 180).

Clear differences in patterns of ownership between trades are apparent from Table 5.8a. Where the exact number of works is not specified on the document, the totals on the table represent a minimum of two books based on the common phrase that noted 'certain' or 'other books'. The testators may well have owned many more. All trades had representatives who owned books, even the poor keelmen, one of whom recorded 'my Service Booke with ye sickmans salve' and 'my short Brief Chronyckles', bequeathed to the son of another keelman (D.P.R. Robinson 1592). Although the number of individuals in the sample is small, taken collectively the figures suggest that there were literate members among all the trades. Well over half the master mariners (72%), almost half the bakers (48%) and mariners (47%), about a third of butchers (28%) and cordwainers (29%), and less than a quarter of keelmen, skinners, smiths, tailors and weavers, all own books, while maps and globes tend to be the exclusive preserve of the seafarers, although a single cordwainer lists a map. Levine and Wrightson found that book ownership in Whickham had escaped 'social confinement', becoming common to all social levels by the later 17th and early 18th centuries (1991: 235), but this situation is evident decades earlier in Newcastle.

Weatherill's figures for 1675–1725 for a selection of these trades show some correlations (1996: Tables 8.1 and 8.4). In the case of master mariners (who she placed among the high-status trades), the figure is close to the 80% of professionals who owned books in the later period, while her figures for the smiths (10%), tailors (20%) and weavers (15%) are a close match. However, the figures for butchers (16%), mariners (18%), and cordwainers (16%) are about half those indicated by the earlier data. Weatherill's observation that virtually all professionals owned books and were literate by the late 17th century can be contrasted with the figures for a majority of master mariners who, according to these criteria were literate by at least the early 17th century (1996: 189). Such an assumption is reasonable, considering what was involved in navigating a ship laden with crew and cargo into several regions of the world.

A steady increase in both book ownership among trades and the numbers of books being acquired over three generations is evident according to Table 5.8b. The most notable increases appear to have been in secular works, rather than in bibles or religious works. Such change is not reflected in Weatherill's data, where only the levels of ownership are recorded, which remained very stable at 23%, with a drop in the figure in the middle of her 50-year time frame (1996: Table 4.4). Her figures do not account for actual changes in the numbers of books per inventory. Overton also found that book ownership changes little between the early 16th and early 18th centuries, but in his analysis of figures for Kent and Cornwall between 1600 and 1659, those for Kent ranged from 19% to 31% (similar percentages to those of Newcastle), whereas those from Cornwall are lower than these levels by one-half to one-third (2004: 113, Table 5.4), again supporting the finding that links to London are an important factor.

Social status and wealth are the explanations that Weatherill gives for ownership patterns, but these do not seem to have been the sole factors within the Newcastle sample (1996: 109, 180). Weatherill includes shopkeepers among the trades with higher ownership levels (1996: 187), and the evidence from Newcastle confirms that the bakers and cordwainers (many of whom had shops), are among those who own a higher percentage of books, but the mariners are an important exception. However, the mean average levels of investment in books varies very little between trades, with a few cordwainers owning a selection of more valuable works, and the more literate bakers, mariners and master mariners all investing 9s or 10s, with valuations for other trades all under the 9s overall mean average (Table 5.8a). A clear correlation between wealth and status, and book ownership, is therefore not demonstrable, contrary to findings elsewhere (Shammas 1990: 173; Weatherill 1996: 108-9). Books are recorded by a keelman whose inventory is valued at about 5li, whilst many wealthy men (who, incidentally, own all sorts of expensive objects), did not list any books, supporting Shammas' finding that those acquiring new commodities were not necessarily the best educated (1990: 180).

Other explanations for ownership patterns can be suggested. The high percentage of seafarers owning books, especially bibles, might be related to the perilous nature of sea voyages, where the reading of such works could act as a source of inspiration in times of trouble, or even help to pass away idle hours on long journeys. The community of literate bakers and brewers is more of a mystery. Weatherill found that the organisational requirements of professional people and clergy were associated with higher levels of book ownership and literacy rates (Weatherill 1996: 180). Certainly, the clergy would have to be able to read the bible, but such associations are more difficult to account for in the case of most tradesmen, such bakers or cordwainers. A wealthy weaver called Oswald Chaitor, for example, also owned a small library containing 42 books, the largest collection in the sample, kept in his study (D.P.R. 1623). The 20s he had invested in books can be compared with the total value of books on Corbett's inventory which was just 13li (D.P.R. 1626). Unfortunately, as no details of Chaitor's books were recorded, what motivated his interest in books cannot be recovered. Was he a great customer of Corbett's West Shop? Chaitor lived on Westgate Street on the west side of town. An overall impression is gained that books were collected by people who took a special interest in reading the Bible and other religious treatises, or who owned works that were of particular use or interest to them, either professionally or for pleasure.

The prices of books are another clue to the patterns of ownership. Relative to many other items, books were fairly cheap (Table 5.8b). The prices of new books listed in Corbett's shops can be compared with the evidence from tradesmen's inventories. The least expensive works mentioned in the inventory of a mariner were four small printed books and a paper book, valued together at 6d (D.P.R. Harrison 1618). In Corbett's inventory, small paper books cost 3d each, but almanacs and little prayer books were a penny a piece (D.P.R. 1626). Spufford discusses small books that cost 2d in 1680, described by their publishers as 'small goodies, small merries and pleasant histories' aimed at urban artisans, or country labourers who could perhaps read but not write (1984: 6). 'The little book', like ribbons or cheap tobacco, were goods created for 'the humble consumer society of the seventeenth century' (Spufford 1981: 111-4). The Newcastle evidence suggests an early 17th century market for such books must have existed. Wealth cannot have been a significant factor in the acquisition of such works, as other items on inventories similarly valued to a penny included cushions, trenchers, earthenware, salt sellers and even glasses, were quite common to almost all households (Table 5.5).

The diversity of books in the tradesmen's inventories means that the prices of most works cannot easily be compared, but the prices of bibles can be recovered to an extent. It is unknown which editions these are, but references to the age and size is sometimes given. Small bibles appear to have been becoming less expensive between the late 16th century and the second quarter of the 17th century. An old bible was appraised at 4s in the later 16th century, but by the second quarter of the 17th century another was valued at just 2s. More expensive editions were valued from 6s 8d to 10s. Testators seem to have cherished old bibles, which were not uncommon. Corbett priced small bibles at 5s and 'one great byble in folio att the two hand' (second hand) at 14s (D.P.R. 1626). Large bibles appear to have been the most expensive item, as seen in the example of a smith who owned a 'Church Bible' in 1619 worth 10s. Spufford found that bibles cost 1s 8d in 1707 in Canterbury, supporting the finding of falling prices (1984: 57). Most religious works and history books in Corbett's shops were priced between 1s and 2s 6d: some cost a few shillings more, some even less, but one could purchase, for example, 'Tullies ovacons in three volumes [bound in] leather & guylt' for just 3s. A cordwainer owned 'A historie Book' and a bible valued at 10s in 1625, and the master mariner owned a testament, a bible and a copy of 'Mr. Dod upon the Commandements' valued at 8s in 1627. In Corbett's shop 'Dod' was valued together with two other religious treatises at 4s 6d. Some information on the cost of maps can also be found in inventories which indicates that these were valued at about 3s 4d to 4s before 1600 but were becoming cheaper in the first quarter of the 17th century, with valuations between 2s 6d and 3s 4d. In the second quarter of the 17th century, a globe with a lantern cost as little as 2s 6d, whereas another model appraised at 1li was far more expensive than any of the books.

The question of the relationship between the ownership of books and literacy is another area of discussion that deserves some attention, although the subject is clearly far beyond the scope of this enquiry. Arkell noted that if books are examined together with other sources, they can provide insights into the extent and type of reading at some levels of society (Arkell 2000: 95), although Erickson argues that the ownership of books cannot prove ability to read (2002: 57), and Shammas contends that education cannot be judged by inventories (1990: 111). Such reasoning, however, cannot be applied exclusively to books, as by this logic any object in a household might not be used in a way implied by design. We have no more reason to doubt reading abilities than to exaggerate them.

A distinction should be made in defining literacy, which has two components - the ability to read and the separate skill of being able to write. Erickson, for example, has confirmed that girls were taught to read, if not to write (2002: 61), and the analysis of writing abilities requires a separate study. Guilds had responsibilities to ensure children were educated, and such provision included basic literacy and numeracy skills (Brooks 1994: 75-6), but the extent to which the guilds and by-trades provided such assistance would require a separate study. Guilds also had written rules governing occasions (King 2001: 49), suggesting literate members.

In assessing reading ability among those tradesmen who owned books, a major factor to consider is the rise of Protestantism and a desire to read the Bible, which stimulated the growth of literacy among the laity (James 1974: 104, Wrightson 1995: 184-5). The Protestant concern, that all should have access to the Word of Scripture promoted an interest in education (James 1974: 63), stimulating such initiatives as the founding of Newcastle's first grammar school in 1540. Patronised by the great Tyne coal-owners, who went on to sent their sons to Cambridge, the opportunity to attend school in Newcastle was not restricted to the wealthiest and most powerful, as free places were also offered to poor boys (James 1974: 100, 103-4). Over the decades, the school headed by markedly successful masters such as Robert Fowberry (1607 -23) and Amor Oxley (1635-45), sent a 'fairly steady stream of boys' to Cambridge before the Civil War (James 1974: 101; Howell 1967: 322-3). Direct evidence that such educational opportunities were being taken up by tradesmen comes from the will of a tanner, who recorded no books on his inventory, but who had sent one son to Cambridge University sometime before 1570 and was preparing to send a second son (D.P.R. Newton 1570). While this is the only such example in this study, the evidence points to educational ambitions beyond those usually associated with provincial tradesmen; as such this was certainly part of a much wider 'educational imperative' witnessed during the Elizabethan and early Stuart reigns, as numbers of students attending universities rose dramatically, as did the numbers of grammar schools (Wrightson 1995: 185). Stone goes so far as to describe an 'educational revolution' taking place between 1560 and 1640 (1964: 73, 78; Burke 1988: 252).

Other evidence supporting the proposition that a sizeable percentage of tradesmen could read, is based on a small sample of deponents who acted as witnesses for the Durham Consistory Court. James found that shopkeepers were a highly literate group, because two-thirds of them could write their names (1974: 105), a finding supported by Weatherill (1996: 187). Spufford discusses signatures on wills of Cambridgeshire villagers of the 16th and 17th centuries noting that 'literacy and prosperity were related' (2000: 192-205). In the case of Newcastle tradesmen, the ability to write was doubtless related to business requirements; however, as has been seen, the low price of books and the variety of owners argues against wealth being a significant factor.

In examining the wills of the tradesmen in this study, increasing efforts to sign names is apparent over successive decades. By the second quarter of the 17th century, more examples of well-formed signatures are evident, whereas earlier efforts often consist of various-shaped marks or initials, indicating greater efforts in learning to write than the mastering of a simple 'x'. Progress in writing abilities appears to have been slow, but steady headway is apparent by the beginning of the 17th century, coinciding with the increased ownership of books. Burke also noted this correlation between the two skills of reading and writing, with the levels of signatures running below, but in close parallel with, reading skills (1988: 251). However, in an examination of the wills of 18 master mariners and nine mariners, who listed books in the accompanying inventory, just one-third of the master mariners and just two of the nine mariners seem to have been able both to read and to write; all these examples were dated from 1623 onwards, a much lower rate than Burke implies. Further detailed analysis of a larger sample of documents would, no doubt, provide useful insights.

There are two other clues to literacy levels in the probate records. The first is the inclusion in some inventories of fees for the education of children, both girls and boys. The presence of unlicensed teachers, a principal source of formal education, was growing in the early 17th century (Levine and Wrightson 1991: 325). Other evidence from inventories includes names of debtors and creditors, along with the places where the various debtors lived, the nature of the debt and the amount owed. The meticulous recording of such information must have required a degree of literacy, and this does suggest that many tradesmen had at least a very rudimentary proficiency in reading, writing and even numeracy. For instance, the appraisers of the inventory of a weaver dated 1636 noted that the man's debts 'good and bad appeareth by bills and booke' (D.P.R. Woodman). Levine and Wrightson have commented on the sheer inconvenience of the inability to write, in an economy that was increasingly involved in complex commercial dealings, highlighting a need for advancing literacy (1991: 324). Everitt's remarks concerning illiterate traders who lost count of transactions owing to a lack of education and an inability to keep accurate records, is in no way apparent in the careful accounting of tradesmen's debts and credits in Newcastle records (1967: 565-7).

James has confirmed that, in the 1620s, an appreciable decline was taking place in the rate of illiteracy, showing that the early injunctions to the clergy (such as that issued in County Durham as early as 1577), to teach children in the parishes to both read and write, were clearly paying dividends (1974: 104-5). Later evidence for increasing literacy comes from the north-west of England, where high levels of book ownership, associated with the value that local religious dissent placed on reading the scriptures, also resulted in higher general literacy (Weatherill 1996: 55). One could add to this body of evidence the fact that many books and maps bequeathed to women as part of their overall inheritance, suggest the presence of even higher numbers of literate people in Newcastle. Literate women there certainly were, as confirmed by a tailor who specifically bequeathed his wife 'her best bible' in 1636, a phrase which acknowledges that the book is hers (D.P.R. Clark). Corbett's wife was specifically bequeathed 'one little cutting presse and one little soweing presse' for the rest of her natural life, and it seems likely that a woman involved in running bookshops and making books was also able to read and probably to write (D.P.R. 1626).

Taken together, what evidence we have indicates that such influences as religious teachings, the requirements of running a business, and the availability of books are all contributing to increased literacy in Newcastle, as well as in the northern region more generally. Wrightson confirms that the period showed a marked advancement in, and provision of, educational facilities that were to provide answers to society's ills and to guarantee social well-being (1995: 184-5). The changing nature of cultural, social and family relationships, and even a fear of the poor, all combined to cause an extraordinary growth of education between 1560 and 1640 (Stone 1964: 73).

It would seem that a reliance on analysis of proportions of signatures in comparison to marks may very much underestimate levels of literacy (Schofield 1968; Levine and Wrightson 1991: 324). In Whickham in the late 16th century, very few individuals were able to sign their names (Levine and Wrightson 1991: 324), while Howell argued for a 'surprising degree of illiteracy' in Newcastle during the Interregnum, extending far down the social hierarchy, based on an ability to sign a name with an 'x', although at the same time he noted 'rather surprisingly' the number of books left to the library of St. Nicholas in the early 1630s by a very wealthy local merchant (1967: 13).

By the time Charles I had brought his printer to Newcastle, the Windsor herald Norgate, writing from the town to his cousin, confirmed that 'a printer with all his trinkets' was 'ready to make new [copies of the proclamation] as occasion may require', a reference to the several hundred printed proclamations directed at the Scottish Covenanters (Welford 1907: 3). Three days later Norgate wrote again to his cousin with the news that 'a proclamation for the importation of butter' was 'now printing' (Welford 1907: 3). Howell confirms that religious and political tracts and pamphlets flooded into Newcastle, that 'a manuscript broadside circulated in Newcastle streets' attacking the Scots, and that in 1642 a 'satirical pamphlet' was aimed at corrupt merchants (1967: 104, 322-3). It is difficult to account for the presence of such printed public announcements if the intended public had no ability to read the hundreds of copies of various broadsides that were being circulated. Sufficient numbers of literate townsmen (and probably women) were clearly a prerequisite for such mass publications. Hunt says that in later decades the output of 'street literature' in the North East was greater than anywhere else in England outside London (1975: xii). The early evidence for printed matter in the form of pamphlets, almanacs, books, and proclamations in Newcastle surely argues for quite extensive literacy at an earlier date.

Assessing levels of literacy by way of the inclusion of books on inventories will have its limitations. Spufford points out that the omission of books does not equate to scarcity but to the fact they were so cheap they may never have been listed (1981: 48, 1990: 149). But problems of under-recording would also have affected such people as Corbett, for example, as he had no books in his own house when he died, although he did have 'certaine parchment for covering books and writing upon' and '4 dozen inkehornes' in his high chamber (D.P.R. 1626). Had his occupation not been specified (as is the case in many documents), and his remarkable inventory not survived, we might have counted him among the illiterate of the town. The unique record of the literature he sold in his two bookshops, together with the detailed accounts in the tradesmen's inventories, create a context for understanding the record of book ownership in the town. A literate community was clearly emerging in Newcastle at least by the early 17th century, one which embraced a much wider social circle than has been suggested.

Household production

5.7 Spinning and sewing

Spinning and sewing are practised by families of all trades, according to the probate evidence. Information on types of spinning wheels, supplies of yarn and cloth, and where this work is carried out, as well as about valuations, is found in the records.

Newcastle inventories list several types of spinning wheels specifically for 'lint' or flax, wool, 'towe' and other coarse yarn, pairs of carding combs for wool, 'yarn wyndle (winding) blades' and other reels. Such useful detail is less common in records from other regions (Shammas 1990: 33). The types of linen yarn and fibres are consistently mentioned and include flax, harden, 'straken' (straiken), 'towe' (tow), and 'ocam' or 'boating towe', a coarse fibre possibly used for caulking ships' seams (D.P.R. Berwicke 1587, O.E.D). Wool and hemp are recorded, the latter used for cordage and stout fabrics, again suggesting usages connected to ships (O.E.D.). Cloth, priced by the yard, includes linen, straken and harden, either bleached or unbleached, wool, 'lynsey wolsey', a linen-wool blend, and russet, a coarse homespun woollen cloth, in white or red. Cotton is recorded by a skinner and glover in 1635, who lists 21 yards priced at 7d per yard. In this period, 'cotton' refers to a woollen fabric manufactured largely in Lancashire, Westmoreland and Wales (www.spintheweb.co.uk). Whether fabrics and yarns are new, fine or coarse is often specified. No other type of cloth or yarn is listed which has not already been made up into garments or soft furnishings.

Spinning wheels and supplies are to be found in virtually every room in the house. Upper chambers and lofts are favoured most for these activities and for storage, but halls, parlours, kitchens and back and brew houses are also frequently mentioned. Occasionally, a separate small room is specified for this purpose. For example, one baker recorded 'a little room over the entry' to his house containing just two spinning wheels (no other goods were listed) (D.P.R. Peacock 1625). Another baker mentions a 'little room on the back side of the kitchen' where there are 'two spynell of linning yarne' (two spinning wheels for linen) (D.P.R. Swynburne 1625). Weatherill has found that, in the houses of tradesmen, most domestic tasks that help to maintain the household (such as spinning), are carried out in separate spaces to those associated with the trade, distinguishing between the workplace and the living space (1996: 144). In Newcastle tradesmen's homes, any such clear delineation will have depended on the principal occupation of the head of the household, as well as the size of the house. For example, weavers and glovers work in the upper chambers of their houses where objects relating to spinning are often found, whereas other trades have no rooms in their houses associated with their work in the first place - as is the case, for example, with keelmen, mariners and master mariners. In contrast, bakers who keep professional brewing equipment in back houses also use this room for washing, cooking and spinning. Documentation is very sparse on this subject (Weatherill 1996: 145, 231), although Overton explores room function in detail for Kent and Cornwall (2004: 130). A more comprehensive analysis of this subject is undertaken in Chapter 6, which examines room function.

Prices per yard, or by pounds or stones, are given for supplies of yarn and cloth, but the sample is too inconsistent to provide a truly reliable guide, and the quality of the fabric or yarn is often unknown. However, the valuations given for spinning wheels can be analysed. Table 5.9a shows a range of prices. The cost of the spinning wheels depends on the type of yarn it is used for, those used for lint (flax) tending to be the most expensive. Prior to 1600, prices are as low as 6d and as high as 3s 4d. One spinning wheel with a stool cost 1s 4d, while the majority are priced at just under 1s. In contrast, a pair of yarn winders is valued at 18s in 1592, showing that some related equipment can be expensive in this period. In the first quarter of the 17th century, the lowest valuations for spinning wheels are still 6d, with others priced up to 6s for a lint wheel complete with a sconce and a chair; but overall, half the items are still valued at about 1s. In the second quarter of the 17th century the lowest valuation is 1s, with spinning wheels in all price ranges - up to 8s for one example, with a pair of carding combs. Although a price rise is evident by the final period, the wide range of valuations suggests that even relatively poor tradesmen could easily acquire equipment that appears to vary considerably in design and quality - a situation, Thirsk has noted, that is true of many consumer goods in the period (1978: 114-5).

Evidence from the households of tradesmen suggests interesting patterns of participation in spinning and sewing, although Overton has questioned whether spinning is prone to under-recording because associated items such as distaffs are of negligible value and are therefore unlikely to be documented. However, he acknowledges that the quantity of items relating to this activity provides some idea of the scale of production (2004: 10, 36). It is of interest to note that the number of spinning wheels listed in the documents decreases in the period when valuations are highest (Table 5.9b), suggesting that the observed under-recording of distaffs may not relate to their value. Instead, perhaps if women are doing all the spinning, testators are simply choosing not to include the distaffs or spinning wheels used exclusively by a daughter or wife on their own inventories.

Table 5.9b gives the percentage figures for the number of households which list, first, spinning wheels, and second, combined spinning wheels, yarn and or cloth, the latter two items being indicative of spinning and sewing activities (Overton 2004: 34). The first figure enables direct comparisons to be made with figures from other studies, which tend to include spinning wheels and/ or yarn, but not cloth.

Looking at the combined figures, it appears that some trades are markedly more involved with these domestic activities than others. Keelmen, mariners, master mariners and shipwrights - trades associated rather exclusively with male employment - show the highest figures, with from 60% to over 70% of households participating. It is possible that the nature of work on the sea and river, and in construction, which likely excluded females, may have allowed the women of these families increased opportunities for spinning and sewing. Overton sees spinning and the presence of wool and yarn as evidence of female employment (2004: 34, 35, 38, 65, 78), and Shammas agrees that only women spun (1990: 33). However, Everitt has found that, in scores of parishes in the early modern period, one-third of the labouring population, both male and female, is involved in spinning and weaving hemp and flax (1967: 426). This finding is echoed in more recent studies, which have highlighted the contributions of men and boys who helped with tasks such as warping, sizing, drying and weaving the warp into cloth (www.spin the web.co.uk).

Overall, the households of butchers show the highest participation of all trades (78%), and one wonders if Shammas is correct in her conclusion that spinners are no more likely to own sheep than non-spinners (1990: 33).

Butchers in Newcastle record more sheep than any other trade, as nearly 80% of the animals listed belong to these men (see Table 5.10a). It is, however, also clear that women could be actively involved in the butcher's trade, both with the slaughter and the sale of animals (Clark 1992: 216-19), a very different situation to that applying to the wives of seafarers.

The low levels of participation in spinning by the weaver's families can be contrasted with these patterns, as well as with corresponding high levels of ownership of looms and related equipment at almost 100% (See section 5.10). The differences in equipment owned seem to indicate that families of weavers are more engaged with the business of weaving than with spinning. Millers are also an interesting statistic, as they record very little in the way of spinning wheels, yarns or cloth. Women are involved with working mills, as witnessed by the wife and the mother of a deceased miller, who ran the Postern mill in the west of the town for over 20 years. The mother is, in fact, already running the mill when her son is still a minor (D.P.R. Reasley 1611, Reasley 1630; Clark 1992: 215-6). The work involved with running a family mill may well have left few idle hands or spare hours for spinning. The percentage figures for the other trades shows that from just over 30% to 50% of households are involved with spinning and sewing.

Clarke found that spinning is but one alternative to some other profitable occupation that could be taken up within the precincts of the home, and that it is not the poorer women, but the well-to-do who could afford to buy wool to spin and sell as opportunities arose (1992: 147). Evidence from Yorkshire shows a connection between the size of a holding and the necessity of taking up occupations such as spinning to support the household (Jennings 2000: 333). But explanations for the varying percentage figures, both among Newcastle tradesmen's households and those from other regions, need to account for differences in employment opportunities rather than on a simple equation between wealth levels and participation in spinning activities. The example of the weavers illustrates this point, as although the majority are not well-off, their relative poverty cannot be linked to a necessity to take up this kind of work. In comparison, the households of wealthy master mariners are very likely to be engaged in spinning. In this context, the historical association between the poor and spinning, especially regarding poor women, and the Legislation in 1576 for the Houses of Correction where such work was undertaken, could be re-evaluated (Thirsk 1978: 19, 65-6). Shammas considers levels of wealth based on inventoried personal estates as a factor in ownership patterns (1990, Appendix 1), illustrated by the finding that in the latter half of the 16th century in Oxfordshire, low-wealth groups in both town and country are slightly more likely to list spinning wheels than are the same group in rural and urban Worcestershire by the later 17th century, where wealthier groups owned marginally more equipment (1990: Tables 2, 3, 2.4). Overall, the majority of Shammas' figures are well below 30% - significantly lower than those for Newcastle for all trades. Everitt's evidence indicates that it is the better-off labourers that carded and spun wool (1967: 426), whereas in Newcastle, whether a trade is found to be associated with high or low wealth levels does not apparently dictate whether the family took up spinning (Levine and Wrightson 1991: 231, 233; Weatherill 1996: 209 – 212).

For Newcastle, the overall average figures pertaining to ownership of spinning wheels is 42%, and for combined spinning wheels, yarn and cloth it is 49%. The figures are comparable to those from Kent and Cornwall in the period between 1600 and 1659. In Kent, the percentage of inventories indicating spinning or potential spinning is 45% overall, whereas the figure for Cornwall is 40% overall, but this is declining over the decades up to the 18th century. The decline of spinning in Cornwall is linked to a general decline in standards of living over the decades. This contrasted with the growing prosperity of Kent (Overton 2004: 47, 171, Table 3.6), which is comparable to the situation in Newcastle (Howell 1967: 2; Lomas 1992: 167; Ellis 2001: 15).

However, widespread involvement in spinning is not as evident elsewhere in the northern region. In an extensive analysis of household production, Shammas has found that, in inventories dated to the late 16th century for rural northern England, only 10-20% list spinning wheels, whereas those dated to the early 17th century for nearby Yorkshire varies between 17% and 38% (1990: 33). Slightly higher figures are found for towns and cities linked to markets throughout England in the late 16th century, ranging from 16% to 33%, with slightly lower figures recorded by the 17th century (Shammas 1990: 33). The evidence seems to suggest that the large markets in Newcastle may be important in explaining the high levels of participation in spinning for some trades, whereas wealth does not seem to have been as important a factor. This conclusion is supported elsewhere, as these figures are higher than those for labourers in the country as a whole, where percentages for weaving and spinning wool are 23%, for flax 15% and for hemp 14% (Everitt 1967: 426).

Whether wealth had a positive or negative effect on the amount of spinning undertaken by a household can also be examined by way of accounts. Weatherill found that in accounts belonging to Richard Latham from the 1730s, increased consumption of decorative objects, suggesting increased prosperity, coincided with increased spinning of cotton and flax (1996: 118). The purchase of raw materials to spin into yarn in the case of this household is for sale and not for family provision (1996: 119). Weatherill highlights the difficulty in establishing figures and relies on evidence for payments recorded in accounts of people undertaking spinning, weaving or dyeing for a family as evidence of market production (1996: 119, 131, 145). One conclusion seems to be that greater wealth provides more opportunity to participate in these activities on a larger scale. Unfortunately, this hypothesis cannot be tested without more accounts, and payments for spinning are not found in the Newcastle inventories.

Taken together the evidence seems to suggest that the poorer members of society may, in fact have done less spinning in this period than those with higher incomes - who were doubtless in a better position to acquire the necessary supplies, as Clark has suggested (above), although basic equipment is very inexpensive (Thirsk 1978: 111; Overton 2004: 36). In Whickham, spinning wheels and harden yarn are found only in the fuller inventories of the later 17th century (Levine and Wrightson 1991: 317-8). Nevertheless, Clark's in-depth analysis of women's work shows that, in town and country alike, the poor took on spinning to survive (1992: 100, 110).

The extent to which a family became involved in spinning and sewing, determined by way of equipment and supplies found in tradesmen's homes, is difficult to assess. It remains unclear how much of this work related to the needs of the family and how much is designated for the market. In the case of one tailor in the sample (who records six spinning wheels, but no other equipment - such as scissors, which are listed by most other tailors), it is clear that the man is spinning professionally. This situation can be compared to Shammas' belief that the most affluent households spun for home consumption, while for poorer households spinning is part of an outwork system (1990: 33). In Newcastle a complex explanation may be required, taking account of household needs, relative wealth, access to markets, and especially provision to the shipping industry. In the case of tradesmen's families, the time available for spinning is clearly linked to other responsibilities associated with helping the head of the household in the principal occupation. Weatherill allowed two hours in every day for making cloth and clothing, noting that cloth and clothing are made at odd times of the day by dependent members of the household (1996: Table 7.1, 145). It is not possible to be certain whether the spinning in a household is for the market or for domestic consumption, because the quantities of yarn and cloth included on the inventories is so variable. The volume of supplies will certainly have fluctuated almost daily as the materials are used up, as is evident in a will belonging to a tailor who left his servant Mary Stokoe 'all the spun yarn which will be in the house at the daie of my death' (D.P.R. Bainbrigge 1642).

In conclusion, it appears that the traditional division of labour between males and females; levels of income; access to, and sufficient means to produce for, a market; and the nature of a family trade, are perhaps all factors that affect levels of participation in the tasks of spinning and sewing. Shammas has concluded that the only places where more than 30% of those inventoried own spinning wheels are those where production is for more than a local market (1990:33) - a situation that will certainly have implications for families living in the provincial capital of Newcastle.

5.8 Livestock

Ideally, a study of livestock should be placed within a broader analysis of household production and access to land. However, in this review the focus is narrowed to specifically consider ownership patterns of animals among urban tradesmen and to ask whether the trade a man practised was an influential factor. Information on where livestock was kept and what sorts of valuations were made by appraisers are also discussed relating to the decades between the 1550s and 1640.

Evidence from the probate records confirms that Newcastle tradesmen owned cattle, oxen, horses, pigs and sheep. No other species of animals were recorded by appraisers, excepting a reference to geese on a regional farm and to beehives located in the Leazes, the common lands to the north of the town. Bee-keeping was apparently quite rare (Everitt 1967: 417). In these northern inventories, specialized names were used for animals depending on an animal's age and sex. Cattle were variously referred to as cows, kine, quyes, whyes, stirks, stottes and calves. A 'Dutch Whye' calf is recorded in 1634, the only evidence of imported breeds. Oxen, sometimes listed in pairs, were owned by very few men. Stallions and geldings were simply called horses, whereas female horses were referred to as nags and mares, and young animals as foals, fillies and colts. A horse's colour was often specified, as well as the size, age and condition of the animal. The millers specifically mention blind horses, most often paired with a sighted horse, as discussed in Chapter 4. For example, one miller had 'two mares the one blinde' which were valued together (D.P.R. Reade 1613). The word pig is not usually found in the documents. Instead these animals were called swine, boars or sows, and piglets were known as 'tuppes'. Some difficulty arises with references to 'hogs': male pigs were sometimes referred to as 'swine hogs' and male sheep were sometimes referred to as 'sheep hogs'. When the word 'hog' is used alone it is taken to mean a pig, unless the animal is specifically listed with ewes and lambs. Ewes were also called 'sheep ewes', and lambs seem occasionally to be referred to as 'tuppes'. The types of animals listed over the decades do not vary.

Information on where animals were kept is recorded, albeit somewhat inconsistently. Documents indicate that, within the town, cows and calves were being kept in stables or back houses attached to dwelling houses in many areas of the town and suburbs (see Chapter 4). Middlebrook mentions numerous byres for cows (1950: 64). A tanner mentions keeping cows in a tan house. Some records refer to animals being grazed on the Leazes, or on nearby farms in, for example, Elswick, Benwell, Jesmond and North Gosforth - separate communities in this period, but all situated close to Newcastle. Other livestock was pastured much further afield at, for example, Wolsingham or Sunderland. These animals were placed in the care of third parties, sometimes kin of the tradesmen. The location of pastures for animals belonging to the tradesmen is not always specified, however, and some with antiquated names may be a challenge to trace. A wide ranging and in-depth analysis would be required to establish many of the place-names listed in the documents. This is beyond the scope of this enquiry, but meadows, lands, farm-holds, closes and wastes are recorded in Northumberland villages north of Newcastle such as Killingworth and Horton, further to the north-west in Ridsdale, to the west in Tindale, and to the south-east at Washington in the Palatine of Durham, indicating wide geographical connections relating to the movement of livestock.

In relation to these regional holdings, a link between animal husbandry and arable farming could be investigated. Weatherill believes that town dwellers had less ready access to land and large gardens (1996: 103), but among those inventories that actually specify a location for property, 40% include landholdings, such as waste grounds or fields with crops, and all trades are about equally represented. If all entries for property in the records were accounted for, the percentage figure would be greater still, providing useful data with which to undertake regional comparisons (Overton 2004: 40-43, 75, Shammas 1990: 20-40). In evidence from Kent and Cornwall, fewer than 50% of inventories showed commercial farming activities, with some crafts more likely to farm than others (Overton 2004: 74-5). However, production activities outside the occupation claimed by a testator were, in the majority of cases, on a small scale, described by Levine and Wrightson as contributing only supplementary income rather than representing a dual-economy (1991: 222-6, 230). As described in Section 5.10 on Objects of the trades, and as discussed in Chapter 2, only a very few tradesmen actually gave up their named occupation to undertake other full-time employment.

In analysing ownership patterns, a degree of under-recording must be considered as all the animals once owned by the testators will not necessarily have been appraised on inventories. Bequests of animals, rather exclusively young cows and sheep, are found in at least 10% of wills (as discussed in Chapter 3), and Spufford noted that expensive horses were frequently sold off before the inventory was made (1984: 40). Nevertheless, Table 5.15a shows that an average of 58% of tradesmen listed animals, but the figures for some trades are much higher than for others. Over 75% of bakers, butchers, cordwainers, skinners, weavers and millers owned animals, whereas the figures for smiths, tailors and tanners were just under the overall average. Significantly lower percentage figures were recorded for keelmen, mariners, master mariners and shipwrights. Only about one-quarter (or fewer) of these men listed animals. However, interpreting the figures requires care as a number of animals tended to be concentrated in the hands of a relatively small number of testators who had herds (notably the bakers and especially the butchers), while millers owned 40% of the recorded horses. The butchers also owned many more horses than average, while the majority of tradesmen who listed livestock at all owned just one or two cows. A few tradesmen had small herds of sheep. However, over one-third of the total cattle and nearly 80% of recorded sheep belonged to the butchers.

Overall, the Newcastle evidence suggests that most tradesmen were not involved with commercial farming of livestock. According to Overton, commercial farming is indicated where more than two cattle or 10 sheep are recorded, and the low percentage figures of under 10% recorded for Kent and Cornwall appear comparable to those from Newcastle (2004: 40-1). Overton also found that those owning more than four cows were likely to be involved with selling butter and cheese on the markets and that, in Kent and Cornwall, one-third of inventories indicated these activities (2004: 53, 60). Unfortunately, such products are markedly absent from Newcastle inventories, as is any specialised equipment indicating these processes - something Shammas had found to be the case elsewhere in the country (1990: 37). Overton notes, however, that large brass and earthenware pans were used in the place of churns in South West England and these items are found in many Newcastle inventories (2004: 61).

Shammas found that, in the 16th century, animal ownership was ubiquitous in the North, averaging between 60% and 90%, noting that most people had cows, and that sheep were very common to the region (1990: 29, Table 2.1). Her figures for Durham and Northumberland in the first half of the 17th century range from 65% for cattle, 65% for sheep and 46% for pigs (Shammas 1990: Table 2.2). The figures in Table 5.15a largely agree with these findings: together, cattle and sheep make up nearly 80% of the total sample, although ownership of pigs is markedly lower in Newcastle than in the region as a whole. Shammas' observations, that inventories in the South are much more likely to record pigs than those in the North, while poultry are in all cases missing or excluded, are also confirmed (1990: 29). Everitt also remarks that pigs are not particularly common in the north (1967: 416). However, Shammas' observations, that ownership of all forms of livestock declines dramatically in urban communities in the early 17th century (1990: Table 2.2, 29-30, 33), echoing Everitt's finding that the percentage of people in the north without cattle rose from 13% to 30% in the early decades between 1610 and 1640 (1967: 417), does not seem to entirely reflect the situation in Newcastle. Table 5.15b indicates that there was initially a rise in ownership at the start of the 17th century, with a decline apparent in the second quarter of the century.

The reasons for the decline in ownership, reflected in a downturn in cow-keeping, together with other livestock holding after 1626, is not clear. Shammas believes that this was related to an increasing population or to rising grain prices (1990: 29), while Everitt believes the determining factors are the diminishing supply of land and population growth (1967: 417). However, if one compares Shammas' figures from towns and cities in the Midlands in the 16th and (especially) the 17th centuries with those from Newcastle, it is apparent that the Newcastle tradesmen retained a much higher percentage of animals than did those in other regions (1990: Table

2.2). For example, the lowest figures from 17th century southern Worcestershire, pertaining to medium and upper wealth groups, show ownership figures under 20% for cows and sheep, and as such are comparable only with the lowest percentage figures for the river and sea trades of Newcastle throughout the study period.

In other regions Shammas, found that sheep-raising was becoming rare in the 17th century, but acknowledges the continued popularity of sheep in the North in the 16th and 17th centuries (1990: 30, 36), a region with extensive pasturing (Everitt 1967: 610). The Newcastle evidence confirms that sheep remained quite common. In the case of pigs, Shammas found that ownership was restricted to the better-off – and indeed most pigs were owned by well-to-do bakers, but poorer trades also continued to list these animals (1990: 36).

Shammas may be correct in her assertion that poor householders retain livestock for longer in the north than elsewhere in the country, but other explanations given for the decline in ownership of livestock are questionable (1990: 41-2). Her suggestion that householders were forced to give up animals in response to changes in household consumption is not corroborated (Shammas 1990: 41-2). In Section 5.3, and in Table 5.3, it is clearly demonstrated that all trades were participating in increasing consumption of household goods, and it seems most unlikely that buying more bedding, for instance, would have led a family to give up their livestock. In other evidence Weatherill's analysis of the accounts from the post-Civil-War period shows consistently high investment figures in livestock relative to other purchases (1996, Tables 6.1, 6.2, 6.3)

Shammas' findings concerning relative wealth and ownership patterns among tradesmen are also not wholly substantiated. Overall, the amalgamated figures for the period show no correlation between the low-wealth trades and ownership patterns as defined by Shammas (1990: Appendix 1), and shown in Table 5.13a. Comparing the percentage of testators listing animals with the average investment levels provides a more useful means of understanding the data.

Butchers were clearly the highest investors, although in interpreting the figures account must be taken of the fact that a handful of these men owned substantially larger herds than others. In terms of the overall investment figure for the combined trades, this is skewed by the butchers, and for purposes of analysis two figures are given, one excluding the butchers. If this trade is removed, the average invested in animals by most trades was just under 4li, although the figure for the bakers at nearly 7li is significantly higher than that for other trades. In cases where a low percentage of testators listed animals, the investment figures can be misleading: for example, few of the wealthy master mariners record animals, thus the investment figure reflects only a few men - one with valuable oxen and others with valuable horses. The same situation applied to the keelmen, mariners and shipwrights, where a minority of men tended to own livestock which were valuable assets, augmenting the figures.

The most obvious pattern of livestock ownership among Newcastle tradesmen unequivocally relates to occupation. In the case of the keelmen - the poorest of all the tradesmen in the study - the low ownership figures are almost certainly related not just to their relative poverty compared with the other trades, but to different investment priorities relating to their trade. This situation can be compared to Everitt's finding for the latter 16th century, where three-quarters of poor farm labourers owned one or two cows (1967: 414), suggesting that income rather than wealth *per se* was the key factor.

The ownership of horses provides a very good example of ownership patterns relating primarily to needs associated with trade and not with wealth. Millers owned the largest numbers of horses, but they were not generally among the wealthiest tradesmen. The expense of horses for milling was mitigated by sharing costs through mutual ownership. Such horses were used at several mills, and the leasing of horses together with mills was quite common (D.P.R Reasley 1611, Story 1636). Further examples of such arrangements can be found among other trades, such as one baker who owned three mill horses 'in Cop[er]tnershipp' (D.P.R. Hoope 1632), and a cordwainer who recorded owning 'the half of two horses & a mare' (D.P.R. Eden 1636). The practice of borrowing plough-animals was also not uncommon generally in the north among farmers (Everitt 1967: 416). Some trades did not, however, share their animals: for instance almost all butchers had horses; some of these men were well-to-do, some were not, but the necessity of travelling to and from the fields to check on herds (and no doubt shepherds as well), which were sometimes kept at distant locations, must be considered a factor in the figures. An example from Whickham underlines the argument that wealth was only part of the explanation for ownership patterns. Although many people had animals in this rural area, poorer cottagers did not buy horses, but better-off copy holders purchased them in increasing numbers despite rising prices at the start of the 17th century. The primary motivating factor in acquiring horses was directly linked to their use with pulling coal wains (Levine and Wrightson 1991: 87, 99). The relative scarcity of horses among tradesmen who would not require them for work can be compared with the master mariner who owned a horse valued at 8li. The man was among the richest in the study and such a horse clearly represented wealth rather than need associated with trade.

In general, it would seem that those involved in provisioning, wool or leather trades are more inclined to acquire animals than are those in the non-food or river and sea trades. However, many men, including nearly 20% of butchers, failed to record any animals at all. Weatherill found that livestock was a very valuable and expensive asset right up to the Civil War (1996: Tables 6.1, 6.2, 6.3). In the 1580s, Harrison wrote that 'In my time a cow hath risen from foure nobles to foure marks' (Furvinal 1877: Part II, 3). The Newcastle evidence, however, indicates that animals were not always expensive and that prices were very dependent on the type and the quality of animal, reflected in wide ranging valuations, and that significant price increases are not apparent in the period. This evidence contradicts Bowden, who found that there was a great increase in the price of livestock in the period between 1500 and 1640 (1967: 604). In Table 5.10b a range of valuations has been traced for cows, oxen, horses, pigs and sheep over three time frames.

Prior to 1600, most cows were, on average, valued at around 1li 10s, with young animals and calves priced as low as 5s and most others costing 10s to 17s each. In this period a very few men had cows worth 2li to 2li 10s. Equivalent valuations were recorded right up to 1625, with the majority of cows still priced between 1li and 1li 10s, with a slightly higher percentage valued at over 2li than had been the case a generation earlier. By 1626 very few young animals were being included in the inventories; but where valuations were recorded, a calf could still be bought for 15s, while about half the cows continued to be appraised at 1li 10s, the same valuation given before 1600. There was, however, a further increase in the overall number of cows valued over 2li, with some now worth 2li 15s. Bowden established that the price of a cow by the early 17th century was c.2li 15s, and that the price of dairy cattle rose by 5% and of calves by 8% between 1585 and 1649 (1967: 604, 647). The Newcastle data confirms that only the most expensive cattle were priced as high as 2li 15s in the final period. Prior to 1600 the most expensive cows had cost as much as 2li 10s. Thus in terms of local price rises, the most expensive cattle showed a 10% increase in the years after 1626, while calves tripled in price if the very lowest valuation of 5s in considered. Overall, however, it seems that an averaged priced cow could be acquired for 1li 10s throughout the decades of this study up to 1642, while the 'Dutch Whye' calf, mentioned above, was worth 1li 13s 4d in 1634, demonstrating that some animals were clearly much more expensive that others. Howell observed a sharp rise in the price of cattle in the second half of the 16th century in Kibworth Harcourt, providing figures of a minimum cost of 13s and the maximum cost of 2li 5s for cows (1983: 267). Such prices are very close to those from Newcastle in this early period. A continual steep rise in the price of livestock up to the Civil War was apparent only for the least expensive animals, according to the Newcastle inventories.

The prices given for horses do not differ significantly from those given for cattle; incidentally, blind horses were just as costly as sighted animals. From the 1550s to 1600, a horse could be purchased for between 13s 4d and 2li 6s 8d, though the majority were valued at between 1li and 1li 10s. In the first quarter of the 17th century, a mare with all her equipment was valued at just 5s, but the majority of horses could still be bought for 1li to 1li 10s, with more expensive horses priced around 2li, and in only one case as high as 3li. By the second quarter of the 17th century, a foal or a small lame horse could be acquired for 10s, marginally less than the cost prior to 1600. In this final period, half the horses continued to be valued from 1li to 1li15s with others priced from 2li to 3li. In an exceptional entry, a master mariner had a horse valued to 8li in 1631, far and away the most expensive animal in the study sample.

A slight trend can be observed towards increasing numbers of more expensive horses. Levine and Wrightson also observed increasing prices for horses in the early 17th century in Whickham (1991: 99). Bowden priced horses at between 2li and 3li in the early 17th century (1967: 621), and Howell observed that mares could cost as much as 3li to 4li in the period up to the Civil War (1983: 267). In comparative evidence from a very large sample of inventories from Hertfordshire, Lincolnshire and Worcestershire, prices from the Newcastle inventories closely follow the mean averages for those counties over the decades of the study (Overton 2000: Figure 6.3, 131). The steep price rises for horses indicated by the *Agrarian History* series (Overton 2000: Figure 6.3), and those suggested by Howell for both cows and horses in other regions, are not evident in Newcastle (1978: 151; 1983: 267).

Oxen were listed on inventories only between 1601 and 1625, and were apparently quite expensive animals. The lowest valuation was for 1li, but another inventory recorded a figure of '9li a yoke' in 1623, a comparable figure to that found in the study of Hertfordshire, Lincolnshire and Worcestershire inventories (Overton 2000: Figure 6.2). Everitt noted that few possessed draught animals (1967: 414). Information on the prices of pigs is limited but most were appraised at between 4s and 6s in all three periods, with one animal worth just 1s in the earliest period. After 1600, some pigs were valued at 8s or 10s. The sample of prices for sheep is also limited, but prices were just as steady as for the other animals: the average cost of a sheep was between 2s and 5s in all periods. In the early 17th century, a price of 1s 6d was calculated for a sheep that was part of a herd, while a single ewe was valued as high as 6s. Sheep were the least expensive animals to acquire (Everitt 1967: 616).

Overall, the prices of animals over the century between the latter 1550s and 1642 did not rise as steeply as has been suggested (Bowden 1967: 604). Prices clearly reflected the quality and, particularly it seems, the age of animals, providing the opportunity for both the less well-off, as well as the wealthy tradesmen to purchase livestock according to their means and needs. Bowden's claim that the increased value of livestock indicated a rise in the numbers of animals being kept, 'not a decline as lamented by a generation of economic historians' (1967: 604), is contradicted by the Newcastle evidence on both valuations and percentage figures.

In considering other explanations for the patterns of ownership, it is not possible to estimate whether the differences or the decline in livestock ownership had anything to do with delayed marriage as suggested by Shammas, as no particular bias has been assumed in the sample (1990: 43). However, the increasing specialisation in trades (Everitt 1967: 432-3, Weatherill 1996: 104), which can be linked to the expansion of the local economy by the 17th century (Howell 1967; Levine and Wrightson 1991: 23-4; Ellis 2001: 9), and the extensive local markets (where better products could perhaps be purchased than could be made at home), provide the most likely explanations for the decline in animal ownership, but only for those trades that did not depend on them for their livelihoods.

5.9 Brewing

Brewing was principally an urban occupation in the early modern period, and Newcastle brewers were particularly well placed to take advantage of the necessity of ale and beer in this prosperous river port, associated with the provision of ships, as well as the local population (Shammas 1990: 31, Overton 2004: 53).

Probate records document the brewing of ale and beer in the town providing information on the type, value and extent of the equipment used in the processes, as well as revealing details about rooms in properties that were used for brewing. The substantial differences in the scale of production between those who brewed commercially and those who produced for the household can also be examined.

The assortment of equipment used in brewing could be quite extensive. The items selected for this analysis were either specifically referred to as 'the brew vessels', or can be clearly identified as such by the description - for example, a 'wort tub'. Many of the wooden and 'stone' (ceramic) tubs, stands, sieves and troughs that were included on inventories may have served several household functions, as well as being used for brewing. However, where it is not clear that the objects were exclusively used for brewing, they have been excluded from the analysis. In most cases such objects, mainly wooden tubs, were valued at only 2d - 8d, and do not therefore markedly alter the overall valuations; however, the number of people who were involved with brewing may have been underestimated as a consequence of the exclusions, particularly perhaps the poorer households with less specialised equipment. Overton found that brewing is prone to under-recording, confirming the problem that households frequently had vessels such as vats, tubs and keeves which could be put to a number of uses (2004: 36). He noted that brewing could be incorrectly identified in his figures for Cornwall and Kent because the vessels could have been used for such other purposes as washing and storage, and thus the high level of brewing he identified could have been an over-estimate (2004: 58-9). In this sample the bias may have been reversed.

The basic equipment listed for either commercial or home brewing included masking tubs, wort tubs and gyle vats for preparing and soaking the grain; and washing tubs, stone troughs, funnels, sieves, buckets and stands or gantries. Brakes were listed for crushing green hops (but these could also have been used for preparing flax or hemp, or as a baker's kneading machine). One must rely on the context to decide the primary function of an object. The beers and ales were stored in casks or 'tuns', firkins, hogsheads and other barrels. 'Tapstones', or stoppers for draining the liquor, possibly in the form of a cylindrical stick, were used to close holes bored into barrels. The occasional inclusion of pairs of 'temes', or chains among the brewing vessels are intriguing, although their function is unclear. Ropes, hooks and slings are also mentioned, and all this equipment may have related to manoeuvring the barrels, although there is an entry by a brewer in 1596 for 'a rope to strike beer' worth 12d.

This simple set-up was substantially augmented by bakers and brewers who, along with a few of other individuals, conducted brewing on a much larger scale, judging by the additional equipment recorded by them, which was not listed by other householders. These individuals owned 'coolers' (vessels designed to cool the wort), pipes for water, 'goats' for channelling water, and multiple 'beer trayes', for which no clear definition has been found. However, it was the investment in 'brew', 'copper' or 'steep' leads, which indicates a clear distinction in the scale of production for sale commercially or for home consumption. Overton recognised this phenomenon in Kent, where it was the commercial brewers who tended to have some specialist brewing equipment (2004: 35). These expensive pieces of equipment were bequeathed in wills and were clearly seen as especially desirable. Sometimes such items were specifically referred to as 'hierloomes of the same house' or as 'belonging to the aforesaid house', indicating that the equipment was attached in some way to the property. The only other equipment listed among the brewing vessels were kiln chimneys and kiln hairs, a cloth on which to dry the grain. This process is described by Harrison (1587), whereby malt was spread on a hair cloth and turned often as it was gently heated until it was dried (Furvinal 1877: 156).

Weatherill found that some households devoted little space to large-scale brewing (1996: 145-6), but such calculations relative to the equipment recorded in individual inventories cannot be recovered from the documentary evidence. However, the documents can be used to identify the location of brewing activities within properties where appraisers have named rooms in the course of taking the inventory. Table 5.11a shows the rooms in Newcastle households where brewing was carried out, although there are certain limitations to be considered.

Because room names are less often provided on the earliest documents (when inventoried items were often simply compiled on a long list), evidence of where the brew vessels were located is slightly skewed in favour of the later inventories, as well as towards those tradesmen with larger houses, where enumeration of rooms was more common (see Table 6.1) (Shammas 1990: 161-3). Occasionally more than one room was used for equipment - as, for instance, when some items were found in the kitchen as well as in the brew house.

References to the 'back house' are sometimes given in place of references to the 'brew house'. Both rooms tend to be included towards the end of the inventories, which suggests that brewing facilities were located towards the rear of properties, as were bake or work houses. Assuming that this was, in fact, the case, the kiln chimneys and kiln hairs were apparently also located towards the rear of the property, as the brew house was also the primary location for grain drying, although upper chambers and lofts were also mentioned.

A 'gyllhouse' with brew vessels and vats is first listed in 1570 by a cordwainer (D.P.R. Robinson), but throughout the 1570s most brew vessels were recorded in kitchens (if the house had such a room), or in halls and chambers. Brew houses begin to appear regularly on inventories from 1580, together with valuable brew leads. On average, about 37% of inventories contained named rooms where brewing equipment was located, although 90% of inventories belonging to bakers and brewers provide this information, 80% of which specify a brew house. The figure is much higher than that for other trades who seldom had special rooms for brewing. Where information on rooms is provided, nearly 60% of the brew vessels were located in a brewhouse and 20% were found in kitchens, with a few other rooms named, probably reflecting the absence of these two rooms in a property. However, over the whole time frame the overall percentage of properties with named brew houses is just over 22%. The figures can be compared with those from Kent, where, in 1600, 6% of households listed a brew house, with the figures rising to 35 - 40% by 1700. The Newcastle figures appear high, and are certainly much greater than those for Cornwall, where only a handful of inventories list brew houses (Overton 2004: 62-3). The low figures for brewing in Cornish inventories may result from the relative poverty of householders who perhaps had very basic multi-functional vessels that were used in whatever space was available in the absence of a brew house (Overton 2004: 63). The situation is probably comparable to that of the keelmen and shipwrights, who list a variety of wooden vessels, and where the percentage of named rooms is very low.

Clearly, brewing activities are more difficult to identify in poorer and smaller homes, whereas more prosperous tradesman employed in large-scale brewing are much easier to recognize, as in the case of bakers and brewers who owned extensive equipment accommodated in brew houses. The type of equipment listed on inventories does not alter over the decades. It seems to have been durable and not often purchased, at least according to evidence from household accounts (Weatherill 1996: 127), as well as the fact that the equipment is treated as an heirloom in a number of wills.

Valuations for brewing vessels provide a means of assessing some of the costs involved with brewing, although appraisers often give a collective valuation for all the relevant equipment. Where prices can be recovered, these are presented in Table 5.11b, covering three time frames. The most expensive pieces of equipment are the brew, copper and steep leads. Although versions of these objects were appraised at around 1li in all decades, other examples were very expensive, with a striking increase in prices in the 1620s, with the highest valuations rising still further in subsequent years. The inventories reveal that three men - two bakers and brewers and a master mariner - were in possession of equipment worth in excess of 30li by this period, indicating increasingly large-scale production. The cost of some steep leads, however, appears to have declined, although the sample is rather small.

Kiln chimneys and kiln hairs were priced both separately and together. Prices for kiln chimneys ranged between 3s 4d and 10s prior to 1600, and then remained at 6s for the duration of the study period. The valuation for kiln hairs prior to 1600 ranged between 3s and 7s and then remained at around 5s to 6s 8d. However, when these objects were priced together, the valuations prior to 1600 were between 4s and 15s 4d, but by the start of the new century prices were rising, with 10s being the lowest valuation recorded in the period 1601 - 1625. After 1626, valuations of between 10s and 1li were recorded, indicating further price rises. At the same time (as Table 5.11b shows) the number of inventories listing these objects was declining over the decades, suggesting changes in where and how malted grain was produced, although the bakers and brewers rarely listed kilns in any decade.

The valuations for the combined masking tubs, gyle vats and wort tubs - which were sometimes listed with stands, shovels or rakes - show slightly different trends. When these objects were appraised together, the price range prior to 1600 was 3s to 6s 8d. In the first quarter of the 17th century, prices were between 2s 6d and 3li, and in the last period the range was between 2s and 1li. The cost of the lower-priced vessels remained steady throughout the whole period, while significant price rises were apparent for high-end valuations of some types of equipment in the 17th century. Overall, it would seem that, although very simple brew vessels continued to be easily purchased, and most wooden tubs can be acquired for as little as 2d, the equipment required for increasingly large-scale production is the preserve of the wealthier investor. Taking the evidence together for both brew houses and expensive specialised equipment (both of which emerge from the 1580s onwards in the hands of the few), a growth in the commercial sector seems to have been taking place, augmenting sharply by the 1620s.

This growth in the scale of brewing appears to coincide with the appearance of hops on the inventories. Overton noted that by the late 16th century, beer made with hops was commonly available in towns and cities (Overton 2004: 59), a finding that is confirmed in the case of Newcastle. Here, hops are first listed on inventories in 1584 and subsequently in all decades thereafter by 30% of the bakers and brewers, but by no other tradesmen. They were stored in cellars, brew houses, upper chambers and lofts, and supplies were occasionally quite extensive. In 1584, one man had one and a half hundredweight of hops worth 20s, kept in a cellar (D.P.R. Berwicke), and in 1596 another listed 1,000 hopes in upper chamber valued at 18s 4d (D.P.R. Peacock).

In evidence from Essex from the 1580s it took a pound and half of hops worth 20d to make 'three hoggesheads of good beere', worth 20s according to Harrison (Furvinal 1877: 158-9). Beer brewing, as opposed to ale making, was more sophisticated and required hops. It was produced on a much larger scale in 'enclosed furnaces', whereas ale was produced with 'basic equipment' in smaller quantities as it deteriorated rapidly with no hops (Overton 2004: 59). Harrison (1587) confirmed that beer 'being well hopped it lasteth longer' and that 'ale that is not hopt, it is thick and soon turns' (Furvinal 1877: 160). The needs of the extensive shipping trade must have been decisive in the growth of beer production in Newcastle, although overall just 3% of inventories actually list hops. In comparison, hops were recorded in fewer than 5% of Kent inventories between 1600 and 1649, whereas Cornwall was very late to adopt beer (Overton 2004: 60 and Table 3.5). Overton's remark that 'Beer was less suited to home production than ale' (2004: 60), is slightly ambiguous, as all brewing, both commercial and domestic, was carried out in rooms attached to a testator's dwelling house. It is clear, however, that only those tradesmen who owned the necessary equipment were able to produce beer rather than ale.

Beer is listed in the documents, mostly by bakers and brewers, together with a handful of other tradesmen, including a master mariner who was probably stocking beer for voyages on his ship. A few brewers had one or two tuns of beer stored in their cellars, 'tun' referring to a large cask. Valuations show one tun of beer priced at 1li 8s in 1584. In 1632 a tun of small (weak) beer cost 1li 10s, but strong beer was appraised at 2li a tun. In 1545 a barrel of beer was 4s, rising to 5s in 1581, and by 1637 half a barrel cost 6s 8d. The slight evidence available is somewhat contradictory, but prices for weak beer (probably referring to ale) were much lower than those for other beers, which had doubled (or in some cases possibly tripled) over the decades. Several wills confirm that beer was valued as it was even bequeathed to friends. Overall, beer is infrequently recorded and it is not possible to determine levels of investment. Whereas commercial brewing was identified within inventories from Kent by the quantity of beer and ale found and from the value of brewing equipment (Overton 2004: 35, 53), the Newcastle documents only provide such clues relating to the extent of equipment. It is possible, however, for substantial quantities of ale to be produced with rather basic equipment. Overton pointed out that 'a tippler or alehouse keeper could make a living from brewing using only the most basic equipment due to the turnover in stock' (2004: 35).

One other clue to the scale of production of beers and ales can be found in the recording of grains that were variously stored in lofts, including 'malt lofts', and upper chambers, back and brew houses, and (in one case) a barn. Inventories list barley, oats, rye, wheat and malted grain. All of these provisions - excepting rye, which was listed in the lowest quantities - were used in brewing, according to Harrison who describes the process and contents of the beer his wife made each month with the help of her maid (Furvinal 1877: 156 - 61). 'Our drinke', he says, was made of barley, water and hops, 'sodden and mingled togither, by the industrie of our bruers, in certeine exact proportions' (1877: 155). Along with the soaked malt, 'headcorne ... sundrie graine, as wheate [and] otes [ground]' were added, along with spices and wheat flour in the last stages (Furvinal 1877: 157-9).

The figures in Table 5.11c show investment in different types of grain represented as percentages, with an average of 35% of inventories listing these provisions. Over half the stores recorded on inventories were malted grain, which, together with barley, made up almost 75% of the grain listed. Every trade except the keelmen and shipwrights listed some malted grain, which correlates to the absence of brewing equipment in named rooms in keelmens' and shipwrights' houses. There is much variability in the scale of grain supplies and, overall, all supplies relating to the making of beer are recorded incidentally, and the valuations reveal not much more than quantities left in the house when the appraisers arrived. Additionally, no account is taken here of seasonal fluctuations in stores, but a similar bias is assumed in all decades, and Harrison confirmed that malt, for example, was available in large towns all year round (Furvinal 1877: 156).

The type of goods used in brewing, their quantity and value are usually sufficient to determine levels of production of beers and ales (Overton 2004: 35); however, a more refined picture can be obtained by separately examining first the average valuations for specialised equipment, second a combination of all types of brewing vessels, and lastly the provisions required for brewing. Table 5.11d shows the average levels of investment, along with the percentage of testators involved with brewing for these three categories. Inventories recording the specialised brew, copper and steep leads required in commercial brewing make up an overall average of 13% of the sample, but 60% of inventories belonging to bakers and brewers listed these objects, with far fewer participants from other trades. The bakers and brewers invested close to 8li in specialised equipment, while the average figure was over 5li, although a single master mariner had 20li worth of brewing copper in 1629, but this was a uniquely high valuation.

When all types of brew vessels are examined together, including the specialised equipment, the figures show that, overall, 44% of testators were involved with brewing on varying scales, with an average level of investment at just over 3li. In comparison, the figures for the bakers and brewers are much higher, with investment levels over four times the average, with at least 80% of these tradesmen participating in production. However, when the high figures for the bakers and brewers are excluded from the calculations, the figures suggest that

38% of Newcastle households were involved with brewing, with an average investment of just 1li 11s. This is not a small sum, and, bearing in mind the fact that an alehouse keeper could make a living from brewing using only the most basic equipment, owing to the turnover in stock (Overton 2004: 35), it seems likely that some tradesmen outside the bakers and brewers were probably producing for the local market. For example, nearly 70% of the weavers had equipment worth over 1li, and three of these men had steep leads.

When provisions are considered, the figures show that investment was about double that for brewing equipment, but only an overall average of 35% of inventories list grain, beer or hops - these stocks were in the hands of a minority of testators, with the bakers and brewers being the exception (as three-quarters of the men listed these provisions). When investment figures for grains (mostly for malt and barley), together with the percentage of inventories with provisions, are compared with the figures for ownership of brew vessels, it would appear that those with both grain and equipment were producing their own beer and ale. Such a conclusion differs from Shammas' finding from 16th century Oxfordshire, where households bought their malt but had their beer brewed elsewhere (1990: 37).

However, when the percentage of testators who did not list equipment or provisions is considered, perhaps 60 - 70% of households were procuring beer and ale on the local markets. Shammas believed that a large portion of those who brewed did so for a living, but she also found that, in cities and towns in the late 16th and early 17th centuries, that the number of inventories with brewing equipment varied widely from 10% to 50% (1990: 31 and Table 2.2). While the Newcastle evidence confirms that 13% of the inventories list specialised equipment for commercial beer production, the extent to which householders with more basic equipment actually brewed for a living is a matter of conjecture. Those c.40% of households with brewing capacity could well have been producing beer or ale to sell to the c.60% of the population without equipment. It is probable, however, that the larger producers of hopped beer dominated the market.

Whether the evidence for an increase in commercial production in Newcastle actually signifies a movement away from home brewing, as observed by Mathias (1983) (Overton 1990: 59), seems unlikely. A late 16th century manuscript on the Revenue of Excise by Rockley (n.d.) confirms that 'all Inhabitants brew for themselves, at least by much the greatest proportion of what they use' (Clark 1919, 1992: 225). Brew vessels continue to be included throughout the study period by all trades, while a decline in the number of kiln chimneys and kiln hairs was observed, suggesting that fewer tradesmen were drying and preparing their own malted grain (Table 5.11c).

One final question can be asked of the evidence for brewing, and that is whether wealth influenced who was involved with the trade. In evidence from 16th century Oxfordshire, brewing was undertaken by less than 10% of low-wealth groups in towns, whereas medium- and high-wealth groups show a figure of 41%; in contrast, by the later 17th century, brewing was virtually absent in all urban southern Worcestershire inventories, with only 4% of the medium- to high-wealth groups represented (Shammas 1990: Table 2.3). In comparing Shammas' figures of total inventoried wealth (1990 Appendix 1: 304), with the amalgamated investment totals for all occupations shown in Table 5.13a, no correlation can be established between participation in production of ale and beer and overall wealth. For example, nearly 70% of weavers, who were not among the wealthiest tradesmen, were involved with brewing, whereas the percentage of poor keelmen involved with brewing was, indeed, low. The percentage of the wealthy master mariners partaking in the activity was also less than that of several trades who were much poorer on average than any of these men.

It was those tradesmen who owned the most extensive specialised equipment, principally the bakers and brewers, who dominated production of beer. Some testators may not have had the means or resources to brew either for the household or for the market, although as the basic equipment did not require much investment, the process was well within the reach of most tradesmen who might choose to involve themselves in the activity.

Occupation was the most important factor relating to brewing, and this fact leads to the question of who actually undertook the work of brewing, which was not wholly the 'servile trade' described by Harrison (Furvinal 1877: 156). Although production was seen as lying within a woman's sphere in the early modern period (Weatherill 1996: 138; Overton 2004: 78), large-scale drink production was a male or mixed occupation (Overton 2004: 38). Clark points out that the position of wives in this trade did not materially differ from that in other trades; although the trade was once 'chiefly, if not entirely, in the hands of women,' their legal right to brew was being eroded after the Act of 1574 - which sought to separate brewing from the sale of beer, with the object of simplifying the collection of taxes (1919, 1992: 221, 223). However, private brewing was not subject to the excise until 1643 (Overton 2004: 60). Attempts to establish a gender divide between the male professionals producing hopped beer primarily for the market, probably with the assistance of members of the household, and the brewsters who carried on the tradition of household ale production, some of which was perhaps sold locally, are clearly problematic. Beer and ale was a staple, described by Harrison as 'excellently well tasted, but strong, and what soon fuddles' (Furvinal 1877: Lxxxiv), and according to Clark both were 'drunk at every meal, and formed part of the ordinary diet of even small children' (1919, 1992: 223).

Trade

5.10 Introduction: Objects of the trades

So far, this chapter has focused primarily on objects associated with the material culture of domestic and household production and consumption. In this section, attention shifts to the objects associated with the tradesmen's named occupations. Investment in tools of a trade, the supplies required to make or to repair objects, and the valuations for wares sold in local shops are analysed. The selection of objects represents only those directly associated with a specialised named occupation. Brew vessels and livestock have been included in the figures where they are deemed essential to the testator's principal trade, as in the case of bakers and brewers, butchers and millers, respectively. Ships or boats recorded by trades who either owned or constructed vessels are included in the analysis. However, vessels recorded by other trades, and all other contributions to the household wealth from activities deemed as by-employment, including spinning, have been excluded from this section. Provisions are also omitted here as these were subject to daily variability, and what is listed is residual (Shammas 1990: 111, 121). It is acknowledged that tradesmen of a given occupation were often involved in procuring income from a great variety of additional sources (Spufford 1990: 144; Levine and Wrightson 1991: 223; Overton 2004: 10, 65), but by concentrating on only those items directly associated with the practice of a named occupation, a more accurate account of production and consumption surrounding the specialised trades can be recovered. Contributions from by-employment are analysed, together with all other objects so far reviewed, in the final conclusion.

Table 5.12a shows the average levels of investment made by testators in running their businesses. The valuations are divided into five categories in an attempt to assess where priorities lay within different occupations. All references to average figures in the following sections pertain to this table. A lack of innovation is apparent in relation to these objects, which hardly alter over the decades of the study. Because of the volume of objects associated with the various trades, an overview of all tools or equipment, personal gear, supplies, wares, and boats and ships listed in the inventories dated between the 1550s and 1642 is given in Appendix 7. Objects associated with each trade will be reviewed in turn.

5.10.1 Bakers and brewers

The brewers, as already described, owned expensive brewing equipment. These men invested almost five times the sums in this kind of equipment compared to those producing beer for the household (Table 5.11d). In sharp contrast, investment in baking gear was minimal and, where prices of objects were recorded, these remained low throughout the study period. For instance, in 1596 a valuation for a moulding board, trough and brake was 7s 6d, and in 1637 the valuation for a kneading chest, moulding board, coal rake, peel and rolling pins was 6s 8d; prices for single brakes show one valued at 1s 6d in 1596, with the same valuation given 21 years later in 1619; and, in 1628, a brake, three tubs and a peel were priced at just 2s. It appears that, whereas investment in brewing equipment continued to rise, this was not the case for baking gear, although additional equipment such as a baking oven is never recorded, as such items were considered to be part of the real property, and baking can be identified only by such items as moulding boards and peels (Shammas 1990: 27; Overton 2004: 58). Many of the items listed among the cooking implements may have been solely used for domestic purposes, thus the total investment for the trade may be underestimated, especially if ovens and fuel costs are considered, as well as stocks of provisions and livestock (points taken up in the conclusion). Procurement of livestock was second only to butchers, and stocks of provisions were significantly higher among bakers and brewers than other trades (see Tables 5.10a and 5.13a).

Weatherill divided bakers and brewers into two separate occupations, with bakers designated as low status, and brewers as intermediate status trades based on wealth (1996: 99, Table 8.1, Appendix 2). The occupations of baker and brewer were practised simultaneously in Newcastle in the early modern period, although in documents dating between 1545 and 1587, both testators and appraisers refer only to bakers, but all the surviving inventories from these dates (as well as one will), include brewing equipment and even brew houses, confirming that the men practised both trades. In all documents dated after 1587, the occupation is referred to as 'baker and brewer' - with one exception from 1627, where the man refers to himself as a 'beer brewer', as do the appraisers. In this case, the inventory lists a brake, tubs and importantly a peel (to remove bread from an oven), as well as very extensive brewing equipment (D.P.R. Taylor).

5.10.2 Butchers

Butchers required minimal investment in tools for butchering, which consisted mainly of cutting implements, weigh scales and tubs or baskets. Valuations remained low for all this type of equipment over 70-odd years, where records survive. In an inventory from 1558, axes, knives, ropes and hooks for carcasses in a shop '& all that appertayning to yt' were valued at 10s. In documents dated between 1601 and 1623, valuations for such assemblages ranged from 3s 4d to 16s and, by 1629, equipment including axes, knives, tubs, baskets and platters of wood and ceramic were valued at just 3s 6d. There is some evidence that shop aprons or 'working days apparel' was worn. The fairly low investment in basic shop tools can be compared with the hefty investment in livestock, which was five times the average (Table 5.10a), and with investment in stocks of provisions, which was also higher than for any other trade (Table 5.13a).

5.10.3 Cordwainers

Evidence for investment patterns for cordwainers is quite complex, as these men had tools for cutting leather and shaping footwear; supplies such as tallow, rosin, pitch and oil to treat a wide range of hides; and stocks of ready-made footwear. Tools, which did not change over the decades and which were usually referred to as the 'working gear belonging to the shop', required the lowest investment; however, where data are available, costs were rising. Valuations ranged from 3s 4d prior to 1600 to over 2li by the early decades of the 17th century, with some shops much more expensively equipped than others. Supplies required the highest investment; however, as shown in Table 5.12b, valuations of products to treat leather remained fairly stable, especially the price of tallow which rose by only 2d a stone between 1553 and 1642. Hides from cattle, horses and sheep of different ages were treated in different ways, including those that were tanned, 'liquored' and 'unliquored'. Valuations for hides remained stable at around 8s to 9s between 1553 and 1625, after which prices ranged from 10s to 2li, indicating substantial increases in the second quarter of the 17th century.

Evidence for footwear in the inventories is fairly extensive, and includes models for men, women and children, as well as single- or double-soled shoes, 'pantofels' (slippers) and wooden-heeled shoes, variously described as pumps, 'sloopes', 'stowpe shoes' and 'falling shoes'. Boots were appraised separately. About 15 designs of footwear are described, including 'dry' leather shoes and 'wet' leather shoes. Table 5.12b confirms that boots were most expensive. Prior to 1600, a pair cost between 1s 9d and 2s 4d and this rose to between 2s 10d and 5s a pair after 1626. The costliness of boots was noted by Shammas, who found that labourers had difficulty in purchasing them in this period (1990: 199). Some boots were even more expensive than the shop prices suggest, as one mariner had a pair among his sea-clothes worth 6s second-hand in 1618. It seems that the price of all shoes was increasing: that of women's shoes rose from 7d - 8d prior to 1600 to between 10d and 1s by the beginning of the 17th century, and that of men's shoes rose from 1s 2d to 1s 8d over the same period. The price of children's shoes can be traced over three periods: prior to 1600, these cost 3d a pair, rising to 8d a pair between 1600 and 1625, with another rise to 10d a pair after 1626, indicating a tripling of prices in less than a generation. Heeled shoes, incidentally, were among the more expensive models, ranging from 1s 4d in the earliest period to 2s 8d by the early 17th century. The great variety of shoes available in the town can be contrasted with Spufford's finding that chapmen, even by the early decades of the 18th century, rarely carried slippers, though these were priced at only 3d a pair, suggesting some shoes, like clothing, may have become less expensive (1984: 94).

Shammas has described cordwainers as a 'low-paying craft' (1990: 34-6), an observation that does not reflect the apparent profitability of the occupation in Newcastle. There were certainly clear differences in wealth between these tradesmen, evidenced most by the differences in the scale of supplies and footwear accumulated. But contrary to Shammas' findings, cordwainers do not appear to have taken up residency with families in order to make or repair shoes, nor to have had to await orders, owing to the substantial expenditure of time and money necessary to create a finished product (1990: 199-200). Instead, the inventory evidence shows that over half the tradesmen had their own shops, well stocked with shoes and boots, and that stocks of ready-made footwear ranged from 30 or so pairs to almost 200 – and, in one case, to over 300 pairs listed in a shop on Middle Street as early as 1587 (D.P.R. Spoore). Overall, investment in tools was minimal, with the greatest investment relating to stocks of leather, which was about double that of ready-made footwear.

5.10.4 Keelmen

Information on keelmen is very limited, as only two wills and three inventories, all dated to before 1600, list boats and objects connected with the trade. The documents describe vessels as 'lightners' (lighters), 'clinker lightners' and 'cavalier lightners', and some of these were, according to the limited evidence, quite elaborately equipped with masts and sails, rudders and 'schelts' (poles), as well as oars and anchors. Planks of wood were listed, apparently used to board-out spaces in order to accommodate loads. Some keelmen may have repaired their vessels, as a few woodworking tools, nails and pitch were listed. The value of these supplies was a fraction of the value of the boats themselves. The relative absence of boats in inventories suggests that perhaps a majority of keelmen were not financially in the position to own vessels themselves. As described below, shipwrights owned more of these vessels than keelmen, according to the documentary evidence. The valuations given to vessels differ hugely: in the decades between the 1550s and 1580s, prices ranged between 3li and 3li 6s 8d; however, in 1592, a fully equipped 'clinker lightner' with all the gear mentioned above was valued at 24li. Some vessels were also owned cooperatively, as evidenced by an entry in 1592 for '1/2 a kurvell lightner' valued at 10li, while the half of another lightner was valued at only 1li 5s in 1594. Even 'an old boat lying on the key', worth only 2s, was included on the inventory of one keelman. The relative poverty of most of these tradesmen is clearly reflected in the slight evidence gleaned from these records, and the picture contrasts sharply with later evidence from 18th century probate records, which suggests that keelmen owned their own keels, as well as shares in a number of ships (Ellis 2001: 12-13). In the later decades of the 16th century, few keelmen owned their own boats, although some men invested in a half-share, but no keelmen recorded owning shares in ships.

5.10.5 Mariners

Tremendous diversity in equipment is the most notable feature of the inventoried objects of mariners relating to their seafaring lives. Investment among the majority of mariners was reflected in 'sea clothes', sometimes stored in 'sea chests', together with silver whistles on silver chains, items of significant value recorded only by these men, master mariners and a few shipwrights. Price per ounce of silver content is given in two inventories, with one whistle valued at 13s 4d and the other at 1li 10s; however, as most were bequeathed to sons on wills few valuations are recorded. These whistles were in quite another category to the those sold by chapmen in the later 17th century which retailed at 5d a dozen in 1680 (Spufford 1984: 94). Various nautical instruments are also recorded, listed together with maps and books (which have been excluded here, but included in the figures for books in section 5.6). A few men owned tools, apparently to repair rather than construct ships, while just two of the 19 mariners whose inventories survive had invested shares in ships (Appendix 8).

The valuations for 'sea clothes', where these were separately appraised, were apparently much lower than those for other apparel. Nautical instruments were listed by several mariners and this specialised equipment was not especially costly. For example, in 1587, two compasses were listed together with over 20 woodworking tools valued at 9s, whereas in 1608 a map and pair of compasses was valued at 2s 6d. In 1597 an astrolabe was valued at 2s, as was a 'dyall for sonne & moone with a case'. By 1621 two little old star globes without a frame were valued at 10s. In comparison, a whip 'appertaining to the office of a boatesman' was valued at 2s in 1618. The valuations for woodworking tools were low, and the equipment recorded by mariners was much less extensive than that of the shipwrights, with just one man listing pitch and timber. The average investment figure for the trade is buoyed up by the significant investment of the two mariners who owned shares in ships totalling almost 100li.

5.10.6 Master mariners

The master mariners invested very substantial sums in objects related to their profession. At sea, these men apparently attired themselves in 'sea apparel' and not in the expensive clothes they wore on land (Section 5.4), though only 'sea gowns' are specifically described, and this clothing was, like that of the mariners, less valuable than land apparel; however, few details providing separate valuations are recorded. These men also invested heavily in silver whistles with silver chains which were, as in the case of mariners, frequently bequeathed in wills, although these versions were more expensive than those listed by the mariners. Valuations reflecting silver content averaged between 3li and 5li, though some men had smaller, cheaper versions. Nautical instruments were recorded (besides the maps and books described in section 5.6), and included cross-staffs, globes, compasses and hour-glasses, as well as unspecified 'instruments of the sea', but separate valuations are rare. A pair of compasses with a book and a cross-staff were valued at 5s in 1587, while a collection of non-itemised instruments, a compass and a map were priced at 1li 5s 8d in 1599. Master mariners did not list tools used to actually construct ships, but they did record fittings and supplies such as masts, pumps, pitch, rosin and tar, and hardware, such as bolts of canvas for sails, cables, ropes, buoys, flags, oars, and anchors. Overall, such items did not account for as substantial a part of investment as personal gear; however, by far the largest investments, overall, were made in the shares the men owned in ships and in the cargoes the vessels carried. Of those master mariners who recorded objects of the trade, 90% owned shares in ships.

Some change in patterns of ownership is evident as the size of shares invested in ships appears to alter over the decades in favour of strategies that spread risks (Appendix 8). Prior to 1600, percentage figures for shares were larger than in later decades, with the clear majority ranging between 25% and 100% of a given vessel. By the early decades of the 17th century, shares ranged between 1/32 and one-quarter. Valuations may have risen as percentage figures of ownership declined. A ship's burden, however, was rarely recorded, and it is difficult to judge whether the cargoes were progressively becoming more valuable. A trend picked up in evidence from the mid-18th century, whereby many investors 'hedged their bets by buying small shares in a large number of vessels' clearly began at a much earlier stage than has been suggested (Ville 1989: 210-3; Ellis 2001: 2).

5.10.7 Millers

Little information survives about objects related to the miller's trade, and most is dated prior to 1613, although almost 90% of these tradesmen record mills. Two documents confirm that millers wore work clothes, in one case described as a 'White Suite ... being my Work Dayes Apperill', complete with a white hat (D.P.R. Huntrish 1613). In a will dated 1585, the testator describes his daughter's 'workeday ranmente', which suggests that other family members involved in milling also wore a particular type of clothing suited to the trade (D.P.R. Grey). Equipment listed in the records included tools for processing flax and hemp, measuring implements for grain, shovels and ropes, basic woodworking tools, and especially gear for horses (notably, harnesses to link animals to the mill). Sails for a mill and a mill stone are also mentioned. None of these objects were expensive, with most ranging from 1s to 4s and others valued at a few pence. Neither the types of equipment nor the valuations altered significantly over the decades. Investment in horses, as discussed in section 5.8, was substantial, whereas millers (unlike bakers and butchers) did not, apparently, have large stocks of provisions (Table 5.13a).

5.10.8 Shipwrights

Shipwrights diversified investment into several areas of their trade. Although only one man described 'working sea cloths' in 1604, several shipwrights owned silver whistles and chains, similar to those listed by mariners and master mariners, and valued from just under 1li to over 3li (again depending on weight), indicating that some shipwrights spent time at sea. One relatively poor shipwright was, in fact, owed 'waidges from the East Country' suggesting that he worked somewhere in the Baltic region (D.P.R. Carnaby 1622). Almost every shipwright owned his own tools. More than 30 types were found in the inventories and almost all were given collective valuations that averaged about 1li in all decades of the study. One shipwright listed buntings, spars, lime for mortar '& other materials for repairing erecting & building of a messuage or tenement' (D.P.R. Colyer 1642), confirming that some individuals were also building houses. In Chapter 4 it was noted that the shipwrights owned multiple properties, especially in Sandgate.

Supplies of many different sorts of wood (some prepared into planking), and trees, including oaks, are listed, together with tar and pitch, and many types of nails and specialised bolts. Some men invested very large sums in these supplies. There is evidence of a trend towards greater investment in timber over the decades. Inventories include references to trees that were 'standing' and to 'sown stock', as well as to 'lying' (fallen) and even 'rotten' trees. At the beginning of the 18th century, Defoe described the large scale importation of timber from Scandinavia (Ellis 2001: 10); however, in the early 17th century, supplies were grown near Newcastle in such places as Denton Wood, Blaydon, Swalwell, Sketer Bank, Lopehaugh, Lemington Point, Stammer Heads and Chopwell Woods (Chaytor 1980:31), all located on or quite near the River Tyne. Some timber was growing in fields or on hills named after the landowner. Wood was also stocked in and around Sandgate, on the Newcastle quay, and on the 'Middle key', just beside the Sandgate Gate. Entries such as 'old timber lying upon John Colyers kast key' and 'Roland Steels key' confirm private ownership of quays in Sandgate that were sturdy enough to support substantial stocks of timber (D.P.R. Colyer 1642).

Valuations for stocks varied hugely, with one man owning timber worth only 2s 8d in 1622, whereas another had interests worth more than 50li in 1642. Large stocks of hardware for boats and ships were also recorded, including anchors, two sizes of masts, and four types of sailcloth – notably, harden and linen, either bleached or unbleached. Shipwrights also invested in boats and ships. There are references to lightners, keel boats, old boats, great boats, and to two- and five-chalder boats (denoting weight carried in coal). Valuations varied, as seen, for example, in the case of a lightner priced at 27li in 1585 (a greater figure than that given to a similar boat belonging to a keelman in 1592), whereas a two-chalder boat was valued at only 3li in 1604 and a five-chalder boat was worth 15li in 1624. Half of an old boat valued at 9s was worth recording in 1633. Joint ownership of small vessels was clearly an option for shipwrights, as was the case for keelmen; 40% of shipwrights had also bought shares in large ships, but all were dated prior to 1604. After this date, shipwrights appear to have invested in timber rather than ships, while retaining ownership of the smaller river vessels throughout the period - an observation that may be relevant to the apparent demise of ownership of small boats among the keelmen. The price of timber was also rising in the 17th century, probably associated with the rising demand for houses and ships, and timber shortages (Bowden 1967: 607; Shammas 1990: 295).

Howell makes several assertions regarding shipwrights, one being that the amount of shipbuilding on the Tyne before 1640 is entirely a matter of conjecture, and that little can be said about the construction of small ships since these could be built by any competent carpenter (1967: 285). Such statements seem exaggerated in view of the inventory evidence, which sheds some light on both the scale of shipbuilding and the specialised nature of the trade. The particular tools and numerous supplies belonging to the tradesmen were not recorded by any other trade. This evidence should be considered alongside the river vessels listed by the shipwrights, and the impressive list of over 60 ships recorded in the total sample of documents, the names of which are listed in Appendix 8. Howell says that 'There were a number of shipwrights in the town before 1640 and a dry-dock was begun in Newcastle in 1641', but believes that any genuine expansion of the trade would appear only as a result of government contracts in the early 1650s (1967: 286). These observations ignore the need for ships in the massively expanding coal trade already evident by the late 16th century (Nef 1932; Ellis 1984; Levine and Wrightson 1991), and the records of the 30 shipwrights in this study, which suggest that the trade was a well-developed and dominant force in Sandgate from at least the early 1600s, judging by the scale of activities evident from the documents.

5.10.9 Skinners and glovers

Quite extensive information has been recorded in the documents belonging to skinners and glovers, relating to three areas of investment. The basic tools listed by the trade include implements to cut, shape and sew articles; scales with weights, probably used to weigh wool or even bark; and a variety of tubs, including an alum tub listed in 1634. Investment in this equipment is small: for example, a pair of shears are valued at 2s in 1588, with entries for all 'workgear' valued to the same figure in the 1620s. Supplies include skins from calves, sheep and lambs, and the pelts of unspecified animals. Leather is described as rough, wrought, wet and 'allomed'. 'Cheverel' or kid leather, white leather, ribbons and laces are mentioned, along with a selection of wool, described as fine, coarse, small and second sort, some dyed black or blue, together with substantial stocks of harden, linen and wool cloth. Not every skinner and glover had the same types or quantities of supplies, indicating differences in what individuals produced. Valuations for supplies are shown in Table 5.12b and, although there are gaps in the records, some trends can be identified. Wool, priced per stone, was becoming more expensive, although the variation in quality must be accounted for. The price of pelts and sheep skins tripled over the time frame, rising from 0.5d to 1.5d, with increases in valuations seen in all other types of leather as well. Supplies accounted for by far the largest percentage of investments.

The wares included in inventories comprise gloves and various bags and purses. Of the two documents that record gloves, only one provides a price of 1d a pair in 1616, but the tradesman had 200 pairs in stock. Purses and bags were listed by more tradesmen, and prices were equally low and do not seem to have risen, in contrast to the prices of supplies. Most of these articles could be purchased for 1d to 2d depending on size. Stocks could be very extensive, but the overall average investment was about one-tenth of that indicated for supplies. There were, however, very large discrepancies in the scale of businesses, with one inventory from 1616 listing hundreds of gloves and purses, as well as over 1,000 hides and very large stocks of wool. In 1635, another tradesman listed over 1,000 'allomed' hides, together with other leather, and hundreds of animal pelts. A growth in the scale of businesses is apparent among a small minority of individuals by the 17th century, but the majority of tradesmen invested more modestly. Weatherill accorded skinners a much higher status than glovers, based on income (1996: 99 and Table 8.1), but such an occupational divide is not apparent in the Newcastle sample, although some tradesmen claimed one or other occupation. One of the wealthiest tradesmen cited above described himself as a glover, whereas the second very wealthy man claimed both occupations. Most inventories list both skins and hides, as well as bags and purses, while very few documents list gloves.

5.10.10 Smiths

Almost every smith listed objects of the trade, and investment in businesses was diverse. More tools were recorded by smiths than by any other trade, and many were unique to the occupation. Some imported tools, such as Danish hatchets and Flemish weighing beams, are mentioned. Valuations for tools, depending on the specific type, show a steady increase over the decades, with the majority of smiths investing from 2li up to 7li. The most expensive equipment were bellows and anvils (referred to as studies or stothies), and these were often given away in wills, a similar practice to that of bequests of expensive brewing equipment.

Wide discrepancies in wealth between these tradesmen are apparent, related to the type of business pursued, which seems to have specialised in two directions in some instances. The majority of smiths produced items such as nails, bolts and horseshoes, agricultural implements, and bill staves (which may have had a military function), and these tradesmen were on average less well-off than those who supplied ships, notably with anchors, stakes and chains. Evidence for production of agricultural implements disappears in the second quarter of the 17th century, whereas supplies for horses, the building trades and for ships continue over the decades, with well stocked shops selling assorted wares, including one with a window display in Sandgate. Differences in wealth are also reflected in the accumulation of large stocks of iron, some described as English or Spanish, or as coming from Denmark. Newcastle's iron market was located in the centre of the town near St. Nicholas church and marked on Corbridge's map (Map 4.16), although as noted in Chapter 4, no smith records operating a shop near this market.

The inventory evidence suggests that the production of steel and iron, and the demand for tools, nails and bolts, anchors and chains, etc., was growing by the early decades of the 17th century, and the market was well established by the time that Ambrose Crowley's ironworks was flourishing in the late 17th century (Ellis 2001: 8). However, the two wealthiest men in the sample, who described themselves as anchorsmiths, were the only members of the trade who owned shares in ships. One man, Edward Lawson, owned shares at 18 ships valued at 1085li (D.P.R. 1641).

5.10.11 Tailors

The occupation of tailor involved very little investment in tools and related equipment. Inventories list shears and pinking shears (1581), pressing or smoothing irons, and shop boards and chests, valued collectively at between 2s 6d and 4s in all decades. Only one tailor appeared to have made a living from spinning, as he owned six spinning wheels, while no other tools were listed on his inventory (Section 5.7). Overton found that tailors were hard to identify, as all that was needed for the trade were scissors, a smoothing iron, cloth, needle and thread - items that were not specific to tailoring (2004: 35). However, items such as shears, smoothing irons, and shop boards are not mentioned in the inventories of other Newcastle tradesmen, and the basic equipment was carefully itemised together, sometimes noted as being in a shop.

Supplies of linen and harden cloth and spun yarn are included in some inventories, but quantities tended to be small, averaging a value of under 1li, with most testators owning much less. The price of linen could be traced, with a yard of cloth of unknown quality valued at 4.5d a yard in 1549, rising to 9d a yard by the 1620s. Such valuations are lower than those from 1641 for 'huswife cloath', a linen that cost 14d a yard, or exceedingly good quality linen that cost 16d to 17d a yard, or 2s for even higher grades (Shammas 1990: 200). Few tradesmen, however, listed any supplies.

Data on the trade are limited, but the evidence suggests that several tailors worked in shops within the town. Shammas' finding, that tailors went to live with families when making and repairing articles of dress (1990: 200), was possible in the case of men who did not own shops, but inventories suggest that individuals without shops used halls and chambers within their homes as places of work, evidenced by the presence of shop boards and shop chests. Such business premises are attested to by the maps showing that tailors lived in busy parts of the town, where custom could be most easily procured (see Chapter 4, Map 4.11).

5.10.12 Tanners

Inventories that survive for tanners provide little information about the types of tools used by the tradesmen, as these were described as 'all the workgeare' or 'the rest of the work tools', with valuations ranging from just over 1s to just over 4s over the decades of the study. A rise in costs is indicated. Some details were recorded about tanning and bark vats and tubs. 'Lecks' (slabs of stone used to line tanning vats) and clap-boards to create vats are mentioned. Valuations for such objects are minimal, but under-recording must be considered, as lime pits are listed separately, along with bark and tan houses which, no doubt, contained vats; however, as these were considered part of the real property, they were not included on the inventory (Spufford 1990: 142; Erickson 2002: 23-7). The most significant investment included in the records reflects the wide range of hides and skins owned by the tradesmen. These were more extensive than those for skinners and glovers, and included hides of horses, oxen and cattle of differing age, including calves. References to white cow hides and veal hides indicate production of fine quality leather. There were early references to 'blacks', which may mean black hides, and to 'sole hides', clearly designated for shoemaking. Skins of sheep and lambs, as well as 'mortes' (the skins of dead sheep and lambs), were listed along with steckleather (hides with the hair still attached). 'Everleather' was listed in 16th century documents, a reference to pig skins ('ever' being the Saxon word for wild boar, an interesting linguistic survival). 'Lork', hair shorn from hides, was itemised, possibly being sold on to the building trades.

Stocks of leather were sometimes extensive, calculated by the 'daker' (ten hides), 'shiftes' or 'blocks'. Individual valuations for items are difficult to recover, as most appraisers provided a single valuation for all stocks. Prices can be recovered to an extent for bark vats, which remained around 3s 4d, and for calf skins, which remained at 6d each for the period 1560 - 1620. There is some indication that horse skins may have declined in price. Changes to the trade are not apparent, according to the documentary evidence. Levels of wealth among the tradesmen differed hugely, based on an individual's ability to stockpile hides and skins; and those that could do this are among the wealthiest tradesmen in the sample.

5.10.13 Weavers

Over 90% of records pertaining to weavers list different types of looms, as well as supplies of cloth and yarn. As early as the 1560s and 70s, woollen and linen looms with separate harden gears are recorded, with the first coverlet loom appearing in 1623. The documents confirm that looms had multiple gears of different sizes, which were interchanged for different yarns - notably wool, harden and linen – as, for example, in the case of one weaver who, in 1580, had 21 different gears for both linen and harden fibres. The types of looms listed in the Newcastle records suggest local specialisation, just as demonstrated by the kersey looms of Cornwall or the broad looms of the Weald of the early 17th century (Overton 2004: 49). A clear majority of Newcastle weavers worked linen looms, which were common at a much earlier date than in Kent (Overton 2004: 49).

Most Newcastle weavers owned two or more looms, according to details provided in both wills and inventories dated from the 1570s, with the number rising in the 1620s, when several weavers recorded between three and five looms in their workhouses. The number of looms is not always specified, but where this information is provided 60% of weavers had more than two looms prior to 1600, 100% between 1611 and 1625, and 75% between 1626 and 1641, suggesting similar figures to those from 17th century Kent, but much higher figures than were evident in Cornwall (Overton 2004: 47). Limited information in wills suggests that each loom was worked by an individual. For example, one weaver bequeathed 'the loom I work upon' to one of his sons, while a second son was bequeathed the 'loom that he works on' (D.P.R. Chaitor 1577). Looms and other work-related gear were frequently bequeathed in wills in all decades.

The looms were listed together with an assortment of other associated equipment, as well as stools. Valuations remained at around 5s for a loom from the 1570s to 1640, with more expensive coverlet looms valued at 10s. However, valuations were often given for 'all the work gear' and the number of looms is not always specified. By the 1620s, a few inventories record work gear in workhouses worth up to 10li, and looms worth between 3li and 5li, suggesting that either production was expanding or that increasingly expensive equipment was becoming available. One inventory from 1611 lists 'work dayes apparel', suggesting that some weavers, similar to tradesmen in other occupations, donned a particular type of clothing for work. Average investment over all decades was 1.62li (Table 5.12a), but the figure was closer to 1li before 1600. By the 1620s, a growing disparity in wealth between weavers is evident, with some tradesmen investing in more extensive equipment housed in workhouses, whereas most weavers continued to invest about 1li or even less as the decades of the 17th century progressed, and these men generally continued to work in chambers within their houses.

Cloth and yarn, including straken, harden, hemp, wool, linsey-woolsey and bleached and unbleached linen are listed. In 1631, silk is recorded in the inventory of the only silk weaver among the sample. This man owed 391li to a merchant in London for items that included silk ribbons, suggesting he was importing ready-made wares as well as producing items locally (D.P.R. Littlepaige). A more extensive range of fabrics was apparently being woven than is evident from descriptions of the types of looms, but the quantities of most of these supplies (especially yarn), were not extensive, as was found to be the case in inventory evidence from Kent and Cornwall (Overton 2004: 47). Only about half the weavers stockpiled any yarn or cloth. Valuations are difficult to assess, as items were appraised together, but prices for linen and harden can be traced. Linen was priced at about 7d a yard in the 1570s and 80s, rising to 12d a yard in the 1620s, slightly higher figures than quoted in the inventories belonging to tailors. But prices remained steady up to 1640, and are lower than those found elsewhere in this period (Shammas 1990: 200). Fewer than 10% of inventories actually listed flax, but quantities were small, and Newcastle weavers do not record smallholdings where they might cultivate their own flax, as was found to be the case in Kent (Overton 2004: 50). One weaver noted that his harden was 'att the weaver' suggesting that processing fibres was sometimes undertaken by specialists within the trade (D.P.R. Woodman 1636), as was the case with the production of yarn (Overton 2004: 47), although the wealthy silk weaver, above, recorded 22lb of hemp among his expensive wares.

Looms are not found in inventories of other trades, as has occasionally been noted elsewhere (Shammas 1990: 27), nor were the wealthy clothier-weavers represented among the Newcastle records (Overton 2004: 49). There were, however, exceptionally well-off weavers, such as Oswald Chaitor, who in 1623 had over 100 yards of cloth stored in his study and a workhouse with 10li worth of unspecified equipment, and whose total inventory was valued at over 460li (D.P.R.), and the silk weaver whose estate was valued at over 600li before his debts were paid (D.P.R. Littlepaige 1631). However, these were exceptionally wealthy men in a trade where most weavers operated on a much more modest scale.

5.10.14 Conclusion: Objects of the trades

Overton noted the significant detail that inventories can provide in identifying production activities (2004: 34). Such activities are certainly evident in the Newcastle records. However, investment trends within individual occupations are more difficult to follow.

There are significant discrepancies in total valuations of trade objects on inventories within any given trade. Some men were apparently running much more successful businesses than others within the same guild or by-trade. Life-cycle factors should perhaps be considered as one explanation for such discrepancies in terms of what was recorded, if, for instance, a man had given up working owing to age or illness. The wills and inventories, however, suggest that testators and their families did not dispose of the objects of the trade until death was imminent, finally giving away key work-related objects in wills to sons or other closely related males, and handing over shops and businesses as going concerns to wives and children, or other relatives (Chapter 3). An idle retirement was not, apparently, a reality for these tradesmen, nor was there any evidence of a move to join the ranks of the gentry upon selling a business as suggested by Earle, who also projected a descent into poverty as the inevitable result of everything being given away to the children at the end of a career (1994:151). Timely bequests appear to be the most common initiative taken by Newcastle tradesmen as death approached (see Chapter 3), reflected in the relatively high percentage of documents containing work-related objects (Table 5.12a). Where discrepancies occur in inventoried wealth, this is apparently a reflection of relative fortunes in business over a life time.

The inventories reveal that such discrepancies in the scale of businesses were growing significantly over the decades in several sectors, and success was not restricted to the dealing sectors as suggested by Weatherill (1996: Appendix 2, A2.3). By examining overall trends, significant differences in the fortunes of individual craft activities can be masked (Overton 2004: 56); the detailed analysis given here therefore provides a more accurate account. Most tradesmen could apparently afford to buy their basic tools of the trade, but it was the ability to accumulate supplies or stocks, or to run a successful shop, that made the fortunes of individuals so disparate. Weatherill noted that people engaged nominally in the same trade might have very different incomes; she cited different sorts of weavers and smiths as examples, while suggesting that professions such as brewers or cordwainers were not as prone to these wide occupational differences (1996: 101, 177). The evidence presented here shows that all trades were subject to such discrepancies in wealth, even the poor keelmen. In the case of the brewers one-third of those whose inventories listed brewing vessels were not brewing on the scale indicated in the other two-thirds of the records; in the case of the cordwainers, investment in tools, stocks and wares for sale showed very considerable differences between businesses, with one man owning a shop containing hundreds of hides and shoes, while another worked from his parlour where he had stocks of soles and a few manufacturing tools.

The extent of objects for sale in shops revealed in some inventories confirms that some businesses were operating on a much larger scale than might be assumed. Shammas' suggestion - that it was not until the latter 17th century that consumer seem to have had direct access to retailers selling pre-processed or ready-made goods, and that it was not until the 18th century that merchandisers carried large stocks - seems to underestimate the scale of the markets witnessed by the inventory evidence (1990: 293). Such evidence supports Spufford's finding that, already by the late 16th century there was an expansion of goods for sale in shops (1984: 62). Cox also holds the opinion that historians have tended to underestimate the extent of retailing activity before the Industrial Revolution (2000a: 55, 2000b). In the 1690s, Celia Fiennes described shops of 'distinctive trades', 'not selling many things in one shop as is the custom' (Ellis 2001: 11). Such specialised shops are evident in Newcastle more than 100 years earlier, selling, for instance, footwear or metal wares, with hundreds of items available.

Overall, evidence of whether various trades were expanding or declining indicates that most trades changed little. Overton noted that prices from inventories provide some of the best evidence for following market trends, and that whether these were for new or second-hand items, the valuations are an accurate reflection of sale prices (2000: 141). According to the Newcastle evidence, investment in tools in particular remained very steady and prices for these objects (with the clear exception of brewing gear) did not apparently alter appreciably. Some livestock became more expensive, and the quantity of timber coming into the town seems to have expanded. The number of looms owned by weavers also increased (and possibly the price of new models). Supplies to businesses, such as hides and pelts, were probably becoming more expensive, but figures were contradictory. It was clear that items such as shoes and linen were becoming more expensive, although purses and gloves remained very inexpensive. The area of greatest expansion with the highest levels of investment, related to the building and provisioning of ships, and ownership of shares in vessels was a key factor in the figures. This evidence supports the idea that the shipping industry in particular was expanding at an earlier period than the 1650s (Howell 1967: 286). Levine and Wrightson confirm that, by the start of the 17th century, those building ships and their fittings were a thriving part of the local economy, as were those in the leather industries (1991: 103).

It is also likely that the prospects for trades involved with shipping were shifting, as evidenced by the decline of boat ownership among keelmen, while a simultaneous expansion of ownership of small vessels was witnessed among shipwrights. But these men were also moving away from purchasing shares in ships and towards investment in timber, although more evidence would be helpful in confirming such trends. The percentages of 'Admissions to Freedom' of the town guilds in the period between 1600 and 1639 showed a decline in clothing, leather and maritime trades, with the figures for building and metal-working trades increasing modestly, whereas figures for those in the food and drink trades doubled (Howell 1967: 353, Table IV). These trends are supported to an extent by the inventory evidence. However, as the analysis has shown, a small elite group of tradesmen in virtually every trade was significantly more prosperous than average, and gradations in wealth are common to all groups.

In order to follow such trends accurately, a mean average for both high and low investment figures for each occupation over three successive time frames would be required, but the sample size precludes this approach. However, when the total average investment figures for the whole time period are examined, a clear hierarchy of relative wealth between occupations emerges. Table 5.12a shows that the wealthiest tradesmen were the master mariners, by a substantial margin, with the shipwrights and, in particular, the anchorsmiths showing the largest investment in businesses. The high figure for smiths includes an anomaly of one anchorsmith who had shares in 18 ships, two of which were still under construction when he died (D.P.R. Lawson 1641). The tanners and butchers showed above-average investment figures, while all other trades invested significantly less in their businesses. The tailors and weavers showed very much smaller levels of investment than average, and the figures for keelmen are buoyed up by just one of 17 testators who owned an expensive boat. It is also of note that 10% of the inventories in the sample indicate the testator died in debt, a figure comparable to that for London in the late 17th century (Earle 1994:151).

French described weavers, tailors and shoemakers as 'poorly capitalised manual trades' (2000: 283-4), and Earle argued along similar lines, by contending that brewers and shipbuilders of 18th century London had considerable fixed capital as well as a large amount of working capital (1994: 143). Such generalisations, however, entirely fail to account for the enormous variability in the scale of production and investment within these occupations evidenced by the Newcastle data. Both large and small concerns were evident among the various businesses and success and failure was possible in any trade.

In the final conclusion to this chapter, the evidence for consumption and production of all the objects that have so far been included for analysis is brought together with further categories of objects not yet discussed.

5.11 Conclusion

In the course of this chapter, unique patterns of consumption and production among the different trades have emerged. In this conclusion, nine of the categories of objects that have been examined individually are amalgamated in a final analysis to reveal the average overall wealth and the related percentage of investment for selected objects. The factors influencing the direction and evolution of the material culture of the tradesmen are discussed in turn.

5.11.1 Occupation

The overall averages presented in Table 5.13a clearly demonstrate significant differences in priorities reflected in material wealth among diverse occupations. Examples of unique patterns of ownership among trades can be found in many types of goods. For instance, animals are owned by almost 60% of testators, but butchers invest five times the amount in livestock relative to other trades. Investment in apparel, which is listed in almost 90% of inventories, ranged from 3.5li to 4.5li for most trades, with the notable exceptions of keelmen, who are very poorly attired, and the master mariners whose valuations are ten times those of these poorer men, and about double the average. Books and maps are listed in about 30% of inventories, and while valuations are generally low, literacy levels are distinctly higher among master mariners, and well above average among mariners and bakers and brewers. Weapons are recorded in about half the inventories and valuations tend to be low, averaging 9s, but master mariners invest almost double the figures of other trades, notably in swords. With their expensive clothes and swords, master mariners must have been the peacocks among the town's population. Nearly 45% of households brewed beer or ale, while 90% of bakers and brewers are practising their trade (evidenced by the recording of vessels and rooms where brewing took place). These professional brewers, who produce hopped beer, invest almost five times the amount in equipment compared with householders.

Household objects are listed in every one of the 257 inventories in the sample. The cordwainers and the master mariners invest the most significant sums in furnishing their homes, with the bakers and brewers being the only other trade with valuations that are above the average figure of over 18li. Three-quarters of inventories include detailed information about objects directly relating to the named occupation of the testator, and investment in businesses is extremely variable. While many trades require minimal investment in basic tools, tanners are found to be the biggest investors, averaging almost five times the overall figure. Cordwainers and shipwrights invest just under double the average, with skinners and glovers, smiths, and bakers and brewers (if account is taken of both their baking and brewing equipment), all investing much larger sums than other trades. However, if shipping interests are added to the accounts of trade-related wealth, the figures are hugely augmented. Shares in ships account for the single most significant figure among the selected objects included in the calculations, but this wealth is in the hands of 35 individuals or just less than 15% of the inventoried sample: most investors are master mariners followed by shipwrights. Shammas confirms that investment decisions depend on those with capital (1990: 42), and among tradesmen this capital is reflected in assets such as ships, stockpiled supplies and ready-made wares. Those men in a given occupation who accumulate such investments are distinctly wealthier than those who did not.

Provisions are included in the final average calculations, representing residual stocks, although there is no reason to assume that, because the testator had died, the household had ceased to function. What is recorded is limited and includes wheat, rye, barley, oats, malted grain and hops, itemised in Tables 5.11c and 5.11d. Quantities of salted meat and fish – notably mutton, beef, cod and herring – 'bay' salt, beans and butter are listed incidentally. Grains are listed in about one-third of inventories overall, the largest stocks being held by bakers and brewers (70%). The other types of provisions are recorded by fewer than 10% of tradesmen of varying occupations, who are apparently involved in marketing or in stockpiling supplies for ships judging by the quantities held by individuals. The overall average invested in provisions is quite substantial, but the figures largely reflect investment by dealers.

The evidence confirms the very significant role played by occupation in patterns of consumption and production, most clearly reflected in investment in businesses. Shammas has observed that occupational status does not have a very great impact on the amount devoted to consumer goods once wealth is held constant, but also notes, that if the value of different types of objects are analysed, the results will be different (1990: 110-12). This has been shown to be the case, as this analysis clearly demonstrates that occupation influenced ownership, and what is included on inventories varies by occupation (Weatherill 1996: 79, Overton 2004: 138). Shammas' assertion, that being in a craft or trade had no impact on the accumulation of any category of good (1990: 180), is not sustainable.

5.11.2 By-employment

The categories of objects in Table 5.13a include figures associated with by-employment, where such activities are recorded. Contributions from such activities to the overall figures are, however, minimal in the majority of cases. Tradesmen who have given up their occupation to wholly undertake other work represent just 3.5% of the sample, although all these men maintain an association with their named trade according to the occupation given on both the will and the inventory. These individuals list no tools or other objects associated with their named occupation on either document, but do specify other means of employment. Examples of such arrangements include two skinners and glovers who are engaged in selling salted and dried fish which they stock in very large quantities. One butcher has taken on running the Pandon Gate Mill, and a smith is similarly running the Chimley Mill on the Bailiff Burn. Both mills are attested to historically (Chapter 4). Five men – three tanners and two weavers – have taken up farming, although one of the tanners continues simultaneously to operate a large tanning house in the town. A single tailor worked as a keelman. Diversification of employment in areas fairly closely associated with the named occupation is much more common than changing occupation entirely: for example, master mariners tend to buy shares in ships; shipwrights may have built the ships in which they have bought shares, they own trees in local woodlands, as well as acting as landlords to properties that they may also have built themselves (Chapter 4). The very wealthy anchorsmith, referred to above, tied all his wealth up in the 18 ships he owned. A baker has bought a share in some mill horses and has acquired a fishing licence, but this man uniquely has also bought shares in two ships, the only man wholly unconnected to the seafaring world to do so.

Contributions from brewing and animal husbandry do indicate other means of by-employment in a few cases. In the 45% of inventories indicating brewing, just 7% of tradesmen, besides the brewers themselves, appear to be producing beer or ale on a commercial scale, attested by the presence of brew leads. Nearly 60% of inventories confirm ownership of animals, although seafarers, shipwrights and keelmen list significantly fewer animals than other trades (Table 5.10a). A clear majority of testators own just one or two cows, while only 5% of documents indicate the ownership of small herds of sheep or cattle. Revenue from spinning has not been included in the calculations, but investment in spinning wheels and the value of residual stocks of yarn are very small and will not have altered the overall figures, as most valuations are around 1s or 2s. Participation in this work is indicated in almost 50% of inventories, with the butchers, master mariners and shipwrights indicating figures closer to 80%.

Overall, the inventory evidence suggests that by-employment, aimed at production for sale, is a significant part of supplementing income for only a small minority of tradesmen's households – an observation based on an examination of the type, quantity and value of goods, which is usually sufficient to determine levels of production (Overton 2004: 35). Where other forms of by-employment are indicated, the vast majority are likely to be connected to production for home consumption (Overton 2004: 7, 66, 171). But most households appear to depend primarily on income from the testator's named occupation and work closely affiliated to the named trade. Levine and Wrightson suggests that we should pause before coming to the conclusion that a 'dual-economy' model has broad applicability, arguing that small-scale supplementing of family income does not constitute a dual economy (1991: 223). The high percentage of households in Kent and Cornwall undertaking two production activities for commercial purposes (Overton 2004: 34, 65-6), contrasts markedly with the situation of Newcastle's urban tradesmen, who follow a single occupation often assisted by family and apprentices.

Overton's finding – that by-employment is associated with higher levels of consumption, more material goods than average, and higher-than-average material wealth (2004: 151) – does not seem applicable to the specialist Newcastle tradesmen. However, the situation in Cornwall whereby specialist production has a negative effect on consumption, leading not to increased material enrichment but to greater poverty, is also not apparent from the Newcastle data (Overton 2004: 171).

Weatherill noted that it is, perhaps, difficult to combine a craft with, for example farming, and that it is rare to gain enough detail to reconstruct the proportions of income that came from each source (1996: 103). Her remarks concerning town dwellers – who, she believes, have less ready access to land and large gardens (Weatherill 1996: 103) - can be examined in the case of the approximately 40% of tradesmen's inventories that confirm ownership of land - such as rigs, closes, meadows and wastes. How such holdings contribute to income is not recorded as much of this information comes from wills; however, as already noted, only one man actually took up farming alongside his tanning business, while a relatively small percentage of other tradesmen, besides butchers, own small herds of animals.

In the clear majority of cases, incomes are apparently derived from the principal occupation of the head of the household, from expansion of businesses (reflected in stockpiling supplies and wares), and from diversification within a trade. Overton's recognition of 'entrepreneurial by-employment' as a way to increase income is evident among tradesmen (2004: 171), but the entrepreneurial drive is focused on opportunities relating to the primary occupation for which they have very specialised skills (Levine and Wrightson 1991: 227). There is also no particular prevalence among any one trade in this study to take up by-employment. Overton found that tradesmen such as cordwainers and tailors are less likely to diversify into farming than those associated with food production and building, arguing that some trades are 'less cyclical' (2004: 72, 74), but none of the Newcastle tradesmen are apparently prone to such trends.

Whether businesses are expanding over the period is not clear, as the data set is insufficient to follow trends, although both small and large concerns are evident in all decades. There is some evidence, however, that home production may have been declining marginally in the period of study. Such fluctuations in household production are evident in inventories from Kent, where a slight rise is evident, whereas by-employment declined in Cornwall (Overton 2004: 63, 172). In comparison, Newcastle inventories indicate a fall of 8% in spinning and 5% in animal ownership, and although brew vessels show no decline, the kiln hairs and chimneys used for drying grain decline by 15% over the decades between the 1550s and 1642.

5.11.3 Wealth

Occupation is a primary factor in consumption and investment patterns, but the question remains as to whether wealth is also a key factor. Table 5.13a shows a clear hierarchy among trades, relative to both wealth invested in a range of selected objects, and wealth levels between trades. The issue is whether the differences in patterns result from consumption choices related to occupation or from differences in wealth.

According to Table 5.13a total average wealth is much higher for some trades than for others. These figures can be compared with those from other studies, but it is important to recognize that the calculations will reflect different assemblages of objects, as well as time periods. Nevertheless, some trends can be examined.

Shammas has created two wealth groups (which do not account for occupations), divided according to those with more, or less, than 20li of total personal wealth, taken from a sample of inventories from Oxfordshire dated between 1550 and 1590, and from a second set of data with the wealth divide set at 40li total personal wealth from other regions of England in the 1660s (1990, Appendix 1: 304-5). All those below the wealth divide are considered to belong to the low-wealth group, and all those above to a medium- and upper-wealth group. Shammas' figures seem fairly low in comparison to the average wealth (from selected objects) for Newcastle tradesmen of about 46li shown on Table 5.13a. If the individual trades are considered, bakers and brewers, butchers, cordwainers, master mariners, shipwrights and tanners all had levels of personal wealth above the average for the significantly later period of the 1660s, with all other trades falling between the wealth divide of above 20li and below 40li. Only the keelmen have less than half the average wealth of the earlier period, and the finding suggests that all but the keelmen belong to a medium or upper wealth group according to Shammas figures.

Weatherill calculated a rough mean value for a selection of some 20 household goods for the period 1675-1725, of 25li for the sample as a whole (1996: 109, 203-7), but she also examined the mean averages of these goods by occupations defined according to three criteria - namely social status based on Brodsky Elliott's research (1978) into occupations and marriage partners, the general criteria classifying occupations using King's (1695) distinctions, and occupations grouped according to economic sector based on Armstrong's (1972) classifications from a 19th - century census (1996: Appendix 2, 212-14).

Weatherill's figures reveal a much more detailed distribution of wealth among the occupations, although the figures prove rather inconsistent when the three different criteria for the groups are applied (1996: Tables A2.1, A2.2, A2.3 and A2.4). To create a more workable comparison with Weatherill's data on average levels of wealth represented in selected goods, the total average of 45.95li in Table 5.13a should be replaced with the figure for household goods taken from Table 5.3 which is 18.51li (or 18.44li, when adjustment is made for variability in sample size). This figure differs from Weatherill's as it includes more furniture, as well as beds, but no hot-drink, tea or coffee utensils, silver or books. In attempting this comparison, the expansion of ownership in goods by 1715 (especially in the decade between 1685 and 1695) must be kept in mind (Weatherill 1996: 39), as must the rise in the real amount of wealth invested in consumer goods over the 17th century (Shammas 1990: 112).

In taking Brodsky Elliott's categories first, based on her social-status designations, we find that she places skinners and mariners among the high-status group, together with the master mariners, who had an average of 39li of the goods selected by Weatherill (Weatherill 1996: Table A2.2). The brewers (but not the bakers), the tanners and the shipwrights have 32li of goods, and all other trades just 19li. Thus, according to Brodsky Elliott's criteria, all the trades in the Newcastle study fall into a low social-status group, precisely the opposite finding to Shammas'. Even accounting for the possible increase in valuations that may have occurred in the post-Civil-War period, such divisions seem too crude.

King's (1695) criteria, which form more general groups (similar to those used by historians in analysing various aspects of social and economic life in the early modern period), prove to be as misleading as Brodsky Elliotts' in relation to the Newcastle data (Weatherill 1996: Table A2.3). In placing the trades in this study into two sectors - those belonging to either crafts or to dealers – bakers (but not brewers), keelmen, master mariners and skinners (but not glovers), are collectively described as dealers, with 33li of household goods, and all other trades are categorised as crafts, with 19li of household goods. The figures cannot be reconciled with those from Table 5.13a, nor with Brodsky Elliott's social-status groups (Weatherill 1996: Table A2.2). Master mariners and cordwainers come closest to trades belonging to King's dealers, but tradesmen such as keelmen and skinners clearly belong in a much lower social bracket according to these calculations (Weatherill 1996: Table A2.3).

Armstrong's classifications (1972: 226-310) seem even more remote from the findings relating to the data from the early modern period and, given that the classifications belong to the 19th century, and mix social and economic criteria, perhaps this is not surprising (Weatherill 1996: Table A2.4). In the 19th century analysis, butchers and mariners are designated as dealers, with 34li of household goods, and are placed among the wealthiest of the trades; master mariners are placed on an equal footing with keelmen in the transport sector with 29li of goods, with all other trades located in the manufacturing sector with 20li of goods. The figure for master mariners, who have just over 30li of goods, agrees with Armstrong's classifications; but the figures for bakers and certainly for brewers, and especially for cordwainers, are too low, while all other the trades which are placed in manufacturing and dealing sectors are too high relative to the Newcastle averages (Weatherill 1996: Table A2.4).

When Weatherill's own average rough mean value for household goods of 25li, with a figure of between 15li and 20li for amalgamated tradesmen and craftsmen (1996: 109, 177), is compared with the mean average of household goods in Table 5.13a, it appears that bakers and brewers, cordwainers and master mariners are above average, and all other trades are below. However, these findings can be further refined when compared with Weatherill's detailed list of averages for individual occupations (1996: Table A2.1). If the mean averages of household objects belonging to Newcastle trades are compared with Weatherill's figures for the same trades in the period 1660-1725 (1996: Table A2.1), we find that the figures for master mariners, the bakers in combination with the brewers, and the skinners in combination with the glovers, are relatively compatible in both data sets. However, the valuations for Newcastle weavers and especially cordwainers are higher for the earlier period, whereas the figures for all other trades are significantly lower than the figures provided by Weatherill.

One final body of evidence on wealth groups, defined according to valuations of household goods from nearby Whickham and based on inventories dated between 1660 and 1719, can be examined. Levine and Wrightson found that a 'variety of craftsmen and tradesmen' emerge as the middling group, described as 'lesser rate-payers' according to the hearth tax analysis, with goods valued from 6li - 7li to l21i - 13li, with a minority of inventories listing less than 5li of goods (1991: 232-34). The Newcastle sample shows that only the keelmen owned less than 5li worth of household goods, with all other tradesmen attaining (and, in most cases exceeding) Levine and Wrightson's figures for Whickham for the later period (1991: 232-34). In fact Levine and Wrightson found that the minor gentry owned just 15li of domestic goods, with the wealthiest of these people listing upwards of 20li of goods in the later period (1991: 234). This calculation will place bakers and brewers, butchers, cordwainers, mariners, master mariners, shipwrights and tanners in the highest wealth group, and all but the keelmen in the upper strata of the middling consumption group. Thus according to these calculations, it would seem that most Newcastle tradesmen are remarkably well endowed with household goods at a significantly earlier period.

Overall, the differing results elicited from these studies, employing various social and economic criteria in establishing a hierarchy of occupations based on inventoried wealth, suggest that those approaches that amalgamate tradesmen into categories are unsatisfactory. French also found that lumping many trades and occupations together, as King (1695) had done, was not satisfactory, but describes Brodsky Elliott's (1978) definitions as the most successful in establishing social boundaries (2000: 279, 283). But the well-established hierarchy proffered by French places 'dirty manual trades', such as tanners and butchers, below shopkeepers, and describes cordwainers and weavers as poorly capitalised manual trades (2000: 283). Earle also identifies weavers and tailors as the poorest of trades (1994: 73). However, where do such conclusions leave the cordwainer with a shop offering 300 shoes for sale (D.P.R Spoore 1587), or the butchers with very substantial and valuable herds of cattle and sheep, or the tanner who owned two rural farms and an extensive urban tan house (Doddes 1594), and another with two sons at Cambridge University (D.P.R. Newton 1570), or the literate weaver with a small library and two lavishly furnished houses (D.P.R. Chaitor 1623) - to name but a few notable individuals?

The dilemma of the relationship of inventoried wealth to occupation, and ultimately to social boundaries, is well illustrated by Tables 5.4a and 5.4b which show the distribution of wealth reflected in three categories of household goods. Table 5.4a reveals that testators with, for instance, over 20li of household goods represent 30% of the sample. When the figures from Table 5.4a are calculated to show what percentage of tradesmen in a given occupation attained this level of wealth, we find individuals from all trades (except the keelmen and skinners and glovers) represented. In descending order, the percentage of those with over 20li of household goods are master mariners (65.4%), bakers and brewers (57.9%), cordwainers (45.2%), tanners (37.6%), butchers (35.3%), mariners (31%), tailors (26.6%), weavers (20.8%), shipwrights (19.1%), smiths (13%) and millers (11.1%). The figures do show that some trades are more profitable than others, while also confirming that wealth levels within an occupation are not uniform. Levine and Wrightson, however, found that occupational and status groups do correspond in general with broad bands of inventoried wealth (1991: 234). In the context of the evidence from the Newcastle records this conclusion has proved generally to be correct in case of the tradesmen included in the study, although some of the often-repeated assumptions regarding the status of certain trades (most notably those working in areas such as shoemaking, butchering and tanning), need to be reconsidered.

Wealth and occupation are clearly related, but how this affected the acquisition of objects is less obvious. Table 5.2a shows that over the three timeframes the number of some 28 selected items recorded in inventories, doubled, and that the increase affected all trades, except the keelmen. Overton believes that wealth as a predictor of the consumption of material goods has been overplayed because, when the volume of goods is considered, there is no significant correlation between a consumption good and wealth (2004: 165). He also found that occupation appears to be more strongly associated with the acquisition of new kinds of goods than wealth (2004: 166). The Newcastle evidence demonstrates the link between occupation and consumption patterns for a great variety of objects regardless of wealth, although in the case of the acquisition of those objects appearing on inventories for the first time (notably after 1625), Table 5.2a suggests that both wealth and occupation were factors. This is best demonstrated in the case of master mariners. These men, who were consistently found to be the wealthiest of tradesmen, were also the first to acquire over half the new items that appear in documents in the early 17th century - notably chinaware, upholstered chairs, court cupboards, pictures and window cushions - but the fact that these men might be the first to encounter such items in the course of their voyages to ports such as London, suggests that occupation played an equally important role in explaining patterns.

Wealth is the key factor in the acquisition of goods in the case of several cordwainers, who were the first to list the new footstools for beds and close stools, of the weaver who listed the first window curtains, and of the tanner who listed the first pair of virginals, as these individuals were all well-to-do men. Thus, in some cases, wealth can be the most important determinant of the value of consumer durables (Shammas 1990: 104, 173).

Schammell has confirmed that higher wealth groups record a higher proportion of goods in all regions of England (2004: 21). However, only by refining the analysis do consumption patterns become clearer. Overton found a positive correlation with material wealth reflected in certain categories of goods, such as upholstered furniture or mirrors, where the wealthy owned more of these items, but with other items such as dairy equipment there was no such correlation (2004: 142-3). Examined from an opposite perspective, the poor material culture of Cornwall was not just a function of its relative poverty, but of investment strategies, where households had more pewter, for example, than did wealthy Kent household (Overton 2004: 144). Such findings, which focus on the numbers of new items (which were the preserve of the few), must be compared with the much greater consumption of items that are listed from the late 1600s throughout the study period, including inexpensive flower pots and cushions, which are increasing exponentially in households of very differing levels of wealth and among tradesmen in all occupations.

Erickson confirms that median wealth doubled over the century 1582 to 1686 (2002: 42), and Shammas found that there appears to be a considerable increase in the real amount spent on consumer goods between the late 16th and late 17th centuries, but that this increase is reflected in bedding, with no other goods showing any positive movement (1990: 88-9, 92). The findings from this study show a clear, and in some cases marked, increase in the wealth represented in many objects selected for analysis, which augmented most significantly in the late 1610s and 1620s. Bedding, beds and table linen indeed show the greatest rise, followed by furniture in a slightly later period, with a more marginal increase in tableware and cookware (Table 5.3). But such trends are also seen in increasing expenditure on apparel (Table 5.6), in the increasing numbers of books (Table 5.8b), in more expensive brew vessels coming into use (Table 5.11b), and with increasing numbers of more valuable animals (Table 5.10b). A larger sample of inventories would have revealed increased wealth in many businesses, especially those involved with shipping and leather manufacture. When the evidence for a doubling of investment is tied to the doubling in the volume of objects (Tables 5.2a, 5.2b, 5.3), it is clear that rapid growth occurred in the early 17th century in Newcastle, a finding that conflicts with Shammas' assertion that the proportion of wealth in consumer goods did not move steadily upwards during the early modern period (1990: 95). The findings also contradict Spufford's assertion that an increase in the quantity of such items as soft furnishings does not pre-date the mid-17th century, although she acknowledges that growth in consumption began prior to the Civil War, (particularly with reference to Harrison's contemporary observations pertaining to the late 16th century), but which, she says, accelerated only after 1680 (1984: 114, 116).

Weatherill has found that, by the 1680s, the most rapid growth in commodities is in goods for entirely new purposes, whereas the acquisition of established goods changes relatively little (1996: 32). In Newcastle, the trend from the late 16th century up to 1625 indicates that the purchase of some goods associated with comfort and decoration of the home expanded very rapidly (as seen with hand basins and ewers, carpet cloths, cushions, Danish pots, glassware and flower pots), whereas established goods such as towels, playing tables, silver objects and salt sellers show no real change. There appears to have been a continued rapid expansion of some of these objects, notably flower pots, in a second wave of consumer change that occurs between the 1620s and 1642. At this time, new goods (most of which are decorative and first appear in small numbers), also expand rapidly. For instance, between about 1620 and 1630 the numbers of pictures and glassware more than doubles, the numbers of mirrors triple, and window curtains increase almost tenfold. The evidence, although limited, suggests that while Overton found a timeframe of 50 years to be too coarse to trace diffusion of new material goods with any precision (2004: 165), the evidence from Newcastle over three generations is unequivocal.

Change and expansion in consumption has, perhaps, too often focused on the introduction of new rituals associated with tea, coffee, and hot drink utensils, as well as on important changes in the increasing availability of decorative goods for use at mealtimes in the late 17th century (Shammas 1990: 183; Weatherill: 1996: 28, 40; Overton 2004: 90). In concentrating on this very restricted group of items, a marked contrast has been highlighted between the allegedly sparse furnishings of the late 16th and early 17th centuries, and the changed situation of the later period (Weatherill 1996: 6-7; Overton 2004: 90). However, the apparent dichotomy between the late 16th and the late 17th centuries fails to account for the tremendous alteration to households in the intervening decades, attested by contemporary historians and catalogued in the probate documents (Furvinal 1877). The acquisition of new goods -which brought about a domestic environment that became richer, more comfortable, and more specialised (Levine and Wrightson 1991: 238; Overton 2004: 118) - is evident at least half a century earlier than has been held to be the case. Observations that people in the late 17th and 18th centuries turned inwards to create living spaces that were more comfortable and aesthetically pleasing, decorated with goods and furnishings that might compensate for the inconveniences of town life (Weatherill 1996: 81-3), are equally valid for those living in Newcastle in the early decades of the 17th century.

Shammas is of the opinion that consumer durables from the 17th century are 'not modish objects', and that items which are recycled for generations indicate a poor standard of comfort - one that continued into the 18th century, where the majority of durables remain decidedly unexciting for all but the very affluent (1990: 209, 293). Such a view seems overly pessimistic, given the evidence suggesting that almost all tradesmen in this study are participating in the consumption of objects that are clearly indicative of efforts to create more comfortable and decorative homes.

Analysis of the change in material culture also tends to focus on a dichotomy between the wealthy who could acquire objects and the poor who could not. It is important to recognise that the new goods are not taken up indiscriminately by all - and some are never taken up, even though they are available to households who could afford them (Overton 2004: 174). For example, taking a wealthy anchorsmith who died in 1641, right at the end of the study period - someone with every opportunity to acquire any of the objects included in the analysis - we find that he lists just five of the 28 decorative or new objects listed in Table 5.2a, and among these are the carpet cloths, cushions and flower pots that have been shown to be items common to many households, and which are owned even by a few keelmen. Furthermore, the anchorsmith listed no books or silver objects (D.P.R. Lawson 1641). There is, nevertheless, every indication that the very poorest tradesmen, especially the keelmen, are wholly unable to acquire the volume of decorative objects listed by other tradesmen, and these men had none of the new items appearing by around the 1620s. In examining the overall total valuations for objects (Table 5.13a), and comparing the figures with the mean averages for selected household goods (Table 5.3), consumption strategies become apparent that demonstrate where priorities lay for different trades. It is clear that, whereas butchers, shipwrights and tanners, for example, recorded less than the average valuations for household goods, the figures for combined categories of objects show the same trades to be above the overall average as a result of the acquisition of objects related to their trades.

Over the period of this study, change is most visible because of the increased quantities of goods, rather than the variety of goods, and cannot be measured only in relation to the adoption of new goods (Overton 2004: 89, 118). It was not the types of goods that differentiated people, but the quantity they possessed (Levine and Wrightson 1991: 91, 103). It should also be noted that no real decline or disappearance of objects is apparent in this period, excepting the slight evidence in terms of goods relating to household production (Tables 5.9b, 5.10b, 5.11b).

When the percentage invested in different types of objects is compared, the mean average valuations for household objects accounts for the largest share of wealth (Table 5.13b). This figure can be added to that for clothes, which account for about 10% of valuations, while for comparative purposes we find that weapons accounted for just 0.5% and books 0.3% of the totals. The figures associated with production activities show that animals and brewing equipment account for about 15% of investments, and objects directly related to production within a trade, together with investments in ships, account for another 30%. The figure for provisions associated with marketing or supplies for ships, contribute about another 7% of figures relating to businesses. It would seem that material wealth is divided about evenly between investments for consumption representing household and personal items, and investment for production relating to objects necessary for business and trade, including by-employment. Shammas found that the proportion of wealth devoted to consumer goods did not change between the late 16th and late 17th centuries (1990: 89), but Table 5.3 shows that over three time frames Newcastle households are devoting an increasing proportion of wealth to bedding, beds and linen goods and, after 1625, to furniture, (an increase of about 5% increase is evident), whereas the relative expenditure on cookware, tableware and decorative objects is declining (by about 10%). Owing to paucity of data relating to specific areas of production activities among differing occupations, such trends can not be calculated over time, but a decline in animal ownership after 1625 of 18%, in relation to the figure prior to 1600, and a corresponding expansion in shipping and brewing interests, suggest an alteration in economic strategies rather than a decline in wealth. It should be noted again that levels of ownership of animals directly associated with a business showed no decline.

Whether those with the greatest wealth unduly influence the percentage figures must be considered (Shammas 1990: 88); however, as already established, wealth did not necessarily dictate consumption patterns. For example, many decorative objects that are more prevalent in the inventories of the better-off tradesmen are, in fact, inexpensive, while the percentage of income devoted to bedding is uniformly high among all trades. The percentage figures, however, omit certain key items such as food - the single most important household expenditure, especially for the poor (Weatherill 1996: 127). The frequency of acquisition also affects the figures, as many goods such as furniture and utensils are purchased irregularly for relatively small amounts, while there is regular expenditure on items that wear out more rapidly, such as clothing and shoes (Weatherill 1996: 134, 136).

Ultimately, the figures in Table 5.13b provide only a guide to expenditure patterns on a selection of objects that reflect inventoried wealth, but not income. Evidence that the poor spent a higher proportion of income on food and clothing than the wealthy (Husbands 1981: 211; Shammas 1990: 159), is not especially relevant to this analysis, which omits food, and where apparel is consistently included in inventories of richer and poorer tradesmen alike. Everitt's calculations show that about 40-50% of wealth is invested in domestic goods between 1560 and 1640, with the increase pertaining to the 17th century (1967: 421), and this figure is broadly in agreement with the Newcastle sample - although Bowden's suggestion that expenditure on industrial goods declined as a result of increased domestic expenditure cannot be sustained (1967: 607-8). Shammas found that, in general, before 1700 slightly more than 25% of inventoried wealth was devoted to consumer goods (1990: 88); this figure appears to be too low, but it should be noted that all calculations omit quantities of goods and food produced in the home, items which are not accounted for or commented on (Weatherill 1996: 103).

The omission of certain items such as cash and silver should also be considered. Such resources are found in inventories belonging to all trades, but the valuations have not been included as these varied enormously, probably partly owing to the residual nature of 'ready money' listed in inventories. Weatherill found the middling ranks did not receive regular sums in cash, but she says that in towns, communities did have cash to spare on consumer goods by 1700, which was not the case in the mid 16th century (1996: 96, 175). In Newcastle, 46% of inventories dated between 1550 and 1600 list both cash and gold coins, or silver in the form of investment, a figure that rises to 61% between 1625 and 1642. Weatherill found no evidence of any increase in hoarding of wealth in silver in the period between 1660 and 1725, although this commodity is recorded in 34% of inventories from the North East in this period (1996: 66); a similar finding is indicated in Table 5.2a relating to silver spoons, where there is no change over the three time frames. The 15% increase in the amount of cash listed in inventories suggests that more is available by the 1620s, but the percentages held by trades varied; 92% of master mariners list the combined assets of cash, gold and silver; over 60% of bakers and brewers and butchers record these assets, while other trades record figures of 30-50%. The keelmen were once again the exception, as just 25% of such men held these assets. These figures accord well with those relating to ownership of silver in regional assessments, where the wealthier members of society held more assets (Shammas 1990: 179; Weatherill 1996: 66).

Any attempt to create figures on expenditure patterns is further complicated when property and debts, both owed and owing, are considered when calculating per capita wealth (Spufford 1990: 151; Shammas 1990: 19). Nevertheless, the percentage figures presented here do provide a useful guide to general priorities among tradesmen, indicating a marked balance between expenditure on household commodities and investment in work-related commodities.

5.11.4 Prices

Clearly, the question of the prices of objects is of importance to these findings. As has been shown in successive tables, prices are not generally rising for most commodities, but the range of valuations for items that are appraised separately, indicate wide discrepancies between both new wares and second-hand objects. Because of the range of valuations, price trends are not always clear cut, but for a number of household items a rise in high-end valuations is apparent after 1625, when new items and more expensive versions of existing items become available, for instance, in the case of upholstered chairs and more expensive glassware and flower pots. Some cookware increases in value, whereas some basic tableware, such as trenchers and earthenware, becomes cheaper. Some prices for linen napkins and table clothes, towels and possibly window curtains declines, although valuations for linen sheets experienced a rise at the low end of price ranges.

It is of interest to find that the ranges of valuations of several items included in the analysis are very similar to valuations given almost a century later in other regions of Britain (Weatherill 1996: Table 5.3). When data from the period 1548-1642 (Table 5.5), are compared with Weatherill's data from the period 1660-1725, we find that the price of pewter doublers and unspecified pewter vessels remained at 1s - 2s throughout all these decades; that earthenware and trenchers could be also be had for 1d in all decades; that many books, including those catalogued in the book dealer William Corbett's shops in 1626 (D.P.R.), could still be acquired for between 6d and 4s by the 18th century. Pictures, which appear after 1600, are worth 1d to 3s in the earlier period and 2d to 9s in the later period, but over both periods most are inexpensive. Mirrors are quite inexpensive in the earliest decades, rising to around 5s after 1625. Such prices are comparable to valuations of between 1s and 5s in the later decades. Linen tablecloths cost between 1s and 6s in the earlier period, compared with 3s for a tablecloth of unspecified fabric in the later period, and linen napkins cost 3d to 2s in both periods, although the type of cloth is not specified in the later period. Valuations for linen were incidentally declining in the early 17th century (Weatherill 1996: Table 5.3).

Valuations for many objects associated with household production show minimal change over the century. Most animals, professional equipment, and spinning wheels are not subject to increased pricing. However, some professional brewing equipment does become much more expensive, as do a few exceptional animals. There is some evidence that more expensive looms may have become available after 1600. Price rises are also observed in some tools, notably those belonging to smiths and shipwrights. Leather, skins and pelts do show notable price increases, and shoes are becoming more expensive.

Overall, however, prices are remarkably steady, but this observation reflects two ends of the market, as there is a consistent divide between more and less expensive versions of the same or similar objects (Overton 2000: 123), and it is the more valuable objects that show the most significant rises over the decades. Shammas notes that the prices of many new commodities are low by the 18th century, and this is also the case in the early 17th century, but she finds that there is not enough information on prices of semi-durables to indicate trends (1990: 185-6, 295). The data from Newcastle suggest that many of such items are not becoming any more expensive, although a decline in prices is certainly not widespread in this period, and it should be acknowledged that there are both very cheap and very expensive versions of many items found in all periods. With the increasing volume of commodities becoming available, such trends probably became more marked. Overton established that the number of goods increased over the 17th century against generally falling prices for most basic items, which he ascribed to the less durable quality of goods associated with cheaper production costs (2004: 8, 118). He also found that the value of non-production goods compared with production goods did not appear to have increased markedly, and in some studies appears to have declined (2004: 8). The Newcastle sample suggests no decline in the price of most household objects, but with production-related goods some increases are, in fact, apparent.

Any link between falling grain prices and increased consumption, as suggested by Bowden (1967: 634), are refuted by Weatherill, who found no such association (1996: 199). Furthermore, the alleged six-fold increase in the cost of living and rising prices in the north of England between the 16th and mid 17th century described by Everitt (1967: 435, 587), and Howell's evidence for sharp rises in the price of cows (1967: 267), is certainly not manifested in the valuations of inventoried objects. Shammas points to the problem that many prices used to understand trends have been taken from an index of goods relating to southern markets (1990: 26); Overton points to the omission of consumer goods, but inclusion of raw material, in the price series compiled by Phelps Brown and Hopkins (1981), and upon which the most frequently used price series depends (2000: 139-140). Bowden's prices from the *Agrarian History* are similarly based chiefly on grain and primary products (1967: 594).

Overton maintains that inventory valuations are a more accurate reflection of prices than are these price series, and that the validity of inventory prices can best be checked by examining the consistency of descriptions (2000: 131, 141). Prices in Newcastle inventories are very consistent, as are descriptions, and evidence of just how reliable inventory prices can be has been found in a unique and extensive accounting of the sale of goods at the death of a wealthy cordwainer called Thomas Spoore (D.P.R. 1587). The document provides a means to test Overton's arguments. Prices paid for items sold to named individuals in a two-day sale of Spoore's possessions, on his death from the plague, match those given by his appraisers on his long inventory. Dozens of people attended the sale, three-quarters of the buyers being local women. When total valuations on inventories could be checked against administrative accounts, where they survive, a similar consistency in valuations is also apparent.

The empirical data presented throughout this analysis confirm that major changes are taking place in the material culture of tradesmen of Newcastle by the early 17th century, evidenced by a very significant augmentation in the volume of objects recorded, and by inventoried wealth levels, which are not accompanied by major price rises in most cases.

5.11.5 Motivations and circumstances

Other motivating factors and circumstances that help to explain the patterns of material culture revealed by the empirical data also deserve attention. First, the urban environment influenced consumption in a number of ways. Market accessibility and town residency show positive correlations with both levels of expenditure and the volume of goods acquired, as townspeople are better exposed to consumer commodities, simply because they were closer to the sources (Shammas 1990: 105, 110, 180). In Newcastle those in trades may have been particularly well placed to take advantage of markets, some more so than others. Seafarers, for example, seem usually to have acquired new commodities before other tradesmen, probably through their access to London markets. The lists of goods first encountered on master mariners' inventories have been mentioned; in addition mariners list the first watch and clocks, and a shipwright the first china cupboard, the only such reference in the documents.

Nevertheless, as Overton points out, the ownership of commodities is by no means a simple function of their availability - reflected, for example, in an urban - rural divide - although he acknowledges that adoption rates of new goods are higher in urban inventories (2004: 118, 167). Weatherill notes that there are many households with just basic utensils and furniture in both rural and urban situations, although she also acknowledges that goods are more readily available in towns with markets at the nodes of transport networks (1996: 83).

Newcastle is at the centre of trade in the early modern period, as the provincial capital of a region that has very advanced aspects to its economy, alongside rather backward rural elements. Weatherill's study of regional patterns of the ownership of goods from the 1660s shows that, although the Metropolis stands out, the North East (together with Kent) are in the vanguard of consumer development in England, linked to the state of economic development (1996: 52, 60). The constant flow of bulky goods (especially coal) to London, in exchange for consumer commodities, which has been dated to the late 17th century (Weatherill 1996: 61), should be correlated to the much earlier continual and rapid expansion of coal-mining operations between 1570 and the 1620s (especially after 1609-10), which did not slow until the 1630s (Levine and Wrightson 1991: 24, 93, 118, 174). The expansion of the coal trade is fundamental to any explanation for the rise in consumption and production among the tradesmen of Newcastle at the beginning rather than the end of the century. It is, after all, the oligarchs of Newcastle who hold the greatest stakes in this wealth (Levine and Wrightson 1991: 21-2) and, as Gray observed, 'this great trade hath made this port to florish in all trades' (1649: 33). Ellis assigns the expansion of Newcastle's trade and economy to the late 17th and early 18th centuries, characterising trade in the late 16th century as an exchange of industrial for agricultural goods, and she suggests that the complex occupational structure of the town, with a growing demand for goods and services, belongs to the early 18th century (2001: 5, 9, 11). The evidence from this study argues for the introduction of consumer goods and services by the late 16th century, coinciding with an expansion of the economy. Levine and Wrightson's observation, that income derived from coal paid for the new domestic trappings of Whickham's copyholders, is analogous to the situation of Newcastle tradesmen (1991: 104).

In trying to establish which factors had the greatest influence on patterns of consumption and production, opinion on the importance of wealth, occupation and urban factors is divided. Glennie and Whyte suggest that consumption changes are earliest and most rapid in towns, over and above the differences expected by wealth and status (2000:188), but Shammas sees no very clear role for occupational status, or market accessibility, which she associates with lifestyle, once wealth and household size are considered (1990: 112, 180). Overton found that, in nearly all cases, county of residence is the greatest influence on ownership, not wealth – although, in his opinion, wealth, status and especially occupation acting together are more significant than the urban factor (2004: 166,168). In Newcastle, the evidence seems to point to occupational and urban factors as being central to the patterns, but other factors are certainly important.

Circumstances surrounding the life-cycle should also be considered in connection to consumption and investment patterns reflected in the overall levels of wealth calculated from inventories. As mentioned above, Earle has suggested that at the end of a man's working life, if he were sufficiently wealthy, he might aspire on selling a business, to join the ranks of the gentry, but in other circumstances a poorer man might face a descent into poverty as the inevitable result of everything being given away to the children at the end of a career (1994: 151); the implication being that any patterns observed in the data are dictated by life-cycle factors. However, it has been clearly demonstrated that timely bequests were common among Newcastle testators, as discussed in Chapter 3, reflected in the relatively high percentage of documents containing work-related objects (Table 5.12a). An idle retirement was unlikely, as families continued to run the household, and businesses were passed on as going concerns on the death of the head of a household. It is suggested here that discrepancies in consumption and investment patterns and in inventoried wealth are manifestly a reflection of relative fortunes in business among middling tradesmen, and that a similar bias – concerning rich or poor, young or old - will be present in all groups included in the sample.

Perhaps in attempting to create a hierarchy, whereby one factor is seen as of greater influence than another in understanding the motivations and the circumstances surrounding patterns of consumption, production and investment, the complexity of the individual circumstances surrounding the development of the material culture of the town is not being adequately acknowledged.

5.11.6 Emulation

French contends that it was a passion for aping the manners and morals of the gentry that unified the middling orders, and he relates this to the observation that the middling sorts are the most conspicuous consumers, with reference to Weatherill's finding that these men own more selected goods than the gentry (2000: 288) - a finding underlined by Overton, who has also found that in Kent professionals embraced new social rituals faster than did the gentry (Overton 2004: 167).

It is difficult to know whether the patterns of consumption among Newcastle tradesmen indicate emulation in some instances. Certain trades (notably the master mariners) did acquire selected goods ahead of others, but many items - such as hand basins and ewers, carpet cloths, cushions, Danish pots, flowerpots, glassware and hand towels, among other items - show up simultaneously on inventories of several trades among both richer and poorer householders. This situation differed, however, in rural Whickham, where only the clergy and lesser gentry had begun to enjoy a new degree of luxury by the mid 17th century, indicated by the appearance of novel items such as mirrors and glassware on their inventories (Levine and Wrightson 1991: 231, 233).

Weatherill believes there is more to consumption than social competition, fashion, emulation or display of personal wealth and status; that a desire to display wealth is not a prime mover behind urban domestic consumption; and that emulation as an explanation shows little regard for practical and social situations or the exact nature of the social hierarchy (1996: 81, 83, 90, 195). Overton concurs, noting that there is no simple trickle-down effect, as the social hierarchy is itself not simple, and he questions who is emulating who as a means of establishing social difference (2004: 174-5). He also notes that, on a practical level, expenditure on familiar items, such as linen, warns against explanations that use fashion or emulation as a primary motive behind consumption, as such purchases may denote status through quality, or are simply related to increased personal comfort (2004: 118-9). The Newcastle data suggest that the latter is the more likely explanation for the growing volume of household objects, evidenced by efforts to improve the comfort (especially that of beds) by almost everyone for whom records survive.

Overton believes that consumption does filter down the social hierarchy, and that social groups distinguish themselves through consumption and material goods; however, items are not adopted wholesale by each social group, but appropriated and refashioned to suit individual needs (2004: 8, 175). This point is well illustrated among the tradesmen of Newcastle, as for instance, in the case of Danish chests which filtered down from master mariner to mariner, or in the example of the expensive attire worn by master mariners (complete with gleaming swords and silver whistles), that was unique to these men; other wealthy tradesmen displayed no such inclination to overtly extravagant daily dress. Cordwainers, on the other hand, made great efforts to decorate their small Middle Street houses, investing sums on a par with the wealthy master mariners, whereas shipwrights showed a marked lack of interest in such goods, choosing to invest in property and boats instead.

Emulation, as an explanation for such consumer behaviour, may be more appropriately applied within, rather than between, various occupations, particularly given the significance of guild association in this period (King 2001: 25, 31), which doubtless resulted in members influencing one another's consumer choices.

5.11.6 Behaviour and identity among the middling sorts

In trying to understand the cultural meaning of material objects, Overton states that goods acquired through inheritance say little about current demand, current fashion or taste, although items that are retained after inheritance do imply consumption choices, illustrating change in household activities, practices and attitudes in relation to the adoption, quality and variety of goods recorded (2004: 87-90). However, such changes are illustrated most particularly in connection with the new social rituals surrounding the acquisition of hot drinks utensils - additions to life that are not evident until the later 17th century (Shammas 1990: 183; Weatherill: 1996: 28, 40; Overton 2004: 90, 167). Therefore, the question here is how changes in behaviour and identity can best be recognized in earlier decades, and how far the middling tradesmen appropriated the changing material culture of their own age. It is also, perhaps, important to consider that the objects upon which judgements are made present a dilemma, in that a distinction should be recognised between the testator's choice to own objects and those of the beneficiaries, who may or may not have kept what they inherited. This consideration also has implications about the time-scale of change in material culture.

By the late 17th century, French claims that material possessions became tokens of the manner of life through which gentility is conferred, noting that genteel tradesmen spend more on furnishings, as can be seen by analysing the value of furnishings in the best bedroom (2000: 46, 147). In Newcastle, both rich and poor alike are spending more on beds and bedding, and it seems unlikely that most of these tradesmen believed that such expenditure denoted genteelness, especially when one considers the situation of the keelmen or millers, for example, or the cordwainers (who indeed spent more than anyone else on such items).

Weatherill found that ownership of selected goods - both quantities and quality thereof - did reflect social status, but that the patterns have inconsistencies and inversions, and that status does not follow a consumption hierarchy (1996:183, 185). In Cornwall, for example, in the first half of the 17th century there is far greater expenditure on mundane goods than on goods for display than is the case in Kent (Overton 2004: 120).

Weatherill continued by noting that the value of moveable estate is a very crude measure of social position, highlighted by her important finding that the gentry possessed fewer of the decorative and new objects than did tradesmen (1996: 169). Although there is a social dimension to the ownership of goods, those higher up the social hierarchy did not necessarily own the goods most often (Weatherill 1996: 195; Overton 2004; 167). In subsequent publications, Weatherill reiterates her finding that there is an association between social position and ownership, between wealth and ownership, and between location in town or country and ownership, but she makes a division between the association of wealth with ownership in all areas, and with social position and ownership, which she says pertains to only certain types of goods, such as books or clocks (Schammell 2004: 15). The Newcastle evidence seems to contradict this, as books and clocks (where they are listed), belong to tradesmen, notably mariners and bakers, who do not traditionally enjoy a high social position, and who are not among the wealthiest trades of the town.

In relation to the North East, Schammell found that social position is not as important a factor in the ownership of goods as is the case elsewhere, but that, by the same token, there is no evidence that domestic aspirations here differed greatly from those in other parts of England; that it was restricted resources, rather than traditional attitudes, that restricted ownership of new things (2004: 20, 23). Social position does not appear to be an important factor in ownership among Newcastle tradesmen, nor is it clear, except in the case of the new upholstered furniture, that the acquisition of objects is related to restricted resources, as many items, particularly the decorative objects such as pictures, flower pots, glassware and cushions, which proliferated over the decades of the study, were not expensive.

The acquisition of these objects seems to have been more dependent on simple personal choice and, perhaps, trade association. For instance, if most of the brethren belonging to the bakers and brewers or the seafaring guilds owned bibles and had learned to read them, then perhaps this encouraged other members to do so. If most master mariners dressed flamboyantly, perhaps others felt obliged to follow suit; and if most cordwainers, who crowded together in Middle Street, chose to purchase a number of decorative objects for their rooms, perhaps it was seen among these men as an appropriate response to the otherwise rather crowded, noisy and smelly conditions on their doorsteps. This argument is tied to that of emulation among men of a given occupation, discussed above.

Perhaps the best explanations for social identity come from nearby Whickham. Levine and Wrightson observed the transformation of social identity in the gentrification of Whickham's copyholders by 1647, a process that began before 1600 (1991: 140, 142), and this transition may well have implications for understanding the status of tradesmen in Newcastle. Levine and Wrightson found that social development in Whickham came about through industrial development, which involved economic, technological, demographic, and social-structural change, which would re-shape social identities and shift patterns of social relationships (1991: 277-8). The close links between the coal-owning oligarchy in Newcastle and their interests in the Whickham pits suggest such forces may have influenced other tradesmen of the town. It can be argued that the development of the material culture of these men is a clear manifestation of these changes, although this thesis does not explore the hierarchical relationships of the population as a whole.

Ellis describes a marked polarisation between an unusually restricted elite and the vast quasi-proletarian multitude of the poor (1984: 197). However, the numerous and increasingly prosperous middling tradesmen must certainly have been a striking feature of this town throughout the early modern period, and especially by the early decades of the 17th century. Weatherill says that understanding the position of the craft trades is crucial to appreciating the limits of the middle ranks in a society, where some craftsmen and small manufacturers are at the bottom end of the scale (1996: 100), whereas shopkeepers and other tradesmen can vie with the lesser gentry in wealth and standard of living (French 2000: 279).

However, the classical social hierarchy of Tudor and Stuart society was a formal social description of the age (Wrightson 1994: 29), and this framework cannot be used as a guide to the consumption and production hierarchy, nor can it be used to conflate occupation and status (Weatherill 1996: 166). Wrightson confirmed that the social order was not unchanging, rigid or uniform, and that social mobility was constant and frankly recognised in the period (French 2000: 277).

Green discusses the importance of material goods in defining social identity in north-east England in the 18th century (2004: 72), and he notes that contemporaries primarily associated the region with coal, characterising the place as provincial and peripheral to the cultural epicentre of London (2004: 85; King 2001: 13). The study of the material culture records of tradesmen living in Newcastle, at least a century earlier, makes clear that this lofty view from the South ignored the flourishing culture of this northern town and people. Although Newcastle coal was a crucial element in the relationship between London and Newcastle, this north-south divide was much more complex and mutually influential than was apparently acknowledged by people of the early modern period - and some might say the same attitudes prevail today.

CHAPTER 6 – Rooms and room function

6.1 Introduction

The previous chapter has dealt extensively with material culture relating to objects in tradesmen's households and this theme is continued here. This chapter has two sections: the first examines the numbers of rooms recorded in inventories in relation to occupation and wealth levels; in the second part, selected objects are used to examine room function, activities and social relations in association with the location of the items in a deceased testator's property. Changes in house size and in the uses of rooms through the decades are traced.

Concerning the analysis of property, the nature of what is recorded on the documents has necessitated a different approach to be taken here than was employed in Chapter 4, principally because wills and inventories contain different information. Just less than 50% of wills provide information on property location, whereas up to 95% of inventories provide information on rooms. This chapter concentrates exclusively on all inventories that specify named rooms, including those that have been excluded from Chapter 4. Those inventories that do not specify rooms have been excluded from the analysis as the reasons for the non-enumeration are a matter of speculation. Contrary to Shammas' assertion, it cannot be assumed that, if no rooms are specified, this denotes a house with only one room (1990: 161). The many limitations inherent in undertaking this type of research have been outlined in Chapter 2, and are acknowledged again here. Of particular relevance are issues relating to the wealth of testators, and the exclusion of rooms on the inventories where there were no objects found by appraisers that were deemed useful to the settlement of the estate (Priestley and Corfield 1982: 99-100; Shammas 1990: 161; Johnson 1991: lxiii-lxiv; Orlin 2002: 57-60; Overton 2004: 122).

However, as highlighted in Chapter 4, the contribution made by this kind of analysis is important, as little evidence survives relating to the interiors of Newcastle houses belonging to the lower and middling sorts for the pre-Civil-War decades of the town. Archaeology normally only recovers ground floor plans; illustrations, maps and the occasional photographs that do survive of the buildings of the early modern period tend to depict the exteriors of later and grander structures that belonged to more elite members of Newcastle society, such as Bessie Surtees House (Heslop et al. 1995). Where aspects of the interiors of houses have survived, these are also confined largely to houses of the elite, such as Alderman Fenwick's House (Heslop et al. 1996). The few standing buildings pre-dating the Civil War, such as the medieval timber-framed house on the Close (Heslop and Truman 1993), or the remains of the White Hart Inn on the Bigg Market (Pevsner et al. 1992) have been much altered over time. All these problems were encountered in the Norwich study by Priestley and Corfield, who endeavoured to incorporate information on existing buildings and archaeological sites with the probate evidence, although exact matches for properties from the diverse sources were not found (1982: 94, 97). Such an approach has not been attempted here. However, a forthcoming study by Graves and Heslop on houses in Newcastle (2003: 38-9), which has not been made available to the writer, will doubtless provide new insight in this area.

The narrow focus of this study, concentrating on the probate evidence, is also justified by constraints of space and because the volume and quality of documentary material available warrants close examination. The properties analysed represent the testator's principal residence or dwelling, named as such on the will (where one survives), and the contents of such houses which appear on the accompanying inventories.

6.2 Rooms in tradesmen's properties 1552 - 1642

It is not possible to recover the architectural layout of properties by assessing numbers of rooms documented in inventories (Overton 2004: 122), and it has been established that inventories are likely to under estimate numbers of rooms (Priestley and Corfield 1982: 100). Johnson confirms that visualising house plans from inventories is impossible, but that generalisations can be made based on recurring patterns of room sequences (1991: lxiv). Despite such limitations, as shown in Chapter 4, much information concerning the location of properties along streets belonging to different trades; the plan, orientation, size and number of storeys of structures; how a building was accessed; and who occupied the premises, can be recovered using both wills and inventories together. This enquiry goes further in attempting an analysis of the interiors of tradesmen's houses over three consecutive time frames.

The types of rooms listed on Newcastle inventories are very consistent throughout the period, as is the order in which rooms are recorded. Halls, butteries, parlours, kitchens, back, lower and upper chambers, lofts, back or brew houses, stables, workshops and shops are the most frequently enumerated rooms. Occasionally, other types of rooms are mentioned, such as a study or, in one case, a barn. In the largest houses, individual names were given to upper chambers, but such references seem to be restricted to houses with more than two or three storeys, and are not at all common in Newcastle documents pertaining to middling tradesmen.

Data on the number of rooms in the properties are collated in Table 6.1a. Besides domestic spaces, shops and workhouses have been added to the figures, although it is not always clear whether these rooms were actually attached to the main house - a problem also discussed by Priestley and Corfield (1982: 100). Such additions will clearly augment house-size figures. In this study, uncertainty over the figures affects the numbers of rooms recorded for cordwainers more than for any other trade, because it is not known whether shops were always incorporated into the home. The evidence presented in Chapter 4 - 4.3.3 strongly suggests designs were similar to those in other parts of the country where small and medium-sized properties on street frontages had a shop as the ground-floor front room (Power 1972: 256; Schofield 1987: 22). Mills are also included as rooms, as they were often described as being adjoined to the rest of the property, as illustrated in Chapter 4, section 4.3.7, and also because the mills were used for both domestic and trade purposes according to room content. Butteries are not included in the figures, as these appear to have been a type of cupboard and not a separate room in Newcastle houses in this period. They can best be treated as a storage facility, although in a few cases, such as that of a baker who recorded a 'buttery chamber', some may well have been rooms, but such references are rare (D.P.R. Hall 1627). More ambivalent entries, such as a 'little buttery attstair head', make a categorical distinction difficult (D.P.R. Browne 1637). Clearly, houses will have been larger in those properties where butteries were separate rooms. The facility is included, however, in the discussion of room function below. Between 60% and 95% of Newcastle inventories specify rooms, although figures differ widely between trades, as shown in Table 6.1a, and the higher percentage figure relates to inventories dated after 1625. The figures are close to those for Kent for the period after 1600, but are much higher than those for Cornwall (Overton 2004: Table 6.1). They are also 10% higher than those in Norwich inventories (Priestley and Corfield 1982: Table 4).

The somewhat lower percentage of inventories recording rooms in the earliest Newcastle inventories probably relates to the fact that these documents listed fewer objects. It is likely that, if the appraisers were dealing with smaller properties housing fewer items, they may not have taken the trouble to name the rooms they were in (Overton 2004: 122). A correlation is therefore indicated between increasing levels of consumption in the first decades of the 17th century, as evident from the findings in Chapter 5, and an augmentation of the number of inventories specifying rooms. However, in terms of the numbers of rooms recorded over the three time frames, it is interesting to find that, although the most substantial increases in consumption occurred between 1600 and 1625, a delay seems to have occurred before appraisers reacted to the sheer volume of objects being acquired, which seems to have necessitated an increase in the enumeration of rooms reflected in the 20% rise in the numbers included in inventories after 1625. Such an increase is not apparent in Norwich inventories (Priestley and Corfield 1982: Table 4), but Overton has observed an increase in the numbers of rooms recorded in inventories from Kent and Cornwall, which he associated with the need to differentiate similar goods in different rooms, and with the overall number of goods in a household that would have an effect on the need for appraisers to differentiate rooms (2004: 122).

This observation can be linked to the question of when and indeed if Newcastle experienced a time of rebuilding, on either a great or a small scale (Hoskins 1953; Shammas 1990: 158-9). Overton concluded that the increasing numbers of rooms in Kent inventories showed that Kent was in the forefront of the so-called 'great rebuilding' in England and was far in advance of the rest of the country (2004: 124). Shammas has also highlighted that houses in the southern half of England grew larger in the course of the 17th century (1990: 161). The evidence for Newcastle is difficult to interpret. There is some evidence of the building of new rooms, either within or on to existing homes, and for construction of new houses in all periods and in several areas of the town. For example, a tanner recorded a 'newe housse at the whit crosse' on Newgate Street in his will dated 1586 (D.P.R. Doddes 1593). A shipwright had built a new house in Sandgate some time before 1609 (D.P.R Wailes 1609) while, in 1636, a baker and brewer described 'a new building in the backside' of his house in Pandon (D.P.R. Hayton 1637). Green uncovered evidence that lawyers were rebuilding houses in the early 17th century to rent out for profit (2000: 333) - a finding echoed in the case of shipwrights, who owned a high percentage of properties which they probably built themselves, and which they subsequently rented to keelmen and mariners, discussed in Chapter 4, section 4.3.8.

In evidence from Norwich, a pattern of ongoing building activity in the early modern period is evident from archaeological work indicating renovation and adaptation rather than a clearly defined period of 'Great Rebuilding' (Priestley and Corfield 1982: 104-5), and this picture may better represent the situation in Newcastle. Newcastle inventories show that, between 1552 and 1642, despite the augmentation in the numbers of objects recorded in inventories and the increasing percentage of inventories specifying the rooms where the objects were found, the numbers of rooms in the majority of tradesmen's houses remained fairly steady throughout this period. Green's finding that, in the late 16th and 17th centuries there was a greater provision of chambers on the first floor 'accommodating the complexities of the middling household' (2000: 321), does not appear to be true for a majority of tradesmen, whereas (as discussed in the second part of this chapter) the percentage of objects found in chambers was, indeed, increasing in the early 17th century. Table 6.1a shows that inventories indicating houses with one to three rooms continued to make up about 30-40% of the sample in all three time frames, and houses with at least four, or up to six rooms, varies from 46% to 54%, with the highest figure falling in the 1st quarter of the 17th century. Throughout the period of this study, the majority of properties with two, three or four rooms specify a hall, a chamber and or a loft, along with a brewhouse or kitchen. The figures for the largest properties suggest that, before 1600, 23% of houses had seven to nine rooms, but this percentage declines, and then recovers to an average of 15% after 1625. Houses with over 10 rooms are not recorded in the earliest period and only appear in any number after 1625. The augmentation of the largest houses, accounting for just less than 10% of the sample, is the only notable change in the relative percentages of the four categories relating to room numbers recorded.

Useful comparisons can be made with evidence from Norwich inventories concerning the period from 1580 to 1654, where house size also changed very little (Priestley and Corfield 1983: 100). However, the percentage of the smallest houses in Norwich is significantly lower than that indicated for Newcastle, which in turn had rather more houses with four to six rooms than were found in Norwich, while houses with seven to nine rooms or more were more common in Norwich (Priestley and Corfield 1983: 100, Table 2). When the Newcastle figures for all houses with more than seven rooms are combined with those with over 10 rooms, the percentages suggest that the differences between the regions mainly concerned the very largest properties, and as the Norwich data included an unspecified number of documents belonging to social groups above the middling sorts, it is unclear whether the figures all relate to the same socio-economic groups (Priestley and Corfield 1983: 94). Nevertheless, the largest properties in these studies were being recorded at an earlier date in Norwich than was apparent from the Newcastle sample for middling tradesmen.

Evidence from other inventories for rooms in houses from Kent and Cornwall in the period between 1600 and 1659 provides further basis for comparison (Overton 2004: 121-136). Relative to Cornwall, Newcastle appears to have had significantly fewer very small houses, featuring lofts, as described in Chapter 4, rather than partitions (as in Cornwall), but a much higher number of houses with up to six rooms or more. In comparison to Kent, Newcastle showed no steep decline in the percentage of small houses, but the town seems to have had a greater number of houses with four to six rooms and fewer with over seven rooms (Overton 2004: Table 6.2) - the same pattern observed in the Norwich data.

The appearance of houses with more than ten rooms, predominantly after 1625, may well mark the beginning of a period of expansion of properties in Newcastle, but inevitably this is linked to the question of wealth as well as function, with certain trades requiring more outbuildings such as stables, workhouses or barns (Barley 1967: 760). Wealthier tradesmen might afford themselves additional chambers, as in the case of the butcher who owned a large house on the Plumber Chare with an upper chamber called the 'Scarborough Castle' and another called the 'Birlington Hall' (D.P.R Ridley 1623). Barley's finding, that the enlargement or rebuilding of houses in the northern counties lagged far behind that in the south, dating this change to after the 1660s, is challenged by the inventory evidence (1967: 757).

An increase in the number of properties with more rooms is evident from the second quarter of the 17th century, and this finding is underlined by the large number of inventories, dated prior to 1600, which do not give room names, and therefore probably indicate small properties, and also by the absence of houses with more than 10 rooms in this period. However, overall almost all tradesmen in the earliest period had houses with either fewer than three, or fewer than six rooms, and this trend continued into the 17th century, following a more general pattern in the rest of the country, where houses with three rooms or less made up one-quarter to one-half of all properties right up to 1700 (Everitt 1967: 442-3; Portman 1974: 152-3; Spufford 1984: 2).

Changes in patterns of house sizes are clearly visible over time, but the wealth of testators must also be considered. Wealth groups are extensively analysed in Chapter 5 (see also Shammas 1990: Appendix 1, 304-5; Weatherill 1996: Appendix 2, 212-14), and the results shown in Tables 5.4a, 5.4b and Table 5.13a, can be compared with the findings shown on Tables 6.1a and 6.1b. Those trades with an average wealth of over 50li as collated on Table 5.13a - which include bakers and brewers, butchers, cordwainers, master mariners and tanners - show the highest percentage of inventories recording rooms, with the poor keelmen showing the opposite trend. The documents belonging to the poorer weavers, especially those belonging to the earliest period, underscore this observation. Many of these inventories give no room headings, and where a hall is specified, all belongings are listed in this one room. However, mariners, and to some extent the smiths, seem to be exceptions, as although they were not among the wealthiest trades their documents nevertheless specify a high percentage of rooms.

In general, however, it appears that those testators belonging to trades with an average of over 35li of inventoried wealth make up almost 90% of those who lived in the largest properties with seven or more rooms, as illustrated in Tables 5.13a and 6.1b - a finding echoed in Green's analysis of the town in the same period (2000: 73). Just two weavers and a miller among those belonging to the five poorer trades record properties with seven or more rooms. However, Table 6.1b also indicates a growth in the percentage of low-wealth tradesmen moving into houses with more than three rooms after 1600, a finding paralleled in Everitt's study of farm labourers in England, who by 1640 had also progressively moved into houses with more than three rooms, which he believes indicated that the 'standard of housing definitely improved' (1967: 442).

It is clear, nevertheless, that a majority of those tradesmen with lower inventoried wealth lived in smaller properties with up to six rooms, while the reverse scenario is not true in all cases. About 70% of tradesmen from the higher wealth trades, including some of the wealthiest men with an average of over 50li of inventoried goods, also apparently lived in fairly small houses - some with three rooms or less, and others with up to six rooms, perhaps even parts of shared buildings (Priestley and Corfield 1982: 100), as multiple occupancy was characteristic of 17th century urban life (Johnson 1991: lxiv); such cases are highlighted in Chapter 4.

The figures can be further compared with findings from Oxfordshire, Worcestershire and East London, where Shammas (1990: Table 6.1, 161-3) argues against the findings by Priestley and Corfield that house sizes changed very little in the period 1580 - 1730 (1990: 163) - a general trend that was manifest in other parts of the country (Portman 1974: 152-3; Spufford 1984: 2; Weatherill 1996: 94-5) and supported by the Newcastle evidence. Shammas acknowledges that a majority of those in her low-wealth group continued to live in one to three rooms right up to the 18th century, but she found that between the 16th and late 17th centuries a majority of those in higher wealth groups moved to houses with more than four rooms, thus apparently meeting the 'Rebuilding criteria' (1990: 163). There may, however, be problems with these calculations, as follows.

If inventories that do not enumerate rooms are excluded from the calculations, the figures for Shammas' southern counties show that, although a greater proportion of low-wealth groups did indeed live in smaller houses of one to three rooms in all periods (as did the higher wealth groups prior to 1600), the percentage of both groups who lived in houses with four to six rooms was quite similar and remained very stable in all subsequent decades (1990: Table 6.1). It was only in the case of houses with over six rooms that a clear wealth divide occurs: although a greater proportion of wealthier individuals owned larger properties, there was also a minority of lower-wealth individuals who came to own these large properties (Shammas 1990: Table 6.1, 163-4). Both these findings are echoed in the Newcastle figures. It would seem that the evidence overwhelmingly points to little change in house sizes for a majority of the population, at least pertaining to those who had the means and the need to record rooms.

The reasons why a minority of individuals in Newcastle owned much larger houses in the early modern period seem to have been motivated either by wealth, or by the need for additional space relating to an occupation, which reflected both the type and the number of rooms that are enumerated in inventories. Shammas believes wealth is important in understanding property size, but argues against occupation being a significant factor (1990: 164-5), and Green also believes house size reflected wealth more directly than occupation, but notes Wrightson's observation that a tight property bracket cannot be ascribed to individuals within an occupation (2000: 73, 333). These findings are contested by the Newcastle evidence, as it was the bakers and brewers, butchers, cordwainers, tanners and smiths who owned the largest houses, often accommodating facilities associated with trade, rather than the wealthy master mariners, the majority of whom had houses of four to six rooms. Spufford (1962) noted the proliferation of service rooms in large houses in Cambridgeshire (Green 2000: 74), and this phenomenon is echoed in tradesmen's houses in Newcastle, where auxiliary structures were required in relation to differing occupations. It is, nevertheless, acknowledged that the poorer tradesmen - especially the keelmen and weavers - often made do with only two rooms, while some of the wealthiest tradesmen were indeed living in large houses as described in Chapter 4.

Crowding within the town may also have had some bearing on property size, as suggested by Shammas (1990: 164). As revealed in Chapter 4, the population in Sandgate lived in low-level buildings with multiple adjoining rooms, but the response to the intra-mural crowding in the Lower East Side of Newcastle was to build taller structures, and this was evident in the case of wealthy tradesmen who added upper chambers to their houses. However, in other parts of town where space was available, a majority of properties were two-storey with multiple adjoining rooms and work spaces. An explanation for the growth in property size relating to demographic change (Shammas 1990: 164) is not evident from Newcastle wills, despite population growth in the town (Howell 1967: 2; King 2000: 337-8).

6.3 Location and function of objects in rooms

Living arrangements in houses in the Northern Counties, according to Barley, evidenced from Durham inventories, were 'largely untouched by the new ideas of comfort and convenience which had flooded over the lowland zone of England' in the late Elizabethan and early Stuart period (1967: 757). Such claims have proved misleading, according to the findings in Chapter 5, as the evidence is overwhelming that there was a great increase in the numbers of objects in the households of Newcastle tradesmen in this period, which clearly indicate improvements in the comfort, if not the convenience, of daily life in this early modern northern town.

In the course of Chapter 5, the location of some objects - notably those associated with hearths and cooking facilities, and spinning and brewing activities – has been discussed. In this section a more in-depth analysis of a selection of objects is undertaken to explore the way rooms were used in tradesmen's households and to discover whether objects provide clues about changes to the function of space over time, and whether wealth and occupation are important factors. The analysis also looks at social relations between household members in connection with mutually shared spaces and household activities associated with the objects listed in specific rooms. Rooms examined in this section include halls, butteries, parlours, kitchens, back or lower chambers, upper or fore chambers, chambers in unspecified locations, lofts and specialised work spaces. Exactly where these rooms are located relative to one another cannot be recovered to any extent, as clues are limited to descriptions such as 'upper', 'lower', 'back', 'fore' 'over' or 'adjoined'; for this type of analysis see Chapter 4. The overall percentage of rooms named in the inventories has not been calculated, although it is noted that such an approach has been successfully undertaken elsewhere by Priestley and Corfield (1982: Table 4), and by Overton (2004: Table 6.3), (albeit on a much larger sample of inventories), whereas approximate house sizes have been calculated in this study.

Tables 6.2a-g illustrate the distribution of selected objects in the households of tradesmen in the period between 1552 and 1642. Percentage figures represent the number of references to any one type of objects in a room, not the number of these objects. A degree of bias in the findings is possible towards more expensive objects, while poorer quality items may be under-represented. However, while objects of little value sometimes cannot be traced, the inventories show the rooms where the greatest investment in objects is being made, and also provide an impression of which rooms are likely to be the most crowded with objects.

Table 6.2a provides an indication of where clothes are kept although, as appraisers often value these items separately, they frequently appear as one of the last items added to the bottom of the inventory (see Chapter 5, section 5.4). Apparel is listed in all rooms in the house, but most items are located in the upper chambers or other unnamed chambers. References to clothes decline for halls and parlours over the decades, but double for upper chambers, while the number of items listed in lofts is halved. Although the sample is rather small, the evidence suggests that tradesmen increasingly dressed in the more secluded parts of houses by the second quarter of the 17th century, but such an observation must account for the other activities that took place in these rooms, discussed below. The disappearance of clothes from lofts might suggest the space is less often used by masters of the household in later decades. An incidental observation is that mirrors are not apparently used for dressing in the homes of tradesmen, as most of these items are located in halls.

In Table 6.2b, the distribution of beds and bedding around the house is examined. Weatherill's belief, that it is virtually unknown to have a bed in a hall in this period, is contradicted by the Newcastle data (1996: 10). Beds are found in halls, as well as parlours and kitchens, although at least half are located in upper chambers and chambers in unspecified locations. Over time, a small increase in the percentage of references to beds in halls is clear, whereas the figure for parlours remains fairly steady, with an increase in the proportion of beds in kitchens and back or lower rooms, with a corresponding decline in references to beds in lofts. In evidence from Norwich, a similar, but slightly more marked increase in the use of halls and kitchens for sleeping is evident up to 1654, whereas parlours and rooms referred to as 'parlour chambers', rather than chambers, are the most frequently mentioned rooms with beds (Priestley and Corfield 1982: Tables 5, 6, 7, 11, p.107). In comparison to evidence from Kent, from the period between 1600 and 1659, halls and kitchens are almost never used for sleeping, whereas parlours and (particularly) chambers were (Overton 2004: Table 6.5).

In Newcastle changes in sleeping arrangements are not particular to any one trade. For example, both the poorer and the better-off tradesmen listed beds in halls - a decision doubtless dictated by necessity in the case of tradesmen with small two-room houses. This situation is echoed in data from Lincoln, where it is the poor who slept in halls (Johnson 1991: lxvi), although many of Newcastle's small houses have beds in lofts. Display may play a role in the wealthier homes, evidenced by increasing valuations in beds and bedding (see Chapter 5 - Table 5.3). An overall average of 14% of families used the hall for sleeping, confirming Overton's finding that, from an early date, halls are not usually a location for beds (2004: 130). However, it is noteworthy that beds described as 'little' or 'small', and cradles for children are mentioned in halls, along with some rare references to children's toys, showing that babies and young children are sleeping in this room, especially perhaps during the day. The hall is also one of the warmest rooms in the house, according to the distribution of hearths illustrated in Chapter 5 - Table 5.1a.

The increasing use of the kitchen for sleeping, by the 17th century, where servant's beds are specially mentioned, could suggest that servants began sleeping in this room rather than in the chambers where the most expensive beds are located. The change may suggest distancing in social relations in some larger households (Weatherill 1996:11). The decline in the use of lofts, where servant's beds are also listed, may indicate progressive change, supporting the evidence that servants are more often sleeping in the kitchen. A more negative reading, however, is that the quality of servant's beds in lofts is so poor that they increasingly did not warrant appraisal. Overall, however, in most homes, old beds, servant's beds, trundle or hurle beds on wheels (which are rolled out from beneath other beds), stand beds and beds of straw or thistledown are to be found in the same rooms as the most expensive feather beds. Social differentiation in sleeping arrangements is not apparent in the majority of inventories. However, in Chapter 5, section 5.3 the doubling of valuations for beds and bedding, reflecting increases in both investment and numbers of beds, suggests that individuals are more often acquiring a bed of their own - or at least one shared with fewer people - as household size, as mentioned, is not apparently growing. It is also interesting to find that the numbers of references to chamber pots rises from 16% listed in documents dated prior to 1600, to 51% between 1601 and 1625, to 74% after 1626 suggesting increasingly personal arrangements - although these items are most frequently located in kitchens and halls, as well as parlours. It appears that a distinction must be made between the designation of an item as personal and the use of the item in communal areas.

The location of cookware, shown in Table 6.2c, as distinct from the iron chimneys, iron bars and appurtenances of the fires, examined in Chapter 5, section 5.1, indicates that, throughout the decades of this study, cooking continued to be done in the hall in a majority of households, or in a kitchen (if the house is large enough to accommodate such a room). When cookware is found in the parlour, most often the inventory lists no kitchen, and therefore both rooms are probably serving the same function and differed only in name. After 1626 there is evidence that in larger houses kitchens (rather than the hall) are becoming the focus of greater investment for cookware, and these items are not those relating to storage or brewing (Overton 2004: 130), although even in these larger households some cooking still took place in the hall. It is very rare to find kitchens that are the exclusive location for the cookware. The very few objects mentioned in upper rooms are likely used for the warming of prepared meals on the upper hearths, rather than for cooking meals, as food would be transferred from the kitchenware to the tableware (Johnson 1991: lxxi) - an observation linked to the change in distribution of tableware, discussed below. A virtual absence of cookware from chambers or parlour chambers is also apparent from Norwich inventories, where a radically different picture is presented: there, cooking did not usually take place in the hall, because kitchens are used by the majority of householders from the 1580s onwards; although parlours are also occasionally mentioned, cooking ceased in such rooms at an earlier date than is the case in Newcastle; however, in both Newcastle and Norwich, a decline in the use of butteries for storing cookware is evident (Priestley and Corfield 1982: Tables 5-7, 9, 11, p.108). Overall, the number of references to cookware remains very steady and the evidence suggests that neither the setup nor the location of the cookware is changing very much in the period of this study. The findings for Newcastle are remarkably similar to those for Kent, especially regarding the figures relating to the use of halls and kitchens, although the use of 'chambers' for cooking appears to be more common in Kent (Overton 2004: Table 6.5, p.130), but whether these chambers are on the upper or ground floor is unclear.

The evidence for distribution of tableware (Table 6.2d) shows increasing references to these objects and some change in where these are located, although it is uncertain if items are stored where they are used (Overton 2004: 131). Throughout the decades of the study, the hall appears to have remained the most popular room for taking meals, a situation echoed in findings from Norwich (Priestley and Corfield 1982: Table 5) and Kent (Overton 2004: Table 6.5). In Newcastle, the use of the buttery to store tableware halves between the beginning and end of the study period. The use of the kitchen for eating is increasing, although figures are higher for both Kent and especially Norwich, whereas Newcastle inventories suggest greater use of the parlour for meals than in either of these other places (Priestley and Corfield 1982: Tables 5, 7; Overton 2004: Table 6.5).

Perhaps the most notable change regarding tableware is the doubling in references to these items in upper chambers, although a close examination of the types of objects listed reveals a selection of the best pewter doublers and banqueting dishes, while wooden trenchers or other cheaper wares are not found here. A similar trend is witnessed in Norwich inventories (Priestley and Corfield 1982: Table 11) and in Kent, where the habit of eating in the chamber is quite common (Overton 2004: Table 6.5).

Changes in social practices within the tradesmen's households are evident from distribution patterns for tableware, notably in the case of the use of upper chambers for meals, which probably appertained to the master and his immediate family, rather than the servants, given the restricted selection of tableware being used. This might indicate distancing in social relations in the household between the servants, who may increasingly have eaten in the kitchen, and other members of the family who chose to have food brought upstairs. However, it is not clear from the location of the tableware which meals are taken in the different rooms, or at what times of the day. Which household members ate together remains a matter of conjecture.

Distribution patterns for furniture, shown in Table 6.2e, provide a guide to the rooms where people consumed meals, worked, relaxed or entertained. The furniture selected for analysis represents the items most commonly mentioned - namely tables, chairs, stools, forms and longsettles (benches with arms and backs). Priestley and Corfield found that in the 16th century there is little provision for sitting, and that only by the 17th century are houses better appointed (1982: 102). An augmentation in furnishings in Newcastle homes is apparent after 1600, with a virtual doubling of references to items over the decades - figures that also reflect increasing expenditure after 1625, as discussed in Chapter 5, and illustrated in Table 5.3. The figures can be contrasted with those for cookware, which show much less change.

Most of the appraised household furniture is found in the hall, especially prior to 1600, while a decline of nearly 20% is evident relative to other rooms after 1625. References to furniture in parlours and kitchens approximately double over the same period, and the volume of furniture in upper chambers also increases quite markedly, whereas the number of items in lofts fall perceptibly, as is also the case for the (few references to) furniture stored in butteries. Prior to 1600, provision of seating in halls is much higher in Newcastle than is the case in Norwich, where kitchens and especially parlours had far more furnishings; however, patterns for Newcastle chambers and Norwich 'parlour chambers' are similar (Priestley and Corfield 1982: Tables 5-7, 11). Some rooms are clearly becoming more crowded with furniture by the early 17th century, and altering patterns of behaviour within the home are implied by these changes in seating arrangements, which are underlined by the steady movement of tableware into parlours and kitchens, and into upper chambers, which although already full of beds, are making space for more seating.

The location of spinning wheels and yarn also provides some (minimal) evidence for seating arrangements. As shown in Table 6.2f, spinning wheels and yarn are to be found in every room in the house, but spinning (according to the distribution of these items), took place mainly in upper or other unspecified chambers and lofts, and secondly in the hall. The figures mirror those from Kent (Overton 2004: Table 6.6). The increasing volume of furniture in the upper chambers, suggests that spinners are being accommodated with more seating, and the growing numbers of cushions in these rooms, discussed below, indicates increasing comfort. There is some evidence that, over the decades, parlours are more often used for spinning, whereas this activity is perhaps declining in halls, as it is in lofts, (a situation echoed by the decline of servant's beds in this room). It is reasonable to presume that servants, if given the opportunity, may have preferred to spin in the warmth of the kitchen rather than remain in the more isolated and unheated lofts.

Another area of interest regarding the distribution of objects relates to the very marked increase in the consumption of decorative items in tradesmen's houses by the early 17th century, as established in Chapter 5. Four of the most popular items have been selected for analysis – namely, cushions, flower pots, mirrors and pictures. Table 6.2g shows that most of these objects are located, first, in halls and, secondly, in upper chambers. Cushions, common to almost all households from the earliest decades, are widely distributed around the home, but by the start of the 17th century many more made their way into parlours and (especially) upper chambers. This finding can be correlated with the observed movement of other furniture into these rooms, indicating increasingly comfortable seating for spinners and diners among others. Flower pots had clearly become a very popular item in many households by the early 17th century. Prior to 1600, those listed are found mainly in halls, which remained the favourite location in subsequent decades, with parlours and upper chambers increasingly mentioned; in the last period, flower pots are making their way into other chambers and, in one case, even into a loft. Mirrors, which are rare before 1600, are usually found in halls and parlours, the opposite finding to households in Kent, where mirrors are more likely to be found in chambers and where (according to Overton) they are 'strictly functional' (2004: 135). This observation perhaps overlooks the possibility that women who sat to spin in chambers, probably in the company of friends and neighbours, enjoyed the mirrors and other decorative objects in this room - an argument supported by evidence from Lincoln, showing women tend to possess many more mirrors than men (Johnson 1991: lxxv). Pictures, also rare in the earliest period, are mostly placed in halls or in chambers. Although their location is seldom mentioned, the patterns are clear and seem fairly similar to those from Kent in the period up to 1659, although here pictures are more often found in parlours (Overton 2004: Table 6.5, p.135). Overall, the huge increase in the volume of decorative objects by the second quarter of the 17th century (see Chapter 5, Table 5.2a), appears to lead to the spread of these items into more rooms. And this development is not confined to those testators with the largest numbers of goods and the largest houses (Green 2000: 73): the cordwainers are a case in point, as these tradesmen tended to have small houses that are particularly well furnished. Overall, Johnson's assertion - that evidence of changes to furniture and of improving standards of comfort is not easily extracted from inventories - has proved too pessimistic (1991: lxxiv).

The distribution of work-related objects also deserves consideration, as the location of tools, stocks and wares associated with individual trades can be recovered to a degree from inventory evidence. It is clear that the nature of the trade is a key factor in the distribution of such objects and in the function of spaces. Weatherill's distinction between 'living space' and 'work place' is not as clear-cut as suggested (1996: 144). Table 6.2h shows that certain trades are much more likely than others to carry out work within rooms that are also used for domestic activities according to room content, whereas other trades confined their business to an area separate from the living quarters (Weatherill 1996: 144), a pattern common to tradesmen with shops in East London in the 17th century (Power 1972: 256).

Relative to other trades, bakers and brewers use more domestic spaces for baking activities and storage, although the figures exclude brewing activities (shown separately in Table 5.11a), which are almost always carried out in an adjoining brewhouse, a room not listed by most other tradesmen. Tailors and weavers are more likely than other trades to use halls, chambers and, occasionally, parlours for work. Weavers, in particular, placed looms in upper chambers (Barley 1967: 761), although both these trades also practised their trades in separate workshops. Mariners and master mariners kept the clothes, navigational equipment, affiliated books and maps mainly in chambers and lofts, although master mariners make use of cellars, including those belonging to the Trinity House, for storing supplies and equipment (Chapter 4 - 4.3.6; Chapter 5 - 5.10.6). Shipwrights also record storing equipment in cellars in Sandgate.

Several trades - including cordwainers, shipwrights, smiths and millers - keep quite substantial numbers of tools and various work-related supplies in chambers, lofts and back houses, while carrying on the bulk of production in shops and workhouses (rooms primarily recorded by butchers, cordwainers, smiths, skinners and glovers, and tanners). The probate evidence suggests that these work spaces are integral to, or adjoined to, the house (as discussed in Chapter 4), fitting the pattern illustrated by Treswell for early 17th century London, where small and medium-sized properties include a ground-floor shop, or a warehouse built as a room attached to a complex of buildings (Schofield 1987: 22). Tanners divide their activities between workhouses that contain vats, and the lime pits on the outskirts of the town. Shipwrights, as outlined in Chapter 4, make use of quayside wharfs and other open spaces around Sandgate to build ships - the same areas where keelmen doubtless keep their boats.

The distribution of those work-related objects associated *only* with the principal occupation is clearly related to the trade practised, and overall about 40% of houses had specialist shops or workhouses (Table 6.2h). This figure is comparable to those in other regions. Evidence from Norwich shows that halls, kitchens, parlours and chambers are not apparently used for working, but about 40% of properties do have shops and workhouses on the ground floor that are exclusively business premises (Priestley and Corfield 1982: Tables 5-8, 11, p.109). The Norwich figures, however, do not specify trade; therefore, no delineation between the needs of varying occupations is made relative to room use. Overton has also examined where work is carried out in houses in

Kent, although here, too, no delineation between occupations has been attempted, and it is not entirely clear if the work-related objects in the figures include items associated with the primary occupation, by-employment, as well as domestic activities, such as spinning, which he examines separately (2004: Tables 6.4, 6.5). As seen in Newcastle households that contain shops or workhouses, the 'service rooms' in Kent households contain about 40-50% of work-related objects, although the percentage of work carried out in halls, chambers and kitchens in Newcastle households is lower than that indicated for Kent (Overton 2004: Table 6.5), but these particular Newcastle figures exclude domestic activities which are taken up separately (see Chapter 5, sections 5.7, 5.9, and above regarding spinning).

However, when the figures from Newcastle and Kent are examined in more detail (especially those relating to small houses), the distribution patterns for work-related objects are similar, with spinning, brewing and baking activities taking place in halls and kitchens (Overton 2004: 130). The figures for chambers, which shows a decline in work in this room in Kent households, is not apparent from the Newcastle sample, especially because in Newcastle weavers, operating looms and spinning, work in chambers. The figures for parlours, from both Kent and Newcastle, indicate this room is rarely used for work (Overton 2004: Table 6.5, p.130, 133).

Generalisations about the distribution of objects around properties - such as Johnson's finding that the presence of a shop on the ground floor would have put pressure on space, resulting in principal chambers being forced upstairs (1991: lxvii) - need to account for the ways in which tradesmen practising different occupations organised room use within properties. The evidence here shows that endeavours to establish any 'national trend' (Johnson 1991: lxvii) must account for occupational specialisation within households.

6.4 Social aspects of room use

Having examined distribution patterns of selected objects in some detail, the question of how social relations within households can be linked to the findings requires comment. It would seem inevitable that some change in the way social relations are being conducted can be inferred from distribution patterns, despite the fact that no objects other than beds and bedding are ever specifically designated in the inventories as being solely the preserve of any one social group within the household - and this exception only concerns servants. All objects in this study of course belong to a deceased male, who is normally the head of a household.

Overton provides plausible examples of how objects can reveal aspects of social relations from Kent inventories, one of which shows how newer and better-quality furniture in a hall is the preserve of certain members of a household, while servants are left to manage with older items in the kitchen, especially in larger households, and another where the taking of meals in more than one room suggests that servants and children might no longer eat together with the head of the household (2004: 130, 134-5). However, the location of furniture or tableware cannot reveal satisfactorily precisely who sat and ate together in rooms. For instance, if several meals are served over the course of the day, these may be regarded differently, some being more and others less formal occasions (Weatherill 1996: 153). Rituals could change, depending on time and occasion. Occasionally, clues to the nature of social relations within households are found. One will in particular, which relates to the family of a tailor and a bequest to a servant sheds light on the question of shared meals and seating arrangements. The testator bequeaths 'his man' Edward money and clothes 'in lew of his mother's love in his entertaining his daughter Margarett att Table' (D.P.R. Clark 1636). The sharing of meals and places at table would seem likely in view of this kind of evidence.

How far social segregation within the house can be inferred from the location of objects within rooms is difficult to access (Overton 2004: 131), but a very prescriptive view by Johnson on the use of chairs, for example, supposedly rare items reserved for male heads of households (1996; 34, 156-7), is not supported by the Newcastle data, or by the records from Lincoln, where the chair has lost its symbolic status by the 1660s (Johnson 1991: lxxii). Green's observations concerning the segregation of spaces for family or servants embodied in the physical form of a house (2000: 322) cannot be ascertained by way of inventories, and social separation within shared living spaces of tradesmen's homes is not evident from the documents. Even the use of upper chambers for spinning by women, which indicates a degree of separation between genders within the home (Overton 2004: 130), and might suggest that women spend more time in upper chambers than men, does not equate to exclusivity of either access to or function of a room. The presence of women spinning, probably with neighbours and friends, does not preclude the presence of other family members or servants who may have sat, eaten, worked or slept in this same room. Evidence from Lincoln shows that chambers are 'far less private than today's bedrooms', functioning as reception rooms for friends, sometimes with lavish provision of seating (Johnson 1991: lxx). This picture is recognisable from the Newcastle evidence and such observations apply equally well to other rooms in the tradesmen's properties that served many functions.

Even in those areas of a property where production activities are undertaken, Weatherill's finding that these were 'done outside the main living space ... often out of sight, 'backstage'' has proven incorrect as several trades worked in rooms where domestic and occupational activities overlapped, while those working in shops, especially on the ground floor facing the street, cannot be described as 'out of sight' (1996: 145). The idea that work-related activities and associated objects are somehow concealed is a highly impractical proposition - one that suggests domestic or trade activities are socially isolated, which would have been a most unlikely situation in the homes of middling tradesmen, considering the collective nature of much employment by master, wife, children and servants (Spufford 1984: 53, 70, 74; Clark 1992: 293-4, 298; Weatherill 1996: 138). The volume and variety of objects in the rooms in tradesmen's houses confirm that exclusive areas, designated for particular activities by some, but not all household members, are not practicable.

Weatherill's other proposal - that a frontstage-backstage dichotomy is useful in understanding the use of space and social behaviour in association with different kinds of goods located in different parts of the house (1996: 9, 145) - can also be challenged. Her idea that 'more attractive and varied goods were associated with the expressive 'frontstage' activities' (Weatherill 1996: 165), cannot be reconciled with the distribution patterns of decorative objects and the increasing comfort in rooms that are simultaneously used for 'backstage' activities (with the possible exception of parlours in a few select homes). Overton noted that, in Kent, many decorative objects such as pictures, mirrors and clocks are, in fact, more likely to be found in rooms designated as 'backstage' areas, and that such simple dichotomies like 'frontstage' and 'backstage', or the idea of private areas, are too crude to capture the usages of rooms and their contents (2004: 135-6).

A more defined use of space by households is perhaps more applicable to the larger households of the later 17th century in connection with the introduction of hot-drink rituals and increased leisure activities (Weatherill 1996: 39, 145), whereas, in the earlier decades of the 17th century, the distribution of decorative objects reveals little about social relations. In Newcastle, such items are found not only in many areas of the homes of tradesmen, but also among those of very differing levels of wealth. Johnson's idea that such objects are 'symbols of distinction' (1991: lxxiii) cannot be sustained, either in the case of individuals or in connection with the rooms where any such objects are to be found. In terms of the concept of privacy, such attitudes or arrangements are also noticeably absent from tradesmen's homes, and an incidental observation cautions against constructing such notions. The inventories reveal that both chamber pots and close stools are most frequently located in halls and kitchens and, increasingly, in the better decorated parlours of larger houses by the mid-1620s. Close stools, when they appear on inventories by the 17th century, are always appraised together with the most valuable beds in halls in wealthier homes, indicating that the new facility is a rather 'public' *en-suite* arrangement.

6.5 Conclusions

This analysis has demonstrated the usefulness of probate inventories for studies of rooms and room function, and for understanding how transitions in material culture are taking place over the decades.

In terms of the size of houses belonging to middling tradesmen, clearly the picture is likely to need revising, owing to omissions in the records. Other social groups and additional sources should be examined, but certain patterns have emerged from the study. The size of houses belonging to middling tradesmen changes very little between the 1550s and 1642, although substantially larger houses are being built by the 1620s. Newcastle may have lagged behind its southern neighbours in such developments, and the percentage of these large properties is apparently greater in places such as Kent and Norwich, where probate evidence could be tied to a period of rebuilding (Priestley and Corfield 1983: 100; Overton 2004: 124). Nevertheless, this analysis has found that rebuilding (albeit on a scale that might not be described as 'great') was certainly experienced in the early 17th century (Green 2000: 333). Both wealth and occupation play a role in determining the size of a property - although wealth may have been of lesser importance than occupation in the case of tradesmen, as trades may have required additional auxiliary rooms to accommodate expanding businesses, augmenting the size of properties.

The analysis of the function of rooms has produced some interesting patterns showing both change and continuity in the location of objects and associated activities in households. Overall, evidence of a move towards functional specialisation of spaces is very limited in the decades of this study, a finding supported by Green's observation that the uses of rooms in houses in County Durham and Newcastle, dated to the late 16th and early 17th centuries, show considerable continuity, especially on the ground floor (2000: 322). The progression to greater specialisation of rooms has been dated to the late 17th century (Green 2000: 323); however, according to the documents, kitchens are an exception, as this room began to supplant the hall as the primary area for cooking by the early 1620s, although only in larger houses. Halls in a majority of households prior to the Civil War remained the primary place for cooking, eating, sitting and (more rarely) for sleeping, and are well decorated, as is also the case in both Norwich and Kent (Priestley and Corfield 1982: 105; Overton 2004: 130). Such arrangements for halls begins to change in Newcastle only by the later 17th century, with the removal of beds and cooking facilities (Green 2000: 323) - a situation echoed in evidence from Lincoln in the Restoration era (Johnson 1991: lxvi).

From the late 16th century onwards chambers are becoming a place to sit and to dine, as evidenced by the increasing references to pewter doublers and banqueting dishes, and by the extra furniture and cushions that are more frequently mentioned in upstairs rooms; but once again, such change is more limited in the smallest houses belonging to poorer tradesmen. Chambers are not, however, generally sparsely furnished (Weatherill 1996: 11), and sleeping is certainly not separated from sitting in this room, as is the case by the end of the 1600s (Green 2000: 323). It should be noted that, in many homes, the function of chambers is diverse, where stores of grain, shop goods and servant's beds are to be found alongside silverware, apparel and the master's bed - a situation echoed in Lincoln households (Johnson 1991: lxvii). During the period of this study, parlours are somewhat more often used for sleeping than are halls, but they are not generally used for eating and rarely for cooking, as is the case in Kent and Lincoln; in Newcastle parlours become progressively better furnished with seating and decorative objects by the 1620s, suggesting changes to the function occur at an earlier date than the late 17th century (Johnson 1991: lxvi; Weatherill 1996: 11; Green 2000: 323; Overton 2004: 132). The evidence for the use of lofts for a variety of functions - notably for storage and servant's beds, (the same uses seen in Lincoln) (Johnson 1991: lxvii) - does appear to decline as references to objects in the room declines, a pattern picked up in Kent inventories which show that the term 'loft' went out of use (Overton 2004: Table 6.3, p.133). However, any such decline is more apparent in the larger households, as the poorer tradesmen continued to use lofts in lieu of chambers as confirmed in Chapter 4.

Room function is apparently dictated by available space, linked to wealth in some cases, and to occupational and domestic requirements, and most rooms have a multiplicity of functions. Overall, in the decades prior to the Civil War, it seems that work-related activities, both professional and domestic, may have been the dominant factor dictating room use in middling tradesmen's households, rather than social considerations, which slowly evolve by the late 17th century. However, evidence for increasing levels of consumption over the decades and the subsequent spread of furnishings and decorative objects into more rooms in houses, does suggest that material life is improving over successive decades. Change is measured, and benefited richer and poorer tradesmen to differing degrees, but almost without exception, the inventories suggest that these changes affected everyone in the sample, even the keelmen, who are so much poorer than other tradesmen.

Truly private rooms in tradesmen's homes are not apparent. There is, however, some evidence for progressively more individual use of certain types of objects, notably beds and chamber pots. However, although the proliferation in objects allowed individuals the opportunity to acquire more personal items, this personalisation of objects did not, apparently, equate to increasing privacy relating to the use of objects within the home. Privacy, in a modern sense, belongs to a later period.

How social relations are conducted among household members, and which rooms visitors to homes are invited to enter remains a matter of conjecture. The overwhelming balance of material cultural evidence suggests that rather informal and practical arrangements predominated in the majority of modest-sized houses belonging to middling tradesmen. Households will have had their own norms and standards. Everitt noted that relationships between master and servant are largely a matter of personality (1967: 438), and such an observation will be equally applicable to all household members. Perhaps this, more than any other consideration, ultimately dictates access both to rooms and to the objects in them, especially if neither the house nor the household is especially large.

This chapter set out to recover a picture of rooms and room function, in association with social relations, examining evidence for transition and change relating to properties belonging to Newcastle's middling tradesmen. The importance of probate records in this kind of research has been demonstrated in this accurate and comprehensive account of the material culture of a group of people whose properties no longer stand and whose possessions are rarely found in museums.

CHAPTER 7 – Discussions and conclusions

The aim of this thesis has been to examine, by way of the Durham Probate Records, the material culture of middling tradesmen who lived in Newcastle in the century between 1545 and 1642. Upon embarking on this analysis, the background to the creation of these documents has been explored and the laws, customs and practices of the town in the early modern period extensively reviewed. Criticisms of studies that utilise probate records have been addressed, and it has been acknowledged that analysis of these records requires care, as there are many limitations and omissions to be considered. However, the exceptional difficulties inherent in such sources for historical analysis can be overcome if careful methodologies are employed in pursuing the aims and objectives of the research.

This empirically based study has demonstrated that probate records remain an invaluable guide to the early modern period, providing one of the few opportunities open to the historian to reconstruct the material culture of the age (Levine and Wrightson 1991: 90). The vast collections of these unique primary sources, surviving for almost every area of Britain, provide immense scope for further analysis. The records pertaining to Newcastle have provided a means to study the people, properties and objects of early modern Newcastle, in a region that has been relatively neglected and in which research has often focused on the great industries, civil war and unrest - aspects of life that in such studies are seen to predominate in this most northern county of England. The particular social group taken up in the study (which excludes those of more elite status) has also tended to be overlooked. The middling tradesmen were not among the rich or powerful, and some were relatively poor, but they do not, however, represent the multitude of the very poor of the town who have left no such records.

In Chapter 3, patterns of bequests have been analysed to understand inheritance practices of middling tradesmen. Life-cycle factors, wealth and occupation have been considered in a local, regional and national context. The ways in which bequests were devised conforms to a nationwide pattern, reflecting laws, customs, and religious duties pertaining to England during the early modern period. Newcastle, and the north more generally, adopted the practices of the rest of the country (Howell 1978; Spufford 1984, 2000; Issa 1986; Levine and Wrightson 1991; Erickson 2002). There is no evidence of a so-called 'Norse influence' (Erickson 2002: 63), or of an 'ancient Germanic method' of transmitting property (Cox and Cox 2000: 19) in northern England. The crucial factor in the disposal of all estates has been family responsibility, relating to the life-cycle stage reached by a family at the time that the head of the household died (Issa 1986: 469-70; Spufford 1976: 171-2). And while the focus has often been on the age of the testators (Howell 1978: 140), it is suggested here that it was both the age and the stage of life reached by beneficiaries on the death of the head of the household that was, in fact, of greater significance.

Primogeniture is apparent, but has been found to be a wholly inadequate explanation for inheritance patterns overall. Sons are almost always bequeathed real property, especially the family home, but take possession only when they have come of age, whereas widows, almost without exception, retain the family property when they have minor children. Widows (if they do not remarry) sometimes retain a right to the family home even once their children have reached the age of majority; otherwise, they are usually given a one-third part of the estate as prescribed by law. Daughters, in lieu of real property, are usually compensated to an extent with cash portions, and they often share in the household 'goods and chattels'. However, sons receive the greater part of the household goods and real property, but not of the cash portions. If a family has multiple properties, these tend to be shared more equitably. Where family members share the household 'goods and chattels', widows together with their sons receive a greater share than widows and daughters. Overall, a clear bias towards males is evident throughout the records, with sons, brothers, nephews, male cousins and apprentices (etc.) all receiving a greater share of bequests than do their female counterparts. However, it is possible that this partiality results from all the testators in the sample being male, as a similar bias has been noted towards female recipients in the wills of widows (Erickson 2002: 77, 215). Even so, the well-attested problem of poverty among women in this period (Levine and Wrightson 1991: 351; Erickson 2002: 154) must surely have been exacerbated by such discriminatory practices, with implications for the distribution of wealth in society as a whole.

Despite these conclusions, it is clear that testators went to great lengths to try to devise estates equitably - a finding illustrated by the detailed testimonies in wills (which have been extensively quoted). Any principal heir, male or female, was given marked responsibilities towards those who did not receive as large a share of the family estate. A preoccupation with principal male heirs has resulted in arguments concerning primogeniture, often ignoring principal female heirs, who were given the same responsibilities as their male counterparts. The different strategies evident in the division of estates, appears to depend partly on the type of bequest and partly on the identity of beneficiaries.

Kin beyond the immediate family, friends, neighbours, and the poor, were often included as legatees, and these people were more important to testators than has been suggested (Cressy 1986; Issa 1986). In Newcastle, although the nuclear family retained up to 90% of both real property and goods, 40% of bequests of cash were distributed to people outside the immediate family. Levine and Wrightson have also found, in nearby Whickham, that although testators concentrated on the well-being of their wives and children, 72% gave at least token bequests to kin outside the nuclear family (1991: 285).

The poor of Newcastle were aided by way of contributions to the churches or clergy, especially in the parish of All Saints (where most of the town's poorer residents lived), and by bequests to other institutions such as almshouses. Assistance was probably more effective and better organised than suggested by Howell (1967: 314, 319), though it would seem that, as only one-quarter of testators specifically bequeathed money to the poor, more could have been done to help these people, whose numbers were prodigious (Bourne 1736, 1980; Langton 1975; Ellis 2001). However, testators increasingly appear, by the early 17th century, to prefer to bequeath money to poor friends and neighbours rather than the unnamed poor - a change that King attributed to the later decades of the century (2001: 62).

Bequests of clothes declined over the decades of this study, as was the case elsewhere in England (Spufford 1984, 1990). The disappearance of clothing from wills marked a notable change in priorities, although clothing continued to be listed on inventories, bequeathed as part of the household goods. A decline in bequests of animals has also been observed, following a wider national trend; this does not, however, apply to children in Newcastle, who continue to be the principal recipients, notably of young cows and lambs, suggesting the survival of traditions that were changing in other regions as cash replaced animal bequests (Everitt 1967: 417; Shammas 1990: 40).

Differences in the division of bequests are apparent between the trades. Several important examples can be cited. Cordwainers, butchers and millers were much more likely than other tradesmen to leave businesses to daughters, and although life-cycle and demographic factors cannot be ruled out, the higher percentage figures for these occupations are significant. Many widows continued to run businesses on their husband's death, but the fact that daughters took over these concerns is noteworthy (Clark 1919, 1992; Erickson 2002: 39, 53). Shipwrights also show unique patterns of bequests, as they owned four times the average numbers of properties and chose to devise these more equitably than is seen among other trades, although the principal dwelling house continued to be left to a son rather than to a daughter (Tables 3.1 and 3.2). Mariners provide another example of distinctive strategies, as they appear to have had fewer children, and may have died younger than other tradesmen. These men bequeathed money far more frequently to their daughters and (especially) to their sisters than was the case with other tradesmen (by a considerable margin). Such findings highlight, once again, the importance of differentiating between the middling trades - an approach that has been neglected in other studies (Howell 1978; Issa 1986; Shammas 1990; Overton 2004).

Although certain differences between the various occupations concerning bequests are clear, wealth is not a significant factor in devising estates, although wealth broadened options for testators (Wrightson 1984: 327), as illustrated in the case of shipwrights, who owned so many properties. However, wealthy testators were no more inclined to primogeniture than the poorer testators to partible inheritance, (as suggested by Howell (1983: 269)). The reverse scenario was equally true.

An overall increase in the wealth of testators has been observed, as evinced by increasing consumption (detailed in Chapter 5 and discussed below), and illustrated by a 20% increase in the number of bequests of cash between the late 16th century and the second quarter of the 17th century (Table 3.8). The findings in this analysis have shown that wills can be successfully used in empirical studies of inheritance patterns and material culture, and that they reveal an intimate picture of the mentality of the period at a time of transition in the life cycle.

In Chapter 4, the contribution that probate records can make to recovering aspects of the built environment, demographics and social geography in urban studies has been demonstrated, confirming that in focusing on the omissions and limitations of what is recorded, the value of this source has been underestimated (Spufford 1990: 142; Erickson 2002: 23 -7), and most especially Orlin (2003).

A uniquely detailed portrait of life in the neighbourhoods of pre-Civil-War Newcastle has been reconstructed, revealing a part of the town's history that would otherwise have been almost entirely lost. With so few standing structures dating from the pre-Civil-War period, the close analysis of properties listed by individual tradesmen makes a significant contribution to our understanding of the urban landscape of that time. The analysis has successfully revealed details of house plans, numbers of storeys and rooms, types of auxiliary buildings, and also the location of wastes, closes and other landholdings along streets and in specific locations around Newcastle and its suburbs. The locations of several mills have also been recovered.

Comparative analysis of the built environment and social geography of both pre- and post-Civil-War Newcastle, incorporating Langton's study (1975), has also been undertaken, highlighting both change and continuity in the town. Newcastle was multi-centred both before and after the Civil War, with occupational zones both concentrated and segregated, a situation that prevailed throughout the decades from the late 16th to the mid-to-late 17th century. However, the occupational groups and occupational zones constructed by Langton for the post-Civil-War town do not concur, in all instances, with the those of the pre-Civil-War town.

Langton's amalgamation of occupations into economic sectors has proved to be unsatisfactory, whereas the delineation of individual trades has resulted in a more accurate assessment of the social geography and occupational zoning of the town. Among Langton's 'shipping trades' (which include the master mariners, mariners and shipwrights), differences in occupational zones were apparent before and after the Civil War. However, in amalgamating the master mariners with the mariners, Langton's methodology has failed to reveal that members of these two trades tended to live together in the

Lower East Side in close proximity to merchants, whereas the shipwrights (and keelmen) resided almost exclusively in Sandgate (1975: 18). Langton noted the predominance of shipwrights in Sandgate, but keelmen have not been included in his analysis. Gateshead has also been excluded from Langton's study; however, prior to 1642, master mariners, mariners and shipwrights, (describing themselves in their wills as residents of Newcastle), resided in properties on the south side of the river, in the Bishopric of Durham, indicating close social-economic ties across the Tyne.

Langton's 'victualling trades', which include bakers and brewers, butchers and millers, are more dispersed around the town than the 1665 data suggest (1975: 17-18). Bakers and brewers predominated (alongside mariners and master mariners) in the Lower East Side in all decades, as confirmed by Langton, but butchers are not confined to a single victualling quarter on Butchers Bank in the early period. They are present in force on the Central Markets and in the Northern Suburbs. Prior to the Civil War, mills operated in many parts of the intra-mural town, as well as in Sandgate. Among the 'metal trades' only the smiths are represented in Langton's sample, and these tradesmen are not concentrated in the central markets and upper east parts of town as the 1665 data suggests. Before 1642 the largest shops are located at the town gates - at Newgate beside the Noult Market and at Sandgate Gate, and in Sandgate itself near the shipbuilding area. Their presence in 1665 in Morden ward is probably associated with the Iron Market, but this was not revealed by the probate sample, which includes only smiths, and not other metal-working trades.

The occupational concentrations of 'clothing and textile trades', revealed by the 1665 data, differed from earlier patterns, as weavers were concentrated in Westgate in the earlier period, listing fewer properties on the Upper Central Markets and Pilgrim ward. Tailors also show a more segregated pattern than is apparent in the 1665 data, appearing to reside primarily along the main arteries of the town, as well as in the Lower East Side. Langton's 'leather trades' also do not correspond well with the post-Civil-War zones, which shows skinners and glovers, tanners and cordwainers concentrated in Pandon and White Friar wards by 1665. Skinners and glovers recorded shops on the Tyne bridge, within White Friar ward, although most are found on the Upper Westside of town. Cordwainers are heavily concentrated on the Central Markets, but also lived and worked all along the central artery of the town from the Sandhill to the Newgate. The tanners listed property in the Upper West Side, Upper Central Market and in Sandgate and its suburbs.

Langton's suggestion, that population pressure is the cause of occupational concentrations in certain parts of the town after the Civil War (1975: 22), is not entirely sustainable, as the earlier probate data reveals concentrated occupational zones in the less built up parts of the town, such as Westgate, in the Upper West Side of town. Densely populated zones are found in the wards of Austin, Pandon, and Wall Knoll (representing parts of the Lower East Side neighbourhood), and in Sandgate, both before and after the Civil War, but the earlier probate data shows that Plummer ward and the Central Markets are also very crowded areas of the town, a finding not well represented by the later Hearth Tax data.

Although Langton has found that merchants were concentrated near their guild hall (1975: 16), trade affiliation did not necessarily translate into concentrations of the tradesmen near such strategic facilities, and it is argued here that there is no reason to assume weaker ties among these guild or by-trades found in occupationally segregated zones. Cordwainers, master mariners and mariners are the only trades that appear to be concentrated near their meeting or guild hall. Occupational zones, both segregated and concentrated, as rehearsed in the conclusions to this chapter, appear to have been dependent on other strategic facilities (such as those associated with markets and traffic along the main arteries of the town), on topography (in the case of shipwrights who required space to construct ships), or on convenience (in the case of master mariners, mariners and keelmen, who chose to live beside the river in close proximity to their ships and boats). Other trades required sufficient space to manufacture and store goods, as evidenced by auxiliary buildings to the rear of properties - listed, for instance, by bakers and brewers on Pilgrim Street and by tanners on Westgate. Historical continuity is also in evidence, as witnessed in by the occupation of the medieval Huckster Booths by bakers and brewers in the 1570s.

Notwithstanding clear evidence of occupational zones, presumed differentiation in status (and certainly in wealth), does not appear to have equated to exclusivity of neighbourhoods. Concerning the Lower East Side, it is often suggested that wealthier sorts, and particularly merchants, predominated in the quayside area (Langton 1975: 16; Ellis 1985: 198-99; Graves 2003), and it has been suggested that the area excluded craft companies (Graves 2003: 40). However, it is clear from the probate records that the neighbourhood was, in fact, extremely mixed, with master mariners, mariners and bakers and brewers forming a community particularly in the vicinity of Trinity House and All Saints Church, while butchers and millers were also very much in evidence, living alongside a wide variety of other tradesmen on the numerous chares and along the quayside. The notion of the dominance of the elite in the quayside area, in close proximity to the Merchant's Guild Hall, is further undermined when one considers that it was a shipwright who, sometime before his death in 1598, let the tenements he owned on Grinden Chare to Alderman Robert Atkinson (D.P.R. Temple). The quayside was certainly not an exclusive domain for those 'of the class' that participated in the processions and civic ceremonies that, on occasion, made their way through the neighbourhood (Graves 2003: 40). The Central Markets and Sandgate, the other most densely populated parts of the town, are also inhabited by a great variety of trades. Middle Street is crowded with the houses of cordwainers and to a less extent those of butchers. Sandgate appears to be a busy autonomous district, home to the shipbuilding industry, and encompassing a variety of local amenities and shops, as well as mills. Although the poor predominate in the neighbourhood, there is clear evidence that Sandgate is not as wholly poverty-stricken as characterised by Gray (1649) or as has been assumed on the basis of Hearth Tax data (Howell 1967; Langton 1975; Graves 2003). Overall, every neighbourhood appears to have had a predominance of certain trades, as outlined above, but all accommodated people of mixed trades, status or wealth designations.

Clearly, there are problems in amalgamating information on properties from different decades, and the individuals mentioned throughout the study are not, of course, all contemporaries. However, in a fair number of documents it is apparent that some of these tradesmen are personally acquainted as colleagues, friends or neighbours, and have acted as witnesses to one another's wills, subsequently acting as appraisers for inventories after the death of a testator.

Further statistically based analysis of the probate records could be pursued in future research of the built environment of Newcastle, but the approach taken here ensures that many of the contemporary descriptions have been preserved, while data has been collated where sample size has allowed for meaningful interpretations. The survival of at least 1,700 documents relating to Newcastle residents before 1659 provides scope for more extensive studies of the early period.

In Chapter 5, thousands of objects listed in the inventories of tradesmen dated between 1545 and 1642 have been examined. Although this investigation did not set out to uncover a 'consumer revolution', careful analysis of a wide assortment of objects belonging to individuals practising one of 13 trades has revealed that significant changes in the material culture of Newcastle took place over the decades included in this study. And although such change has been observed in the late 17th and 18th centuries (McKendrick 1982; Spufford 1984; Weatherill 1988, 1996; Shammas 1990; Barry et al. 2004), this study has revealed much earlier precedents.

Factors that influenced the material culture of the tradesmen have been explored in connection with three categories of objects – those associated with the household, with household production and with objects of the trades – which have revealed detailed patterns of consumption and investment among different trades.

The importance of retaining occupational designations has been demonstrated, and the problems of defining a socio-economic hierarchy relating to inventoried wealth has been discussed. All the tradesmen in the study (apart from most keelmen) can be said to have belonged to the 'middling sorts'. It is argued here that the amalgamation of distinct specialised trades into occupational sectors fails to account adequately for the levels of prosperity within a specialised occupation, and has resulted in stereotypical views of the relative wealth or poverty of certain trades (particularly concerning cordwainers) going unchallenged,. This amalgamation of trades has also failed to reveal the distinctive strategies of consumption and investment of men practising different occupations.

The study has revealed that only 3.5% of testators actually gave up practicing the trade that they claimed on their wills (which accorded in 100% of cases with the trade named on the accompanying inventory, where one survives), while diversification and expansion into areas of business closely associated with the principal occupation of the testator was more common. Half the wealth represented in the inventories was tied up in objects directly related to the running of a business, in by-employment activities, and in objects associated with household production. By-employment for production outside the home does not appear to have been a significant factor, whereas animal husbandry, spinning and brewing for household consumption is evident in at least half the inventories, although differences among trades is evident. For instance, seafarers own significantly fewer animals than land-based trades, and butchers, who own more sheep than other tradesmen, recorded the highest levels of spinning. Many similar examples have been cited.

The other half of inventoried wealth is represented by consumption of objects for the household in general. There was a very marked increase in the acquisition of objects for the home between the 1550s and 1642, with the most significant rise taking place between the 1610s and 1620s. Overwhelmingly, the increasing consumption concerns objects that had been available since at least the late 16th century in various forms, and often reflect efforts to make homes more comfortable. This change was most apparent in the increasing numbers of beds and in greater investment in bedding, which more than doubles during the period of study. Such improvements in home comfort are evident among all trades, including some poor keelmen. A very substantial increase in the number of decorative objects is also visible from the late 16th century, as numbers of objects doubled by the second quarter of the 17th century, with even greater increases recorded for items such as flowerpots, Danish pots, cushions, carpet cloths and foot stools, which would have added comfort and decoration to homes.

Truly new objects start to appear on inventories only after 1619, when the first clock is listed by a mariner; a few years later, upholstered furniture is becoming available; in 1636 a pair of virginals is recorded by a tanner. Although the numbers of these items - and of others such as mirrors, pictures, glassware and window curtains - continues to expand (sometimes rapidly), the great change during the decades covered by this study is in the volume of objects rather than in their variety.

Whereas remarkable changes to the material culture in the late 17th and early 18th centuries is evidenced primarily by the appearance of new commodities (Weatherill 1996), the focus of change in the early 17th century must be on increasing comfort and decoration to the home. The increasing numbers of items such as beds, furniture, and decorative objects, are in striking contrast with the unchanging situation of many of the more mundane household items, such as towels, salt sellers, and mortars and pestles, the numbers of which remain steady. A focus on rituals surrounding the drinking of tea and coffee, or the introduction of forks for dining in the later 17th century, has meant that rapid and significant change to households in the early decades of the 17th century has been largely overlooked.

The observed changes to material culture in Newcastle applied to all tradesmen, richer or poorer in varying degrees, but wealth alone is not dictating consumption (Weatherill 1996; Overton 2004), as people participated in consumption of items selectively. It is nevertheless the case that wealthier testators tend to be the first to acquire the newer commodities, but there are equally well-to-do individuals who do not acquire such items. Whereas traditional and new objects continue to increase in number, there is also no clear evidence, in this study, of a corresponding decline in any category of object.

It is acknowledged that the inventoried sample represents tradesmen with sufficient goods and chattels to warrant an inventory being made (Shammas 1990: 20, 23; Erickson 2002: 41), although contrary to Weatherill's view, many of the individuals included in this study cannot be described as 'better-off' (1996: 177), as the term is relative. The tradesmen included in the study are not among the very poor, but some men are (relatively speaking) poor, especially the keelmen, and some died in serious debt. The focus on the 'middling sorts' confirms that the assumption, that only the well-off made wills and inventories, cannot be sustained, a finding echoed in the wills of Cambridgeshire villages where poorer landless peasants wrote more wills than the richer men (Spufford 1978: 169).

Nevertheless, wealth levels vary considerably both between and within trades, but most of the inventoried population are reasonably well endowed with material objects, notably in comparison with the copyholders in nearby Whickham (Levine and Wrightson 1991). Wealth is always a factor in consumption and investment patterns, as is occupation, but the relationship is not straightforward. The accumulation of stocks and wares associated with businesses is a key factor in relative wealth levels (in trades where such assets are acquired) and in the consumption of new household objects. However, other factors deserve consideration.

Prices of objects in inventories indicate that, although there is a high and a low end to the second-hand valuations made by appraisers, most remain very steady over the decades of this study, indicating that inflation has not affected the types of commodities listed, despite evidence that price rises elsewhere in the country are affecting other types of commodities (Bowden 1967; Howell 1967; Phelps Brown and Hopkins 1981). Many objects, especially the increasingly popular decorative items, were inexpensive; before 1642 carpet clothes cost less than 1s, flowerpots and cushions were priced as low as 4d, and pictures could be had for 1d. Price should not have been an obstacle to acquisition for most tradesmen, as valuations for these items were among the lowest on the inventories. Overall, the very significant augmentation in the volume of objects recorded, and the increasing levels of inventoried wealth are not accompanied by price rises – although, by around the 1620s, the inclusion of a few exceptional objects (such as watches, clocks, upholstered chairs and pairs of virginals), indicate new and expensive objects are becoming available.

In coming to an understanding of the circumstances and motivations behind the patterns of consumption and investment revealed by the empirical data, it is argued here that, in the case of Newcastle, urbanisation and occupation are probably the most important factors, although wealth, household size, and lifestyle must also be considered. A hierarchical approach to deciding which factors were most important may underestimate the complexity of factors driving changes in the material culture.

Emulation, as an explanation for consumption patterns, appears to be inadequate. There is no empirical evidence suggesting one trade is following the lead of another in the acquisition of household objects: many of the more decorative objects show up simultaneously on inventories of different trades. Nevertheless, as acknowledged previously, master mariners (who were not only the wealthiest of the tradesmen but also probably the best travelled), do list many of the decorative and new objects earlier than testators of all other trades. It has been suggested here that men within a given occupation may have felt some pressure to compete with one another, in the light of strong guild and by-trade associations (King 2001); this may have resulted in emulation among tradesmen of a given occupation, rather than among the population as a whole. Whether emulation was a factor relating to the acquisition of trade-related objects among men practising the same trade has not been explored. Trade secrets were certainly shared among members (Brooks 1994: 75).

It is questionable whether patterns of consumption and investment can be used to construct a regional identity. Schammell found no evidence that domestic aspirations differed greatly in the northern region from those in other parts of Britain (2004: 20, 23). For instance, when categories of objects from Newcastle inventories are compared with similar collections from Kent, marked similarities are apparent in the consumption patterns for household goods (Overton 2004).

There is little evidence that tradesmen sought social status through selective consumption, (perhaps with the notable exception of the expensive apparel and swords worn by master mariners). Those social markers of the later 17th century - the hot drinks utensils for tea and coffee - were absent in the earlier decades. Social identity will certainly have been associated with wealth, occupation, and urbanisation, but such factors cannot generally be linked to select objects in inventories. Instead, the acquisition of objects seems to have been more dependent on simple personal choice (often associated with efforts to create more comfortable and decorative living spaces) and, certainly, on trade association relating to investment strategies. Levine and Wrightson found that social development in Whickham came about through industrial development (1991), and there is no doubt that the changes to the material culture of Newcastle were inextricably linked to the expanding economy of the region (Ellis 1984). However, a consumption hierarchy (if one existed at all among Newcastle tradesmen), was not synonymous with the social hierarchy, as far as could be determined from the inventory evidence. Neither the social hierarchy of Tudor and Stuart society, nor patterns of consumption and investment, can be portrayed as rigid or unchanging (Wrightson 1994; Weatherill 1996).

In summary, the developing material culture of Newcastle in the early modern period is very much part of the wider nationwide change, that was affecting some regions more than others (Weatherill 1996), just as Harrison (1587) had observed, although his opinion that such changes 'were not verie amended as yet ... further off from our Southerne parts' (Furvinal 1877: 239-40), perhaps underestimated the speed of change in the northern provincial capital of Newcastle. Transition and change is apparent, but existing objects are not generally being superseded by entirely new goods, (of which there are few in the period before the Civil War). Instead, there is a marked increase in consumption of items that had been around in the 16th century (in one form or another). Such objects were widely available at prices the middling sorts could afford - and reflect the growing consumption by tradesmen for homes and businesses.

In Chapter 6, the analysis of material culture extents to the size of houses and the function of space in tradesmen's properties, based on recorded objects in named rooms. As outlined in Chapter 4, there are few standing structures belonging to the pre-Civil-War period in Newcastle. Properties that once belonged to the middling sorts are all but lost to history. The surviving buildings from the early 17th century belong almost exclusively to the elite of the town, and where aspects of the architecture of other early properties exists, these are entombed in the much altered buildings of later periods (Pevsner 1992; Heslop et al. 1995, 1996). Given this situation, information on properties from probate records on interiors of the houses of the middling sorts is central to gaining a better understanding of the built environment and the material culture of the town. However, significant omissions from probate records must also be accounted for (Orlin 2002; Overton 2004), and the inclusion of a larger segment of the inventoried population in this kind of study would be advantageous.

The question of whether Newcastle experienced a period of 'great rebuilding' has been considered. There is evidence of testators adding rooms to properties, and of new buildings being erected in all periods. Properties acquired extra halls, parlours or chambers for domestic purposes, while change to other properties is reflected in the addition of auxiliary buildings to accommodate expanding businesses. Most properties, however, remained modest in scale, the majority having either one to three or four to six rooms - figures that come with the proviso that all the rooms in such properties may not have been enumerated. Houses with seven to nine rooms comprise rather less than one-quarter of properties; houses with over 10 rooms are not recorded prior to 1600 and only appear in any number after 1625. The augmentation of the largest houses, accounting for just less than 10% of the sample, is the only notable change in the relative percentages of the four categories relating to room numbers in properties. The growth in house sizes seems to suggest that change on a modest scale is occurring in the second quarter of the 17th century, affecting most especially the largest properties.

It has been proposed here that there is probably a correlation between the increase in size of the largest homes, and the huge augmentation in household objects listed in inventories by the 1610s and 1620s, although the decades of change in house size do not entirely coincide with the tremendous growth in consumption. A slight delay in the accommodation of the increasing number of objects, for those who could afford larger premises, is suggested. However, it is also clear that wealth in inventoried objects does not necessarily correlate with the ownership of the largest properties, as the wealthiest individuals among the tradesmen are the master mariners, who did not own the largest houses. The relatively prosperous cordwainers were also great consumers of household objects for their modest Middle Street houses.

In relation to the use of space in properties, the location of selected objects within named rooms has been examined to determine whether inventory evidence can reveal the nature of activities taking place in different areas of a house. In reviewing the evidence, it can be confirmed that, over the decades of this study, there is both change and continuity in the function of spaces. It appears that the testator dressed most often in an upper chamber, where a clear majority of the beds and bedding used by both master and servant, are located. Although there is evidence that, after 1600, servants' beds are increasingly to be found in kitchens and less often in lofts, evidence of social distancing relating to the location of beds, is very minimal in the early decades of the 17th century, when these changes to furnishings in rooms have been observed. However, there is very clear evidence that items such as beds and chamber pots are becoming increasingly personalised. A transition period seems to have occurred, during which objects became more personal, whereas the private use of space within the house, in a modern sense, is not apparent in this period.

The location of cookware and tableware has also been examined. Cooking continued to be done in the hall in tradesmen's homes over the whole timeframe of this study. However, after 1626 the evidence suggests that in the largest properties this activity was increasingly taking place in the kitchen, although some cookware often remained in the hall. Changes in the location of tableware was more marked: throughout the decades of this study, the hall remained the most popular room for taking meals, whereas, by the 17th century, parlours become a focus for meals (but once again, only in the larger houses that have such rooms). There are increasing references to tableware in upper chambers, which coincides with the movement of more furniture into these rooms. However, the inference that social distancing is taking place between the master and his family, who begin to take meals upstairs, and the servants, who are confined to the kitchen, is difficult to sustain (Overton 2004), especially as rituals will doubtless differ, depending on the type of meal and the time of day (Weatherill 1996). Arrangements for seating are also experiencing transition: prior to 1600, most furniture is located in the hall, but over the decades the relative percentages alter, as more furniture, together with cushions, is moved into upper chambers, as well as into parlours and kitchens. The spread of furnishings into more rooms in houses includes decorative objects - notably pictures, mirrors and flowerpots. Nevertheless, throughout the pre-Civil-War era, halls continue to be the most heavily decorated rooms, with a majority of the seating.

Of considerable importance to these discussions is the finding that the location of objects associated with the principal occupation of testators demonstrates that the use of space within properties is ultimately determined by the nature of the trade practised, underlining the importance of retaining trade designations in this sort of analysis. In the properties of some trades, the location of work-related objects is congruent with those objects associated with household production, indicating that domestic activities and specialist occupations are carried out in the same rooms. Other trades have specialist shops or workhouses that are separate from domestic rooms but integral to the property (Schofield 1987). The domestic life of the household had to accommodate the need for space to carry out work-related activities.

As a result of the multiple function of most rooms, social distancing is not apparent in the household of middling tradesmen. The majority of tradesmen living in Newcastle in the 100 years between the mid-16th century and the outbreak of the Civil War resided in generally modest-sized properties, where relations between householders are likely to have been informal and sociable, and where work life and home life were congruous - a situation dictated by occupational activities and the need for space, as well as social expectations.

A final word

This empirically based research of the Durham Probate records pertaining to Newcastle, which includes the earliest surviving documents for the middling tradesmen, has shown that significant changes to the material culture in the town occurred much earlier in the 17th century than has previously been held to be the case. Dramatic growth in the urban sector began in the mid-16th century and continued apace in the early decades of the 17th century.

Gray quotes Camden's (d.1623) description of Newcastle, as 'Ocullus, the eye of the North, the Harth that warmeth the South parts of the Kingdome with fire; An AEgypt to all the Shires in the North (in times of famine) for bread' (1649, 1970: 37), and such observations perfectly encapsulate this dynamic period of the town's history. The constant flow of bulky goods (especially coal) to London, in exchange for consumer commodities, which has been described in the late 17th century (Weatherill 1996: 61), should be correlated to the much earlier, continual, and rapid expansion of coal-mining operations between 1570 and the 1620s (especially after 1600), which did not slow until the 1630s (Ellis 1984, 2001; Levine and Wrightson 1991). The expansion of the coal trade is fundamental to any explanation for the increase in consumption and production among the middling tradesmen of Newcastle at the beginning (rather than the end of the 17th century). Wrightson has described the coal industry and ancillary industries of Tyne and Wear in this period as 'utterly exceptional' (2000: 171), and Newcastle's place is clearly pivotal.

The picture created by the probate records certainly suggests that the tradesmen in this study were very much a part of the 'entrepreneurial climate' described by Levine and Wrightson, but the characterisation of the people as driven by 'ruthless opportunism and obsession with gain' (1991: 107), focused on the coal trade, seems too narrow an interpretation. The wills and inventories suggest a far more diverse society, an argument supported by King who found that the flourishing urban culture of the late 17th century, associated with many sporting and cultural activities, was actually already present in the town by the early 17th century (2001: 320). It is acknowledged that further study of other important primary sources and the archaeological records of the town, which have not been included in this thesis, would certainly help to both support and refine this interpretation on the material culture of the town.

Gray noted that the 'town hath been famous in foure ages of the world' - 'in the time of the Romans'; for its 'famous monasteries'; as 'a bulwarke against the Scots' and 'the great trade of Coale, White Salt, Grindstones', and he also mentions the town walls with gates and towers, the steeple of St Nicholas Church, the Tyne Bridge and the 'long and faire key' (1649, 1970: 38-9). Such areas of research have had, and continue to have, a marked influence on both the direction of research and on interpretations of life in the north. This thesis shows that the material culture of the provincial capital Newcastle in the early modern period is also deserving of the attention that it has received in this lengthy and detailed analysis.

Chapter 2 - Table 2.1 – Document survival – Durham Probate Records wills and inventories of Newcastle upon Tyne trades 1545 - 1642

Numbers of documents	Bakers &/or brewers	Butchers	Cordwainers	Keelmen	Mariners	Master mariners	Millers	Shipwrights	Skinners &/or glovers	Smiths	Tailors	Tanners	Weavers	Total numbers of documents
Wills: 1545-1600	8	4	10	10	10	18	7	10	8	13	14	8	10	**130**
Wills: 1601-1625	7	11	11	5	7	3	8	9	6	8	6	2	6	**89**
Wills: 1626-1642	11	5	12	1	1	11	5	4	4	2	6	6	9	**77**
Total no. of wills	26	20	33	16	18	32	20	23	18	23	26	16	25	**296**
Inv.'s: 1549-1600	4	3	10	6	7	10	2	9	5	8	5	8	7	**83**
Inv.'s: 1601-1625	6	10	10	5	10	7	9	11	5	12	5	2	7	**99**
Inv.'s: 1626-1642	10	5	11	1	2	8	7	3	3	3	5	6	10	**75**
Total no. of inv.'s	20	18	31	12	19	25	18	23	13	23	15	16	24	**257**
Total no. of testators	27	22	34	17	23	37	26	30	18	29	27	20	29	**(339)**
Overall total documents in sample	-	-	-	-	-	-	-	-	-	-	-	-	-	**553**

Chapter 3 - Table 3.1 – Bequests of real property: Percentage of beneficiaries of all properties listed in wills and inventories including all testator's houses, shops, mills and lands - 1543-1642

Group		Baker/ brewer	Butcher	Cordwainer	Keelman	Mariner	Master mariner	Miller	Shipwright	Skinner/ glover	Smith	Tailor	Tanner	Weaver	Overall average
1	Wife	38%	25%	30%	50%	38%	31%	24%	24%	47%	42%	36%	25%	54%	**33%**
	Son	45%	41%	41%	22%	14%	31%	29%	25%	47%	21%	46%	50%	31%	**34%**
	Daughter	6%	1%	13%	16%	23%	26%	16%	24%	5%	24%	7%	15%	-	**16%**
2	Brother		4%		5%	9%		2%	4%		3%	4%	5%	8%	**3%**
	Sister		4%	2%		14%	2%	4%	4%		3%				**3%**
	Grandson							6%	2%		3%	7%		8%	**2%**
	Granddaughter							6%	4%						**1%**
	Nephew	3%							2%						**<1%**
	Niece	3%						4%	2%						**<1%**
3	Other relative*	3%	4%	2%			2%	8%	4%		3%				**3%**
4	Non-relative**	6%	4%	9%	5%		5%		5%						**3%**
Total properties		**c.59**	**c.70**	**c.97**	**c.38**	**c.49**	**c.73**	**c.68**	**c.161**	**c.22**	**c.62**	**c.52**	**c.51**	**c.40**	**c.842**
Avg. no. of properties ***		**3**	**5**	**4**	**3**	**4**	**4**	**4**	**8**	**2**	**3**	**3**	**4**	**2**	**2**
Total beneficiaries		33	24	43	18	21	41	51	55	19	33	28	20	26	**412**
Avg. no. of beneficiaries		**2**	**3**	**2**	**2**	**2**	**3**	**1**	**3**	**1**	**2**	**2**	**3**	**2**	**2**
Total no. testators bequeathing property		18	15	23	11	12	19	16	19	14	18	16	12	20	**213 (72%)**

* **Other relatives**: male and female cousins, all in-laws and mothers ** **Non-relatives**: male and female 'friends' and their children, executors and supervisors *** **(bequeathed per testator)**
Figures have been rounded to nearest number. Bracketed figures beside percentage figure indicate numbers of properties per group.

Chapter 3 – Table 3.2 – Bequests of real property: Percentage of beneficiaries of the Testator's Principal Residence (TPR) or 'dwelling house' 1543-1642

Group		Baker/ brewer	Butcher	Cordwainer	Keelman	Mariner	Master mariner	Miller	Shipwright	Skinner/ glover	Smith	Tailor	Tanner	Weaver	Overall average
1	Wife	60%	30%	45%	86%	71%	67%	40%	46%	71%	76%	55%	34%	63%	**57.2%**
	Son	27%	55%	27%	14%	-	17%	30%	21%	29%	-	36%	50%	31%	**25.9%**
	Daughter	13%	11%	18%	-	29%	11%	10%	17%	-	6%	-	-	-	**8.8%**
2	Brother	-	-	-	-	-	-	-	4%	-	6%	9%	8%	-	**2.07%**
	Sister	-	-	-	-	-	-	10%	8%	-	-	-	-	-	**1.38%**
	Mother	-	-	-	-	-	-	5%	-	-	-	-	8%	-	**1%**
3	Grandson	-	-	-	-	-	-	-	-	-	6%	-	-	6%	**0.92%**
	Male relative	-	-	5%	-	-	-	-	-	-	6%	-	-	-	**0.84%**
	Son of friend	-	-	5%	-	-	5%	-	-	-	-	-	-	-	**0.76%**
	Daughter in law	-	-	-	-	-	-	5%	-	-	-	-	-	-	**0.38%**
	Male friend	-	-	-	-	-	-	-	4%	-	-	-	-	-	**0.30%**
Beneficiaries		15	9	22	7	7	18	20	24	7	17	11	12	16	**185**
TPR's bequeathed		13	7	18	7	5	17	11	17	7	17	11	12	16	**154**

Chapter 3 – Table 3.3 – Bequests of real property: Percentage of beneficiaries of shops 1543-1642

Group		Baker/ brewer	Butcher	Cordwainer	Keelman	Mariner	Master mariner	Miller	Shipwright	Skinner/ glover	Smith	Tailor	Tanner	Weaver	Overall average %
1	Wife	-	14%	39%	-	-	-	-	-	66.5%	75%	50%	40%	67%	**27%**
	Son	-	57%	28%	-	-	50%	-	100%	33.5%	17%	50%	60%	16.5	**31%**
	Daughter	-	29%	28%	-	-	-	-	-	-	-	-	-	-	**4%**
2	Grandson	-	-	-	-	-	-	-	-	-	-	-	-	16.5%	**<1%**
	Gr. daughter	-	-	-	-	-	-	100%	-	-	-	-	-	-	**<1%**
	Brother	-	-	-	-	-	-	-	-	-	8%	-	-	-	**<1%**
	Male friend	--	-	-	-	-	50%	-	-	-	-	-	-	-	**<1%**
	Son of friend	-	-	5%	-	-	-	-	-	-	-	-	-	-	**<1%**
	Unspecified	-	-	-	-	-	-	-	-	-	-	1			
Number of beneficiaries		-	7	19	-	-	2	1	1	3	12	3	5	6	**55**
Number of bequeathed shops		0	6	22	0	0	1	1	1	3	12	3	5	6	**55**

Chapter 3 – Table 3.4 – Bequests of real property: Percentage of beneficiaries of mills 1543-1642

Group		Baker/ brewer	Butcher	Cordwainer	Keelman	Mariner	Master mariner	Miller	Shipwright	Skinner/ glover	Smith	Tailor	Tanner	Weaver	Overall average %
1	Wife	100%	100%	-	-	-	100%	29%	100%	-	-	-	-	-	**33%**
	Son	-	-	100%	-	25%	-	33%	-	-	-	100%	-	-	**20%**
	Daughter	-	-	-	-	25%	-	19%	-	-	-	-	-	-	**3%**
2	Grandson	-	-	-	-	-	-	-	-	-	100%	-	-	-	**<1%**
	Brother	-	-	-	-	50%	-	-	-	-	-	-	-	-	**<1%**
	Mother	-	-	-	-	-	-	5%	-	-	-	-	-	-	**<1%**
	Cousin m/f	-	-	-	-	-	-	14% (m)	-	-	-	-		-	**<1%**
Beneficiaries		1	1	1	-	4	1	21	1	-	1	1	-	-	**32**
Bequeathed mills		1	1	1	0	3	1	18	1	0	1	1	0	0	**28**

Chapter 3 – Table 3.5 – Individual bequests of objects: The percentage of objects* or 'goods and chattels' bequeathed 1545 - 1642

The table includes bequests of household objects and furniture, silver, work gear and work products, grain, pieces of gold, and gifts of rental payments to tenants. It excludes bequests of clothes, animals and those given to the poor which are analysed separately.

Group		Baker/ brewer	Butcher	Cordwainer	Keelman	Mariner	Master mariner	Miller	Shipwright	Skinner/ glover	Smith	Tailor	Tanner	Weaver	Overall average
1	Wife	41%	45%	27%	47%	60%	45%	20%	21.5%	25%	24.5%	22.5%	12%	19%	**31.5%**
	Son	25%	28%	27%	20%	16%	21%	23%	23%	25%	19%	30%	29%	35%	**25%**
	Daughter	9%	24%	29%	20%	12%	21%	22%	28%	17%	26%	27.5%	29%	13%	**21%**
2	Friend (male)	7%	-	13%	3%	4%	1.5%	12%	-	17%	5%	4%	16%	5%	**7%**
	Servant/apprentice (male)	-	-	3%	-	-	-	-	4%	6%	9%	-	6%	5%	**2.5%**
	Brother	-	-	-	-	4%	1.5%	2%	5.5%	2%	1.5%	1%	4%	3%	**2%**
	Friend (female)	2%	-	1%	-	4%	-	8%	1%	2%	-	7%	-	-	**2%**
3	Others*														**1% or less**
No. recipients of 'objects'		44	29	79	30	25	58	60	75	48	74	77	35	78	**712 beneficiaries****
No. wills		26	19	33	16	18	32	20	23	18	23	26	16	25	**296**

* Group 3: includes parents, sisters, unborn children, grandchildren, godchildren, in-laws, nieces, nephews, cousins, children of friends, female servants, executors, supervisors.
** Average 2.4 beneficiaries per will

Chapter 3 – Table 3.6 - Bequests of Objects: Principal beneficiary of "All the rest of my goods and chattels, debts, legacies and funeral expenses paid' 1545 - 1642

Social group	Percentage average	Number of recipients
Wife	39%	112
Wife & all children	11%	32
Wife & daughters	5%	15
Wife & sons	10%	29
Wife & non-nuclear &/or non-family member*/**	4%	10
Daughters & sons	5%	15
Daughters	2%	6
Sons	8%	22
Brothers	2%	6
Non-nuclear family member (excluding brothers)*	2.5%	7
Non family member**	1.5%	5
Combined non-nuclear & non-family members	2.5%	7
No person specifically named	7%	20
Totals	**100%**	**286**

* Non-nuclear family members include son or daughter in law, grandchildren, parents, nieces or nephews, kinsmen, male and female cousins.
** Non-family members include male and female friends, executors, work colleagues and apprentices.

Chapter 3 – Table 3.7 – Bequests of cash: Percentage figures for principal beneficiaries of cash bequests 1545 -1642

Group		Baker/ brewer	Butcher	Cordwainer	Keelman	Mariner	Master mariner	Miller	Shipwright	Skinner/ glover	Smith	Tailor	Tanner	Weaver	Total beneficiaries	Overall percentages
1	Wife	3	3	-	12	7	2	-	4	-	4	7	-	7	(12)	**3**
	Son	18	20	27	6	13	26	7	17	5	9	14	11	36	(66)	**18**
	Daughter	50	36	39	12	13	19	50	9	5	35	39	34	21	(107)	**29**
2	Brother	3	11	2	6	13				15			3	3.5	(14)	**4**
	Sister	9		7		40	11	7	26	10	4	3.5			(28)	**8**
	Grandson		8	2	12							3.5	3	3.5	(9)	**2**
	Gr.daughter			2	12			7		5		7			(7)	**2**
	Mother	3				7				5					(3)	**1**
	Father									5					(1)	**1**
3	Friend m			2			6.5	7	9	20	4		11		(16)	**4**
	Friend f		5.5	2	6		4		4	5		3.5	3	3.5	(11)	**3**
	Cousin m	6		4.5						5	9		6		(9)	**2**
	Cousin f						2					3.5	6		(4)	**1**
4	Others A		3	2	6		15	7	4	10	30	14	17	18	(36)	**9**
5	Clergy	4	3	7				7				3.5	3		(8)	**2**
	Poor	9	3	7	6		4	7	9	10				7	(14)	**4**
	Others B		8	9	23	7	8.5		17		4		3		(20)	**5.5**
	Total beneficiaries	(34)	(36)	(44)	(17)	(15)	(46)	(14)	(23)	(20)	(23)	(28)	(35)	(28)	(365)	**100**
	Number of wills	(26)	(20)	(33)	(16)	(18)	(32)	(20)	(23)	(18)	(23)	(26)	(16)	(25)	(296)	-

All figures, except those in brackets, are percentages.**Group 4**: Others A: brothers-in-law:1% (4), sisters-in-law: <1% (3), sons-in-law: <1% (3), daughters-in-law: <1% (2), nephew: >1% (5), nieces: 1% (4), son of friend: 1% (4), daughter of friend: 1% (2), male servant or apprentice: >1% (5), female servant: 1% (4) = 36. – **Total male recipients = 21 – Total female recipients = 15 Group 5:** Others B: stepson: 1% (1), great grandson: <1% (1), great nephews: <1% (2), great niece: <1% (1), uncle: <1% (2), clerk: <1% (2), scrivener: <1% (2), executor: <1% (2), supervisor: <1% (2), tenants: 1% (4) and a chapel: <1% (1) = 20. **Total male recipients = 14 – Total female recipients = 1 – Unknowns = 5**

Chapter 3 – Table 3.8 - Percentage of beneficiaries receiving cash bequests relative to total beneficiaries of all bequests over three periods 1545 -1642

Period: 1545-1600 (130 wills)	Baker/ brewer	Butcher	Cordwainer	Keelman	Mariner	Master mariner	Miller	Shipwright	Skinner/ glover	Smith	Tailor	Tanner	Weaver	Overall totals
Beneficiaries of cash*	89	23	48	23	22	63	7	39	47	56	66	87	26	596
Total beneficiaries	118	35	80	47	46	119	59	83	71	110	126	128	66	1088
Percentage of beneficiaries of cash	**75%**	**66%**	**60%**	**49%**	**48%**	**53%**	**12%**	**47%**	**66%**	**51%**	**52%**	**68%**	**39%**	**55%**

Period: 1601-1625 (89 wills)	Baker/ brewer	Butcher	Cordwainer	Keelman	Mariner	Master mariner	Miller	Shipwright	Skinner/ glover	Smith	Tailor	Tanner	Weaver	Overall totals
Beneficiaries of cash*	44	72	73	14	17	17	44	52	19	52	52	14	44	514
Total beneficiaries	54	110	112	26	35	20	71	87	29	82	67	20	62	775
Percentage of beneficiaries of cash	**81%**	**65%**	**65%**	**54%**	**49%**	**85%**	**62%**	**60%**	**65.5%**	**63%**	**78%**	**70%**	**71%**	**66%**

Period: 1626-1642 (77 wills)	Baker/ brewer	Butcher	Cordwainer	Keelman	Mariner	Master mariner	Miller	Shipwright	Skinner/ glover	Smith	Tailor	Tanner	Weaver	Overall totals
Beneficiaries of cash*	56	20	126	0	3	45	4	5	4	27	40	65	53	448
Total beneficiaries	80	24	156	3	4	72	16	14	8	33	67	90	72	639
Percentage of beneficiaries of cash	**70%**	**83%**	**80%**	**0%**	**75%**	**62.5%**	**25%**	**36%**	**50%**	**81%**	**60%**	**72%**	**74%**	**70%**

* Beneficiaries of cash bequests may also have received other types of bequests

Chapter 3 – Table 3.9a – Bequests to the poor: 1545 – 1600, 1601 – 1625, 1626 – 1642 (Sample: 296 wills)

Period: 1545 – 1600				**Period: 1601 – 1625**				**Period: 1626 – 1642**		
Group 1	**Totals**	**Percent./ Averages**		**Group 2**	**Totals**	**Percent./ Averages**		**Group 3**	**Totals**	**Percent./ Averages**
All Saints	11	24%		**All Saints**	14	42%		**All Saints**	4	18%
St. Andrew	2	4%		**St. Andrew**	0	-		**St. Andrew**	2	9%
St. John	3	6.5%		**St. John**	2	6%		**St. John**	3	14%
St. Nicholas	2	4%		**St. Nicholas**	1	3%		**St. Nicholas**	2	9%
Clergy	9	19.5%		**Clergy**	9	27%		**Clergy**	6	27%
Other	19	41%		**Other**	7	21%		**Other**	5	23%
Bequests per trade	46	1.3 per person		**Bequests per trade**	33	1.5 per person		**Bequests per trade**	22	1.8 per person
Number of testators	35	27%		**Number of testators**	22	25%		**Number of testators**	12	16%
Number of wills	130	100%		**Number of wills**	89	100%		**Number of wills**	76	100%

Group 1

Clergy: includes minister or curate of All Saints Church (2), preacher (1), curate (4), parson of Standell Church (1), vicar for forgotten tithes (1)
Other: includes poor widows (2), 'the poor'- unspecified (7), poor of Sandgate Ward (1) Chapel at Easter Dale, Arrendale (1), Almshouse 'beside my house'(1), Poorman's box (1), Poor householders (1), Two poor women of Maison Dieu (1), 'Preparing a house of provision for the poor' (1), Poor neighbours (2), Poor of Spittel Almshouses (1)

Group2

Clergy: includes preacher (6) curate All saints (1), curate St. Andrews (1), vicar (1)
Other: includes the poor- unspecified (4) poor of Trinity House (1), poor man's box (1), cloth for communion table of St. John (1)

Group 3

Clergy: including minister St. John (2), preacher (2), curate (1), Right Worshipful Doctor (1)
Other: including poor – unspecified (2) poor of all parishes (1), poor of Ponteland (1), poor of Ovingham (1)

Chapter 3 –Bequests to the poor (continued)

Table 3.9b - Combined figures of bequests to the poor 1545 -1642

	Bakers &/or brewers	Butchers	Cordwainers	Keelmen	Mariners	Master mariners	Millers	Shipwrights	Skinners &/or glovers	Smiths	Tailors	Tanners	Weavers	Totals	Percent./ Averages
All Saints	5	2		1	1	6		5	2	2	3	1	1	29	**29%**
St. Andrew									1			2	1	4	**4%**
St. John			3				1					3	1	8	**8%**
St. Nicholas		1	2			1							1	5	**5%**
Clergy	1	2	3				1	2		1	7	4	3	24	**24%**
Other		3	3	1	1	1	3	3	3	2	6	3	2	31	**31%**
Bequests per trade	6	8	11	2	2	8	5	10	6	5	16	13	9	101	**1.4 bequests per person**
Number of testators	5	7	5	2	1	8	3	8	6	5	8	6	5	69	**23%**
Number of wills	26	20	33	16	18	32	20	23	18	23	26	16	25	296	**100%**
Average percentage	19%	35%	15%	12.5%	5.5%	25%	15%	35%	33%	22%	31%	37.5%	20%	-	-

Chapter 3 – Table 3.10 – Bequests of clothing: 1545 - 1600, 1601 -1625, and 1626 - 1642

	Baker &/or brewer	Butcher	Cordwainer	Keelman	Mariner	Master mariner	Miller	Shipwright	Skinner &/or glover	Smith	Tailor	Tanner	Weaver	Total bequests	Total wills	Percentage	Average bequests per person
Pre-1600	21	1	13	3	8	21	12	10	9	8	11	5	15	137	130	57.8%	1.05 pp
1601-1625	0	10	5	0	3	1	2	5	3	3	5	3	6	46	89	19.4%	0.51 pp
1626-1642	4	0	10	0	0	1	1	1	2	0	17	16	2	54	77	22.7%	0.70 pp
Total bequests	25	11	28	3	11	23	15	16	14	11	33	24	23	237	296	100%	-
Total wills	26	20	33	16	18	32	20	23	18	23	26	16	16	-	-	-	-
Bequests per person	.96	.55	.84	.18	.61	.71	.75	.69	.77	.47	1.2	1.5	1.4	-	-	-	0.80 pp overall

Chapter 3 - Table 3.11 - Bequests of animals 1545-1642

	Cattle	Sheep	Horses	Pigs	Total animals	Number of recipients	Overall percentage
Group 1							
Wife	19	2+	2	-	23	12	13%
Son	15	-	2	-	17	14	16%
Daughter	16	54 (2 bequests*)	-	-	70 (including 2 anomalies*)	11	12%
Group 2a							
Male relatives	5	81 (1 bequest*)	8	-	94 (including 1 anomaly*)	15	17%
Group 2b							
Female relatives	11	13	-	-	24	14	15%
Group 3a							
Male non-relatives	5	9	4	-	18	14	16%
Group 3b							
Female non-relatives	4	4	-	1	9	9	10%
Total animals including anomalies	75	163	16	1	255	89	100%
Total animals excluding anomalies	75	28	16	1	120	-	
Percentage of animals inc. anomalies	29%	64%	6%	<1%	100%	-	-
Percentage of animals excl. anomalies	60%	26%	14%	<1%	100%	-	-

Group 2a: Male relatives – includes brothers, grandsons, father, nephews, father in-law.
Group 2b: Female relatives – includes sisters, granddaughters, mothers, nieces.
Group 3a: Male non-relatives – includes male friends, sons of friends, servant
Group 3b: Female non-relatives - includes female friends, daughters of friends.

* Two bequests of 54 sheep and one bequest of 81 sheep are anomalies, as most beneficiaries received one or two animals. The totals show figures including and excluding these three anomalies.

Chapter 4 – Table 4.1 - Property Distribution: A – Z of place names and streets from Durham Probate Records indicating the number of properties owned or leased by tradesmen in Newcastle upon Tyne and Gateshead 1549 –1642. Properties specified as let to tradesmen by other tradesmen within the study group are enclosed in brackets and record where the leaseholder lived not the landlord. See Table 4.4 for the 24 ward names that correspond to numbers following Welford's serialization (1911).

Street name or location	Neigh'hood/ Wards	Baker /brewer	Butcher	Cord-wainer	Keelman	Mariner	Master mariner	Miller	Ship-wright	Skinner /glover	Smith	Tailor	Tanner	Weaver	Totals
All Hallows/ Butcher Bank	N2 – W19,20		2				1								3
All Saints Church Yard	N2 – W19	2				5		3							10
Back Row	N6 – W5											1			1
Bailey Gate	N6 – W3					2				3		2			7
Magdalene Meadows	N8 – W16													1	1
Bigg Market	N4 –W 9,15											1			1
Blind Chare	N1 –W 22		1												1
Bourne Bank	N1 – W23					3									3
Broad Chare	N1 – W22					1	2	2							5
Broad Garth	N1 - W20	9					2								11
Byker Chare	N1 – W23			7		(+1 let)	7		3						18
Carliol	N2 – W18							2							2
Castle Field/ Leazes	N8 – W12,13		2					1					1	1	5
Castle Garth	N6 – W2 (?)7													1	1
Chimley Mill, Castle Leazes	N8 - W13 (?)										3				3
Close	N3 – W1, 2						2							1	3
Cloth Market	N4 - W14						1					1			2
Cow Gate	N2 – W19	(+1 let)					2								3
Dark Close, Without Pilgrim Gate	N8 – W17, 18	3													3
Denton Chare	N4 – W3, 5, 10	1		1											2
Flesh Market	N4 – W14		5	1								1			7
Flesher Rawe (East side of Side)	N3 –W 6											1			1
Forth Hills	N7 – n.a.							1							1
Gallowgate	N8 – W12		5	2				1							8
Gateshead	N10 – n..a.				6	2 (+ 2 lets)	6		2						18
Grinden Chare	N1 - W20								1						1
Head of Side	N3 – W4		1	1 (+ 1 let)						1					4
High Friar Chare	N5 – W16										4				4
Hornsby Chare	N1 – W20	5 (+ 2 lets)		1		9 (+1 let)						3			21

Table 4.1 Property Distribution (continued)

Street name / location	Neigh'hood/ Ward	Baker /brewer	Butcher	Cord-wainer	Keelman	Mariner	Master mariner	Miller	Ship-wright	Skinner /glover	Smith	Tailor	Tanner	Weaver	Totals
Huckster Booths, Newgate	N5 – W13							3							3
Quayside, Newcastle	N1 – W21	2 (+1 let)	4				1				1	(+2 lets)			11
Lime Kilns, Ewse Burn	N9 – W24 (?)										2		3		5
Long Stairs	N3 – W1, 2			4											4
Low Friar Chare	N5 – W9	1		2								5			8
Lowe Kirke Chare, Gateshead	N10 – n.a.						1								1
Maison Dieu, Sandhill	N3 – W19			2											2
Meale or Groat Market	N4 – W10		4	3 (+ 1 let)										1	9
Middle Street	N4 – W11		4 (+1 let)	13 (+ 5 lets)				1	2		2	1 (+ 1 let)			30
Newgate Street	N5– W9,12,13,16	2											3		5
Noult (Horse) Market	N5 – W12, 13		3	2							1	2	1	1	10
Pandon Street	N1- W19(?)22,23	8	2		2	(+1 let)	2	1	2	1	3	4			26
Pepper Coleman's (Corn) Chare	N1 –W 20		2												2
Pilgrim Street	N2 – W17,18,19	4		2		4			2			1			13
Pipergate, Gateshead	N10 – n.a.												2		2
Plummer Chare	N1 – W20	1	4			(+1 let)		1	1						8
Postern	N6 – W8							4							4
Pudding Chare	N4 – W10						1	2							3
Pullen/Poultry Market	N4 – W14			2											2
Sandgate	N9 – W23, 24	2	5	2 (+1 let)	11 (+ 7 lets)	6 (+ 9 lets)	8	5	54		3 (+1 let)				114
Sandgate Gate	N1 - W21										2				2

Table 4.1 Property Distribution (continued)

Street name or location	Neigh'hood/ Ward	Baker /brewer	Butcher	Cord-wainer	Keelman	Mariner	Master mariner	Miller	Ship-wright	Skinner /glover	Smith	Tailor	Tanner	Weaver	Totals
Sandhill	N3 – W 7,19			3											3
Shield Field	N2 – W18,23 (?)	2													2
Side	N3 – W4,6,7			3			1								4
Sidgate	N8 – W13, 16		5	6				2							13
Silver Street	N2 – W19		1					1			3	2			7
St. John's Church Yard	N6 – W 8,10		4	4											8
Stackgarth, Ouse Burn	N9 – W24(?)						1	2							3
Swirle, Sandgate	N9 – W24												2		2
Trinity House	N1 – W20						2								2
Trinity House Chare	N1 – W20	(+1 let)						5							6
Tyne Bridge	N3 – W2						1			2					3
Upper Dean/ High Bridge	N4 – W15, 17	2		4						1				4	11
Wall Knoll	N1 – W23					1		(+1 let)			1	1			4
Westgate Street	N6 – W8	1	(+1 let)				1	3		2		1	4	4 (+ 1 let)	18
Without Pandon Gate	N1 – W23(?)		1												1
Without Pilgrim Street Gate	N8 – W 17, 18	7		4						2					13
Without Westgate	N7 - W 8		1					2				1	2	(+1 let)	7
Total number of properties specified as let to third parties	-	**5**	**2**	**8**	**7**	**15**	**0**	**1**	**0**	**0**	**1**	**3**	**0**	**2**	**44**
Total number of properties owned or leased by testators	-	**52**	**56**	**69**	**19**	**33**	**42**	**42**	**67**	**12**	**25**	**28**	**18**	**14**	**477**
Total combined properties	-	**57**	**58**	**77**	**26**	**48**	**42**	**43**	**67**	**12**	**26**	**31**	**18**	**16**	**521**

Chapter 4 – Table 4.2 - Occupation of Property: A –Z Place names and streets from the Durham Probate Records listing properties specified as occupied by a named trade in Newcastle upon Tyne and Gateshead 1549 –1642. Properties specified as let to tradesmen by other tradesmen within the study group are enclosed in brackets and record where the leaseholder lived, not the landlord.

Street name or location	Baker &/or brewer	Butcher	Cordwainer	Keelman	Mariner	Master & mariner	Miller	Shipwright	Skinner &/or glover	Smith	Tailor	Tanner	Weaver	Totals
All Hallows / Butchers Bank		1				1								2
All Saints Church Grounds					1									1
Bailey Gate									2		1			3
Bigg Market											1			1
Broad Chare						1	2							3
Broad Garth	1					1								2
Byker Chare			2		(1let)	4								7
Castle Field/ Leazes		2												2
Castle Garth													1	1
Chimley Mill, Castle Leazes										3				3
Close						2							1	3
Cowgate	(1 let)					1								2
Flesh Market		2	1											3
Flesher Rawe (East side of Side)											1			1
Gallowgate		5												5
Gateside					(2 lets)									2
Head of Side		1	(1 let)						1					3
High Friar Chare										4				4
Hornsby Chare	2 (+2 lets)				1 (+1 let)									6
Huckster Booths, Newgate							3							3
Lime Kilns/ Pits												1		1
Low Friar Chare											5			5
Lowe Kirke Chare, Gateside						1								1
Meale Market		2	1 (+1 let)											4
Middle Street		1 (+1 let)	8 (+5 lets)								(1 let)			16
Noult Market/ White Cross											1	4	1	6
Pandon Street	1	2		1	(1 let)		1	1	1		1			9
Pilgrim Street	2		2		1						1			6
Plummer Chare	1	2			(1let)									4
Postern							4							4
Pudding Chare							2							2
Pullen/Poultry Market			1											1
Quayside	2 (+1 let)	(1let)									(2 lets)			5
Sandgate	2		(1 let)	10 (+7 lets)	3 (+9 lets)	1	5	16		2 (1let)				57

Table 4.2 Occupation of Property (continued)

Street name or location	Baker &/or brewer	Butcher	Cordwainer	Keelman	Mariner	Master & mariner	Miller	Shipwright	Skinner &/or glover	Smith	Tailor	Tanner	Weaver	Totals
Sandgate Gate										2				2
Sandhill			3											3
Side			3											3
Stackgarth, Sandgate							2							2
Trinity House Chare	(1 let)													1
Tyne Bridge									2					2
Upper Dean/ High Bridge	2		3						1				4	10
Wall Knoll							(1let)							1
Westgate		(1 let)					2		2			3	3 (+1 let)	12
Without Pandon Gate		1												1
Without Pilgrim Street Gate	4	1												5
Without Westgate		1									1		(1 let)	3
Total number properties specified as let to tradesmen by other tradesmen in the study	**5**	**2**	**8**	7	**15**	**0**	**1**	**0**	**0**	**1**	**3**	**0**	**2**	**44**
Total number of properties where testator confirms specifically location of trade	**18**	**21**	**24**	**11**	**6**	**12**	**21**	**17**	**9**	**11**	**12**	**8**	**10**	**225**

Chapter 4 -Table 4.3 - Distribution of properties: The table shows the number of properties owned or occupied by trades located within the ten neighbourhoods shown on Map 4.15 - 1549 – 1642

Location of neigh'hood	No.	Baker /brewer	Butcher	Cord-wainer	Keelman	Mariner	Master mariner	Miller	Ship-wright	Skinner /glover	Smith	Tailor	Tanner	Weaver	Total Prop.	% figures
Lower east side	**1**	25 (4lets)	14	8	2	14 (4lets)	16	9 (1let)	7	1	7	8 (2lets)	-	-	122	23.4%
Upper east side	**2**	8 (1let)	3	2	-	9	3	6	2	-	3	3	-	-	40	7.7%
Lower west side	**3**	-	1	13 (1let)	-	-	4	-	-	3	-	1	-	1	24	4.6%
Central markets	**4**	3	13 (1let)	24 (6lets)	-	-	2	3	2	1	2	4 (1let)	-	5	67	12.9%
Upper central markets	**5**	3	3	4	-	-	-	3	-	-	5	7	4	1	30	5.8%
Upper west side	**6**	1	4 (1let)	4	-	2	1	7	-	5	-	4	4	5 (1let)	39	7.5%
Western suburbs	7	-	1	-	-	-	-	3	-	-	-	1	2	(1let)	8	1.5%
Northern suburbs	**8**	10	12	12	-	-	-	4	-	2	3	-	1	2	46	8.8%
Sandgate & suburbs	**9**	2	5	2 (1let)	11 (7lets)	6 (9lets)	9	7	54	-	5 (1let)	-	5	-	124	23.8%
Gateshead	**10**	-	-	-	6	2 (2 lets)	7	-	2	-	-	-	2	-	21	4.0%
Let properties	-	5	2	8	7	15	0	1	0	0	1	3	0	2	44	8.5%
Properties owned/leased by tradesmen	-	52	56	69	19	33	42	42	67	12	25	28	18	14	477	91.4%
Overall total properties	-	57	58	77	26	48	42	43	67	12	26	31	18	16	521	100%
Percentage of total properties		10.9%	11.1%	14.8%	5.0%	9.2%	8.1%	8.3%	12.9%	2.3%	5.0%	6.0%	3.5%	3.1%	100%	-
No. testators specifying location of property	-	14	12	15	9	8	17	13	15	11	11	13	7	11	156	46.1%
Average no. of properties excluding lets		3.5	4.6	4.6	2.1	4.1	2.4	3.1	4.4	1.0	2.0	2.2	2.5	1.2	-	-
Total testators	-	27	22	34	17	22	37	26	30	18	29	27	20	29	338	100%
Overall % of testators listing properties	-	51.8%	54.5%	44.1%	52.9%	36.3%	43.2%	50%	50%	61.1%	37.9%	48.1%	35%	37.9%	45.8 %	46.1%

Chapter 4: Table 4.4 - Wards and neighbourhoods

Ward/ Number	Corresponding Neighbourhood/ Number
Close Gate (1)	Lower West Side (3)
White Friar Tower (2)	Lower West Side (3), Upper West Side (6)
Denton (Neville) Tower (3)	Lower West Side (3), Upper West Side (6)
West Spittle Tower (4)	Lower West Side (3), Upper West Side (6)
Stank Tower (5)	Central Markets (4), Upper West Side (6)
Gunner Tower (6)	Upper East Side (2), Lower West Side (3)
Pink Tower (7)	Lower West Side (3)
Westgate (8)	Upper West Side (6), Western Suburbs (7)
Durham Tower (9)	Central Markets (4), Upper Central Markets (5)
Herber Tower (10)	Central Markets (4)
Mordon Tower (11)	Central Markets (4)
Ever Tower (12)	Upper Central Markets (5), Northern Suburbs (8)
Andrew Tower (13)	Upper Central Markets (5), Northern Suburbs (8)
Newgate (14)	Central Markets (4)
Bertram Monboucher Tower (15)	Central Markets (4), Upper Central Markets (5)
Ficket Tower (16)	Upper Central Markets (5), Northern Suburbs (8)
Pilgrim Tower (17)	Upper East Side (2), Central Markets (4), Northern Suburbs (8)
Carliol Tower (18)	Upper East Side (2), Northern Suburbs (8)
Plummer Tower (19)	Upper East Side (2), Lower West Side (3)
Austin Tower (20)	Lower East Side (1)
Corner Tower (21)	Lower East Side (1)
Pandon Tower (22)	Lower East Side (1)
Wall Knoll Tower (23)	Lower East Side (1), Eastern Suburbs (9)
Sandgate (24)	Eastern Suburbs (9)

Neighbourhood	Corresponding wards
Lower East Side	Austin Tower, Corner Tower, Pandon Tower, Wall Knoll Tower (part)
Upper East Side	Pilgrim Tower (part), Carliol Tower (part), Plummer Tower (part), Gunner Tower (part)
Lower West Side	Close Gate, White Friar Tower (part), West Spittle Tower (part), Gunner Tower (part), Pink Tower (part), Plummer Tower (part), Denton (Neville) Tower (part)
Central Markets	Stank Tower (part), Durham Tower (part), Herber Tower, Mordon Tower, Newgate, Bertram Monboucher (part), Pilgrim Tower (part)
Upper Central Markets	Durham Tower (part), Ever Tower (part), Andrew Tower, Ficket Tower (part)
Upper West Side	White Friar Tower (part), Denton (Neville) Tower (part), West Spittle Tower (part), Stank Tower (part), Westgate (part), Herber Tower (part)
Western Suburbs	Westgate (part)
Northern Suburbs	Ever Tower (part), Andrew Tower (part), Ficket Tower (part), Pilgrim Tower (part), Carliol Tower (part)
Eastern Suburbs	Wall Knoll (part), Sandgate
Gateshead	n.a.

Chapter 4: Table 4.5 - Concentrations of trades in Newcastle wards – Heley 1549 – 1642 and Langton 1665

The concentrations are derived from observations on density of properties shown on Maps 4.1 -4.13, which can be cross-referenced to Figures 4.1a - 4.1m, Figures 4.4a – 4.4e, and to Map 4.15B

* Square brackets indicate concentrations were spread over two or more wards

Occupational categories (Langton)	**Wards within neighbourhoods** (Heley)	**Wards described by Bourne** (Langton)
B1: Mariners	Sandgate, Wall Knoll, Plummer, Austin	Sandgate, Wall Knoll
B1: Master Mariners	Sandgate, Wall Knoll, [Pandon, Austin], Gateshead	
B1: Shipwrights	Sandgate, Wall Knoll	
n.a. Keelmen – (excluded by Langton)	Sandgate	

B2: Bakers/Brewers	Austin, [Carliol, Pilgrim], Pandon	Plummer, Austin, Carliol, Pandon
B2: Butchers	Austin, [Newgate, Mordon], [Ever, Andrew, Ficket]	
B2: Millers	Plummer, Pandon, West Gate, Sandgate	

C1: Smiths/ anchorsmiths	Wall Knoll, Pandon, Ficket, Sandgate	Mordon, Pilgrim, and Carliol as shown in Table IV [1]

C3: Tailors	No concentrations[2]	Mordon, Denton (Neville), West Spittle, Pilgrim
C3: Weavers	Westgate, [Bertram Monboucher, Pilgrim]	

C4: Cordwainers	Mordon, [Pilgrim, Carliol, Andrew, Ficket], [Plummer, Pink, West Spittle, White Friar, Gunner]	Pandon , White Friar
C4: Skinners/Glovers	[White Friar, Denton (Neville), West Spittle][3]	
C4: Tanners	[Durham, Ever, Andrew], Westgate, Sandgate.	

1: Langdon's occupational category C1 includes eight metal trades and therefore the concentration is not necessarily applicable to smiths, which are the only trade in this group represented in Heley's data.
2: Tailors appear to be distributed along the three main arteries of the town, in particular through the central markets to the Newgate, but there are no concentrations attributable to individual wards.
3: Sample size too small to confirm concentrations.

Chapter 5 – Table 5.1a - Heating and cooking: Location of iron chimneys and iron bars in Newcastle houses according to inventoried rooms 1549 -1642

IC = Iron chimney, IB = Iron bars in pairs - Sample size:189 testators

Location	Type	Baker /brewer	Butcher	Cord-wainer	Keelman	Mariner	Master mariner	Miller	Ship-wright	Skinner /glover	Smith	Tailor	Tanner	Weaver	Total IC/IB
Hall	IC	15	10	19	3	13	18	5	13	5	15	9	12	13	**150**
	IB	4	3	2	-	-	1	4	2	2	2	-	1	4	**25**
Kitchen	IC	7	5	11	-	6	9	1	7	1	5	3	5	2	**62**
	IB	2	2	2	-	-	4	-	2	1	1	2	1	1	**18**
Parlour	IC	3	4	8	-	4	6	2	2	-	3	1	5	2	**40**
	IB	2	1	8	-	-	-	2	1	1	-	1	3	2	**21**
Chamber*	IC	6	1	6	1	9	3	-	3	1	2	3	3	5	**43**
	IB	7	6	8	-	3	14	-	7	4	5	2	3	6	**65**
Brew house	IC	1	-	1	-	-	2	-	-	-	1	-	-	-	**5**
	IB	-	-	2	-	-	-	-	-	-	1	-	-	-	**3**
Loft	IC	-	1	-	-	-	1	3	1	-	-	-	-	1	**7**
	IB	-	1	-	-	-	-	-	-	-	-	-	-	-	**1**
Misc. rooms**	IC	-	-	1	-	-	-	1	-	-	-	-	1	-	**3**
	IB	2	1	-	-	-	-	1	-	-	-	1	-	-	**5**
Average number of IC/ IB per trade	-	**2.52**	**2.69**	**2.72**	**1.33**	**2.69**	**2.63**	**1.72**	**2.11**	**1.87**	**2.05**	**2.44**	**2.42**	**2.35**	**2.36**
No. of testators listing IC/IB in specified rooms	-	19	13	25	3	13	22	11	8	18	17	9	14	17	189
Total IC/ IB per trade	-	48	35	68	4	35	58	19	38	15	35	22	34	40	447

Chapter 5 – Table 5.1b- Combined percentages showing distribution of iron chimneys and iron bars within Newcastle houses1549 -1642

Location	Baker/ brewer	Butcher	Cord-wainer	Keelman	Mariner	Master mariner	Miller	Ship-wright	Skinner/ glover	Smith	Tailor	Tanner	Weaver	Total
Hall	100%	100%	84%	100%	100%	86.4%	81.8%	83.3%	87.5%	100%	100%	92.9%	100%	**92.5%**
Kitchen	47.4%	53.8%	52%	0%	46.2%	59.1%	9.1%	50%	25%	35.3%	55.6%	42.9%	17.6%	**42.3%**
Parlour	26.3%	38.5%	64%	0%	30.8%	27.3%	36.4%	16.7%	12.5%	17.6%	22.2%	57.1%	23.5%	**32.3%**
Chamber*	68.4%	53.8%	56%	33.3%	92.3%	77.3%	0%	55.6%	62.5%	41.2%	55.6%	42.9%	64.7%	**57.1%**
Brew house	5.3%	0%	12%	0%	0%	9.1%	0%	0%	0%	11.8%	0%	0%	0%	**4.2%**
Loft	0%	15.4%	0%	0%	0%	4.5%	27.3%	5.6%	0%	0%	0%	0%	5.9%	**4.2%**
Misc. rooms**	10.5%	7.7%	4%	0%	0%	0%	18.2%	0%	0%	0%	11.1%	7.1%	0%	**4.2%**

*** Includes upper, lower, fore, side and unspecified chambers ** Includes: room over entry, buttery, shop, old house, bake house, work house, ever house**

Chapter 5 – Table 5.2a - Acquisition of selected objects 1549 – 1642; figures show total number of objects in inventories, the date when the object was first recorded and which trade listed the object first.
Total sample of inventories: 1549-1599: 83 inv.'s – 1600-1625: 99 inv's – 1626-1642: 75 inv.'s.
*The abbreviation for a hand basin and ewer is 'b&e', hand basin: 'hb' ewer: 'e'. ** Salt sellers were also referred to as 'kits' and 'vats' and were either 'single' or 'double'

Objects	**First recorded: date/ trade**	**1549-1599**	**1600-1625**	**1626-1642**
Hand basin &/ or ewer*	All periods/ trades	5 b&e/ 3 hb/ 3 e	25 b&e/ 10 hb/ 7 e	33 b&e/ 4 hb/ 4 e
Carpet cloths	All periods/ trades	79	144	170
Chinaware	1634 (master mariner)	-	1	15
Clocks	1619 (mariner)	-	2	3
Closet stools	1616 (cordwainer)	-	5	5
Covered chairs	1629 (master mariner)	-	-	29
Cushions	All periods/ trades	360	672	751
Danish chests, coffers, trunks	1570 (master mariner)	58	41	33
Danish pots	1570 (several trades)	68	159	183
Desks	1587 (master mariner)	4	11	11
Flower pots	1585 (several trades)	53	211	603
Footstools for beds	1587 (cordwainer)	4	15	35
Glass bottles	1593 (skinner/ glover)	1case/ 2 bottles	2 cases/ 9 bottles	3 cases/ 1 bottles
Glass cases or glasses	1572 (several trades)	7 cases	18 cases/ 5 drinking/ 3 beer	30 cases/ 2 drinking
Towels/ hand towels	All periods/ trades	229	169	220
Livery/ court cupboards	1619 (master mariner)	-	3 livery/ 1 court	10 livery/ 3 court
Mirrors	1573 (master mariner)	3	10	34
Mortar &/ or pestle	All periods/ trades	4 mortars/ 39 pestles	11 mortars/ 40 pestles	13 mortars/ 35 pestles
Musical instruments	1596 lute(master mariner)-1636 virginals (tanner)	2	-	4
Pictures	1616 (master mariner)	-	20	50
Playing tables	1573 (several trades)	9	8	11
Querns – pepper or mustard	1587:pepper/1570: mustard (several trades)	6 pepper/ 2 mustard	2 pepper/ 2 mustard	2 pepper
Salt sellers**	All periods/ trades	140	195	144
Silver spoons	All periods/ trades	217	180	211
Spice boxes	1587 (master mariner)	1	8	5
Window cloths	1554 (smith)	12	4	2
Window curtains	1623 (weaver)	-	3	25
Window cushions	1616 (master mariner)	-	3	9
Total number of objects	-	**1311**	**1999**	**2693**

Chapter 5 – Table 5.2b - Acquisition of selected objects 1549 – 1642; figures show mean average for the ownership of 28 selected objects listed on Table 5.2a

	Baker /brewer	**Butcher**	**Cord-wainer**	**Keelman**	**Mariner**	**Master mariner**	**Miller**	**Ship-wright**	**Skinner /glover**	**Smith**	**Tailor**	**Tanner**	**Weaver**	**Meanaverage/ #objects**
Mean average 1549-1599(83 inv.'s)	36.7	10.3	19.1	4	16.5	27	8	14.2	15	11	13.5	18	4.2	**15.7 (1311)**
Mean average 1601-1625(99 inv.'s)	23.8	22.6	26.1	2	23.4	44.5	12.4	17.8	12.8	15	20.8	13.5	23.2	**20.1 (1999**
Mean average 1626-1642(75 inv.'s)	41.6	37.4	52.8	2	50.5	56.5	16.5	27	20.3	20	21.6	37.8	24.5	**35.9 (2693**
Mean average of objects per trade 1549-1642	35.2	24.6	33.3	3	23.7	41.8	13.5	17.6	15.3	14.2	19.1	24.8	18.2	**23.3**
Total inventories 1549-1642	20	18	31	12	19	25	18	23	13	23	15	16	24	**257**
Total objects 1549-1642	705	444	1033	36	451	1046	244	405	200	328	287	398	438	**6003**

Chapter 5 – Table 5.3 - Mean average valuations for three categories of household objects 1549 -1642 (£)
1: Furniture & soft furniture 2: Beds, bedding & table linen 3: Tableware, cookware & decorative objects

Period: 1549-1600 – Sample size 80

Type of object	Baker &/ or brewer	Butcher	Cordwainer	Keelman	Mariner	Master mariner	Miller	Shipwright	Skinner &/or glover	Smith	Tailor	Tanner	Weaver	Percentage of objects per category	Overall mean average
1:Furniture. etc.	6.58	2.95	3.08	1.72	3.70	7.08	2.78	2.90	3.23	2.45	3.66	2.95	1.22	25.57%	3.35
2:Beds etc.	16.21	3.69	6.35	.99	6.91	11.69	3.55	4.79	6.87	3.03	3.37	5.04	1.01	42.43%	5.56
3:Tableware etc.	7.88	5.99	4.85	1.74	4.30	7.57	5.05	4.46	4.32	2.89	3.97	3.86	1.80	32.00%	4.19
Mean average for combined objects	30.67	12.63	14.28	4.45	14.92	25.51	11.39	12.17	10.11	8.00	9.48	11.86	4.04	100%	13.10

Period: 1601 – 1625 – Sample size 99

Type of object	Baker &/ or brewer	Butcher	Cordwainer	Keelman	Mariner	Master mariner	Miller	Shipwright	Skinner &/or glover	Smith	Tailor	Tanner	Weaver	Percentage of objects per category	Overall mean average
1:Furniture. etc.	5.71	4.51	5.49	.82	3.90	9.12	2.19	3.80	2.82	3.09	5.18	4.80	4.51	24.22%	3.99
2:Beds etc.	10.99	8.03	17.40	.88	5.85	16.46	6.16	6.97	3.61	4.12	8.54	7.02	9.48	49.25%	8.12
3:Tableware etc.	5.42	13.37	6.05	1.11	3.90	6.80	4.16	3.80	2.89	3.50	5.72	3.57	3.84	26.53%	4.37
Mean average for combined objects	22.12	18.58	26.60	2.82	13.66	32.39	12.09	14.57	9.30	10.08	19.45	15.40	17.83	100%	16.49

Period 1626 – 1642 – Sample size 75

Type of object	Baker &/ or brewer	Butcher	Cordwainer	Keelman	Mariner	Master mariner	Miller	Shipwright	Skinner &/or glover	Smith	Tailor	Tanner	Weaver	Percentage of objects per category	Overall mean average
1:Furniture. etc.	13.18	6.48	12.69	1.00	6.78	11.87	2.63	9.36	4.83	6.20	3.44	8.46	5.21	30.90%	8.32
2:Beds etc.	9.28	14.34	26.56	2.71	15.68	16.02	7.16	14.44	5.31	12.21	7.77	11.53	9.08	47.77%	12.87
3:Tableware etc.	5.16	5.31	8.87	1.39	6.79	7.41	3.23	4.92	3.94	5.56	2.40	6.41	5.70	21.34%	5.75
Mean average for combined objects	27.63	23.27	48.13	5.10	29.26	35.30	13.03	28.73	13.91	23.98	13.61	26.41	19.90	100%	26.94

Combined figures for all periods 1549 – 1642 – Sample size 253

Type of object	Baker &/ or brewer	Butcher	Cordwainer	Keelman	Mariner	Master mariner	Miller	Shipwright	Skinner &/or glover	Smith	Tailor	Tanner	Weaver	Percentage of objects per category	Overall mean average
1:Furniture. etc.	9.78	2.68	7.27	1.29	4.13	9.37	2.79	4.26	4.45	3.28	3.85	5.25	3.81	27.39%	5.07
2:Beds etc.	10.92	8.56	16.53	1.09	7.28	14.66	5.92	7.21	5.22	4.49	6.56	7.72	6.85	47.09%	8.71
3:Tableware etc.	5.67	5.79	6.47	1.45	4.36	6.99	3.67	4.22	3.69	3.41	3.77	4.79	4.02	25.52%	4.72
Mean average for combined objects	26.3	17.0	30.2	3.8	15.7	31.0	12.3	15.6	12.3	11.1	14.1	17.7	14.6	100%	18.51 (median: 12.78)
Sample size	19	17	31	12	19	25	18	21	13	23	15	16	24	(253)	-

Chapter 5 - Table 5.4a – Range of valuations for three categories of combined household objects:
1 - Furniture & soft furniture - 2 - Beds, bedding & table linen – 3 -Tableware, cookware & decorative objects.

Figures show range of valuations (£), sample size and the percentage of combined objects listed per trade 1549 -1642

Sample size: 253

	Bakers and brewers		Butchers		Cordwainers		Keelmen		Mariners		Master mariners	
£'s	#	%	#	%	#	%	#	%	#	%	#	%
0-5	2	10.5	2	11.8	4	12.9	8	66.7	5	26.3	2	7.7
5-10	2	10.5	1	5.9	2	6.5	4	33.3	4	21.1	1	3.8
10-15	3	15.8	5	29.4	6	19.4	0	0.0	2	10.5	4	15.4
15-20	1	5.3	3	17.6	5	16.1	0	0.0	2	10.5	2	7.7
20-30	3	15.8	3	17.6	5	16.1	0	0.0	3	15.8	4	15.4
30-40	2	10.5	2	11.8	2	6.5	0	0.0	1	5.3	7	26.9
40+	6	31.6	1	5.9	7	22.6	0	0.0	2	10.0	6	23.1

	Millers		Shipwrights		Skinners & glovers		Smiths		Tailors		Tanners		Weavers	
£'s	#	%	#	%	#	%	#	%	#	%	#	%	#	%
0-5	8	44.4	1	4.8	4	30.8	9	39.1	3	20.0	3	18.8	7	29.2
5-10	1	5.6	6	28.6	3	23.1	3	13.0	4	26.7	4	25.0	9	37.5
10-15	5	27.8	7	33.3	2	15.4	6	26.1	2	13.3	2	12.5	2	8.3
15-20	2	11.1	3	14.3	4	30.8	2	8.7	2	13.3	1	6.3	1	4.2
20-30	0	0.0	2	9.5	0	0.0	1	4.3	2	13.3	2	12.5	2	8.3
30-40	0	0.0	1	4.8	0	0.0	2	8.7	2	13.3	3	18.8	1	4.2
40+	2	11.1	1	4.8	0	0.0	0	0.0	0	0.0	1	6.3	2	8.3

Overall figures for combined trades and objects

£'s	#	%
0-5	58	22.9
5-10	44	17.4
10-15	45	17.8
15-20	28	11.1
20-30	27	10.7
30-40	23	9.1
40+	28	11.1
Totals	253	100

Table 5.4b - Overall distribution of valuations for three categories of combined household objects 1549 - 1642

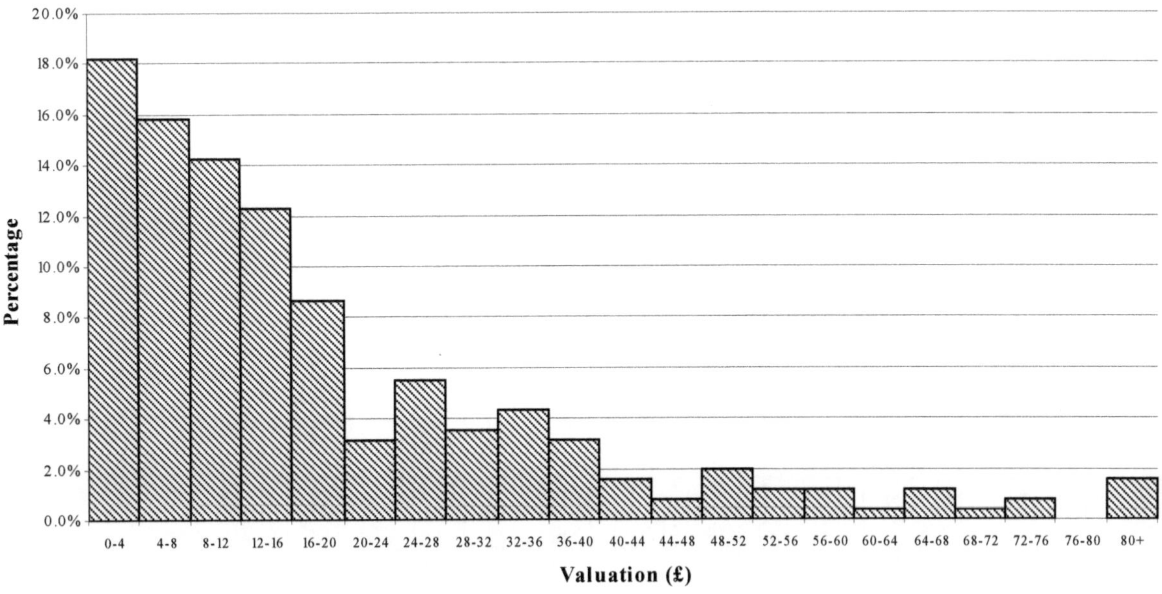

Chapter 5 – Table 5.5 – Valuations of furniture and household wares 1549 - 1642

Furniture and soft furnishings	**1549 -1580**	**1581 – 1600**	**1601 – 1625**	**1626 – 1642**
Buffet stools	4d (single entry)	6d – 1s 6d	3d – 1s 3d	6d – 1s (little)
Carpet cloths	6d (old) – 10s	5d – 10s	4d (old) – 6s 8d	1s (old) – 1li
Chairs (unspecified)	4d – 1s 3d	3d (old) – 1s 8d	3d – 6s 8d	4d (old) – 6s
Cushions	1d (old) – 1s 11d	1d – 6s 8d	3d – 6s	4d – 6s 4d
Cushions (window)	none	none	1s (both entries)	1s – 13s 4d
Danish chests/ coffers	2s 8d – 6s (great)	1s 6d – 1li (set work)	2s 3d – 1li 10s	5s – 4li (with frame)
Longsettles	2s 6d (1 entry)	1s 6d – 6s 8d (wainscot)	8d – 3s	6d – 10s
Bed and table linen				
Codpillowbers	3d – 1s 10d	4d – 3s 5d	6d – 1s 8d	6d – 1s 2d
Hand towels (unspecified)	6d – 8s	2d - 6s 8d	2d (old) – 2s	3d – 3s 4d
Linen napkins	none	3d – 2s	3d – 6d	6d – 1s 2d
Linen table cloths	6d (old/ 2 yards long) (single entry)	1s (old) – 6s	1s 10d – 4s 5d	2s 2d – 5s
Linen sheets (pairs)	1s 8d (old) – 5s	1s – 10s 8d	2s 6d – 10s	3s – 10s
Cookware				
Dropping pans	6d & 1s	6d – 1s 4d	6d – 1s 4d	1s & 4s
Frying pan	6d – 8d	4d – 2s	6d – 1s 4d	6d (old) (single entry)
Mortar & pestle	1s – 5s	1s – 6s 8d	1s – 6s 8d	2s – 5s 6d
Tableware				
Doublers (pewter)	6d – 1s 7d	6d – 2s 6d	7d – 2s	1s 3d – 2s
Earthenware (all types including dishes, platters, jugs, pots	1d (all)	1d (all)	1d – 6d 10d (pitcher)	1d (all)
Glass bottles	none	4d each	6 for 2s	2d each
Glass cages/ cases	2d – 6d	4d & 1s	3d – 5s (wainscot cage)	3d – 13s 4d (wainscot cage)
Glasses: drinking	none	1d each	1d – 4d	none
Salt sellers (unspecified)	1d – 9d	2d – 10d	3d – 10d	4d (old) – 1s
Salt sellers (pewter)	4d (single entry)	3d – 1s	4d -6d	none
Spoons (tin)	none	2 for 1d (all)	10 for 1d – 1d each	.5d – 1d
Trenchers (wooden)	1.5d (single entry)	6 for 1d – 1d each	5 for 1d – 2d each	6 for 1d – 2 for 1d
Decorative and miscellaneous objects				
Chamber pots (unspecified)	10d (single entry)	8d – 1s 8d	4d – 1s	9d – 1s 6d
Close stools	none	none	2s – 14s (lead)	1s (old) & 5s
Flower pots	none	3d – 6d	4d – 10d	4d – 10s
Mirrors	4d & 6d	none	4d – 2s 4d	6d – 5s
Pictures	none	none	3d – 1s (in a frame)	1d – 1s (in a frame)
Window cloths	6d – 2s 6d	2s & 2s 8d	1s	none
Window curtains	3s 4d (fleers for window) (single entry)	2s 6d (single entry)	1s 6d & 3s	1s 1d – 7s

Chapter 5 – Table 5.6 – Average valuations of apparel (£s) 1549 - 1642 (Sample: 257 inventories)

	Baker & brewer	Butcher	Cordwainer	Keelman	Mariner	Master mariner	Miller	Shipwright	Skinner & glover	Smith	Tailor	Tanner	Weaver	Overall average (£)	No. inv.'s listing apparel	Percentage inv.'s listing apparel
1549-1600	8.92	2.05	4.10	.55	3.05	7.30	2.76	2.45	2.20	2.35	2.30	2.35	1.20	**2.92**	**65**	**87%**
1601-1625	4.60	5.05	4.85	1.35	6.60	9.30	3.80	3.30	4.75	3.95	5.80	4.00	3.95	**4.76**	**90**	**91%**
1626-1642	7.15	5.95	5.20	-	-	10.40	3.60	4.25	2.25	8.85	4.05	7.55	4.00	**6.08**	**68**	**91%**
Overall averages per trade	**6.46**	**4.80**	**4.78**	**.87**	**5.18**	**9.20**	**3.61**	**3.09**	**3.49**	**4.04**	**4.18**	**4.54**	**3.42**	**4.62**	-	-
Percentage inv.'s listing apparel	80%	100%	81%	83%	79%	84%	56%	83%	77%	96%	93%	94%	83%	-	-	**87%**
No. inv.'s listing apparel	16	18	25	10	15	21	18	19	10	22	14	15	20	-	223	-

Chapter 5 – Table 5.7a – Valuations and ownership patterns of weapons and armour 1558 – 1642 (Total sample: 257 inventories)

Type of weapon/ armour	Baker & brewer	Butcher	Cordwainer	Keelman	Mariner	Master mariner	Miller	Shipwright	Skinner & glover	Smith	Tailor	Tanner	Weaver	Total weapons	Overall Percentage
Bow	1	-	1	-	-	-	-	3	1	2	-	1	-	9	2.3
Quiver of arrows	1	-	1	-	-	-	-	2	-	2	2	-	-	8	2.0
Stuff jacket	-	-	3	-	-	-	-	1	-	1	-	2	-	7	1.8
Head piece (helmet)	1	-	4	-	4	3	1	2	-	1	-	1	1	18	4.6
Steel/ plate cape	-	3	1	-	2	-	-	-	1	1	1	4	-	13	3.3
Halberd staff	7	2	10	1	3	7	4	5	2	12	2	2	3	59	15.2
Bill staff	3	-	3	1	2	2	3	-	1	13	2	1	-	31	7.9
Sword	9	1	5	2	3	18	3	7	6	5	4	3	3	69	17.7
Dagger	-	-	-	1	3	5	1	1	1	3	1	1	1	17	4.3
Rapier	-	-	-	-	2	2	-	1	-	3	1	-	1	10	2.5
Musket	4	4	6	-	1	11	1	3	1	2	2	2	4	40	10.3
Caliver	4	3	7	-	3	9	1	6	1	6	2	1	4	46	11.8
Bandolier	2	1	2	-	1	3	-	1	1	1	2	1	3	18	4.6
Bird/ fowling piece	-	-	-	-	2	2	-	-	-	1	-	1	-	6	1.5
Pistol/ gun	3	1	-	-	-	-	-	2	1	1	1	1	1	11	2.8
Other weapons	5	1	2	-	2	8	-	6	-	-	1	1	-	26	6.7
Total weapons	40	16	45	5	28	70	14	39	16	54	16	22	21	388	100%
Weapons per person	3.3	2.2	3.2	2.5	4	4.3	2.3	3	3.2	3.8	1.7	3.1	3	3.2	-
Percentage	63%	39%	45%	17%	37%	64%	33%	57%	38%	60%	60%	44%	29%	-	46%
No. inv.'s listing weapons	12	7	14	2	7	16	6	13	5	14	9	7	7	119	-
Total valuation of weapons/ armour (£)	7.26	3.47	3.97	0.02	3.20	13.32	1.89	2.96	1.88	5.45	2.78	3.42	4.12	53.62	-
Overall mean average valuation (£)	0.60 (12s)	0.49 (10s)	0.28 (6s)	0.01 (2d)	0.45 (9s)	0.82 (17s)	0.31 (6s)	0.22 (5s)	0.37 (8s)	0.38 (8s)	0.30 (6s)	0.48 (10s)	0.58 (12s)	0.45 (9s)	-

Table 5.7b – Range of valuations for weapons and armour

Type of object	Pre 1600	1601 -1625	1626 -1642
Bill staff	4d – 1s 7d	1s (single entry)	(no valuations)
Halberd staff	8d – 4s 8d	8d – 4s	1s 2d – 2s 4d
Musket	6s 8d (single entry)	3s 4d (old) – 16s	2s 6d – 20s
Caliver	3s – 26s 8d	1s (old) – 10s	(no valuations)
Sword	1s 8d – 6s	8d (old) – 10s	(no valuations)
Dagger	1s (long – single entry)	6d (single entry)	(no valuations)
Bow & arrows	2s – 6s 8d	(none recorded)	(none recorded)

Chapter 5 – Table 5.8a – Ownership of books, maps and globes 1580 – 1641 (Total sample: 257 inventories)

	Baker &/or Brewer	Butcher	Cordwainer	Keelman	Mariner	Master mariner	Miller	Shipwright	Skinner &/or glover	Smith	Tailor	Tanner	Weaver	Totals	Percentage
Bibles	14	4	7	0	6	16	0	1	3	2	4	1	2	61	29.6%
Religious works	4	2	5	2	1	4	1	0	1	0	1	0	0	21	10.1%
Other works	7	0	5	1	13*	22	0	2	0	1	0	0	44**	95	46.1%
Maps & globes	0	0	1	0	12	16	0	0	0	0	0	0	0	29	14%
Combined total books & maps	25	6	18	3	32	58	1	3	4	3	6	1	46	206	100%
Total inv.'s with books & maps	12	5	9	2	9	18	1	1	3	3	3	1	4	71	-
Percentage	48%	28%	29%	17%	47%	72%	5%	4%	23%	13%	20%	6%	17%	-	28%
Overall total valuation (£)	5.15	1.37	7.08	(unreliable valuation)	4.07	8.88	(unknown)	0.33	0.65	0.73	0.33	0.25	2.10	31.95	-
Overall mean average valuation (£)	0.43 (9s)	0.27 (6s)	0.79 (16s)	-	0.45 (9s)	0.49 (10s)	-	0.33 (7s)	0.22 (4s)	0.24 (5s)	0.11 (2s)	0.25 (5s)	0.53 (11s) (6s)**	0.45 (9s)	-

* 8 owned by 1 mariner
** 42 books were owned by 1 weaver called Oswald Chaytor valued at 20s in 1623. The second bracketed figure for overall mean average valuations excludes Chaytor.

Chapter 5 – Table 5.8b –Range of valuations for bibles and ownership patterns for books, maps and globes 1580 -1641

	1580 -1600	1601 -1625	1626 -1641
Range of prices for bibles	4s (old) – 6s 8d	3s 4d (old) – 10s	2s – 10s
Number of bibles recorded in inv.'s	8	25	28
No. of other religious & secular books	15	74 **	58
No. of maps & globes	10	17	2
Overall total no. of works recorded	33	116	88
No. of inv.'s in sample	83	99	75
Average number of books/ maps/ globes per inv.	.39	1.17 (0.76)**	1.17

** See note above

Chapter 5 – Table 5.9a– Range of valuations for spinning wheels 1558 – 1642

Type of spinning wheel	1558 – 1600	1601 -1625	1626 -1642
Coarse/ harden yarn	-	6d	5s
Linen	1s – 2s	8d – 4s	2s & 5s
Towe	-	8d & 1s	-
Wool	9d	8d	2s
All specified & unspecified types	6d – 3s 4d	6d – 6s	1s – 5s
Total sample of priced spinning wheels	20	17	12
Percentage	24%	17%	16%
Total no. inv.'s in sample	83	99	75

Chapter 5 – Table 5.9b – The number and the percentage of inventories recording spinning wheels, yarn and cloth 1549 -1642 (Sample: 257 inventories)

	Baker	Butcher	Cordwainer	Keelman	Mariner	Master mariner	Miller	Shipwright	Skinner & or glover	Smith	Tailor	Tanner	Weaver	Totals
Spinning wheels	10	14	13	3	8	19	2	17	4	7	2	4	4	107
Percentage	50%	78%	42%	25%	42%	76%	11%	74%	31%	30%	13%	25%	17%	42%
Spinning wheels, yarn and cloth*	10	14	13	7	11	19	4	17	6	8	5	7	4	125
Percentages	50%	78%	42%	58%	58%	76%	22%	74%	46%	35%	33%	44%	17%	49%

***Potential spinning and sewing is indicated by supplies of yarn and cloth**

Chapter 5 – Table 5.10a – Ownership patterns of animals 1553 – 1642

	Baker & brewer	Butcher	Cordwainer	Keelman	Mariner	Master mariner	Miller	Shipwright	Skinner & glover	Smith	Tailor	Tanner	Weaver	Total animals/ inv.'s	Overall percentage of animals
Cattle	42	156	64	4	3	9	29	9	40	17	19	17	38	447	**35%**
Oxen	5	37	4	-	-	6	-	-	-	-	-	4	-	56	**4%**
Horses	16	30	8	-	-	8	50	1	3	2	3	2	8	131	**10%**
Pigs	28	11	9	1	10	-	10	6	-	6	-	-	5	86	**7%**
Sheep	6	427	46	3	-	-	-	2	17	7	28	-	8	544	**43%**
Total animals	97	661	131	8	13	23	89	18	60	32	50	23	59	1264	**100%**
Inv.'s listing animals	15	15	26	3	3	6	16	7	12	10	8	9	18	148	-
Percentage	75%	83%	84%	25%	16%	24%	84%	30%	92%	42%	53%	56%	75%	58%	**(257 inv.'s)**
Average (£)	**6.66**	**33.44**	**4.08**	**2.32**	**2.05**	**3.97**	**4.65**	**2.74**	**3.40**	**3.19**	**2.61**	**3.68**	**3.49**	**7.47**	-

* The average level of investment excluding butchers is £3.96.

Chapter 5 – Table 5.10b – Range of valuations for animals 1553 -1642

Type of animal	Pre 1600	1601 -1625	1626 -1642
Cattle	5s (calf) – 2li 10s	10s (calf) – 2li 10s	15s (calf) – 2li 15s
Oxen	-	1li – 4li 10s	-
Horses	13s 4d – 2li 6s 8d	5s – 2li 13s 4d	10s – 8li
Sheep	3s 8d & 5s	1s 6d – 6s	3s (single entry)
Pigs	1s – 5s 5d	4s – 10s	4s 2d – 8s
No. of inv.'s recording prices for animals	58	82	49
Percentage of inventories recording animals	70 %	83%	65%
Total no. of inv.'s in sample	83	99	75

Chapter 5 – Table 5.11a – Inventories listing brewing equipment in named rooms 1549 – 1642 (Sample: 257 inv.'s)

Room	Baker & brewer	Butcher	Cordwainer	Keelmen	Mariner	Master mariner	Miller	Shipwright	Skinner & glover	Smith	Tailor	Tanner	Weaver	Totals	Averages
Back house	-	-	-	-	-	-	-	2	-	-	-	-	-	**2**	**2%**
Bake house	1	-	-	-	-	-	1	-	-	-	-	-	-	**2**	**2%**
Brew house	16	2	7	-	3	6	3	-	2	5	3	7	3	**57**	**59%**
Cellar	1	1	-	-	-	-	1	-	-	-	-	-	1	**4**	**4%**
Chamber	-	-	1	-	1	-	-	-	2	1	-	-	-	**5**	**5%**
Hall	-	-	-	-	-	-	1	-	-	-	-	-	1	**3**	**3%**
Kitchen	-	2	1	1	2	5	-	2	-	-	3	1	3	**20**	**21%**
Parlour	-	-	2	-	-	-	-	-	-	-	-	-	1	**3**	**3%**
Work house	-	-	-	-	-	-	-	-	-	-	-	-	1	**1**	**1%**
No. of named rooms	18	5	11	1	6	11	6	4	4	6	6	8	10	**96**	**100%**
Percentage	90%	28%	35%	8%	32%	44%	33%	4%	31%	26%	16%	50%	42%	**37%**	-
Total inventories	20	18	31	12	19	25	18	23	13	23	15	16	24	**257 inv.'s**	-

Chapter 5 – Table 5.11b – Range of valuations for brew, copper & steep leads & basic brew vessels

Range of valuations	1570 - 1600	1601 - 1625	1626 - 1640
Brew or copper lead	1li – 6li 13s 4d	1li – 22li	1li 10s – 24li
Steep lead	4li – 5li	4li	1li 10s – 2li 6s (old)
Kiln chimney	3s 4d – 10s	6s	6s
Kiln hair	3s – 7s	5s - 6s	6s 8d
Kiln chimney & kiln hair	4s -15s 4d	10s	10s – 1li
Combined wort, gyle, & masking tubs	3s – 6s 8d	2s 6d – 3li	2s – 1li
Percentage of inventories listing kiln chimney/ hair	20%	7%	5%
Sample of inventories	83	99	75

Chapter 5 – Table 5.11c –
Percentage of grains recorded in inventories

Grains	Percentage
Barley	22.39%
Oats	13.46%
Rye	1.82%
Wheat	10.62%
Malted grains	51.73%
Total	100%
No. of inv.'s listing grain	**89 (35%)**

Table 5.11d – Average valuations (£) for brewing equipment, kiln chimneys and kiln hairs, grains (malted grain, barley, wheat, oats, rye), beer and hops 1549 – 1642

	Baker & brewer	Butcher	Cordwainer	Keelmen	Mariner	Master mariner	Miller	Shipwright	Skinner &/or glover	Smith	Tailor	Tanner	Weaver	Averages (£)
BREW, COPPER & STEEP LEADS														
Average valuation (£)	7.69	4.00	2.13	-	2.00	20.00	3.50	1.00	-	1.20	4.50	6.00	4.89	**5.45**
No. of inv.'s	12	1	5	-	1	1	2	1	-	1	1	1	3	**(30)**
Percentages	60%	6%	16%	-	5%	4%	11%	4%	-	4%	7%	6%	13%	**13%**
COMBINED EQUIPMENT														
Average valuation (£)	12.94	1.01	1.42	.15	.76	4.60	2.49	1.78	.62	.92	.92	1.34	1.39	**3.18***
No. of inv.'s	16	7	16	2	6	9	7	5	5	8	8	8	17	**(114)**
Percentages	80%	50%	52%	17%	32%	36%	41%	38%	22%	35%	53%	50%	68%	**44%***
GRAIN, HOPS & BEER*****														
Average valuation (£)	10.87	12.71	4.38	.88	8.68	8.62	5.58	3.83	2.58	2.13	8.33	2.75	7.54	**7.17**
No. of inv.'s	15	8	13	1	4	9	10	4	4	5	6	3	8	**(90)**
Percentages	75%	44%	42%	8%	21%	36%	56%	31%	17%	22%	40%	19%	33%	**35%**

* Without bakers and brewers the average valuation is 1li 11s and the percentage of inventories listing brewing equipment is 38%.
**Hops were recorded only by the bakers and brewers.
*** Beer was recorded by six bakers and brewers, one cordwainer, one master mariner and one weaver.

Chapter 5 – Table 5.12a – Average investments for objects of the trades (£) Sample: 257 inventories)

Figures include only those items associated with a named occupation, and do not include contributions from by-employment, which are presented in the conclusion.

	Baker & brewer	Butcher	Cordwainer	Keelman	Mariner	Master mariner	Miller	Shipwright	Skinner & glover	Smith	Tailor	Tanner	Weaver	Averages
Tools/ equipment/ clothes	13.11 12.94* / 0.52**	.32	.92	.08	.77	2.48	.14	.99	.10	3.68	.17	.03	1.62	-
Supplies for making/ repairing objects	-	-	8.89	.09	.46	4.23	.08	13.27	9.34	6.70	.93	46.08	1.03	-
Wares for sale	-	-	5.39	-	-	-	-	-	.68	6.29	-	-	-	-
Ships/ boats	-	-	-	13.78	8.70	74.70	-	38.02	-	58.35	-	-	-	-
Animals for trade	-	33.44	-	-	-	-	4.65	-	-	-	-	-	-	-
Overall average investment	13.46	33.76	15.2	13.95	9.93	81.41	4.87	52.28	10.12	75.02 (26.13)***	1.1	46.11	2.65	**32.36**
Percentage	85%	72%	77%	25%	53%	77%	82%	87%	69%	96%	53%	75%	92%	**75%**
Inv.'s with objects of trade	17	13	24	3	10	20	14	20	9	22	8	12	22	**(194)**

* Total average investment for brewing equipment. ** Total average investment for baking equipment. *** Bracketed total excludes anomaly of single anchorsmith with £1085 of shipping interests.

Chapter 5 - Table 5.12b - Valuations of wares

CORDWAINERS			
Type of object	**1553 - 1600**	**1601 -1625**	**1626 -1642**
Oil (per gallon)	1s – 2s	2s - 17s	1s 8d (single entry)
Tallow (per stone)	2s	3s (single entry)	2s 2d
Tanned, liquored, 'unliquored' & unspecified hides	8s	8s (Yarm) / 9s (Beverley)	10s – 2li
Boots	1s 9d – 2s 4d	2s – 5s 4d	2s 10d – 5s
Women's & lesser/ little shoes	7d – 8d	10d – 1s	-
Men's & greater shoes	1s 2d	1s – 1s 8d	-
Children's shoes	3d	8d	10d
Various heeled shoes	1s 4d (pumps)	2s 8d (falling shoes)	1s 6d (wooden heel)
SKINNERS & GLOVERS			
Type of object	**1589 - 1597**	**1616 - 1625**	**1634 - 1635**
Coarse wool	2s 6d per stone	-	3s 10d per stone
Blue wool/ Black wool	-	-	3s 2d per stone/ c.7s per stone
'Second sort' wool	-	-	6s 6d per stone
Pelts	.5d each (half penny)	-	1.5d each
Cheveral leather	2d each	-	-
Wet leather	.5d each (half penny)	1.2d each	-
Wrought/ made leather	-	2d each	4d each
Alumed leather	-	-	3d
Sheepskin	1.5d each	-	3d each
Lambskins	1.5d each	-	2d each
Calf skins	-	-	4d & 6d each
Gloves	-	1d each	-
Purses/ small bags	3d each	1.5d each	2d each
Leather bags for women	-	-	1d each
Lambskin money bags	-	-	1.5d each
SMITHS			
Type of object	**1570 - 1600**	**1601 -1625**	**1626 - 1631**
Horse shoes	1d – 1.5d	1.2d – 7d (new)	-
Shoe irons	1d	1.5d – 2d	-
Shovels	-	4d – 4.5d	3d – 3.5d
Hammers (variety)	2.5d – 1s 4d	10d – 1s 6d	-
Hammers (small)	.5d	3d – 6d	-
Nail hammers	4d	4d	-
Bores (variety)	2d (small) – 14s (stand)	4d (small) – 1s 6d	-
Bellows (variety)	6s – 1li	3s 6d (old) – 1li 6s 2d	1li 6s
Anvils	8s – 10s	9s -15s 2d	-
Anvils (small)	2s - 13s 4d	-	
Anvils (great)	1li 14s – 2li 10s	-	1li 6s

Chapter 5 – Table 5.13a - Mean overall average investment for combined categories of objects (£) 1548 – 1642

Type of object	Bakers &/or brewers	Butchers	Cordwainers	Keelmen	Mariners	Master mariners	Millers	Shipwrights	Skinners &/or glovers	Smiths	Tailors	Tanners	Weavers	Overall averages*
Animals	6.66	33.44	4.08	2.32	2.05	3.97	4.65	2.74	3.40	3.19	2.61	3.68	3.49	**6.94**
Apparel	6.46	4.80	4.78	.87	5.18	9.20	3.61	3.09	3.49	4.04	4.18	4.54	3.42	**4.58**
Books	.43	.27	.79	-	.45	.49	-	.33	.22	.24	.11	.25	.53	**0.44**
Brew vessels	12.94	1.01	1.42	.15	.76	4.60	2.49	1.78	.62	.92	.92	1.34	1.39	**3.17**
Household ojects	26.3	17.0	30.2	3.8	15.7	31.0	12.3	15.6	12.3	11.1	14.1	17.7	14.6	**18.44**
Objects of trades	.52	.32	15.2	.17	1.23	6.71	.22	14.26	10.12	16.64	1.1	46.08	1.03	**9.56**
Provisions	13.44	14.09	4.54	0.88	10.21	11.79	5.58	7.04	9.92	2.28	8.33	1.37	8.44	**8.59**
Ships	30.0	-	-	13.78	8.70	74.70	-	38.02	-	58.35	40.0	-	-	**53.13**
Weapons	.60	.49	.28	.01	.45	.82	.31	.37	.22	.38	.30	.48	.58	**0.45**
Total averages*	**60.49**	**59.16**	**52.24**	**8.69**	**24.90**	**102.74**	**24.39**	**47.57**	**31.24**	**35.88**	**26.27**	**59.74**	**25.07**	**45.92**
Sample size	19	17	31	12	19	25	18	21	13	23	15	16	24	**253**

Table 5.13b – Overall mean average and related percentage figures for all trades (£) 1548 – 1642

Type of object	**Overall average (£)***	**Percentage of objects***
Animals	4.05	8.84%
Apparel	4.20	9.18%
Books	0.12	0.27%
Brew vessels	1.42	3.11%
Household objects	18.44	40.05%
Objects of trades	7.30	15.96%
Provisions	3.01	6.58%
Ships	7.14	15.55%
Weapons	0.21	0.47%
Total average	**45.92**	**100.00%**

* The individual figures for each trade presented for each category of objects are the same as those given in the tables accompanying the relevant sections in Chapter 5. The total average figures account for the variable sample size among the categories of objects and among tradesmen's inventories, which cannot be directly compared with each other. The figures assume that every inventory included in the total sample listed at least one object in at least one of the nine categories of objects.

Chapter 6 – Table 6.1a – Numbers and percentage figures of rooms recorded in houses 1552 – 1642 (Sample: 257 inventories)

Date	%inv.'s w/rooms	No. of rooms	Baker/ brewer	Butcher	Cordwainer	Keelman	Mariner	Master mariner	Miller	Shipwright	Skinner/ glover	Smith	Tailor	Tanner	Weaver	Totals	%
1552 -	**62.6%**	1 - 3	-	-	2	2	3	1	-	2	1	1	1	1	2	16	**30.7%**
1600		4 - 6	2	-	4	-	2	5	-	3	1	2	1	4	-	24	**46.1%**
(83		7 – 9	1	1	3	-	-	2	2	1	-	1	-	1	-	12	**23%**
inv.'s)		10+	-	-	-	-	-	-	-	-	-	-	-	-	-	-	-
1601 -	**67.6%**	1 - 3	2	4	3	1	2	1	2	4	1	4	1	1	2	29	**40.2%**
1625		4 - 6	4	3	2	1	5	4	3	4	2	5	3	-	-	36	**53.7%**
(99		7 – 9	-	-	-	-	-	1	-	-	-	1	-	1	-	3	**4.4%**
inv.'s)		10+	-	1	-	-	-	-	-	-	-	-	-	-	-	1	**1.4%**
1626 -	**80%**	1 – 3	3	3	3	-	-	1	2	2	1	-	1	1	2	19	**31.6%**
1642		4 – 6	3	1	3	-	1	4	1	1	2	1	2	4	4	27	**45%**
(75		7 – 9	2	-	2	-	-	2	-	-	-	1	-	1	1	9	**15%**
inv.'s)		10+	2	-	2	-	-	-	-	-	-	-	-	-	1	5	**8.3%**
% inv.'s w/rooms	-	-	**95%**	**77%**	**83%**	**25%**	**68%**	**84%**	**55%**	**73%**	**61%**	**69%**	**60%**	**87%**	**54%**	**180**	**70.0%**

Chapter 6 – Table 6.1b - Percentage of tradesmen in low and high wealth groups with above and below £35 inventoried wealth (Sample: 257 inventories)
High wealth group: Bakers and brewers, butchers, cordwainers, master mariners, shipwrights, smiths, tanners
Low wealth group: Keelmen, mariners, millers, skinners and glovers, tailors, weavers

Date	Number of rooms	Totals: Low wealth	Percentages: Low wealth	Totals: High wealth	Percentages: High wealth
1552 -1600	1-3	9	**60.0%**	7	**18.9%**
	4 - 6	4	**26.7%**	20	**54.1%**
	7 – 9	2	**13.3%**	10	**27.0%**
	Over 10	0	**0.0%**	0	**0.0%**
	Total	**15**	**100.0%**	**37**	**100.0%**
1601 -1625	1-3	9	**39.1%**	19	**42.2%**
	4 - 6	14	**60.9%**	22	**48.9%**
	7 – 9	0	**0.0%**	3	**6.7%**
	Over 10	0	**0.0%**	1	**2.2%**
	Total	**23**	**100.0%**	**45**	**100.0%**
1626 -1642	1 – 3	6	**33.3%**	13	**31.0%**
	4 – 6	10	**55.6%**	17	**40.5%**
	7 – 9	1	**5.6%**	8	**19.0%**
	Over 10	1	**5.6%**	4	**9.5%**
	Total	**18**	**100.0%**	**42**	**100.0%**
1552-1642	1 – 3	24	**42.9%**	39	**31.5%**
	4 – 6	28	**50.0%**	59	**47.6%**
	7 – 9	3	**5.4%**	21	**16.9%**
	Over 10	1	**1.8%**	5	**4.0%**
	Total inventories	**56**	**100.0%**	**124**	**100.0%**

Chapter 6 - Tables 6.2a – 6.2g– Distribution of objects in named rooms (percentages) (Sample: 257 inventories)
Figures refer to numbers of references not numbers of objects

Table 6.2a - Distribution of apparel

Period	Halls	Butteries	Parlours	Kitchens	Lower/ back chambers	Upper/ fore chambers	Chamber - location unspecified	Loft	Totals
1552 – 1600 (83 inv.'s)	17%	-	17%	-	-	22%	33%	11%	100% (36 ref.'s)
1601 – 1625 (99 inv.'s)	14%	-	14%	3%	3%	28%	33%	5.5%	100% (36 ref.'s)
1626 – 1642 (75 inv.'s)	12%	-	-	-	12%	47%	23.5%	6%	100% (17 ref.'s)
Totals (all periods)	15%	-	12%	1%	3%	29%	31%	8%	100% (89 ref.'s)

Table 6.2b - Distribution of beds and bedding

Period	Halls	Butteries	Parlours	Kitchens	Lower/ back chambers	Upper/ fore chambers	Chamber - location unspecified	Loft	Totals
1552 – 1600 (83 inv.'s)	10%	-	17.5%	4%	1%	24%	28.5%	14%	100% (91 ref.'s)
1601 - 1625 (99 inv.'s)	12.5%	-	16%	8%	4%	30%	22 %	8%	100% (144 ref.'s)
1626 - 1642 (75 inv.'s)	14%	-	17%	8%	4%	26%	20%	9%	100% (159 ref.'s)
Totals (all periods)	14%	-	17%	7%	3.5%	27%	23%	10%	100% (394 ref.'s)

Table 6.2c- Distribution of cookware

Period	Halls	Butteries	Parlours	Kitchens	Lower/ back chambers	Upper/ fore chambers	Chamber -location unspecified	Loft	Totals
1552 – 1600 (83 inv.'s)	52%	4%	6%	34%	-	-	2%	1%	100% (82 ref.'s)
1601 – 1625 (99 inv.'s)	55%	3%	3%	37%	0.9%	0.9%	-	-	100% (110 ref.'s)
1626 – 1642 (75 inv.'s)	52%	1%	6%	40%	1%	-	-	-	100% (88 ref.'s)
Totals (all periods)	53.5%	2.5%	5%	37%	0.3%	0.3%	0.3%	0.3%	100% (280 ref.'s)

Table 6.2d - Distribution of tableware

Period	Halls	Butteries	Parlours	Kitchens	Lower/ back chambers	Upper/ fore chambers	Chamber - location unspecified	Loft	Totals
1552 – 1600 (83 inv.'s)	48%	20%	9%	9%	3%	5%	5%	1%	100% (100 ref.'s)
1601 – 1625 (99 inv.'s)	44%	14%	9%	18%	0.7%	9%	5%	1%	100% (139 ref.'s)
1626 – 1642 (75 inv.'s)	45%	11%	11%	14%	1%	11%	6%	1%	100% (141 ref.'s)
Totals (all periods)	45%	14%	9%	14%	1.5%	8%	5%	1%	100% (380 ref.'s)

Table 6.2e - Distribution of furniture (tables, chairs, stools, forms and longsettles)

Period	Halls	Butteries	Parlours	Kitchens	Lower/ back chambers	Upper/ fore chambers	Chamber - location unspecified	Loft	Totals
1552 – 1600 (83 inv.'s)	51%	3%	9%	5%	-	15%	10%	8%	100% (102 ref.'s)
1601 – 1625 (99 inv.'s)	40%	1%	13%	10%	0.6%	20%	13%	2%	100% (165 ref.'s)
1626 – 1642 (75 inv.'s)	33.5%	1%	16%	12%	2%	22%	11%	3%	100% (185 ref.'s)
Totals (all periods)	40%	1.5%	13%	10%	1%	19%	12%	4%	100% (452 ref.'s)

Table 6.2f – Distribution of spinning wheels and yarn

Period	Halls	Butteries	Parlours	Kitchens	Lower/ back chambers	Upper/ fore chambers	Chamber - location unspecified	Loft	Total references
1552 – 1600 (83 inv.'s)	8	-	2	2	2	4	9	11	38
1601 – 1625 (99 inv.'s)	7	-	2	3	3	8	12	10	45
1626 – 1642 (75 inv.'s)	7	1	6	4	1	9	5	9	42
Totals	22	1	10	9	6	21	26	30	125
Percentages	17.6%	0.8%	8%	7.2%	4.8%	16.8%	20.8%	24%	100%

Table 6.2g- Distribution of selected decorative objects

Period: 1552 -1600 – (83 inventories)

Object	Hall	Buttery	Parlour	Kitchen	Lower/ back chambers	Upper/ fore chambers	Chamber - location unspecified	Loft	Total references
Cushions	30	-	1	-	-	6	8	2	47
Flower pots	7	-	1	-	-	1	-	-	9
Mirrors	3	-	-	-	-	-	-	-	3
Pictures	-	-	-	-	-	-	-	-	-
Totals	40	-	2	-	-	7	8	2	59
Percentages	67.7%	-	3.3%	-	-	11.8%	13.5%	3.3%	100%

Period: 1601-1625 – (99 inventories)

Object	Hall	Buttery	Parlour	Kitchen	Lower/ back chambers	Upper/ fore chambers	Chamber - location unspecified	Loft	Total references
Cushions	34	1	10	1	2	19	11	3	81
Flower pots	19	4	5	-	-	3	1	-	32
Mirrors	6	-	-	2	-	2	-	-	10
Pictures	5	-	-	-	-	2	-	-	7
Totals	64	5	15	3	2	26	12	3	130
Percentages	49.2%	3.8%	11.5%	2.3%	1.5%	20%	9.2%	2.3%	100%

Period: 1626 -1642 – (75 inventories)

Object	Hall	Buttery	Parlour	Kitchen	Lower/ back chambers	Upper/ fore chambers	Chamber - location unspecified	Loft	Total references
Cushions	36	-	5	1	1	18	11	3	75
Flower pots	34	4	14	1	-	13	5	1	72
Mirrors	20	-	4	1	-	3	1	-	29
Pictures	4	-	1	-	-	4	-	-	9
Totals	94	4	24	3	1	38	17	4	185
Percentages	50.8%	2.1%	12.9%	1.6%	0.5%	20.5%	9.1%	2.1%	100%

Table 6.3 – Distribution of work related objects (tools, supplies, wares) in named rooms 1552 – 1642 (Sample: 257 inventories)

Rooms	Baker /brewer*	Butcher	Cordwainer	Keelman	Mariner	Master mariner	Miller	Skinner/ glover	Shipwright	Smith	Tailor	Tanner	Weaver	Total references	%
Back House	2					2		1	1	1		1		8	**4.9%**
Bake House	1													1	**0.6%**
Brew House	2													2	**1.2%**
Cellar			1			6			2					9	**5.5%**
Chamber	2				1	10			4	4	1		6	28	**17.3%**
Hall					1					1	3			4	**2.4%**
Kitchen	2								1				1	4	**2.4%**
Loft	2		3		1	3	3		4	3				19	**11.8%**
Parlour			1**										2	2	**1.2%**
Shop/workshop/ work house		7	24					2		18	5	9***	2	66	**40.9%**
Other						1 (quayside)	2(stables) 3(mills)		7 (quayside/ suburbs)			3 (Lime Pits)		16	**9.9%**
Totals	11	7	29	-	3	22	8	3	19	27	8	13	11	161	**100%**

* Figures represent references to baking equipment <u>only</u>. For distribution of brewing equipment see Chapter 5 – Table 5.11a .** Cordwainer listed supplies of 'leather soles' only.
** *Total references include bark houses and tan houses.

Appendix 1

Examples of transcribed wills and inventories from the Durham Probate Records: The documents are transcribed verbatim. The transcription of the wills does not follow the layout of the original document. The transcription of the inventories does follow the original layout of the document to assist the reader in finding items on the original documents.

Armstronge, Marke
Skinner & Glover
(Will and probate inventory survive in copy in Register of Wills, Vol.VI, f.153)

Will dated 30th May, 1588

In the name of god Amen the 30th day off November Anno 1588 I marke armstronge of the Towen of Newcastell upon Tyne Skinner & glover sicke in bodye & yett of good and perfect memorie prased be god maketh this my last will & testament in maner and forme ffollowinge ffirst I give and bequith my soule unto almightie god & my bodye to be buried in the church yearde of Saint Andrewes as neare my children as may be Item I give to the porre 10s Item I give & bequyth to my sonne henrye Armstronge my best flanders chist and a danske chist which was my shope chist & faylinge him to his sister Isabell armstronge Item I give to my daughter Isabell armstronge my best cobord & 4 new chargers and ffalinge hir to her brother henry armstronge aforsaid Item I give to John armstronge my brother my brother John armstronge sone, when he comes to lawfull years 40s.// Item I give & bequith all my lands & Tenements to my sone henrye armstronge and to his years lawfullye begotten & falinge him & his hears lawfullye begotten I give and bequieth all my said landes and Tenimentes unto my daughter Isabell armstronge & to her eires of bodye lawfullye begotten & failinge her & her heires lawfully begotten I give and bequieth my said landes and Tenamentes unto John armstronge my brother John armstronge sone & to the heires of his bodye for ever Item I give to my brother Thomas wiggham my best sworde Item I give to cuthbert armstronge my halbord staff, Item I bequieth unto my cosynge george armstronge laite sone of william armstronge my unkle 5 L of the condicion /. yt if my hieres in joye the house which I tooke in lease of hym in west gaite / which was there fathyers william armstronge Item I do constitute and make my wif margerit armstronge and my forsaid sone henrye armstronge & my daughter Isabell armstronge my full and soll Executors of this my last will and testament And ffalinge my 2 children I bequieth the said implements to my wife margerit armstronge with all there portions if they dye before they come to lawfull years of age Supervisors of this my last will & testament John burdes weaver Thomas wiggam afore said Item I give to the said John burdese 5s and to the said Thomas wiggam a france crowne in gold for A token or remembrance of my good will Witnesses of this my last will & testament John lecke tailer, John Barker glasier & Robert Dalton baker and Thomas wigghm with others

Marke Armstronge
Inventory dated 12th June, 1589

The Inventorie of all the goods and chattels moveable and unmoveable of marke armstrong Skinner and glover deceased prased the 12th day of June 1589 by John burdess John lecke Robert dalton & Thoman wiggham

In the hall

Imprimis an yron chymney with thappertinances 10s
Item 1 table with aioyned forme 6s 8d
Item one short table
and two short formes 4s
Item apressor almery 2s 8d
Item a letell almery 4s
Item 17 peace of pewder 20s
Item pece of powder vessell 6s
Item 9 sawsers 2s 4d
Item potendisses 3s 4d
Item 2 pottell pottes
one quart pott & 4
pynt pottes 6s 8d
Item 5 saltes of powder 16d
Item 2 dringkinge peaces
of powder 12d
Item A basinge , a laver , 6
candlstickes of brass 5s
Item one copper cawdron 10s
Item 4or pans 5s
Item 3 brass pottes 14s
Item 2 old chaires 6d

In the chambers

Item 1 letell counter 20d
Item 2 olde carpettes
and 6 qiusshions 3s
Item two old chistes 3s 4d
Item two letell coffers 12d
Item all his apparell 40s
Item one twilte 2s 6d
Item 9 coverletes 18s
Item two happins 2s 4d
Item 3 part of blanketes 9s
Item 4 paire of linninge
sheetes 16s
Item 4 paire of harden
sheetes 8s

Item 6 codd pillibers	4s
Item two head sheetes	2s
Item two tabelclothes and 6 napkinges	4s
Item one fedder bedd	10s
Item two old mattresses	2s
Item 11 feather codes	7s 4d
Item one paire of woollen cortens	3s 4d
Item 7 bedsteades	8s
Item a linte wheale & a paire of old tables	12d
Item a halbort a Bill saffe 2 swordes and a bowe	6s 8d
Item 9 bowels of malte	3li
Item 6 bowels of Rye	30s
Item the kilhaire & kill chimney	13s 4d
Item one nagg	30s
Item one cowe	20s
Item 3 quyes	30s
Item the brewinge vessell & a brake	10s
Item two stone of lynt	6s 8d
Item an olde bible & a service booke	6s

Soma 22li 15s

Debtes owne to the said marke armstronge

Item Lent to the towne	10s
Item To Jerrard burne	6s
Item to david gray	6s
Item to John moore marchant	10s

Suma totalis 24li 7s

John Almry
Milner (Miller)
D.O.P. 8th July, 1606

Will dated 3rd March, 1605

In the name of god amen. I Iohn Almry of the towne and countie of newcastle upon tyne milner sick in body, but sound and perfect in minde thankes be to god, doe make and ordeine this my last will and testament in forme followinge. ffirst I give and bequeath my soule to almightie god, and to Iesus Christ my redeemer by whose death and blood shed, am whont any myne <owne> meritt I hope to be saved, and my body I will to be buried in St Iohns Churchyeard nere unto the thorne tree their and of my worldly goods I thus dispose. viz : to my welbeloved wife Iaine Almry, and Robert Almry my sonne I give my housholde <stuffe> and all my <other> goods and lands whatsoever equally to be divided betwixt them, yet so as she the said Iaine Almry, my debts thereout deducted and payd, shall have the free use of all my houshold stuffe and other goods soly undivided, duringe her naturall life, and also the one half of <my> lands duringe the said Iaine her life tyme, All which said goods and lands and all other my dedts, leases and reversions of leases after her decease my will is that they shall descend and come <whole and undivided> to my said Sonne Robert Almry to use and occupie duringe his naturall life, and to the heires of his body lawfully begotten or to be begotten, and for defalt of issue all my fore said lands and goods wholy and undivided i give and bequeath unto Dorothie Douglas the daughter of Thomas Douglas and her heires for ever. Provided alwyes that my will is, that if the <said> Dorathie Douglas shalbe prefered in marriage before she shall reape any benifit by this my givft in reversion, that my said wife Iaine Almry or Robert my sonne, or the heires of the said Robert, or which of them shall then survive, at the tyme of ther the said Dorathies sure marriage shall give unto her the said Dorathie one fetherbed <and a standinge bedstead> with sheets blankets, coverings, courtins and all things unto a fetherbed belonginge, And of this my said will and testament I doe make and ordaine my said welbeloved wife, and Robert my sonne Ioynte and full executors, appointinge for supervisors of the same my welbeloved freinds Thomas Douglas and Archbald Dodds Cordiners. In witnes whereof I herunto set my hand and seale the third day of march in the third of the reigne of our Soveraigne lord Iames by the grace of god kinge of Great Brittaine ffrance and Ireland defender of the faith Etc annoque salutis secundum cursum et computacionem ecclesia Anglicane 1605/6
the signe and seale of the said
Iohn Almry
In the presence of us
Edward Wigham Clerici
The marke of
Archbald Dodes
the marke of
Thomas Douglas
the marke of

Robert Mautland

Iohn Almry
Inventory dated 5th July, 1606

An Inventorie of all the goodes and chattells moveable and unmoveable of Iohn Almery desesed in the parish of St Iohnes praysed the fifth day of Jully 1606 by theis four men Steven potes William Kirkis Archbauld dodes Thomas douglas \ Etc

In the hall

Imprimis one Iron chemney and four Irone speates praised	xvj s
Item one latten bason	xviij d
Item vj putter playteres price	vj s
Item x putter dishes	v s
Item v pynt potes and a quarte pot of putter	iiij s
Item iiij white candellstekes	ij s
Item viij brase candelstekes	ij s
Item iij saultes and A gell pot	i s
Item in putter vessell the which goeth About the howse xxxij peac of putter	xv s
Item A dosen sausers	iij s
Item ij putter bassons xiiij tyn spunes	i s vj d
Item iiij quarte pottes and one pottell pote	iij s
Item two tables and A fourme	vj s viij d
Item two chistes	v s
Item two pair of playinge tables	viij d
Item ij unsketes & A callener	x s
Item v chamber pottes	i s viij d

Some is iiij li iij s x d

In the kitshen

Item one Irone chemney and one Irone pore	iij s iiij d
Item one fryen panne	vi d
Item ij crankes	viij d
Item ij skumeres	vj d
Item iij Laydles	vj d
Item one chopinge knife one mynching knife	iiij d
Item one morter and a pestell	ij s vj d
Item ij beasteres	ij d
Item one payr of beefe crannkes	ij d
Item iiij panes and a kettell	vj s
Item three pottes and A posnet	x s
Item one dreping panne	i s
Item one payr of pott clipes	ij d

Some is i li v s x d

In the hey chamber

Item one feder bed & a boulster a cod	vj s viij d
Item one blanket one happing and A coverled	vj s viij d
Item one bedstead	iij s iiij d
Item iiij bufett Stulles	ij s vj d
Item one chaire	viij d
Item one table	i s

Some is i li x d

In the myddell Chamber

Item one fether bed A boulster and A Cod	xvj s
Item ij blankettes one happening & A coverled	xs
Item one fether bed A boulster & A code	viij s
Item one blanket one happing & A coverled	v s
Item thre courtinges of flaninge & fleres	v s
Item one bed stead	viij s
Item three wollen courtinges and flers	iij s iiij d
Item one stand bed and a tr[]mell bed	x s
Item ij tables vj s viij d	vj s viij d
Item v ould bufet stulles	i s viij d
Item ij chayres	i s vj d
Item one dresser table	ix d
Item ij carpinge clothes of plading	iij s vj d

Some is iij li xviij s iiij d

In the kytchinge chamber

Item iij matresses and A flock bed	iiij s
Item iiij boulsteres	iiij s
Item viij hand napkinges & viij ould happinges	vj s viij d
Item iiij bed steades	v s

Some is xix s viij d

In the parler

Item one chemney	i s vj d
Item ij fether bedes	xvj s
Item ij boulsters and A cod	iij s
Item blankates ij hapinges ij coverleds	viij s
Item the courtens & a pair of fleeres	iiij s
Item ij bed steades	vj s viij d
Item ij tables two fourmes	x s
Item x whishinges	iij s iiij d

Some is ij li xij s iiij d

Bruinge vessell in the Bruinghowse

Item viij tubes	iiij s vi d
Item iiij weshinge tubes	viij d
Item ij beefe tubes	i s vi d
Item vj dayles	ij s
Item one flishe stole & A bracke	viij d
Item ij seas for caringe watter	i s
Item ij [sic]	

Some is x s viij d

His Apperell

Item one cloke	v s
Item ij dublates and A Ierkinge	vj s viij d
Item ij pair of bryches	iij s iiij d

Some is xv s

A true notes of the debtes owinge to the
said Iohn Almry as flloweth.

Christopher Hodshon of newcastell within said taylor	iiij li x s
Edward Cranie of Lonndon maister and mariner	x li
Steven pottes of newcastell afforesaid Cordiner	xxxviij s
william Almry of newcastell afforesaid mariner	xxviij s
daniell hilles	xviij s
Roger Cockson and william Brady as appeareth by a bound for twlne poundes and which is parcell of the said twelne poundes	iij li
Mathew denwillis of newcastell aforesaid Chepman	x s
Elizabeth Browne one fifeside in Scotland	iiij li xvij s
one hallyday for which Eilles wallis & Thomas Grene ar surties	xxxx s

A true note also of such debtes as I the
said Iohn am at this instannt indebted
unto others as followeth

Imprimis to nycholas Armstronge	vij li
Item to henery Browne	iij li
Item to william pattison due at Easter next	xxvj s viij d
Item to Robert Orwine due at lammas next	xx s
Item to Anthony french	x s
And which I Recieve of the portion of Christabell Grene	viij li

Henrie Atkinson
Cordwainer
D.O.P. 13th November, 1616

Will dated 27th May, 1616

In the name of god Amen the xxvij th daie of Maie Anno domini 1616 I Henrie Atkinson of the towne of Newcastle upon tyne in the countie of the same cordiner being sicke in bodie but in good & perfectt memorie god be praised therefore doe maike this my last will & testament in maner & forme followinge. ffirst I give & bequeath my soule in to the handes of almightie god my maker & redemer and my bodie to be buried in the parish church of St Andrews. And as concerninge my worldlye landes goods & chattels wherwith it hath pleased god to indowe me I give & bequeath the same as followeth. first I give & bequeath unto my sonne william Atkinson all that burgaige or tenement with thappurtenances wherin Robert winter my father in lawe dwelleth, situate and beinge in the noult markett in Newcastle bye tyne aforesaid To have and to holde the said burgaige or tenement with thappurtenances unto the said william Atkinson and to the heires of his bodie lawfullie to be begotten for ever: and for default of such issew then to remaine & come to my sonne Henrie Atkinson and to the heires of his bodie lawfullie to be begotten for ever. And for default of such issuethen to remaine & come to my daughter Margaret Atkinson and to the heires of her bodie lawfullie to be begotten for ever. And for default of such issew then to remaine and come to the right heires of me the said Henrie Atkinson for ever. Item I give & bequeath to my said sonne William Atkinson all that my close lyinge & beinge att Pandon Cawsey head with thappurtenances which I purchased of mr Anthonye Swinburne and his wife, and the litle house without the newe gate in sidgate and the garth on the back side thereof now in the occupation of Andrew dove. To have and to holde the said close at Pandon Cawsey head the said litle house & garth in sidgate aforesaid unto the said william Atkinson and the heires of his b[o]d[ie] lawfullie to be begotten for ever. And for default of such issew then to remaine & come to my said sonne Henrie Atkinson and the heires of his bodie lawfullie to be begotten for ever. And for default of such issew then to remaine & come to the said margaret Atkins[on] and to the heires of her bodie lawfullie to be begotten for ever. And for default of such issue then to remaine & come to the right heires of me the said Henrie Atkinson for ever. Item I give and bequeath unto my said sonne Henrie Atkinson all that my burgaige or tenement with thappurtenances wherein I now dwell scituate and being in Pilgram streete in Newcastle upon tyne aforesaid. To have & to holde the said burgaige or tenement with thappurtenances unto the said Henrie Atkinson my sonne and to the heires of his bodie lawfullie to be begotten for ever and for default of such issew then to remaine & come unto the said william Atkinson his brother and to the heires of his bodie lawfullie to be begotten for ever. And for default of such issew then to remaine & come to the said Margaret Atkinson and to the hieres of her bodie lawfullie to be begotten for ever, And for default of such issew to remaine & come to the right heires of me the said Henrie Atkinson for ever. Item I give to my said daughter Margaret Atkinson one hundred markes in monie. Item I give to my father in lawe Robert winter xx s to my mother his wife xx s to my brother Iohn Atkinson xx s and his wife x s to Ellinor Goodwin v s to Gilbert Newton v s to Margaret Lynn v s to Heugh maison v s to Henrie Whitfeild v s to Lawrance Carr v s to Thomas watson v s Item I give to George Best and Margaret Best the rent of the house that Raph Scurfeild dwelleth in duringe the life tyme of my mother equallie emongst them. And the residue of all my goods & chattels unbequeathed I give to my wife marie Atkinson whom I maik & ordaine sole executrix of this my last will and testament And alsoe I will that the said marie shall give to my said sonnes William and Henrie Atkinson x li a peece to brin[]e them prentices. And xl s to Henrie Atkinson my brothers sonne. Witnesses hereof Robert winter George Newton. Iohn Atkinson Heugh maison Lawrence Carr meique Thome Watsonn

Henry Atkinsone
Inventory dated 11th November, 1616

An Inventory of all the goodes and Chattells of
Henry Atkinsonne of the parish of Alsaintes in the
towne of newcastell upon tyne Cordewayner deseased
praysed the xj the daye of November Anno domini
1616 : by Robert Winter gentleman John Stobbs marchant
Hewe Masone yeoman and Iohn Atkinsone Cordwayner

In the Hall

Item One Chimney and a littell porr	x s
Item two tables: vj stooles a forme a fireane & a chare	xl s
Item two Carpetes six new Cusshons and nyne olde Cusshons	xxvj s viij d
Item A booke of martyers and a byble	xl s
Item A Costlet ffurnishedd	xx s
Item one Cubbert and a pulke	xxxiij s iiij d
Item one basone and ewer with other forty peace of puter smale and great and three brasse candellstickes	iij li
Item one Cusshon and one lantrone	ij s
	10 li - 11 s - 7 d

In the Buttry

Item ffowrteene peece of Pewter iiij banketting dishes six sawsers two hande basons	xxiij s
Item One stone Iugg tipt with sillver	iiij s
Item three peace of plate and a xj silver spoones	vj li
Item xj pewter spoones	xviij d
Item six table Clothes thre dussen napkins and xij towells all Course and on worne	xxx s
	8 li - 18 s - 6 d

In the lyttle Parler
within the hall

Item One standing bedd a trundle bedd & a Chiste	xiiij s
Item one fetherbed one boulster and two pillowes two	

Curtins a redd Coveringe a Coverlid and a blanket	xl s
	2 li - 14 s
In the fore Chamber on the Hall	
Item One paire of littell barrs and a porr	iij s iiij d
Item one stand bedd and a truckell bedd	xxx s
Item one longe settellbed, a littell Counter, a forme, a Chist and a Chare	xx s
Item two fetherbeddes two boulsters and fowre pillows five say Curtins, with vallance one oversey Coveringe, iij Coverlidds a Carpet, iij blanketes and iij Cusshons	vj li
	8 li - 13 s - 4 d
In the Porche Chamber	
Item one bedd stead with a footstoole	vj s viij d
Item one fetherbed a boulster two pillows one old Greane Rugg a Coverlid thre old Curtins and two blanketes	xl s

Henry Atkinsone
Inventory dated 11th November, 1616 (continued)

	2 li - 6 s - 8 d
In the Middle Chamber	
Item fowre firr beddsteades thre Chists	xxv s
Item thre fether bedds a flock bed fowre bowlsters eight pillowes and a mattris	v li
Item six Coverlids and fowre balnketes	xx s
Item xij paire of lynn sheetes	vj li
Item eight paire of Course sheets	xl s
Item tenn payre of ould lin sheetes &: x: paire of Course	iiij li
Item xvj Pillobers of Lyne	xvj s
Item one dussen of fine pillobers	xiij s
Item iij diper table Clothes & a dusen diper napkins	xxx s
Item iij sewed seme sheetes	xxs
	24 li - 12 s - 8 d
In the High parler	
Item A Chimney and a porr	vj s viij d
Item one table a dresser vj stooles a Chare two Chistes six Cushones and a Carpett	xxxv s
Item one longe Cushon and a shorte	vj s
Item two standing beddes a trundle bed & a pulke	iij li x s
Item thre fetherbeddes thre bowlsters vj pillowes	vj li
Item two ruggs a twilt thre Coverlides five blanketes two pair of Curtins and two paire of vallences	v li
	16 li - 17 s - 8 d
In the chamber over the Kitchin	
Item one payre of smale Barrs a porr & a paire of Bellowes	iij s
Item two bedsteades one trunell bed a long settell bed a Close stoole a Chare and one Chiste	xxiij s
Item iij fetherbeds a flock bed a mattris thre bowlsters five pillowes two paire of blanketes eight Coverlides and two Curtins	iiij li
Item one skeene	ij s vj d
	5 li – 18 s- 6 d
In the Barrons chamber	
Item one paire of Barrs and a porr	vj s
Item one table a dresser six stooles a Carpet	

a dresser Clothe vj Cushons	xxx s
Item one standing bedd and a trundle bedd	xx s
Item two fether bedes thre bowlsters iij pillowes one Rugg two Coverlids thre blanketes A payre of Curtins and vallins	v li
	7 li - 16 s - 0 d
In the Roome on the seller	
ffowre old firr bedsteades & thre Caff beds	6 s 8 d
In the lowe parler	
Item one paire of Iron barrs & a porr	viij s
Item one Cubbert A table and a forme	xv s
Item thre firr beddsteades with foot stooles	xij s
Item thre fetherbedes thre bowlsters ix pillowes	iiij li
Item five Coverlides thre blankets & Curtins	xxx s
	7 li - 5 s
In the stable	
Item one nagg	xxvj s viij d
Item two kye with Calve	iij li vj s viij d
Item Haye	xxxij s
	6 li - 5 s - 4 d
In the Kitchin	
Item one Irone Chimney a porr a paire of rackes a fier shovell a payre of tongs a paire of lyeng Irons a payre of Crankes one frieng pan two dripping panns thre spittes two shering knyfes a Chafing dishe	iij li
Item six bras potts a morter viij panns vij brass candelstickes a warming pann two brasladells a hanging Candelsticke two dripping spoones	l s
Item sixteene smale peece of pewter six pottin dishes thre sawsers a Iill and halfe Iill (Gill) pott thre Custerd Cases a laver a scumer a hand basone ix Chamber pottes one old Cubbert and a stoole	xl s
	7 li - 18 s - 0 d
Item ffive and thirty bowles of Bigg at 8 s per bowle	xiiij li
Item xl bowles of blawen Malt	xvj li
Item the third parte of one Close in lease for one yeare	xl s
Item A lease of a Mylne and Certayne howses yett to come	xx li
Item Apparell	x li
	62 - li - 0 s
	debts due to the testator by bondes and bills
Item By Gawen Oyell	xl li
Item By Sir Effrom Withrenton	iiij li i s
	Some of the goodes and Chattells praysed as above said is 215 li - 16 s - 6 d
	debtes oweing by the testator
Item To Georg Nicholsone by bonde	xxij li
Item To Mr ffoscrop upon bonde	v li
Item To Georg Nicholsone Iunier by bond	xxj li x s
Item To Myghell waterhowse by bonde	vj li xiij s iiij d
Item To Hewe Masone	iiij li

	81 li - 3 s - 4 d
	Legesies by his will
Item To William Atkinsone his sonne	x li
Item To Henry Atkinsone his younger sonne	x li
Item To Margret Atkinsonne his daughter	xlvj li vj s viij d
Item To other legesies as by the will appeareth	vj li
	92 li - 6 s - 8 d
Item ffunerall expencis	xv li
	Some of the debtes Legesies and funerall expencis 188 li - 10 s
So the goodes and chattells Amounteth to more by the praysinge then the debtes Legesies and ffuneralles to	27 li - 6 s - 6 [ ]

Appendix 2 - Mills: Part 1

The location of mills shown on Map 4.14 and recorded in the Durham Probate Records 1584 – 1641

* Mills with an asterisk denote those which may be the same mill showing up in different documents

Mill reference number	Date of document	Location/ description of mill	Name of testator	Trade
1	1638	'Chimley Mill', Bailiff Burn, Castle Leazes	Thomas Nicholson	Smith
2	1613	Westgate Street	John Huntrish	Miller
3	1611 1630	Postern	Thomas Reasley John Reasley	Miller Miller
4*	1592	Pudding Chair and Groat market	Robert Johnson	Master mariner
5*	1613	Pudding Chair	Thomas Reade	Miller
6	1634	'Barrow Mills', Magdalene Meadow	Anthony Foster	Weaver
7	1603	West end All Saints Church	Robert Reasley	Miller
8	1623	Head of Hornsby Chair	John Patteson William Patteson,	Mariner Miller
9*	1605	Broad Garth	Cuthbert Wymphery,	Baker & brewer
10*	1632	Broad Garth	Robert Hoope	Baker & brewer
11*	1585 1587	Broad Chair	John Patteson William Patteson	Mariner Miller
12*	1617	Broad Chair	William Anderson	Miller
13	1641	'Pandongate Mill', Pandon gate	Henry Scott	Butcher
14*	1622	'Walke Mill', Wall Knoll	John Holbourne	Mariner
15*	1604	'Behind' Wall Knoll	Richard Kell	Tailor
16	1603 1604 1611 1633	Sandgate	Robert Reasley Walter Reasley Thomas Reasley William Reasley	Miller Miller Miller Shipwright
17	1603 1604 1611	Stackgarth, Ouse Burn	Robert ReasleyMiller Walter Reasley Thomas Reasley	Miller Miller Miller

Appendix 2 - Mills: Part 2 –

Inheritance of mills - Tracing family history

Several of the mills that appear in the records of the millers can be traced through generations of occupiers, passing either to other millers, or to close relatives in other trades. Sufficient information about the location of some mills, and the people who inherited the properties were recorded to confirm that some were the same properties showing up in different documents. One family in particular stands out and provides an interesting insight into the workings of property bequests, and endorses the finding that millers tended to retain control of mills for generations.

The Reasley family must have owned many of the mills of Newcastle in the period under study, and their records show just how complex the patterns of bequests could become. In 1581 a miller called George Reaslie recorded three mills left to his large family, including his wife, four sons and four daughters. Unfortunately, the location of the mills was not specified, but George did record owning property right next to All Saints Church on Silver Street, left to his son Thomas, and a second property in Gallowgate left to his brother Roger, who may also have been called Richard as the names 'Roger' and 'Richard' were sometimes confused by clerks in the Durham Probate Records.

Property belonging to the Reasley's emerged again twenty years later. In 1603, a miller called Robert Reasley, left his son William the Elder the mill "on the west end of All Hallows church and all houses belonging to it" bordering Silver Street. The mill may have been one of the properties that had belonged to George Reasley (1581). In the same will Robert also left his eldest son Roger his "dwelling house" in Sandgate where he lived. He bequeathed a second son, Walter, a mill & all her furniture "in the garth", which is a reference to the 'Stackgarth' in Sandgate, discussed below (D.P.R. Reasley 1603).

Just a year later in 1604 Walter appeared to have acquired both Sandgate properties, as he bequeathed a 'horse mill and seate house' located in Sandgate to his wife, daughter and a son called John, suggesting that his brother Roger might have died within the year. Walter himself was also dying the same year. Walter named Thomas and Anthony Reasley, the sons of one Richard Reisley, miller, as second in line to his own wife and children, together with William, the younger brother of Thomas and Anthony as third in line. This 'Richard' Reasley was probably 'Roger' Reasley, Walter's dead brother, as nephews were often next in line for property when the natural children of the testator had died. Walter also left the same nephews Thomas and Anthony the "water corne mill" "att the Stackgarth", the same property he was left by his own father, Robert, in 1603.

When Thomas, one of the three brothers, died in 1611 he left "half of a water corne mylne lying and being in a place called Ewse (Ouse) burne being the lowest mylne of and in that burne", to another relative Thomas, son of another George Reisley, a cordwainer. He noted that the other half of the mill was still "in the occupation of Anthony Reasley, miller", his brother. Attached to this mill was "a tenement thereto belonging" which was to be given to "Janet, wife to Thomas Brown' miller", "after (a period of) 21years", and this woman was living in the tenement at this time. In 1633, about twenty-one years later, the water corn mill appears on the third brother William Reasley's testament, together with a house "in Sandgate in the forestreet", where he then was living. He was the youngest brother of Thomas and Anthony and had become a shipwright. He had been third in line to the property to begin with in 1604, according to their father Walter's 1604 will. When William died in 1633, "Jane Brown, widow", almost certainly the 'Janet' Brown above, was still occupying the same tenement. Her husband had obviously passed away.

Thomas Reasley, who had inherited the mills in Sandgate and Stackgarth, who died in 1611, had been married, and had a son called John and a wife called Margaret. He had subsequently acquired another mill with two tenements on the Postern, where he was living, at the foot of Westgate Street. He left the property to his wife and his son. When John died nineteen years later in 1630 he passed this mill back to his mother Margaret, who had actually been joint beneficiary in the first place, and to his own wife Barbara, leaving these two women to run the mill. Margaret must have been running the mill for at least twenty years (D.P.R. Reasley 1630). It is also possible that the Postern mill was one of the mills that had belonged to George Reasley some fifty years earlier (D.P.R. 1581).

When taken together, the Reasley family properties seem to have passed between perhaps a dozen family members in thirty years, thus securing the livelihoods of this extensive family for generations. The inventory of the testator Robert Reasley recorded an eighty-year lease on his properties in Sandgate, which helps to explain why these properties, and perhaps other mills belonging to this family, remained in their hands for so many decades (D.P.R. Reasley 1603, 1604, 1611, 1633).

Appendix 3 - Imported Objects – The objects recorded are listed A –Z by country. The date denotes the first time the object appears in the Durham Probate Records 1574 - 1641

Country of origin	Date recorded in document	Type of object
Baltic region – 'From the East Country'	1622	Drinking cups
	1622	Wages for a shipwright
	1633	Cushions of leather gilt
	1634	Painted coffer with a frame
Denmark	1570	'Dansk' chest
	1579	'Dansk' dales
	1587	'Dansk' pot
	1587	'Dansk kannes' (cups)
	1587	'Dansk' cassock
	1592	'Dansk' desk
	1592	'Dansk' trough
	1592	'Dansk' iron
	1593	'Dansk' set chest
	1593	'Dansk' pottel pot/ quart pot/ pint pot
	1610	'Dansk' hatchet
	1618	'dansk' coverlet
Flanders	1588	Flanders chest
	1586	Flanders balk, scales, weights
France	1587	French grate (for fire)
	1592	French 'twilt' (quilt)
	1623	French cup
Germany	1615	'German piece' (gun)
Holland	1634	Dutch whye (calf)
	1641	Pictures
New world/ Unknown	1579	Sugar loaves
	1587	Pepper (in grinders)
	1622	Tobacco ('Blowkicke' tipped with silver)
	1634	China platters & dishes
	1634	Tobacco (trencher with knife)
Norway	1587	Norway dales
Scotland	1625	Scot's cloth
	1628	Scot's work cushions
Spain	1574	Spanish leather jerkin
	1587	Spanish cushions
	1587	Spanish iron
	1613	Carpet of Spanish work
Turkey	1599	Turkey carpet

Appendix 4: Furniture and household objects: A selection of items appearing on Newcastle upon Tyne wills and inventories 1545 -1642

The dates that appear in brackets provide the approximate date of the earliest record of an object in the Durham Probate Records. Objects without dates were ubiquitous to the whole period. (See also Chapter 5 – Table 5.5 'Acquisition of objects' over three time periods for further information on selected objects, and Appendix 3: Imported objects).

Category 1 – Furniture and soft furnishings

Furniture

- Chairs: wainscot (1592), wanded (1593), turned (1597), Falling (1619), wicker (1613), round (1625), covered (1629), leather (1634)
- Chests/ coffers/ trunks: small, little, great, barred/ bound in iron, with frames, painted, Danish (1570), Danish set chest, Flanders (1583), Types of wood: oak, fir, wainscot
- Close stool (1616)
- Counter
- Cupboards, buttery, almery, almery- cupboard, presser-cupboard, presser-almery, livery cupboard (1619), court cupboard, cupboard with fleers – Type of wood: oak, fir, wainscot
- Cushions: filled, unfilled, stuff, painted (1623), needlewrought (1623), thrumb, Spanish (1587), leather, sewn, laidwork, embroidered, setwork (1631), Scots needle work (1629)
- Desks (1587), Danish desk (1592)
- Dressers
- Forms: joined form
- Longsettles, longsettlebeds
- Playing tables (pairs) (1573)
- Pulk, woman's pulk
- Stools: high, low, lesser, leather, joint buffet, backstool,
- Tables: long, short, round square, wainscot draw leaf, wainscot draw table (1584), tables with frames, draw table with frame, thrumb table – Type of wood: fir, oak

Soft furnishings

- Carpet cloths: stripped, green, thrumb
- Cushions: filled, unfilled, stuff, painted, needle wrought, thrumb, Spanish, leather, sewn, laid work, embroidered, set work, Scots needle work, long, window (1616)
- Dresser cloths/ Painted cloths
- Fleers for cupboards

Category 2 – Beds, bedding and linen

Beds

- Bedsteads/ Standing beds/ hurle or truckle beds/ case beds/ cradles & child's bed- Types of wood: fir, oak
- Mattresses, feather, flock beds, chaffe beds, thistledown beds, straw
- Testers

Bedding

- Bed 'covers'
- Blankets: white
- Codpillowbers/ codwares/ head sheets
- Cods/ hapins/ boulsters: feather, flock
- Coverlets, 'oversea' coverlets
- Curtains, valances, fleers with rods/ poles/ hangers: green, stripped, linen
- Quilts, 'twilts'
- Rugs: green, yellow, red, white
- Sheets (pairs): linen, straken, harden, course

Table linen

- Napkins: Linen, straken, harden, course, damask, diaper, laidwork
- Tablecloths: Linen, straken, course, damask, diaper, laidwork
- Towels, hand towels, towel pins

Category 3 – Cooking ware, table wares, decorative objects and imported objects

Cookware

- Basins: Latten, brass
- Beef tubs
- Bottles: tin, leather, glass, stone
- Bread grate
- Buckets: wood
- Cauldrons: copper
- Chaffing dishs, warming pans
- Chopping knives
- Dropping pans
- Fish panyers
- Flagging pots
- Frying pans
- Kettles: copper
- Ladles/ fish ladles: brass, tin
- Lavers: latten
- Mortar & pestle: brass, stone
- Pans
- Pots: iron, brass, pint, quart, gill, pottel
- Rolling pins
- Sieves
- Skimmers (skummer)
- Stewing pans
- Troughs: wood, stone
- Weigh scales
- Yetlings

Tableware

- Banqueting dishes
- Basins & ewers
- Baskets: wanded, wicker, cloth
- Candlesticks, hanging candlesticks, lanterns, sconces & 'snuffers' (1616): pewter, wood, latten, brass, copper, 'white', silver
- Chargers
- Chinaware (1634)
- Custard coffin
- Doublers: wood, pewter, stone, ceramic
- Drinking pots
- Glasses: cages, cases, drinking
- Hand basins
- Mugs, cups: earthen ware, wood, tin
- Mustard querns
- Pepper querns, pepper box, pepper tin
- Perry pans
- Pewter wares
- Pie plates
- Platters: earthen ware
- Porringers
- Posnet pots
- Potting dishes
- Salt sellers: tin, pewter, glass salt (1629)
- Saucers: pewter
- Spice boxes
- Spice boxes
- Spoons: tin, pewter, wood, 'Apostle', silver
- Trenchers: pewter, wood, red, white
- Troughs: stone, wood
- Tuns/ cups: tin, wood
- Water bowls
- Wooden vessels

Decorative objects and miscellaneous wares

- Chamber pots: pewter, glass
- Clocks (1619)
- Flower pots: pewter(1584)
- Hour glasses
- Pictures (1616)
- Virginals (1636)
- Window curtains (1580), window cloths

Category 4 – Silver objects

- Silver 'pieces' (unspecified)
- Silver bowls/ wine bowls
- Silver cups/ wine cups
- Silver goblets/ beakers
- Silver salts/ double salts
- Silver spoons

Appendix 5: Apparel – Types of material and colours of garments belonging to Newcastle tradesmen 1549 – 1637

Type of material	'Bowdagg'	Shipwrights
	'Budge'	Tanners
	Broadcloth	All trades
	Canvas	Cordwainer, Master mariners, Millers
	Damask	Master mariners
	Felt	Bakers
	Fustian	Mariners, Master mariners, Smiths
	Kerseye/ Jersey	Mariners, Millers
	'Knit'	Millers
	Linen (bleached and unbleached)	All trades
	Mockadoo	Tanners
	Russet	All trades
	'Sangwyne'	Tailors
	Satin	Cordwainer, Master mariners
	Satin russet	Master mariners
	Serge	Master mariners
	Silk grograne/ Turks grograne	Mariners, Tailors
	Silk ribbons	Weavers
	Silk russet	Mariners
	Taffeta	Master mariners, Shipwrights, Tanners
	Velvet	Butchers, Mariners, Master mariners, Smiths
	Velvet lace	Mariners
	Wool	Butchers, Keelmen, Master mariners
	Worsted	Mariners, Master mariners, Smiths
Colours	Ash colour stockings	Keelmen
	Beggars grey	Millers
	Black	Bakers, Keelmen, Mariners, Master mariners, Millers, Shipwrights, Smiths, Tailors, Tanners, Weavers
	Blue	Bakers, Butchers, Keelmen, Tailors
	Lace	Master mariners
	Red	Millers, Shipwrights, Smiths, Tailors, Weavers
	Red thrumb "of the old fashion" (1604)	Shipwrights
	Sky (blue?) & clay	Millers
	Striped (canvas)	Master mariners
	Silver	Mariners
	Tawney	Bakers
	Violet	Mariners, Master mariners, Millers, Shipwrights
	White	Keelmen, Mariners, Millers, Smiths, Tailors, Tanners, Weavers
Fur & leather	Black lamb	Bakers
	Buckskin	Butchers
	Chamlet	Butchers, Cordwainers, Master mariners, Millers, Smiths, Tanners
	Conny fur	Smiths
	Fox fur	Cordwainers, Tanners
	Leather	Butchers, Millers, Tanners, Tailors
	Wild leather	Tanners
Imported items	Belgium Lace	Master mariners
	Danish cassock	Cordwainer
	Friese jerkin & jacket	Shipwrights, Smiths
	London russet	Shipwrights
	Spanish leather	Tanners

Appendix 6 - Books

Titles or names of books provide by appraisers which were recorded in the Durham probate inventories for Newcastle tradesmen, excepting bibles 1584 - 1637

Date	Title/ name of book	Trade of owner
584	'Englishe book'	Mariner
588	Service book	Skinner & glover
1585	'Pray book'	Son of miller
1592	'Service booke'	Keelman
1592	'ye Sickmans salve'	Keelman
1592	'My short Brief Chronyckles'	Keelman
1593	'Pissels'	Cordwainer
1593	'Gospals'	Cordwainer
1593	'Common prayer'	Cordwainer
1597	'Testament booke'	Mariner
1599	'a book upon thexosetione of the foure evangilistes'	Master mariner
1616	'Sea books'	Master mariner
1616	'Book of Martyrs'	Cordwainer
1618	'Printed books'	Mariner
1619	Prayer booke	Master mariner

Date	Title/ name of book	Trade of owner
1619	'Church Bible'	Smith
1622	Testament	Butcher
1623	'Book of Martins'	Butcher
1625	'Booke of Martyres'	Baker
1625	'Communion Booke'	Baker
1625	'A booke of Mr. Smith's sermons	Baker
1625	'A historie booke'	Cordwainer
1627	'Mr. Dod upon the Commandements'	Master mariner
1627	'Testament'	Master mariner
1628	'A booke of pres[ ]dentes for wills	Baker
1636	'Service book'	Cordwainer
1636	'Prayer book'	Tailor
1637	'Service Book'	Baker

Appendix 7: Tools, personal gear, supplies and wares of the trades 1549 -1642

Bakers and brewers (excluding brewing equipment: see Table 5.11d)

- **Tools:** Coal rakes, shovels, bowls, pecks, bushels, scoops, peelers , sieves, rolling pins, moulding boards, brakes, tubs, troughs, chests, boulting chests, leven tubs, buckets, cawells (baskets)
- **Ships:** 2 ships listed by 1 baker and brewer (See Appendix 8)

Butchers

- **Personal gear:** Working days apparel (1605), shop aprons (1623)
- **Tools:** Hammer axes, hand axes, lychen knives (for removing protrusions), flaying knives, hand knives, ropes, flange with crook (hooked tool), balks, beams, weights, scales, tubs, baskets, platters of wood and stone (ceramic)
- **Animals:** Cattle, oxen, horses, pigs, sheep (see Table 5.10a)

Cordwainers

Tools: Lasts, boot trees (wooden model on which to shape boots and shoes), cutting boards, hammers, knives, chests, tubs
Supplies: Tallow, 'rended' tallow, rosin, oil, 'traine' oil, pitch, leather (dry, wet, liquored, red, broken, unwrought, wrought, Spanish (1634)), tanned hides of horses, sheep and cattle of different ages
Wares: Boots, lesser, little and greater shoes (men's and women's), children's shoes, wet leather shoes, dry leather shoes, single and double soled shoes, pantofels (slippers), and heeled (wooden) pumps, sloopes, stowpe and falling shoes

Keelmen

Tools: Tree nails, hammers, sledge hammer, womels (drill), shaver, gimlets, axe, chisels

Supplies
Planks of wood and timber, pitch
Hardware for vessels
Cables, anchors, masts, sails, lines, ropes, oars, swapes (rudder), shelts (poles), shewels (scarecrows/ hanging objects)
Boats
Keelboats, lightners, (clinker and cavalier)

Mariners

Personal gear
Clothes: 'sea apparel', 'sea doublet', 'sea britches', 'sea stockings', jacket of 'unwater chamlet' (water-proofed leather), silver chains with silver whistles, silver toothpick, whip, nautical instruments (compass, sea maps, standeye (telescope?), star-globe, astrolabe, a dial for the 'sonne and moone with a case', cross-staff)
Tools
Mallets, clinking hammers, saw, chisel, wombles, gimlets, caulking irons, axes, shaves
Supplies
Pitch, timber
Ships
3 ships listed by 2 mariners

Master mariners

Personal gear
Sea clothes, sea gowns, sea chests for clothes, unspecified nautical instruments, sea cards, compasses, cross-staff, hourglass, globes, silver whistles with silver chains
Supplies
Tar, pitch, rosin, pumps, timber, planks, 'cleven' boards, dales and spares for masts, bolts of canvas for sails, Amish iron
Hardware for vessels
Oars, ropes, cables, flags, buoys, anchors, fishing nets
Ships
33 ships listed by 18 master mariners (See Appendix 8)

Millers

Personal gear
'Work days apparel' (1585, 1613)
Tools
Axes, iron chisels, wombles, crow bars, saws, picks, hatchets, hammers, swingles and heckles (for scraping hemp and flax), bucklers (for compressing material), bushels, shovels, pecks, ropes, trusses, saddle-bags, 'horse gear', iron gear, links for horses, sails (1613), mill stones (1637)
Animals
Horses for milling (see Table 5.10a)

Shipwrights

Personal gear
"Working sea cloths" (1604), silver whistles with silver chains
Tools
Axes, caulking irons, chisels, files, fir dale presser, fire fork, gimlets, grind stones, hacks, hammers, great hammers, hand spikes, hatchets, hole gage, melyards, planes, pliers, ring bowls, saws (whip, quart, hand, toward), shaves, sledges, square, wedges, womble (wimbles), pitch kettles, tree nail wedges, weigh balks & scales, weigh hooks
Supplies
Boards (clap, Norway, ship), buntings, crooked pieces of wood, gunwale, dales, fir dales, planks (floor, inch), spars, swales, trees (oak, short, long, bottom, standing, lying, rotten) pitch, tar, tree nails, bolts (keel, iron, long, ring, set, prange), iron gear
Hardware for vessels

Anchors, anchor stakes, cloth for sails (linen & harden, bleached & unbleached), masts, small masts, oars, ropes, slings
Ships
8 ships listed by 7 shipwrights (See Appendix 8)

Skinners and glovers

Tools
Shears, knives, hatchet, 'parkin iron and wethe' (to stretch and soften leather), tubs, alum tubs, points or punts (needles), scales & weights
Supplies
Sheep skins, lambskins, calf hides, pelts (unspecified animals), leather (rough, wrought, made, wet, cheverel (kid), 'allomed', 'white'), wool (small, course, fine, 'second sort', blue, black, tails and shanks of wool), ribbons, laces, bark (single reference), cloth (linen, harden, white 'cotton' (wool))
Wares
'Madeware', gloves, purses (little, small, men's), leather bags for women, small bags, money bags (two sizes), lamb's leather bags

Smiths

Tools
Bags, bellows, old bellows, bolsters, small bolsters, iron bolsters, bores (stand, small, sand spike, spike, double take, single take, hechy nail, nail, tenge, tabett, caulking iron), bow for making nails, chests, iron boxes, chisels, files, grind stones, hammers(nail, hand, fore, little, up & down, set, boat, upward), hand nail tools, hatchets, Danish hatchets, hewing irons, hewers, hoare bowls, hooks (iron, little), mandrel, axe mandrel, mell mandrel, pattel irons, pincers, pors, punches, scoffets, skummers, iron sledge with iron 'byker', ship sledge, drudge, spades, spade irons, shovels, sloops & forks, wood shovels, stakes (iron), spike (iron), staples, studies (anvils) (crooked, pope, small, little, great, casting), tongs (fire, smith, churching, plain, axe), troughs, coal troughs (stone, wood), vices, wain-clouts, weights (lead, yetling), Flanders balk/ beam, scales, wooden scales
Supplies
'Pan work', iron (English, Spanish, Danish, old, new, unwrought)
Wares
Bills (bill staves), bolts, chains (iron), coulters, shackles for plough, hacks, yolk harnesses & socks for horses, horse shoes, shoe irons, plough shoes, nails (broad, hetch, spike, double tack, single tack, scapper, seam, rawfe), 'nails of all sorts', roves, visor of iron, anchors (new and old), cross for anchor, broken anchors, anchor hooks
Ships
19 ships listed by 2 anchorsmiths (See Appendix 8)

Tailors

Tools
Shears, pinking shears (1581), pressing irons, smoothing irons, shop boards, shop chests
Supplies
Cloth (linen, harden), spun yarn

Tanners

Tools
Tanning vats, tubs, 'leck' (slab of stone to line vat), clap-boards (to create vats)
Supplies
Bark (new, old), hides (raw, tanned) (horse, cattle, calf, oxen), skins (raw, tanned), 'white' cow hide, veal hides, 'blakes' (black) hides, 'sole' hides, 'mortes', 'stecke' leather (hides with rough hair still attached), 'lork' (shorn hair), ever leather (pig or boar)

Weavers

Personal gear
Work day apparel
Tools
Linen looms, harden looms, wool looms, new 24 inch wool loom (1577), 21 gear loom for linen and harden (1580), coverlet loom (1620), multiple gears of different sizes for linen, harden and wool looms, horn wheels, loom wheels, bartrees (?), beams, sleighs (for linen and harden looms), stone weights, 'lambs' (wool, linen), tubs, vats, warp vats, stools for working at loom
Supplies
Yarn (linen, harden, hemp, straken)
Wares
Cloth (linen, harden, hemp, straken, linsey-woolsey (linen-wool blend -1620), linen (bleached, unbleached), silk (1631)

Appendix 8: Ships – Vessels owned by tradesmen of Newcastle and listed in the Durham probate records 1569 - 1641
(Blank cell indicates no information recorded)

Date	Names of ships of Newcastle	Burden	Share of ownership	Valuation	Owner's name	Owner's trade
1569	Mary Galland		1/4		John Hawton	Master mariner
1571	Prommose (Promise)			+ 10li	Nicholas Maddison	Master mariner
1580	Speedwell			35li	John Taillor	Master mariner
1580	John Bonadventure		1/3	120li**	(same)	(same)
1581	Jesus		100%	100li	Jhon Readeheade (Eld.)	Shipwright
1582	Nightingale		1/4		Anthony Wilkinson	Shipwright
1585	Jesus		1/4	195li	Thomas Smith	Shipwright
1586	Mary Grace		100%	200li	(same)	Shipwright
1587	Jesus		1/4	30li	Thomas Fife	Master mariner
1589	Jonas	100 ton	1/4		Edward Bell	Master mariner
1592	Daniell		1/3	110li	Robert Johnson	Master mariner
1592	Barke Rawes		1/4	60li	(same)	(same)
1592	Grace of God		2/3	60li 13s 4d	Thomas Redhead	Shipwright
1594	New John		1/8	35li	Edward Johnson	Master mariner
1595	Nightingaile				Thomas Nicholson	Master mariner
1596	Christopher & John*	56 tons	1/2	70li	John Tucker	Master mariner
1596	Faith		1/3	20li	Richard Herrisone	Mariner
1596	Maria Katherine		2/3	22li	Richard Herrisone	Mariner
1598	Robert		1/4		Henry Temple	Shipwright
1604	Emmanuall	149 tons	1/4	100li	Richard Bulman	Shipwright
1604	A ' greate bote'				(same)	(same)
1616	Peter		1/8	50li	Robert Chrysoppe	Master mariner
1619	Consent		1/6	26li	Rober Heley	Master mariner
1622	Welcome		1/8	45li	John Holborne	Mariner
1623	Maieflower	160 tons	1/4 & 1/16	50li	James Nicholson	Master mariner
1625	Salamander of Ncl.		1/12	24li	John Swynburne	Baker & brewer
1625	Mayflower of Ncl.		1/16	16li	(same)	(same)
1625	Thomas & a " barke "		1/4 & 1/8	200li	John Carr	Master mariner
1629	End Voyage		1/8 & 1/16		John Peacock	Master mariner
1631	Unitie of Newcastle		1/8	100li	George Comyn	Anchor smith
1634	Woodbind		1/16	20li	Richard Fell	Master mariner
1634	Pincke		1/16	40li	Oswold Nixon	Master mariner
1634	Eastland Venture		1/16	30li	(same)	(same)
1634	Porpoise		1/16	16li	(same)	(same)
1634	Hope		1/4	100li	(same)	(same)
1636	John		1/8	45li	John Reed	Master mariner
1639	May Flower		1/4 & 1/32	39li	Robert Browne	Master mariner
1639	Consent		1/12	35li	(same)	(same)
1639	William		1/16	35li	(same)	(same)
1639	Susan		1/12	40li	(same)	(same)
1639	Consent		1/16	40li	(same)	(same)
1639	Mary Merchant		1/16	31li	(same)	(same)
1639	Mary		1/16	45li	(same)	(same)
1639	Violet		1/4	80li	(same)	(same)
1639	Fortune		1/8	5li	(same)	(same)
1641	Abigaile		1/16		Edward Lawson	Anchor smith
1641	Constant		1/16	43li 15s	(same)	(same)
1641	Debora		1/8	68li 5s	(same)	(same)
1641	Dolfin		1/16	37li 10s	(same)	(same)
1641	Eagle		1/12	54li 3s 4d	(same)	(same)
1641	Elsabeth		1/8	100li	(same)	(same)
1641	Endeavor		1/16	45li	(same)	(same)
1641	Fortune		1/8	60li	(same)	(same)
1641	Jane		1/8	37li 10s	(same)	(same)
1641	John		1/16	32li 10s	(same)	(same)
1641	Marie		1/8	110li	(same)	(same)
1641	Mayflower		1/8	118li 15s	(same)	(same)
1641	Nathan		1/8	130li	(same)	(same)
1641	Seaventer		1/8	125li	(same)	(same)
1641	Tryal		1/6	23li 6s 8d	(same)	(same)
1641	Unknown		1/8	100li	(same)	(same)
1641	A new ship being built		1/8		(same)	(same)
1641	A new ship being built		1/16		(same)	(same)

*Lost at Elsinore, Denmark
** Plus cargo 22li 19s 2d of cargo

Bibliography

Manuscript Collections

Durham Probate Records 1545 – 1642

Printed and contemporary sources

Brand, J. 1789. *The History and Antiquities of the Town and County of Newcastle upon Tyne, including an Account of the Coal Trade*, Vol. I & II. London: B. White & Sons, T. & I. Egerton.

Bourne, H. 1980 (1736). *The History of Newcastle upon Tyne.* Newcastle upon Tyne: Frank Graham.

Furvinal, F.J., (ed.) 1877. *Harrison's Description of England in Shakespere's Youth: Being the second and third books of his Description of Britaine and England/ Edited from the first two editions of Holinshed's Chronicle, A.D. 1577 - 1587.* London: Trubner.

Gardiner, R. 1655. *England's Grievances Discovered.* London: R. Ibbitson.

Gray, W. 1970 (1649). *Chorographia, or a Survey of Newcastle upon Tyne.* Newcastle upon Tyne: Frank Graham.

Morris, C., (ed.) 1983. *The illustrated journeys of Celia Fiennes 1685 – c.1712.* London: Macdonald.

Schofield, J., (ed.) 1987. *The London Surveys of Ralph Treswell.* London Topographical Society, Publication 135.

Rogers, P. 1983. *A tour through the whole island of Great Britain / Daniel Defoe.* London: Folio Society.

Secondary Sources

Arkell, T. 2000. 'The Probate Process', in T. Arkell, E. Nesta, N. Goose (eds.), *When Death Do Us Part: Understanding and Interpreting the Probate Records of Early Modern England.* A Local Populations Studies Supplement.

Arkell. T. 2000. 'Interpreting Probate Inventories', in T. Arkell, E. Nesta, N. Goose (eds.), *When Death Do Us Part: Understanding and Interpreting the Probate Records of Early Modern England.* A Local Populations Studies Supplement, pp. 72 – 102.

Arkell, T., Nesta, E., Goose, N., (eds.) 2000. *When Death Do Us Part: Understanding and Interpreting the Probate Records of Early Modern England.* A Local Populations Studies Supplement.

Barley, M.W. 1967. 'Rural Housing in England', in J. Thirsk (ed.), *The Agrarian History of England and Wales*, Volume IV 1500 -1640. Cambridge University Press, pp.696 – 761.

Barnard, J., Bell, M. 1994. *The Early 17th century York Book Trade & John Foster's Inventory of 1616.* Leeds: The Leeds Philosophical & Literary Society Ltd.

Barnes, A. 1867. *The Memoirs of the Life of Mr. Ambrose Barnes, Late merchant and sometime Alderman of Newcastle upon Tyne*, Surtees Society, Vol. L. Durham: Andrew's & Co.

Barry, J. 1994. 'Introduction', in J. Barry and C. Brooks, (eds.), *The Middling Sort of People: Culture, Society and Politics in England 1550 – 1800.* Macmillan Press, pp. 1 - 27.

Barry J., Brooks, C., (eds.) 1994. *The Middling Sort of People: Culture, Society and Politics in England 1550 – 1800.* Macmillan Press.

Barry, J. 1994. 'Bourgeois Collectivism? Urban association and the Middling Sort', in J. Barry and C. Brooks, (eds.), *The Middling Sort of People: Culture, Society and Politics in England 1550 – 1800.* Macmillan Press, pp. 84 - 112.

Berry, H., Gregory, J., (eds.) 2004. *Creating and Consuming Culture in North-East England, 1660 – 1830.* Ashgate.

Berry, H., Gregory, J. 2004. 'Introduction', *Creating and Consuming Culture in North-East England, 1660 – 1830.* Ashgate, pp. 1-11.

Bowden, P. 1967. 'Agricultural Prices, Farm Profits, and Rents', in H.P.R. Finberg (ed.), *The Agrarian History of England and Wales*, IV, 1500 – 1640. Cambridge: Cambridge University Press, pp. 593 – 695.

Braudel, F. 1992. *Civilization and capitalism, 15th-18th century.* Berkeley: University of California Press.

Braudel, F. 1973. *Capitalism and Material Life, 1400-1800.* London: Weidenfeld & Nicolson.

Brewer, J., Porter, R., (eds.) 1993. *Consumption and the World of Goods.* London: Routledge.

Brewer, J., Porter, R. 1993. 'Introduction', in J. Brewer and R. Porter (eds.), *Consumption and the World of Goods.* London: Routledge, pp.1 – 15.

Brooks, C. 1994. 'Apprenticeship, Social Mobility and the Middling Sort, 1550 – 1800', in J. Barry and C. Brooks, (eds.), *The Middling Sort of People: Culture, Society and Politics in England 1550 – 1800.* Macmillan Press, pp. 52 - 83.

Burke, P. 1988. *Popular Culture in Early Modern Europe.* Wildwood House.

Byrne, D. 2001. 'The Reconstruction of Newcastle', in R. Colls and B. Lancaster (eds.), *Newcastle: A Modern History.* Phillimore, pp.1 – 26.

Cambell, C. 1996. The Meaning of Objects and the Meaning of Actions, in D. Miller and C. Tilley (eds.), *Journal of Material Culture*, Vol.1. Sage Publications, pp. 93-128.

Chalklin, C.W., Havinden, M.A. 1974. *Rural change and urban growth, 1500-1800: essays in English regional history in honour of W. G. Hoskins*. London: Longman.
Charleton, R.J. 1885. *Newcastle Town*. Newcastle upon Tyne: Frank Graham.
Chaytor, M. 1980. 'Household and kinship: Ryton in the late 16th and early 17th centuries', History Workshop Jounal, Vol. 10, pp.25 – 60.
Clair, C. 1965. A History of Printing in Britain. London: Cassell.
Clark. A. 1992 (1919). *Working life of Women in the Seventeenth Century*. London: Routledge.
Clark, P., (ed.) 2000. *The Cambridge Urban History of Britain*, Vol. II, 1540 – 1840. Cambridge University Press.
Clark, P., (ed.) 2000. 'Introduction', in P. Clark (ed.), *The Cambridge Urban History of Britain*, Vol. II, 1540 – 1840. Cambridge University Press, pp.1-24.
Clark, P. 1976. *The Early Modern Town; A Reader*. Longman, Open University Press.
Clark, P., Slack, P. 1972. *Crisis and Order in English Towns: Essays in urban history*. Routledge and Kegan Paul.
Clephan, J. 1891. 'Windmills', in *The Monthly Chronicle of North Country Lore and Legend*, Vol. V, No. 58.
Colls, R., Lancaster, B., (eds.) 2001. *Newcastle: A Modern History*. Phillimore.
Cooper, J.P. 1978. 'Patterns of inheritance and settlement by great landowners from the fifteenth to the eighteenth centuries', in J. Goody, J. Thirsk, E.P.Thompson (eds.), *Family and Inheritance: Rural Society in Western Europe, 1200 – 1800*. Cambridge University Press.
Corfield, P. 1972. 'A provincial capital in the late seventeenth century: The case of Norwich', in P. Clark and P. Slack (eds.), *Crisis and Order in English Towns: Essays in urban history*. Routledge & Kegan Paul.
Cox, J., Cox, N. 2000. 'Probate 1500 -1800: A system in transition', in T. Arkell, E. Nesta and N. Goose (eds.), *When Death Do Us Part: Understanding and Interpreting the Probate Records of Early Modern England*. A Local Populations Studies Supplement, pp. 14 – 37.
Cox, N. 2000 *The Complete Tradesmen: a study of retailing*, 1550 – 1820. Ashgate.
Cressy, D. 1986. 'Kinship and kin interaction in early modern England'. Past and Present, No. 113 (Nov.), pp. 33 – 69.
Cressy, D. 1997. *Birth, Marriage and Death: Ritual, Religion and the Life-Cycle in Tudor and Stuart England*. Oxford: Oxford University Press.
De Vries, J. 1993. 'Between purchasing power and the world of goods: understanding the household economy in early modern Europe', in J. Brewer and R. Porter (eds.), *Consumption and the World of Goods*. London: Routledge, 85 – 132.
Dendy F.W. 1921. 'Gilds and their survival', in F.W. Dendy (ed.), *Three lectures on Old Newcastle, its suburbs and its gilds*. Newcastle, pp. 46 -7.
Dobson, M.J. 1997. *Contours of Death and Disease in Early Modern England*. Cambridge: Cambridge University Press.
Duffy, E. 2001. *The Voices of Morebath: Reformation and Rebellion in an English Village*. New Haven & London: Yale University Press.
Duffy, E. 1992. *The Stripping of the Altars: Traditional Religion in England 1400 – 1580*. New Haven & London: Yale University Press.
Dyer, A. 1973. *The City of Worcester in the Sixteenth Century*. Leicester University Press.
Dyer, C. 1989. *Standards of Living in the Later Middle Ages: Social Change in England 1200 – 1520*. Cambridge: Cambridge University Press.
Dyer, C. 1984. 'Changes in the size of peasant holdings in some west Midland villages, 1400 – 1540, in R. M. Smith, (ed.), *Land, kinship and life-cycle*. Cambridge University Press, pp. 277 – 294.
Dyer, C. 1984. 'Changes in the link between families and land in the West Midlands in the 14th and 15th centuries', in R. M. Smith (ed.), *Land, kinship and life-cycle*. Cambridge University Press, pp. 305 - 311.
Earle, P. 1994. *A City Full of People: men and women of London, 1650 -1750*. London: Methuen.
Earle, P. 1994. 'The Middling Sort in London', in J. Barry and C. Brooks (eds.), *The Middling Sort of People: Culture, Society and Politics in England 1550 – 1800*. Macmillan Press, pp. 141 - 157.
Earle P. 1989. *The Making of the English Middle Class: business, society and family life in London 1660 – 1730*. Methuen.
Ellis, J. 2001. ' The Black Indies: Economic Development of Newcastle, c. 1700 – 1840, in R. Colls and B. Lancaster (eds.), *Newcastle: A Modern History*. Phillimore, pp.1-26.
Ellis, J. 1984. 'A Dynamic Society: Social Relations in Newcastle upon Tyne 1660 -1760, in P. Clark (ed.), *The Transformation of English provincial towns, 1600-1800*. London: Hutchinson, pp.190-227.
Ellison, M., McCombie, G., MacElvaney, M., Newman, A., O'Brien, C., Taverner, N., Williams, A. 1993. Excavations at Newcastle Quayside: waterfront development at Swirle. Archaeologia Aeliana, Series 5, Vol. 23, pp.145-214.
Epstein, S.R. (ed.) 2001. *Town and country in Europe, 1300-1800*. Cambridge: Cambridge University Press, 2001.
Erickson, A.L. 2002. *Women and Property in Early Modern England*, 2nd Edition, London: Routledge.

Everitt, A. 1967. 'Farm labourers', in J. Thirsk (ed.) *The Agrarian History of England and Wales*, IV, 1500 – 1640. Cambridge: Cambridge University Press, pp. 396 – 465.

Everitt, A. 1967. 'The Marketing of Agricultural Produce', in J.Thirsk, (ed.), *The Agrarian History of England and Wales*, IV, 1500 – 1640. Cambridge: Cambridge University Press, pp. 466 – 592.

Garrard, R. P. 1980. 'English probate inventories and their use in studying the significance of the domestic interior 1570 – 1700', in A. Van der Woude and A. Schuurman, (eds.), *Probate inventories: a new source for the historical study of wealth, material culture and agricultural development.* Afdeling Agrarishe Geschiedenis, Bijdragen 23, Landbouwhogeschool: Wageningen, pp.55-82.

Glennie, P. 1995. 'Consumption within historical studies', in D. Miller (ed.), *Acknowledging Consumption.* London and New York: Routledge, pp. 164 – 203.

Glennie, P., Whyte, I. 2000. 'Towns in an agrarian economy 1540 -1700', in P. Clarke (ed.), *The Cambridge Urban History of Britain 1540 -1840.* Cambridge: Cambridge University Press.

Goody, J., Thirsk, J., Thompson, E.P. 1978. *Family and Inheritance; Rural Society in Western Europe 1200-1800.* Cambridge University Press.

Goose, N., Evans, N. 2000. 'Wills as an Historical Source', in T. Arkell, E. Nesta, N. Goose (eds.), *When Death Do Us Part: Understanding and Interpreting the Probate Records of Early Modern England.* A Local Populations Studies Supplement.

Graves, C.P. (forthcoming). *North Sea Capital: Newcastle, the Making of a Mercantile Community*, With an Inventory of the Archaeology by David Heslop, Oxford, English Heritage/Oxbow Books.

Graves, P. 2003. 'Civic ritual, townscape and social identity in seventeenth- and eighteenth-century Newcastle upon Tyne, in S. Lawrence (ed.), *Archaeologies of the British: Explorations of identity in Great Britain and its Colonies 1600 – 1945.* Routledge, pp. 31 – 54.

Graves, C.P., Heslop, D. (forthcoming) *Ritual and townscape in Newcastle upon Tyne.*

Green, A. 2004. ' "A Clumsey Countrey Girl": The material and Print Culture of Betty Bowes', in H. Berry & J. Gregory, J. (eds.), *Creating and Consuming Culture in North-East England, 1660 – 1830.* Ashgate, pp.72 – 97.

Green, A. 2003. 'Houses in north-eastern England: regionality and the British beyond, c.1600-1750, in S. Lawrence (ed.), *Archaeologies of the British: Explorations of identity in Great Britain and its Colonies 1600 – 1945.* Routledge, 55 – 75.

Harris, R. 1999. *Discovering Timber-Framed Buildings.* Shire Publications.

Harrison, J.K. 2001. Eight centuries of milling in North East Yorkshire. Thirsk: North York Moors National Park Authority.

Harbottle, B. 1987. 'Black friars, Newcastle-upon-Tyne, after the dissolution of the monasteries. Archaeologia Aeliana, Vol. 15, pp. 23-150.

Harbottle, B. 1981. 'An Excavation in the Castle Ditch, Newcastle upon Tyne, 1974 – 1976', Archaeologia Aeliana, Series 5, Vol. 11, pp. 75 – 250.

Hey, D. 1981. *The History of Myddle: Richard Gough.* Harmondsworth: Penguin Books.

Helmholz, R.H. 1990. *Roman Canon Law in Reformation England.* Cambridge: University of Cambridge.

Heslop, D., C.P. Graves (Forthcoming) *An Archaeological Assessment of Newcastle-upon-Tyne up to 1650.* English Heritage.

Heslop, D., Jobling, B., McCombie, G. 2001. *Alderman Fenwick's House : the history of the seventeenth-century house in Pilgrim Street, Newcastle upon Tyne, and its owners.* Newcastle upon Tyne : Society of Antiquaries of Newcastle upon Tyne.

Heslop, D., McCombie, G., Thomson, C. 1995. *Bessie Surtees House: two merchant houses in Sandhill, Newcastle upon Tyne.* Newcastle upon Tyne: Society of Antiquaries of Newcastle upon Tyne.

Heslop, D., Truman, L. 1993. *The Cooperage, 34 – 4, The Close.* Archaeologia Aeliana, Forth Series, 21, 1 – 12.

Hodder, I. (ed.) 2001. *Archaeological Theory Today.* Cambridge Polity.

Hodder, I., (ed.), 1987. *The Archaeology of Contextual Meaning.* Cambridge: Cambridge University Press.

Holderness, B.A. 1984. 'Widows in pre-industrial society: an essay upon their economic functions', in R. M. Smith (ed.), *Land, Kinship and Life-Cycle.* Cambridge University Press, pp. 423 – 442.

Hoskins, W.G. 1961. 'The Elizabethan merchants of Exeter', in S. Bindoff and J. Hurstfield, (eds.), *Elizabethan government and society : essays presented to Sir John Neale.* Imprint London: Athlone Press.

Hoskins, W.G. 1957. *The Midland peasant: the economic and social history of a Leicestershire village.* London: Macmillan ; New York : St. Martin's Press.

Hoskins, W.G. 1953. 'The Rebuilding of Rural England, 1570 – 1640', Past and Present, 4, pp. 44-59.

Houlbrooke, R. 2000. Death, Religion and the Family in England 1480 – 1750. Clarendon Press: Oxford.

Houlbrooke, R. 1995. *The English Family 1450 – 1700.* London: Longman.

Howell, C. 1976. 'Peasant inheritance customs in the Midlands, 1280 – 1700', in J. Goody, J. Thirsk and E. P. Thompson (eds.), *Family and Inheritance: Rural Society in Western Europe, 1200 -1800.* Cambridge University Press.

Howell, C. 1983. *Land, Family and Inheritance in Transition: Kibworth Harcourt 1280 – 1700.* Cambridge University Press

Howell, R. 1967. *Newcastle upon Tyne and the Puritan Revolution.* Oxford: Clarendon Press.

Howell, R., (ed.), 1978. *Monopoly on the Tyne, 1650 – 58: Papers relating to Ralph Gardiner.* The Society of Antiquaries of Newcastle upon Tyne

Hoyle, R.W. 2001. *The Pilgrimage of Grace and the Politics of the 1530s.* Oxford: Oxford University Press.

Hugman, J. 2001. 'Print and Preach: The Entrepreneurial Spirit of Nineteenth-Century Newcastle', in R. Colls and B. Lancaster (eds.), *Newcastle: A Modern History.* Phillimore, pp.113 - 132

Hunt, C.J. 1975. *The book trade in Northumberland and Durham to 1860; A Bibliographical Dictionary.* Newcastle upon Tyne: Thorne's Student Bookshop Ltd.

Hurst, J.G., Neal, D.S, Beuningen, H.J.C., (eds.) 1986. *Pottery produced and traded in North-west Europe 1350 -1650.* Rotterdam Papers VI. Rotterdam.

Husbands, C. 1981. 'Standards of living in North Warwickshire in the Seventeenth Century', Warwickshire History, 4, pp. 211.

James, M.E. 1974. *Family Lineage and Civil Society; politics and mentality in the Durham region 1500-1640.* Clarendon Press: Oxford.

Jennings, B. 2000. 'Beyond the Probate Line: Probate evidence and related sources in Early Modern Yorkshire', in T. Arkell, E. Nesta, N. Goose (eds.), *When Death Do Us Part: Understanding and Interpreting the Probate Records of Early Modern England.* Local Populations Studies Supplement.

Johnson, J.M. 1991. *Probate Inventories of Lincoln Citizens 1661- 1715.* Lincoln Record Society, The Boydell Press.

Johnson, M. 1996. *An Archaeology of Capitalism.* Oxford: Blackwell.

Kenyon, G.H. 1958. 'Petworth town and trades 1610 – 1760, Part 1', Sussex Archaeological Collections, 96.

King, R. 2004. 'The Sociability of the Trade Guilds of Newcastle and Durham, 1660 -1750: The Urban Renaissance Revisited', in H. Berry and J. Gregory (eds.), *Creating and Consuming Culture in North-East England, 1660 – 1830.* Ashgate, pp. 57-71.

Knowles, W.H., Boyle, J.R. 1890. *Vestiges of Old Newcastle and Gateshead.* Newcastle: A. Reid; London: E. Stock.

Kitching, C. 1976. 'Probate during the Civil War and Interregnum', in Journal of the Society of Archivists, 5.

Langton, J. 1975. 'Residential patterns in pre-industrial cities: some case studies from seventeenth century Britain'. Transactions of the Institute of British Geographers, 65, pp.1-27.

Lawrence, S., (ed.) 2003. *Archaeologies of the British: Explorations of identity in Great Britain and its Colonies 1600 – 1945.* Routledge.

Lomas, R. 1996. *County in Conflict: Northumberland from Conquest to Civil War.* East Lothian: Tuckwell Press.

Lomas, R. 1992. *North East England in the Middle Ages.* Edinburgh: John Donald.

Malcolmson, R. W. 1980. 'A Set of Ungovernable People: Kingswood Colliers in the Eighteenth Century', in J. Brewer and J. Styles (eds.), *An Ungovernable people: The English and Their Law in the Seventeenth and Eighteenth Centuries.* London

Margeson, S. 1993. 'Norwich Households: Medieval and Post Medieval Finds from the Norwich Survey Excavations' 1971 – 78. East Anglian Archaeology 58. Norwich: Norwich Survey.

Marsh, C. 2000. 'Attitudes to Will-Making in Early Modern England, in T. Arkell, E. Nesta, N. Goose (eds.), *When Death Do Us Part: Understanding and Interpreting the Probate Records of Early Modern England.* A Local Populations Studies Supplement

McCombie, G. 1985. 'The Buildings of Trinity House, Newcastle upon Tyne'. Archaeologia Aeliana, Series 5, Vol. 13.

McKendrick, N., Brewer, J., Plumb, J.H. 1982. *The Birth of a Consumer Society: the commercialisation of eighteenth-century England.* Europe Publications: London.

McKenzie, E. 1827. *A Descriptive and Historical Account of Newcastle upon Tyne.* Newcastle upon Tyne: McKenzie & Dent.

Middlebrooke, S. 1950. *Newcastle upon Tyne; Its Growth and Achievement*, Kemsley House, Newcastle upon Tyne

Munby, L. 2002. *Reading Tudor and Stuart Handwriting.* Chichester, British Association for Local History.

Myers, A. 2001. 'Winged Words: Literature of Newcastle', in R. Colls and B. Lancaster (eds.), *Newcastle: A Modern History.* Phillimore, pp.293 – 318.

Nef, J.U. 1932. *Rise of the British Coal Industry.* London: G. Routledge & Sons Ltd.

Nolan, J. (forthcoming). 'Excavations at Bottlebank, Gateshead'.

O'Brien, C., Brown, L., et al. 1988. *The Origins of the Newcastle Quayside: Excavations at Queen Street and Dog Bank.* Royal Commission on the Historical Monuments of England.

Orlin, L.C. 2002. 'Fictions of the Early Modern English Probate Inventory', in H.S. Turner (ed.), *The Culture of Capital: Properties, Cities, and Knowledge in Early Modern England.* Routledge, pp. 51 – 84.

Overton, M., Whittle, J., Dean, D., Hann, A. 2004. *Production and Consumption in English Households, 1600 – 1750.* Routledge.

Overton, M. 1996. *Agricultural revolution in England : The transformation of the agrarian economy, 1500-1850.* Cambridge, Cambridge University Press.

Overton, M. 1983. *A Bibliography of British Probate Inventories.* Newcastle upon Tyne: University Department of Geography.

Overton, M. 1980. 'English probate inventories and the measurement of agricultural change', in A. Van der Woude and A. Schuurman,(eds.), *Probate Inventories: A new source for the historical study of wealth, material culture and agricultural development.* Afdeling Agrarishe Geschiedenis, Bijdragen 23. Landbouwhogeschool: Wageningen, pp. 205-216.

Palliser, D.M. 1992. *The Age of Elisabeth: England under the Later Tudors 1547 – 1603.* London: Longman.

Pevsner, N., Richmond, I., Grundy, J., McCombie, G., Ryder, P., Welfare, H. 1992. *The Buildings of England: Northumberland.* Penguin Books.

Phelps-Brown, H., Hopkins, S.V. 1981. *A Perspective on Wages and Prices.* London: Methuen.

Pirenne, H. 1969. *Medieval cities: their origins and the revival of trade.* Princeton: Princeton University Press.

Platt, C. 1994. *The great rebuildings of Tudor and Stuart England: revolutions in architectural taste.* London: UCL Press.

Portman, D. 1974. 'Vernacular Building in the Oxford region', in C.W. Chalkin and M. A. Havinden (eds.), *Rural Change and Urban Growth, 1500-1800: Essays in English Regional History in Honour of W.G. Hoskins.* London: Longman, pp.135 -168.

Power, M. J. 1972. 'East London housing in the seventeenth century', in P. Clark and P. Slack (eds.), *Crisis and Order in English Towns: Essays in urban history.* Routledge & Kegan Paul, pp.237 - 262.

Priestley, U., Corfield, P. 1982. 'Rooms and room use in Norwich housing, 1580-1730. Post-medieval Archaeology 16, pp. 93-124.

Rollason, D. 2003. *Northumbria 500 – 1100: Creation and Destruction of a Kingdom.* Cambridge University Press.

Scammell, L. 2004. 'Was the North-East different from other areas? The property of Everyday consumption in the late seventeenth and eighteenth centuries', in H. Berry and J. Gregory (eds.), *Creating and Consuming Culture in North-East England, 1660 – 1830.* Ashgate, pp. 12 - 23.

Schofield, R.S. 1968. 'The Measurement of Literacy in Pre-Industrial England', in J. Goody (ed.), *Literacy in Traditional Societies.* Cambridge University Press, pp. 311-325.

Shammas, C. 1990. *The Pre-Industrial Consumer in England and America.* Clarendon Press, Oxford.

Smith, P. 1967. 'Rural Housing in Wales', in J. Thirsk (ed.), *The Agrarian History of England and Wales,* Volume IV 1500 -1640. Cambridge University Press, pp.767-813.

Smith, R., (ed.) 1984. Land, Kinship and Life-cycle. Cambridge University Press.

Smith, R. 1984. 'Some issues concerning families and their property in rural England 1250 -1800', in R. Smith (ed.), *Land, Kinship and Life-cycle.* Cambridge University Press, pp. 1 - 86.

Snape, M., Bidwell, P. 2002. 'The Roman Fort at Newcastle upon Tyne', Archaeologia Aeliana, Series 5, Vol. 31, Part 2, pp. 1 - 295.

Spufford, M. 2000. *Contrasting Communities: English Villagers in the Sixteenth and Seventeenth Centuries.* Sutton Publishing.

Spufford, M. 2000. 'Religious Preambles and the Scribes of Villagers' Wills in Cambridgeshire, 1570 – 1700, in T. Arkell, E. Nesta, N. Goose (eds.), *When Death Do Us Part: Understanding and Interpreting the Probate Records of Early Modern England.* A Local Populations Studies Supplement.

Spufford, M. 1990. 'The Limitations of the Probate Inventory', in D. Hey (ed.), *English Rural Society, 1500 – 1800: Essays in honour of Joan Thirsk.* Cambridge University Press.

Spufford, M. 1984. *The Great Reclothing of Rural England: Petty Chapmen and their Wares in the Seventeenth Century.* The Hambledon Press.

Spufford, M. 1981. *Small Books and Pleasant Histories: Popular fiction and its readership in seventeenth-century England.* London: Methuen.

Spufford, M. 1976. 'Peasant Inheritance Customs and Land Distribution in Cambridgeshire from the sixteenth to the eighteenth centuries', in J. Goody, J. Thirsk and E.P. Thompson, (eds.), *Family and Inheritance: Rural Society in Western Europe, 1200 – 1800.* Cambridge University Press.

Stone, L. 1979. *Family, Sex and Marriage 1500 – 1800.* Harmondsworth: Penguin.

Stone, L. 1964. 'The Educational Revolution in England, 1560-1640'. Past and Present, Number 28.

Stow, J. 1987 (1598). *The Survey of London,* (ed.) H.B. Wheatley. Everyman's Library.

Thirsk, J., (ed.) 1984. *The Agrarian History of England and Wales: Regional Farming Systems.* Vol. 5. I, 1640 – 1750. Cambridge: Cambridge University Press.

Thirsk, J. 1978. *Economic policy and projects: The development of a consumer society in Early Modern England.* Oxford: Clarendon Press.

Thirsk, J. 1978. 'The European debate on customs of inheritance, 1500 -1700', in J. Goody, J. Thirsk, E.P.Thompson (eds.), *Family and Inheritance: Rural Society in Western Europe, 1200 – 1800.* Cambridge University Press.

Thirsk, J., ed., 1967. *The Agrarian History of England and Wales*. Vol. 4, 1500-1640. Cambridge: Cambridge University Press.

Trinder, B., Cox, J. (eds.) 1980. *Yeomen and Colliers in Telford.* Chichester.

Turner, H.S. (ed.) 2002. *The Culture of Capital: Properties, Cities, and Knowledge in Early Modern England.* Routledge.

Van der Woude, A., Schuurman, A., (eds.) 1980. *Probate Inventories: A new source for the historical study of wealth, material culture and agricultural development.* Afdeling Agrarishe Geschiedenis, Bijdragen 23. Landbouwhogeschool: Wageningen.

Ville, S.P. 1989. 'Patterns of shipping investment in the port of Newcastle upon Tyne 1750 -1850', Northern History, Vol. 25, pp. 210-13.

Wake, T. 1936. 'Isaac Thompson's plan of Newcastle upon Tyne, 1746, Archaeologia Aeliana, 4th Series, Vol. XIV, pp. 110 -122.

Wales, T. 1984. 'Poverty. Poor relief and the life-cycle: Some evidence from 17th century Norfolk, in R. Smith (ed.), *Land, Kinship and Life-cycle.* Cambridge University Press, 351 – 388.

Walton, J. 2000. 'North', in P. Clark (ed.), *The Cambridge Urban History of Britain*, Vol. II, 1540 – 1840. Cambridge University Press, pp.111 - 131.

Weatherill, L. 1996. *Consumer Behaviour and Material Culture 1660 – 1760*, Second Edition. London: Routledge.

Weatherill, L. 1986. 'A Possession of One's Own: Women and Consumer Behaviour in England 1660 – 1740. The Journal of British Studies, Vol. 25, Number 2 (April), pp. 131 – 156.

Welford, R. 1911. 'Newcastle Householders in 1665; Assessment of Hearth or Chimney Tax', Archaeologia Aeliana, Series 3, Vol. VII, pp. 49 -76.

Welford, R. 1907. *Early Newcastle Topography: 1639 – 1800.* Newcastle upon Tyne: Andrew Reid & Co. Ltd.

Welford, R. 1884. *History of Newcastle and Gateshead*, Vol. I, Sixteenth Century. London: Walter Scott.

Welford, R. 1885. *History of Newcastle and Gateshead*, Vol. III, Fourteenth and Fifteenth Centuries. London: Walter Scott.

Welford, R. 1887. *History of Newcastle and Gateshead*, Vol. I, Sixteenth and Seventeenth Centuries. London: Walter Scott.

Wheatley, C. 2002. 'The Pocket Books of Early Modern History', in H.S. Turner (ed.), *The Culture of Capital: Properties, Cities, and Knowledge in Early Modern England.* Routledge, pp. 183 – 202.

Whiting, C.E. 1934. *The Rising of the North in 1569.* Durham: Durham University Journal.

Wrightson, K. 2000. *Earthly Necessities: Economic Lives in Early Modern Britain.* New Haven and London, Yale University Press.

Wrightson, K. 1995. *English Society 1580 -1680.* London: Routledge.

Wrightson, K., Levine, D. 1991. *The Making of an Industrial Society: Whickham 1560 – 1765.* Clarendon press, Oxford.

Wrightson, K. 1994. 'Sorts of People in Tudor and Stuart England', in J. Barry and C. Brooks (eds.), *The Middling Sort of People: Culture, Society and Politics in England 1550 – 1800.* Macmillan Press, pp. 28 – 51.

Wrightson, K. 1984. 'Kinship in an English Village: Terling, Essex 1550 – 1700', in R. M. Smith (ed.), *Land, kinship and the life-cycle*, Cambridge, Cambridge University Press. pg 327

Wrightson, K., Levine, D. 1979. *Poverty and Piety in an English Village: Terling 1525 – 1700.* New York: Academic Press.

Wrigley, E.A., Schofield, R.A. 1989. *The population history of England 1541-1871: a reconstruction.* Cambridge: Cambridge University Press.

Unpublished Theses

Green, A. 2000. *Houses and households in County Durham and Newcastle c.1570 – 1730.* PhD Thesis, University of Durham.

Issa, C. 1986. *Obligation and Choice: Aspects of family and kinship in 17th century County Durham.* PhD Thesis, University of St. Andrews.

King, R. 2001. *Aspects of Sociability in the North East of England 1600 – 1750.* PhD Thesis, University of Durham.

Maps

Armstrong, A. (1769) Northumberland with 'A Plan of Newcastle' inset. Newcastle Public Library, Local Studies Collection.

Corbridge, J. 1984 (1723). Newcastle. In *Maps of Newcastle*, ed. F. Graham. Newcastle: Frank Graham.

Hutton, C. 1984 (1772). A Plan of Newcastle upon Tyne and Gateshead. In *Maps of Newcastle*, ed. F. Graham. Newcastle: Frank Graham.

Mercator, G. 1636 (1970) Northumbria, Cumberlandia et Dunelmensis Episcopatus. Amsterdam: Koeman ME 41; A, no. 7; Skelton.

Oliver, J. 1984 (1838). Plan of Newcastle upon Tyne and Gateshead. In *Maps of Newcastle*, ed. F. Graham. Newcastle: Frank Graham.

Speed's plan of Newcastle 2000 (1610). In *Tudor Townscapes: The Town Plans from Speed's 'Theatre of the Empire of Great Britaine' 1610.* Buckinghamshire: Map Collector Publications.

Tallis, J. 1984 (c.1851). Newcastle upon Tyne. In *Maps of Newcastle*, ed. F. Graham. Newcastle: Frank Graham.

Thompson, I. (1746) Town Plan of Newcastle upon Tyne, in Archeaologia Aeliana

Cotton Manuscript 1984 (c.1590). In *Maps of Newcastle*, ed. F. Graham. Newcastle: Frank Graham.

Unpublished pamphlet

Durham Probate Records: Index 1600 -1660: General Introduction. University of Durham: Palace Green Library, Special Collections.

Websites

EEBO – Early English Books Online: http://eebo.chadwyck.com

Images of England – Number 304504 – White Hart Inn, Cloth Market, Newcastle upon Tyne: www.imagesofengland.org.uk

Spinning the web – www.spinningtheweb.co.uk

Figures 4.1a – 4.1m: Distribution of trades over neighbourhoods.

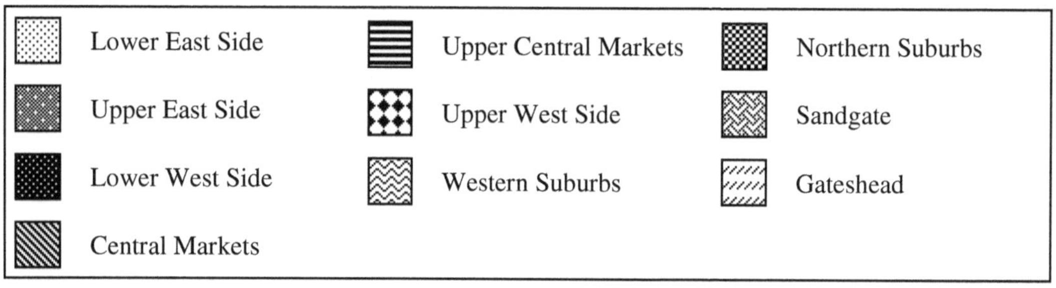

Figure 4.1a – Bakers and/or brewers

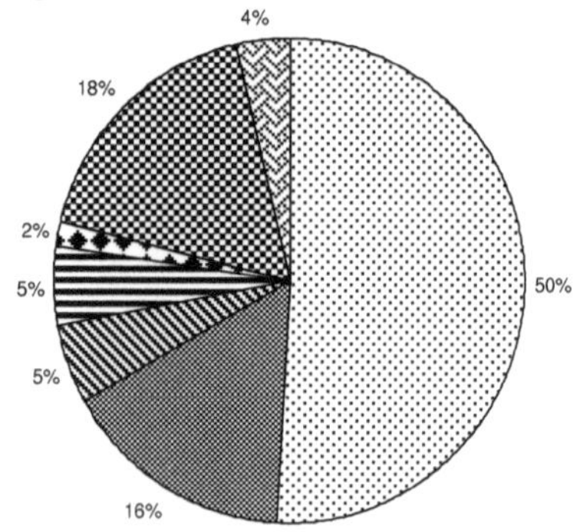

Figure 4.1b – Butchers

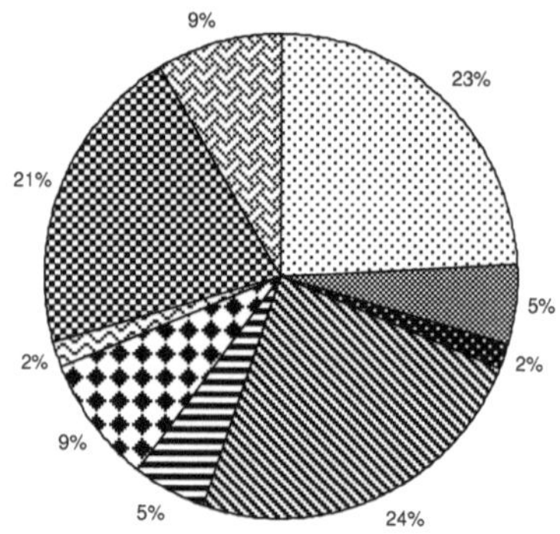

Figure 4.1c – Cordwainers

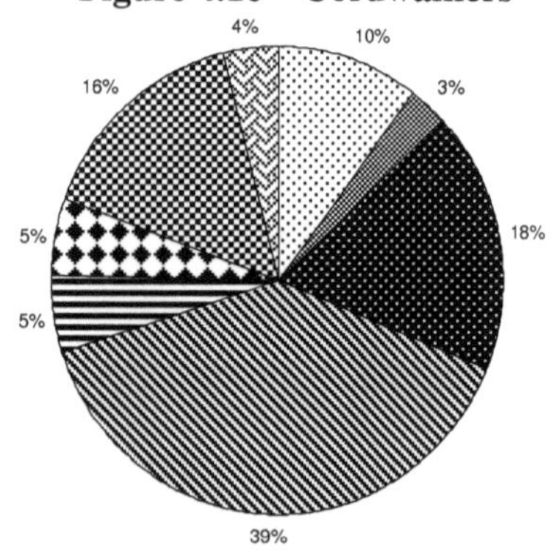

Figure 4.1d – Keelmen

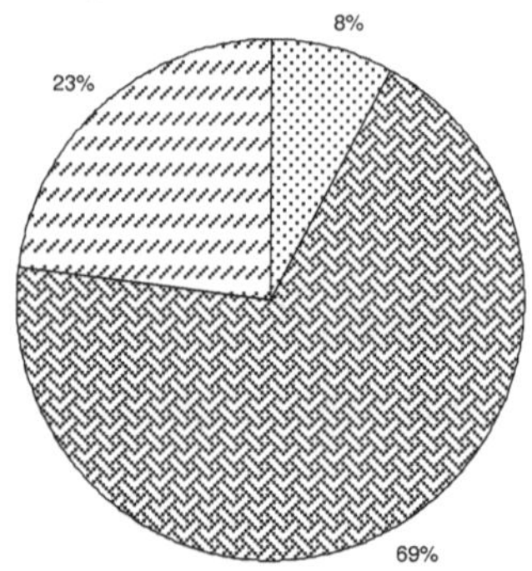

Figure 4.1e – Mariners

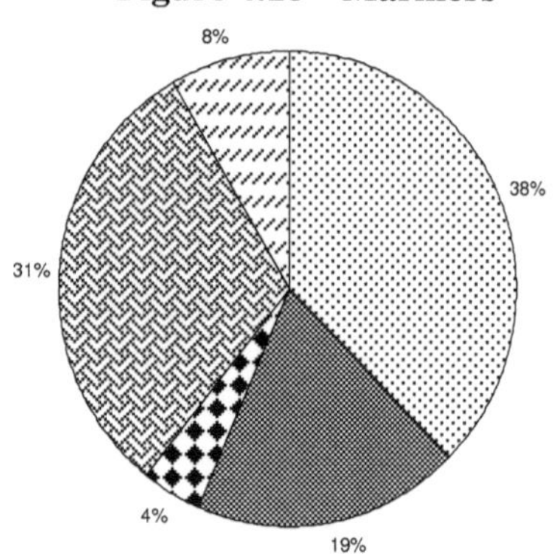

Figure 4.1f – Master Mariners

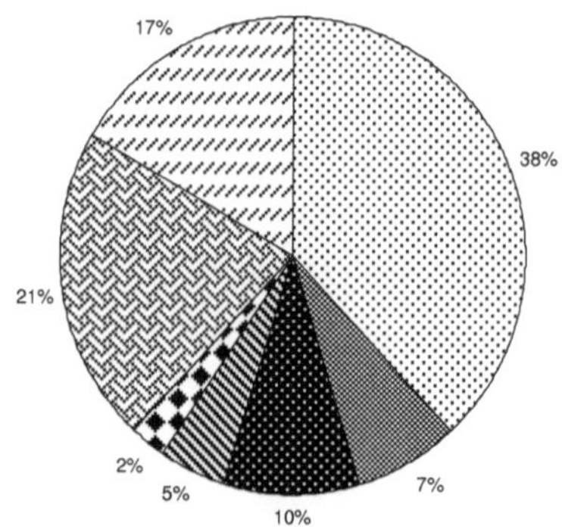

Figure 4.1g – Millers

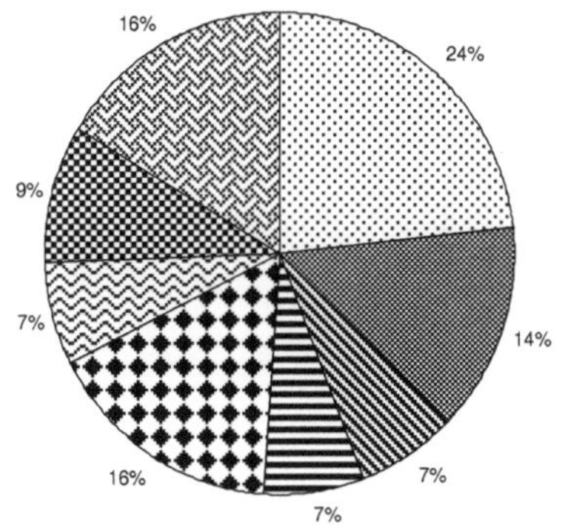

Figure 4.1h – Shipwrights

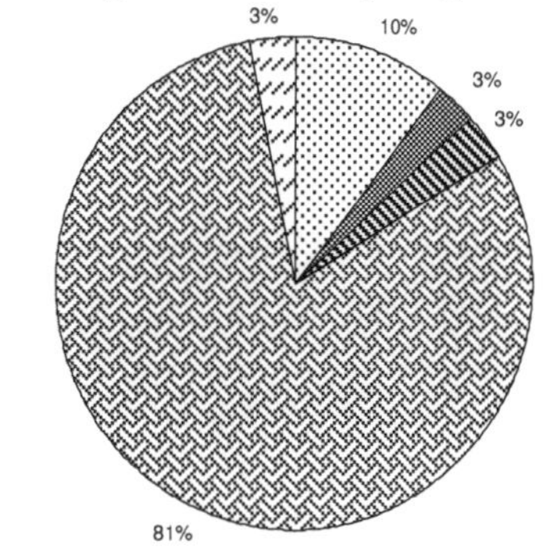

Figure 4.1i – Skinners and/or Glovers

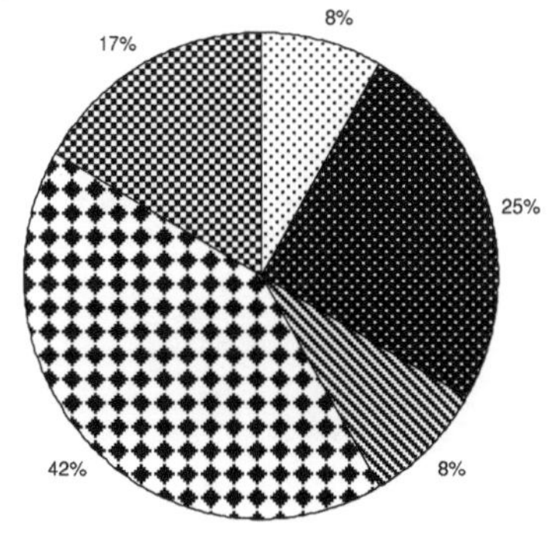

Figure 4.1j – Smiths

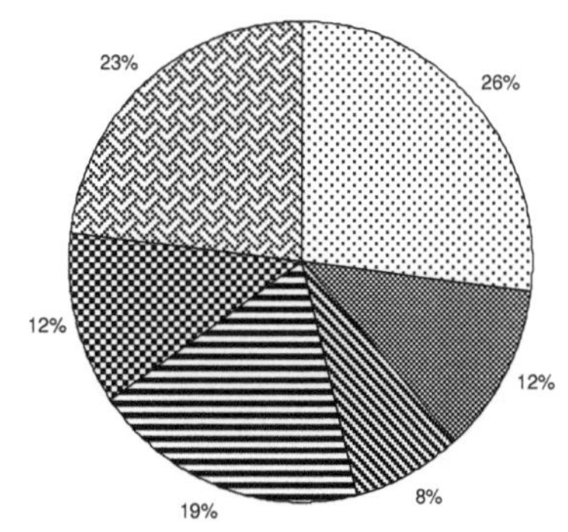

Figure 4.1k – Tailors

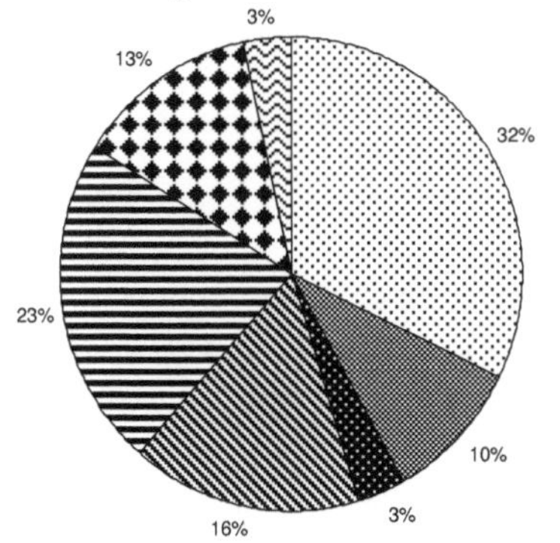

Figure 4.1l – Tanners

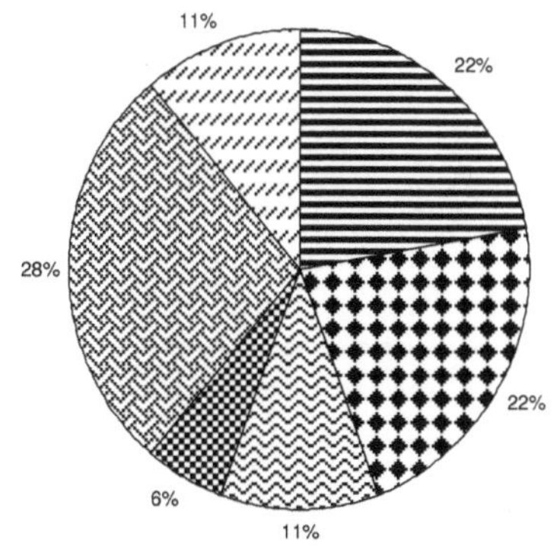

Figure 4.1m – Weavers

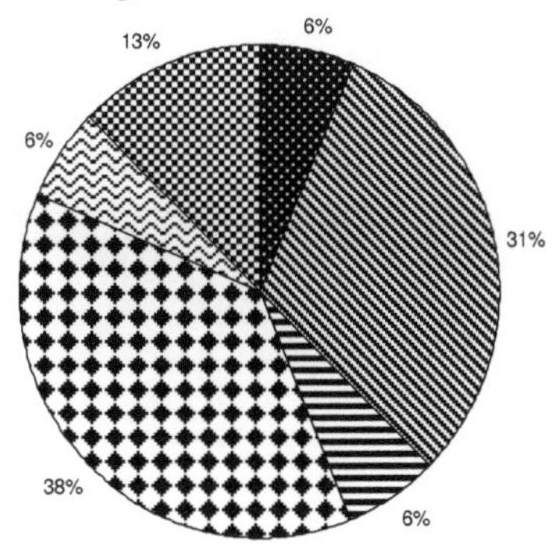

Figures 4.2a – 4.2j: Distribution of trades within neighbourhoods.

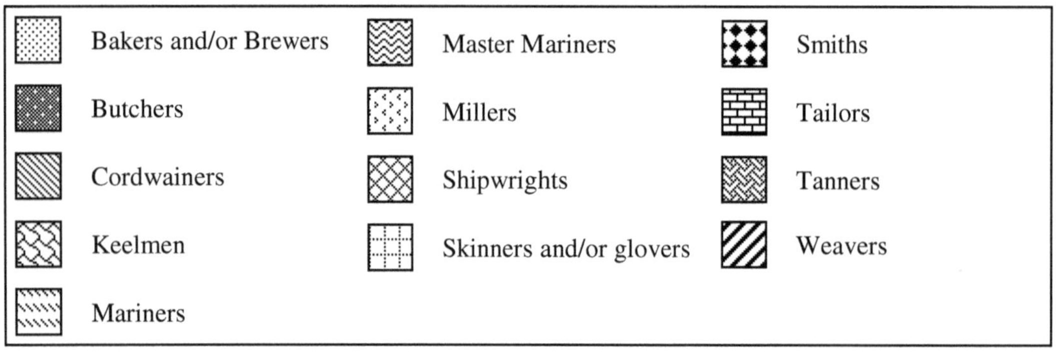

Figure 4.2a – Lower East Side

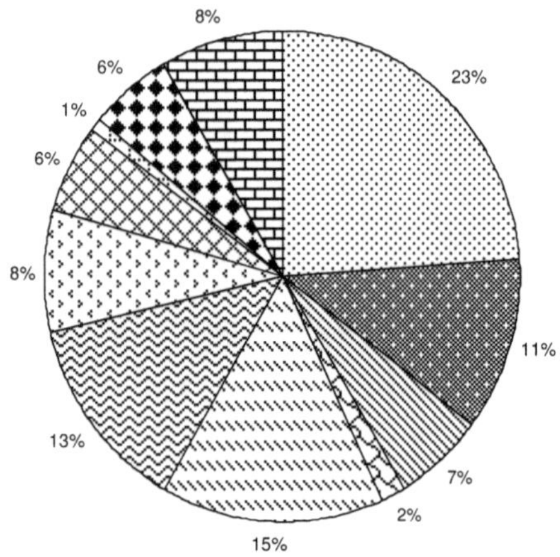

Figure 4.2b – Upper East Side

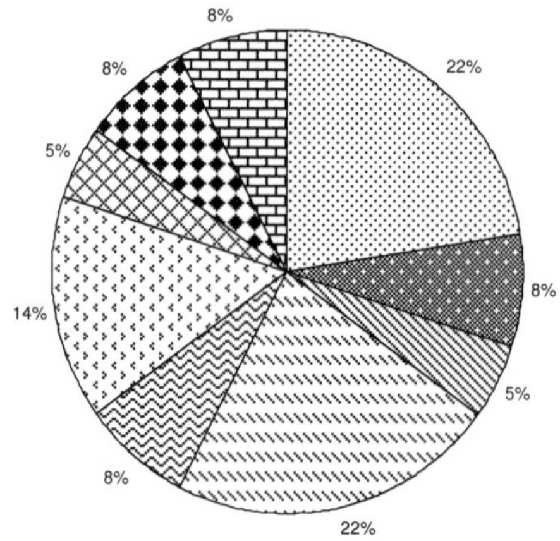

Figure 4.2c – Lower West Side

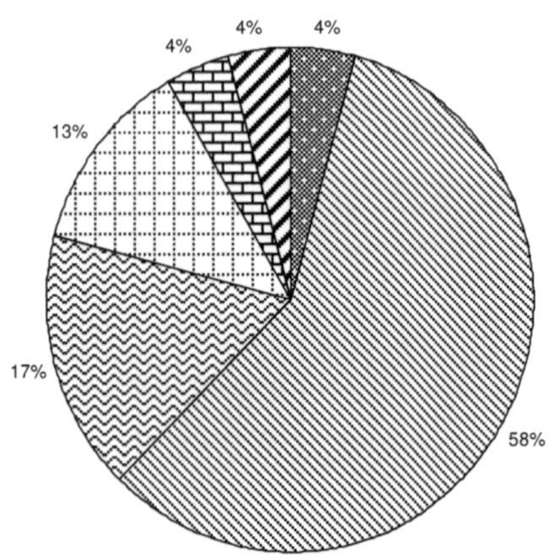

Figure 4.2d – Central Markets

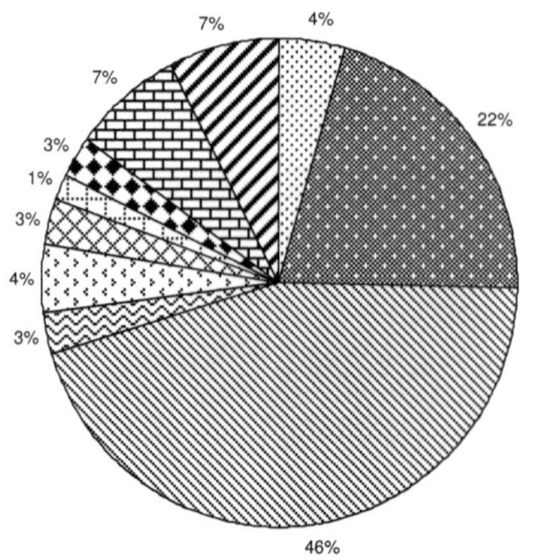

Figure 4.2e – Upper Central Markets

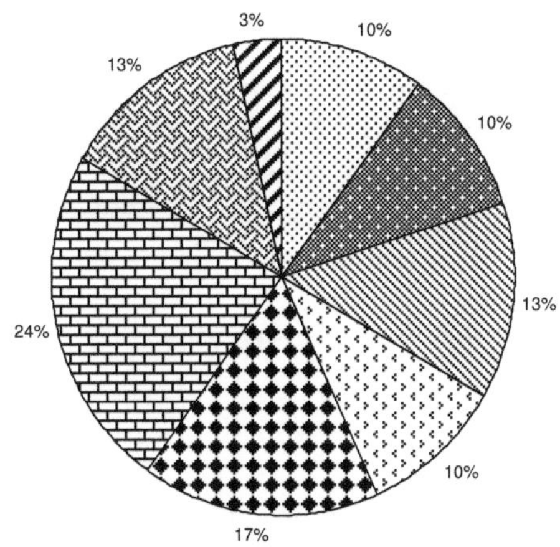

Figure 4.2f – Upper West Side

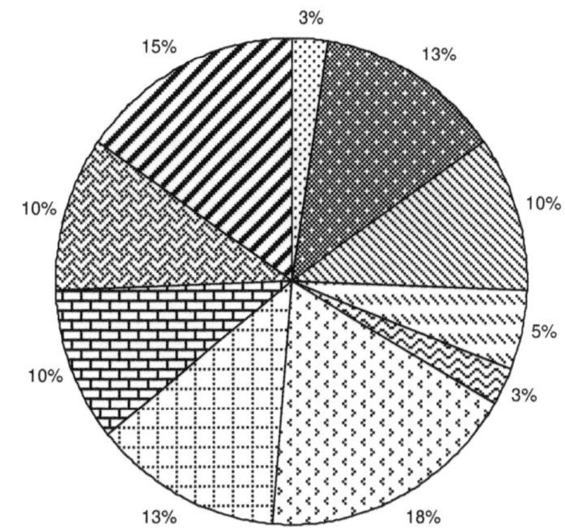

Figure 4.2g – Western Suburbs

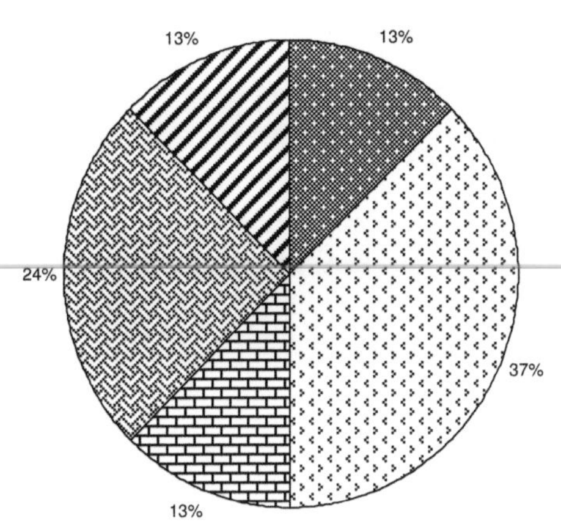

Figure 4.2h – Northern Suburbs

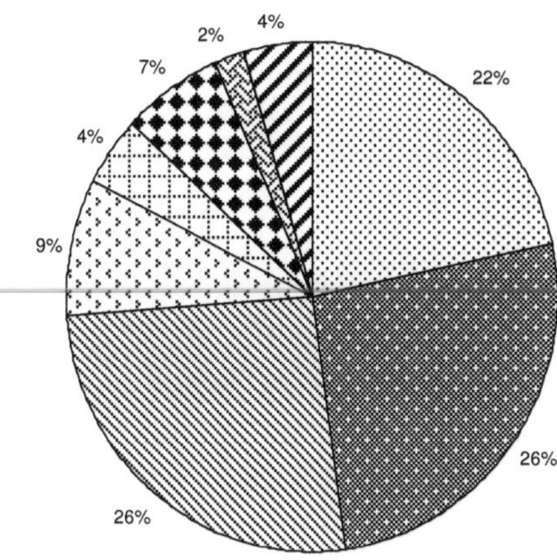

Figure 4.2i – Sandgate

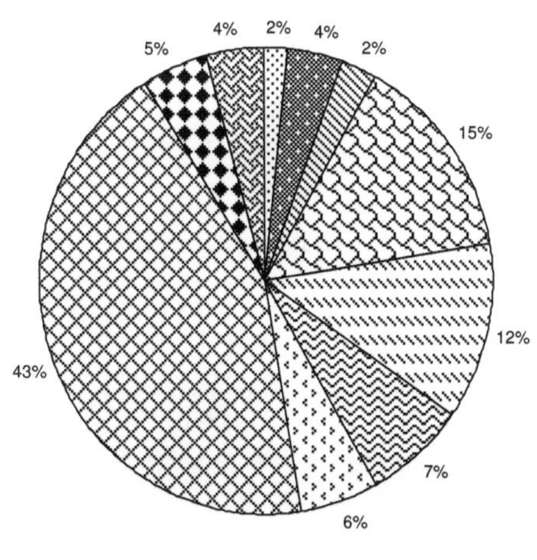

Figure 4.2j – Gateshead

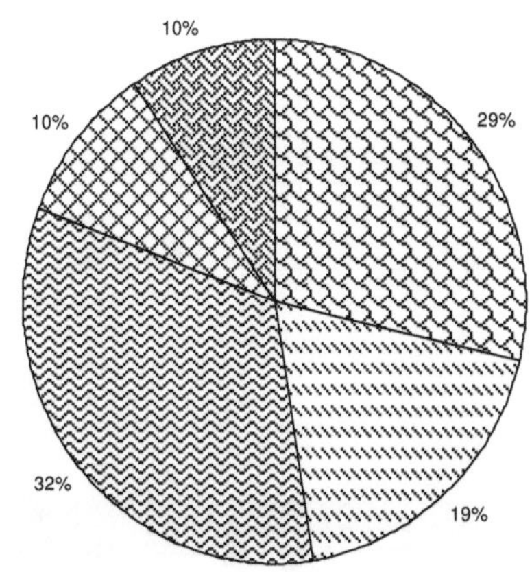

Figures 4.3a: Distribution of properties over trades (1549-1642)
Sample: 520 properties

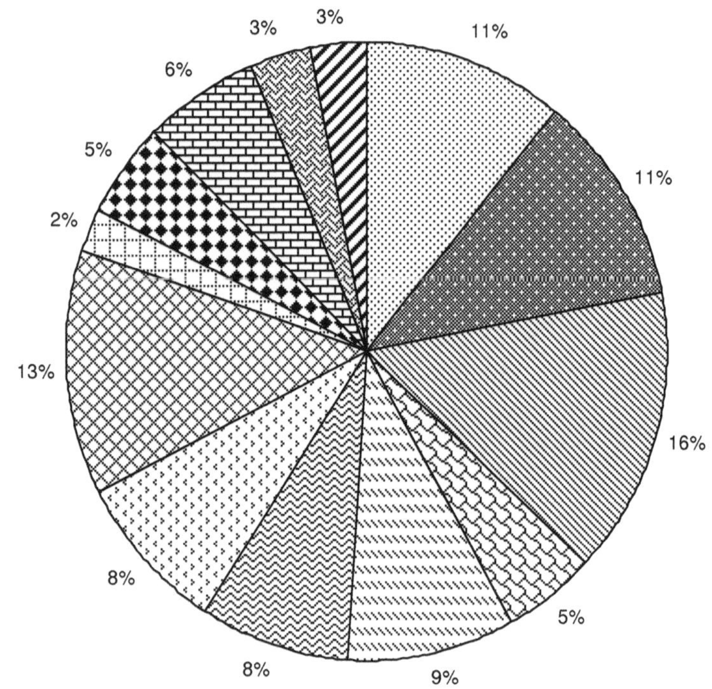

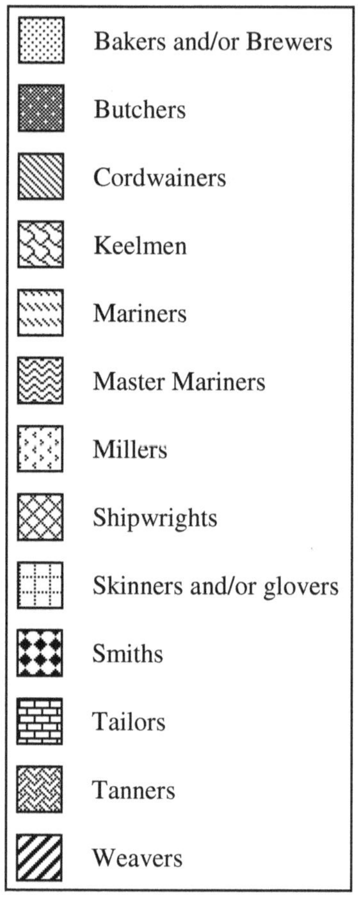

Figures 4.3b: Distribution of properties over neighbourhoods (1549-1642)
Sample: 520 properties

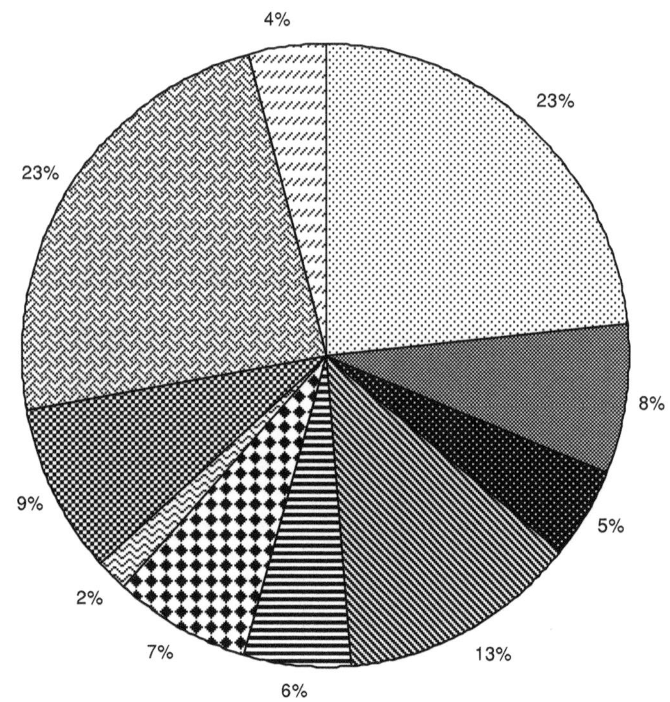

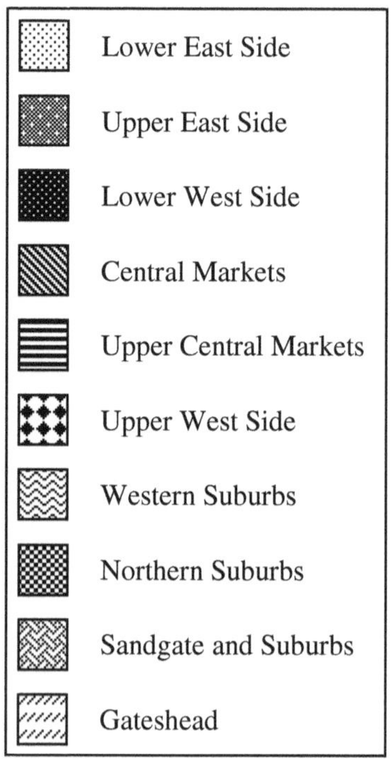

Chapter 4 Figures 4.4a – 4.4e: Distribution of trades over neighbourhoods within Langton's sub-groups (B1/B2/C1/C3/C4)

Figure 4.4a (Langton B1 – Includes keelmen from probate data)

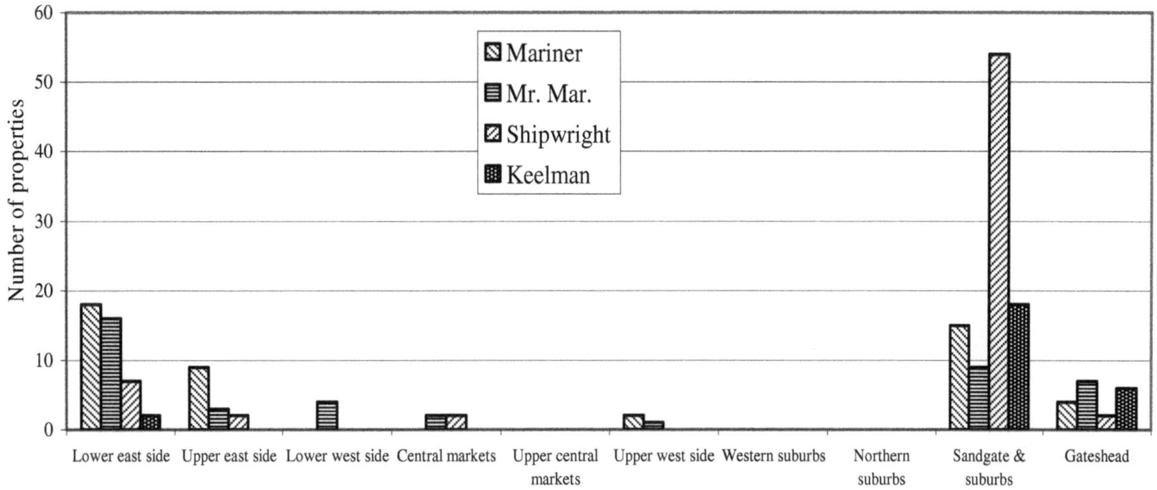

Figure 4.4b (Langton B2)

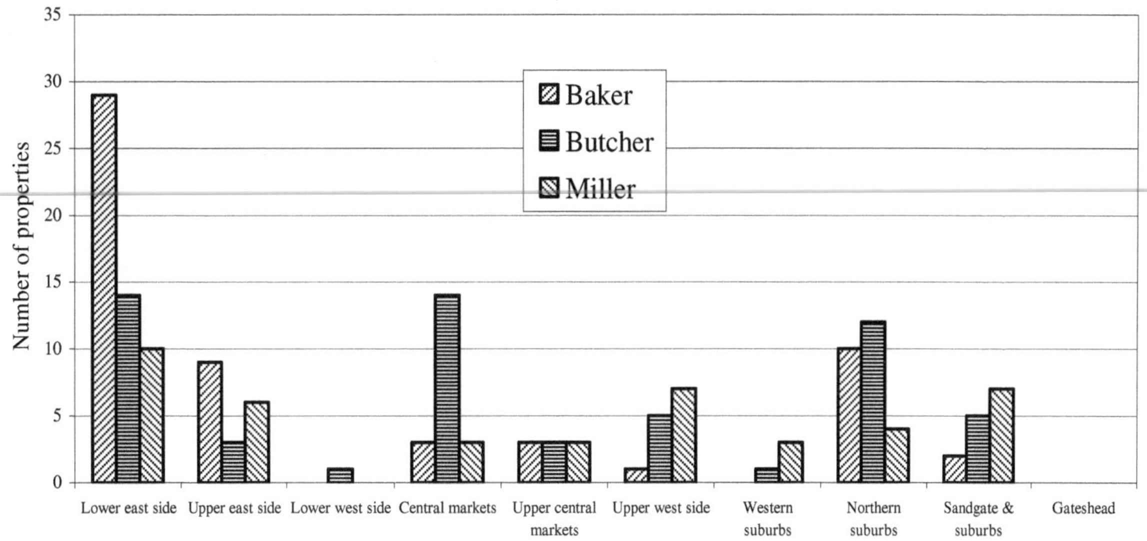

Figure 4.4c (Langton C1 – Excludes all other metal trades)

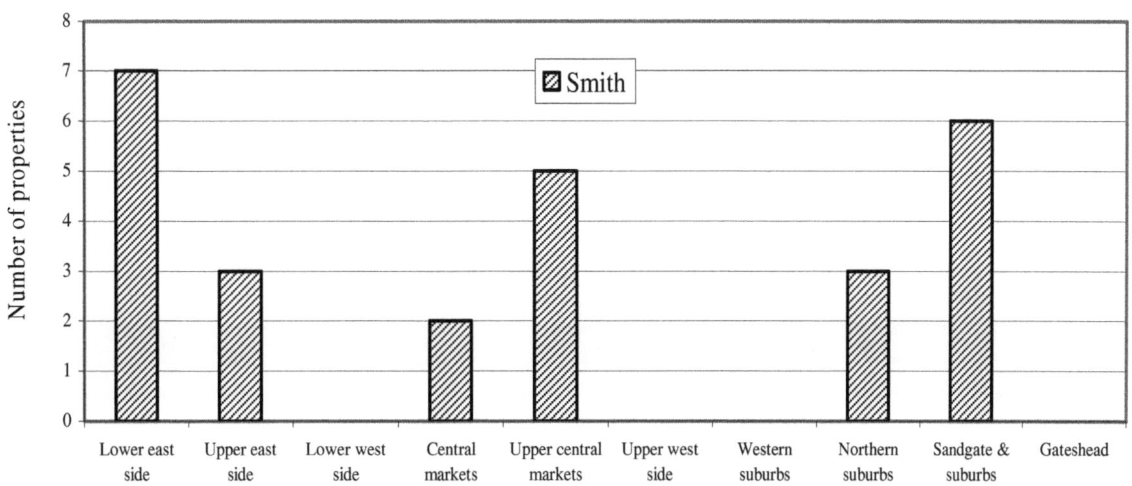

Figure 4.4d (Langton C3)

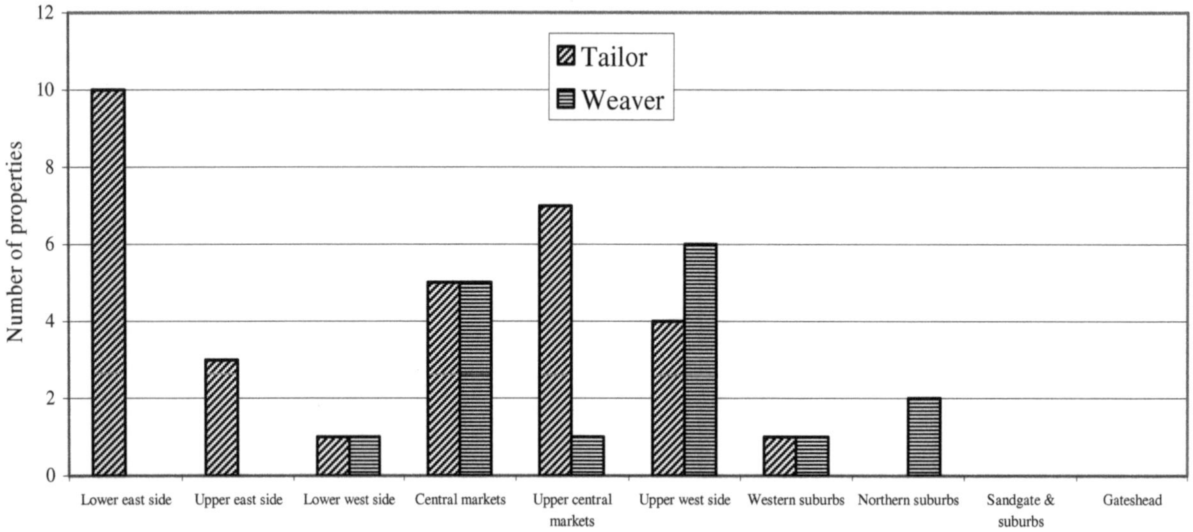

Figure 4.4e (Langton C4)

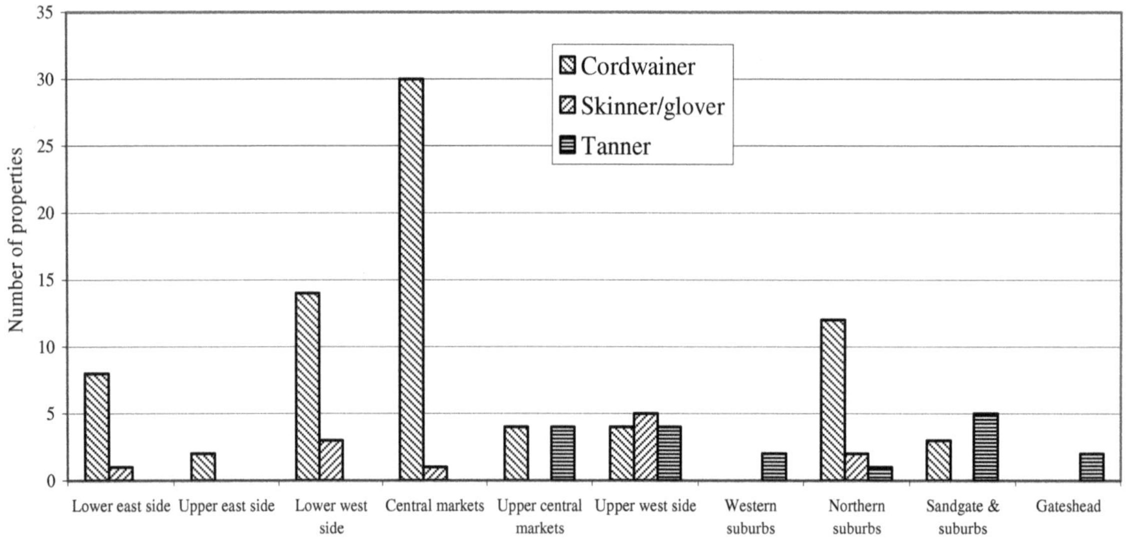

Map	4.1
Trade	Bakers and/or Brewers
Property dates	1549-1639

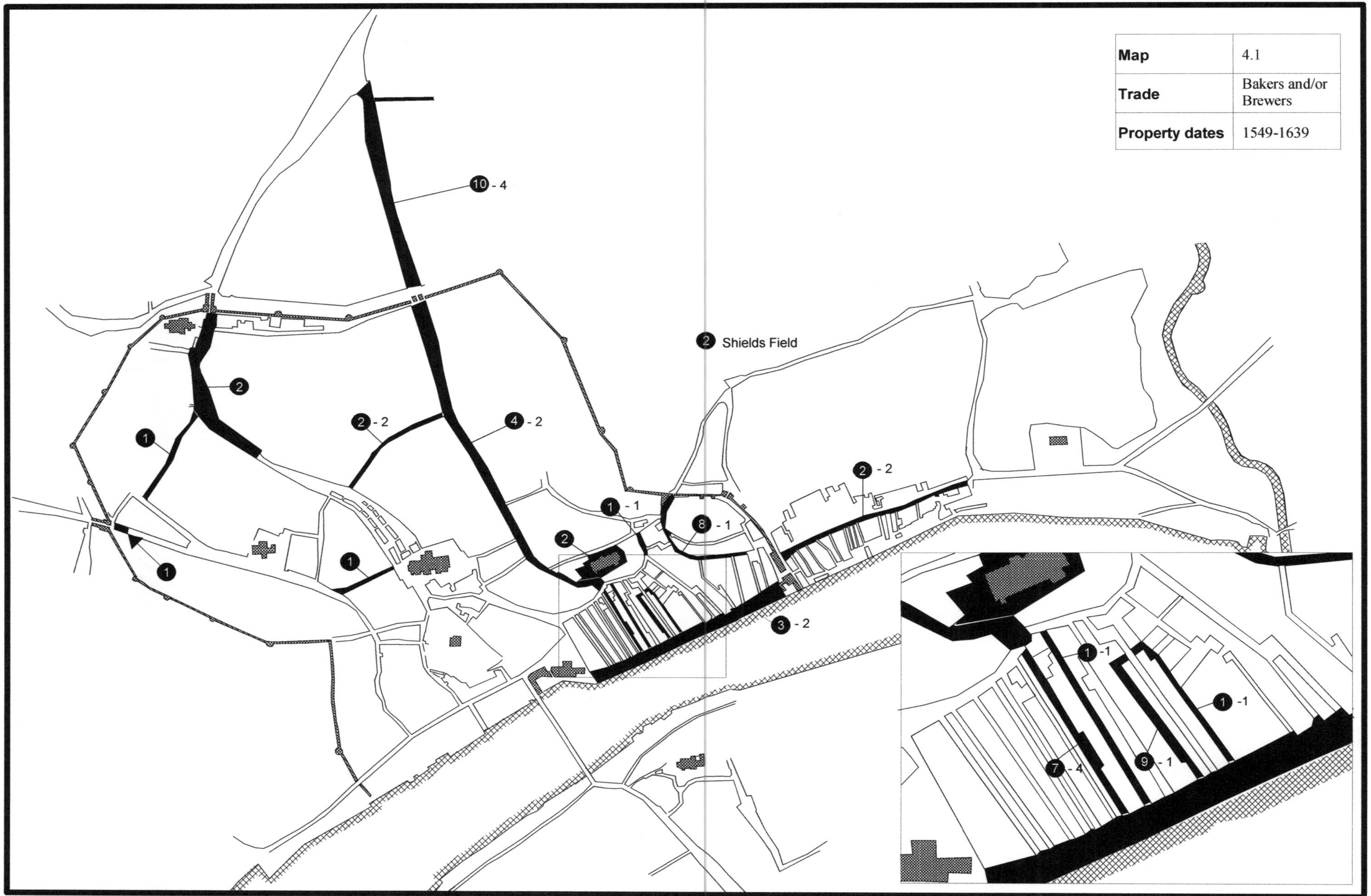

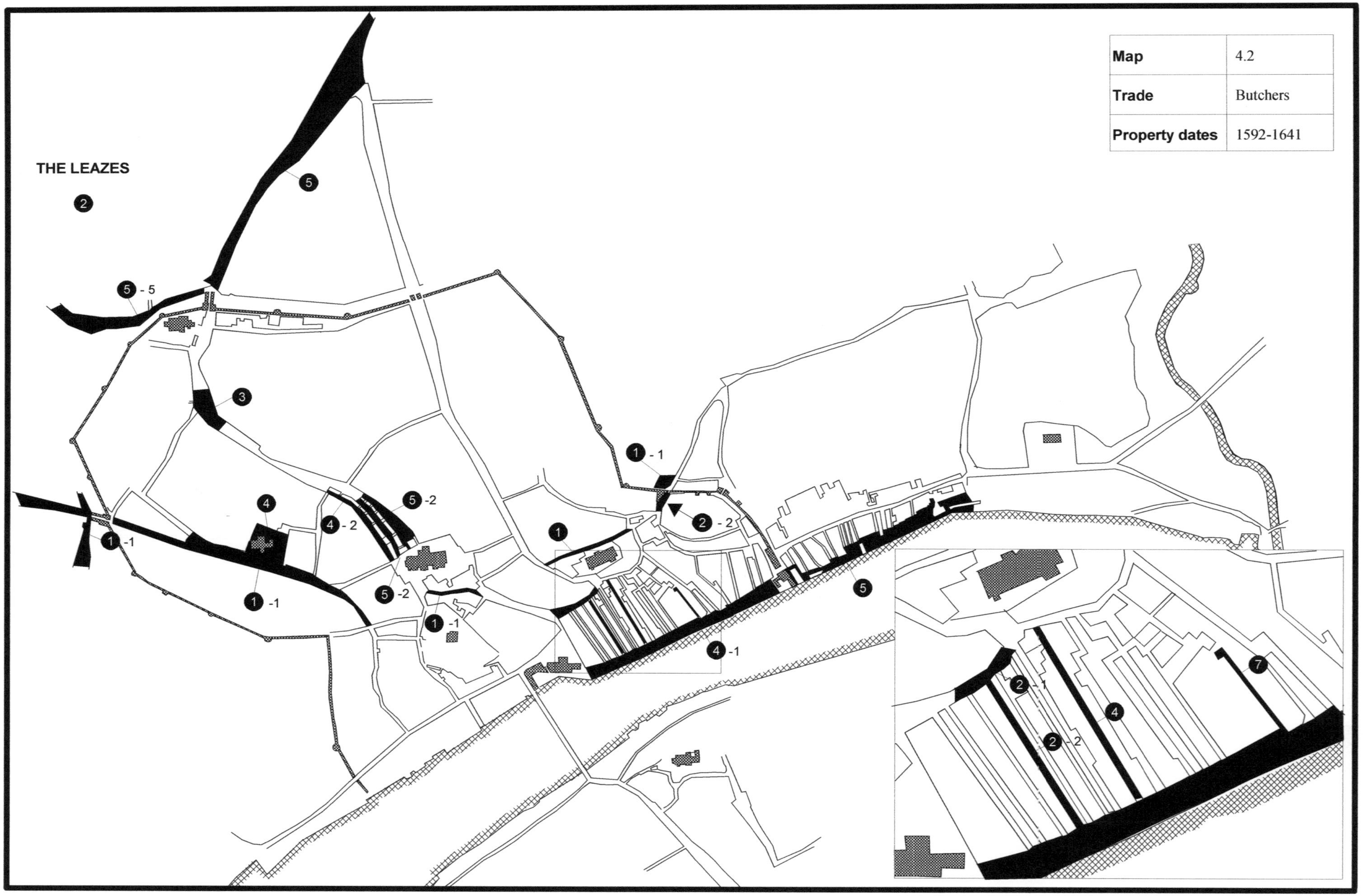
Map 4.2
Trade Butchers
Property dates 1592-1641
THE LEAZES
2
5
5 - 5
3
1 - 1
4
4 - 2
5 -2
5 -2
1 -1
1 -1
1
1 - 1
2 - 2
5
4 -1
7
4
2 -1
2 -2

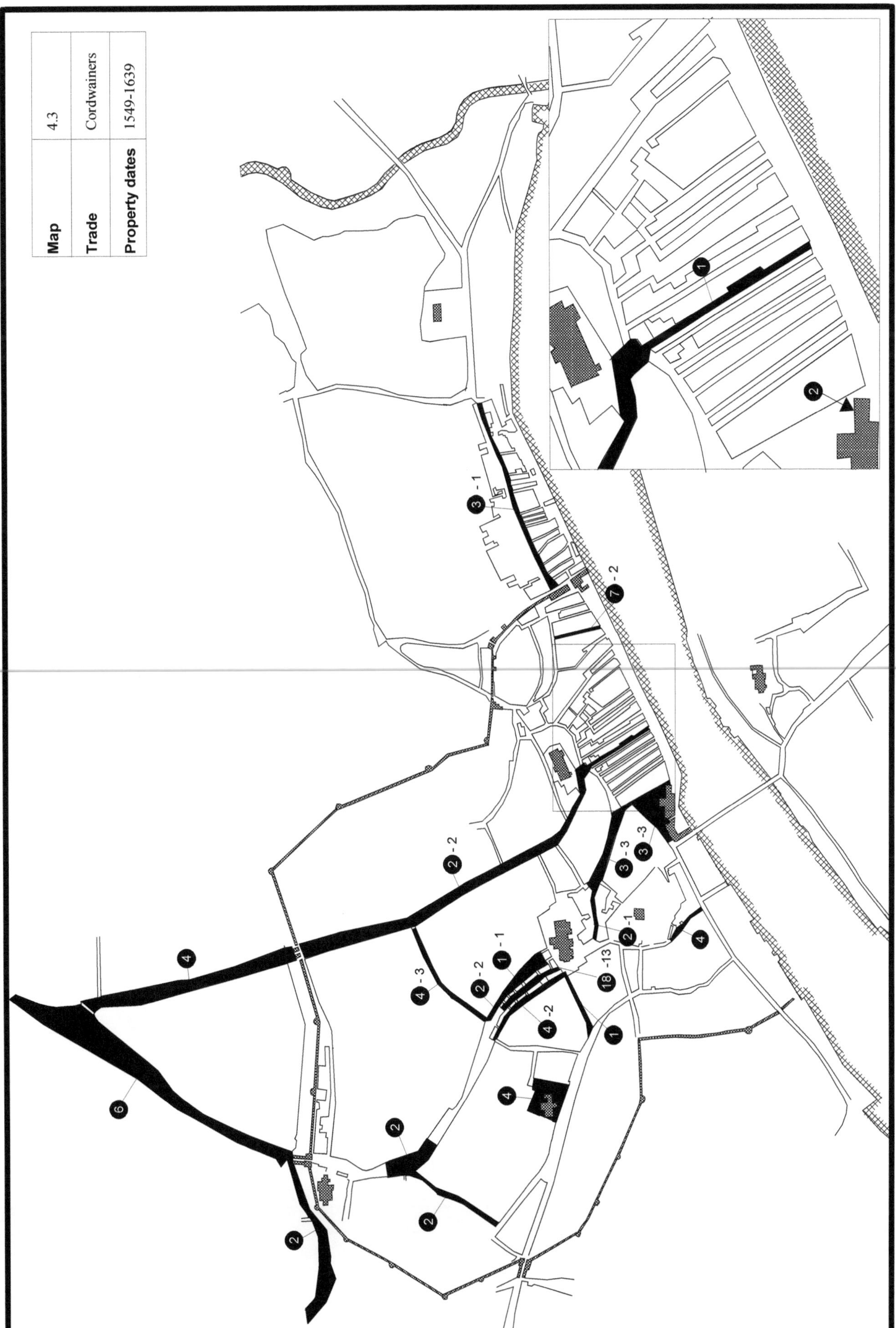
Map 4.3
Trade Cordwainers
Property dates 1549-1639

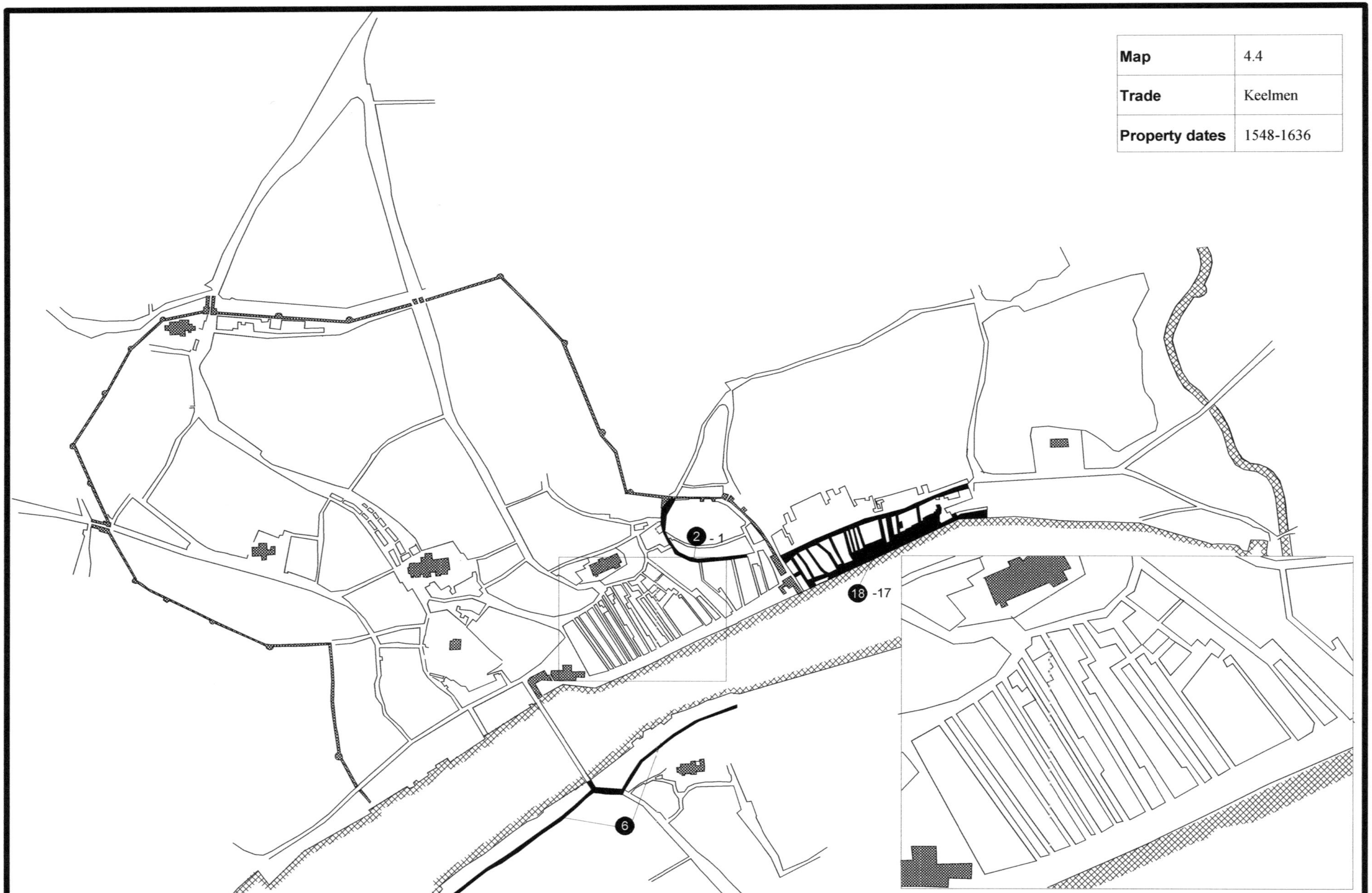

Map	4.4
Trade	Keelmen
Property dates	1548-1636

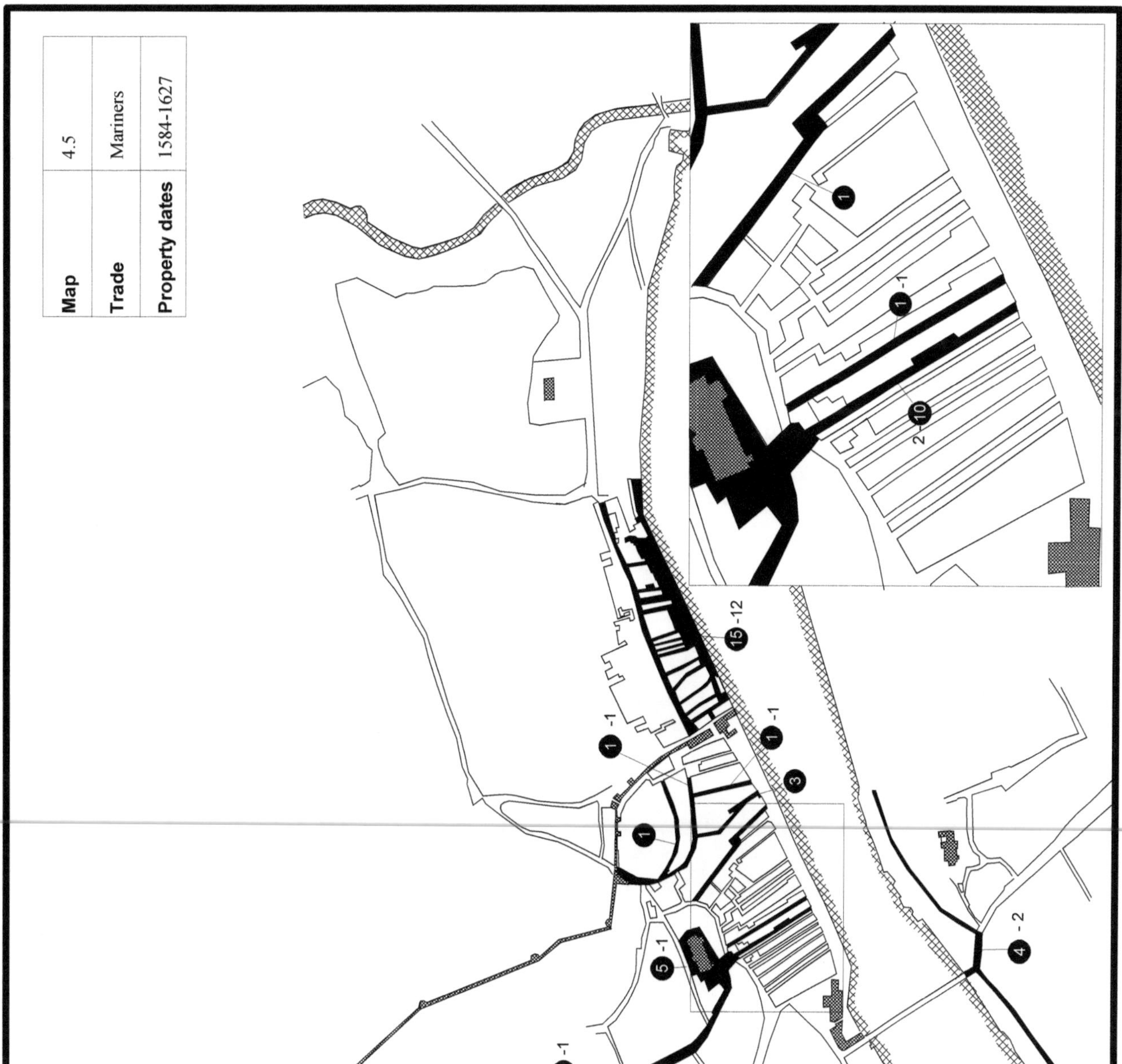
Map 4.5
Trade Mariners
Property dates 1584-1627
1
1 -1
1 -1
1 -1
2
2 10
3
4 -1
4 -2
5 -1
15 -12

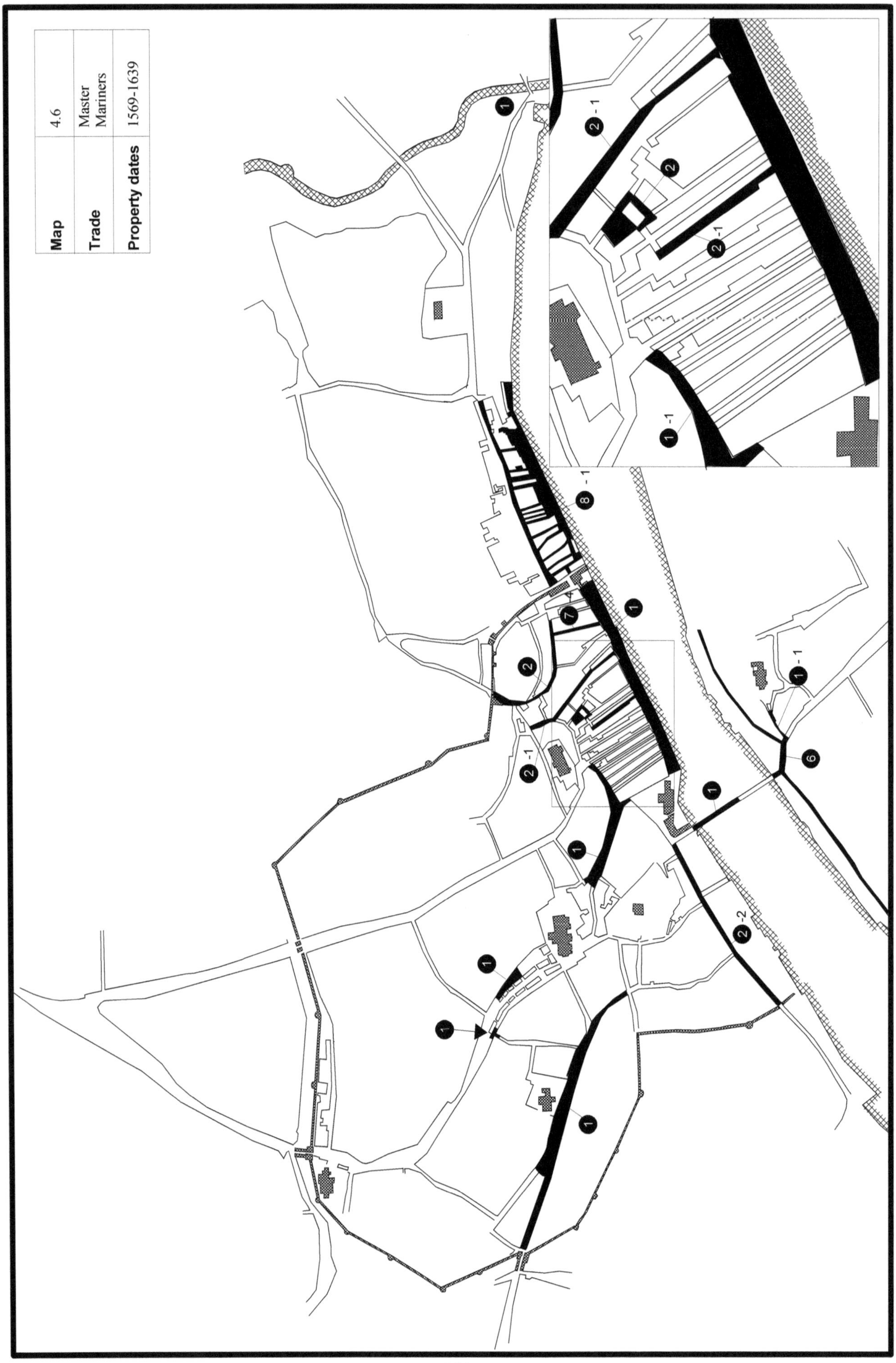
Map
4.6
Trade
Master Mariners
Property dates
1569-1639

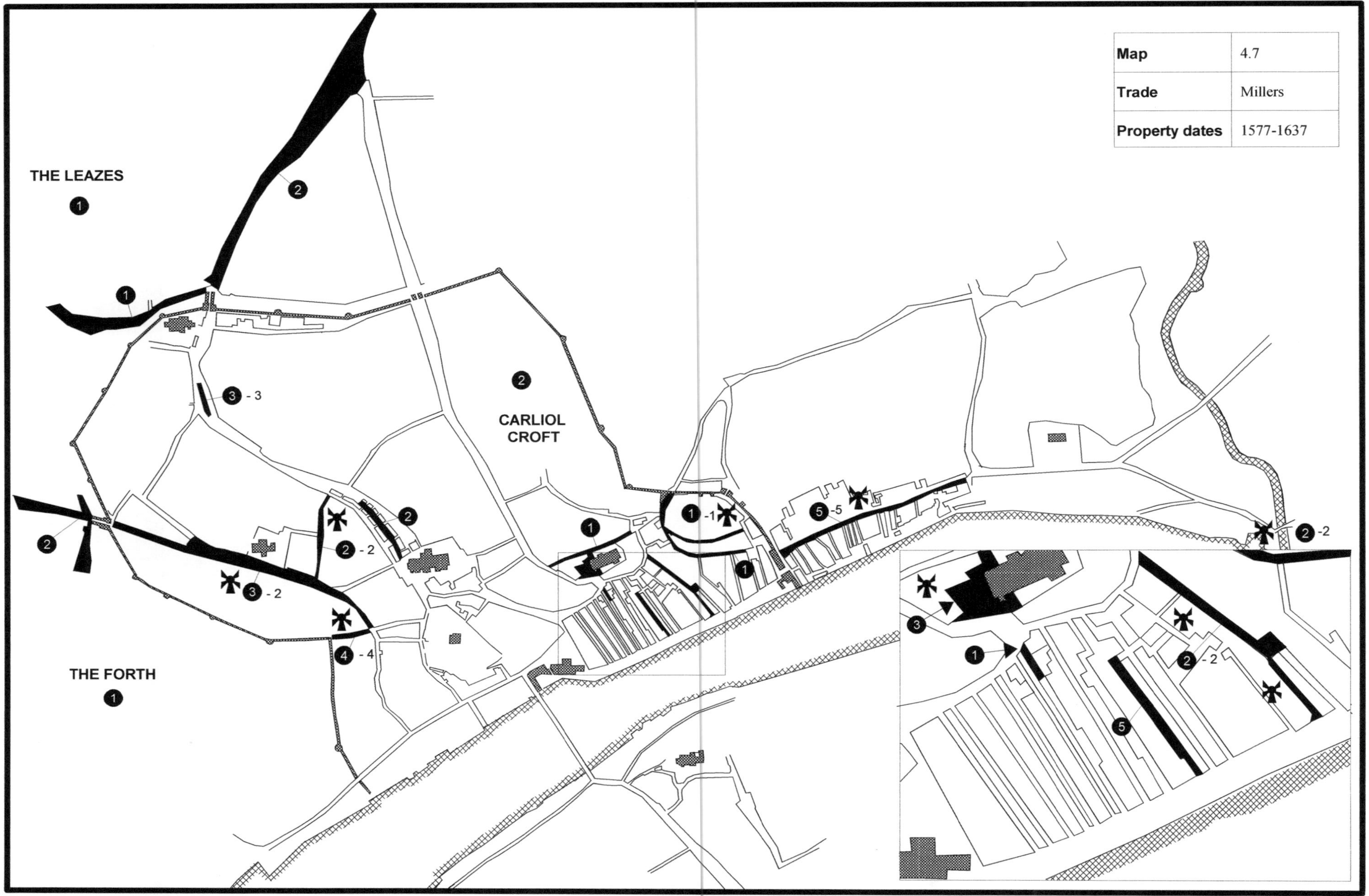
Map 4.7
Trade Millers
Property dates 1577-1637
THE LEAZES
CARLIOL
CROFT
THE FORTH

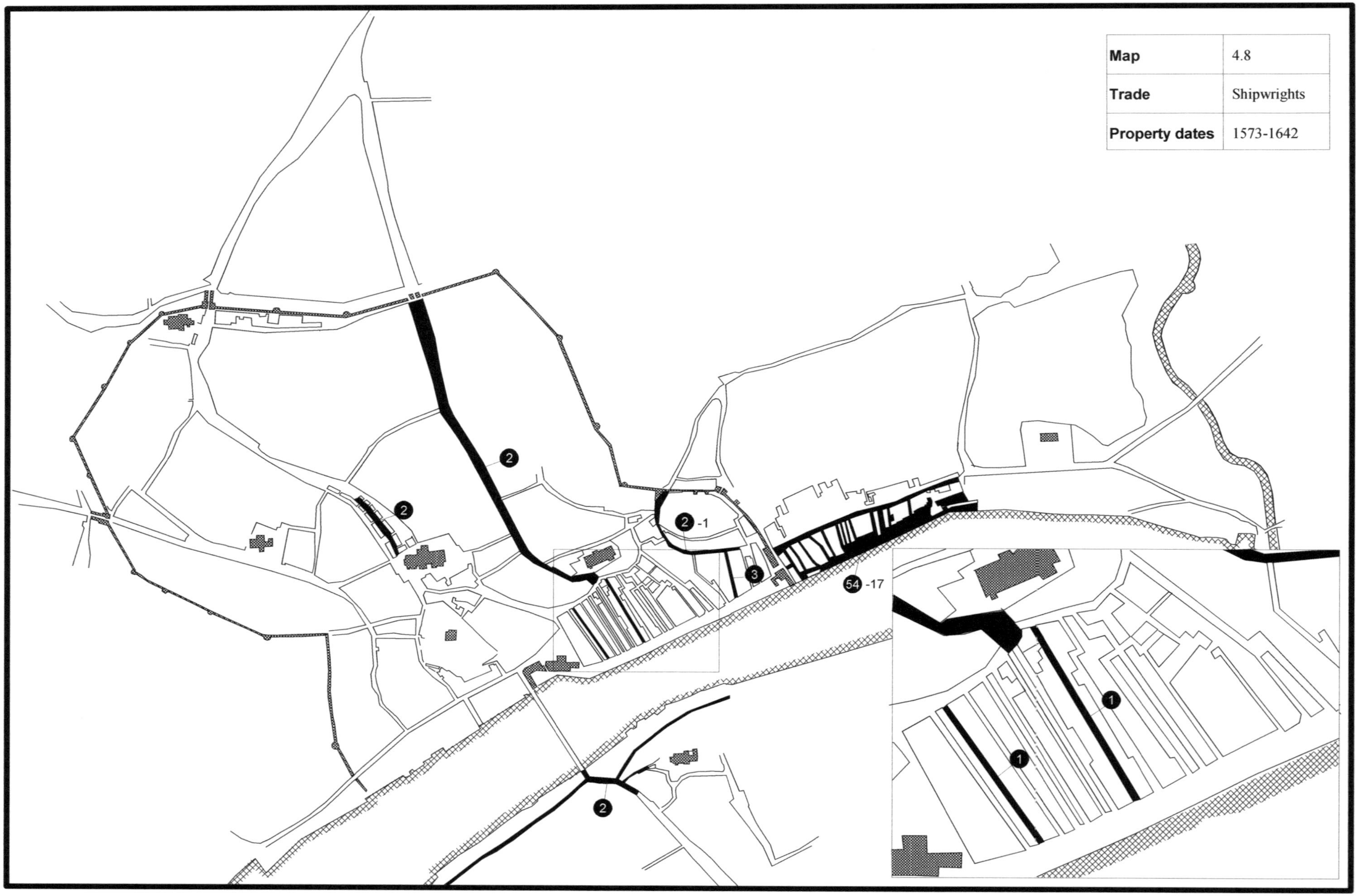
Map 4.8
Trade Shipwrights
Property dates 1573-1642
2
2
2 -1
3
54 -17
2
1
1

Map	4.9
Trade	Skinners and/or glovers
Property dates	1570-1634

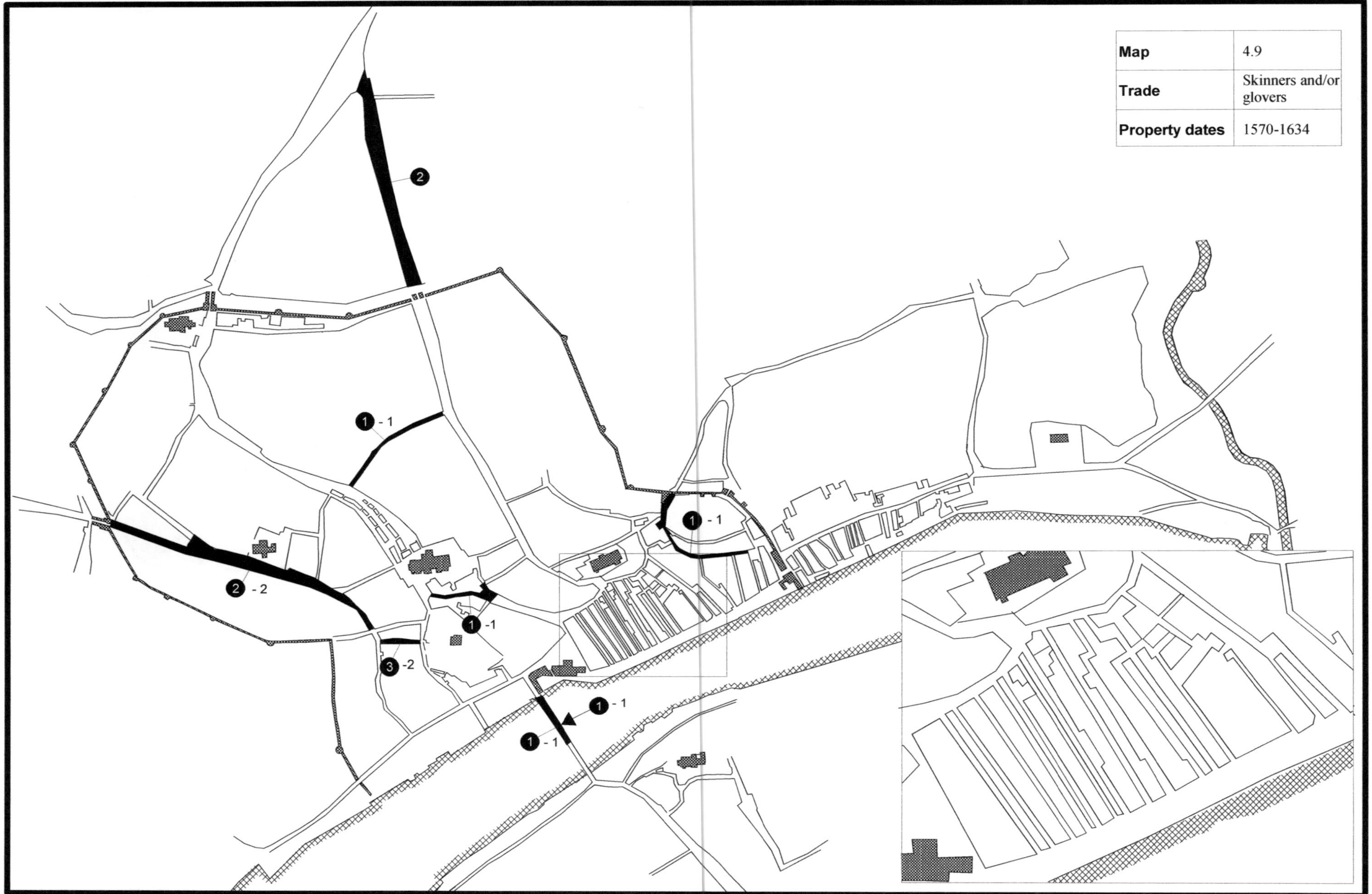

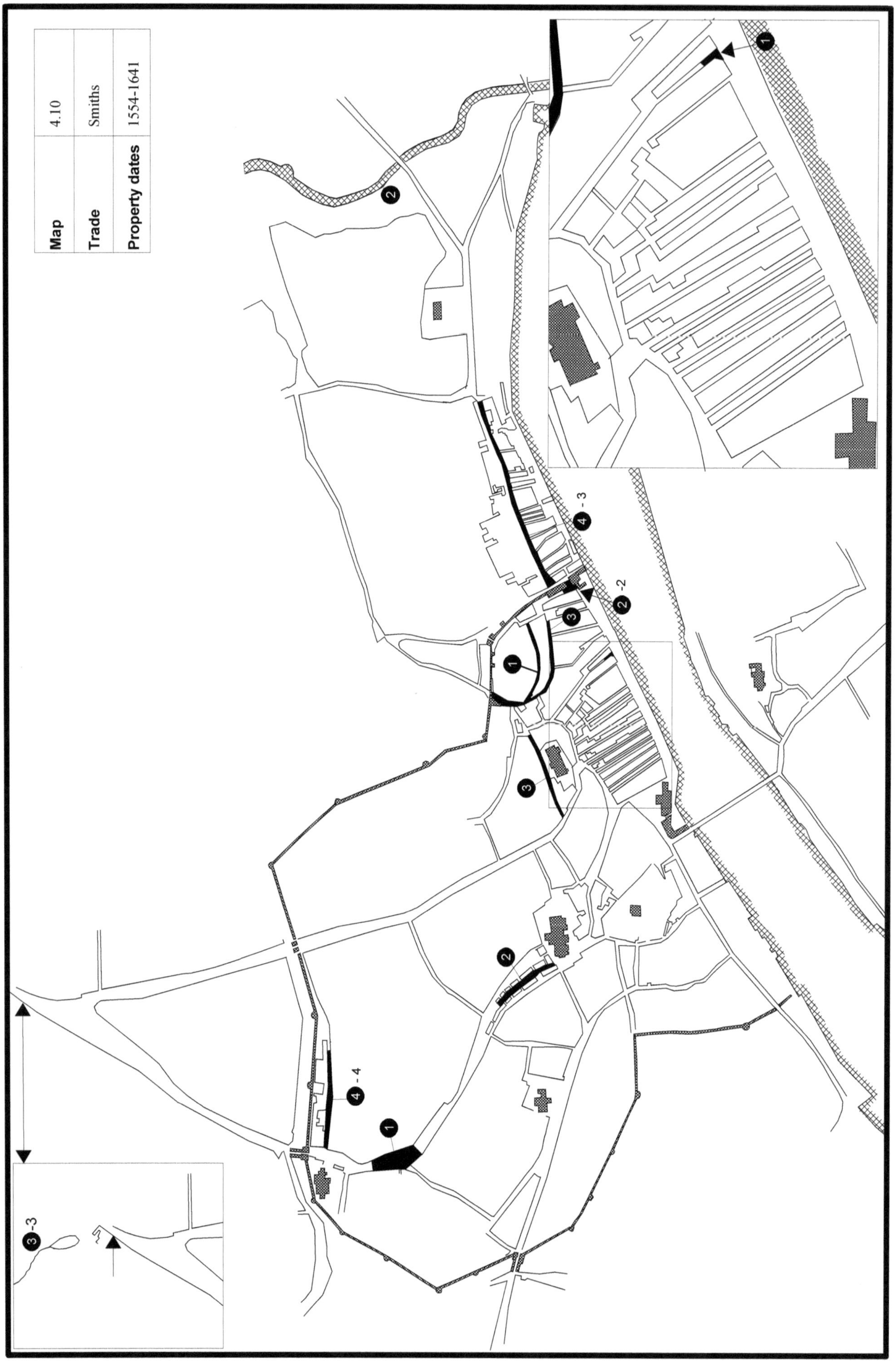
Map
4.10
Trade
Smiths
Property dates
1554-1641

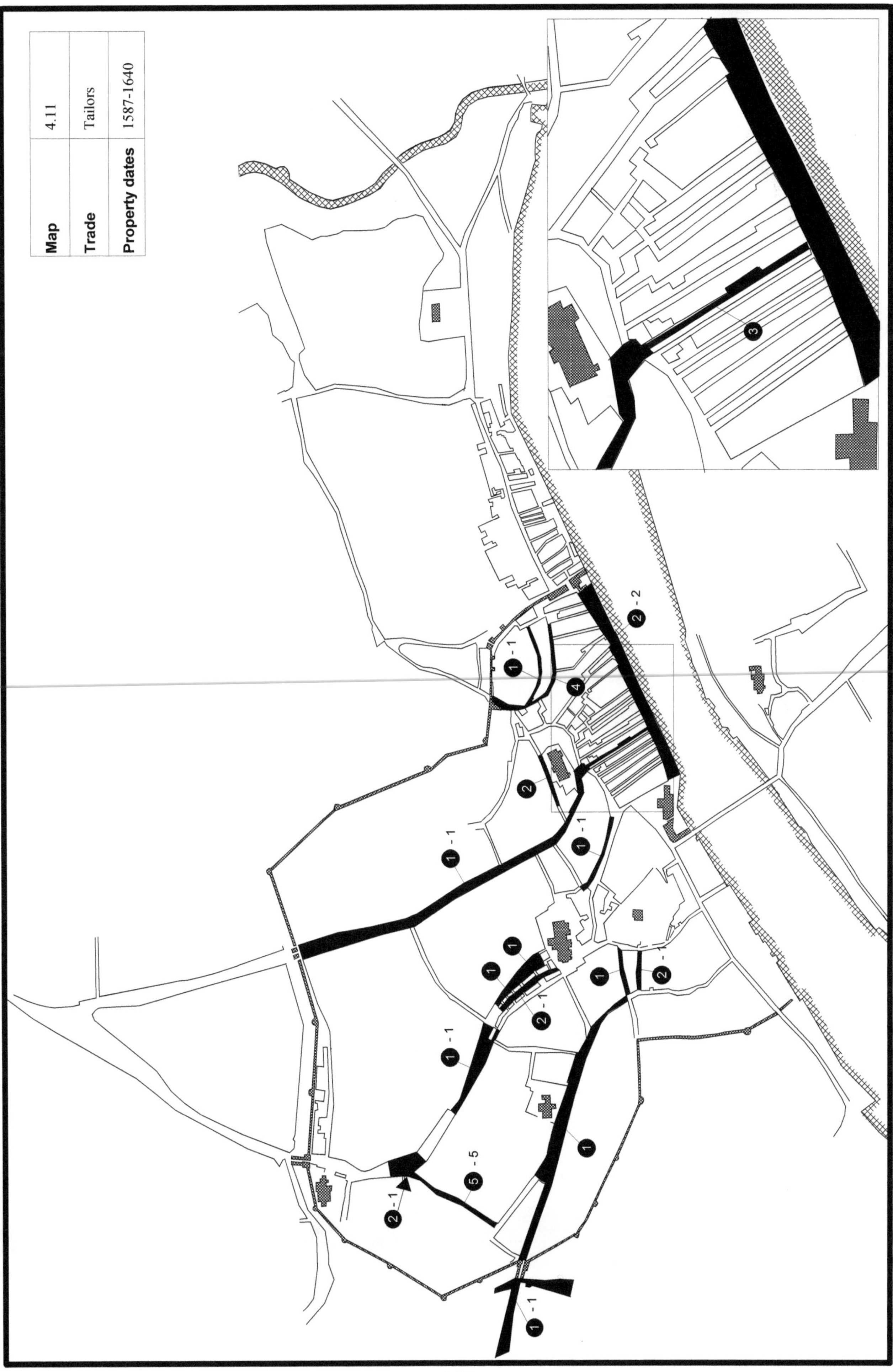
Map
4.11
Trade
Tailors
Property dates
1587-1640

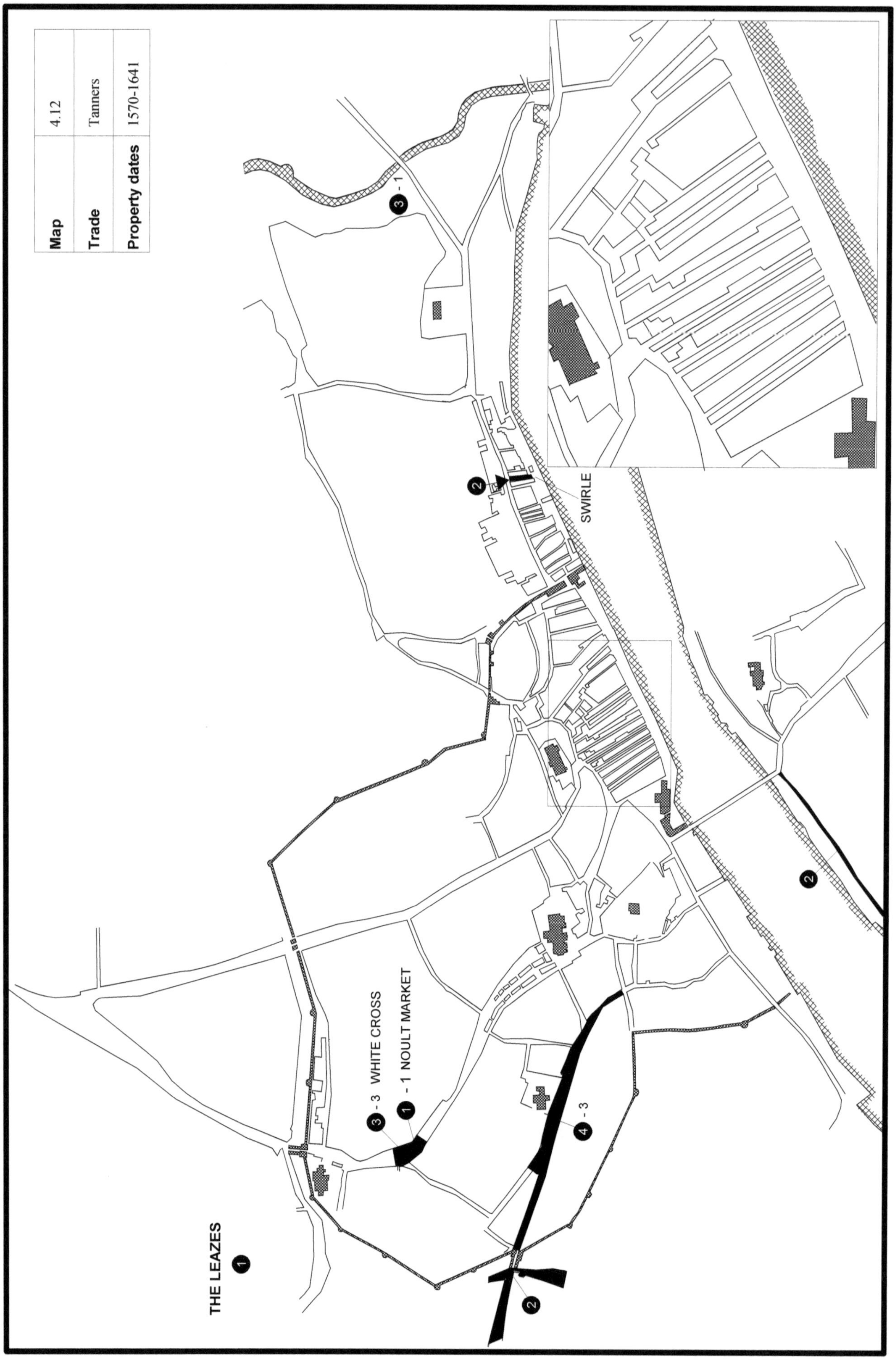
Map 4.12
Trade Tanners
Property dates 1570-1641
THE LEAZES
1
3 - 3 WHITE CROSS
1 - 1 NOULT MARKET
4 - 3
2
SWIRLE
2
3 - 1
2

Map	4.13
Trade	Weavers
Property dates	1577-1641

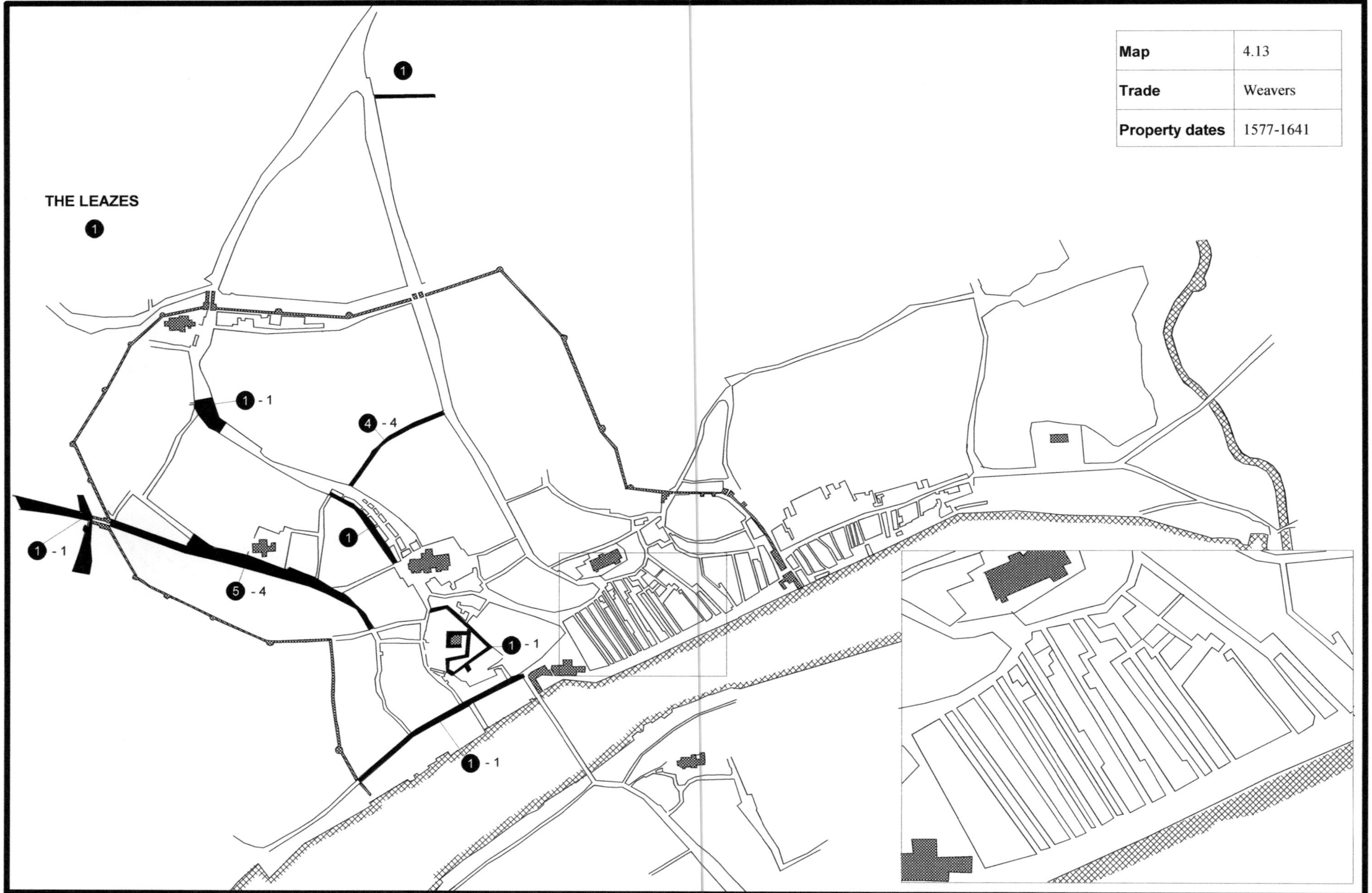

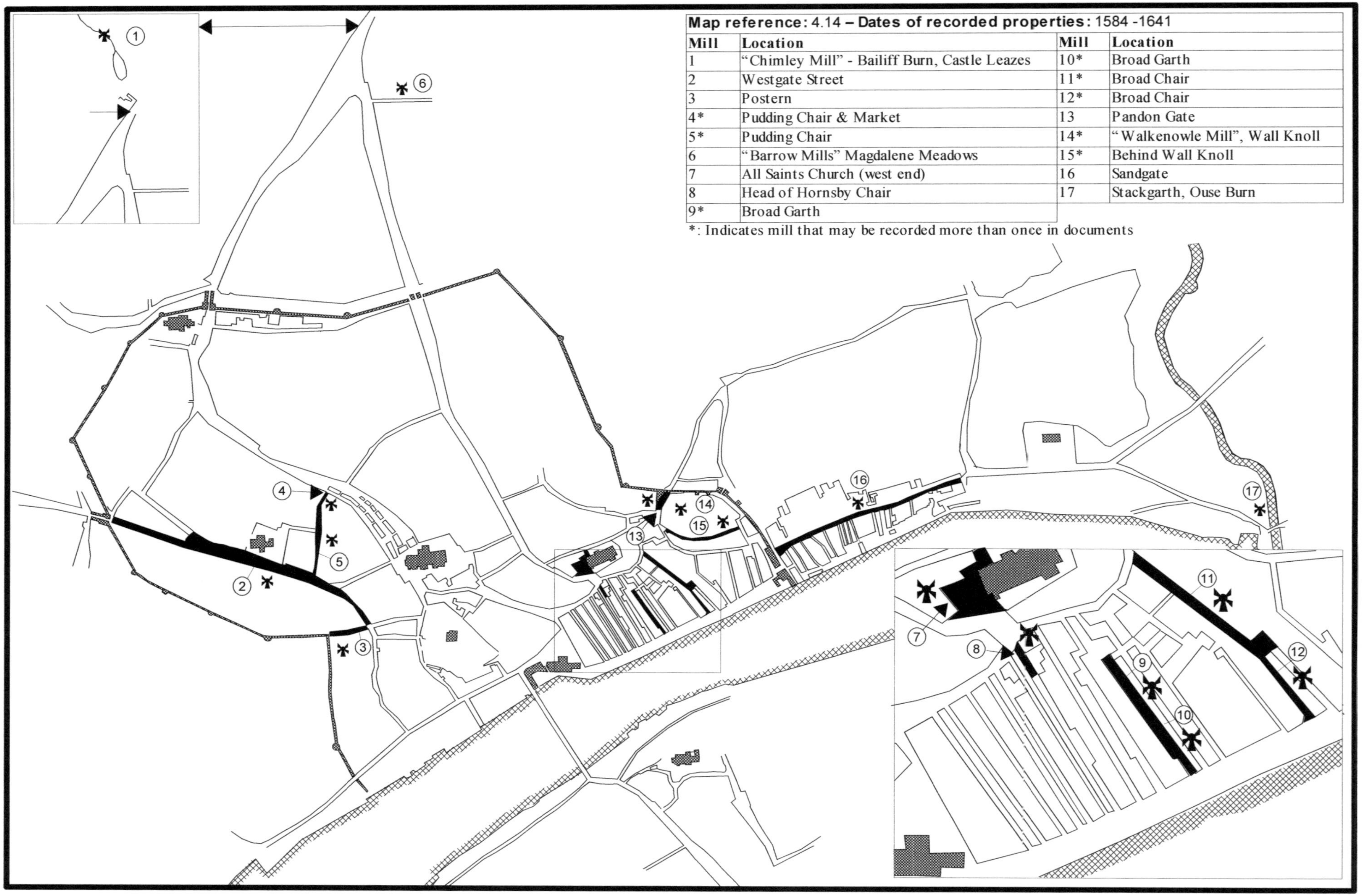

Map reference: 4.14 – Dates of recorded properties: 1584 -1641

Mill	Location	Mill	Location
1	"Chimley Mill" - Bailiff Burn, Castle Leazes	10*	Broad Garth
2	Westgate Street	11*	Broad Chair
3	Postern	12*	Broad Chair
4*	Pudding Chair & Market	13	Pandon Gate
5*	Pudding Chair	14*	"Walkenowle Mill", Wall Knoll
6	"Barrow Mills" Magdalene Meadows	15*	Behind Wall Knoll
7	All Saints Church (west end)	16	Sandgate
8	Head of Hornsby Chair	17	Stackgarth, Ouse Burn
9*	Broad Garth		

*: Indicates mill that may be recorded more than once in documents

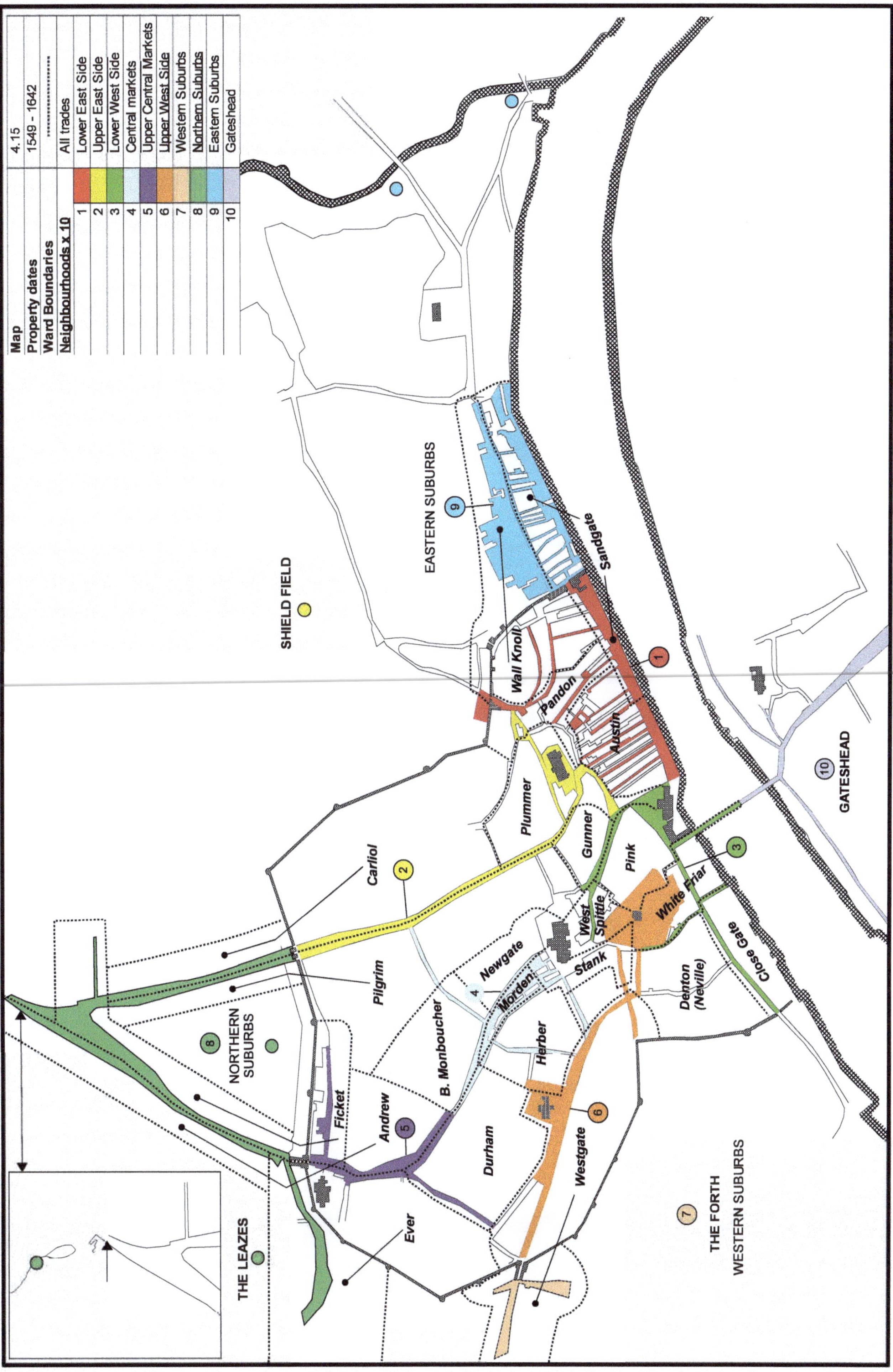

Map 4.15
Property dates 1549 - 1642
Ward Boundaries
Neighbourhoods x 10
All trades
1 Lower East Side
2 Upper East Side
3 Lower West Side
4 Central markets
5 Upper Central Markets
6 Upper West Side
7 Western Suburbs
8 Northern Suburbs
9 Eastern Suburbs
10 Gateshead
SHIELD FIELD
EASTERN SUBURBS
Sandgate
Wall Knoll
Pandon
Austin
Plummer
Gunner
Pink
White Friar
West Spittle
Stank
Newgate
Morden
Carliol
Pilgrim
B. Monboucher
Herber
Denton (Neville)
Close Gate
NORTHERN SUBURBS
Ficket
Andrew
Durham
Westgate
Ever
THE LEAZES
THE FORTH WESTERN SUBURBS
GATESHEAD

NOTE

A larger version of the map on the previous page is available for download at:
www.barpublishing.com/additional-downloads.html

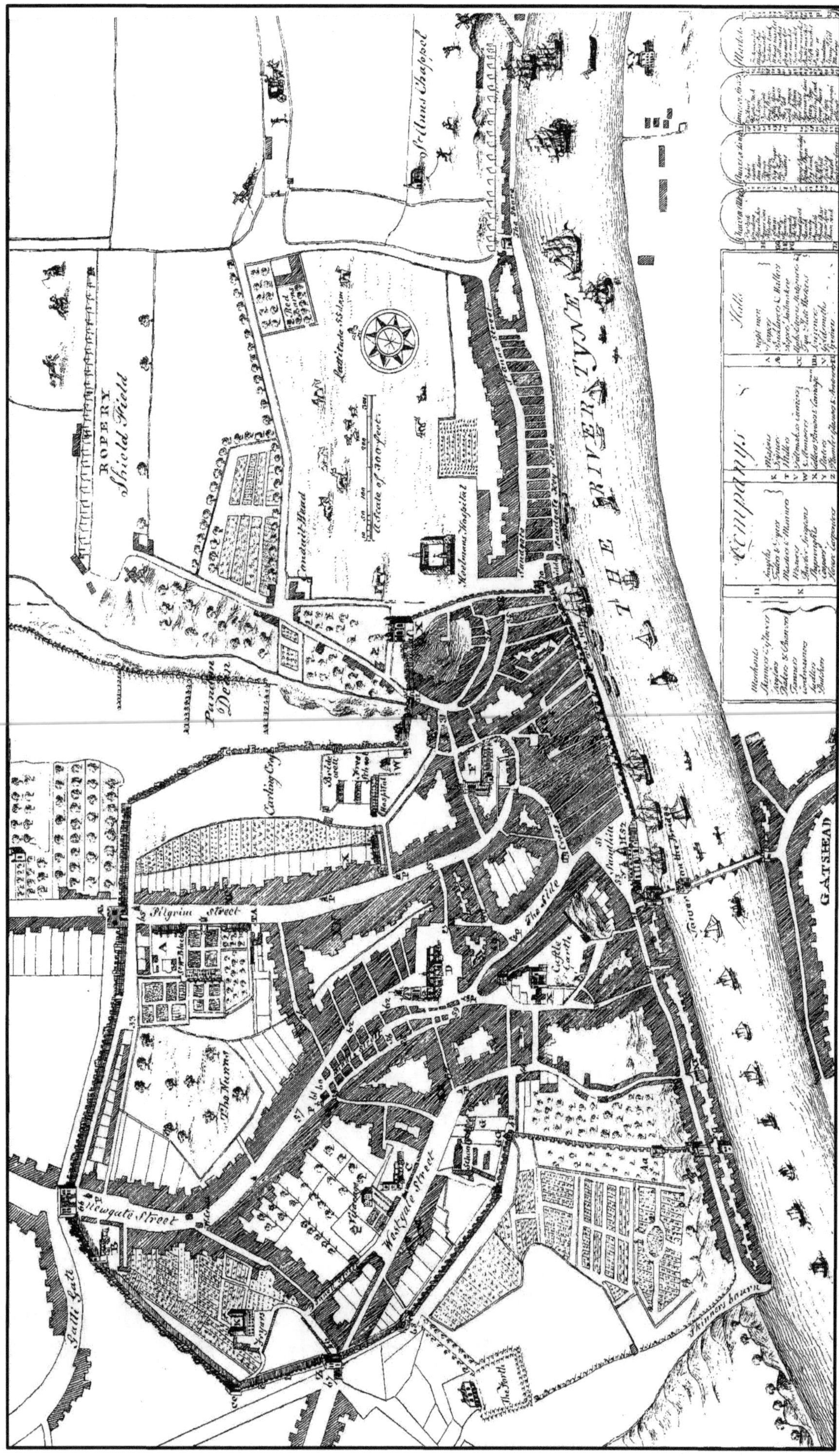

Map reference 4.16: James Corbridge (1723)

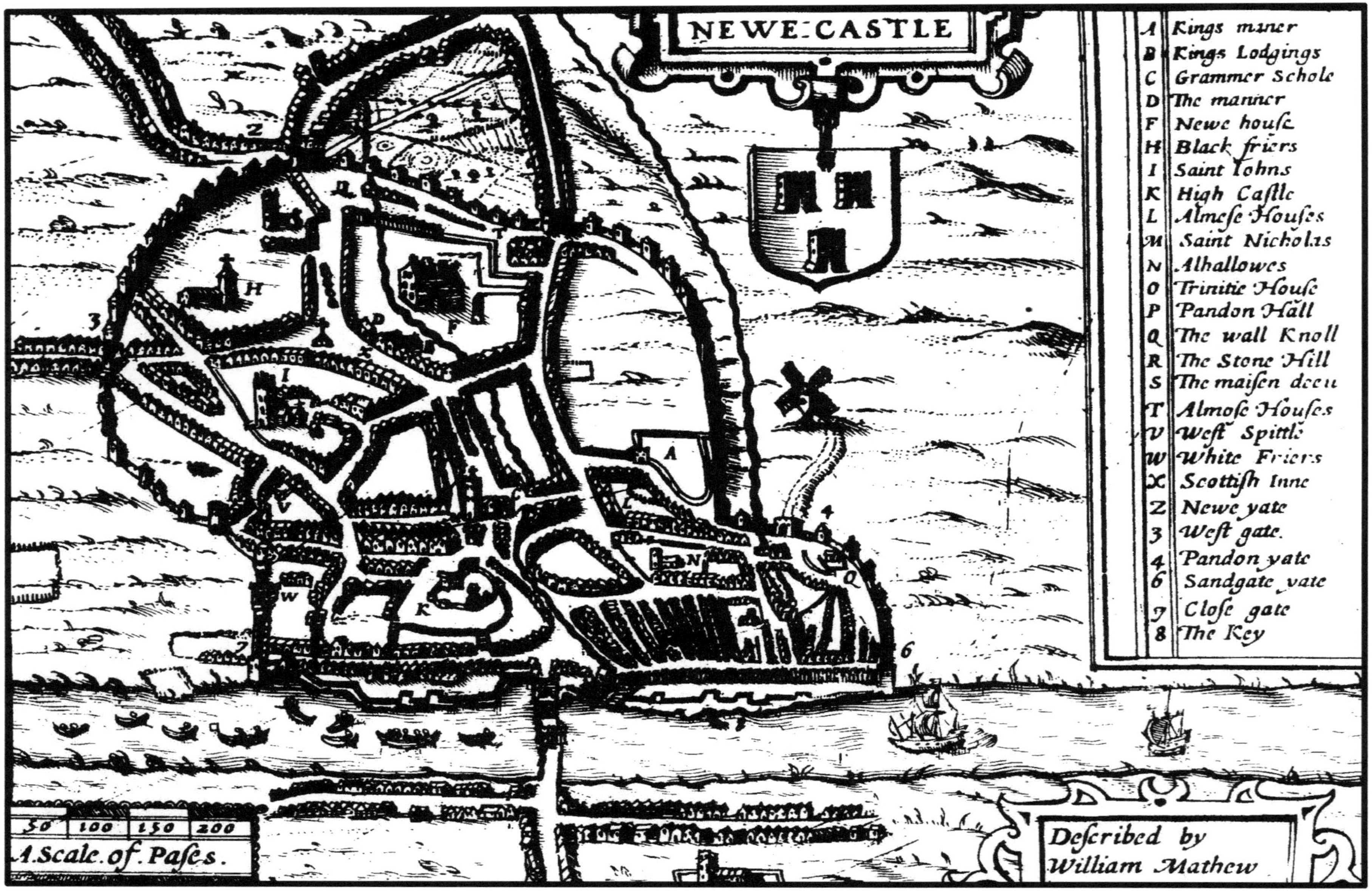

Map reference 4.16: John Speed (1611)

www.ingramcontent.com/pod-product-compliance
Lightning Source LLC
LaVergne TN
LVHW072253300926
849160LV00018B/1657
* 9 7 8 1 4 0 7 3 0 6 0 1 8 *